From Empire to Republic: Post-World War I Austria

Günter Bischof, Fritz Plasser (Eds.)
Peter Berger, Guest Editor

CONTEMPORARY AUSTRIAN STUDIES | Volume 19

innsbruck university press

Printed in the United States of America.

Cover photo: A severely wounded soldier from the battle on the Isonzo front awaits transport to the hospital on 23 August 1917. (Photo courtesy of Picture Archives of the Austrian National Library)

Published in the United States by
University of New Orleans Press:
ISBN: 9781608010257

Published and distributed in Europe
by Innsbruck University Press:
ISBN: 9783902719768

iup

Contemporary Austrian Studies

Publication of this volume has been made possible through generous grants from the Austrian Ministries of European and International Affairs through the Austrian Cultural Forum in New York as well as the Ministry of Science and Research. The Austrian Marshall Plan Anniversary Foundation in Vienna has been very generous in supporting CenterAustria at the University of New Orleans and its publications series. The College of Liberal Arts at the University of New Orleans and the Auslandsamt of the University of Innsbruck provided additional financial support as did the Cultural Office of the City of Innsbruck.

Preface

Günter Bischof

The breakup of the Habsburg Dual Monarchy and the redrawing of the political map of East Central Europe constituted a major experiment in "destroying the old, and creating the new" (O. Hwaletz). Historians are more inclined to study the rise of empires than their demise and aftermath. The eighteen essays in this volume offer fresh perspective and innovative scholarship on the difficult *transition from empire to republic* for the small state of Austria, newly created by the Allied peacemakers in Paris in 1919. These essays also deal with complex challenges of *nation building after a major war* as well as the ambiguity inherent in the creation of new institutions in politics, economics, social life and culture. In 1919 the government of the instable and fledgling Republic of Austria faced the task of integrating more than a million of returning war veterans and taking care of 110,000 wounded veterans returning from the frontlines. The government was also confronting revolutionary turmoil in the streets of Vienna, a near-total collapse of the agricultural and industrial economies and near-mental breakdown from the trauma of defeat. Hyperinflation produced a financial crisis in the early 1920s and major economic challenges in the banking and industrial sectors. The redrawn borders produced loss of German ethnics and major demographic shifts. Pan-Germanism was an ideology popular in all political camps. "Austrians"—no longer dominant in a vast empire—were searching for a new identity. After four years of war, Austrians had to confront defeat and constructed a national memory from painful personal remembrances. Most families were dealing with family members returning from a long and destructive war with limbs missing and souls deranged. In spite of ideological conflict between the major political camps, a national cultural revival ensued and new educational institutions were born.

The idea for this volume arose after a reception by the Austrian Cultural Forum at the end of a long day during the annual German Studies Association Meeting in St. Paul, Minnesota, in early October 2008. Over a beer, I conversed with John Deak, Patrick Houlihan and Ke-chin Hsia—all of them very bright PhD students mentored by John Boyer at the University of Chicago. They told me excitedly about their fascinating dissertation research. As it happened, all of them worked on topics of the immediate post-World War I period. That same evening I began to map out in my mind a CAS volume on Austria dealing with the consequences and legacies of World War I. CAS had covered the "Dollfuss/Schuschnigg Era" in volume 11 (2003); individual essays had covered the two decades between the wars in various other volumes (on identity and memory, foreign policy, sexuality). But we had never covered the end of the war and the 1920s as a distinct era. I had just been reading Tony Judt's *Postwar*, his marvelous history of post-World War II Europe. Of course, I knew that our canvas would be more modest than Judt's. But his grand depictions of confronting the challenging political, social, and economic impacts of the Great War were there in the case study of Austria after World War I too. Also, the memory of the war—so prominent in Judt's work—would need to be addressed. A few weeks after the St. Paul meeting I invited John Boyer to pen the introduction, and he generously agreed to do it. In a way, then, this is a volume that takes its intellectual origins in Boyer's University of Chicago seminar. This core group of Boyer's "Chicago boys" had met other researchers in the Vienna archives and were well connected to the community of international scholars working on post-World War I Austria; they asked some of them to contribute, too. I would like to thank them all for making this a volume of Austrian Studies that nicely demonstrates that there is a tightly woven *global* Austrian Studies community from Chicago via Oxford and Austria to Jerusalem in the Middle East and Taiwan and Australia in the Far East.

My friend and colleague Peter Berger at the Vienna University of Economics and Business generously agreed to serve as the guest editor. He has been working on the 1920s throughout his distinguished career and brought contributors through his contacts in the Viennese scholarly community to this volume. Peter also contributed the chilling concluding essay to this volume. This intricate Jewish family portrait illustrates in a tight dramatic family saga the tergiversations and bloody culminations of twentieth century Austrian history that is usually the stuff of fiction. Sam Williamson contacted me about a piece he was writing on Count Berchtold and his role in the tragic origins of World War I—not quite a book but more than a regular journal article. I eagerly invited him to contribute it to this volume to set the stage about the prewar era, a period to which he had been making major scholarly contributions throughout his illustrious career both as a scholar and high university administrator. We cannot thank these far-flung scholars enough for the timely submissions of their contributions, along with their kind patience with our copy-editing team.

This is the first volume produced "in house" from scratch at UNO and the second volume to be published jointly by UNO and iup presses. Bill Lavender at UNO Press was helpful at every step of the way from copy-editing to producing photo-ready copy to printing and distribution. Lindsay Maples worked very hard in copy-editing the entire volume and also type-setting it. At iup Birgit Holzner cooperated promptly whenever asked. Klaus Frantz, Franz Mathis and Mathias Schennach of the University of Innsbruck helped make the cooperation with iup possible. They each contributed in their own way to make this volume come together. Hans Petschar and Michaela Pfunder of the Picture Archives of the Austrian National Library were more than helpful in the search for pictures to illustrate this volume. The Austrian Federal Ministry of Science and Research in Vienna finances an annual "Ministry Fellow" at CenterAustria who assists me with my CAS work load. I could not have asked for a more congenial and hard-working fellow than Alexander Smith. He maintained daily contacts with some two dozen authors and shepherded every manuscript from submission to type-setting. In spite of some ups and downs along the way, he never lost his cool and good cheer. This volume would not have come together in time without his keen engagement. Whether we were working on CAS or other matters, as always Gertraud Griessner kept CenterAustria running. This volume could not have been published without the generous financial support of the University of New Orleans and the University of Innsbruck, as well as the Austrian Ministry of Science and Research and the Austrian Ministry of European and International Affairs via the Austrian Cultural Forum in New York. Florian Gerhardus, Christoph Ramoser, Josef Leidenfrost, Martin Rauchbauer, Andreas Stadler and Emil Brix all deserve our gratitude for making this financial support possible. The Austrian Marshall Plan Foundation has been the most important institutional sponsor of all the work we do at CenterAustria, including the publication of CAS. Eugen Stark, the Executive Director, has been a marvelous friend and supporter over the years. Thank you all.

Table of Contents

II. Costs of War: Social/Mental/Cultural Legacies

III. Habsburg Successor States: Economic Legacies

Coda: A Twentieth Century Family

BOOK REVIEWS

ANNUAL REVIEW

INTRODUCTION

Boundaries and Transitions in Modern Austrian History

John W. Boyer

In thinking about the kind invitation to write a short introduction to this year's edition of the *Contemporary Austrian Studies*, which focuses on the history of the Austrian First Republic, I was struck by the fact that on both sides of the First Republic a great deal of fascinating scholarly work has emerged in the last fifteen to twenty years.[1] For example, the historiography of the Habsburg Empire has been enriched recently by historians interested in identity and memory—highly topical in the age of post-Maastricht Europeanisms—who are concerned with the often oblique and obtuse quality of ethnic-national personhood. Other scholars of the Empire have emphasized the sturdiness and success of regional politics in the late Empire, emphasizing how precocious and creative local, regional, and even state-level politicians and political organizations were in expanding the sphere of political communications and public interest articulations relating to vital civic issues between 1880 and 1914 and in ramping up the effectiveness of administrative institutions to respond to those issues.

The work of both groups of scholars has suggested that the resilience of civic institutions under the Empire may have been underestimated by past scholars who alleged the inevitability of the Empire's demise, and that large numbers of citizens in the Empire, many of whom shared self-identities that merged class, confession, and ethnicity in surprising malleable ways, were willing to tolerate different forms of cultural diversity under a rule of administrative-parliamentary state that sought to reconcile the robust authority of the Crown with the pragmatic policy needs of a rapidly changing civil society, a society that both needed and demanded stronger forms of self-government under the umbrella of Imperial administrative rule. As Professor Gary Cohen has recently argued, "in the last decades before World War I, a vibrant civil society developed in each side of the Monarchy, with multiple mass parties and popularly based interest groups" and that there was "a greater possibility of evolutionary change in the relationship between society and government during the late nineteenth century than many older views allowed."[2] I would also add that these recent historiographical interventions about the late Empire parallel, in ironic and surprising ways, the hopes (and illusions) that surrounded the semi-constitutional project of the creation of universal manhood suffrage in 1907. And they accord well with the more general proposition that the Habsburg Empire only collapsed after a long and protracted effort by the Imperial war state to wage war against its own civil society between 1914 and 1918.[3]

Second, in contrast to the more confident tone of recent late Imperial historiography, the post-1945 historical world has been subject to several overlapping analytical perspectives, and many of them are not particularly flattering. What might be called the "Waldheim Affect" in post-World War II Austrian historiography has generated skepticism about the traditional view that a sharp break in Austrian public life took place between 1944 and 1946, about the ambivalent motives of the founders of the Second Republic, about the very nature of the democratization of Austrian civil society in the 1950s and even the 1960s, and about a seemingly self-conscious and unflattering amnesia on the part of many Austrians about their complicity in the terror state of 1938-1945. In the views presented by Robert Knight, Gerhard Botz, and many other scholars, for example, the leaders who steered the early Republic are seen as at best indifferent, and at worst deeply as mendacious toward the question of the guilt in which many Austrians were implicated during the *Nazizei*t. Other historians, most prominently Gerald Stourzh, have continued to insist that whatever their personal or professional failings, the leaders who found themselves thrust into power in 1945 did preside over a *Stunde Null*, and that 1945 was profoundly disjunctive and transformational turning point in Austrian history.[4]

Robert Knight is surely correct when he scoffs at the idea that Red and Black collaboration after 1945 was hatched out of the egg of joint suffering in Nazi concentration camps (the so-called "*Geist der Lagerstrasse*"), insisting that this collaboration was an ad hoc, patch work process, one marked by a "cautious and provisional agreement which had to be developed and confirmed by post-war political practice."[5] This sober and pragmatic political practice was only able to succeed because important structural disabilities created in the late Empire and distorted in the First Republic had been stripped away from the grid of everyday political exchange, but in a way that preserved treasured partisan myths about the self and the other, myths that expressed a still living frustration and anger over the "bad outcomes" after 1918 that had resulted from the fully sanctioned partisanships set loose in the political system in 1907. The continued fascination with 1934 in both of the big party *Lager*—in 1945 the American diplomat Martin F. Herz rightly predicted that the conundrum of 1934 was a kind of "white-heat" that would "plague the Austrian democracy for a long time"—demonstrated that Austrian leaders in 1945 were still reliving the chronic pathologies that afflicted the First Republic while also coping with the catastrophe of 1938 to 1945.[6] The "white- heat" of the Interwar period continued to be identity-shaping after 1945 precisely because it signified the palpable existence of vital unfinished business from the First Republic, above all, how to (finally) make the Constitution of 1920 work.

This historiographical disjunction between a civilized and reputable Empire and a duplicitous and amnesiac Second Republic is fascinating, but it also raises the logical question of what are we supposed to do with the First Republic? Much of the modern scholarly history of the First Republic in Austria remains to be written, and it clearly has to be connected to some kind of perspective on the Empire and some kind of perspective on the early Second Republic. Certainly, the continued fascination with the events of February 1934 is fully understandable, but focusing only or primarily on 1934 and its aftermath does not easily resolve the challenges of constructing an adequate portrait of the significance of the whole of the First Republic.

1. The emergence of a critical historiography relating to the immediate post-1945 period should draw our attention to special importance of connecting what happened before 1914 and what happened after 1918, and also to the need to reach back into the past in order to understand the broader structures and systems that defined Austrian political culture in the later twentieth century. For example, the classic stand-off between the Social Democratic and Christian Social camps of the First Republic cannot be understood without a serious interrogation of the late Imperial period. The Christian Socials began as a rag-tag oppositional *kleinbürgerlich* movement, but Karl Lueger made them far more than that. By 1907 they had become the largest party in the Austrian parliament, and the impact of

this self-proclaimed Christian Reichspartei was of enormous consequence for the general political and administrative system in the last two decades of the Monarchy's existence. Granted that they often deployed their anti-authoritarian "democratic instincts" for hyper-partisan purposes and for ill as opposed to good, still, if Gary Cohen's argument about the emergence of a "vibrant civil society" in the last decades of the Empire are plausible and correct, then the emergence of that vibrant civil society is in part owing to the impact of the Christian Socials under Lueger. As my colleague Margaret L. Anderson has asserted about the systemic impact of German Zentrum on Wilhelmine political culture, "religion—its rhetoric and its leadership—... provided for Catholic under-dogs in Upper Silesia the emancipatory tool kit that rules might supply in other milieus: a knife to cut the existing vertical lines of authority and the thread to weave horizontal lines of solidarity. Not least, religion, like rules, provided voters with civic courage, the gumption—of which Germans are traditionally said to be in such short supply—to stand up for one's rights, human and civil, against authority."[7]

Inevitably, much of Christian Socials' attention after 1897 came to be focused on the dangers posed by the Austrian Social Democrats. The Austrian Social Democratic party had a magnificent history, indeed a heroic history, between 1889 and 1914, but much of that early history was not simply reacting to and thinking about the nationalities question—pace Hans Mommsen's excellent studies—but to reacting to Karl Lueger and the Christian Social party. It is certainly true that the Social Democrats were an Empire-wide party, but they were also a preeminently Viennese party, and the party "grew up" (if I may use a biological-developmental metaphor) in the shadow of Karl Lueger. It was of critical importance that Vienna was ruled after 1895 not by an elite of Liberal notables, but by a large popular party representing lower and middle bourgeois social forces who, for all their suspicions of the very wealthy, were even more suspicious of and antagonistic toward the representatives of the working class. The Christian Socials were a mass party, but a mass party with a particularly aggressive *kleinbürgerlich* hue, and their grasp of power made them both an attractive target and an alluring model for the nascent Social Democrats. The city's competitive political culture thus functioned as an immense school of civic participation and political identity formation by providing an intense and dynamic network of collision points over which rival groups struggled for hegemony.

Rather than "killing off" alternate views of polity and society, as they claimed they could and would do, the Christian Socials seemed to generate new oppositional forms at every turn.[8] The striking presence of Lueger's power—his arrogance, ruthlessness, and ostentatiousness—begged for challenges. That these challenges occurred in a reasonably free political environment, at a time when governmental censorship was slowly withdrawing its control over political expression, testified both to the mediatory power of the Imperial administration and to the pleasure which all sides took in the theatricality of the new rhetoric. One of the most vital components of the political revolution in Vienna between 1897 and 1914 was the new anticlericalism. Indeed, for the *Jungen* like Karl Seitz and Otto Glöckel and for those who joined the *Los von Rom* and *Freie Schule* movements, anticlericalism assumed a life of its own. The Austro-Marxist preoccupation with religion and anticlericalism reflected two wider differences from the Marxism of their German comrades to the north.[9] The first lay in the propensity of younger Austrian Socialists to privilege theories of political personality development in a multi-ethnic empire, applauding strategies that would enhance cultural and ethnic individuality while maintaining legal and economic solidarities. The second lay in their equally strong instrumental evaluation of ethical forces as being able to shape the context in which class struggle would be pursued. The impassioned front mentality that the younger Austro-Marxists practiced with such zeal was a component of their larger quest to empower "new men" and "new women" with revolutionary cultural identities. For some, like Max Adler, a new society of purely secular, humanistic values in which religious expression would be erased from the public (and perhaps also from the private) scene might accompany and perhaps even precede a fundamental transformation in the relations of material production. Since bourgeois culture and religious morality seemed to affirm existing class relations in Austria, their Socialist counterparts should be turned against those class relations. They might help to modify, if not overcome, class repression, since Socialist humanism could be offered not merely to the proletariat but also to Austrian society at large, including the middle and lower bourgeoisie.

One of the most fundamental characteristics of interwar Austro-Marxism was the revolutionary value that the Viennese Socialists accorded to changes in education (*Bildung*) and in manners (*Gesittung*), as opposed to mere reconstruction of tax codes and housing systems. Coming out of an epoch of prewar political conflict in Vienna, in which the primal enemy of the party was an ostentatiously "Christian" movement that blandished religion as a tool for spectacle and political combat, the younger Socialists understandably defined political success in counter-religious terms. Catholicism functioned for the Austro-Marxists in much the same way as the bogeyman of the "*Junkers*" served for their German counterparts. The intellectual and political world of the younger Socialists was that of Karl Lueger triumphant; of Albert Gessmann, the Imperial Hofrat and Cabinet Minister; of the *Piusverein* and networks of politicizing Catholic clerics, who condemned Socialism from the pulpit on Sunday and in catechism classes during the school week; of the *Reichspost*, prosperous and confident of financial help from conservative Court circles and from Austrian industry, mediated through Rudolf Sieghart. Their world was also one of nationalist crisis, in which their own party threatened to degenerate into feuding national wings. The level of brilliant theory which this generation of Socialists attained was not a little owing to the gap between expectation and concrete achievement wrought by earlier generations' political and institutional strategies. This gap invited new experiments in national-cultural mediation, among the most notable of which were Karl Renner's and Otto Bauer's contributions, but also a new emphasis on anticlerical culture and on mass education as positive and unifying modes of progressive Socialist politics that some hoped would constitute a bridge between rival Social Democratic ethnic factions and a way of reaching out to more progressive *bürgerlich* voters as well.

Moreover, an ironic parallel between the Christian Social and Social Democratic experiences seems obvious, for the Christian Socials sought to exploit anti-Socialism before 1914 as a bridge over bourgeois nationality squabbles, in much the same way that the Social Democrats exploited anti-clericalism. Friedrich Gaertner, a young assistant to Albert Gessmann, argued in 1907 that two great blocs would eventually dominate Austrian parliamentary life, one led by the Christian Socials, the other by the Social Democrats. In the former ensemble the other German bourgeois parties would have to cooperate, as would Slavic *bürgerlich* politicians. Gaertner was sure that in such an atmosphere of *intrabourgeois* economic cooperation "a *Kulturkampf* appears to be virtually excluded."[10] Gaertner's utopian assumptions were at least plausible before 1914, but after 1918 they had become completely irrelevant. After the loss of the German- and Czech-speaking areas of Bohemia and Moravia in 1918-1919, the Christian Socials lost any need to use anti-Socialism as a bridge over Imperial nationality squabbles, and their own appreciation of anti-Socialism became even more Vienna-centered and much more intensely and more exclusively targeted on the Viennese agents of the new anti-clericalism, many of whom now had prominent political positions in the Rathaus in the 1920s. This change of framework came at the same time as the shift in power within the Christian Social party to a much more openly Catholic profile—Ignaz Seipel and Richard Schmitz as opposed to Karl Lueger and Albert Gessmann—and both of these changes converged after 1918 to help create the supercharged cultural-political battles of the 1920s.

The evolutionary development of these powerful cultural formations—Social Democratic anti-clericalism and Christian Social anti-Socialism—may thus provide useful threads to connect politics under the Empire with politics under the First Republic. They originated in one set of complex circumstances long before 1914, but gained a second and even fiercer lease on life after 1919, after the great divide of the political Revolution of 1918.

2. If the world before 1914 took hostages for the decades to come, the War and the Revolution were equally salient ventures in shaping the First Republic. The Revolution was a truly democratic and liberal revolution in structural terms, but it was also a revolution with profoundly unresolved ethical and cultural tensions. This may explain why both the Left and the Right, as Professor Margarete Grandner has shrewdly observed, soon refused to claim genuine paternity with that Revolution.[11] In another venue I have called attention to the powerful disruptive effects of the Revolution in destroying the semi-secular *bürgerlich* wing of the Christian Social party, and it is impossible to understand Ignaz Seipel's career and the enormous impact that he had on Austrian politics in the 1920s and early 1930s without appreciating the simple fact that his version of Christian Socialism was not only profoundly different from that of Karl Lueger and Albert Gessmann, but that this difference was only made possible because of the savage impact of the War and the Revolution.[12]

Like the crushing geopolitical losses that resulted from the disaster of July 1866, in their further amputations of the known world of Austrian civic institutions and social imagination the events of November 1918 also left deep and painful scars. Geoffrey Wawro has recently called attention to the fact that the preeminent Austrian historian of the catastrophe of 1866, Heinrich Friedjung, wrote "far more a Liberal critique of Franz Josephan Austria than a serious study of Austria's war effort," and, in its deep-seated German nationalism and evident frustrations over the failure of the Anschluss, something similar might be said for Otto Bauer's great book, *Die österreichische Revolution*, on the catastrophe of 1918.[13]

When the Revolution took place in 1918, traditional nationalist issues did not immediately disappear—the Provisional National Assembly that met in Vienna in November 1918 had more *Deutscher Nationalverband* deputies than either Christian Socials or Social Democrats, with many of them having been elected from Bohemian, Moravian, or Silesian electoral districts in 1911.[14] The Revolution thus began as a tripartite exercise in which the German Nationalists enjoyed a major parliamentary presence.

The mirage of Wilsonian democracy seemed to give to the German Bohemian politicians what decades of Cabinet-level and parliamentary infighting before 1918 was unable to achieve, namely, a national partition of German-speaking areas of Bohemia and Moravia. Czech political leaders in Prague steadfastly ignored any concessions or negotiations, however, using their status as a new small nation basking (so they fervently hoped) in the sun of Entente approval to encourage ad hoc military units to occupy the German-occupied territories in Bohemia and Moravia, sometimes using force.

Once the Czechs forced the new Austrian state to back down on its claims to the northern territories, many German Nationalist deputies were forced to abandon the new Republican parliament in Vienna and the small contingent of remaining German Nationalists who had been elected in electoral districts in Vienna or the Alpine lands shrunk into what Lothar Höbelt has called a "third Lager" by 1919.[15] The *Grossdeutschen* were in fact double orphans—they lacked the larger structural legitimacy and leadership that their faction enjoyed before 1918, and they lacked compelling issues. Yet they were sufficiently fearful of Red Vienna to make them a plausible junior coalition partner with Seipel's Christian Socials, and throughout most of the 1920s they allied with the Christian Socials in a junior-senior partner alliance for lack of plausible alternatives.[16] The contingent particularities of the Revolution, as it played out between November 1918 and February 1919, fundamentally over-determined the structural landscape of Republican politics.

3. Finally, on the other end of the temporal divide of the 1920s, there lies the murky challenge of how to connect the ruins of the First Republic itself with the complex events of April 1945. Critical questions about guilt and memory are certainly valid and necessary, especially within the conceptual framework of 1934 to 1945. But if one broadens the framework, and tries to work through the thorny problem of what actually changed in Austrian society between 1900 and 1918 and how those changes affected the history of Austria between 1918 and 1945, other perspectives may also emerge. This is clearly the case with Karl Renner. Working in the Ballhausplatz immediately after the collapse of Nazi rule, the Austrian diplomat Josef Schöner was flabbergasted by Karl Renner's tirades invoking 1934 as a kind of beacon with which to guide his personnel choices in the summer and fall of 1945.[17] But what one must remember is that for Renner 1934 had not simply been an attack on the Socialist Party and its unions and secondary organizations, and not even just an attack on the constitutional state established in 1920. It was also an attack on the fundamental principles

that had guided the Social Democratic Party since the early 1890s and confirmed by the success of Social Democrats in achieving universal suffrage in 1907. In defending the Constitution of 1920 against Christian Social attacks in November 1929 Karl Renner interpreted the 1880s and 1890s as a time of struggle of the SPÖ to guarantee the lawful behavior of the state, to force the Austrian *Rechtsstaat* to honor its own claims. The party did this even before winning the full and equal right to the vote in 1907, enabling Renner to read Social Democracy's role as the guarantor of a parliamentary *Rechtsstaat* deep into the nineteenth century. 1934 was so bitterly shocking to the Left because it was a direct abrogation of the rules of a game that had been established constitutionally in 1907. In Renner's mind, the Christian Socials bore a heavy and almost unredeemable burden of guilt, because they systematically repudiated the system of open, no-holds-barred democratic partisanship that 1907 had sanctioned and to which they themselves had originally assented.

One sees thus two sides to Karl Renner in 1945: the ardent proponent of a kind of popular front of various classes—his famous bi-partisan rhetoric of "*Bürger, Bauern und Arbeiter*" as constituting a sturdy platform for the newly revived Republic—and the ardent partisan of 1934, who felt that the Austro-Fascists were as bad and perhaps even worse than Austrian Nazis. Renner believed that free and universal suffrage in a robust parliamentary framework was the best guarantee for that mixing up of economic, social, and cultural interests, which he considered essential to the stability of the modern state. For Renner, the achievement of 1920 had been to create a liberal constitutional framework worthy of the code of democratic partisanship inaugurated in 1907. His outrage was genuine when he saw Seipel and Dollfuss attacking not only the 1920 Constitution, but also the logic of the system of civil liberties created in 1867 and the democratic parliamentary values and practices established in 1907. It is hardly surprising that in his remarkable study of the Austrian state problem in 1918 Renner would quote James Madison's Tenth Federalist Paper to the effect that "the regulation of these various and interfering interests forms the principal task of modern legislation and involves the spirit of party and faction in the necessary and ordinary operations of government."[18] Bruno Kreisky caught this side of Renner when he gently observed in his autobiography that Renner was held in suspicion among many in his own party because "they felt his reformism placed too heavy an emphasis on the transformative potential of parliamentary representation."[19]

The various essays in this edition of *Contemporary Austrian Studies* provide many insightful perspectives about the fascinating history of the

First Republic. They confirm the fact that the First Republic was deeply shaped by memories, traditions, and institutional practices from the Empire, and that the Republic was hard pressed to extricate itself from, much less to overcome, the stunning collapse of the Empire. Taken as an ensemble, these essays also suggest that the field of First Republican studies will continue to offer Austrian historians on both sides of the Atlantic a rich and fruitful domain for future scholarly research.

Notes

1. These comments are in part drawn from a longer essay on Austrian politics in the Twentieth Century, "Power, Partisanship, and the Grid of Democratic Politics: 1907 as the Pivot Point of Modern Austrian History," which was the keynote address presented at a conference on "Austria and Europe after 1989" at Stanford University, 5 March 2009.

2. Gary B. Cohen, "Neither Absolutism Nor Anarchy: New Narratives on Society and Government in Late Imperial Austria," *Austrian History Yearbook 29* (1998): 59, 61; as well as "Nationalist Politics and the Dynamics of State and Civil Society in the Habsburg Monarchy 1867-1914," *Central European History 40* (2007): 241-78. Among the historians whose work is relevant in this regard, I would include Gerald Stourzh, Helmut Rumpler, Gary Cohen, Pieter Judson, Lothar Höbelt, Jeremy King, Tara Zahra, James Shedel, Maureen Healy, David Good, Laurence Core, John Deak, Larissa Douglass, and myself.

3. See John W. Boyer, "Silent War and Bitter Peace: The Austrian Revolution of 1918," *Austrian History Yearbook 34* (2003): 1-56; and Maureen Healy, *Vienna and the Fall of the Habsburg Empire: Total War and Everyday Life in World War I* (Cambridge: Cambridge University Press, 2004).

4. Among a huge literature, see Robert Knight, "The Politics of Memory in Post-Nazi Austria," in *The German-Jewish Dilemma: From the Enlightenment to the Shoah*, ed. Edward Timms and Andrea Hammel (Lewiston: Mellen, Edwin Press, 1999), 291-203; and idem., ed., *"Ich bin dafür, die Sache in die Länge zu ziehen": Die Wortprotokolle der österreichischen Bundesregierung von 1945 bis 1952 über die Entschädigung der Juden*, 2nd ed. (Vienna: Böhlau, 2000); Gerhard Botz and Albert Müller, "'1945': 'Stunde Null': Historischer Bruch oder Kontinuität mit der NS-Zeit und der Ersten Republik?," *Jahrbuch 1995 des Dokumentationsarchivs des Österreichischen Widerstands*, 6-27; Gerhard Botz and Gerald Sprengnagel, eds., *Kontroversen um Österreichs Zeitgeschichte: Verdrängte Vergangenheit, Österreich-Identität, Waldheim und die Historiker* (Frankfurt: Campus, 1994); Barbara Kaindl-Widhalm, *Demokraten wider Willen? Autoritäre Tendenzen und Antisemitismus in der 2. Republik* (Vienna: Verlag für Gesellschaftskritik, 1990); Günter Bischof, *Austria in the First Cold War 1945-1955: The Leverage of the Weak* (New York: St. Martin's Press, 1999), ch. 1; and Gerald Stourzh, *1945 und 1955: Schlüsseljahre der Zweiten Republik* (Innsbruck: Studienverlag, 2005).

5. Robert Knight, "Narratives in Post-war Austrian Historiography," in *Austria 1945-1955: Studies in Political and Cultural Re-emergence*, ed. Anthony Bushell (Cardiff: University of Wales Press, 1996), 15.

6. Reinhold Wagnleitner, ed., *Understanding Austria: The Political Reports of Martin F. Herz, Political Officer of the US Legation in Vienna 1945-1948*, Quellen zur Geschichte des 19. und 20. Jahrhunderts Bd. 4 (Salzburg: Neugebauer, 1984), 53.

7. Margaret L. Anderson, "Voter, Junker, Landrat, Priest: The Old Authorities and the New Franchise in Imperial Germany," *American Historical Review 98* (1993): 1466; as well as Anderson's excellent book, *Practicing Democracy: Elections and Political Culture in Imperial*

Germany (Princeton: Princeton University Press, 2000).

8. For more detail, see John W. Boyer, *Culture and Political Crisis: Christian Socialism in Power, 1897-1918* (Chicago: University of Chicago Press, 1995), esp. chs. 2 and 4.

9. For a comparative perspective between the "cultural socialist" orientations of the two movements which focuses on the interwar period, see Michael Scholing and Franz Walter, "Der 'Neue Mensch': Sozialistische Lebensreform und Erziehung in der sozialdemokratischen Arbeiterbewegung Deutschlands und Österreichs," in *Solidargemeinschaft und Klassenkampf: Politische Konzeptionen der Sozialdemokratie zwischen den Weltkriegen*, ed. Richard Saage (Frankfurt: Suhrkamp, 1986), 250-73, esp. 259.

10. *Germania*, 26 May 1907, 1. This article is untitled, but Gaertner is the likely author.

11. Margarete Grandner, *Kooperative Gewerkschaftspolitik in der Kriegswirtschaft: Die freien Gewerkschaften Österreichs im ersten Weltkrieg* (Vienna: Böhlau, 1992), 441-42.

12. John W. Boyer, *Karl Lueger (1844-1910): Christlichsoziale Politik als Beruf: Eine Biografie* (Vienna: Böhlau, 2009), 413-56.

13. Geoffrey Wawro, *The Austro-Prussian War: Austria's War with Prussia and Italy in 1866* (Cambridge: Cambridge University Press, 1996), 3. William J. McGrath has shrewdly observed of Friedjung's classic book, *The Struggle for Supremacy in Germany*, that "[d]isappointed by his exclusion from the German nationalist cause, Friedjung's energies found an appropriate substitute in tracing what he saw as the historical tragedy of Austria's exclusion from the Germanic homeland." *Dionysian Art and Populist Politics in Austria* (New Haven: Yale University Press, 1974), 206.

14. Wilhelm Brauneder, *Deutsch-Österreich: Die Republik entsteht* (Vienna: Amalthea, 2000), 41, 193-207; Boyer, "Silent War and Bitter Peace," 27-33.

15. Lothar Höbelt, "Deutschnationale – Nationaldemokraten – Grossdeutsche – Bauernpartei: Das 'nationale Lager' 1918-1922," *Studien und Forschungen aus dem Niederösterreichischen Institut für Landeskunde 39* (2007): 101-14.

16. "Die Bindung an die Christlichsozialen wurde in Anbetracht der zurückgehenden Unterscheidbarkeit der beiden Parteien immer grösser und die Akzeptanz bei den Wählern immer geringer." Richard Voithofer, *Drum schliesst Euch frisch an Deutschland an...: Die Grossdeutsche Volkspartei in Salzburg 1920-1936* (Vienna: Böhlau, 2000), 178.

17. Josef Schöner, *Wiener Tagebuch 1944/1945*, ed. Gerald Stourzh et al., Veröffentlichungen der Kommission für Neuere Geschichte Österreichs Bd. 83 (Vienna: Böhlau, 1992), 237, 254, 256-57, 295, 319, and 323.

18. Karl Renner, *Das Selbstbestimmungsrecht der Nationen in besonderer Anwendung auf Oesterreich* (Leipzig: Franz Deuticke, 1918), 275.

19. Matthew P. Berg, ed., *The Struggle for a Democratic Austria: Bruno Kreisky on Peace and Social Justice* (New York: Berghahn, 2000), 489.

Leopold Count Berchtold: The Man Who Could Have Prevented the Great War

Samuel R. Williamson, Jr.

19 July 1914: "Berchtold came at 6 and stayed to dine. He was very human and pleasant but with M [aurice de Bunsen, her husband and the British Ambassador] as secretive as he always is with all Ambassadors and let no word fall as to his intentions towards Serbia."[1]

Only later would Berta de Bunsen learn that her dinner guest had earlier that same day given final approval of an ultimatum designed to provide a pretext for war with Serbia. Her secretive guest was the one person who could have prevented the outbreak of war.[2] Had he counseled Emperor Franz Joseph to continue a policy of militant diplomacy instead of a policy of hostile, military confrontation, peace would have been preserved, regardless of German pressures. But after the assassination of the Archduke Franz Ferdinand and his wife Sophie, Leopold Berchtold, the Habsburg foreign minister, almost immediately resolved for a military showdown; no German pressure was needed.[3]

Berchtold's performance as foreign minister before July 1914 and during it has drawn much criticism. Some of the foreign minister's associates scorned him and some of his contemporaries judged him as not up to the task of directing the monarchy's diplomacy. For example, in May 1914, Habsburg ambassador to Italy Kajetan Meréy de Kapos-Mére accused Berchtold of "dilettantism" and Josef Redlich, a university professor who moved easily among the policymakers, often wrote critical diary entries about him as inadequate to the task.[4] Nor have some historians been kind. Sidney Fay noted he had been called "a mere 'rubber stamp'" for his subordinates, but also saw him taking a "very active and sinister part" in the

July crisis. Bernadotte Schmitt wrote: "He appeared never to know his mind and to have no intelligible policy" though he was "shrewd" in the July crisis. Luigi Albertini routinely criticized his performance, at one point writing, "By temperament he was certainly not inclined to shoulder responsibilities and face storms of the kind [the July crisis]."[5] On the other hand, Hugo Hantsch, his only biographer, while acknowledging Berchtold's limitations, consistently sought to refute the more severe criticism. And in the 1990s John Leslie, Manfried Rauchensteiner, and Williamson sketched a more assertive, effective Berchtold who had had modest success during the two Balkan Wars and their aftermath and who pressed his policy persistently and effectively, if with disastrous results, during July. Given these divergent opinions about Berchtold, he clearly deserves more attention.[6]

Who was this minister? How did he view Austria-Hungary's position and its future in European politics? Why did he so quickly opt for a "final reckoning"? How did he manage to bring a united set of Habsburg ministers to support a clash with neighboring Serbia? What did he and his colleagues hope to gain? With a relentless focus on just Berchtold, much as John Röhl has recently done on Kaiser Wilhelm II, this essay seeks to answer these questions and open a new discussion about Berchtold's role in the July crisis. Perhaps this might prompt further needed research into this key decision-maker on the road to war.

On the Eve

Leopold Berchtold von und zu Ungarschitz became the *kaiserliche und königliche Minister des kaiserlichen und königlichen Hauses und des Äusseren* on 17 February 1912. One of the three candidates recommended to Franz Joseph by the dying Alois Lexa von Aehrenthal, the count had earlier refused—on grounds of inexperience—the Kaiser's plea to become his chief minister. "Count Berchtold had his faults," a critic once noted, "but ambition was not among them." But when pressed anew in mid-February, Berchtold yielded, he later wrote, because of the emperor's profession of confidence, because of his age, and because of the total impact of his "being."[7]

Upon his appointment Berchtold became, at age forty-nine, Europe's youngest foreign minister. Compared not only with other foreign ministers, but also with his contemporaries in the Habsburg diplomatic establishment, his career had been meteoric. Entering the service in 1893 after a six-year stint in Moravian administration, he succeeded Aehrenthal as ambassador to St. Petersburg just thirteen years later in 1906. This key embassy—second only to Berlin in importance—he retained until the spring of 1911 when

Count Leopold von Berchtold (1863-1942), Austrian-Hungarian Foreign Minister, 1912-1915 (Photo courtesy of Picture Archives of the Austrian National Library, Vienna)

he effectively retired from the foreign service to return to his estates in Moravia and Hungary. When Franz Joseph summoned Berchtold to head the Ballhausplatz, he brought back an individual with only eighteen years of diplomatic experience. By comparison, the ambassadors working for Berchtold had served over thirty years and the ministers at lesser capitals twenty-six years. Not surprisingly a number of his diplomatic subordinates (and presumed rivals) were less than charitable toward Berchtold, first of his appointment, and subsequently of his performance as foreign minister.[8]

Berchtold personified the world of "old diplomacy." His social and political assets were not insignificant. A noted sportsman, especially fond of horse racing, the new minister also enjoyed hunting—as did Franz Joseph and Franz Ferdinand. An avid collector of art, he moved comfortably in the world of the secessionist movement in Vienna.[9] Berchtold's Moravian title, moreover, assured his place in the upper circles of Viennese society. And his Hungarian wife not only buttressed this social position, she helped his political position in Hungary as well. Countess Ferdinandine Károlyi de Nagy-Károly, called Nandine by Berchtold and friends, was the daughter of the former Habsburg ambassador to Berlin and London, Count Alois Károlyi. Their 1893 marriage reinforced Berchtold's own Hungarian connection, while linking his wife's considerable land holdings with the already sizable Berchtold estates and led him in 1911 to opt to sit in the Hungarian upper house. Conversant in Czech and Slovak, Berchtold spoke Hungarian well enough to address the Budapest Delegation in the language. Certainly, Franz Joseph considered Berchtold's Hungarian associations strong, for in 1912 he ousted his Hungarian Common Finance Minister, István Burián, lest there be two Hungarians among the three common ministers. The Hungarian connection, therefore, provided Berchtold with considerable flexibility, while his political instincts remained more Austrian—or to be more precise—more Habsburg than Hungarian.[10]

Despite his Magyar ties, Berchtold managed early and easily to establish a close working relationship with Franz Ferdinand, who was notorious for his anti-Magyar views. The count managed far more effectively than his predecessor to deal with the whims and moods of the *Thronfolger* and his Belvedere group. When they differed over policy, Berchtold took a more evasive, less confrontational stance than Aehrenthal and on war-peace issues they presented with minor exceptions a united front against the more bellicose General Franz Conrad von Hötzendorf, chief of the General Staff. Their productive association would continue right down to Sarajevo.[11]

But Berchtold brought more than social and political credentials to the Ballhausplatz. Eight years in St. Petersburg had exposed him to Tsar Nicholas II, the Russian court, and the leading Russian political figures. Moreover, since he had also served in London and Paris, Berchtold was no stranger to the Triple Entente or to the problems it posed for Berlin and Vienna. And, curiously, in his only tour at the Ballhausplatz, he had worked on Albanian issues. Still there were gaps. He lacked any first-hand knowledge of the Balkan situation. Unlike Aehrenthal and most senior members of the Habsburg diplomatic service, he had never served in one of the Balkan states or in the Ottoman Empire. He had no first-hand contact with any of the Balkan royal houses (or their chief ministers), and possibly failed to appreciate the passions and deviousness of Balkan politics.

Behind these political and social assets, and his brief but intensive diplomatic experience, was a complex and contradictory personality. Berchtold's etched face, distinguished by a sharp pointed nose and receding hairline, suggested at first glance weakness. He looked more the dapper, dissolute nobleman than the resolute custodian of the monarchy's sagging international fortunes. Yet these physical features often characterized the genteel courtesy of an aristocratic age fast receding, an era in which trust, loyalty, honor, and a sense of discipline were admired and emulated. If Berchtold brought something of a reputation for dilettantism from his earlier posts, he would as foreign minister be unceasingly attentive to the demands of office. If he was often unimaginative and disinclined to take the initiative, he was, once committed to an approach or a point-of-view, tenacious and relentless in pursuing his position. Though refreshingly self-deprecating about his own limitations, as for example his knowledge of domestic politics, he also worked to repair his deficiencies. Moreover, he possessed a coherent, unambivalent view of himself: He was an Austrian-Habsburg (though he held a seat in the Hungarian House of Magnates), dedicated to the perpetuation of a viable multinational state and the social system that characterized it. Finally, whatever weaknesses Berchtold displayed as a leader—such as occasional passivity and sometimes patience to a fault—must be contrasted with his repeated resistance to the siren songs of the Austrian military between September 1912 and July 1914. Indeed, it was his conversion to their viewpoint in July 1914 that became a major variable in the monarchy's decision for war. Until then he had stubbornly refused to abandon peace for war to resolve the Serbian issue.[12]

Sunday, 28 June 1914, 9 a.m., Buchlau, Moravia

Berchtold and Nandine had come to their Buchlau estate, some 125 miles from Vienna, for the weekend. Had the foreign minister paused that Sunday morning to reflect upon his stewardship of Habsburg foreign policy and upon the monarchy's longer-term prospects, his assessment would have necessarily included the following data.[13] First, despite his renewed efforts to leave office, Franz Joseph had repeatedly pressured him to stay while praising his performance.[14] With the more erratic *Thronfolger*, the minister enjoyed comfortable access. Indeed, he and Nandine had just visited the archducal couple two weeks before at their estate at Konopischt.[15] While all could worry about the emperor's health, a monarchical transition process—even with potential friction with Budapest—was in place. With his fellow ministers on the Common Ministerial Council, Berchtold was clearly the first among equals as the *de facto* chancellor of the monarchy. But the sway that he had had the first fourteen months had been challenged since mid-1913 by István Tisza's appointment as the minister president of Hungary and thus a seat on the Common Ministerial Council. From the start Tisza had left no doubt that he intended to use the provisions of the *Ausgleich* agreement of 1867 to ensure his input into the monarchy's foreign policy. He even went a step further, appointing Burián as his Viennese envoy with an office just minutes from the Ballhausplatz. There had even been press hints that Tisza might succeed Berchtold.[16] Still, even with this robust Magyar personality, Berchtold had cooperated more often than not. With the Habsburg military, relations had often been fractious, whether in resisting the pleas of Conrad for war with Serbia or with General Alexander Krobatin, the war minister, and his insistent demands for more men and more money.[17] Perhaps equally significant, the minister had survived the May meetings of the Austrian and Hungarian delegations, with some criticism to be sure but generally more praise than barbs. In short, Berchtold could feel personally confident about his place and his political future in the senior leadership.[18]

But he could be far less certain about the two consistent issues that had vexed Habsburg diplomacy for decades: relations with Russia and control of the western Balkans against the machinations of Serbia. In the six years since Aehrenthal's dramatic demarche of annexing Bosnia-Herzegovina, relations with Russia had become increasing fragile.[19] The success of the Russian inspired Balkan League and the Austro-Russian war-scare of January-February 1913 left enduring bitterness. While Tisza and even Franz Ferdinand talked of the need for improved ties with the eastern empire, the openings did not appear. And by late June 1914 what especially worried Berchtold were reports of Russian success in wooing Rumania away from its long, if covert, ties with the Triple Alliance. Still, more disturbing, Tsar Nicholas had visited Rumania earlier in the month and more unforgivable, Foreign Minister Serge Sazonov had actually crossed into the contested land of Transylvania held by Budapest. This was a deliberate provocation, as were the Russian propaganda activities among the monarchy's restive

Ruthenian population. For all of his experience in St. Petersburg, Berchtold was unable to blunt the ceaseless Russian pressure.[20]

Paradoxically, in the western Balkans, relations with Serbia were almost quiescent, in part thanks to the political upheaval in Belgrade pitting the army against the civilian leadership. The main issues with Serbia centered on a possible trade of spies, on resolving the question of damages suffered by the Oriental Railway Company during the Balkan wars, and on loose talk of a possible fusion of Montenegro and Serbia. Far more worrisome was the mounting struggle with erstwhile ally Italy for control and/or influence in the newly created Albanian state; friends could be even more trouble than enemies.[21]

That same perspective about troublesome allies certainly influenced Berchtold's analysis of Vienna's relations with its most important ally: Germany.[22] While the generals in both countries might glibly do what generals do—talk of war—the relationship had a series of problems. Throughout the Balkan crises of 1912 and 1913, Berlin had blown hot, usually Kaiser Wilhelm II in bellicose terms of supporting Vienna, and cold, usually Chancellor Theobald von Bethmann Hollweg urging caution and restraint. Each time Vienna wanted to be decisive, Berlin had objected and Vienna had demurred. In the October 1913 showdown with Serbia over Albania's territorial frontier, Berchtold had more or less presented the Germans with a *fait accompli.* Adding further uncertainty was Berlin's resolute failure to take the Serbian threat to Austria-Hungary seriously and Wilhelm's refusal to accept that Rumania was drifting away from the Triple Alliance. Even face-to-face conversations, such as those in late March 1914 with the German ruler, had little impact.[23]

Within this overall political framework, Berchtold that Sunday morning could also reflect on a new Ballhausplatz policy memorandum completed just four days earlier.[24] This lengthy assessment of the monarchy's foreign policy advocated a new strategic approach to the Balkans: the diplomatic containment of Serbia by a revival of the Rumanian alignment and a new agreement with Bulgaria. This assertive policy would seek to create a new balance of power in the Balkans and indirectly check Russia's ability to manipulate the situation. To succeed, the policy would require German cooperation and possibly financial inducements to Bulgaria. These proposals embodied a new militancy and aggressiveness to regain control of the situation, an assertiveness not seen in years from Vienna. If successfully implemented, Berchtold could reasonably believe the monarchy might move from its current defensive posture to one that regained control of the Balkan situation. And he could hope the new moves would convince doubters in Berlin and Budapest that the venerable monarchy remained a major power.[25]

Hours later came the news from Sarajevo. Almost immediately, Berchtold's staff asked him by a telegram at 3:30 p.m. to return to Vienna; he took a train at Ungarisch-Hradisch near Buchlau, reaching Vienna at 9:32.[26] All of the earlier certainties were suddenly suspect.

Berchtold Seeks to Gain Control of Habsburg Foreign Policy

On the train ride back to Vienna, Berchtold surely reflected upon his abrupt change of fortune. Personal grief, worries about the monarchy's future (Archduke Karl, the new heir, was not impressive), concern for the dead couple's children, anger at the terrorists, genuine concern for the old emperor, and worry about the monarchy's future were certainly some of his thoughts.[27] He now faced a major decision: whether to engage in more militant diplomacy with Serbia or simply go to war with the neighboring kingdom? After all, twice during the crises of May and October 1913 he had been ready to accept actual combat. Thus, despite the assessment by Albertini and others that Berchtold would be captured in July 1914 by the "war party," the foreign minister entered the crisis in a less tolerant, less patient mood. Earlier he had threatened war and first the Montenegrins and then the Serbs had capitulated. But what had those diplomatic victories brought? Threats had not prevented the terrorism; was it now time for war? This option he could no longer evade.

The enormity of the murders would not have escaped the minister. Rulers had been assassinated before, including Tsar Alexander II in 1881 in Russia. But this was the first time that terrorists had moved across state borders to murder a leading figure in another country.[28] From the start, evidence linked some of the assassins with individuals employed by the Serbian government. And now historians recognize that the senior leadership in Belgrade, including Prime Minister Nikola Pašić, were aware of a conspiracy and even tried to block it.[29] Berchtold, not unlike American leaders after 9/11, could believe he would have support from other European governments for action against Serbia if he could show that the murderers were linked to Serbia. Dynastic interests alone, he could believe, would make the difference.

Berchtold also realized that the archduke's death dramatically altered the decision matrix for him. In the months since 1912 Franz Ferdinand had been a force for peace and restraint, a person with whom the minister had to reckon but who could also be an ally for peace. Now the archduke's murder became the possible occasion for a war the archduke had so greatly feared. If the victim at Sarajevo had been General Oskar Potiorek, the Governor General of Bosnia-Herzegovina who was also in the car, the odds of a war with Serbia would have been greatly reduced. But that was not the situation, and Berchtold immediately grasped that.

In the past war-peace crises, Berchtold had had to consider three independent variables: the views of Franz Joseph and Franz Ferdinand, those of his fellow ministers, including the generals and Tisza in October 1913, and those of the ruling elite in Berlin. Those variables would be minus the archduke in 1914. But now there was a fourth, new, unprecedented variable: alarming reports of unrest in Bosnia and Herzegovina generated by the murders and by assertions, exaggerated to be sure, that the monarchy's control of the two provinces was severely threatened. The seamless web of the monarchy's external and internal problems once more came to the fore.[30]

Dinnertime: Tuesday, 30 June 1914

By late afternoon on Tuesday, 30 June, Count Berchtold had concluded that war with Serbia had become a political necessity. In the first hours after returning to Vienna on Sunday the minister appears to have been careful not to commit himself, though others were pressing for immediate war with Serbia. And when Berchtold saw Conrad late on 29 June, the general just back from the Bosnian maneuvers, he heard the familiar refrain: "*Krieg, Krieg, Krieg.*" The minister at this point told the military commander that he had to meet with Kaiser Wilhelm when he arrived for Franz Ferdinand's funeral and to see what the German reaction would be; then they would decide.[31]

Just after noon on Tuesday, 30 June, Berchtold saw a shaken, worried Franz Joseph at Schönbrunn where they met for an hour and discussed the dangers of passivity. In his memorandum notes, Berchtold says he told the emperor of his fear of the consequences of further inaction. If reports linked Belgrade with Sarajevo, then an "action program" would be necessary.[32]

Later that afternoon, the foreign minister saw Tisza, who had earlier seen the emperor. Indeed, Franz Joseph appears to have conveyed to the Magyar leader an impression that Berchtold was determined to settle accounts with Serbia. From the start of their discussion Tisza, while agreeing about the dangers of inaction, pressed for a more resolute diplomatic approach, a strategy that Berchtold resisted as taking too long and with scant prospects of success. This meeting so disturbed Tisza that the next day, back in Budapest, he wrote Franz Joseph and expressed grave doubts about using the Sarajevo events "as the occasion for a reckoning with Serbia." He wanted more proof of Belgrade's role and assurances from Kaiser Wilhelm of German support for the monarchy's Balkan plans. Given these differences, Berchtold immediately realized that he and the Magyar leader were in a struggle to shape the direction of Habsburg policy. The other members of the Common Ministerial Council and, of course, the military were for a "reckoning," and as soon as possible. The bureaucratic struggle between Berchtold and Tisza would continue for another two weeks, with Berchtold the ultimate victor.[33]

In any event, by late afternoon on 30 June Berchtold had committed himself to a belligerent approach. A steady stream of reports from Sarajevo and Belgrade also buttressed his conviction of the need to act, as did the views of his own subordinates.[34] And his decision was his decision, not forced by the Germans or by a war party. It did not take the famous conversation of Viktor Naumann of 1 July with Berchtold's *chef de cabinet*, Alexander Hoyos, to prod the Habsburg minister to action; he was already there. Indeed, German ambassador Heinrich Tschirschky's own celebrated dispatch of 30 June reported that "even … serious people" were glad that "at last a final and fundamental reckoning should be had with the Serbs."[35]

On 1 July Conrad once more saw Berchtold, again pressing for action. This time he found the minister ready to agree and that he believed the emperor shared this view. But Berchtold wanted, as did others, he told Conrad, to have the results of the investigation in hand before moving against Serbia. Still, Berchtold was convinced that this information would justify a war with Serbia.[36]

On Thursday, 2 July, Berchtold once more saw Franz Joseph. Again they reviewed the situation; the old emperor again wanted more proof of links to Belgrade and assurances of German support. But even with these caveats, the veteran ruler was prepared for action. Still, Berchtold knew that he must have clear evidence of German support. For this purpose the 24 June memorandum was edited to give it a sharper focus; at the same time they drafted a personal letter from the emperor to the Kaiser. It was planned to give both to the German monarch when he arrived for the funeral of Franz Ferdinand. But their plans were interrupted when security concerns in Berlin about Wilhelm's safety in Vienna led to a cancellation of his trip. Now Berchtold had to move quickly to catch Wilhelm before he left on his annual North Sea cruise, all the more since Ambassador Tschirschky on 2 July, while expressing general support for the Habsburg position, had observed that Vienna had never presented Berlin with a definite plan of action.[37]

Berchtold read his cues well. He knew he needed evidence of German support to gain the emperor's approval. With German backing he could hope to convince Tisza as well. Thus he quickly decided to send his earlier, now revised memorandum calling for action and a personal letter from Franz Joseph to Berlin, along with an oral explanation of Vienna's intentions. Almost certainly with deliberate guile, he sent Tisza the proposed materials going to Berlin so late to prevent him from making changes in the text before Hoyos actually left on the overnight train to Berlin on Saturday, 4 July. And, as Berchtold had anticipated, Tisza did want to soften the tone of the emperor's letter, but it was too late. [38]

In arranging the approach to Berlin Berchtold took two interesting precautions in addition to outmaneuvering Tisza: he ordered Ambassador Ladislaus Szögyény to give both items personally to Wilhelm II, and he wanted the ambassador to see Chancellor Bethmann Hollweg in person. Having had ample experience of the Kaiser's expansive promises and their reversal or softening by the German chancellor, Berchtold wanted clear assurances of actual German support from the two key principals in Berlin.[39]

The celebrated "Hoyos Mission" achieved its desired goal.[40] Wilhelm II pledged his support to the Habsburg ambassador on Sunday afternoon, 5 July, while fully recognizing some of the dangers posed by Russia. Late that day he discussed this pledge with Bethmann and some of his senior military officers. The first news of the Kaiser's support reached Vienna at 10 p.m. that Sunday night. The key sentence read: "but if we had really recognised the necessity of warlike action against Serbia, he (Kaiser Wilhelm) would regret if we did not make use of the present moment, which is all in our favour."[41]

The next day Szögyény and Hoyos met with Bethmann and Arthur Zimmermann, Undersecretary at the Foreign Ministry. Once again the Germans pledged support (if in their own documents there were doubts Vienna would actually act). The key sentence in the Szögyény telegram that reached Vienna at 8 p.m. that night read: "I ascertained that the Imperial Chancellor like his Imperial master considers immediate action on our part as the best solution of our difficulties in the Balkans."[42]

With these telegrams, Berchtold had received the "blank check" of German support. When he returned early Monday morning to Vienna after a brief weekend respite at Buchlau, the foreign minister met with Franz Joseph for forty minutes, letting him know of the German support and winning his agreement for strong action. Later at noon Berchtold met with Conrad and Count Johann Forgách, the second section chief in the Foreign Ministry. In one of the few surviving fragments of his July diary, the minister wrote: "Spoke about eventual action against Serbia on the basis of the telegrams received from Szögyény about yesterday's conversation with Kaiser Wilhelm. 4 p.m. Saw Tschirschky." Conrad concluded, with assurances of German support in hand, that war would come. But at this meeting, when pressed on what the army planned to do and when, Conrad became evasive, perhaps because he knew that much of his army was scattered across the monarchy on "harvest leave." There could be no question of an immediate surprise attack; nothing could happen before 21 or 22 July at the earliest, when the troops had returned to their duty stations. Curiously, but typical of the entire slide to war, there was no discussion of what Russia might do. Finally, though Berchtold now had German backing, he still needed more proof linking Belgrade to the crime and he needed to sideline Tisza. Initially, Berchtold hoped German support would convince the Magyar leader, thus he telegraphed him at noon on 6 July with Wilhelm's view: "We should not leave the present favorable moment unused. Russia is not ready to fight and Germany stands in total alliance loyalty on our side."[43]

But despite the German pledge of support, Berchtold soon discovered on 7 July that it was not enough to convince Tisza. To buttress his efforts, the minister had invited German Ambassador Tschirschky to a private briefing of Tisza and Karl Stürgkh, the Austrian premier, about the German position. But Berchtold's efforts got off to a terrible start when the Hungarian leader learned that Hoyos had discussed a possible partition of Serbia while in Berlin. Tisza was so angry that Berchtold had to force Hoyos to say that it was only his private opinion. Things went just slightly better in the actual meeting of the Common Ministerial Council.[44]

Berchtold, even after the lengthy meeting of the Council, still had not convinced the Magyar of the need for an ultimatum that virtually assured war. Berchtold, at the very opening of the meeting, had put the question squarely: "whether the moment has not come when a show of force might put an end to Serbia's intrigues once and for all." Further, Berlin had promised support "in the eventuality of a warlike complication with Serbia." While Berchtold noted the problem of Russia, he did not believe it would intervene. For his part, the Hungarian leader asked repeatedly: What would war achieve? He wanted no surprise attack and only diplomatic pressure at first, though he did agree that there would be no attempt to use mobilization as a diplomatic weapon as had been the case during the Balkan wars. The only glimmer of concession came when Tisza said that if war came, no territory could be added to the monarchy. While there were discussions of security measures in the two provinces of Bosnia-

Herzegovina, no martial law, as Potiorek preferred, was declared. Still, after the briefings by Conrad and Admiral Karl Kailer, few could doubt that war was not far off. In fact, the final sentences of the minutes said bluntly: "still an agreement had been arrived at, since the propositions of the Hungarian Premier would in all probability lead to a war with Serbia, the necessity of which he and all the other members of the Council had understood and admitted." Nevertheless, Tisza still objected and his objections would carry weight. Berchtold had to overcome the Magyar's resistance if he wanted his sovereign to agree as well.[45]

Indeed, after the meeting Berchtold sent Franz Joseph a telegram that outlined Tisza's position and reported that the rest of the ministers wanted to use the opportunity for "warlike action against Serbia." Such action would deal with the Serbian problem while also protecting the monarchy's control in the two provinces. He had desired, he told his ruler, to come immediately to see him at Bad Ischl but would wait so that he could bring a memorandum from Tisza. Meanwhile, the Foreign Ministry began discussion of possible demands on Serbia while German hints of the need for action were quickly sent to Budapest. Meanwhile, Tisza drafted a letter that once more argued for diplomacy and no certainty of war; German considerations, he wrote, should not dictate Habsburg policy. Berchtold took this memorandum with him when he traveled overnight to Bad Ischl late on Wednesday night, 8 July.[46]

The minister arrived at the emperor's favorite resort at 7 a.m. on Thursday morning in a driving rain. Later in the morning he met with Franz Joseph for more than an hour. Once again Berchtold's brief diary entry captures it well: "I read the Tisza memorandum to the emperor. I pleaded for conditions that would humiliate Serbia and create practical control for us [over Serbia.] The emperor approved. He was concerned that a weak stance would discredit our standing with Germany." Still, the old monarch wanted proof of Serbia's involvement in the murders and pressed Berchtold to bridge the differences with Tisza.[47]

Over the next five days, from 9 to 14 July, Berchtold supervised the preparatory steps to war. A Foreign Ministry official, Friedrich Wiesner, was sent to Sarajevo to gather more evidence linking the conspiracy to Belgrade. Steps were taken to control press comments. Alexander Musulin started the first drafts of the eventual ultimatum.[48] At the same time, Berchtold fended off repeated German queries of when would something happen, answering in ten days or so and citing the need to gather more evidence of the crime. He did not reveal that Conrad's "harvest leave" policy had made immediate mobilization impossible.[49]

Simultaneous with these efforts Berchtold got Tisza's ally, Burián, to travel to Bad Ischl to judge for himself the attitude of the emperor/king. The former common finance minister left the resort on 12 July confident that Franz Joseph wanted action. Two days later, on 14 July, Tisza reversed course and agreed to war against Serbia. Why he altered his stance remains less clear. Almost certainly Franz Joseph's views had some sway as did assurances that the Habsburg army could protect Transylvania from any possible Rumanian attack. In addition, Berlin's strong support must have had some influence, as did the argument that an unchastened Serbia might turn its attention to Hungary or help Rumania against Hungary. In any event, Tisza agreed to hard demands, a forty-eight hour term limit, and possible action no later than 25 July.[50]

With Tisza's *volte-face* Berchtold had secured two of his necessary conditions for war: German support and Hungarian agreement. And, of course, he also believed he had Franz Joseph's sanction as well. At the same time, reports from the two provinces left few doubts that domestic unrest in Bosnia and Herzegovina remained a threat to Habsburg rule. At the end of Tuesday, 14 July, Berchtold had secured full control of Habsburg foreign policy. Now the next, most dangerous steps were on the horizon; soon blissful assumptions would be transformed into deadly reality.[51]

Days to War

Nine days passed between Tisza's agreement to confront Serbia with hard demands (and probably war) and the actual delivery of the ultimatum. This nine-day hiatus, coupled with a week to convince Tisza, meant that memories of the Sarajevo murders were fading. It also meant that Europe had to be deceived about future Habsburg intentions, even as the danger of leakage increased. Nor could Berchtold ignore the fact that French leaders President Raymond Poincaré and Premier René Viviani would soon be in St. Petersburg on a long-planned state visit, a not happy coincidence given Poincaré's strident anti-German views. Moreover, the continual delays worried German officials at the Wilhelmstrasse. Not surprisingly, Berlin feared the delay endangered the chances for a local war; the delay also gave the Russians more time to plan a response. Still, Berchtold continued to assure Berlin that the ultimatum would soon be finished. Finally, on 15 July he told Tschirschky that the delivery would come on 25 July, obviously adjusted later.[52]

Later, historians would use the inquiries from Berlin as further evidence of Germany pushing the Habsburgs to war. For them, Berchtold was a mere pliant minister who had to be urged on to war. The evidence strongly suggests otherwise. Berchtold reached his own decision for war by 30 June and no German pressure was needed. But from the start he knew he could not proceed without clear evidence that Berlin would back Vienna and act, it was hoped, as an effective deterrent against Russia. He preferred, as did the German ally, quick action: that had proved impossible. But he needed no German pressure; he only needed time. Later, when the German Kaiser got "cold feet," Berchtold had no hesitance in accelerating the declaration of war to present a "*fait accompli*" to his ally. Moreover, he repeatedly rebuffed all German pressures after 20 July to reach a deal with Italy and thus bring the "allied enemy" into the fray. Berchtold kept control of his policy, even as some of its assumptions by late July were thoroughly suspect.[53]

By mid-July the Habsburg foreign minister had another reason for caution vis-à-vis Berlin. On 16 July he learned for certain that the German Foreign Office had informed its ambassador to Italy, Hans von Flotow, of Vienna's intentions. Flotow, who was at an Italian spa, then told Italian Foreign Minister Antonino San Giuliano of Vienna's plans. The Italian wasted no time in telegraphing this intelligence to his envoys in Belgrade, St. Petersburg, and even Vienna where the ciphers had been quickly broken. Berchtold concluded (correctly) that St. Petersburg knew of his intentions and possibly even Belgrade. Henceforth a virtual wall of silence descended upon Austro-German communications, even to the point of refusing to give Berlin a copy of the ultimatum until almost the eve of its delivery. Berchtold would thwart, if at all possible, further indiscretions from Berlin.[54]

On Sunday, 19 July, now three weeks after Sarajevo, the Common Ministerial Council met incognito at Berchtold's private residence in Vienna. Once more the ministers reviewed the ultimatum and some of the supporting documentation that accused low-ranking Serbian officials of complicity in the murder. Berchtold told the group that the ultimatum would be handed over at 5 p.m. on 23 July. General Conrad gave some information on his war plans, though he focused his chief attention on mobilization details and not the larger question of what Russia might do. Not surprisingly, there were no references about German pressure to act; this was a Habsburg decision, pure and simple. The main topic in fact centered on Tisza's persistent demand that the monarchy agree to take no territory from Serbia save possibly a few border modifications. The ministers agreed to his demand, though probably few thought the condition would be honored—certainly not Conrad. Later that afternoon, Berchtold went to the residence of British ambassador Maurice de Bunsen where, as Berta noted in her diary, he was as secretive "as always."[55]

Two days later, on Tuesday, 21 July, after another overnight trip from Vienna, Berchtold and Hoyos met with Franz Joseph at Bad Ischl at 9 a.m. With bright sunshine streaming outside his modest villa, the monarch reviewed the demands of the forty-eight hour ultimatum, some of which he thought were "very sharp" though the document remained intact. After lunch with the eighty-one-year-old ruler, the two officials traveled back to Vienna. Late that same evening, Vienna transmitted the terms of the ultimatum to its German ally; the Italians got no such extra notice.[56]

Even as the ultimatum was delivered, officials in Vienna continued a last-minute effort to complete the dossier against Serbia. They wanted to buttress the demands contained in the harsh ultimatum; that effort would fail. News of the severe demands shocked most across the continent and in Britain. The long delay since Sarajevo now hurt, nowhere more so than Russia, where some preliminary steps toward mobilization began on the afternoon of 24 July. And Serbia began mobilizing on the same date, not waiting for the ultimatum to expire with full mobilization on 25 July.[57]

As Serbia began to mobilize, the foreign minister was once again on his way to Bad Ischl, ordered by Franz Joseph to be there by Sunday, 26 July; instead he came on the Saturday. En route that Saturday at Lambach, Berchtold was handed a Russian plea to extend the deadline for a Serbian response; he refused.[58]

When Berchtold arrived at Bad Ischl, there was no news from Belgrade and the monarch was preoccupied and uneasy. The minister went for a walk, only to be summoned from the Hotel Bauer just after 6 p.m. with news that Giesl had rejected the Serbian response as inadequate and had left Belgrade. The foreign minister hurried back to Franz Joseph's villa, now finding him calm and displaying a strong military posture. While the two turned aside Tisza's hurried request for immediate mobilization, the emperor did sign the order to mobilize troops for action against Serbia, the first day to begin on 28 July.[59]

Berchtold and his colleagues now confronted two interlocking issues: when to declare war on Serbia and how to assess the situation with Russia? The mobilization orders and a proclamation from the emperor went out on 26 July. Over the next two days the mobilization preparations proceeded without many delays.[60] Berchtold's decision on the declaration of war showed the true steel of intent that he pursued throughout the crisis. By 26 July he recognized that the leadership in Berlin had once more begun to have reservations, almost certainly because it appeared that Russia and now Britain might not stand aside. Indeed, over the next two days and later Berchtold received information that suggested a German hesitancy to move forward, yet there were no formal demands to stop though Berlin's proposal for a "Halt in Belgrade" came close.[61] For his part, Conrad wanted to mobilize first and then declare war later. Berchtold profoundly disagreed with the general on 26 July, correctly assessing that any delay would lead to more German reflection and also strong pressure from Sir Edward Grey to accept an European conference, a proposal he had no intention of accepting. Indeed, Hoyos wrote Baron Franz Schiessl von Perstoff, the emperor's senior cabinet secretary, on 26 July that Berchtold wanted the war declared on Tuesday, 28 July, "to prevent a possible intervention of a third power or an incident that would cause postponement."[62]

Finally, the next day, 27 July, Conrad relented as Berchtold and Hoyos pressed anew for a declaration of war to prevent foreign interference with Habsburg plans. Berchtold apparently still hoped that the clear, limited war against Serbia might deter the Triple Entente from intervention, an illusion not reality. On 28 July, Emperor/King Franz Joseph, at his desk in Bad Ischl signed, not without misgivings, the declaration of war against Serbia. Later that evening shots were fired between Serbian and Habsburg troops near Belgrade. The war had started.[63]

After the Great War, critics accused Berchtold of pressing the old emperor to war or even deceiving him. As evidence, they often cited Berchtold's inclusion in a letter of 27 July to Franz Joseph of an erroneous report about Serbian troops firing on Habsburg soldiers near Temes-Kubin. They viewed this as an attempt to rush the monarch's decision. Yet as Rauchensteiner has conclusively shown, the foreign minister on learning that the report was erroneous had immediately informed the emperor that he was mistaken and deleted any reference to the incident from the actual war declaration. Despite the harsh evaluations of Berchtold, most contemporary witnesses suggest that the monarch and the minister, though not happy with the prospect of war, saw it as the only way to resolve the Serbian issue.[64]

With the declaration of war against Serbia, few chances for peace remained. To be sure, delays between mobilization and actual, sustained fighting offered a chance for mediation which is exactly what Berchtold feared. But the military exchanges on the night of 28-29 July effectively closed that window, since exaggerated reports of the skirmish soon reached St. Petersburg. This news immediately influenced the Russian decision for general mobilization on 30 July, a move that effectively closed off all chances for a local war as St. Petersburg moved to protect its Serbian client.

During the last chaotic week of July 1914, Berchtold had, at least theoretically, three chances to change his mind and block the momentum to war. The best chance came on 25 July when he was at Bad Ischl. The emperor's obvious discomfort with the Serbian rejection of the ultimatum offered a chance for Berchtold to ask for a reconsideration of their proposed actions. Almost certainly had he told the monarch that they needed to wait and see what the Russians would do, Franz Joseph would have agreed, though Conrad would have been almost hysterical and the newly converted Tisza difficult to handle. Still, the emperor's confidence in Berchtold would have kept the foreign minister in charge. But, of course, Berchtold did not change his mind, nor did he ask his sovereign to reconsider.

A less likely chance to reconsider came on 27 July as numerous reports were now reaching Vienna about Russian actions that suggested a pending Russian mobilization. But again, rather than reconsider basic premises and especially Russia's position, the minister plunged ahead. After the war he suggested to historian Bernadotte Schmitt that had Sir Edward Grey appealed directly to him instead of via Berlin, there might have been a chance for further negotiation at this point. But by treating Austria-Hungary as a satellite of Germany, Grey had centered all his attention on Berlin and wasted valuable time. And, in any event, by 28 July, Berchtold wanted a war declared to thwart just this kind of intrusion.[65]

A third, possibly final chance to reverse course came on Thursday, 30 July, when Bethmann proposed that Habsburg forces "Halt in Belgrade." This proposal, which confirmed anew the changing views in Berlin, got only modest consideration from Berchtold. Neither he nor the emperor would stop the mobilization against Serbia, but they would pledge no action against Russia and repeated that the monarchy would take no Serbian territory. For his part Conrad had no plans for such a logical move as occupying Belgrade, even though the Serbian capital was just across from Habsburg territory and had by this date been evacuated by the Serbian government. The general wanted a war of annihilation and glory, not a chess board game move that would have put the monarchy in a strong diplomatic position. So Berchtold brushed the German proposal aside and in any case Russia's general mobilization that same day must have always rendered it a "will of the wisp" possibility.

Still, Berchtold, Conrad, and Krobatin met with Franz Joseph that day to reconsider the situation; when it was over, Conrad noted: "The war with Serbia would continue; the English proposals would receive an obliging answer without taking any position; general mobilization would be ordered on 1 August with the 4th of August the first day." The next day, Friday, 31 July, when the Common Ministerial Council met once more on the eve of general war, there was no longer talk of possible peace but only of war.

Berchtold, the man who could have prevented the war, became the man who made it possible.[66]

Why War?

What led Berchtold, the emperor, the other ministers, and eventually even Tisza, to agree to go to war with Serbia? For nearly a century, historians have returned to this central question, hoping to find reliable, thoughtful documentation to answer it. Instead, historians have found contradictory information, fragmentary detail, and vague, almost fantasy discussions of what the war would achieve. Now, several generations later and after Vietnam and two Iraq wars, historians are perhaps less surprised to see how vague, almost negligible such discussions can be at the highest levels of government. The pressures to reach a decision often pre-empt any attempt to reflect more carefully on the consequences. And, as political scientists tell us repeatedly, the 1914 situation, with its time-bound character and need to act before the anger over the assassinations waned, left a very narrow time frame for serious considerations of "what if" the assumptions were wrong. [67]

Yet some answers to this question and to Berchtold's role are possible. A successful, cross border terrorist attack with murders did challenge the dynastic system. Evidence linking these acts to Belgrade, while not wholly conclusive at the time, required a forceful Habsburg response if Austria-Hungary wanted to retains its status as a great power. If none of the Habsburg leaders would have used the words "The Sick Man of Europe," the thought of being the new Ottoman Empire was never far distant. Each time Vienna had sought to reach a deal with the Serbian government—in 1909 and again repeatedly in 1913 during the Balkan wars—it received promises of respect for certain understandings only to see Belgrade immediately renege. The steady stream vituperation from the Belgrade press never seemed to ease, or efforts by such groups as the *Narodna Odbrana* to stir discontent among the South Slavs wane. Vienna and Budapest believed the monarchy was under siege, ceaselessly plummeted with challenges from Belgrade. Patience was now in short supply. A "regime change" in Belgrade, to use a more contemporary term, with the ouster of the Karadjordević dynasty would be a start.[68]

Nor could Berchtold ignore the domestic political import of the murders on the monarchy's position in the Balkans. For decades Habsburg foreign ministers had warned about the South Slav threat, a threat that posed a constant challenge to its imperial control of Bosnia and Herzegovina. The Serbian acts put the challenge front and center, but so also did the unrest that had spread across the provinces in the wake of the Sarajevo shootings. Even allowing for General Potiorek's self-interest in inflammatory reports, the murders and the unrest provided visible reminders of the dangers of inaction. For months Berchtold had heard Conrad complain about the failure to settle with Serbia in 1909 when the chances of a Habsburg victory had been almost assured. Now, in 1914, he agreed with Conrad on the need to act, but now the chances were, as the general realistically admitted, like betting the bank; and so it would be.

Tisza had secured a pledge of no Serbian territory after victory. But in fact officials at the Ballhausplatz wasted little in starting to think aggressively and expansively about new territorial arrangements. For sure, the monarchy wanted to control the Mount Lovcen height that dominated the Bay of Kotor, for another some way geographically to prevent any possible union between a "rump" Serbia and Montenegro. Nor would the diplomats be timid about rewarding Bulgaria and Romania with slices of Serbia for their neutrality and possible military assistance.[69]

In late June, before Sarajevo, Berchtold and his colleagues were considering a new policy to isolate troublesome Serbia; a war would make this happen even sooner. And there might be other advantages as well: an economic Anschluss with Serbia and a predominant position in the western Balkans would help check their ever-troublesome Italian ally. In the future Vienna, not St. Petersburg, would become the pivot point for the western Balkans. Above all, a successful war with Serbia would bestow a renewed sense of self-confidence to the monarchy.

To achieve this welter of goals required military success against Serbia and non-intervention from Russia. Berchtold believed both of these assumptions were realistic. But he, and his advisers, never deceived themselves entirely; they knew there was always the risk of a more general war. With the strong and open German pledge of support, Berchtold hoped St. Petersburg would set more store with the principle of dynastic solidarity than the actions of a group of Serbian regicides. This assumption rapidly vanished in the last days of July; still, Berchtold was willing to run the risk.

Perhaps Berchtold really believed General Conrad and his confident, bellicose militarism.[70] Though he did not know of Conrad's own pessimistic calculations at mid-point in the crisis, neither the foreign minister nor his ministerial colleagues ever critiqued the general's bland assurances. Even the ever-difficult Tisza did not force a more significant explanation of the plans once he had Conrad's assurances about the defense of Transylvania. In his failure to press Conrad, Berchtold merely joined the ranks of the other civilian ministers in Europe that July 1914 (President Poincaré was the rare exception) in their failure to examine the respective war plans of their military and naval staffs. For his part, Leopold Count Berchtold accepted the general's confident assessment even if by 30 July those assessments were open to serious challenge. Once mobilization started, the general had control; not even the emperor could prevent the next steps, as Kaiser Wilhelm II would also soon discover.

Berchtold opted for war because he believed the monarchy could quickly defeat Serbia, bring regime change in Belgrade, and quell the challenge to Habsburg rule in Bosnia and Herzegovina. In reaching that conclusion assurances of German support had been crucial. But Germany did not push Berchtold to war; he used Germany to get the war he believed would rescue Austria-Hungary from the Serbian menace. War would achieve what his militant diplomacy of the last eighteen months had not: security against a troublesome, intriguing Serbia. He got his war; he did not get his victory.

Notes

1. Diary entry, 19 July 1914, in Christopher H.D. Howard, "The Vienna Diary of Berta de Bunsen, 28 June-17 August 1914," *Bulletin of the Institute for Historical Research 51* (1978): 215.

2. The standard biography of Berchtold remains Hugo Hantsch, *Leopold Graf Berchtold: Grandseigneur und Staatsman*, 2 vols. (Graz: Styria, 1963); for general surveys of his foreign policy, see F.R. Bridge, *From Sadowa to Sarajevo: The Foreign Policy of Austria-Hungary, 1866-1914* (London: Routledge & Kegan Paul, 1972); his *The Habsburg Monarchy among the Great Powers, 1815-1918* (New York: Berg, 1990); and his "Österreich(-Ungarn) unter den Grossmächten," in *Die Habsburgermonarchie*, 1848-1918, vol. 4, pt. 1, *Die Habsburgermonarchie im System der Internationalen Beziehungen*, ed. Adam Wandruszka and Peter Urbanitsch (Vienna: Verlag der Österreichischen Akademie der Wissenschaften, 1989), 196-373. Also the author's *Austria-Hungary and the Origins of the First World War* (New York: St. Martin's Press, 1990), and with Russel Van Wyk, *July 1914: Soldiers, Statesmen, and the Coming of the Great War: A Brief Documentary History* (Boston: Bedford/St. Martin's Press, 2003), 42-72. Berchtold's diary (with virtually no entries for July 1914 possibly as a result of deliberate cleansing) and his carefully crafted memoir notes are in the Nachlass Berchtold, Haus-, Hof-, und Staatsarchiv, Vienna. The official documents of the Foreign Ministry for this period are in the same archive. After the war Berchtold made occasional efforts to defend his actions in July 1914. See, e.g., Berchtold's comments (probably 1919) on Roderich Gooss, *Das Wiener Kabinett und die Entstehung des Weltkrieges* (Vienna: L.W. Seidel, 1919) in the Nachlass Aehrenthal, Haus-, Hof-, und Staatsarchiv, Karton 5. I am grateful to Dr. Peter Broucek for this citation. Also see Berchtold's review of Serge Sazonov's memoirs in "Russia, Austria, and the World War," *Contemporary Review 131* (April 1928): 422-32; and his interview with Bernadotte E. Schmitt, "Interviewing the Authors of the War," (privately printed for the Chicago Literary Club, 1930), (www.chilit.org), 26-30. I am grateful to my research assistant, Tracey Omohundro, for discovering this interesting document.

3. The most recent restatement of the "Berlin pushing Vienna" thesis can be found in John C. G. Röhl, *Wilhelm II: Der Weg in den Abgrund 1900-1914* (Munich: Beck, 2008), chs. 37-41; also see the earlier work by Fritz Fischer, *War of Illusions: German Policies from 1911 to 1914*, trans. Marian Jackson (New York: W.W. Norton, 1975), chs. 19-22. The celebrated work of Luigi Albertini repeatedly made this point in *The Origins of the War of 1914*, trans. and ed. Isabella M. Massey, 3 vols. (London: Oxford University Press, 1952-57). In contrast, see Samuel R.

Williamson, Jr., "Aggressive and Defensive Aims of Political Elites: Austro-Hungary Policy in 1914," in *An Improbable War: The Outbreak of World War I and European Political Culture before 1914*, ed. Holger Afflerbach and David Stevenson (New York: Berghahn, 2007), 61-74. For a superb overall account, balanced and nuanced, see Hew Strachan, *The Outbreak of the First World War* (Oxford: Oxford University Press, 2004) which is also the first part of *The First World War*, vol. 1, *To Arms* (Oxford: Oxford University Press, 2001), 1-102. Also see David Stevenson, *Armaments and the Coming of the War: Europe 1904-1914* (Oxford: Clarendon Press, 1996), 366-421, and his *Cataclysm: The First World War as Political Tragedy* (New York: Basic Books, 2004), 3-35.

4. On Merey's views, see Fritz Fellner, "Die 'Mission Hoyos,'" in idem., *Vom Dreibund zum Völkerbund: Studien zur Geschichte der Internationalen Beziehungen, 1882-1919* (Munich: Oldenbourg, 1994), 119; the essay appeared originally in 1976. On Redlich, see Hantsch, *Leopold Graf Berchtold*, vol. 1, 249-51; on Redlich's views during the July crisis, see *Schicksalsjahre Österreichs, 1908-1919: Das politische Tagebuch Josef Redlichs*, vol. I, *1908-1914*, ed. Fritz Fellner (Graz: Verlag Hermann Böhlaus, 1953), 233-45.

5. Sidney B. Fay, *The Origins of the World War*, 2 vols. (New York: Macmillan, 1928), vol. 2, 198; Bernadotte E. Schmitt, *The Coming of the War 1914*, 2 vols. (New York: George Scribner's Sons, 1930), vol. 1, 264; Albertini, *The Origins of the War of 1914*, vol. 2, 125.

6. Hantsch, *Leopold Graf Berchtold*; John Leslie, "The Antecedents of Austria-Hungary's War Aims," in *Archiv und Forschung: Das Haus-, Hof-, und Staatsarchiv in seiner Bedeutung für die Geschichte Österreichs und Europas*, ed. Elisabeth Springer and Leopold Kammerhofer (Vienna: Verlag für Geschichte und Politik, 1993), 375-94; Manfried Rauchensteiner, *Der Tod des Doppeladlers: Österreich-Ungarn und der Erste Weltkrieg* (Graz: Styria, 1993), 63-85; Williamson, *Austria-Hungary and the Origins of the First World War*, 43-44, and ch. 10.

7. The quote is from G.P. Gooch, "Berchtold," in *Before the War: Studies in Diplomacy*, vol. 2 (London: Longmans, Green, 1938), 373. On the appointment, see Hantsch, *Leopold Graf Berchtold*, vol. 1, 247-48; also Solomon Wank, "The Appointment of Count Berchtold as Austro-Hungarian Foreign Minister," *Journal of Central European Affairs 23* (July 1963): 143-51.

8. On the Habsburg foreign policy establishment, see William D. Godsey, Jr., *Aristocratic Redoubt: The Austro-Hungarian Foreign Office on the Eve of the First World War* (West Lafayette: Purdue University Press, 1999). Also see the historical essay on the Foreign Ministry by Helmut Rumpler in *Die Habsburgermonarchie im System der Internationalen Beziehungen*, 1-121.

9. On Berchtold's early career, see Hantsch, *Leopold Graf Berchtold*, vol. 1, 1-48.

10. On his language skills, see ibid., 9-10.

11. On the relationship, Hugo Hantsch, "Erzherzog Thronfolger Franz Ferdinand und Graf Leopold Berchtold," *Historica* (Vienna, 1965), 175-98; Robert A. Kann, "Erzherzog Franz Ferdinand und Graf Berchtold als Aussenminister, 1912-1914," *Mitteilungen des Österreichischen Staatsarchivs 22* (1969): 246-78; Samuel R. Williamson, Jr., "Influence, Power, and the Policy Process: The Case of Franz Ferdinand, 1906-1914," *The Historical Journal 17* (June 1974): 417-34.

12. This assessment of Berchtold is based on a detailed study of his diary, his memoir notes, and from an analysis of his diplomatic correspondence, first when in St. Petersburg and later as foreign minister.

13. On the overall situation from Berchtold's perspective, see Rauchensteiner, *Der Tod des Doppeladlers*, 27-36; Williamson, *Austria-Hungary and the Origins of the First World War*, 164-89. On the monarchy as a whole, see Steven Beller, *Francis Joseph* (London: Longman, 1996), 200-19; Robin Okey, *The Habsburg Monarchy: From Enlightenment to Eclipse* (New York: St. Martin's Press, 2001), 369-80.

14. For example, see the diary entry for 16 February 1914 in which the emperor praised his

efforts and conferred on him the order of St. Stephen; Nachlass Berchtold, Karton 2.

15. On the visit, see Berchtold's diary entry, 14 June 1914, ibid; Hantsch, *Leopold Graf Berchtold*, vol. 2, 544-45.

16. On Tisza, see Gabor Vermes, *István Tisza: The Liberal Vision and Conservative Statecraft of A Magyar Nationalist* (New York: East European Monographs, 1985), and on Burián, the valuable diary extracts for the summer of 1914 in István Diószegi, "Aussenminister Stephan Graf Burián: Biographie und Tagebuchstelle," *Annales Universitatis Scientiarum Budapestinensis de Rolando Eötvös Nominatae, Sectio Historica 7* (Budapest, n.p., 1966): 161-208. For a view of Tisza as a foreign policy player, see "Der Dirigent: Tisza und die äussere Politik," *Graz Tagespost*, 18 Apr. 1914; a copy of this is, interestingly, in the Militärkanzlei des Generalinspektors der gesamten bewaffneten Macht [Franz Ferdinand], fasz. 198b, Österreichisches Staatsarchiv-Kriegsarchiv, Vienna (hereafter KA).

17. On Berchtold's relations with the Habsburg military, see Günther Kronenbitter, *"Krieg im Frieden": Die Führung der k.u.k. Armee und die Grossmachtpolitik Österreich-Ungarns, 1906-1914* (Munich: Oldenbourg, 2003), 369-519; also William D. Godsey, Jr., "Officers vs. Diplomats: Bureaucracy and Foreign Policy in Austria-Hungary, 1906-1914," *Mitteilungen des Österreichischen Staatsarchivs 46* (1998): 43-66.

18. On Berchtold at the Delegations in Budapest, see his diary entries from 28 April to 27 May 1914, Nachlass Berchtold, Karton 2.

19. The first volume of Solomon Wank's biography of Aehrenthal provides new insights into the elite thinking on the question of Russia in the years before the annexation crisis: *In the Twilight of Empire: Count Alois Lexa von Aehrenthal (1854-1912), Imperial Habsburg Patriot and Statesman* (Vienna: Böhlau, 2009).

20. On Tisza's irritation at the Russian actions, see Tisza to Berchtold (tel.), 14 June 1914, in *Österreich-Ungarns Aussenpolitik von der bosnischen Krise 1908 bis zum Kriegsausbruch 1914*, ed. Ludwig Bittner and Hans Uebersberger, 8 vols. (Vienna: Österreichischer Bundesverlag, 1930) [hereafter cited *ÖUA*, with volume and document number]: 8, no. 9861; see the explanation of the visit given by Ottokar Czernin, the Habsburg minister in Bucharest, on 17 June 1914, ibid., no. 9875. On the earlier tensions, Samuel R. Williamson, Jr., "Military Dimensions of Habsburg-Romanov Relations During the Era of the Balkan Wars," in *East Central European Society and the Balkan Wars*, ed. Béla K. Király and Dimitrije Djordjevic (New York: East European Monographs, 1987), 316-37. On Russian machinations among the Ruthenians, see Z.A. B. Zeman, *The Break-up of the Habsburg Empire, 1914-1918* (London: Oxford University Press, 1961), 1-35.

21. For Vienna's knowledge of the Serbian political situation, see, e.g., the report from Minister Wladimir Giesl to Berchtold, 12 June 1914, *ÖUA*, 8, no. 9844. Also Barbara Jelavich, "What the Habsburg Government Knew about the Black Hand," *Austrian History Yearbook 22* (1991): 131-50.

22. On the overall issue of Austro-German relations, see Jürgen Angelow, *Kalkül und Prestige: Der Zweibund am Vorabend des Ersten Weltkrieges* (Cologne: Böhlau, 2000) and on the larger alliance, Holger Afflerbach, *Der Dreibund: Europäische Grosssmacht- und Allianzpolitik vor dem Ersten Weltkrieg* (Vienna: Böhlau, 2002). For the problems of alliance relationships, see Patricia A. Weitsman, *Dangerous Alliances: Proponents of Peace, Weapons of War* (Stanford: Stanford University Press, 2004).

23. Berchtold's diary entries recount his conversation with Kaiser Wilhelm and his subsequent briefing of Franz Joseph on 26 March 1914, Nachlass Berchtold, Karton 2; also the entry for 16 May 1914 when Berchtold complained that Habsburg ambassador to Berlin, Ladislaus Szögyény-Marich, had been unable to convince Berlin of the threat from Serbia, ibid. Also Berchtold to Szögyény, 16 May 1914, *ÖUA*, 8, no. 9674. See Röhl, *Wilhelm II*, 1038-66, for the

German perspective.

24. Hantsch, *Leopold Graf Berchtold*, vol. 2, 545-51. Berchtold had been thinking about these issues since the summer of 1913; see Erlass nach Berlin, 1 August 1913, *ÖUA*, 7, no. 8157. Tisza had also peppered him with suggestions; e.g., his memorandum, 15 March 1914, that stressed a coordinated German-Habsburg effort in the Balkans, ibid., no. 9482. Also see the insightful memos from Ludwig von Flotow, a senior Ballhausplatz official, May 1914, ibid., 8, no. 9627, and Count Heinrich Apponyi, a Habsburg attaché in Berlin and great friend of Wilhelm II, dated May 1914, in the Politisches Archiv, Haus-, Hof-, und Staatsarchiv, Vienna, PA I/582 [hereafter PA].

25. The original memorandum was drafted by Baron Franz Matscheko and edited by Count Johann Forgách by 24 June 1914; Matscheko and Berchtold then re-edited it before 28 June. The document would be edited again, altered slightly, and then sent with Count Alex Hoyos to Berlin on 4 July. The first draft is in *ÖUA*, 8, no. 9918; the revised is no. 9984. For a very useful summary of the history of the document and the changes made before its dispatch to Berlin, see H. Bertil A. Petersson, "Das österreichisch-ungarische Memorandum an Deutschland vom 5. Juli 1914," *Scandia 30* (1964): 138-90.

26. Franz Kinsky to Berchtold (tel.), 28 June 1914, PA I/810/(82).

27. Berchtold wrote a brief memoir account of the fallen archduke; see Hantsch, *Leopold Graf Berchtold*, vol. 2, 552-56.

28. For a somewhat sympathetic view of the murders, see Vladimir Dedijer, *The Road to Sarajevo* (New York: Simon and Schuster, 1966). See also David James Smith, *One Morning in Sarajevo 28 June 1914* (London: Weidenfeld & Nicolson, 2008).

29. On this see Mark Cornwall, "Serbia," in *Decisions for War 1914*, ed. Keith Wilson (New York: St. Martin's Press, 1995), 55-96; David MacKenzie, *Apis, the Congenial Conspirator: The Life of Colonel Dragutin T. Dimitrijevic* (Boulder: East European Monographs, 1989); and Williamson and Van Wyk, *July 1914*, 15-42.

30. See the analysis in Kronenbitter, "*Krieg im Frieden*", 462-74; Rudolf Jerábek, *Potiorek: General im Schatten von Sarajevo* (Graz: Styria, 1991), 88-96. On the unrest in Bosnia-Herzegovina, see Potiorek to Krobatin, 29 June and 2 July (tels.) 1914, *ÖUA*, 8, nos. 9948, 9993; Potiorek to Leon von Biliński (the Common Finance Minister in charge of the two provinces), 30 June and July 3 (tels.), ibid., nos. 9961, 9974, 9993, 10020-21, 10025. Potiorek had come to detest Biliński; see Conrad to Berchtold, 7 July 1914, ibid., no. 10113.

31. For Conrad's account of the conversation, see Franz Conrad von Hötzendorf, *Aus meiner Dienstzeit, 1906-1918*, vol. 4 (Vienna: Rikola, 1923) [hereafter, Conrad, *AMD*], 30-32; also see Conrad to Berchtold, 30 June 1914, PA XL, 188; Hantsch, *Leopold Graf Berchtold*, vol. 2, 557-58. War Minister Krobatin also pressed the military solution when he met with the foreign minister on 30 June 1914. In addition, Berchtold was soon receiving a steady stream of reports from Belgrade on the belligerent, almost joyful attitude of the Serbian press about the assassinations; Wilhelm von Storck to Berchtold, 29 June (tel.), 1 July (tel.) 1914, *ÖUA*, nos. 9941 and 9963.

32. Hantsch, *Leopold Graf Berchtold*, vol. 2, 558-60, based on the memoir accounts.

33. Ibid., 560-61; Tisza to Franz Joseph, 1 July 1914, *ÖUA*, no. 9978. For insights into Tisza's concerns during the July crisis, see the correspondence in *Count Stephan Tisza: Prime Minister of Hungary: Letters* (1914-1916), trans. Carvel de Bussy (New York: Peter Lang, 1991), 1-16. On Vienna's early knowledge of the investigation into the plot, Potiorek to Biliński, 2, 3, and 5 July (tels.) 1914, *ÖUA*, 8, nos. 9991-92, 10023, 10066-68.

34. Potiorek, sensitive to the security failures in Sarajevo, sent copious and numerous memoranda on the volatile situation in Sarajevo and by implication throughout Bosnia and Herzegovina and

with any tidbit that linked the assassins to Belgrade; see, e.g., Potiorek to Krobatin, 29 June (tel.) 1914, ibid., no. 9948; Potiorek to Biliński, 30 June (tel.) and 3 July 1914, ibid., nos. 9962, 10021. The Potiorek files in the Kriegsarchiv contain a full set of the July reports; KA, A12:A: 1914(323B). The Habsburg military attaché in Belgrade, Otto Gellinek, filed numerous reports as well; see, e.g., Gellinek to Conrad, 4 July (tel.) 1914, PA I/811; a complete set are in the KA, MA/Belgrad, fasz. 8.

35. For Hoyos' record of his talk with Viktor Naumann on 1 July 1914, see *ÖUA*, no. 9966; it has been widely reprinted as evidence of German pressure on Vienna. Tschirschky's report of 30 June 1914 in which he urged Vienna to move cautiously drew Wilhelm's famous retort, "Who authorized him to act that way?" and this is often cited as part of the pattern of German pressure on Vienna rather than a not surprising reaction to the comments of an ambassador; the full report is in *Outbreak of the World War: German Documents Collected by Karl Kautsky*, ed. Max Montgelas and Walther Schücking (New York: Oxford University Press, 1924) [hereafter Kautsky, *Outbreak*], no. 7; this document has been reprinted many times. The July reports from the German military attaché, Count Karl von Kageneck, to Berlin offer further insights into the decision process in Vienna; see Günther Kronenbitter, "Die Macht der Illusionen: Julikrise und Kriegsausbruch 1914 aus der Sicht des deutschen Militärattachés in Wien," *Militärgeschichtliche Mitteilungen 57* (1998): 519-50.

36. Conrad, *AMD*, 34.

37. On the interview with the emperor, see Hantsch, *Leopold Graf Berchtold*, vol. 2, 562-64; for copies of the revised memorandum and the personal letter of 2 July 1914, see *ÖUA*, 8, no. 9984. For the report of the conversation with Tschirschky, see ibid., no. 10006; the report is dated 3 July 1914. Also see Hantsch, *Leopold Graf Berchtold*, vol. 2, 568-69.

38. On Tisza's proposed changes, see his 5 July 1914 telegram that reached Vienna at 11:50 a.m. that Sunday; *ÖUA*, 8, no. 10070.

39. Berchtold to Szögyény, 4 July (tel.) 1914, ibid., no. 10037. That same day Berchtold was forcibly reminded of the need for clarity from Berlin, for Tschirschky now talked of the need for immediate action, while Szögyény from Berlin reported that Undersecretary Arthur Zimmermann (who was acting for honeymooning Foreign Minister Gottlieb von Jagow) urged no humiliating demands on Serbia; ibid., nos. 10038 and 10039.

40. Fellner's "Die 'Mission Hoyos'" remains a valuable introduction to this controversial mission. He cites evidence to suggest that Hoyos seized the chance to go because he wanted a military solution to the Serbian issue. In his article he reprints a 1917 memoir note by Hoyos of the trip.

41. The translation is from *July 1914: The Outbreak of the First World War: Selected Documents*, ed. Imanuel Geiss (New York: Charles Scribner's Sons, 1967), 77; the original is Szögyény to Berchtold, 5 July (tel.) 1914, *ÖUA*, 8, no. 10058. Also see Röhl, *Wilhelm II*, 1082-86; Hantsch, *Leopold Graf Berchtold*, vol. 2, 567-71; Rauchensteiner, *Der Tod des Doppeladlers*, 70-73.

42. The translation is from Geiss, ed., *July 1914*, 79; the original is Szögyény to Berchtold, 6 July (tel.) 1914, *ÖUA*, no. 10076; Hoyos claimed to have done most if not all of the drafting of the telegram.

43. The diary fragments are in Hantsch, *Leopold Graf Berchtold*, vol. 2, 569-70; Berchtold to Tisza, 6 July (tel.) 1914, *ÖUA*, 8, no. 10091. See Conrad's record of the discussion with Berchtold, Conrad, *AMD*, 39-40; on the harvest leave issue, Williamson, *Austria-Hungary and the Origins of the First World War*, 199-200, and his "Confrontation with Serbia: The Consequences of Vienna's Failure to Achieve Surprise in July 1914," *Mitteilungen des Österreichischen Staatsarchivs 43* (1993): 168-77.

44. Tschirschky to Jagow, Kautsky, *Outbreak*, no. 18; Hantsch, *Leopold Graf Berchtold*, vol. 2, 572-76.

45. These lines are taken from Geiss, ed., *July 1914*, 80-86. The full minutes of the meeting are in *ÖUA*, 8, no. 10118, and in Miklós Komjáthy, ed., *Protokolle des Gemeinsamen Ministerrates der Österreichisch-Ungarischen Monarchie (1914-1918)* (Budapest: Akadémiai Kiadó, 1966), 141-50; also see Williamson, *Austria-Hungary and the Origins of the First World War*, 197-200; Hantsch, *Leopold Graf Berchtold*, vol. 2, 574-82. Press leaks about the conference and its aftermath led to a confrontation between Berchtold and Biliński over the issue; see, e.g., Berchtold to Biliński, 11 July and Biliński to Berchtold, 13 July 1914, *ÖUA*, 8, nos. 10209 and 10211. One article in the *Neue Freie Presse* on 8 July 1914 noted the conference had lasted six hours and discussed the threat posed by Greater Serbdom to the monarchical principle, while the article that offended Berchtold of 9 July had talked of "Imminent Steps in Belgrade," ibid.

46. Berchtold to Franz Joseph, 7 July (tel.) 1914, *ÖUA*, 8, no. 10116; diary entry, 8 July 1914, in Hantsch, *Leopold Graf Berchtold*, vol. 2, 570; Berchtold to Tisza, 8 July 1914, *ÖUA*, 8, no. 10145. On 8 July at 6 p.m. Berchtold met with Conrad, Forgách, Burián, Hoyos, and Karl von Macchio, first section chief of the Foreign Ministry, to discuss the terms of the ultimatum and its delivery in fourteen days after the harvest leaves and investigation were ended. At the meeting the foreign minister expressed the desire for Conrad and War Minister Krobatin to go on leave "to give the appearance that nothing was happening," Conrad, *AMD*, 61-62. Yet even as Berchtold pushed ahead, one of his chief aides, Forgách belittled the foreign minister and wondered if he would really act; Forgách to Merey, 8 July 1914, Nachlass Merey, Haus-, Hof-, und Staatsarchiv, Vienna. The Habsburg press chronicled Berchtold's travels to and from Bad Ischl; see, e.g., *Fremdenblatt*, the semi-official press organ of the Foreign Ministry, 9 and 21 July 1914.

47. Diary entry, Hantsch, *Leopold Graf Berchtold*, vol. 2, 570-71, 586-89; Tisza to Franz Joseph, 8 July 1914, *ÖUA*, 8, no. 10146. On 10 July Conrad reported that Berchtold, just back from Bad Ischl, had found the ruler to "be for action against Serbia and only had concerns about unrest in Hungary," Conrad, *AMD*, 70; also see Tschirschky to Jagow, 10 July (tel.) 1914, Kautsky, *Outbreak*, no. 29.

48. On the Wiesner mission, the study by Friedrich Würthle, *Die Spur führt nach Belgrad: Die Hintergründe des Dramas von Sarajevo 1914* (Vienna: Molden, 1975) remains valuable. On 13 July Wiesner reported by telegram as settled fact that three of the conspirators had been armed in Serbia and smuggled across the border and that two Serbian officials had been responsible for the weapons; he would name them in the dossier as among those to be punished; *ÖUA*, 8, no. 10253. On the drafting of the ultimatum, see the memoir account by Musulin, *Das Haus am Ballhausplatz: Erinnerungen eines österreichisch-ungarischen Diplomaten* (Munich: Verlag für Kulturpolitik, 1924), 222-34. General Potiorek disagreed with Wiesner's decision not to describe Serbian governmental participation in the plot; there must have been someone, he argued, in a message to Krobatin, 14 July 1914, Kriegsministerium Präs., 1914, 81-10/60, KA.

49. Szögyény to Berchtold, 9 July (tel.) and 12 July 1914, *ÖUA*, 8, nos. 10154, 10214. For the files on "harvest leave" and the operational war plans against Serbia, see KA, Gstbs., Operationsbüro, fasz. 43.

50. Burián diary extracts, 9, 10, 12, and 14 July 1914, "Aussenminister Stephan Graf Burián," 206; on Burián's role in the crisis, see Leslie, "The Antecedents of Austria-Hungary's War Aims," 342-44. On Tisza's change of views, see Berchtold to Franz Joseph, 14 July 1914, *ÖUA*, 8, no. 10272; Vermes, *István Tisza*, 228-31; József Galántai, *Die Österreichisch-Ungarn Monarchie und der Weltkrieg* (Budapest: Corvina Kiadó, 1979), 251-77; also Tschirschky to Bethmann Hollweg, 14 July 1914, Kautsky, *Outbreak*, nos. 49-50.

51. Hantsch, *Leopold Graf Berchtold*, vol. 2, 591-96; Williamson, *Austria-Hungary and the Origins of the First World War*, 200-01. One sign of the shift in attitudes: on 12 July Redlich doubted war would come and on 15 July the bellicose Hoyos assured him it would, Redlich, *Schicksalsjahre Österreichs*, vol. 1, 236-38.

52. Berchtold to Szögyény, 15 July (tel.) 1914, *ÖUA*, 8, no. 10276; Berchtold to Merey, 15 July (tel.) 1914, ibid., no. 10289. For Berlin's irritation at the delays, see Szögyény to Berchtold, 16 July (tel.) 1914, ibid., no. 10296.

53. Berchtold's memoranda of conversations with Tschirschky about Italy, 20 and 26 July 1914, ibid., no. 10398, 10715; Tschirschky's reports are in Kautsky, *Outbreak*, nos. 94 and 212. Also, e.g., Berchtold to Merey and Szögyény, 28 July (tel.) 1914, *ÖUA*, no. 10909; Röhl, *Wilhelm II*, 1090-166.

54. Merey to Berchtold, 18 July (tel.) 1914, *ÖUA*, 8, no. 10364, and Berchtold to Merey, 20 July (tel.) 1914, ibid., no. 10418; also see Albertini, *The Origins of the War of 1914*, vol. 2, 222-26.

55. The minutes of the meeting of 19 July 1914 are in *ÖUA*, 8, no. 10393, and also in Komjáthy, ed., *Protokolle des Gemeinsamen Ministerrates*, 150-54; reprinted in part in Geiss, ed., *July 1914*, 139-42. Conrad also reprints the minutes and then at the end noted that during the Balkan wars the governments had pledged no territorial changes and that "after the war no one concerned himself with it," Conrad, *AMD*, 92, 87-91; also Hantsch, *Leopold Graf Berchtold*, vol. 2, 599-602.

56. Ibid., 602-03. Berchtold gave Tschirschky a copy of the ultimatum late on 21 July 1914; Szögyény would deliver the formal copy to Berlin on 24 July 1914, *ÖUA*, 8, nos. 10478, 10400.

57. The terms of the ultimatum are in ibid., no. 10395; the belated dossier, dated 25 July (tel.) 1914, ibid., no. 10654. Also see Hantsch, *Leopold Graf Berchtold*, vol. 2, 605-16. On the Russian actions on 24 July 1914, see Samuel R. Williamson, Jr. and Ernest R. May, "An Identity of Opinion: Historians and July 1914," *Journal of Modern History 79* (June 2007): 367-68. On 23 July Biliński and Potiorek queried Berchtold on what would happen if Belgrade accepted all of the demands; would they ask for more? Berchtold replied that he would wait and see what happened in Bosnia and Herzegovina; Berchtold to Tisza, 23 July (tel.) 1914, PA I/810.

58. Macchio to Berchtold, 25 July (tel.) 1914, Berchtold to Macchio, 25 July (tel.) 1914, *ÖUA*, 8, nos. 10703-05.

59. Hantsch, *Leopold Graf Berchtold*, vol. 2, 612-16; also Albert von Margutti, *The Emperor Francis Joseph and His Times* (New York: George H. Doran, 1921), 312-20, where he portrays a less belligerent ruler than other accounts; Albertini, *The Origins of the War of 1914*, vol. 2, 374-76.

60. For an official summary of the mobilization actions taken, some as early 24 July 1914 (moving the Danube naval flotilla), see the official record in the papers of General Conrad von Hötzendorf, KA, Conrad B 1450/114, prepared by Rudolf Kundmann, one of his aides; also Kronenbitter, "*Krieg im Frieden*", 504-19; Rauchensteiner, *Der Tod des Doppeladlers*, 87-99.

61. For the most recent review of the German actions, see Röhl, *Wilhelm II*, 1097-175; also Annika Mombauer, *Helmuth von Moltke: The Origins of the First World War* (Cambridge: Cambridge University Press, 2001), 182-226.

62. Hoyos to Schiessl, 26 July 1914, *ÖUA*, 8, no. 10772.

63. Conrad, *AMD*, 131-34; Hantsch, *Leopold Graf Berchtold*, vol. 2, 617-20; on the first fighting, see the draft article by Kurt Peball, "Die Beschiessung Belgrads zu Beginn des Ersten Weltkrieges," no date but mid-1980s, KA, E/1755/58. On British views and Berchtold's pushing back, see Ambassador Albert Mensdorff to Berchtold, 27 and 28 July (tels.) 1914, *ÖUA*, 8, nos. 10812-13, 10893-94; Berchtold to Mensdorff, 28 and 29 July (tels.) 1914, ibid., nos. 10891-92, 10972.

64. Rauchensteiner, *Der Tod des Doppeladlers*, 92-94; Robert A. Kann, *Kaiser Franz Joseph und der Ausbruch des Weltkrieges* (Vienna: Böhlau, 1971).

65. On 27 July Conrad still thought that Germany would deter Russia; the next day he told Berchtold he had to know by 1 August whether Russia would be in the war. On 30 July Conrad learned of Russian mobilization in Warsaw, Kiev, Odessa, and Moscow, but nonetheless sent the troops southward. That same day Franz Joseph authorized full mobilization to start on 1

August; Conrad, *AMD*, 132-48; Kronenbitter, "*Krieg im Frieden*", 498-505; Hantsch, *Leopold Graf Berchtold*, vol. 2, 636-38.

66. Röhl, *Wilhelm II*, 1126-49; Hantsch, *Leopold Graf Berchtold*, vol. 2, 630-34; Conrad, *AMD*, 151; Williamson, *Austria-Hungary and the Origins of the First World War*, 205-08. The minutes of the Common Ministerial Council are in *ÖUA*, 8, no. 11203 and Komjáthy, ed., *Protokolle des Gemeinsamen Ministerrates*, 154-58; reprinted in part in Geiss, ed., *July 1914*, 318-22. For German reports from Vienna, see Tschirschky to Jagow, 30 July (tel.) [actually sent at 1:35 a.m., 31 July 1914], Kautsky, *Outbreak*, no. 465, and Franz Joseph's letter to Wilhelm, 31 July (tel.) 1914 in which he indicated the war with Serbia would proceed, ibid., no. 482; Kronenbitter, "*Krieg im Frieden*", 507-09.

67. Scott D. Sagan, "1914 Revisited: Allies, Offense, and Intractability," *International Security 11* (Fall 1986): 151-75, and Jack S. Levy, "Preferences, Constraints and Choices in July 1914," *International Security 15* (Winter 1990/91): 151-86; Williamson and May, "An Identity of Opinion," 383-87.

68. Joseph Baernreither, a Habsburg foreign policy expert, expressed this view in October 1913 after a visit to Sarajevo said: "We have got either to annihilate Serbia, or, if we cannot do that, learn to live with it. *Tertium non datur*"; Joseph M. Baernreither, *Fragments of a Political Diary*, ed. Joseph Redlich (London: Macmillan, 1930), 246. Also Solomon Wank, "Desperate Counsel in Vienna in July 1914: Berthold Molden's Unpublished Memorandum," *Central European History 26* (Sept. 1993): 281-310.

69. Leslie, "The Antecedents of Austria-Hungary's War Aims," 307-94, remains indispensable. For what the principals thought about the war, see Hantsch, *Leopold Graf Berchtold*, vol. 2, 644-47; Conrad, *AMD*, 114-21, and for an insightful analysis later, Kronenbitter, "*Krieg im Frieden*", 516-30.

70. For the most recent summary of Habsburg military plans and Conrad's role in them, see Günther Kronenbitter, "Austria-Hungary," in *War Planning 1914*, ed. Richard F. Hamilton and Holger H. Herwig (Cambridge: Cambridge University Press, 2010), 24-47.

I. END OF EMPIRE/EARLY REPUBLIC: POLITICAL (DOMESTIC AND FOREIGN) LEGACIES

Utopian Perspectives and Political Restraint: The Austrian Revolution in the Context of Central European Conflicts

Wolfgang Maderthaner

It seems like an irony that the Republic of German-Austria (*Deutsch-Österreich*) was born precisely on the day of the seventieth anniversary of field marshal Prince Windischgraetz's victory over the Viennese revolution of 1848.[1] By the end of October 1918 the Habsburg Empire, a first-rate European power for more than four centuries, had ceased. The events unfolding against the backdrop of its demise—until 12 November 1918—are known by the name of "Austrian Revolution." Primarily of a political nature, this revolution sparked a process of de-feudalization and social upheaval. At the same time it marked the spectacular arrival on the historical scene of the proletarian masses.

An article in a Vienna daily of 3 November 1918 written by Paul Busson gives a vividly emotional description of the capital city besieged both by social unrest and a particularly vicious epidemic of Spanish flu:

> Burning fever has befallen many of its [Vienna's, W.M.] inhabitants, raging through their bodies, impairing their senses. Their limbs refuse to obey; their heads are full of the 'painful mass' which suggests wild nightmares and agonizing visions. And just like the individual citizen, the whole 'huge sick body' of the town is smitten by a fever attack,

> sapping the vigour that enabled it to carry its heavy burden for so long. Like a 'red flag' the feverish blaze is flickering, finding its expression in a cry mouthed by hundreds of thousands: Revolution![2]

Two weeks later, columnist Carl Marilaun, writing for the same paper, located the revolution in those "great and terrible cauldrons" where hundreds of thousands of strong arms are at work to transform old Vienna into the metropolis of a new human generation, of a new mankind. "Revolutions that change the world are always being prepared in some Ottakring or Favoriten. [Revolutionen, die das Antlitz der Erde verändern, bereiten sich immer in irgendeinem Ottakring oder Favoriten vor]."[3]

It was indeed an attack generated by revolutionary fever that hit the former Habsburg metropolis. The masses, exposed to the terrors of war and its aftermath, had been transformed in their thinking, their minds and their whole lives, to acquire a new consciousness of themselves. When the front began to dissolve in a spectacular manner without precedent in the history of earlier armed conflicts; when the combat troops refused further obedience and the rear echelons were in full anarchy; when chaotically retreating soldiers plundered depot facilities and seized trains to bring them home, military defeat and social revolution became inextricably intertwined.

As a product of the war, the revolution originated not so much in the factories but in the barracks. The disproportionally high percentage of soldiers appearing at political manifestations signalled the total incapacity of the military authorities, the total breakdown of military discipline in the garrisons of Vienna. This collapse was epitomized in an episode, symptom and symbol at the same time: During mass demonstrations on 30 October 1918, soldiers appeared in the streets wearing red cockades, while others wore cockades in black, red and gold. Some officers still sported the rosette with the imperial insignia, but they risked violent attacks by marauders snatching the emblems of those who remained conspicuously loyal to their princely ex-commander-in-chief. Among those who were stripped of their rosettes were a former minister of war, Rudolf Stöger-Steiner von Steinstätten, and Field Marshall Lieutenant Karl Bardolff. In ever increasing numbers, soldiers and officers succumbed to the fascination of political upheaval, assuming prominent roles in the revolutionary movement both in Vienna and in Budapest. Those twenty of them who appeared before the first president of the National Assembly, Karl Seitz, on 31 October 1918, to declare themselves representatives of the Soldiers' Council (*Soldatenrat*), had destroyed their cockades and military decorations themselves.[4]

One day earlier, the same Provisional National Assembly enacted Austria's first republican constitution, an event accompanied by impressive manifestations of workers as well as soldiers. The sweeping demonstrations of 30 October 1918 dissolved into a series of mass meetings all over town, calling for the proclamation of the republic and the release from prison of Friedrich Adler.[5] The situation came to a head in the evening when 2,000 men—the "wildest mob"—turned up from the middle of nowhere and rallied in front of the military gaol in the Rossauer barracks. They were dispersed in the last minute. At the same time, thousands of demonstrators from the Leopoldstadt district, shouting slogans like "peace now," gathered on the square in front of the war ministry. In the streets lining the House of Parliament a crowd of "three thousand from Ottakring" demanded the immediate abdication of the emperor. The repeated attacks on imperial insignia culminated in the removal of the double-headed eagle adorning the entrance to the Imperial Hotel in downtown Vienna by a group of young workers from the suburbs. The next day looting started again and impassioned mass meetings of revolutionary soldiers were held in places formerly utilized as recruitment and examination sites for army freshmen. *Oberpolizeirat* Dr. Franz Brandl, a high police official, wrote in his diary:

> One notes that amidst all the meaningless talking and acting of our days Bolshevism is being ushered in. The mood becomes more and more agitated. One hears calls to form a Red Guard; the soldiers', workers' and farmers' councils along the lines of the Russian example begin to haunt the minds. Two thousand soldiers, led by officers, marched to the war ministry, waving red flags. From Budapest there is news that Tisza (the Hungarian Prime Minister) was murdered by soldiers in his apartment.[6]

No doubt, Austrian ex-POW's returned from Russia played an important part in the mobilization of soldiers' gangs who gathered near the Rossauer barracks in Vienna's ninth district. These gangs came to be known under the name of "Red Guard"; they marched through town carrying weapons and requisitioned vehicles and food. Intellectuals like the journalist Egon Erwin Kisch or the writer Franz Werfel, who embraced a self-assured, deterministic Bolshevik ideology and banked on putsch activism, were drawn into the Red Guard. Petty delinquency took advantage of the self-dissolution of the garrisons, of barbarization by war and starvation. Otto Bauer, commenting on the immediate post-war situation, wrote:

> The wildly agitated home comers, the desperate men and women out-of-work, the militants rejoicing in a romantic revolutionary ideal joined with those disabled by the war, who wanted to take revenge for their personal destiny on a blameworthy social order. They joined with

The unruly streets of Vienna: social unrest 1919 (Photo courtesy of Picture Archives of the Austrian National Library, Vienna)

> morbidly excited women whose husbands had languished as prisoners of war for years, with intellectuals and writers of all kind, who all of a sudden, confronted with Socialism, were full of the utopian radicalism of the neophyte. They joined with the Bolshevist agitators sent home from Russia.[7]

Early in November 1918, Vienna's town-major (*Stadtkommandant*) Johann Ritter von Mossig had only four companies at his disposal. The most important ammunition depots and magazines were left unguarded, most of the guardsmen having returned to their villages. Each train arriving at Vienna's railroad stations was crammed with half-starved, angry home comers, brutalized by the war and, above all, carrying weapons. The danger of looting by demobilized Magyar or Slavic front soldiers on their way home was omnipresent. Shootings at train stations were a daily occurrence. The inmates of the Möllersdorf military prison all fled since the guards had deserted their posts. Italian prisoners of war had seized the arms deposits at the Sigmundsherberg POW camp and marched on to Vienna, provoking serious alarm, albeit for a few hours only.

A secret organization of Social Democratic soldiers and officers, already operative during the last months of the War, formed the nucleus of Austria's new republican army. But the *Volkswehr*, as this army came to be called, did not really seem a reliable peace-keeping power during the first period of its existence. The ranks of the newly formed volunteer corps were filled by unemployed workers who had lost their jobs due to the collapse of the armaments industry; by those who returned from the front and had given up hope for any other future perspective; by revolutionary romanticists and political adventurers; and by petty criminals and subproletarians.[8] Otto Bauer, the Social Democratic leader and state secretary (i.e. minister) of foreign affairs, was highly suspicious of the political adventurism displayed by mercenaries in the service of the *Volkswehr*: A considerable portion of the freshly recruited troops were, as he wrote, "convinced that with a few machine guns and with a few hundreds of armed men, gathering in strongholds of the revolutionary movement such as the provincial towns of Ternitz or Traisen, the social order of Europe might be knocked over."[9] The situation indeed looked dramatic, political revolution constantly threatening to be transformed into a social one. This "terrible catastrophe of cosmic dimensions, this haze of despair, revolt and craving for revenge"—as Paul Szende, in a contemporary analysis of the *Crisis of the Central European Revolution*, put it—formed the context of the rise of the masses to history. Their actions were determined by economic, political and social disruption.[10]

But the Red Guard did not, as feared by the Lammasch government, imprison the emperor at Schönbrunn palace to force him to abdicate, nor was the republic proclaimed as a result of masses fighting in the streets.[11] Rather, social unrest and agitation, the elementary commotion which had struck these masses, found significant expression in a gigantic demonstration while the provisional national assembly met in the premises of the old Upper House on 12 November 1938. Seemingly unending processions of Social Democratic workers marched from the Viennese suburbs to the houses of parliament, the ramps of which were occupied and secured by 2,000 hand-picked shop stewards from Floridsdorf, the electoral district of Karl Seitz. When the State Council ordered to hoist the red-white-red colours of the republic for the first time, demonstrators stripped them of the white middle part, and a red flag was flown before parliament. Shortly afterwards, communist soldiers rushed to the entrance, shooting at random—an incident which, apart from costing two lives, produced no further consequences.

This, too, should be seen both as a symbol and a symptom. Out of the demonstrations of the early revolutionary phase there evolved an instinctive, elementary, archaic movement, effective until the summer of 1919. Progress, form, direction and finally the limits of this movement depended to a large extent, if not exclusively, on external factors, such as the severing of supply lines between Vienna and the Austrian provinces, the blockade and the permanent threat of intervention kept up by the Entente, and the course taken by the Central European revolution in Germany, especially during the short lifespan of the Soviet Republic of Munich. More important than all these factors, however, were the events in Hungary.

***

Hungary's decision in October 1918 to part ways with Austria sealed the fate of Habsburg's reign. The power of the Magyar ruling oligarchy had been further strengthened during the War, to the point that Hungarian Prime Minister István Tisza was thought to actually run the Monarchy. At the same time, the War helped inaugurate Hungary's democratic movement headed by Count Miklós Kàrolyi, a freedom-lover and pacifist whose ideas were rooted in the tradition of the Hungarian Kuruc rebels and of Lajos Kossuth, the revered icon of 1848. Károlyi's political program aimed at Hungarian independence, and thus revocation of the compromise (*Ausgleich*) between Greater Austria and Greater Hungary concluded in 1867. He also advocated universal suffrage and land reform. In order to achieve his goals, Kàrolyi envisioned an alliance of Hungary's radical bourgeois intelligentsia which endorsed the West's democratic principles, and the Social Democratic labor movement of Budapest. This was not an entirely new idea. During the War, a similar coalition had appealed successfully to the masses, gaining widespread support. In October 1918, the Democratic Union, as it came to be called, agreed with the representatives of the old regime in that the last and only chance to retain the frontiers of historical Hungary would consist in repealing the constitutional union with Austria, in breaking away from Germany, and in concluding a separate peace treaty with the Entente. Parliament, dominated by the landed aristocracy, was confronted with a newly formed democratic National Council. At the end of October a mutiny in the name of the National Council resulted in a complete reversal of the power structure hitherto existing. Kàrolyi became prime minister "based on the law of the revolution", and on 31 October 1918 Hungary acquired the status of a de facto republic.

In close collaboration with the Social Democratic Party, Kàrolyi established his democratic regime, whose explicit aim was to entertain friendly relations with the Entente. But Hungarian democracy, and the multi-national state it claimed to represent, faced a serious dilemma when confronting the explicit territorial demands of the Czechs (claiming Slovakia and Ruthenia), the Romanians (who claimed Transylvania and some Hungarian counties adjacent to it) and the Yugoslavs (claiming Bačka and Banat). Against these intentions of annexation the entire Magyar population held up the principle of *historical integrity* of the country. As in German-Austria, the democratic-national revolution in Hungary had quickly assumed a social dimension, resulting in a temporary dominance of the political scene by the workers and their elected representatives. But whereas in Vienna and the surrounding industrial areas the Social Democrats used all their authority and their highly developed organizational skills to canalize revolutionary energies into the promotion of political democracy and social *reform*, Hungary's communist leaders despised bourgeois democracy, and their fight for territorial integrity became coterminous with the fight for the dictatorship of the proletariat.[12]

On 20 March 1919, France's Colonel Vyx, on behalf of the Entente, presented the Hungarian government a twenty-four-hour ultimatum, asking for the withdrawal of Hungary's armed forces behind demarcation lines well advanced into Hungarian territory. The Vyx-memorandum caused the immediate resignation of the Károlyi government. Károlyi himself asked the Social Democrats to come to an understanding with the Communists based on the complete rejection of Allied demands. A proclamation addressed "*To All!*", and publicized in the night of 21 March 1919 established a Soviet republic under communist hegemony. The masses of the country, deprived of their hopes for a peace in compliance with President Wilson's principles, reacted "with a national Bolshevism of staggering impact"—to quote Vilmos Böhm, a prominent Social Democratic party executive, minister of war under Károlyi, and now commander-in-chief of the Hungarian Red Army.[13] From the very first day of its existence, Soviet Hungary, a product of the fight for the country's national borders, was at war with Romania and Czechoslovakia. No wonder it overreached its economic and military limits precisely at the moment when its Red Army, reorganized by the aforementioned Böhm, in a sweeping offensive conquered large parts of Slovak territory. The communists' ultimate downfall, however, was mainly due to their inadequate handling of the agrarian question.

In German-Austria, strong particularistic tendencies of the Alpine provinces (whose economic interests widely differed from those of the central government), and their refusal to keep up food deliveries to hunger-ridden Red Vienna, clearly indicated the boundaries no revolutionary movement would be capable of transgressing. Budapest suffered from the same lack of loyalty on the part of Hungary's agrarian population, setting off a vicious circle of forced requisitioning and ever renewed resistance that hastened the end of the revolutionary experiment, the success of which depended almost exclusively on the support of the industrial workforce and of Budapest's intelligentsia, radicalized during the War. Left-leaning urban intellectuals took it for granted that the peasants, who were often illiterate, exposed to miserable living conditions, and politically apathetic, would acquiesce in the policies decreed by the capital, and accept the rule of the proletariat. Leo Lania, a journalist writing for the Viennese "*Arbeiter-Zeitung*" and later a stage director for Piscator and Brecht, was aghast at the ignorance displayed by the Hungarian leadership when he returned from a fact-finding mission on behalf of the executive board of the Austrian Communist Party (KPÖ): "The farmers' verdict was bound to decide the future of the government. But the Council of the People's Commissaries presided over by Béla Kun did not include one single peasant representative, while there were many young men of letters and radical bohemians. (...) They all came from Budapest and had no affinity whatsoever to country life. Peasant thinking and feeling remained alien to them."[14]

In the Hungarian countryside, prior to 1918, feudalism was the dominant mode of socio-economic organization. Slavic and Romanian peasants, many of them illiterate, faced a Magyar landowning class, which exposed everyone of non-Magyar ethnic extraction to rigorous politics of cultural assimilation. Members of the Hungarian Parliament were elected according to a census-based suffrage, and usually belonged to the aristocracy, gentry, or, to a smaller extent, the commercial and financial bourgeoisie. In contrast to the agrarian provinces, Budapest (grown out of a merger of two cities in 1872 and since then the undisputed and unrivaled political, economic and cultural capital of the country) had become a focus of modernization and a stronghold of industrial civilization and urban lifestyle. The political significance, the ambition, and the authority of the Hungarian capital were not least derived from the fact that it housed, on the eve of the Great War, sixty percent of the financial capital and more than one third of the large industries of Hungary (meaning also the majority of the industrial labor force). The monopolistic position of the city in the import and export trades corresponded with a sophisticated banking and financing sector.[15]

The Communists' advent to power in March 1919 had taken place amidst an atmosphere of national self-assertion and euphoria. But soon the complexities of Hungary's social fabric, fraught with tension, brought about paradoxical results. A majority of the gentry, poverty-stricken and deprived of its privileged status as a leisurely semi-aristocracy, joined with the peasants—who in turn were irritated and embittered by the refusal of the Soviet regime to distribute estate land among them—to form an anti-modernistic and anti-urban coalition. Claiming to speak for the whole nation, the gentry-peasant alliance heaped scorn on the metropolitan outlook of the city of Budapest, which in the nineteenth century still had been a reason for pride in gentry circles. Now agrarian resentment and petty aristocratic prejudice against the *big town* were allowed vivid expression. Budapest was denounced as cosmopolitan, revolutionary, socialist, Jewish and Bolshevist, in short, as a vicious antithesis to authentic Magyar culture. It is in this sense that the phrase, coined by Dezső Szabó, of the *city of sin* waiting for Magyarization must be understood.[16] Admiral Horthy, seizing power after the collapse of Soviet Hungary, continued on Szabó's note, talking of Budapest as the sinful city which he had come to punish and to purify.

***

Against the backdrop of persistent destitution and mass unemployment, revolutionary activities in Vienna started to pick up again following the proclamation of the Soviet Republic at Munich on 7 April 1919, and the victories of the Hungarian Red Army in Southern Slovakia in May 1919. For the communist regime in Budapest, Austrian developments were crucial. Its chances for survival depended on the fortunes of war, and Austria possessed sizeable amounts of weapons formerly belonging to the Austro-Hungarian military. Austria also had armaments and ammunition industries superior to those of Hungary, and Vienna was the site of the headquarters of the Austro-Hungarian Bank. Thus, on 22 March 1919, the Hungarians appealed to the executive committee of the Vienna Workers' Council to proclaim a "Soviet Republic of Austria," and to enter into an alliance with Hungary. But Vienna's Social Democrats politely declined this "invitation of the Austrian labor movement to commit suicide," as Julius Braunthal put it in his *History of the Socialist International*.[17] Hungary's Communist leader Béla Kun reacted by trying to force a putsch.

Twice in the course of the first half of 1919, attempted coups d'état shook the foundations of the infant Austrian Republic. The chief instigators of these revolts were men without work, disabled war veterans, or deracinated soldiers. Many belonged to the intelligentsia. On Thursday, 18 April 1919, shortly before Easter and a few days after the proclamation of the Bavarian Soviet Republic, several hundreds of desperate, starving men—deprived by the War of their health and their jobs—stormed the Parliament building on Vienna's Ringstrasse and set it on fire. Police and militia were called to quell the riot. Six members of the security forces were killed in the shooting that ensued. Put to the test for the first time, the volunteer militia of the *Volkswehr* demonstrated its ability to defend the lawful order.

About one month later Ernst Bettelheim, an envoy dispatched by Béla Kun, arrived in Vienna. In the name of the Communist International, which he claimed to represent, he dismissed the entire leadership of the Austrian Communist Party (KPÖ) and charged a newly appointed executive board with preparations for another putsch attempt. Communist propaganda was now directed chiefly at the *Volkswehr* itself. *Volkswehr* soldiers were encouraged to take part in an armed street demonstration planned for 15 June, the deadline set by the inter-Allied armistice commission for a substantial downsizing of the Austrian army. Revolutionary Soldiers' Committees distributed to their comrades written instructions for street-fighting and for the occupation of public buildings. At the same time, the Hungarian Trans-Danubian corps was ordered to occupy the frontier to German-Austria prior to 14 June.

In the morning of June 13, the newly elected Viennese District Workers' Council (*Kreisarbeiterrat*) held its first session. Following a speech by Friedrich Adler, the Council unanimously condemned Communist preparations for a putsch, calling them an inexcusable infringement of the Council's "revolutionary authority." In addition, the secretary of state in charge of military affairs (*Staatssekretär für das Heereswesen*), Julius Deutsch, who had in time been informed about Communist-inspired subversive activities, ordered a *Volkswehr* battalion known for its outstanding discipline to encircle the barracks of the ex-Red Guard Battalion No. 41. During the night of 14 to 15 June, a group of Communist leaders was arrested. When in the course of the following day a few thousand demonstrators marched to the police jail in order to free the prisoners, a city guard detachment opened fire. In the shooting, twenty were killed and eighty injured. The *Volkswehr* then proceeded to occupy strategically important sections of the Ringstrasse, Vienna's famous boulevard; deployment of the Communist 41st battalion thus became impossible, and the putsch attempt was doomed to failure.[18]

Among those who participated—without arms—in the manifestations of 14-15 June was Karl (later Sir Charles) Popper, then a seventeen-year-old member of the Marxist and pacifist Association of Socialist High-School Students (*Freie Vereinigung Sozialistischer Mittelschüler*). One of Popper's fellow-members in the association was Eugenia Schwarzwald, who was about to gain repute as a pioneer of feminism and educational reform. Like most of the other demonstrators, Popper was completely unaware of his role in a hazardous action directed against the state, but later he was to count the experience of June 1919 among the most formative ones of his life. In retrospect, he associated the events of 1919 with the beginning of his lifelong intellectual crusade against "historicism" culminating in his publication of *The Open Society and Its Enemies*. Also, he aptly characterized the crisis of the Central European Revolution already apparent at the time of the putsch of June 1919. Little was left of the euphoria of rebellion, adventure, romantic social utopia, of something new and fascinating, of something different, of the promise of a better world.

If the logics of violence and terror are accepted for the sake of a future ideal, then the consequences for mankind must be fatal, according to Popper. Everyone who underwrites these premises compromises his or her moral and intellectual autonomy, commits an act of mental self-immolation in the name of an envisioned historical mission.[19] With this interpretation, Popper follows a strand of thought influential or even hegemonic in Central Europe after the turn of the twentieth century, a way of thinking that seemed to open a meaningful way to understand the phenomenon of "the masses," a phenomenon mysterious and threatening at the same time.

In his novel of 1929, *Barbara und die Frömmigkeit*, the writer Franz Werfel, having parted with his youthful radicalism long ago, deals with these masses that so profoundly influenced the course of history. Referring to the demonstrations of 12 November 1918, he speaks of a flood of hundreds of thousands who, by "inexorably extinguishing both corporeality and self-determination of the individual," assumed "a collective persona of their own" commanding "infinite spontaneity and sovereignty." Endowed with a "mysterious, superior self-consciousness," the crowds had turned a day of extreme destruction of power into a day of ultimate display of power. The joy of collective self-consciousness, the unanimous will of hundreds of thousands had engulfed the whole city in an irresistible flood of what was *New*.[20] Following Gustave Le Bon (and his principal work *Psychologie des foules*, published in 1895), Werfel thus presented an apocalyptic view of the modern masses in the light of the theory of decadence, according to which the masses are governed and directed by a type of collective soul. The crowd is highly susceptible to emotional and passionate appeals, it is easily seducible and dirigible, capable of either pursuing the highest ideals or giving in to the most basic instincts. It transforms the individual into an automaton with no will of its own. The crowd acts unconsciously, following the logics of passion, and therefore needs a leader to submit to. In the light of emerging mass politics, a collective social pathology is being sketched out here.[21] Le Bon's theories impressed a significant portion of the Viennese intelligentsia and had a long-lasting impact even upon the élite of the labor movement. Sigmund Freud's indebtedness to the French philosopher can be traced in his *Massenpsychologie und Ich-Analyse*, an essay published in 1921 (and inspired by the events of the Great War), just as in Elias Canetti's *Masse und Macht*, which appeared in 1960. Adolf Hitler's writings may be seen as epitomizing the pathological, paranoid and totalitarian side of Le Bonian thought.

***

What has been termed the Austrian Revolution owed its peculiar character—and its limitations—to the swift and disastrous liquidation of the communist experiments in Budapest and Munich, and to political impotence, continued economic disintegration and social distress working together to destabilize the newly formed Austrian state from inside. Obliged to clip their own wings, Vienna's revolutionaries could hardly boast of heroic deeds or exult in dramatic episodes. As Otto Bauer wrote in a brilliant essay of 1923, subversion of the social fabric could take place only within very narrow limits. But this may have exactly been the reason for the greatness of Austria's revolution: "Just because destitution and powerlessness prevented us from developing a powerful revolutionary force, we could rule the masses only by intellectual means. Just because destitution and powerlessness required the revolution to exercise self-restraint, self-conquest and the containment of mass-passion by mass-insight had to be enforced in a desperate intellectual struggle with the masses themselves. [Gerade weil Not und Ohnmacht uns hinderten, eine starke revolutionäre Gewalt aufzurichten, konnten wir nur mit geistigen Mitteln die Masse beherrschen. Gerade weil Not und Ohnmacht die Revolution zur Selbstbeschränkung zwangen, mußte die Selbstüberwindung, die Zügelung der Massenleidenschaften durch die Masseneinsicht im schweren geistigen Ringen mit der Masse selbst durchgesetzt werden.]"[22]

Out of the collapse of all values, standards and authorities, only the Social Democratic Labor Party had emerged with flying colors. In conformity with its historical traditions, the party began at once to canalize the revolutionary energies of the masses, which had been uprooted by the war, into the establishment of a parliamentary democracy and the enactment of sweeping social reforms. Promoting mass-education and mass-discipline was a project of the *late enlightenment*. Under conditions of revolutionary turmoil and socio-romantic adventurism, the Workers' Councils grew into a decisive factor of social and political stability.[23] Under the leadership of Friedrich Adler, they succeeded in subjecting the *Volkswehr* militia to their authority, and engaged in a highly difficult and controversial discussion to arrive at a position broadly in line with the Social Democratic vision: renewal of production, establishment of a bourgeois parliamentary democracy, elimination of war absolutism and the vestiges of feudalism, comprehensive social reforms.[24] Since the councils themselves refuted dictatorship, as Otto Bauer put it, dictatorship had become non-enforceable. The councils, originally conceived of as instruments of a revolutionary intervention into the economic order and administration, had become organs of political consolidation, thus ensuring that the Social Democratic Party had enough leeway and freedom of action, especially in Vienna.

The Party's prime goal still was the establishment of a *social republic*, along the lines of the Jacobin republican state of the French Revolution, adapted to the conditions of a modern industrial society. The sovereignty of the people was to be attained by complementing and correcting parliamentary democracy with a "functional" extra-parliamentary system, in which all citizens should be able to participate and exert their influence via the media and representation.[25] The corresponding economic model envisaged extensive socialization measures to ensure collective ownership of production means. The provisions of the peace treaty of St. Germain, however, made these concepts obsolete. The denial of the right of self-determination and above all the economic reprisals imposed on Austria had fatal consequences. They dramatically changed the objective framework of domestic political action and the balance of power between the actors on the social and political stage. On 17 October 1919 the Constituent National Assembly ratified the peace treaty. This day witnessed not only the resignation of the first coalition government; it also marked the end of the Austrian Revolution.

Notes

1. The political, social, economic, and cultural aspects of the Austrian Revolution are treated extensively in Helmut Konrad and Wolfgang Maderthaner, eds., ... *Der Rest ist Österreich: Das Werden der Ersten Republik*, 2 vols. (Vienna: Gerold, 2008).

2. *Neues Wiener Tagblatt*, 3 Nov. 1918, 3.

3. Ottakring and Favoriten are suburbs of Vienna with a predominantly working-class population. The quote is from *Neues Wiener Tagblatt*, 16 Nov. 1918, 3.

4. See Francis L. Carsten, *Die Erste Österreichische Republik im Spiegel zeitgenössischer Quellen* (Vienna: Böhlau, 1988), 11ff.

5. Friedrich (Fritz) Adler, son of the founder of the Social Democratic Party, Victor Adler,

professor of physics at ETH Zurich, and close friend of Albert Einstein, had returned to Vienna as party secretary in 1911. In 1916 he chose to commit an act of individual terrorism, shooting the Prime Minister Count Karl Stürgkh on 21 October while the latter dined at Hotel Meißl&Schadn, in Vienna's Neuer Markt. When the trial started about half a year after the murder, the political climate had changed considerably. In the run-up to the legal proceedings, a strike movement, which at its peak was carried by more than 48,000 workers, had snowballed from the ammunition production plants at Vienna. Its prime goal was Adler's release. In fact, the underlying reason for his action was revealed by Friedrich Adler, expert in cognitive psychology, only at the trial – which figures among the most important of its kind in the course of the 20th century. In a spectacular reversal of roles, his speech of defense turned into a flaming accusation of the crimes of mass destruction, war dictatorship and the lethargic and defeatist policy of tolerance practiced by the Social Democratic party leaders. See Michaela Maier and Wolfgang Maderthaner, eds., *Physik und Revolution: Friedrich Adler – Albert Einstein: Briefe, Dokumente, Stellungnahmen* (Vienna: Löcker, 2006).

6. Cit. in Rudolf Neck, *Österreich im Jahre 1918: Berichte und Dokumente* (Munich: Oldenbourg, 1968), 97-98.

7. Otto Bauer, *Die österreichische Revolution* (Vienna: Wiener Volksbuchhandlung, 1923), 121.

8. Francis L. Carsten, *Revolution in Mitteleuropa 1918-1919* (Cologne: Kiepenheuer & Witsch, 1973), 61ff.

9. Bauer, *Die österreichische Revolution*, 99.

10. Paul Szende, "Die Krise der mitteleuropäischen Revolution: Ein massenpsychologischer Versuch," *Archiv für Sozialwissenschaft und Sozialpolitik 47* (1920/21): 341.

11. "Tagebuch Josef Redlich," cit. in Neck, *Österreich im Jahre 1918*, 133.

12. For a contemporary analysis see Béla Szanto, *Klassenkämpfe und Diktatur in Ungarn* (Vienna: Verlagsgenossenschaft Neue Erde, 1920).

13. Wilhelm Böhm, *Im Kreuzfeuer zweier Revolutionen* (Munich: Verlag für Kulturpolitik, 1924), 297. A large number of documents concerning the Hungarian Soviet Republic is attached to the personal archives of Vilmos (Wilhelm) Böhm, Verein für Geschichte der Arbeiterbewegung, Vienna, Mappe 103.

14. Leo Lania, *Welt im Umbruch: Biographie einer Generation* (Frankfurt: Forum Verlag, o. J. 1954), 156.

15. See the introduction of the editors, "Budapest and New York Compared," in *Budapest and New York: Studies in Metropolitan Transformation 1870-1930*, ed. Thomas Bender and Carl E. Schorske (New York: Russell Sage Foundation, 1994), 4ff.; as well as Peter Csendes and Andreás Sipos, eds., *Budapest und Wien: Technischer Fortschritt und urbaner Aufschwung im 19. Jahrhundert* (Budapest: Deuticke, 2003).

16. Miklós Lackó, "The Role of Budapest in Hungarian Literature 1890-1935," in *Budapest and New York*, 352ff.

17. Julius Braunthal, *Geschichte der Internationale*, vol. 2 (Hannover: J. H. W. Dietz, 1963), 160.

18. For a detailed outline see Hans Hautmann, *Die Geschichte der Rätebewegung in Österreich 1918-1924* (Vienna: Europaverlag, 1987), 329ff.

19. Malachi Haim Hacohen, *Karl Popper: The Formative Years, 1902-1945: Politics and Philosophy in Interwar Vienna* (Cambridge: Cambridge University Press, 2000), 82-83.

20. Cit. in Ulrich Weinzierl, ed., *Versuchsstation des Weltuntergangs: Erzählte Geschichte Österreichs 1919-1938* (Vienna: J&V, 1983), 22ff.

21. Wolfgang Maderthaner and Lutz Musner, "Der Aufstand der Massen – Phänomen und Diskurs im Wien der Zwischenkriegszeit," in *Stadt. Masse. Raum: Wiener Beiträge zur Archäologie des Popularen*, ed. Roman Horak et al. (Vienna: Turia+Kant, 2001), 32ff.

22. Bauer, *Die österreichische Revolution*, 194-95.

23. See Hans Hautmann, "Die Arbeiter- und Soldatenräte," in *Handbuch des politischen Systems Österreichs: Erste Republik 1918-1933*, ed. Emmerich Tálos et al. (Vienna: Manz, 1995), 245-60.

24. For the social reforms of the era Hanusch see Emmerich Tálos, "Sozialpolitik der Ersten Republik," in ibid., 577ff.

25. Richard Saage, *Demokratietheorien: Historischer Prozess – Theoretische Entwicklung – Soziotechnische Bedingungen: Eine Einführung* (Wiesbaden: VS-Verlag, 2005), 219-20.

Was There an Austrian Stab-in-the-Back Myth? Interwar Military Interpretations of Defeat

Patrick J. Houlihan

Introduction

One of the most baleful legacies of the Great War was the legend that the German Army had been stabbed in the back by traitors on the home front. The myth helped to undermine the legitimacy of the fledgling Weimar Republic, becoming a cornerstone of right-wing ideology in Germany, most infamously though not exclusively championed by the Nazi Party. All of this has been thoroughly investigated for the case of Germany but not for its Habsburg ally in defeat, which is surprising for four main reasons: first, the increasing degree to which Austria-Hungary became enmeshed with the German military effort during the course of the Great War; second, the gravitation of elements in Austrian society, especially among the authoritarian right, toward union with Germany during the interwar period; third, the extreme animosity even to the point of paramilitary violence between Austrian political parties during that same time frame; and fourth, the virulence of traditional anti-Semitism in Central and Eastern Europe, which the war exacerbated.

The previous observations might seem to suggest that a similar stab-in-the-back myth obviously occurred in Austria, too. The title of this paper, however, poses in binary form the question of an Austrian stab-in-the-back myth in order to emphasize that the answer is not as deceptively simple as the historiography would lead one to imagine. On the contrary, this essay will argue that the answer to the question depends on conventions of narrative framing regarding historiographies that are not intertwined with each other but should be. There are at least three different strands: military history, authoritarian politics, and the history of anti-Semitism. Overall, what unites these historiographies is a sense of military history as cultural history,[1] underscoring the legacies of empire reformulated in the new context of an Austrian Republic.

This essay begins by recapitulating key elements of the stab-in-the-back myth in its German context and then exploring those features comparatively, highlighting important differences in the respective collective interpretations of the war's outcome. Much of the argument here would seem to diminish the importance of the Austrian myth compared to Germany—at least in a largely quantitative sense. The final section of the essay, however, outlines elements of an Austrian stab-in-the-back myth and its qualitative implications for readings of twentieth-century Austria in transnational perspective as an "entangled history."[2] Thus, a comparative conceptual history of Germany and Austria on the issue of the stab-in-the-back myth can help to illuminate the similarities and differences of a "culture of defeat."[3]

The *Dolchstoss* in Comparative Context

The concept of a stab-in-the-back myth antedates the Great War, with shadowy origins in the nineteenth-century literary imagination in Central Europe that became more feverish as the imagined community became more exclusionary. As Wolfgang Schivelbusch has noted, national mythologies of this era depended heavily on "medieval or pseudomedieval" epics to establish the rubrics by which nations judged heroes and villains, and furthermore, "the connections between these fictional narratives and historical reality merit close attention."[4] As a theoretically supranational entity, however, the Habsburg monarchy posed considerable conceptual difficulties for nationalists, and the tension between a national abstraction and a multinational experiment forms one of the main tropes of Habsburg history since the French Revolution.[5]

One of the most eminent Habsburg historians, Robert Kann, once remarked that "probably the first known reference to the *Dolchstosslegende*" occurred in the "aesthetic dream-world, in which literary aestheticism was over-emphasized to the point of absurdity, and political criticism survived in the emasculated form of literary criticism." For Kann, this was traceable to Wolfgang Menzel's *Biedermeier* philosophy of a Christian-German synthesis that animated the *Burschenschaften* movement of the early nineteenth century.[6] The immense destruction and social reordering of the Great War, however, would ensure that "aesthetic dream-worlds" had a political dimension that was all too real.

The myth that the German Army during the Great War had been "unbeaten in the field" abroad (*im Felde unbesiegt*) and thus "stabbed in the back" (*Dolchstoss*) by subversive elements at home was one of the most pernicious beliefs of the authoritarian right. The stab-in-the-back myth was a denial of culpability, reflecting an inability to accept German defeat in war and the consequent realities of the postwar world. Across a wide spectrum of the political right-wing, responsibility for German defeat and postwar misery was foisted upon a projected conspiracy of Jews and Bolsheviks. In the right-wing imagination, these shiftless, alien, deceitful, cosmopolitan groups had undermined the German war effort and betrayed the nation in a shameful dictated peace treaty. The "betrayers" continued to put their narrow economic self-interest ahead of the well-being of the German nation, even by fomenting international revolution associated with the developments in Soviet Russia. Although the seeds of this myth were planted during the conflict itself around 1916-17, the legend of a "stab-in-the-back" became politically consequential during the interwar period. The myth was disseminated by two German Army commanders whose political importance in the Wilhelmine Kaiserreich as well as the Weimar Republic was absolutely crucial: Paul von Hindenburg and Erich Ludendorff. The legend became central to Nazi ideology, which proclaimed a mission to avenge the perceived treachery.[7]

German histories of the *Dolchstoss* present the phenomenon in an exclusively German context with no mention of an Austrian counterpart. Even less-studied is a more autonomous Austrian stab-in-the-back myth, which is surprising given the numerous complaints about the supposed disloyalty of the Habsburg monarchy's increasingly centrifugal ethno-national groups as well as the socio-political chaos of the interwar period. To return to the conceptual history of the *Dolchstoss* noted earlier, Robert Kann was certainly attuned to the possibility of a stab-in-the-back myth in Austrian history. Yet, Kann failed to mention an Austrian example of the phenomenon rooted in the military events of the Great War. Kann explicitly dealt with what he termed a "kind of second *Dolchstoss* legend" where he used the term as his personal label for the ascribed nefarious diplomacy of Wilson, Lloyd George, and Clemenceau during the Paris Peace Conference regarding the Habsburg polity's intentional dissolution. Kann contrasted this imagined *Dolchstoss*, which he rejected, with the "original German stab-in-the-back myth," thus underscoring his dichotomy of a German *Dolchstoss* concept and its Austrian absence.[8]

Later histories of Austria, however, have briefly asserted that there was indeed a *Dolchstoss* legend, but these histories are elusive regarding the myth's content, diffusion, and significance. Histories of Austrian authoritarian movements and anti-Semitism in the twentieth century briefly mention the existence of an Austrian "stab-in-the-back" myth but do not explore it in detail.[9] A more recent conceptually innovative work on collective memory has argued that a *Dolchstoss* myth did exist in the memoir literature of certain segments of the Austro-Hungarian elite, particularly high-level former military officers.[10] Especially in a comparative context, however, the idea of an Austrian *Dolchstoss* remains unknown compared to its German counterpart, both historically and historiographically.

At first glance, the military history of Austria-Hungary during the Great War would seem to stand in extreme contrast to the German war effort and lend strength to the case that no Austrian *Dolchstoss* existed. In the war's opening stages, Austro-Hungarian forces were embarrassingly repulsed in their attempt to invade a minor power, Serbia, the declared cause of the war. The effort to subdue Serbia only succeeded with substantial German and Bulgarian aid in 1915. Furthermore, massive Russian territorial incursions into Galicia in the war's opening phase and again during the shattering Brusilov offensive of 1916 represented substantial defeats on Habsburg home soil. In contrast to Germany, Austro-Hungarian military elites could not seriously claim that the k.u.k. Army was "unbeaten in the field."[11] Furthermore, as the war progressed, increased German intervention not only became a prerequisite for successful Austro-Hungarian offensives, but also staved off the collapse of the Austro-Hungarian military as a fighting unit.[12]

The military historiography of the First World War varied enormously between the Central Powers, with implications for how the "stab-in-the-back" legend did or did not become a dominant social myth. Rudolf Jeřábek has noted that Austrian military historians of the interwar period, rooted in the long traditions of Habsburg history, were much more accustomed to (one could say, became experts in) retaining glory while chronicling and rationalizing military defeats.[13] This fit well with a pre-modern conception of politics focused on the preservation of dynasties, where the Army was the "Shield of the Dynasty" and military conflicts were agreements between monarchs, not totalizing wars fought to threaten the existence of enemy polities.[14]

The collective Austro-Hungarian social experience of war also seems more suited to a bygone era. As Mark Cornwall has argued, unlike the other European great power combatants in the First World War, the necessary "secondary mobilization" of the Habsburg state never took place. Weakened by the change of imperial leadership after the death of the popular and long-serving Kaiser Franz Joseph in November 1916, the monarchy pursued a course of action that, even in grim economic conditions, was more politically permissive. In essence, this exacerbated the inefficiency of the Habsburg state in managing total war, especially in contrast to the other states engaged in the conflict.[15]

The official Austrian military history of the Great War did not subscribe to a *Dolchstoss* myth, which was incompatible with the Habsburg grand narrative of decline premised on a large-scale vision of history: the honorable and traditional dynasty unsuited to a conflict dominated by mass warfare and commercial empires. Though perhaps seeming like sour grapes, the official military history is quite clear in its judgment: the Central Powers were geo-strategically doomed from the outset of the conflict, and, highlighting its tragic nobility, the Army remained loyal to the Habsburg cause until the war had ended.[16] In this view, the Army played an honorable role in defending the State even after the State technically ceased to exist. The history speaks of the k.u.k. Army possessing an "existential will" (*Daseinswille*) of "astounding power" that "gave up only when the foundation of the State (*Staatsfundament*) was already destroyed."[17] Even though the official history was a self-justificatory rationalization dominated by ex-k.u.k. loyalists, it became the dominant paradigm in the recorded military history of Austria-Hungary's participation in the war.[18] Even much later, secondary scholarship on the Army essentially upholds this view. Gunther Rothenberg's closing cadences to his eminent work on the Imperial Army argue the view that, "While it existed, the army carried out its mission, did its duty, and remained faithful, and in the bitter end the army outlived the empire and the dynasty it had been meant to defend."[19] Even during the last years of the war, when ethno-national movements concretely began to realize their plans for independence outside of the imperial framework, scholarship generally agrees that the Army, symbolically encapsulated by its officer corps, remained loyal to the Habsburg dynasty.[20]

Some contemporary leaders of the k.u.k. Army, however, were willing to rationalize impending doom by blaming others for the dismal course the war had taken—even if this meant calling the military's performance into question. Even if the Army was ultimately loyal until the end, military commanders pointed the blame at home front agitation that, in their view, had destroyed the Army's discipline. The last Chief of the General Staff, General Arthur Arz von Straussenburg, was a prolific advocate of such views, claiming that disaffection on the home front directly undermined the performance of the Army at the front. In his post-war history of the conflict, Arz claimed that on the eve of the January 1918 labor strikes, he told an unspecified member of the high command that collapse in the rear, not battlefield defeat, would cause the monarchy to lose the war.[21] In his later analysis of the Central Powers' performance in the war, Arz succinctly wrote, "Who bears the guilt? Certainly not the Army. … The Army did its duty. At the downfall of the Empire, the Army is not guilty."[22] So who, according to Arz, was guilty? Arz blamed first and foremost the material odds weighed against the Central Powers from the outset. He also wrote of the "excessive propaganda" that "awakened national sentiment" (*nationales Empfinden*) and caused the "political agitation" (*politische Verhetzung*) of the "Slavic, Italian, and Romanian" inhabitants of the empire, which began on the homefront early in the war and increased throughout to the point that "disadvantageous influences of this kind entered the Army and poisoned the co-national troops." Arz contrasted these developments with the "absolutely dependable" (*absolut verlässlich*) behavior of "German-speaking and Hungarian regiments."[23]

Arz's predecessor as Chief of Staff, Franz Conrad von Hötzendorff, also attributed the defeat to a *Dolchstoss* of ethnic disloyalty to the monarchy, which began before the war and which the Entente powers deliberately exacerbated. Conrad's Social Darwinist fatalism inclined him to see the war, at least retrospectively, as a group struggle between nation-states that the Habsburgs were bound to lose. Nevertheless, he voiced his opinion in the waning days of the war that the Austro-Hungarian war effort had been an attempt to rally the "loyal elements" within the Empire, and he ultimately judged the failure due to a "stab-in-the-back" on the home front. In a letter to a close friend on 23 November 1918, Conrad wrote that "from the rear, our monarchy and our army were brought to ruin (*sind von rückwärts zugrunde gerichtet worden*)." He added that the beginnings of the disloyalty could be dated to ethno-national movements before the war, i.e., with the "Czech, Slovak, Serbian, Ruthenian, Romanian, and…also Polish propaganda" though he also heaped blame on the "deluded (*verblendeten*) independence strivings of Hungary."[24]

A closer examination of Conrad's correspondence shows just how quickly military interpretation of defeat could shift once the final outcome of the war became clear. In a previous letter to the same friend written just a few weeks earlier on 3 November 1918, Conrad had affirmed his belief that, though he had long ago given up hope of a "breakthrough victory," yet he had "reckoned on a holding of all fronts that finally would bring both sides to the view of the inefficacy of further struggle and therefore would bring peace." Conrad wrote that the surprising Bulgarian withdrawal from the war had disabused him of this assessment.[25]

The search for blame continued among many Austro-Hungarian officers. Especially among former commanders of *großdeutsche* sentiments, most notably Edmund Glaise von Horstenau and Karl Bardolff, the *Dolchstoss* myth was a prominent part of their interpretation of military collapse viewed retrospectively. As director of the Austrian Military Archives, Glaise's influence on a military collective memory should not be underestimated, even if the official military version solidified the verdict of collective military loyalty.[26]

Military commanders' ex post facto rationalizations that strive to secure a personally favorable judgment in the annals of history are nothing new, of course.[27] Individual self-justificatory grievances of high-ranking commanders aside, however, this highlights another difference between Germany and Austria-Hungary. For the most part, high-ranking Austro-Hungarian military officers did not dominate the political scene in interwar Austria as was the case for their counterparts in Germany, particularly Hindenburg and Ludendorff who were prime disseminators of the *Dolchstoss* myth.

Furthermore, the role of the monarch helped to reinforce the notion of treachery's absence in the late Habsburg Empire. With the death of Kaiser Franz Joseph in November 1916, the embodiment of bureaucratic stability since the 1848 Revolution, it seemed more plausible that the Empire had come to an end. Much of the Habsburg monarchy's symbolic capital passed away with Franz Joseph.[28] Whatever his familial ambitions for hereditary succession, the new Kaiser Karl sought a separate peace, renounced his participation in the affairs of state, and helped transfer power to a more democratic government.[29] These actions made it harder to believe that "November criminals" had betrayed the monarchy.

The different corporate military reactions to defeat played an enormous role in framing interpretations of the conflict. The nineteenth century wars of unification had deceptively accustomed the German officer class to a continual series of decisive and influential victories. It was simply beyond the collective political imaginary of the highest military leaders that they bore a large degree of responsibility for the German defeat in the Great War. If, as they believed, the German military machine was destined for victory, only home front politics could explain the loss. The role of the German military's corporate ethos, unconstrained by external political control, was fundamental in creating a radicalizing dynamic of "absolute destruction" that exacerbated the ideological enmity and violent methods of German military planning in the twentieth century.[30] In contrast, the corporate role of the Habsburg military was structurally different, subject to much greater political checks and balances.[31] Furthermore, the interwar Austrian *Bundesheer* as a successor institution engineered by the Austrian Social Democrats in the negotiations around St. Germain, was politically moderate, and thus different from its conservative and aggrieved counterpart in Weimar Germany.[32]

The myth of the *Dolchstoss* also calls attention to the differences in ascribed ideological development narratives between Germany and Austria-Hungary. There were fundamentally different religiously loaded collective projections of the experience of the First World War. One should emphasize here the historical-philosophical dimensions of a societal reading of state development. In the German case, numerous scholars have noted the virulent influence of religiously charged Protestant Prussian nationalism. Germany's Protestant clergy as a corporate group helped to sacralize the German nation in a story of linear and indeed teleological historical development throughout the course of the nineteenth century.[33] When the stagnation of the Great War set in, the consequences of disillusion were more precipitous for Protestant Germany than for Catholic Austria-Hungary.[34]

A focus on the war theology, and indeed, jingoism, of many bishops and higher clergy in the public sphere has obscured everyday experiences of the war for many religious believers, especially from the losing Central Powers.[35] An all-too-convenient teleology of collective religious disillusionment in the First World War tempts many historians to explain the rise of Nazism in Germany as a sublimation of spiritual energy, eventually channeled into the substitute messianism of Nazism. Although this was certainly one historical course for many German-speaking Central Europeans, the alternative tracks are much more convoluted and historically interesting.[36] One of the major areas of research on the First World War remains an attempt to tease out such implications of the everyday war experiences of Central and Eastern Europe. These geographic areas have been long neglected in favor of focus on the disenchanting slaughter on the Western Front.

At a micro-level, one can approach this everyday experience through the reports of Catholic military chaplains, critically examined in the context of other sources. It is true that many prominent religious figures, primarily those safely ensconced on the home front who suffered no personal deprivation, expounded an exclusionary just-war theology to the end of the conflict.[37] However, the broader social religious projections of collective experience, especially at the battlefront, were not nearly as simplistic. Contrary to the stereotype of hypocritical fire-breathers found in the literary works of authors such as Karl Kraus and Jaroslav Hašek, Catholic chaplains did not reify the nation-state to the extent that their Protestant counterparts in Germany did. Thus, when the war stagnated, the Austro-Hungarians could more easily drop the Old Testament "chosen people" rhetoric and focus on New Testament discourses of peace and healing. For instance, chaplain Bruno Spitzl of the k.u.k. 59th Infantry Regiment went off to war full of the hurrah patriotism that infected both religious and non-religious soldiers.[38] Chastened by the actuality of war, by 1917 Spitzl's sermons, as reported back to the Apostolic Field Vicariate in Vienna, reflected themes such as "Love of God and charity (*Nächstenliebe*): two poles of Christian faith" and "God's offer of peace."[39]

By contrast, in his thorough study of the *Dolchstoss* phenomenon, Boris Barth has noted the central role of the Protestant Church as a social-moral milieu for the "origin, dissemination, and reception" of the *Dolchstoss* myth as well as other myths rationalizing German defeat.[40] In the immediate post-war period, the Austrian Catholic bishops and leading clergy accepted the radically changed political circumstances much more so than their German Protestant counterparts did. The Austrian bishops, despite their avowed preference for monarchist hierarchy as supposedly more organically democratic, nonetheless supported the legitimacy of the fledgling republic. On the very day of the First Republic's founding, 12 November 1918, Cardinal Piffl of Vienna underscored to Austrian Catholics that Kaiser Karl's proclamation granting a determination of government to the people had enabled a transfer of loyalty to the new democratic republic. On its first anniversary, the new Austrian First Republic was officially recognized by the Holy See.[41]

The shattering of the throne-and-altar alliance was less traumatizing for Austrian Catholics than grand narratives of Habsburg history indicate. It was precisely the Catholic natural law philosophy of the universal magisterium, which did not sanctify any one form of government, that allowed Catholics to transfer their political allegiances from one legitimately constituted polity to another—and to keep their options open for transferring loyalty from the new republic to other more authoritarian forms of state. As Cardinal Piffl maintained, Kaiser Karl's proclamation enabled precisely this transfer. On the day of the First Republic's founding, the preeminent Catholic paper *Reichspost* championed the new republic in words that could scarcely have been more different from the political sentiments of Wilhelmine Protestants. On 12 November 1918, a *Reichspost* editorial read that, "For the Christian peoples of German Austria, the foundations are clearly indicated," and that "no one would be a lesser Catholic" for believing in "the republican form of state that comes about through legal means." Conveniently leaving open the possibility that a democracy could choose to constitute itself in forms other than a republic, the article argued that Catholics would be "loyal to the lawfully achieved order" in which the "legal forms of democracy remained defended." The article closed by enjoining

Austrian Catholics to display, "calm, patience, and loyal tolerance in face of convictions that were not [their] own."[42] Of course, for Austria's Catholic clergy, official proclamations of loyalty were one thing, and more private and widespread feelings of treachery were quite another matter. In the public sphere, however, Austrian perceptions of treason did not quickly seize on the shadowy figure of the "Jewish-Bolshevik" as was the case in Germany.[43]

Turning to the postwar settlements that helped fuel the hatred of the stab-in-the-back theory, in Austria, as in Germany, there was widespread animosity toward the results of the Paris Peace Conference. Citizens in both countries railed against the supposedly dictated nature of a victor's peace completely at odds with the idealism embodied in Woodrow Wilson's Fourteen Points. German Austrians in particular were outraged at Article 88 of the St. Germain Treaty that forbade union with Germany. More generally, the Austrian populace felt indignation at being held accountable for the misdeeds of the Habsburg regime.[44] In the Austrian case, however, much of the outrage was directed at improprieties of international relations, not supposed intra-Austrian traitors who had sold out the state.[45]

Some Austrians in the German National camp, however, could not get over the dictated nature of the treaty, and it is remarkable how their fury survived into even the post-World War II era. Indeed, as late as 1969, the notorious Taras Borodajkewycz was still fulminating against the supposed sins of Saint Germain.[46]

Austrian Implications of a *Dolchstoss* Phenomenon

The comparative history sketched above points in many ways to substantial collective differences between Germany and Austria-Hungary on the issue of the stab-in-the-back as a social myth. One would be tempted to write off the *Dolchstoss* as a German phenomenon, with a few exceptions of defensive former Habsburg military commanders attempting to salvage their reputations. Nevertheless, the myth of a stab-in-the-back was part of a discourse in 1920s Austria. It remains an important research desideratum to probe just how much this sentiment permeated beyond isolated figures of the high command.

It is important to underscore at the outsets that stab-in-the-back sentiments, even if not directly articulated in the *Dolchstoss* phrase, began to emerge during the Great War and continued to escalate during the interwar period, reaching a crescendo during the initial period after the Anschluss. During the Great War, Jews were blamed for the deteriorating economic conditions on the home front. The situation was exacerbated by the increasing presence of Orthodox Jewish refugees from Eastern regions in Galicia fleeing the advancing Russian armies in 1914 and again in 1916.[47] Following the relaxation of censorship after 1917, Leopold Kunschak, the Christian Social labor leader, was only one of the most visible who made increasingly vicious speeches denouncing Jews for the conduct of the war. Kunschak even went so far as to advocate Jewish expulsion or internment in concentration camps.[48]

During the war, the Habsburg state lost legitimacy due to its failure to provide its citizens with enough food.[49] As Maureen Healy has argued, this politics of food had repercussions that continued into the postwar period: "Among Christian, German-speaking Viennese, Jews and Czechs were the choice targets of those looking for an internal enemy."[50] Indeed, precisely because their former Czech antagonists were geographically excluded in the new Austrian rump state created after the Treaty of St. Germain, German Nationals in Austria concentrated their focus on Jews who seemed to embody an alien outsider in the new state.[51] However, as Peter Pulzer has noted, this postwar surge of belief in the Jew as outsider in Austria was hardly confined to the German National camp.[52]

The anti-Semitism of the war years had certainly survived into 1920s Austria, clustering around *Dolchstoss* resentments. On the eve of the signing of the St. Germain Treaty, the *Reichspost* commented on the Third Congress of Christian trade unions in Austria with words similar those of Leopold Kunschak. The paper declared a desire for a "permeating mood of peace, directed at the people and the State," which would lead toward "bridging the opposition between classes, equal rights, equal freedom for all." This, the paper held in contrast to the "class warfare cry of Jewish leaders that during this fight live prosperously in the rear staging areas (*die bei diesem Kampf in der Etappe wohl leben*)."[53] It is especially important here to note the militarized language of supposedly self-serving Jewish interests, and the identification of socialist agitators as Jews pulling the strings from their comfortable positions on the home front while real warfare occurred elsewhere. This was a *Dolchstoss* sentiment in everything but name, and it was a trope from the very beginning of the First Republic. Only now, the militarized language provided a frame of reference that essentialized "true" war experience, identified traitors to the cause, and symbolically applied this understanding to current Austrian politics.

Especially in the German National camp of Austrians, the stab-in-the-back myth was a key part of the belief system.[54] At the height of Anschluss euphoria, Robert Körber wrote one of the most widely circulated of the texts expressing an Austrian *Dolchstoss*. Along with Anton Jerzabek of the Christian Social Party, Körber was the pan-German co-chair of the

Antisemitenbund,[55] and he gave expression to these deep-seated feelings when he wrote that, "Jewry's stab in the back against the German people in its most difficult and vulnerable hour is not a legend or discovery, but rather a historical fact, documented and proven, psychologically clear and well-founded."[56] Körber continued,

> Even before the collapse, still in the midst of the war, Jewish politicians, journalists, and writers in the hinterland began to appeal to the people for "peace at any price" and to nurture their defenselessness and dishonor. Their writings and flyers also poisoned the front and destroyed the military powers of defense (*Wehrwillen*), and all this was methodically continued in the state after they seized power. The Revolution of 1918 was never an uprising of the German people against its oppressors, but rather a rebellion of the Jewish subhuman (*Untermensch*). This hate-filled conqueror used the time of emergency of his host (*Gastgeber*), in order to stab him in the back. Instead of the pretended "dictatorship of the proletariat," he established the compulsory leadership of Jewish powerbrokers over the German working man also in his Austrian homeland (*ostmärkische Heimat*).[57]

The increased association between the Christian Social movement and the German National camp during the interwar years in Austria is a topic deserving of further research in terms of mutual ideological influences. This is especially the case given the Christian Social reliance on the *Heimwehr* as paramilitary formations to combat the Social Democrats.

Viewed from the perspective of the fragmented Austrian right-wing, the Justice Palace fire of 15 July 1927, was the "great stroke of luck" that helped to unite the right-wing movements in Austria in the face of a seemingly impending "red revolution."[58] During the tenure of Chancellor Ignaz Seipel of the Christian Socials, the *Heimwehr* became the critical force for the Christian Social paramilitary attacks on the Social Democrats in the increasing bouts of political violence that culminated in civil war of February 1934.[59] One of Seipel's best biographers, Klemens von Klemperer, referred to Seipel as "altogether irresponsible and, in the last analysis dishonest in his position toward the radicalism from the Right"; it is difficult to disagree with this assessment.[60] The slide of the *bürgerlich* camp toward the clerico-authoritarian Dollfuss-Schuschnigg Regime would see increased reliance on the so-called front generation as Christian-social, *völkisch*, and *Heimwehr* groups began to blend together.[61]

A cultural history of military-political sentiments focused on the legacies of the war can help to illuminate the social circumstances of the diffusion of a stab-in-the-back myth. One can say at this point that ideological sentiments clustering around the notion of an Austrian *Dolchstoss*, even if not always expressed in that term, were embraced by influential political figures of the authoritarian right in Austria, especially associated with the *Heimwehr* movement.[62] Ernst Rüdiger Starhemberg, the former *Freikorps* veteran and participant in the Beer Hall Putsch, became a leader of the Austrian *Heimwehr* movement, and he described encounters with revolutionary crowds in Linz in November 1918 in words that reflect sentiments of betrayal and retribution. On his return from the front, people in the crowd beat Starhemberg until they drew blood, then threw his military decorations in the mud, and smashed his saber. In his memoirs, published posthumously in 1971, Starhemberg's account was still tinged with bitterness. He recounted thinking, "Damned rabble...there will be a day of reckoning for you."[63] Starhemberg's memoirs demonstrated not only personal grievance but much more an interpretation of history that focused on collective betrayal and retribution, a notion that was common to many figures with reactionary and indeed counterrevolutionary sentiments. In hindsight, however, Starhemberg focused on the mutual incomprehensibility of the political camps, and the empathetic inability of later generations:

> Those who never experienced the break-up of their Fatherland, like the Austrian patriots did with the collapse of the Austro-Hungarian Monarchy in 1918, can scarcely empathize with the heavy spiritual destitution (*seelische Not*) under which the young patriotic Austrians had to suffer in view of this frightful event. They also cannot measure the embittered fury (*verbitterte Wut*) that dominated the young war participants of a centuries-old and even in recent battles victorious army—an army that, despite all casualties, despite all victories, had to experience a shameful downfall. One must somewhat understand and not take it amiss that young fighters of a generation, which saw all their hopes and successes betrayed, opposed those who harshly and unjustly reviled and dragged through the mud the sacred ideals and honored concepts and institutions. Similarly, one may not rightfully resent others who were animated by a fanatical radicalism for the new, when they branded and persecuted any emotional attachment to the old as "reaction." In this reciprocal incomprehension (*gegenseitiges Nichtverstehen*) lie the roots of the tragic fate that has burdened the political development of the Austrian Republic until its downfall.[64]

As John Boyer has argued, such sentiments well represented political attitudes of a fundamentally new liberal democratic state that was born in the relatively bloodless Revolution of 1918-20 but whose citizens would have to acclimate to a "political culture of tolerance and respect worthy of that state" in a process that was "slow, arduous, and deeply painful."[65]

In the meantime, however, resentment, feelings of betrayal, and the hope of union with Germany loomed large in the conceptions of many of the front-generation. Another former junior officer, Emil Fey, would become a *Heimwehr* leader and eventual vice-chancellor of Austria. Fey's postwar reminiscences, published in 1937, reflect the nostalgic fanaticism that longed for a Germanic confraternity dating back to the Middle Ages. His service with the k.u.k. Infantry Regiment "Hoch- und Deutschmeister Nr. 4" during the Great War would be the frame of reference that determined his interpretation of the interwar Austrian Republic. Fey wrote of the regiment's return to Vienna in November 1918 as a "return home to a foreign city…that betrayed [us]…not a hometown…only the center of a false idea (*die Zentrale einer falschen Idee*)."[66] Especially from Austrians outside of Vienna, the symbolic incongruity of the socialist bastion would dominate the imagination of *Heimwehr* participants.

This sense of betrayal, illegitimacy, and retribution, which was a key part of the *Dolchstoss* myth, became a central component of the ideology of groups associated with the ambition to counteract the perceived menace of the socialist revolution that had swept Central and Eastern Europe in the wake of the Bolshevik Revolution. Elucidating these political-ideological exchanges, Robert Gerwarth has recently argued that Germany, Austria, and Hungary shared a common transnational experience of paramilitary units bent on counterrevolution through the use of redemptive violence against perceived political enemies. The frustration of defeat and the chaos of revolution and political reordering spawned a relational network of association among the authoritarian right that transcended clear national boundaries.[67] In particular, Gerwarth has argued that the stab-in-the-back myth existed as a transnational phenomenon in Germany, Austria, and Hungary in the interwar period.[68] Studies of Hungarian disillusionment would seem to confirm this notion.[69]

Indeed, the combined German-Austro-Hungarian war effort on the Eastern Front, and the bitter fruits of a frustrated "victory" in that geographic area, remains one of the burgeoning fields of research on the Great War. The experience of occupation and destruction during the war years set an ominous precedent for military utopias drawing on the fear of Bolshevism generated by the Russian Revolution and its possible importation into Central Europe. The failed colonial administration of Eastern Europe, blending into the Bolshevik Revolution and Russian Civil War, remained an unsettled legacy of the Great War that was a crucial source for the ideological escalation of violence against the Eastern regions during the Second World War.[70] Especially compared with the German dynamics of military colonialism, it remains a subject of contention whether Habsburg occupations in Italy and the Balkans, for instance, were conceptually traditional or in fact, governed by the brutalizing dynamic of twentieth-century warfare.[71]

Conclusion

The memory boom in Austria continues. Drawing on earlier monographic work, recent Austrian efforts modeled on French and German research have used the concept of collective memory to produce increasingly sophisticated collaborative studies of the phenomenon.[72] As always, the concept of collective memory must focus on a plurality of collectives, thus emphasizing the disparate degrees of agency and identity among groups. This is especially the case for the legacies of the Great War.[73] In a suggestive work drawing on the earlier studies of Maurice Halbwachs, Jan Assmann has argued that studies of collective memory depend on the interconnected social structures between "memory (or: relationship to the past), identity (or: political imagination), and cultural continuation (or: the cultivation of tradition)."[74] This insight, coupled with narrative patterns of comparative history, does much to lay the theoretical framework for a further examination of the *Dolchstoss* phenomenon.

The legacy of the Great War is too often a convenient narrative frame that ends the outdated Habsburg mystique and begins the story of the modern Austrian state. The material deprivations and territorial losses of the war have been well-documented in the history of twentieth century Austrian history.[75] Beyond the generic concept of the formation of oppositional political camps, much less studied are the mentalities, emotions, and frustrations that began during the war, specifically as a result of the war, and carried over into the postwar period and its new socio-political context.

This essay began with a binary question, "Was there an Austrian stab-in-the-back myth?" The principle of Chekhov's gun necessitates an answer: This essay argues for a qualified "Yes." No, there was not a *Dolchstoss* in the sense of a unifying vision that animated the collective right-wing in Austria as a political force during the 1920s, as was the case in Weimar Germany. There were two main reasons for this: first, the comparative political insignificance of a military elite that was incapable of admitting defeat and taking responsibility for it, and second, the dominant religious institution in Austria, the Catholic Church, did not seek blame for the destruction of the Habsburg throne-and-altar alliance.

Nevertheless, yes, such a myth did exist in the sense of motivating sectors of the interwar right in Austria who were searching both for scapegoats and for grounds to legitimate fundamental opposition to the political system, which increased during the period of the 1920s and 1930s, especially after the Justice Palace fire of 1927. The Austrian *Dolchstoss* phenomenon, though deserving of further study, began to emerge during the years of the Great War and into the First Republic as political frustration increased. Indeed, as the years went by, the German *Dolchstoss* myth became inextricably intertwined with Austrian sentiments that had emerged during the Great War. Most notably, these included the German National camp, many of whom were junior officers from the Great War, who drew on their war experiences in order to express their dissatisfaction with the current political system. It is in this area that a blended pan-German political animosity most resembled its German counterpart, even if sometimes expressed in more specifically Austrian terms. In Assmann's collective memory conceptualization, increasing numbers of Austrians viewed their identity as culturally German. Consequently, they cultivated a tradition that selectively looked to a vision of the Great War that identified an ethnic enemy responsible for their current socio-political misery.

The nature of selective remembrance and forgetting is crucial in the construction of social collective memories associated with national mythmaking. As time progressed in the Austrian First Republic, the supranational Habsburg mystique was quickly forgotten as a source of useful social myth for a military-based collective memory of the war. Earlier *Dolchstoss* visions about disloyal national groups, especially from high-ranking Habsburg military commanders, fell by the wayside because those national groups were no longer effectively represented in the political scene of the First Republic. In the small Austrian state, the political imaginary of a catch-all inner enemy responsible for postwar memory was reduced to the Jewish-Bolshevik figure identified with the cosmopolitan socialist bastion of Red Vienna, seemingly incongruous in the new rump state.[76] This also merged quite efficiently with Nazi visions of membership in a German community.

Yet one must not overstate the case. Even within right-wing and anti-Semitic politics in Austria throughout most of the 1920s, an Austrian *Dolchstoss* remained marginalized in comparison to its German counterpart. In reference to disparities between the harsh rhetoric of anti-Semitism and its lack of concrete political effects in Austria, Peter Pulzer has argued that, "All in all, the only consistent characteristic of official anti-Semitism under the Republic and the Dollfuss-Schuschnigg regime was *Schlamperei*."[77]

Although generally accurate as a statement of official policy, scholars must analyze the deeper social diffusion of noxious ideas, especially when those ideas helped to bolster the ideology of the Nazi movement that eventually conquered Austria—both from outside and inside of the Austrian state's borders.

In line with broader patterns of historiography, the turn to cultural history has shown a remarkable outpouring in recent years, and the cultural history of the Great War is a part of this trend. Only relatively recently, historians of the conflict have begun to discover the autonomous power of the mentalities of ordinary soldiers and civilians.[78] The war's participants constructed complex worldviews based on their individual experiences, which highlights situational contingency as well as the broader social patterns involved in the construction of identity formation.

The military history of the Great War and its legacy for the Austrian First Republic must stop focusing on generals and field marshals as well as the literary output of undeniably talented modernist writers like Kraus and Hašek. Instead, scholarly effort must concentrate on ordinary participants,[79] especially junior officers and enlisted men who became political players of importance during the interwar period. Thus, the broader societal resonance of the stab-in-the-back myth as *ex post facto* rationalization is a topic worthy of further consideration, especially among the groups that would play important roles in the intertwined political, military, and paramilitary history of the Austrian First Republic.

If one discards convenient narrative frames, dominated by an Austrian military historiography that ends the war conveniently in 1918 with a collective verdict of the Army's tragic but noble loyalty, the picture becomes much more complicated. An Austrian stab-in-the-back legend represents an "entangled history" that one cannot so easily unravel.

Notes

1. Thomas Kühne and Benjamin Ziemann, "Militärgeschichte in der Erweiterung: Konjunkturen, Interpretationen, Konzepte," in *Was ist Militärgeschichte?*, ed. Thomas Kühne and Benjamin Ziemann (Paderborn: Ferdinand Schöningh, 2000), 9-46. For their comments and suggestions to improve this paper, I would like to thank Günter Bischof, John Deak, Thomas Grischany, Jonathan Gumz, Bettina Houlihan, Ke-chin Hsia, Nicole Phelps, Aviel Roshwald, and Gregory Weeks; I bear full responsibility for errors that remain.

2. Jürgen Kocka, "Comparison and Beyond," *History & Theory 42* (Feb. 2003): 39-44.

3. Wolfgang Schivelbusch, *The Culture of Defeat: On National Trauma, Mourning, and Recovery*, trans. Jefferson Chase (New York: Picador, 2003).

4. Ibid., 15. Foremost among these for German-speaking Central Europe, of course, was the *Nibelungenlied*. See ibid., 203-15, 247.

5. Ernst Bruckmüller, *Nation Österreich: Kulturelles Bewußtsein und gesellschaftlich-politische Prozesse*, 2nd ed. (Vienna: Böhlau, 1996), 27-34. See also Friedrich Heer, *Der Kampf um die österreichische Identität* (Vienna: Böhlau, 1981); Félix Kreissler, *Der Österreicher und seine Nation: ein Lernprozess mit Hindernissen* (Vienna: Böhlau, 1984). For an excellent conceptual overview of recent revisionist trends against a teleology of inherent Habsburg decline and fall, see Gary B. Cohen, "Nationalist Politics and the Dynamics of State and Civil Society in the Habsburg Monarchy, 1867–1914," *Central European History 40* (Jun. 2007): 241-78.

6. Robert A. Kann, "Wolfgang Menzel: Pioneer of Integral Nationalism," *Journal of the History of Ideas 6* (Apr. 1945): 213-30, here 218, 213. For the concept of "Verräter an der gemeinsamen Sache des Vaterlandes," see Panajotis Kondylis, "Reaktion, Restauration," in *Geschichtliche Grundbegriffe: Historisches Lexikon zur politisch-sozialen Sprache in Deutschland*, ed. Otto Brunner et al. (Stuttgart: Klett-Cotta, 1984), 5:207.

7. Boris Barth, *Dolchstoßlegenden und politische Desintegration: das Trauma der deutschen Niederlage im Ersten Weltkrieg* (Düsseldorf: Droste, 2003). See also Gerd Krumeich, „Die Dolchstoß-Legende," in *Deutsche Erinnerungsorte*, ed. Etienne François and Hagen Schulze (Munich: C.H. Beck, 2001), 1:585-99. Or, more briefly, Gerd Krumeich, "Dolchstoßlegende," in *Enzyklopädie Erster Weltkrieg*, ed. Gerhard Hirschfeld et al., 2nd ed. (Paderborn: F. Schöningh, 2004), 444-45.

8. Robert A. Kann, *The Habsburg Empire: A Study in Integration and Disintegration* (New York: Praeger, 1957), 164.

9. Most recently, see Steven Beller, *A Concise History of Austria* (Cambridge: Cambridge University Press, 2006), 209. See also Francis L. Carsten, *Fascist Movements in Austria: From Schönerer to Hitler* (London: Sage, 1977), 95; Bruce F. Pauley, *From Prejudice to Persecution: A History of Austrian Anti-Semitism* (Chapel Hill: University of North Carolina Press, 1992), 159.

10. Gergely Romsics, *Myth and Remembrance: The Dissolution of the Habsburg Empire in the Memoir Literature of the Austro-Hungarian Political Elite*, trans. Thomas J. DeKornfeld and Helen D. Hiltabidle (Wayne: Center for Hungarian Studies and Publications, distributed by Columbia University Press, 2006), 37-43.

11. The most definitive work to date on Austria-Hungary during the Great War remains Manfried Rauchensteiner, *Der Tod des Doppeladlers: Österreich-Ungarn und der Erste Weltkrieg* (Graz: Styria, 1993).

12. Rauchensteiner has argued that after the Brusilov offensive of 1916, German troops were the "corset strings" that held Austro-Hungarian forces together. See ibid., 372.

13. Rudolf Jeřábeck, "Die österreichische Weltkriegsforschung," in *Der Erste Weltkrieg: Wirkung, Wahrnehmung, Analyse*, ed. Wolfgang Michalka (Munich: Piper, 1994), 953-71, here 956.

14. Gunther E. Rothenberg, "The Shield of the Dynasty: Reflections on the Habsburg Army, 1649-1918," *Austrian History Yearbook 32* (2001): 169-206.

15. Mark Cornwall, "Morale and Patriotism in the Austro-Hungarian Army, 1914-1918," in *State, Society, and Mobilization in Europe during the First World War*, ed. John Horne (Cambridge: Cambridge University Press, 1997), 173-91. See also John W. Boyer, *Culture and Political Crisis in Vienna: Christian Socialism in Power, 1897-1918* (Chicago: University of Chicago Press, 1995), 369-443.

16. Bundesministerium für Heerwesen und Österreichisches Kriegsarchiv, ed., *Österreich-Ungarns letzter Krieg* (Vienna: Verlag der Militärwissenschaftlichen Mitteilungen, 1930-1938), 7:809-12.

17. Ibid., 7:833.

18. Jeřábeck, "Die österreichische Weltkriegsforschung," 953-71; see Peter Broucek and Kurt

Peball, *Geschichte der österreichischen Militärhistoriographie* (Cologne: Böhlau, 2000).

19. Gunther E. Rothenberg, *The Army of Francis Joseph* (West Lafayette: Purdue University Press, 1976), 221.

20. István Deák, *Beyond Nationalism: A Social and Political History of the Habsburg Officer Corps, 1848-1918* (Oxford: Oxford University Press, 1990).

21. Artur Arz von Straussenburg, *Zur Geschichte des Grossen Krieges, 1914-1918* (Vienna: Rikola, 1924), 222. More objective recent research has confirmed the extent to which an "inner front" in the last year of the war helped to cause the collapse of the Habsburg polity. See Richard Georg Plaschka et al., *Innere Front: Militärassistenz, Widerstand, und Umsturz in der Donaumonarchie 1918* (Vienna: Verlag für Geschichte und Politik, 1974), 1:159-66.

22. Arthur Arz von Straussenburg, *Kampf und Sturz der Kaiserreiche* (Vienna: Johannes Günther, 1935), 122, 130.

23. Ibid., 128-29.

24. Quoted in Karl Friedrich Nowak, *Der Weg zur Katastrophe*, 2nd ed. (Berlin: Verlag für Kulturpolitik, 1926), cviii-cix. See also Lawrence Sondhaus, *Franz Conrad von Hötzendorf: Architect of the Apocalypse* (Boston: Humanities Press, 2000), 214-15.

25. Quoted in Nowak, *Der Weg zur Katastrophe*, cii.

26. Karl Bardolff, *Soldat im alten Österreich: Erinnerungen aus meinem Leben* (Jena: E. Diedrichs, 1938); Edmund Glaise von Horstenau, *Die Katastrophe: Die Zertrümmerung Österreich-Ungarns und das Werden der Nachfolgestaaten* (Zürich: Amalthea, 1929); Edmund Glaise von Horstenau, *Ein General im Zwielicht: die Erinnerungen Edmund Glaises von Horstenau*, ed. Peter Broucek, 3 vols. (Vienna: Böhlau, 1980-1988).

27. Michael Epkenhans et al., eds., *Militärische Erinnerungskultur: Soldaten im Spiegel von Biographien, Memoiren, und Selbstzeugnissen* (Paderborn: Ferdinand Schöningh, 2006).

28. Laurence Cole and Daniel L. Unowsky, eds., *The Limits of Loyalty: Imperial Symbolism, Popular Allegiances and State Patriotism in the Late Habsburg Monarchy* (New York: Berghahn, 2007).

29. For the contested symbolic importance of Franz Joseph, see Daniel L. Unowsky, *The Pomp and Politics of Patriotism: Imperial Celebrations in Habsburg Austria, 1848-1916* (West Lafayette: Purdue University Press, 2005). For views on Karl, see Elisabeth Kovács et al., eds., *Untergang oder Rettung der Donaumonarchie?*, 2 vols. (Vienna: Böhlau, 2004).

30. Isabel V. Hull, *Absolute Destruction: Military Culture and the Practices of War in Imperial Germany* (Ithaca: Cornell University Press, 2005).

31. Adam Wandruszka and Peter Urbanitsch, eds., *Die bewaffnete Macht*, vol. 5, *Die Habsburgermonarchie 1848-1918* (Vienna: Verlag der Österreichischen Akademie der Wissenschaften, 1987).

32. Peter Broucek, "Heerwesen," in *Österreich 1918-1938: Geschichte der Ersten Republik*, ed. Erika Weinzierl and Kurt Skalnik (Graz: Styria, 1983), 1:209-24; C. Earl Edmondson, *The Heimwehr and Austrian Politics, 1918-1936* (Athens, GA: University of Georgia Press, 1978), 16-17; Ludwig F. Jedlicka, *Ein Heer im Schatten der Parteien: Die militärpolitische Lage Österreichs, 1918-1938* (Graz: H. Böhlaus Nachf., 1955).

33. For an overview of the nineteenth century track, see Wolfgang Altgeld, *Katholizismus, Protestantismus, Judentum: Über religiösbegründete Gegensätze und nationalreligiöse Ideen in der Geschichte des deutschen Nationalismus* (Mainz: Matthias Grünewald, 1992). For the experience of the First World War as a shattering of this Protestant Prussian-led imaginary, see Gerd Krumeich and Hartmut Lehmann, eds., *"Gott mit uns": Nation, Religion, und Gewalt im 19. und frühen 20.*

Jahrhundert (Göttingen: Vandenhoeck & Ruprecht, 2000), especially the essays by Hübinger, Krumeich, and Mommsen.

34. For comparative examples of the religious dimensions of nationhood and historical time, see Aviel Roshwald, *The Endurance of Nationalism: Ancient Roots and Modern Dilemmas* (Cambridge: Cambridge University Press, 2006).

35. Michael Snape, "The Great War," in *World Christianities, c.1914-c.2000*, ed. Hugh McLeod (Cambridge: Cambridge University Press, 2006), 131-50.

36. Michael Burleigh, *Sacred Causes: The Clash of Religion and Politics from the Great War to the War on Terror* (New York: HarperCollins, 2007).

37. Wilhelm Achleitner, *Gott im Krieg: Die Theologie der österreichischen Bischöfe in den Hirtenbriefen zum Ersten Weltkrieg* (Vienna: Böhlau, 1997); Karl Hammer, *Deutsche Kriegstheologie, 1870-1918* (Munich: Deutscher Taschenbuch Verlag, 1974).

38. Bruno Spitzl, *Die Rainer: Als Feldkurat mit IR 59 im Weltkrieg*, 2nd ed. (Innsbruck: Tyrolia, 1938). For reminiscences by other Catholic chaplains, see Karl Drexel, *Feldkurat in Sibirien, 1914-1920*, 3rd ed. (Innsbruck: F. Rauch, 1949), Karl Egger, *Seele im Sturm: Kriegserleben eines Feldgeistlichen* (Innsbruck: F. Rauch, 1936).

39. Pastoralbericht for August 1917, IR 59, Apostolisches Feldvikariat, Ktn. 232, Österreichisches Staatsarchiv-Kriegsarchiv. For more on the comparative aspects of German and Austro-Hungarian Catholic military chaplaincy, see my dissertation, Patrick J. Houlihan, "Clergy in the Trenches: Catholic Military Chaplains of Germany and Austria-Hungary during the First World War," PhD. diss., University of Chicago, forthcoming.

40. Barth, *Dolchstoßlegenden und politische Desintegration*, 150-71, 340-59; quote from 555.

41. Maximilian Liebmann, "Von der Dominanz der katholischen Kirche zu freien Kirchen im freien Staat— vom Wiener Kongreß 1815 bis zur Gegenwart," in *Geschichte des Christentums in Österreich*, ed. Rudolf Leeb et al., Österreichische Geschichte (Vienna: Ueberreuter, 2003), 361-456, esp. 393-97; Karl R. Stadler, "Die Gründung der Republik," in *Österreich 1918-1938*, 1:72. It was also relatively quickly, on the second anniversary of the First Republic's founding, 21 November 1921, that the Holy See approved the allocution of the famous Concordat of 1855.

42. "Große Entscheidungen," *Reichspost*, 12 Nov. 1918.

43. Most indications are that outbursts of traditional Catholic anti-Semitism, at least from the Church hierarchy and prominent priests in the public sphere, were largely ideological instead of biological—at least in the pre-Anschluss era. Pauley, *From Prejudice to Persecution*, 158-64; see John Connelly, "Catholic Racism and Its Opponents," *Journal of Modern History 79* (Dec. 2007): 813-47.

44. Erich Zöllner, *Geschichte Österreichs: Von den Anfängen bis zur Gegenwart*, 8th ed. (Vienna: Verlag für Geschichte und Politik, 1990), 499.

45. Isabella Ackerl and Rudolf Neck, eds., *Saint-Germain 1919: Protokoll des Symposiums am 29. und 30. Mai 1979 in Wien* (Vienna: Verlag für Geschichte und Politik, 1989); Fritz Fellner, "Der Vertrag von St. Germain," in *Österreich 1918-1938*, 1:85-106; Lorenz Mikoletzky, "Saint-Germain und Karl Renner: Eine Republik wird 'diktiert,'" in *Das Werden der Ersten Republik: der Rest ist Österreich*, ed. Helmut Konrad and Wolfgang Maderthaner (Vienna: Carl Gerold's Sohn, 2008), 1:179-86.

46. Taras Borodajkewycz, *Saint-Germain: Diktat gegen Selbstbestimmung* (Vienna: Österreichische Landsmannschaft, 1969).

47. Albert Lichtblau, "Integration, Vernichtungsversuch und Neubeginn: Österreichisch-jüdische Geschichte 1848 bis zur Gegenwart," in *Geschichte der Juden in Österreich*, ed. Eveline

Brugger et al., Österreichische Geschichte (Vienna: Ueberreuter, 2006), 487-91.

48. Karl Stubenvoll, "Die christliche Arbeiterbewegung Österreichs 1918 bis 1933: Organisation, Politik, Ideologie," PhD. diss., University of Vienna, 1982, 606, 610; Hermann Holzmann, "Antisemitismus in der österreichischen Innenpolitik 1918-1933: Der Umgang der drei politischen Lager mit diesem Phänomen," Diplomarbeit, University of Vienna, 1986, 51, 109, quoted in Pauley, *From Prejudice to Persecution*, 159.

49. Boyer, *Culture and Political Crisis in Vienna*, 419-43.

50. Maureen Healy, *Vienna and the Fall of the Habsburg Empire: Total War and Everyday Life in World War I* (Cambridge: Cambridge University Press, 2004), 27, 145-46.

51. Lichtblau, "Integration, Vernichtungsversuch und Neubeginn," 492. For ethnic politics during the collapse of the Habsburg Empire, see Aviel Roshwald, *Ethnic Nationalism and the Fall of Empires: Central Europe, Russia, and the Middle East, 1914-1923* (London: Routledge, 2001).

52. Peter Pulzer, *The Rise of Political Anti-Semitism in Germany and Austria*, revised ed. (Cambridge, MA: Harvard University Press, 1988), 308-12.

53. "Eine Voraussetzung der Arbeit," *Reichspost*, 10 Sept. 1919.

54. Adam Wandruszka has written about the difficulty of finding a mean between the "overemphasis and under-emphasis" of the German Nationals in Austria as a socio-political force. See Adam Wandruszka, "Das 'nationale Lager,'" in *Österreich 1918-1938*, 1:277-315, esp. 277-78.

55. Pulzer, *The Rise of Political Anti-Semitism in Germany and Austria*, 310.

56. Robert Körber, *Rassesieg in Wien: der Grenzfeste des Reiches* (Vienna: Braumüller, 1939), 202. "Der Dolchstoß des Judentums gegen das deutsche Volk in seiner schwersten und verwundbarsten Stunde ist nicht eine Legende oder Erfindung, sondern geschichtliche Tatsache, urkundlich belegt und bewiesen, psychologisch klar und begründet."

57. Ibid., 206. "Die schon vor dem Zusammenbruch noch mitten im Kriege im Hinterlande begonnene Aufforderung des Volkes zum 'Frieden um jeden Preis' und dessen Erziehung zu Wehr- und Ehrlosigkeit durch jüdische Politiker, Journalisten und Literaten, die dann durch Schriften und Flugblätter mit Millionenauflagen auch die Front vergifteten und den weiteren Wehrwillen zerstörten, wurde nach Eroberung der Macht im Staate planmäßig fortgesetzt. Die Revolution 1918 war niemals ein Aufstand des deutschen Volkes gegen seine Bedrücker, sondern ein Aufruhr des jüdischen Untermenschen, der als haßerfüllter Eroberer die Notzeit seines Gastgebers benützte, um ihm in den Rücken zu fallen und an Stelle der vorgetäuschten 'Diktatur des Proletariats' die Zwingherrschaft jüdischer Gewaltherrscher über den arbeitenden deutschen Menschen auch in seiner ostmärkischen Heimat zu errichten."

58. Franz Schweiger, "Geschichte der niederösterreichischen Heimwehr von 1928 bis 1930," PhD. diss., University of Vienna, 1964, quoted in Carsten, *Fascist Movements in Austria*, 111; more generally, see ibid., 105-40.

59. Edmondson, *The Heimwehr and Austrian Politics, 1918-1936*; Bruce F. Pauley, *Hitler and the Forgotten Nazis: A History of Austrian National Socialism* (Chapel Hill: University of North Carolina Press, 1981); Walter Wiltschegg, *Die Heimwehr: Eine unwiderstehliche Volksbewegung?* (Munich: R. Oldenbourg, 1985); Michael Wladika, *Hitlers Vätergeneration: Die Ursprünge des Nationalsozialismus in der k.u.k. Monarchie* (Vienna: Böhlau, 2005).

60. Klemens von Klemperer, *Ignaz Seipel: Christian Statesman in a Time of Crisis* (Princeton: Princeton University Press, 1972), 436.

61. Heinrich Benedikt, ed., *Geschichte der Republik Österreich* (Vienna: Verlag für Geschichte und Politik, 1954), 336ff.; see Emmerich Tálos et al., eds., *Austrofaschismus: Politik—Ökonomie—Kultur 1933-1938*, 5th ed. (Vienna: Lit, 2005).

62. Alois Götsch, *Die Vorarlberger Heimwehr: Zwischen Bolschewistenfurcht und NS Terror* (Feldkirch: Rheticus Gesellschaft, 1993).

63. Ernst Rüdiger Starhemberg, *Memoiren* (Vienna: Almathea, 1971), 37-38.

64. Ibid., 38: "Diejenigen, die nie den Zusammenbruch ihres Vaterlandes erlebt haben, wie es der Zerfall der Österreichisch-Ungarischen Monarchie 1918 für die österreichischen Patrioten war, können kaum die schwere seelische Not nachempfinden, unter der gerade die jungen, patriotischen Österreicher angesichts des furchtbaren Ereignisses zu leiden hatten. Sie können auch nicht die verbitterte Wut ermessen, von der junge Kriegsteilnehmer einer jahrhundertealten und auch in den jüngsten Schlachten siegreichen Armee beherrscht wurden, die trotz aller Opfer, trotz aller Siege einen schmählichen Untergang miterleben mußten. Daß junge Kämpfer einer Generation, die sich um alle Hoffnungen und Erfolge betrogen sehen, gegen diejenigen hart und ungerecht werden, die geheiligte Ideale und verehrte Begriffe und Einrichtungen schmähen und in den Kot ziehen, muß man einigermaßen verstehen und darf man nicht übel nehmen. Ebenso darf man es gerechterweise den anderen, die von einem fanatischen Radikalismus für das Neue beseelt sind nicht verübeln, wenn sie jede gefühlsmäßige Anhänglichkeit an das Alte als Reaktion brandmarken und verfolgen. In diesem gegenseitigen Nichtverstehen wurzelt das tragische Schicksal, das auf der politischen Entwicklung der Republick Österreich bis zu ihrem Untergange lastete." See Karl Renner: "We all have failed, all without exception. By the force of things, by the dialectics of the civil war psychosis were we driven, all of us, to commit follies." Stenographisches Protokoll, 56. Sitzung III, G.P., 3 Oct. 1928, 1624, quoted in Klemperer, *Ignaz Seipel: Christian Statesman in a Time of Crisis*, 435. For a comparative exploration of the phenomenon of defeat, see Schivelbusch, *The Culture of Defeat.*

65. John W. Boyer, "Silent War and Bitter Peace: The Revolution of 1918 in Austria," *Austrian History Yearbook 34* (2003): 56; see Wolfgang Maderthaner, "Die eigenartige Größe der Beschränkung: Österreichs Revolution im mitteleuropäischen Spannungsfeld," in *Das Werden der Ersten Republik*, 1:187-206

66. Emil Fey, *Schwertbrüder des Deutschen Ordens* (Vienna: J. Lichtner, 1937), 218-19.

67. Robert Gerwarth, "The Central European Counter-Revolution: Paramilitary Violence in Germany, Austria and Hungary after the Great War," *Past and Present 200* (Aug. 2008): 175-209.

68. Ibid.: 181.

69. Paul A. Hanebrink, *In Defense of Christian Hungary: Religion, Nationalism, and Antisemitism, 1890-1944* (Ithaca: Cornell University Press, 2006).

70. Günter Bischof et al., eds., *New Perspectives on Austrians and World War II* (New Brunswick, NJ: Transaction, 2009); Wolfram Dornik and Stefan Karner, eds., *Die Besatzung der Ukraine 1918: Historischer Kontext—Forschungsstand—wirtschaftliche und soziale Folgen* (Graz: Verein zur Förderung der Forschung von Folgen nach Konflikten und Kriegen, 2008); Thomas R. Grischany, "The Austrians in the German Wehrmacht, 1938-45," PhD. diss., University of Chicago, 2007; Vejas Gabriel Liulevicius, *War Land on the Eastern Front: Culture, National Identity, and German Occupation in World War I* (Cambridge: Cambridge University Press, 2000); Mark Von Hagen, *War in a European Borderland: Occupations and Occupation Plans in Galicia and Ukraine, 1914-1918* (Seattle: University of Washington Press, 2007).

71. Jonathan E. Gumz, *The Resurrection and Collapse of Empire in Habsburg Serbia, 1914-1918* (New York: Cambridge University Press, 2009); see Stéphane Audoin-Rouzeau and Annette Becker, *14-18: Understanding the Great War*, trans. Catherine Temerson (New York: Hill and Wang, 2002); Alan Kramer, *Dynamic of Destruction: Culture and Mass Killing in the First World War* (Oxford: Oxford University Press, 2007).

72. Emil Brix et al., eds., *Memoria Austriae*, 3 vols. (Vienna: Verlag für Geschichte und Politik, 2004).

73. Jay Winter has called attention to the need to displace the term "collective memory," which tends to obscure the agency and identity of disparate collectives of social actors. Winter's concept of "historical remembrance" seems better suited to the task. See Jay Winter, *Remembering War: The Great War between Memory and History in the Twentieth Century* (New Haven: Yale University Press, 2006), 4-9, quote from 9. Historical remembrance, in Winter's words, "overlaps with personal or family remembrance on the one hand and religious remembrance, so central to sacred practices, on the other. But the overlap is only partial. Historical remembrance is a way of interpreting the past which draws on both history and memory, on documented narratives about the past and on the statements of those who lived through them."

74. Jan Assmann, *Das kulturelle Gedächtnis: Schrift, Erinnerung, und politische Identität in frühen Hochkulturen* (Munich: C.H. Beck, 1992), 16; see Romsics, *Myth and Remembrance.*

75. Ernst Bruckmüller, *Sozialgeschichte Österreichs* (Vienna: Herold, 1985), 448-514.

76. Helmut Gruber, *Red Vienna: Experiment in Working-Class Culture, 1919-1934* (New York: Oxford University Press, 1991); Anson Rabinbach, *The Crisis of Austrian Socialism: From Red Vienna to Civil War, 1927-1934* (Chicago: University of Chicago Press, 1983).

77. Pulzer, *The Rise of Political Anti-Semitism in Germany and Austria*, 312.

78. Jay Winter and Antoine Prost, *The Great War in History: Debates and Controversies, 1914 to the Present* (Cambridge: Cambridge University Press, 2005).

79. In addition to Maureen Healy's path-breaking work on Vienna noted earlier, studies of the everyday experience of the war in Tirol have seen remarkable advancement in recent years. See e.g., Hermann J. W. Kuprian and Oswald Überegger, eds., *Der Erste Weltkrieg im Alpenraum: Erfahrung, Deutung, Erinnerung / La Grande Guerra nell'arco alpino: esperienze e memoria* (Bozen: Athesia, 2006); Matthias Rettenwander, *Der Krieg als Seelsorge: Katholische Kirche und Volksfrömmigkeit in Tirol im Ersten Weltkrieg* (Innsbruck: Wagner, 2006); Oswald Überegger, ed., *Zwischen Nation und Region: Weltkriegsforschung im interregionalen Vergleich: Ergebnisse und Perspektiven*, Tirol im Ersten Weltkrieg (Innsbruck: Wagner, 2004). For a superb photo collection with accompanying essays, see Anton Holzer, *Die andere Front: Fotografie und Propaganda im Ersten Weltkrieg: Mit unveröffentlichten Originalaufnahmen aus dem Bildarchiv der Österreichischen Nationalbibliothek* (Darmstadt: Primus, 2007).

"A Status Which Does Not Exist Anymore": Austrian and Hungarian Enemy Aliens in the United States, 1917-21

Nicole M. Phelps

When exactly did Habsburg sovereignty in Central Europe end, and when did that of the successor states begin? Those seem like questions that should have succinct and precise answers, and, indeed, many scholars have provided answers of that nature. Their answers have not been the same, however. Some scholars, many of whom work in international and diplomatic history, take a "the king is dead; long live the king" approach: When Emperor Karl abdicated in November 1918, sovereign authority passed immediately and neatly to the governments of the successor states. Others put the end of Habsburg sovereignty several weeks earlier, when the Czecho-Slovak National Council received Allied approval to raise an army and then recognition as the "trustee" of a future independent Czechoslovak government; in this scenario, Habsburg sovereignty was rendered impotent and thus irrelevant, even if it still persisted in name. Another group argues that the transition occurred when the various successor governments declared their independence and authority. Still others—in particular, those who are most interested in what was happening day-to-day on the ground in Central Europe—see weeks and months of confusion after the armistice when people were largely without government, running on the institutional fumes of the empire, but without clear, widely recognized alternative authority figures. Yet another group might place the end of Habsburg sovereignty at the points in 1919—or 1921, in the case of Hungary—when the successor governments signed the various treaties emanating from the Paris Peace Conference. This version stresses the intergovernmental construction of sovereignty, rather than a social contract approach between government and governed.[1]

This dissent among scholars suggests that the end of Habsburg sovereignty and the transition to new Central European sovereignties was not a quick and neat development, but rather a messy and drawn-out affair, in which multiple claims to sovereignty—over individual people and specific physical territory—coexisted, each vying for sufficient support to confirm their legitimacy and carve out stable territorial and social borders. The multiplicity of sovereign claims belies the contemporary rhetoric of U.S. President Woodrow Wilson and many Central European nationalist leaders, which, in keeping with the scientific thought of the times, posited the existence of stable national communities with clearly defined, natural boundaries derived from biology and geography and manifested in language.[2]

While Wilson was positing the existence of clearly recognizable national social borders, however, other agents of the U.S. government, including officials in the departments of State, Justice, War, and Labor, were confronted with the practical problem of determining the citizenship status of those former Habsburg subjects who were located on U.S. soil when the fighting ended, particularly those individuals who had been interned or jailed as dangerous enemy aliens after the United States entered the war. It took these officials nearly three years and a considerable amount of correspondence to figure out what to do with the enemy aliens, demonstrating that national identity was hardly self-evident. The debates surrounding the status of these enemy aliens also demonstrate that national identity and citizenship status were not matters of individual choice; the vast majority of the claims made directly by enemy aliens were ignored. Nor were identity and citizenship determined through a domestic social contract between an individual and a single government: the successor state governments had relatively little say in the matter, and, as we will see, the claims they did make were often ignored, too—especially those of the Austrian Republic.

Instead, it was agents of the U.S. government who made the key decisions, and they communicated those decisions not through the governments of the successor states, but rather through the agents of a persistent Habsburg sovereignty: the Swedish Legation in Washington. The Swedish government had accepted the responsibility of protecting Habsburg subjects in the United States when the U.S. and Habsburg governments broke diplomatic relations in April 1917, and it continued to protect those individuals in the name of the Habsburg government until late 1921. The story of these enemy aliens demonstrates the complexity and duration of the transition from Habsburg to successor state sovereignty after World War I, as well as the role of human agency in the construction of national borders.

Before World War I, citizen protection had been a key aspect of U.S.-Habsburg relations, especially from the 1880s, when changes in the international economy and transportation technology produced an explosion in the number of individuals moving back and forth between the two countries.[3] The U.S. and Austro-Hungarian governments, acting through their foreign ministries, diplomatic corps, and consular services, each worked to establish and maintain their claims to sovereign authority over their citizens traveling or living abroad, and they did that by assisting those citizens when they ran into trouble. For U.S. citizens in Austria-Hungary, that trouble most often consisted of impressment into the armed services or arrest for violating the empire's laws; these were problems that were exacerbated by ambiguities in the U.S.-Habsburg treaty that governed naturalization and the fact that passports—which would clearly mark a person's citizenship—were unnecessary for international travel. For Habsburg subjects—Austrian and Hungarian citizens—in the United States, problems typically involved work-related injuries and deaths, financial swindles, and violence motivated by racism and xenophobia. Habsburg representatives in the United States worked tirelessly to aid their fellow citizens in the United States, but they were handicapped by the relatively small size of the staff and the large number of people in need of assistance. More importantly, Habsburg efforts to get Americans to pass, obey, interpret, and enforce laws and policies consistently and in a racially unbiased manner met with little success.[4]

The problems of racism and xenophobia persisted and proliferated with the outbreak of World War I in August 1914, and they continued to escalate as the United States moved closer and closer to entering the fray on the Allied side. Because international travel became much more difficult as borders were closed, passports were required, and transportation infrastructure was given over to military uses, thousands of people got stuck in foreign countries, often without the financial assets needed to survive. All of the belligerents in the conflict followed the norms of post-1815 diplomatic culture and entrusted their citizens and other interests in enemy countries to the protection of neutral governments.[5] Before the United States entered the war, American diplomats and consuls were the primary people providing services to stranded foreigners, as governments on both sides of the conflict entrusted their interests abroad to the comparatively large and well-staffed U.S. diplomatic corps and consular service.[6] As the official U.S. position became more and more favorable to the Allies and especially when the United States joined the war, those responsibilities shifted to other governments that remained neutral. Austro-Hungarian interests in the United States were entrusted to the Swedish government, while the Swiss handled those of the German government, and U.S. interests in Austria-Hungary became the responsibility of the Spanish.

As the trustees of Habsburg sovereignty in the United States during wartime, members of the Swedish legation had a great deal to do. The war caused deep-seated American racial prejudices to erupt in particularly virulent forms, and violence—including lynchings and near lynchings—was common throughout the United States. As one historian has noted, "Immigrants ... learned it was expedient to carry Liberty Bonds at all times."[7] Austrian and Hungarian citizens were very much caught up in these trends. For example, in 1917, Joseph Kovath, a thirty-five-year-old Austrian citizen and Cambria Steel Company employee who resided in Johnstown, Pennsylvania with his wife and three children, was "escorted through several of the streets of Johnstown after having been rolled in a cement bed and grease applied to his hands and face" because he would not buy a Liberty Bond; "his escorts consisted of some 40 or 50 workmen of the mill who had him attached to a rope about the waist." According to the U.S. Department of Justice agent reporting on the incident, this could not be considered "cruel or violent treatment." He wrote, "the exhibition of him on the streets was more as a matter of ridicule or shame, with a notice perhaps to other aliens that they might expect the same treatment unless they exhibited enough loyalty to assist the Government with the Liberty Loan .... [I]t is believed that the morals established was of considerable benefit to the alien population [sic]." After his exhibition in the streets, Kovath bought a $100 Liberty Bond and was allowed to return to work; his "escorts" received no punishment.[8]

In this climate of public and officially sanctioned racial prejudice, the U.S. government formulated policies for dealing with citizens of the Central Powers located on U.S. soil. Following the 1798 Alien Act, the Justice Department had jurisdiction over enemy aliens during wartime. Prior to U.S. entry into World War I, Justice Department employees began compiling lists of Austrian, Hungarian, and German citizens in the United States, noting especially those that might prove somehow dangerous to American national security. Those lists included more than 11,000 names by 1917.[9] War Department personnel also began planning what they would do with prisoners of war once the United States was involved in the fighting.[10] They decided that they would keep prisoners of war and any civilian internees at a number of camps, the largest being at Fort Douglas, Utah, and Fort Oglethorpe, Georgia.

Once Congress passed a declaration of war against Germany on 6 April 1917, a series of special wartime legislation came into effect. Press censorship was effected via strict postal codes, and commerce was blocked through the Trading with the Enemy Act. In addition to these laws, President Wilson made several proclamations regarding the activities of enemy aliens on U.S. soil. The first set of restrictions were issued on 6 April 1917 and applied to "all natives, citizens, denizens or subjects of a hostile nation or Government being male of the age of 14 years and upward who shall be within the United States and not actually naturalized." Wilson's statement forbade enemy aliens from possessing weapons and signaling equipment and operating airplanes, and it restricted their movements and allowed for their registration, arrest, and confinement. In November 1917, more restrictions were added, further limiting the freedom of mobility of aliens and obliging all enemy aliens to register and carry their registration cards with them at all times. Finally, in the spring of 1918, these restrictions were again expanded, this time to apply to female enemy aliens, as well as male.[11]

Between April and December 1917, these restrictions on enemy aliens were supposed to apply only to German citizens, as the United States was only at war with Germany. Wilson made the point that Austrian and Hungarian citizens were not to be affected by these restrictions. This was not merely an effort to adhere to international law: Austrian and Hungarian citizens made up large portions of the workforce in vital war-related industries, including iron, steel, coal, and munitions. Even when Congress finally declared war on Austria-Hungary in December 1917, Wilson issued yet another proclamation that limited the applicability of the enemy alien restrictions on certain citizens of Austria and Hungary who were vital to war production, but these provisions did not prevent many Austrian and Hungarian citizens from losing their jobs or from being harassed by members of the public.[12]

Indeed, the limits of the presidential proclamation did not stop the Justice and War departments from arresting and interning Austrian citizens, even before the American declaration of war against Austria-Hungary. Assistant Attorney General Charles Warner, commenting on potential espionage charges against Julius Preleuthner, an Austrian citizen, wrote, "Of course, he cannot be taken up by this Department under the President's proclamation, but I feel that it is very unsafe to have him, as well as many other Austrians, wandering around loose here. Many of them are unquestionably in the pay of Germany and are acting here as German spies."To get around the proclamation, Warner asked the State Department to inform the War Department of the case "and ask them if they could not take up men of this character under the provisions of the present Articles of War relating to spies."[13] The War Department took Preleuthner into custody less than a week later and interned him "pending an investigation for sufficient evidence to warrant his court martial." Sufficient evidence was never found, but Preleuthner was still in the camp when war against Austria-Hungary was declared, making him eligible for detention under the president's new proclamation of December 1917.[14]

Between April 1917 and February 1919, the Justice Department and various local jurisdictions arrested approximately 6,000 enemy aliens. Of these, approximately 2,300 were interned. The civilian internees were a very diverse group of people. As historian Gerald H. Davis has observed, "The common bond was [their] arbitrary concentration ... in a remote location because someone with authority regarded them as 'dangerous enemy aliens.'"[15] Department of Justice officials opted to define threats to national security very broadly. There were working-class people with socialist, communist, and/or anarchist tendencies among the internees, including members of the International Workers of the World. There was also a white-collar group that included businessmen, engineers, scientists, professors, editors of ethnic newspapers, and musicians, among others. The internees were almost exclusively male, although approximately fifteen women were also interned. Some of the internees were relatively long-term residents in the United States, while others were travelers who got stuck in the United States once opportunities for international travel became scarce and dangerous.[16]

Extant records make it a challenge to parse out the Austrian and Hungarian citizens from the Germans, but there were at least 150 of them.[17] Among the white collar group, those who wrote letters to the Swedish Legation included Erich Pohl, a Viennese mining engineer; Dr. E. E. Werber, a Galician-born biologist who had worked at Princeton and who had held a prestigious fellowship at Yale just prior to his internment; and Dr. Ernst Kunwald, the director of the Cincinnati Symphony Orchestra. Kunwald's wife was also interned, as was at least one other Austrian woman, Margarethe Weiss-Wikins. Repatriation and deportation records in the State Department files also reveal more than fifty alleged anarchists from Austria-Hungary.[18]

The Habsburg and German governments did not take issue with

the U.S. government's right to intern their male civilian citizens. It was a widespread practice of the time, although in World War I it was most common in Britain, Australia, Canada, and the United States—countries further removed from the battlefields and with more resources to spare.[19] The specific circumstances that brought individuals to the camps in the United States were often problematic, however, and the staff of the Swedish Legation spent much of their time calling for investigations into the legality of individual internment cases at the request of the internees.

The majority of the civilian internees had no idea what the specific charges against them were, and they repeatedly asked the Swedish Legation to try and find out.[20] The one relatively concrete charge that Department of Justice officials frequently mentioned was espionage, but very little, if any, solid evidence was ever found in these cases.[21] As Austrian laborer Valentin Reibel told the Swedish ambassador, "I am as much a spy or plotter as a ship is the moon." He went on to say, "I am put into an interment camp for absolutely nothing except being austrian born [sic]."[22] In most cases, when the Swedish Legation pressed to get a clear statement of the reasons for individual internments, the Department of State could only offer vague statements from the Department of Justice, such as, "his continued presence at large was considered as constituting a menace to the peace and safety of the United States in its successful prosecution of the war."[23] The Department of Justice was equally unforthcoming about denying parole, usually meeting such requests with phrases like, parole is "inadvisable at the present time," or "your being at large would be incompatible with the best interests of the United States."[24] The basic Department of Justice policy was to intern people first and then undertake investigations—investigations that rarely produced sufficient evidence. John Lord O'Brien of the Department of Justice went so far as to comment on three Austrian citizens that "until innocence has been definitely established, the presumption against these persons is such that it would not be the part of wisdom to release them."[25] This stance went against the constitutionally sanctioned American legal notion that people are to be presumed innocent until proven guilty.

Department of Justice officials also responded to public demand for arrests; such demand usually appeared in the newspapers. In describing the Department of Justice's investigation of Ernst Kunwald's case—which was led by J. Edgar Hoover—historian Allan Howard Levy wrote, "Finally, admitting no solid evidence existed but holding that public outcry must be met, [Hoover] ordered Kunwald arrested."[26] Department of Justice officials commented in some of the cases where press feeling was high that they were acting to protect the aliens from mob violence, but not everyone was convinced by that line of argument.[27] Alvo von Alvensleben, a prominent German-born businessman with significant property in Canada and the United States, accused the Department of Justice of colluding with the press to destroy alien enemies: "You arrested and gave no reasons, the press did the rest. It vilified, exaggerated, invented, insinuated, in short it did the dirty work and you remain 'The Department of Justice.' Your part was to appear lenient, just, broadminded, liberal—the press was vindictive, unscrupulous, sensational, untrue and to use your own words: 'Your department was not aware of any means at your disposal to control public opinion.'"[28]

Local grievances that had absolutely nothing to do with the war or the Department of Justice could also land people in internment camps.[29] For example, in early December 1917, Mr. Schoppe, a deputy sheriff in Salt Lake City, arrested Mr. Erich Pohl, an Austrian citizen and mining engineer who resided in Salt Lake City with his pregnant wife and three children. Apparently, Schoppe was interested in Mrs. Pohl, and he had been harassing the entire family for months, trying to get her to divorce her husband and take up with him. After Pohl spent several weeks in jail, Schoppe met with a local U.S. district attorney and arranged for Pohl's internment. Once interned, Pohl met with a U.S. marshal about his case, and that marshal told Pohl that, prior to Schoppe's meeting with the district attorney, he "was not even known to the federal authorities to be an alien, much less dangerous."[30]

Cases like these were symptomatic of a broader racism and xenophobia, as well as wartime disregard for civil liberties on the part of many American officials and members of the public. The abuses, along with numerous others, sparked a broader movement for civil liberties protection, including the founding of the American Civil Liberties Union.[31] Appeals to legal rights were not particularly effective in getting enemy aliens released from internment camps, however. Internees—German as well as Austrian and Hungarian citizens—tried a number of other lines of argument, though the majority of these proved equally ineffective when the Swedish Legation presented them to the Department of Justice.

After protesting one's innocence, one of the most common strategies was to claim ill health. This strategy, however, was not at all effective. In at least one case, a camp doctor was prevailed upon to change his diagnosis to keep a prisoner incarcerated.[32] More commonly, though, the Department of Justice and the medical staff at the camps consistently argued that the medical care and facilities for the internees were more than adequate to meet the needs of the prisoners. The poor health argument was especially ineffective for those interned at Fort Douglas because the doctors usually argued that internment was in fact a health benefit, especially for internees with tuberculosis. One doctor did note that camp conditions could cause nervous disorders, but that was not seen as grounds for release.[33] As internment dragged on into late 1919 and early 1920, however, the Justice Department was increasingly lenient in granting medical transfers—particularly to St. Elizabeth's in Washington, DC, the federal government's primary mental health facility.[34]

The Swedish Legation, in conjunction with the War Prisoners Relief Committee, a private organization headquartered in New York City, worked to find jobs and supervisors for internees so they could be released on parole.[35] Various businessmen around the country did volunteer to employ and supervise paroled internees, but the Department of Justice usually found reasons to deny parole. Mr. Reichert, an Austrian internee, made arrangements through the Swedish Legation to work for August Cornelius, a farmer in Minneapolis, Minnesota. The Department of Justice deemed this location "inadvisable," and Reichert stayed in the camp.[36] In the case of Friederich Woehrer, the Relief Committee found him a job at New York's Sullivan County Creamery Company and also provided his rail passage to the job. The Department of Justice had already sent Woehrer to work at the Katterjohn Construction Company in Cedar Bluff, Kentucky, with several other internees, and they decided that it was better for Woehrer to stay at that location, where he would be more heavily supervised.[37]

Existing records do not reveal exactly how each individual internee came to be released from the camps, so conclusions about what arguments were most persuasive can not be made decisively. From the available records, however, it does appear the appeals to gender responsibilities—providing economic support for women and children—did resonate with the Department of Justice. For example, Dr. E. E. Werber wrote to the Swedish Legation that his wife, who was living in the United States, was receiving relief payments from the War Prisoners Relief Committee, but those payments were insuffiencient. He asked to be released in order to provide for her.[38] He was released two months later in October 1918, making him one of the earliest parolees.[39] The effectiveness of this argument may also be attributable to the fact that immigrants with wives and children in the United States were more apt to become U.S. citizens and were therefore seen as safer and more desirable than those who had left their families in Europe and thus had potentially powerful ties to the enemy.

When the camps were first opened, the Austro-Hungarian experience there was not particularly different from the German experience. Austrian and Hungarian internees became distinctly different from their German counterparts with the partial recognition of Czechoslovak sovereignty in the fall of 1918, however. While German internees were still clearly German and there was still a Germany that they might go back to, the fate of the Habsburg Empire was called dramatically into question, creating new confusion and new possibilities for the Austrian and Hungarian internees. In March 1919, Frank Daniš, an internee at Fort Oglethorpe, wrote to the Department of State via the Swedish Legation "as spokesman of the internees of Slavic nationality," asking for release on the grounds that those internees born in Bohemia and Moravia were now citizens of the "Tsechco-Slovakian Republic," which had been recognized by Allies. "They have been interned as Austrians," he wrote, "a status which, in their particular case, does not exist anymore." He added that he and his fellow internees wished to stay in the United States "for the time being at least," and that "not a single one has been indicted for an offence against the United States."[40] Daniš wrote for the group again a few days later, this time sending an excerpt from a *New York Times* article on "Britain's Interned Aliens." According to the article, of Britain's 18,607 interned enemy civilians, approximately 6,000 had been repatriated, and 113 had been released from the camps; two thirds of this latter number were released "on being duly recognized as Czechoslovaks and therefore ceasing to be enemies."[41] Daniš observed, "As we presume you are going to treat subjects of the Czecho-Slovak Republic similarly we trust you will recognize our present status."[42]

State Department officials duly forwarded the letters on to the Department of Justice. In response, a Justice Department official addressed his comments to the Department of State, writing that the Justice Department had "informed the internees that in the absence of any notice from you [the Department of State] that the status of natives, citizens, denizens or subjects of a hostile nation or government has been changed they must still be considered alien enemies ...."[43] When put to the Office of the Solicitor at the Department of State, official opinion held that, although the Czecho-Slovak National Council had been recognized as "a de facto belligerent government clothed with proper authority to direct the military forces of the Czecho Slovaks," no specific territorial rights came with that recognition. Therefore, the territory of Bohemia retained its status as enemy territory, and as a result the internees were still enemy aliens.[44] With this answer, the Solicitor was sticking by nineteenth-century conceptions of territorial sovereignty, rather than making a leap to a Wilsonian future in which ties of blood were to be more salient than physical location for determining national identity and citizenship.

When Daniš heard the Justice Department's decision, he wrote to the

Department of State again, encouraging them to notify the Department of Justice of his group's change in status. He argued:

> ever since [the Czecho-Slovak Republic's] establishment we unequivocally considered ourselves citizens of the New State. We were born in districts which undoubtedly compose the Czecho-Slovak Republic, our nearest relatives are living there, some of whom have meanwhile become official members of Boards instituted by the new Czech authorities, we own property and business there, and some of us have there permanent residence there. In the present state of affairs we know of no other reasons which could prove our present status as citizens of the Czecho-Slovak Republic more clearly since we cannot be citizens of Austria-Hungary which does not exist anymore, and therefore also ceased to be technical alien enemies.[45]

Daniš managed to get out on parole after an investigation of his particular circumstances, but the rest of his group was still interned. Their new spokesman was Erich Posselt, and he wrote to both the Department of State and Department of Justice via the Swedish Legation several times over the following months. He repeated the argument that Austria-Hungary no longer existed and thus could not have citizens and again drew attention to the recognition of the Czechoslovak government by the Allies and Czechoslovak participation in the peace negotiations. He again requested that the Department of State inform the Department of Justice of their change in status.[46] He then went further with his arguments, stating that he and those he represented had all taken out their first citizenship papers, thus demonstrating their intention to become U.S. citizens. This likely hurt Posselt's case, rather than helping it: Admitting a desire to stay in the United States went against Justice Department efforts to repatriate or deport as many internees as possible, and a claim on U.S. citizenship undermined his claim to Czechoslovak citizenship.

By August 1919, Posselt was writing on his own behalf.[47] He wrote to the Swedish Legation:

> In view of the fact that it is my intention to become a citizen of this country—I have taken out my so-called First paper more than five years ago—I respectfully ask you once more to intervene in my behalf to bring about my discharge from the internment camp. As I have pointed out before I happen to be born in, and am still a subject of Bohemia. As you know Bohemia, under the protection of the Allied powers, and more especially under the protection and with the aid of the United States, has become an independent republic even now represented

in Washington. I have never had any connections with German or Austrian subjects who were in the pay of the respective Governments, and have never received any penny out of any German or Austrian fund. I am far from being an anarchist or a believer in the doctrins [sic] of bolshevism. I am not a propagandist. And I know myself absolutely innocent of any overt act against this country. I am a married man, and my wife is living here. I have no near relatives abroad, and have no business interests in Europe. It is my wish to stay permanently in the US, and I am willing to give any guarantee required for my bona fide intentions. May be these points, if presented by you to the proper authorities, will help to finally settle my case in my favor.[48]

The Department of State, apparently ignoring previous correspondence from the Department of Justice that told them the issue of release from camps for such persons depended on a statement from the Department of State, forwarded Posselt's letter on to the Department of Justice. This time, however, the Department of Justice's story changed. Rather than laying the blame for continued internment at the Department of State's door, the Department of Justice responded that, "while it is fully cognizant of certain appealing aspects in Mr. Posselt's case, it has thus far, notwithstanding a most careful review of the record of his activities in this country, not deemed it expedient to release him. The Department will, however, give Mr. Posselt's case further attention."[49]

In November 1919, Posselt changed his story. He had an interview with a Department of Justice representative, who informed him that the department believed him to have been engaged in espionage, a charge which Posselt hotly denied. He asked for a trial on those charges.[50] He did not wait for a response before writing to the Swedish Legation again. In this next letter, he announced that his wife was ill and without funds and thus in need of his assistance and release.[51] This last, of course, had helped others get out of the internment camps. It did not provoke a quick response in Posselt's case, however, and he wrote again in December 1919, this time saying that he had "instructed my lawyers to start habeas corpus proceedings ... as it is contrary to all national and international law to hold in confinement without legal charge any person. (See Article-Amendment VI of the Constitution)."[52] This letter—and, more importantly, the passage of time— yielded the desired results, and Posselt was paroled on 8 January 1920.[53] The combination of a desire to remain in the United States, presumed espionage activities, and the Department of State's decision not to announce to the Department of Justice that the status of Czechoslovaks had changed kept people in internment camps for more than a year past U.S.

recognition of the Czecho-Slovak Republic and the end of all hostilities.

> At least one internee was successfully able to claim Czecho-Slovak citizenship, however. Felix Zweig wrote to the Department of State in May 1919 that "Under date of April 21st, 1919 I have been informed by my lawyer ... that the Czecho-Slovak Minister has recognized me as a citizen of his country and that he has stated this fact to the Department of State. I am asking you herewith to kindly officially notify the Department of Justice of said change in my status ...."[54] Shortly thereafter, a New York City attorney wrote to the Department of State requesting a passport for Zweig, as the Department of Justice had agreed to his release.[55] Apparently the combination of official Czecho-Slovak recognition—and the desire to leave the United States—were enough to secure release.

On the whole, however, the successor states were in no rush to claim responsibility for the internees, and Habsburg subjects were still instructed to write to the Swedish Legation for help, rather than to representatives of the successor governments. In March 1919, the Swedish Legation informed the State Department that relief payments to internees and their families from the Austro-Hungarian government had to stop, "since the Governments of the various states of the former Austro-Hungarian Monarchy are not disposed to furnish the necessary funds." The Swedish minister went on to request the immediate release of internees with families to support, or, failing that, to adjust the Relief Committee's powers so that they could provide relief payments in lieu of those from the Austro-Hungarian government.[56] The Justice Department replied that the release of all such internees was "not deemed advisable," but a half a dozen were released under this initiative, and the Relief Committee was allowed to provide funds.[57]

Not only were the successor states unwilling to make relief payments, they were also generally unwilling to accept repatriates or deportees from the United States. Both the Department of Justice, which had jurisdiction over the repatriation of internees, and the Department of Labor, which housed the Bureau of Immigration and had jurisdiction over enemy aliens who had been arrested, jailed, and slated for deportation, were committed to removing enemy aliens from U.S. soil. Their approaches differed, however. The Department of Justice was willing to hold people in camps indefinitely, waiting on repatriations until the successor governments agreed to take the individuals who were rightfully "theirs," as the Zweig case demonstrates; officials would also release internees from the camps on parole, which did not alter their status as enemy aliens or Habsburg subjects. Department of Justice officials were waiting on the Department of State to inform them of status changes, and the Department of State staff was waiting on developments in Europe—namely, the formal, legal acceptance of the Paris treaties by all interested parties.

The Department of Labor, however, was unwilling to wait, and Immigration officials moved quickly to deport people into the confusion that was Central and Eastern Europe, much to the dismay of the enemy aliens, the successor governments, and the Swedish Legation. The Department of Labor's deportation practices were directly at odds with Wilsonian rhetoric and the spirit of the peace treaties, which aimed at creating a peaceful Europe through the introduction of nation-states and the alignment of individuals' biologically based national identity with their political citizenship and their physical location. In short, the Wilsonian vision was that all Poles, for example, would live in Poland and hold Polish citizenship, allowing them to express their common political goals in their own democratic state. Immigration officials did not worry about that alignment, however.

The heart of the problem was this: the official diplomatic name of Austria-Hungary while it existed was "Austria," so when people had given their place of birth to Immigration officials before the war, they usually named a town, a province, and then "Austria," or, in many cases, merely "Austria." Thus, when Immigration officials wanted to deport people after the war, they planned on sending all these people back to where they came from: Austria. However, most of these deportees had not come from the territory that was now the independent Republic of Austria; at least one-third of them were from the province of Galicia, which had become part of the newly independent Poland, and, ethnically, they were either Polish or Ruthenian (Ukrainian). The government of the Austrian Republic did not want to accept the anarchists, nor did it want to have to deal with them traveling through Austrian territory en route to other locations—an understandable position for a fledgling government trying to establish its authority.[58]

For example, one of the potential deportees, Mike Podolak, was identified as "a native and subject of Austria, ... of the Ukrainian race, [who] gives his place of birth as Sambor, Lonevich, Galicia, Austria."[59] To the Swedish Legation, the most relevant part of that statement was either Galicia, which meant that he should be sent to Poland, or Ukrainian, which meant he should be sent to Ukraine—at the time occupied by Soviet forces. The Labor Department, however, kept focusing on Austria, much to the consternation of the Austrian Republic. Ultimately, what was most important to immigration officials was Sambor, but they did not clearly convey that to the Swedes or the Austrians. In defending the deportations, Louis F. Post, assistant secretary of labor, wrote, "It seems immaterial whether the homes of these aliens are included in States other than Austria under the geographical rearrangement effected in Europe, and notwithstanding they were ordered deported to Austria, the Commissioner at Ellis Island invariably secures transportation in deportations at Government expense to the aliens' respective homes, and it would seem that this is all that is necessary under the present unsettled conditions."[60] Post apparently failed to realize that Labor Department policy was contributing to those "unsettled conditions."

The head of the Swedish Legation wrote to the Department of State to try and enlist the help of the State Department in putting a halt to the deportations. The minister requested "the kind intermediary of the Secretary of State with a view that the Department of Labor, before issuing the warrants for deportation, may kindly establish positively the present citizenship of subjects of the former Austro-Hungarian Monarchy, in order that they be deported to the State of which they are subjects at the present time, and that the deportation of subjects of the former Austro-Hungarian Monarchy be held in abeyance until their present citizenship has been positively ascertained."[61] In making this request, the Swedish minister was following the Habsburg tradition in dealing with the U.S. government: he was calling for consistency in American policy. He was also attempting to act in the best interests of the individuals the Habsburg government had charged him with protecting, trying to make sure those individuals ended up in a place where they could maximize their political rights and personal safety. Through the Swedish Legation, Habsburg sovereignty—and particularly the responsibility of the government to provide protection to those it governed—persisted for a considerable amount of time after Karl's abdication, playing a role the successor governments were not yet strong enough to assume.

Notes

1. Accounts that end with Karl's abdication include Wilfried Fest, *Peace or Partition: The Habsburg Monarchy and British Policy, 1914-1918* (New York: St. Martin's Press, 1978); Paul M. Kennedy, *The Rise and Fall of the Great Powers: Economic Change and Military Conflict from 1500 to 2000* (1987; New York: Vintage Books, 1989); and many surveys of the empire's history, including Robert A. Kann, *A History of the Habsburg Empire, 1526-1918* (Berkeley: University of California Press, 1974); and Alan Sked, *The Decline and Fall of the Habsburg Empire, 1815-1918* (New York: Longman, 1989). Czech-centered accounts include Victor S. Mamatey, *The United States and East Central Europe 1914-1918: A Study in Wilsonian Diplomacy and Propaganda* (Princeton: Princeton University Press, 1957); as well as the view of Czech nationalist leaders themselves; see

Tomás G. Masaryk and Henry Wickham Steed, *The Making of a State: Memories and Observations, 1914-1918* (New York: Frederick A. Stokes Co., 1927). On-the-ground accounts include John W. Boyer, "Silent War and Bitter Peace: The Revolution of 1918 in Austria," *Austrian History Yearbook 34* (2003): 1-56; Maureen Healy, *Vienna and the Fall of the Habsburg Empire: Total War and Everyday Life in World War I* (New York: Cambridge University Press, 2004); and Dagmar Perman, *The Shaping of the Czechoslovak State: Diplomatic History of the Boundaries of Czechoslovakia, 1914-1920* (Leiden: E. J. Brill, 1962). Treaty-focused accounts include Frederick Dumin, "Self-Determination: The United States and Austria in 1919," *Research Studies 40* (3/1972): 176-94; and Ivo J. Lederer, *Yugoslavia at the Paris Peace Conference: A Study in Frontiermaking* (New Haven: Yale University Press, 1963). My understanding of sovereignty and its complexities is based on Stephen Krasner, *Sovereignty: Organized Hypocrisy* (Princeton: Princeton University Press, 1999).

2. For Wilson's personal perspective, see Ray Stannard Baker, ed., *Woodrow Wilson: Life and Letters*, 8 vols. (Garden City: Doubleday, Page & Co., 1927-39). For supporters of Wilson, including the staff of the Inquiry, see, among numerous others, Leon Dominian, *The Frontiers of Language and Nationality in Europe* (New York: Henry Holt and Company for the American Geographical Society of New York, 1917); and Charles Seymour, *Geography, Justice, and Politics at the Paris Conference of 1919* (New York: American Geographical Society, 1951). The Inquiry's relationship with Wilson and the members' expertise and worldviews are explored in Lawrence E. Gelfand, *The Inquiry: American Preparations for Peace, 1917-1919* (New Haven: Yale University Press, 1963). The idea of fully formed national groups just waiting to be freed from Habsburg rule also found a home in a great deal of subsequent scholarship on the empire; a key text that bridges the divide between participant accounts and subsequent historiography is Oscar Jászi, *The Dissolution of the Habsburg Monarchy* (Chicago: University of Chicago Press, 1929).

3. On migration between the two countries—including return migration to the empire—see Mark Wyman, *Round-trip to America: The Immigrants Return to Europe, 1880-1930* (Ithaca: Cornell University Press, 1993).

4. I elaborate on these problems in my dissertation: Nicole M. Phelps, "Sovereignty, Citizenship, and the New Liberal Order: US-Habsburg Relations and the Transformation of International Politics, 1880-1924," PhD. diss., University of Minnesota, 2008.

5. On this practice, see David D. Newsom, *Diplomacy Under a Foreign Flag: When Nations Break Relations* (Washington, DC: Institute for the Study of Diplomacy, School of Foreign Service, Georgetown University, 1989).

6. U.S. officials protected the interests of Britain, France, Italy, Russia, Japan, Serbia, Montenegro, Romania, San Marino, and Belgium in Austria-Hungary, as well as Habsburg interests in Britain, France, Japan, Russia, and Belgium. See No. 46, "Closing of the Budapest Consulate General," Coffin to the Secretary of State, Christiania, Norway, 24 July 1917, file no. 125.2432/54; "Conduct of the Consulate General at Budapest, Hungary, since July 4, 1914," Mallett to the Secretary of State, Budapest, 14 September 1914, file no. 125.2436/32; "Work of the Budapest Consulate General during the war," Coffin to the Secretary of State, Budapest, 6 January 1916, file no. 125.2436/42; and Penfield's telegram to the Secretary of State, Vienna via Berne, 29 December 1915, file no. 124.63/4, all in U.S. National Archives and Records Administration, College Park MD, General Records of the Department of State, Record Group 59 (hereafter cited as NARA). On the efficacy of the U.S. Consular Service, see Phelps, "Sovereignty, Citizenship, and the New Liberal Order," ch. 4; and Charles Stuart Kennedy, *The American Consul: A History of the United States Consular Service, 1776-1914* (New York: Greenwood Press, 1990).

7. Helen Z. Papanikolas, "Immigrants, Minorities, and the Great War," *Utah Historical Quarterly 58* (Fall 1990): 351-70, esp. 361. On other instances of wartime violence, see, among numerous others, Jörg A. Nagler, *Nationale Minoritäten im Krieg: "Feindliche Ausländer" und die amerikanische Heimatfront während des Ersten Weltkriegs* (Hamburg: Hamburger Edition, 2000); and Christopher Capozzola, "The Only Badge Needed Is Your Patriotic Fervor: Vigilance,

Coercion, and the Law in World War I America," *Journal of American History 88* (March 2002): 1354-82.

8. J. C. Rider, "Alleged Cruelties and Violence to Austrians and Germans," 19 November 1918, file no. 311.63/351, in NARA.

9. There is some debate among historians as to when the list-making began. The date 1914 is given in Mitchell Yockelson, "The War Department: Keeper of Our Nation's Enemy Aliens during World War I," Presented to the Society for Military History Annual Meeting, April 1998, available at: <http://www.lib.byu.edu/~rdh/wwi/comment/yockel.htm> (8 July 2005); 1916 is listed in Mark Ellis and Panikos Panayi, "German Minorities in World War I: A Comparative Study of Britain and the USA," *Ethnic and Racial Studies 17* (April 1994): 238-59.

10. William B. Glidden, "Internment Camps in America, 1917-1920," *Military Affairs 37* (Dec. 1973): 137-41, esp. 138.

11. See Woodrow Wilson, "Proclamation 1364: Declaring That a State of War Exists Between the United States and Germany," 6 April 1917; and Wilson, "Proclamation 1408: Additional Regulations Prescribing the Conduct of Alien Enemies," 16 November 1917; both available through *The American Presidency Project*, ed. John T. Woolley and Gerhard Peters, available at: <http://www.presidency.ucsb.edu/ws/>; and Nagler, *Nationale Minoritäten im Krieg*, 14.

12. Nagler, *Nationale Minoritäten im Krieg*, 250-60; and E. E. Werber to the Swedish Legation, Fort Douglas UT, August 1918, file no. 311.63/230, in NARA.

13. Charles Warner to the Secretary of State, Washington, 14 September 1917, file no. 311.63/49, in NARA.

14. O'Brien to the Secretary of State, Washington, 26 January 1918, file no. 311.63/75, in NARA.

15. Gerald H. Davis, "'Orgelsdorf': A World War I Internment Camp in America," *Yearbook of German-American Studies 26* (1991): 249-65, esp. 257.

16. On internees and camp conditions, see Nagler, *Nationale Minoritäten im Krieg*; Ellis and Panayi, "German Minorities in World War I," 238-59; Nagler, "Enemy Aliens and Internment during World War I: Alvo von Alvensleben in Fort Douglas, Utah. A Case Study," *Utah Historical Quarterly 58* (Fall 1990): 388-405; Davis, "'Orgelsdorf'"; Glidden, "Internment Camps in America"; Richard B. Goldschmidt, *In and Out of the Ivory Tower: The Autobiography of Richard B. Goldschmidt* (Seattle: University of Washington Press, 1960); Yockelson, "The War Department"; and Howard Levy, "The American Symphony at War: German-American Musicians and Federal Authorities during World War I," *Mid-America: An Historical Review 71* (Jan. 1989): 5-13.

17. There were 150 Austrian and Hungarian citizens held at Fort Ogelthorpe, Georgia; the number held in other camps has not been separated from the statistics on Germans; see Davis, "'Orgelsdorf.'"

18. See Erich Pohl to the Swedish Ambassador, Fort Douglas, 10 February 1918, file no. 311.63/95; Werber to the Swedish Legation, August 1918; Dr. Ernst Kunwald to the Royal Swedish Legation, Fort Oglethorpe, 11 February 1918, file no. 311.63/94; and Margarethe Weiss-Wikins to the Swedish Legation, Fort Oglethorpe, 2 March 1919, file no. 311.63/435, all in NARA. It is likely that the anarchists mentioned in these records had been interned, but it is also possible that they had merely been arrested; the Department of State records do not clarify this point. See the files in group 311.6324, in NARA.

19. On internment in other countries, see especially Gerhard Fischer, *Enemy Aliens: Internment and the Homefront Experience in Australia, 1914-1920* (St. Lucia: University of Queensland Press, 1989); and Bill Waiser, *Park Prisoners: The Untold Story of Western Canada's National Parks, 1915-1946* (Saskatoon: Fifth House Publishers, 1995). See also Mary Stenning, *Austrian Slavs:*

Internment Camps of Australia, 1914-1918 (Australia: Fast Books, 1995); Rudolf Rocker, *An Insight into Civilian Internment in Britain during WWI*, new ed. (Maidenhead: Anglo-German Family History Society, 1998); and Desmond Morton, "Sir William Otter and Internment Operations in Canada during the First World War," *Canadian Historical Review 55* (March 1974): 32-58.

20. See, for example, Giuseppe Webber and the Lega Tirolese Trentina di Greater New York to Lansing, New York City, 16 June 1919, file no. 311.63/519, in NARA: "Not one of [Cirio Lucki's] people knew just why he was arrested and up to the present are in the dark on this subject." O'Brien to the Secretary of State (re: Julius Preleuthner), Washington, 26 January 1918, file no. 311/63/75, in NARA; Nagler, "Enemy Aliens and Internment."

21. See, for example, O'Brien to the Secretary of State, 26 January 1918; and Valentin Reibel to the Swedish Ambassador, Fort Douglas, 15 March 1918, file no. 311.63/134; and file no. 311.63/140, all in NARA.

22. Reibel to the Swedish Ambassador, 15 March 1918.

23. O'Brien to the Secretary of State, 26 January 1918.

24. Goldschmidt, *In and Out of the Ivory Tower*, 178.

25. O'Brien to the Secretary of State, Washington, 12 February 1916, file no. 311.63/89, in NARA.

26. Levy, "The American Symphony at War," 9.

27. O'Brien to the Secretary of State, Washington, 1 May 1918, file no. 311.63/134, in NARA.

28. Alvo von Alvensleben to the Attorney General, 2 May 1919, quoted in Nagler, "Enemy Aliens and Internment," 402.

29. On this phenomenon, see Mark Sonntag, "Fighting Everything German in Texas, 1917-1919," *The Historian 56* (Winter 1994). There is also evidence of this type of opportunism in Australia and Canada. There is a discussion of local businessmen pressing to have their competitors interned in Fischer, *Enemy Aliens*. Localities in Canada sent the destitute to internment camps to avoid having them become local public charges; see Waiser, *Park Prisoners*; and Morton, "Sir William Otter and Internment Operations."

30. Pohl to the Swedish Ambassador, 10 February 1918.

31. On wartime civil liberties and efforts to protect them, see Thomas C. Lawrence, "Eclipse of Liberty: Civil Liberties in the United States during the First World War," *Wayne Law Review 21* (Nov. 1974): 33-112; Donald Oscar Johnson, *The Challenge to American Freedoms: World War I and the Rise of the American Civil Liberties Union* (New York: Oxford University Press, 1980); Paul L. Murphy, *World War I and the Origin of Civil Liberties in the United States* (New York: Norton, 1979); and Harry N. Scheiber, *The Wilson Administration and Civil Liberties, 1917-1921* (Ithaca: Cornell University Press, 1960).

32. See E. E. Werber to the Swedish Legation, Fort Douglas, August 1918, enclosing William F. Beer (surgeon) to the Commandant, War Prison Barracks, Fort Douglas, 12 August 1918, file number 311.63/230, in NARA.

33. Acting Secretary of State to Ekengren, Washington, 12 June 1919, file no. 311.63/516, in NARA.

34. John Hanna to the Secretary of State, Washington, 24 March 1920, file no. 311.63/596, in NARA.

35. See, for example, No. 5255/21, Ekengren to Lansing, Washington, 28 October 1918, file no. 311.63/294; and O'Brien to the Secretary of State, 2 November 1918, file no. 311.63/324, both in NARA; as well as the other cases listed below.

36. O'Brien to Secretary of State, 31 October 1918, file no. 311.63/321, in NARA.

37. No. 3875/21, Ekengren to Lansing, Washington, 9 August 1918, file no. 311.63/219; and O'Brien to Lansing, 14 October 1918, file no. 311.63/238, both in NARA.

38. Werber to the Swedish Legation, August 1918.

39. O'Brien to Secretary of State, 16 October 1918, file no. 311.63/285, in NARA.

40. Daniš et al. to the Department of State, Fort Oglethorpe, 9 March 1919, file no. 311.63/436, in NARA.

41. "Britain's Interned Aliens," *New York Times*, 16 March 1919, quoted in Daniš et al. to the Department of State, Fort Oglethorpe, 21 Mach 1919, file no. 311.63/449, in NARA.

42. Daniš et al. to the Department of State, 21 Mach 1919.

43. O'Brien to Lansing, Washington, 27 March 1919, file no. 311.63/450; see also O'Brien to Lansing, Washington, 3 April 1919, file no. 311.63/457, both in NARA. In a similar case, an ethnic Romanian from Transylvania was denied release because Transylvania was still considered enemy territory, despite the fact that it had passed into the possession of Allied Romania. See O'Brien to Lansing, Washington, 24 February 1919, file no. 311.63/430, in NARA.

44. Department of State Solicitor to Coffin, "Memorandum," Washington, 7 January 1919, file no. 311.636/6, in NARA.

45. Daniš et al. to the Department of State, Fort Oglethorpe, ca. 9 April 1919, file no. 311.63/458, in NARA.

46. Posselt to Department of State, Ft. Oglethorpe, 4 June 1919, file no. 311.63/515; see also Posselt to Department of State, Ft. Oglethorpe, 23 May 1919, file no. 311.63/504, both in NARA.

47. It is not clear from the available records what became of the others represented in this correspondence.

48. Posselt to the Swedish Legation, Ft. Oglethorpe, 2 August 1919 [forwarded to the Department of State on 14 August 1919], file no. 311.63/534, in NARA.

49. Creighton to the Secretary of State, Washington, 10 September 1919, file no. 311.63/543, in NARA.

50. Posselt's letter, enclosed in No. 4500/21, Ekengren to the Department of State, Washington, 8 November 1919, file no. 311.63/559, in NARA.

51. Posselt's letter, enclosed in No. 4581/21, Ekengren to the Department of State, Washington, 11 November 1919, file no. 311.63/560, in NARA.

52. Posselt to the Department of State, Ft. Oglethorpe, 7 December 1919, file no. 311.63/567, in NARA.

53. Hanna to the Secretary of State, Washington, 9 January 1919, file no. 311.63/574, in NARA.

54. Zweig to Adee, Ft. Oglethorpe, 9 May 1919, file no. 311.63/495, in NARA. Note that his letter is filed under Austria-Hungary, not Czechoslovakia. A search of the Czechoslovak protection of interest files yielded no documents relating to internment.

55. Wachtell to the Department of State, New York City, 31 May 1919, file no. 311.63/509, in NARA.

56. No. 1011/21, Swedish Legation to the Secretary of State, Washington, 19 March 1919, file no. 311.63/447, in NARA.

57. O'Brien to the Secretary of State, Washington, 9 April 1919, file no. 311.63/455, in NARA.

58. See file 311.6324, in NARA.

59. All anarchist deportations are filed under 311.6324, in NARA. The classic historical work on anarchist and communist deportations is Robert K. Murray, *Red Scare: A Study in National Hysteria, 1919-1920* (Minneapolis: University of Minnesota Press, 1955).

60. Post to the Department of State, Washington, 30 July 1920, file no. 311.6324P26/2, in NARA; see similar statements from Post: Post to the Department of State, Washington, 21 May 1920, file no. 311.6324B49/4; and Post to the Department of State, Washington 9 July 1920, file no. 311.6324R96/2, both in NARA.

61. No. 1986/21, Ekengren to the Department of State, Washington, 1 May 1920, file no. 311.6324B86/2, in NARA.

Selectively Perceived Legacies of World War I: The Little-Known Halstead Mission in Austria, 1919

Siegfried Beer

[In 1919] the cards of history were stacked against Austria and Hungary.

—Nicholas Roosevelt, member of the Coolidge Mission, 1919[1]

The Great Powers who had insisted on a new artificial [Austrian] state, if they wished to maintain it, would have to pay for it. It would have been difficult, but it might have been possible to make another "Switzerland", permanently neutralized, with democratic institutions, guaranteed externally and internationally by the League of Nations (who might have put their capital in Vienna), and financed by the Great Powers. The Great Powers have never been willing to do anything except hand out doles.

—FO minute, A.W. Leeper, March 3, 1934[2]

Most historians would agree that the role and attitude of the United States in the dissolution process of the Habsburg Empire during the last war year, 1918, was crucial if not decisive.[3] While and when U.S. President Wilson gave up the idea of keeping the Dual Empire intact, the faltering war-leadership in Vienna could only grasp the prospect of a fair peace, based largely on Wilson's Fourteen Points. During the bloodless "Austrian Revolution," which accompanied the transition from empire to republic, i.e. the first few months after the armistice and of the establishment of the new German-Austrian state,[4] the New Austria in 1918/19 more or less started out under auspices and conditions of a "failed" state. It could not provide for its safety; it could not feed its population; it could not offer sufficient jobs for its people; and its citizens did not identify themselves with it; nor did they believe in its viability as a new state entity; similarly in 1945, as a state to be re-constructed. Contrary to 1945, however, in 1919 the victorious Allies at first chose not to ponder the Austrian dilemma much. The peacemakers in Paris were wholly occupied with Germany, as the British peace conference participant James Headlam-Morley was later to remember: "in Paris it was very difficult to have attention paid to Austrian matters."[5]

Despite the preparatory work of the Inquiry on dozens of questions concerning the Habsburg Monarchy, when war finally ended and armistice arrived, the U.S. government was ill-prepared for peacemaking and ill-informed on what was really going on in the territories having been ruled and governed by the Habsburgs, in most cases over centuries. The belated start of the Paris Peace Conference, due mainly to Wilson's delayed arrival in the French capital, did not help either.[6] When the American Commission to Negotiate Peace was finally set up in Paris it soon became clear to Secretary of State Robert Lansing and to Colonel Edward House, the American Plenipotentiary and Wilson's most influential adviser, that new sources of information about developments in (former) enemy territory and particularly in Central Europe were needed.[7] Thus he called for political intelligence from "secret agents" under cover of semi-official missions similar to Herbert Hoover's American Relief and Food Administration and several study or field missions like the Dresel Mission to Germany, the Lord Mission to Poland or the Coolidge Mission to the successor states of Austria-Hungary.[8] Their essential tasks included the forwarding of news, observations and reports to the Commission to Negotiate Peace at Paris and the State Department in Washington. Most of these missions have been researched and analyzed, among them the aforementioned mission of Professor Archibald C. Coolidge, former diplomat, member of the Inquiry, and professor as well as head librarian at Harvard College, whose centre of activity was to be in Vienna. The Coolidge Mission consisted mainly of various specialists, territorial or subject-related to Central Europe, mostly university professors and journalists, or military intelligence personnel.[9] The United States still had no civilian intelligence service then.

The Coolidge Mission worked from December 1918 to May 1919

and produced hundreds of reports, dispatches and telegrams. However, its influence on the opinion-making processes and the decision-making patterns at Paris is difficult to gauge. It was certainly over-estimated by the Austrians, who frequently courted the mission members and fed them with astute information, often secret and targeted. Coolidge, though generally well-disposed towards the New Austria, was not easily fooled. Not by the Austrians, nor by his colleagues or superiors in Paris. He was painfully aware of his limited influence, even importance. To Wilson's interpreter on a visit to Vienna he would complain in April 1919 that "a letter to Santa Claus has a better chance of being answered than an inquiry sent to the delegation."[10]

Coolidge's successor in Vienna was to be Albert Halstead (1867-1949), a former newspaper editor and career consular officer, who had been U.S. Consul General in Vienna from 1915 to 1917 and was recalled from Stockholm in May 1919. He arrived in Vienna via Paris in early June of 1919 and stayed in his position as American Commissioner for Austria until mid-October 1920. He reported to the Commission to Negotiate Peace in Paris until late July 1919 and from then on to the Secretary of State on the latter's return to Washington. By then the Austrian treaty had been finalized.[11]

This analysis will concentrate on the Halstead Mission in the crucial year 1919 during which Halstead wrote dozens of reports, many of them published in the official documentary series Foreign Relations of the United States (FRUS), Paris Peace Conference (PPC), Volume XII. Contrary to published opinion, Halstead's mission was no more official than the Coolidge Field Mission had been before him. However, while Coolidge and his various field teams were to provide information and intelligence on all regions of the former Habsburg Empire, Halstead's focus was mainly on German-Austria and until about mid-August 1919 also on Hungary.[12] As former consul general he was seen by the Austrians as the official and permanent representative of the U.S. government. Legally the Austrian status as enemy country was ended only in mid-1921, when a bilateral peace treaty between the New Austria and the United States was signed.[13] Furthermore, American representation in several commissions in Austria was limited in size and number, altogether probably no more than a dozen people before 1921.

In many ways, British and American positions were perceived by the Austrians as being similar. When State Chancellor Karl Renner spoke of Austria's new orientation to the West, he meant London and Washington, less so Paris. Yet it was clear that Washington mattered infinitely more than London. This was most obvious in the area of food politics. During the first

After the war, the Austrian population, especially the destitute Viennese, were kept alive by American food aid. (Photo courtesy of Picture Archives of the Austrian National Gallery)

year after the war and beyond, the Austrians were only kept alive by allied, mainly American, food aid, administered by Herbert Hoover's American Relief Administration.[14] Since the New Austria was considered a (former) enemy state, this aid could only be secured by an indirect loan of the U.S. Treasury to Great Britain, France and Italy for the designated purpose of securing food shipments to Vienna.[15] Thus Austria profited from the food crisis because developments in Hungary, where Bela Kun's communists had come to power in March, led to the lifting of the war blockade against Austria.[16] The primary reason for that, of course, was containment of Bolshevism in Central Europe. Even after Bela Kun's demise, the American Relief Administration continued food and technical support with the assistance of private programs by charity organizations with food and dollar packages for children and with intelligentsia relief.[17]

By the time Coolidge left Vienna in mid-May 1919, very little had yet been known about the conditions of the treaty for Austria.[18] Some border issues had been discussed, some even resolved, and a compromise agreement was reached among the Big Four about forbidding the Anschluss, analogous to the German treaty. But generally speaking, Austria was very much on the backburner in Paris, for both London and Washington. Like Hungary, Austria did not have its own commission. And it was seen in a dreary and pessimistic light. Harold Nicolson, FO expert on Central Europe, remembers gloomily that "in regard to [Habsburg] Austria I had a 'de mortuis' feeling. [...] My attitude towards Austria was a rather saddened reflection as to what would remain of her when the new Europe had once been created. I did not regard her [the New Austria] as a living entity, I thought of her only as a pathetic relic."[19] It was generally seen as a "strange misshapen orphan."[20] And there was a curious basic flaw in dealing with Austria. Both Great Britain and the United States lacked real experts on German-Austria who could grasp the full range of issues regarding the new republic. Once more Headlam-Morley sagaciously recognized the problem in terms of enemy-ally categorization and admonished in early retrospect (probably at the end of 1919) that "sound policy requires that we should [have been] as fully informed as to the point of view of the enemy as that of our friends."[21] Even though this point of view was continuously addressed and commented upon by the respective allied agents in the field (in the case of Great Britain by Col. Sir Thomas Montgomery Cuninghame and in the case of America first by Professor Coolidge and then by Commissioner Halstead and several others in various other commissions)[22] it hardly ever reached or impacted the negotiators in Paris, as again Headlam-Morley points out: "When the different committees and sections turned their attention to the Austrian Treaty, what they did, in fact, was to adopt almost 'en bloc' the clauses of the relevant sections of the German treaty and apply them to Austria, simply eliminating the word Germany and putting in Austria."[23] In other words, the German treaty was more or less used as a template. And apparently confusion reigned, as a decision was difficult to reach even on the exact status of the New Austria. Headlam-Morley noted in his diary at the end of May 1919, "the Austrian treaty is in a [sic] awful mess."[24] It so happened that "the financial clauses were drafted on the assumption that Austria is a new state; [...] the commercial clauses on the assumption that it is an old state."[25] The British diplomat Maurice Hankey called the document handed over to the Austrians on 2 June "a simulacrum of a treaty."[26] There had not even been time to check its articles for accuracy and consistency in phrasing.[27]

One of Halstead's first reports to Paris dealt with the general feeling of dissatisfaction, despair, anxiety, and impotence felt by Austrians about the initial terms revealed in June 1919. They were seen as "a death sentence to what remains of old Austria."[28] Halstead argued that the treaty for Austria should not unduly punish but encourage her so as not to "inculcate despair."[29]

He also kept in close contact with probably all members of the allied missions to Austria, particularly with the British Military Representative Col. Cuninghame and asked for concerted action against Hungarian Bolshevism, which in his opinion targeted Austria as its next victim.[30] Again and again he asked for clear instructions and guidance by his government in regard to U.S. policy vis-à-vis the Bela Kun regime. Finally, he was told that the Commissioners in Paris and the State Department wanted him to stay out of any involvement. Practically all allied representatives stationed in Austria and Hungary asked for an active policy for overturning the Kun government;[31] yet the American Commission in Paris and the governments in London and Washington refused to think in terms of direct military action.[32]

While open U.S. military intervention in Hungary was ruled out, American officers in the field were involved in covert measures of destabilizing the revolutionary regime of Bela Kun. At least two of these involved Austria. In June 1919 Czechoslovakia was in need of weapons for her military conflict with Hungary over Slovakia, while Austria was in desperate need of coal deliveries for which she could not pay. U.S. officers arranged a secret deal which actually brought Austrian shipments of weapons to Czechoslovakia by the end of July.[33] The second incident concerned secret negotiations during the summer between T.T.C. Gregory of the American Relief Administration and Hungarian Red Army General Vilmos Böhm in Vienna on toppling the Kun government. Gregory was called back and only allowed to keep informal contact.[34] Washington shied away from a counter-revolutionary intervention. By the first of August the Bela Kun episode was over anyway.[35]

Who did Halstead consult and confer with? Not surprisingly, Halstead had frequent discussions with Chancellor Karl Renner, Foreign Minister Otto Bauer and also the Vienna Police President Johannes Schober,[36] significantly less so with Christian-social politicians.[37] All of them kept stressing the politically undisputed Austrian orientation towards the West and the need for help from the United States, even beyond food and coal requirements. America was seen as the only country without "selfish interests and schemes."[38] Halstead also stressed the excellent opportunities for American investments in Austria, pointing to British, French and Italian investments already undertaken.[39] He found it regrettable that American capital had been totally indifferent to these chances.[40] Chancellor Renner regularly expressed thankfulness for support given to Austria by Great Britain and the United States, kept stressing that "Austria looked to the United States and England for help" and ensured that Austria would live up to the treaty.[41]

In September Halstead's deputy, Consul A.W. DuBois, a coal expert, warned of Austria's precarious coal situation for the upcoming winter. Already in May he had suggested to the American Commission that the Entente should take over the distribution of coal. Now he reiterated his concern: "If the Conference has an interest [...] in the future and stability of Austria, drastic action must be taken to forestall disaster."[42] A few days later Viennese newspapers published stories about possible pogroms on account of the influx of Hungarian and Galician Jews into Vienna. Halstead warned Renner that "any mistreatment of the Jews in Vienna would have an unfortunate effect on public opinion in the United States." When no attacks occurred, he intimated that it may have been due to his intervention with the State Chancellor.[43]

By October 1919, when the treaty had been signed, Halstead spoke of "a pressing need of Austria, standing on the verge of utter destruction" and that the condition of Austria is "that of a convict sentenced to a lingering death" while "the fate of Central Europe is at this moment at stake."[44] He urged that "the people of Austria should be able to rebuild themselves. The Austrians naturally are a self-respecting, self-supporting people brought into distress by those who ruled them in the past. [...] With raw materials, with coal and food Austria can gradually rebuild, but she must be given time."[45] When Halstead argued that "without raw material and food from the other states no peace can come to German-Austria," he referred mainly to the difficult attitude of Czechoslovakia.[46] He saw particularly the Austrian capital in peril: "The gravest anxiety prevails into Vienna's immediate future. Without coal, with reduced food rations [...] it is apprehended that the population in desperation may proceed to plunder. [...] The majority of the poor are in a desperate state."[47] When asked what would follow the breakdown in Vienna, Renner "with a jerk of his shoulders" answered: "probably the entrance of the Czechs into Vienna."[48] In conversation with Halstead, Renner frequently argued that foremost the Czechs "were prepared to go to the extent of wholly breaking up Austria [...] to obtain a predominant influence in Southern Central Europe."[49] In retrospect, these warnings and intimations of 1919 by the Austrian head of government appear unsubstantiated. Nevertheless, Halstead saw fit to report them to Paris and Washington.

After the peace treaty was accepted by the Austrian National Assembly on 17 October, Halstead stressed the need for basic reforms concerning Austria's finances, the creation of a steady currency and of a reliable republican army, and most importantly, the drafting of a new constitution.

It was a huge plate of problems while the general situation "appear[ed] still to be going from bad to worse." Remarkably, he also noticed "comparatively little respect for the law anywhere." As the one strong force for real order, he again pointed toward the police of Vienna.[50] By the end of November 1919, Renner professed to Halstead that his colleagues in the government "were at their wits' ends [sic]." Alone the United States with its wealth would be "in position to help."[51] Even though the situation, Renner continued, would not permit the U.S. government "to help directly," as in the past, the United States could "advance money which the other three powers would loan to Austria. [...] Austria could pledge her water power, her woods, her state property to an American financial group which could save seven million people by advancing for example 200 million US dollars and subsequently be in a position of practical control of the future of this country at an immense profit."[52] This in effect amounted to a kind of sell-out by design, but help "must be immediate," or by Christmas "the whole country would fall to pieces."[53]

In early December 1919 Renner again appealed to all four allied missions for immediate aid without which "a catastrophe could not be avoided."[54] In mid-December 1919, Viennese newspapers reported that salvation of Austria would come from the United States and that American capital had agreed to take over all of Austria's public services. "America alone could save the Austrian people from death from freezing and starvation and from utter anarchy, and that it was the duty of America to be that life-saver."[55] Thereupon Halstead protested at the Ballhausplatz and demanded that these statements be withdrawn and that the officers of the Austrian Correspondence Bureau immediately correct these unfounded reports and point out how much America had already helped. Towards Christmas 1919 Halstead again reported that the outlook had become even more serious, the cold weather increasing the strain.[56] There was also "a demand in many quarters for a stronger government" and "the people are really hopeless." Anything may happen; even "demonstrations against Americans are not impossible."[57] Halstead's admonitions and warnings fell on deaf ears. There was hardly any response from Washington.

The published record of the Halstead Mission during 1919 proves a mostly favorable attitude toward, and an acute awareness of, the Austrian predicament by the few Americans in the field, seconded by similar sentiments by the other Western representatives in Vienna, particularly by Col. Cuninghame and the head of the French Military Mission, Henri Allizé. Of the three, the latter may have had the most influence on his government.[58] But neither Paris nor London and Washington really shared the views and concerns of their experts on the premises.[59] There remains the question whether these various food, military and civilian experts and commissioners were sufficiently knowledgeable about Central Europe. In the record we find indications that their reporting and insights at times came under suspicion.[60] Their power and influence on the spot and with their governments was clearly limited.[61] And as Margaret MacMillan reminds us, "unlike Germany and Hungary, Austria was too small and too poor to be a threat" to anybody.[62] Only in combination with fascist neighbors did she later pose a serious problem for the international system.

As to the Wilson government, it chose not to recognize a specific responsibility toward the New Austria as long as she proved immunized against turning communist and exhibited a generally Western democratic outlook. As we now know, somehow Austria survived the crisis of 1918/19, as it did again in 1945/46. And forbidding the Anschluss was soon to be reinforced by international conditions for providing the much-needed loan in 1922, the so-called Geneva Protocol.[63] Already in June 1919, Headlam-Morley had foreseen that "the policy pursued towards German-Austria is of such a nature as to drive them straight into the arms of Germany."[64] March 1938 at the latest proved him right.

Beyond these two issues the inner consolidation of a newly democratic Republic of Austria was never a real concern or commitment during the last 18 months of the Wilson administration, less of course of the American Congress, dominated by the Republicans. The parameters of making the world safe for democracy were geared towards the then current interests of American diplomacy. The New Austria did not occupy a significant place in the European sphere of American interests. This was to change only in 1945, after another global conflagration and only because of significantly altered geopolitical conditions. By the summer of 1919 Washington could not decide about getting into Central Europe, less about staying in it. Wilsonian internationalism was of limited duration, even in politically and ideologically precarious regions. American diplomacy after the Paris Peace Conference never really developed a sensitiveness for the basic needs of an emerging democratic state like the New Austria; American awareness of Austria was at the most selective, both of the legacies of empire and the difficulties of a new and struggling democratic body politic.

In the long term of about two more generations, as we know today, the story ended well. Certainly by the end of the 20th century Austria belonged among the ten most stable and affluent countries in the world. This is in no small part due to American aid and support after World War II. The food and moral support given in 1918/19, however, was soon forgotten, by and large even by historians.[65] It apparently was not enduring enough to help sustain a momentum for building a new state. Austrian nation-building was, anyway, then on nobody's agenda.

Notes

1. Nicholas Roosevelt, *A Front Row Seat* (Norman: University of Oklahoma Press, 1953), 118.

2. National Archives/Public Record Office, FO 371, 18351, R 2190/37/3, cited in: Siegfried Beer, *Der "unmoralische" Anschluß: Britische Österreichpolitik zwischen Containment und Appeasement 1931-1934*, Veröffentlichungen der Kommission für Neuere Geschichte Österreichs 75 (Vienna: Böhlau, 1988), 464.

3. Surprisingly, there has been very little research on US-policy towards the New Austria before, during and immediately after the Paris Peace Conference, except for several dated and documentarily mostly weak doctoral dissertations: see Simone Meisels, "Die Beziehungen zwischen Österreich-Ungarn und den Vereinigten Staaten 1917 bis November 1918," PhD. diss., University of Vienna, 1961; Astrid Hausmann, "Amerikanische Außenpolitik und die Entstehung der österreichischen Republik von 1917-1919," PhD. diss., University of Vienna, 1973; Ursula Freise, "Die Tätigkeit der alliierten Kommissionen in Wien nach dem Ersten Weltkrieg," PhD. diss., University of Vienna, 1963; and more reliable: Georg E. Schmid, "Die amerikanische Österreichpolitik zur Zeit der Pariser Friedenskonferenz 1919: Die Coolidge Mission," PhD. diss., University of Salzburg, 1968; Peter E. Schmidt, "The Relief of Austria, 1918-1922," PhD. diss., Case Western Reserve University, 1977; and Wolfgang Pucher, "Die Beziehungen Österreichs zu den Vereinigten Staaten 1918-1932," PhD. diss., University of Vienna, 1981.

4. Early analyzed by Otto Bauer, *The Austrian Revolution* (London: L. Parsons, 1925); Carlile A. Macartney, *The Social Revolution in Austria* (Cambridge: Cambridge University Press, 1926); Kurt Trampler, *Deutschösterreich, 1918-1919* (Berlin: C. Heymann, 1935); David F. Strong, *Austria: October 1918 – March 1919* (New York: Columbia University Press, 1939); Mary MacDonald, *The Republic of Austria 1919-1934: A Study in the Failure of Democratic Government* (London: Oxford University Press, 1946); and Charles Gulick, *Austria from Habsburg to Hitler* (Berkeley: University of California Press, 1948).

5. James Headlam-Morley, "Note on the Austrian Treaty," undated, in *British Policy on Hungary 1918-1919: A Documentary Sourcebook*, ed. M. Lojkó (London: School of Slavonic and East European Studies, 1995), 365.

6. James Headlam-Morley, *A Memoir of the Paris Peace Conference 1919*, ed. A. Headlam-Morley et al. (London: Methuen&Co., 1972), 161.

7. See Pucher, "Die Beziehungen Österreichs zu den Vereinigten Staaten," 54-55.

8. A central telegraph office of the Hoover operation was eventually set up in Vienna, of which the food administrator later boasted: "Within a short time we had spread our organization over thirty-two countries and had included tens of thousands of nationals in our service. We had the only connected telegraph system over all Europe." Herbert Hoover, *The Ordeal of Woodrow Wilson* (New York: McGraw-Hill, 1958), 90.

9. See Georg E. Schmid, "Die Coolidge-Mission in Österreich 1919: Zur Österreichpolitik der USA während der Pariser Friedenskonferenz," *MOESTA 24* (1971): 433-67.

10. Stephen Bonsal, *Unfinished Business* (Garden City: Doubleday, 1944), 90; for another version of the Santa Claus reference see Roosevelt, *A Front Row Seat*, 117.

11. Halstead was a journalist and newspaper editor by profession, had worked on the staff of

Governor, soon to be President William McKinley in the mid-1890s and acted as U.S. consul in Birmingham from 1906 to 1915. After his second Vienna assignment he held consular jobs at Montreal (1920-1927) and London (1929-1932).

12. From summer 1919 onwards there was a special American mission to Hungary, headed by General Bandholtz. See Papers Relating to the Foreign Relations of the United States (FRUS), The Paris Peace Conference (PPC), Volume XII (Washington, DC: U.S. Government Printing Office, 1947), 635ff. and Harry H. Bandholtz, *An Undiplomatic Diary: By the member of the Inter-Allied Military Mission to Hungary, 1919-1920*, ed. F.-K. Krüger (New York: Columbia University Press, 1933).

13. The state of war between the U.S. and Austria-Hungary was terminated by Congressional Resolution on 21 July 1921. The bilateral peace treaty between Austria and the United States was signed on 24 August 1921 and was ratified by Austria on 8 October 1921.

14. Already in early 1919 Woodrow Wilson was convinced that "the real thing to stop Bolshevism is food." See Woodrow Wilson Papers, Series 5B, Wilson to Lansing, 10 Jan. 1919. Cited in: Peter Pastor, *Hungary Between Wilson and Lenin: The Hungarian Revolution of 1918-1919 and the Big Three* (New York: Columbia University Press, 1976), 166.

15. FRUS, PPC, X, 158.

16. See Hanns Haas, "Die Vereinigten Staaten von Amerika und die alliierte Lebensmittelversorgung Österreichs im Winter 1918/19," *MOESTA 32* (1979): 233-55.

17. See Hanns Haas, "Die Pariser Friedenskonferenz und das Ende der Ungarischen Räterepublik," *MOESTA 29* (1976): 363-410; and Franz Adlgasser, *American Individualism Abroad: Herbert Hoover, die American Relief Administration und Österreich, 1919-1923* (Vienna: Verbund der wissenschaftlichen Gesellschaften Österreichs, 1993).

18. Already by 1935 two political scientists from Stanford University submitted an authoritative edition of materials on the treatment of the Austrian question in Paris: N. Almond and R.H. Lutz, eds., *The Treaty of St. Germain: A Documentary History of Its Territorial and Political Clauses*, Hoover War Library Publications 5 (Stanford: Stanford University Press, 1935).

19. Harold Nicolson, *Peacemaking 1919* (New York: Harcourt, Bross&Co., 1965), 34.

20. MacDonald, *The Republic of Austria 1919-1934*, 247.

21. Headlam-Morley, "Note on the Austrian Treaty," 362.

22. See Robert Hoffmann, "Die Mission Sir Thomas Cuninghames in Wien 1919: Britische Österreichpolitik zur Zeit der Pariser Friedenskonferenz," PhD. diss., University of Salzburg, 1971.

23. Headlam-Morley, "Note on the Austrian Treaty," 364.

24. Headlam-Morley, *A Memoir of the Paris Peace Conference 1919*, 30 May 1919, 131.

25. Ibid., 26 May 1919, 126.

26. Maurice P. Hankey, *The Supreme Control at the Paris Peace Conference 1919: A Commentary* (London: Allen&Unwin, 1963), 160.

27. Nicolson, *Peacemaking 1919*, 356.

28. Halstead to Commission to Negotiate Peace (CNP), 13 June 1919, FRUS, PPC, XII, 530.

29. Halstead to CNP, 6 July 1919, ibid., 539.

30. See Robert Hoffmann, "Die wirtschaftlichen Grundlagen der britischen Österreichpolitik 1919," *MOESTA 30* (1977): 251-87.

31. See Franz Adlgasser, "The Roots of Communist Containment: American Food Aid in Austria and Hungary after World War I," in *Austria in the Nineteen Fifties*, ed. Günter Bischof et al., Contemporary Austrian Studies 3 (New Brunswick, NJ: Transaction, 1995), 171-88.

32. See Hanns Haas, "Österreich und die Alliierten 1918-1919," in *Saint-Germain 1919: Protokoll des Symposiums am 29. und 30. Mai 1979 in Wien* (Vienna: Verlag für Geschichte und Politik, 1989), 31-33.

33. The coal for weapons deal in numbers: 20,000 rifles, 40,000 shells, 1,500,000 cartridges in the value of 21,515,375 German-Austrian crowns. See Adlgasser, *American Individualism Abroad*, 68-69.

34. See Wilhelm Böhm, *Im Kreuzfeuer zweier Revolutionen* (Munich 1924), and Adlgasser, "The Roots of Communist Containment," 178-79. Gregory, a lawyer and investment banker from California, proved one of the most influential American operatives in Central Europe in 1919. See Pucher, "Die Beziehungen Österreichs zu den Vereinigten Staaten," 74.

35. See Alfred D. Low, "The First Austrian Republic and Soviet Hungary," *Journal of Central European Affairs 20* (July 1960): 174-203.

36. Who in Halstead's opinion ran "the one really efficient organization for the protection [of Vienna] – 5000 police." He praised its head as "a man of unusual force and ability." Halstead to SoS, 5 Sept. 1919, FRUS, PPC, XII, 564.

37. However, Halstead held regular contact with an assortment of business, industry and bank management personnel, many of which belonged to the conservative camp.

38. Halstead to the Secretary of State (SoS), 12 Aug. 1919, FRUS, PPC, Vol. XII, 561.

39. See Herbert Matis, "Disintegration and Multi-national Enterprises in Central Europe During the Post-war Years, 1918-23," in *International Business and Central Europe, 1918-1939*, ed. A. Teichova and P.L. Cottrell (New York: St. Martin's Press, 1983), 73-100.

40. Halstead to SoS, 9 Sept. 1919, in: FRUS, PPC, Vol. XII, 566-67.

41. Halstead to SoS, 15 Sept. 1919, ibid., 571.

42. A.W. DuBois to SoS, 21 Sept. 1919, ibid., 575.

43. Halstead to SoS, 26 Sept. 1919, ibid. 576. When in mid-October the new coalition cabinet was presented Halstead's deputy made a point of stressing that it included four Jews. A.W. DuBois to SoS, 18 Oct. 1919, ibid., 582.

44. Halstead to SoS, 10 Oct. 1919, ibid., 579.

45. Ibid., 580.

46. Halstead to SoS, 18 July 1919, ibid., 548.

47. Halstead to SoS, 7 Nov. 1919, ibid., 584-86.

48. Halstead to SoS, 26 Nov. 1919, ibid., 591.

49. Halstead to SoS, 27 Nov. 1919, ibid., 593.

50. Halstead to SoS, 21 Nov. 1919, ibid., 587-89.

51. Halstead to SoS, 26 Nov. 1919, ibid., 590.

52. Ibid.

53. Ibid., 591.

54. Halstead to SoS, 3 Dec. 1919, ibid., 598.

55. Halstead to SoS, 12 Dec. 1919, ibid., 602. Another American observer detected a kind of

victim attitude among most Austrians and noticed a "complete assumption that [the Americans] were free from resentment and filled with a sympathetic desire to put them on their feet." See Margaret MacMillan, *Paris 1919: Six Months that Changed the World* (New York: Random House, 2002), 249. The victim card would be played again after the next World War, that time perhaps with more initial success.

56. During these days, Halstead was the private guest of Josef Redlich, the renowned professor of constitutional law at the University of Vienna and former minister of finance, who on this occasion commented in his diary on December 9, 1919: "Daß ich so viel Trauriges miterleben muß: das verhungernde Wien, der mit Blödsinn vermischte Haß und die konfuse Gleichgültigkeit, mit der die Entente das ganze österreichische Problem behandelt." ("That so many sad things have to happen to me: a starving Vienna, hatred paired with stupidity and this confused apathy with which the Entente is treating the whole Austrian Problem"). in F. Fellner, ed., *Schicksalsjahre Österreichs 1908-1919: Das politische Tagebuch Josef Redlichs*, II. Band (Vienna: Hermann Böhlau, 1954), 349.

57. Halstead to SoS, 12 Dec. 1919, FRUS, PPC, Vol. XII, 604-06.

58. See Henri Allizé, *Ma Mission à Vienne, mars 1919-août 1920* (Paris 1933).

59. See Hanns Haas, "Henri Allizé und die österreichische Unabhängigkeit," in *Austriaca. Cahiers universitaires d'information sur l'Autriche*, 3ème Spécial Colloque: Deux fois l'Autriche après 1918 et après 1945, Actes du colloque de Rouen 8-12 novembre 1977, 3e volume (Rouen: Centre d'Etudes et de Recherches Autrichiennes, 1977), 241-84.

60. As, for example, Headlam-Morley complained: "There is practically no one on the spot who has really sound knowledge and experience." Headlam-Morley, *A Memoir of the Paris Peace Conference 1919*, 147.

61. Halstead was fully aware of this when early in his mission he pleaded that "it is earnestly hoped that the views of those on the spot who should understand the situation best will receive noted consideration." Halstead to CNP, 7 July 1919, FRUS, PPC, XII, 540. Almost a month later he qualified his stance: "I fully appreciate that writing from Vienna I must to a degree be influenced by my situation and that from this single angle it is absolutely impossible to view the grave problems presented to the Peace Commission as broadly as it is viewed by those upon whom the responsibility rests in Washington and Paris." Halstead to SoS, 3 Aug. 1919, ibid., 557.

62. MacMillan, *Paris 1919*, 247.

63. See Duane Myers, "The United States and Austria, 1918-1919: The Problem of Self-Determination," *Proceedings of the South Carolina Historical Association*, 1975, 5-15.

64. Headlam-Morley, *A Memoir of the Paris Peace Conference 1919*, 25 June 1919, 163.

65. Even though Austria had become the fourth largest beneficiary of allied aid, after Germany, Poland and Belgium. See MacMillan, *Paris 1919*, 249.

Dismantling Empire: Ignaz Seipel and Austria's Financial Crisis, 1922-1925*

John Deak

The German-Austrian Republic was proclaimed on the steps of the Vienna Parliament building on 12 November 1918. The Allied Powers, through the Treaty of Saint-Germain, had carved Austria out of the Habsburg Empire's hereditary lands following the First World War. The internal contours of the new Austrian Republic, however, would take shape over the next few years as Austria's leadership, its political parties, and its citizens responded to the new republic's smallness, its reduced economic base, and its new geopolitical position in Central Europe. It is the argument of this paper that Austria's financial crisis and subsequent bailout by the League of Nations in the early 1920s was crucial in Austria's transition from the core lands of an empire to a republic. It was largely a result of the financial crisis, and the response to it by Ignaz Seipel's government between 1922 and 1925 that the administrative structures of the Habsburg Empire were finally dismantled, clearing the path for a new republic. In other words, the Austrian Republic was forged over time and this creation of a new state had as much to do with dismantling the structures of the empire as it did with the active creation of a new state.

In 1922, after four successive winters in which Austria had to beg the allied powers for credits to purchase food and coal, Chancellor Ignaz Seipel successfully negotiated a major loan with the League of Nations. This loan, totaling upwards of 650 million gold crowns (i.e., an amount pegged to the pre-war value of the Austrian crown), was to cover the Austrian government's budget for two years. This major loan would be floated in the international currency market and guaranteed primarily by the governments of Great

Britain, France, Italy, and Czechoslovakia. But the large loan would come with significant strings attached to it and would do much in the way of reforming Austria into a new, smaller republic.[1]

The chief negotiator in both securing the loans with the League of Nations, as well as reforming the Austrian state, was the recently-appointed chancellor, Iganz Seipel. Seipel, born in Vienna in 1876, came to the chancellorship of Austria less than four years after the proclamation of the republic and the fall of the Habsburg Monarchy. He had risen to prominence as a political thinker in the First World War. By 1918 Seipel was both a Catholic priest and a *Professor Ordinarius* at the University of Vienna. Though he taught theology, Seipel's intellectual energy had been directed toward political and constitutional reform in the Habsburg Monarchy. His work brought him into contact with the Christian Social Party and found him a place in public service: He became minister of social welfare in the last imperial-Austrian cabinet and presided over the dissolution of the Habsburg Monarchy. By 1922, Seipel had been promoted to the prelature in the Catholic Church (he even had been considered as a candidate for Archbishop of Salzburg); he had also become the Chairman of the Christian Social Party. It was under Seipel's leadership that Austria would secure funds under the tutelage and supervision of the League of Nations. It was thus under Seipel that Austria would financially secure its existence in a new Europe consisting of nationalizing "nation-states" and that Austria would dismantle the structures and vestiges of its imperial past to re-forge itself as a republic.

The League of Nations bailout of Austria is generally considered as the League's first test-case and its first success as an international organization.[2] Moreover, within Austria, the *Sanierung* is seen (though this can depend on one's political affiliation/commitments) as the moment when Austrian independence and statehood was both guaranteed and put on proper footing through a balanced budget and a stable currency. Beyond this, the subsequent need to create new "Austrian" historical narratives, ones which emphasize Austria's status as a small republic—disconnected from its imperial origins and existing separately and distinctly from Germany—have naturally led to views of Austria's financial reconstruction as a milestone on the path to Austrian statehood. In a sense, then, the international dimensions of Austria's financial crisis lend themselves to Whiggish histories of the Second Republic—the one that appears democratic, liberal, and free. But such a view does not help to explain the period in Austria after 1927, when democratic institutions began to fail. It certainly does not provide much insight into the Catholic-corporatist/clerical-fascist (terms which follow

Ignaz Seipel (1876-1932), Austrian Chancellor, 1922-1924, 1926-1929 (Photo courtesy of Picture Archives of the Austrian National Library, Vienna)

Red or Black political ideologies) regime that followed the Austrian civil war in 1934.

However, if we choose to focus on Austria's financial reconstruction in the early 1920s as a domestic and constitutional issue—and a moment when long-standing debates on the role of democratic and bureaucratic governance in society came to a head—a quite different story emerges. In essence, we should see the financial reconstruction not only as an international issue, and not only as a financial issue, but as part of a decisive process about the functioning of governmental power in Austrian society. This process was the result of long-standing debates that emerged with the growth of representative and parliamentary government in the Habsburg Monarchy and which concerned the interplay of bureaucratic authority and democratic (and party-political) institutions.

The financial reconstruction of Austria, from the standpoint of 1955 or 2010, might have set the stage for an independent Austria in Central Europe, but it also made a major intervention into Austria's administration. This intervention was particularly important for the way policy making was divided between ministerial bureaucrats and political parties. Financial reconstruction disrupted the traditional relationship between the civil service and the state; it remapped the lines of authority in the bureaucratic apparatus itself. The once-imperial bureaucrats, stationed in the provinces and districts and answering to the Interior Ministry in Vienna, would now be forced to answer to elected officials in the provinces. The once enlightened absolutist bureaucracy would now come under the control of Christian Social or Social Democratic party politicians.

Postwar Austria, then, is really a constitutional story. It tells us much about the delicate nature of democracy and its susceptibility to failure. The immediate years following the fall of the Habsburg Monarchy were by nature years of transition. The republic was not founded overnight: The legal institutions and the relationship between the state and citizen developed between the initial proclamation of the republic and the political crises in the 1930s. In many ways, however, it was in the midst of a great financial crisis and the eventual bailout of the Austrian government, that the republic was forged.

But the Austrian Republic was not formed of new metals; rather the vestiges of the Empire, its political leaders, its administration, but also the legal and constitutional debates that structured the internal developments of the last twenty years of the monarchy, provided the stuff of the new state. The way Austria responded to its financial crisis as it secured a major loan from the League of Nations in 1922 actually reflected political, administrative, and institutional debates that stretched well back into the nineteenth century. Moreover, the process of implementing the loan proved most important for establishing the governmental shape of the Austrian Republic. The policies of Chancellor Ignaz Seipel—while in their most immediate sense they responded to a state financial crisis—also worked to dismantle the administrative vestiges of the Habsburg Monarchy and to forge a new, decentralized republic.

Austria's Imperial Inheritance

There are a few major characteristics of the First Republic that we must keep in mind so that we may properly evaluate the way the financial crisis would shape the new state. The first is that the Austrian Republic, founded in 1918 at the close of the First World War, was in a state of administrative and constitutional transition at least until 1925—after the country had weathered the financial crisis that accompanied its new statehood. Second, the young republic had inherited the central bureaucratic ministries—and the legions of officials who staffed them—in the months immediately following the First World War.

In the ongoing transition process from the empire to the republic, financial crises accompanied administrative uncertainty. As a successor to the Empire, the Austrian Republic inherited not only German-speaking politicians and bureaucrats from the Empire, but also the institutions, norms, and administrative ideals of the central offices that were located in Vienna. In addition to this, however, the Austrian Republic quickly found itself containing the still intact provincial diets and their ever-loyal provincial bureaucracies. In a sense, then, Austria's imperial inheritance would contain not only the centralizing enlightened absolutism that the state bureaucratic apparatus embodied. This inheritance also came with a well-established tradition of provincial autonomy.

On 22 October 1918, one day after the National Assembly of the future German-Austrian Republic met in the Lower Austrian *Landhaus*, a new body constituted itself in the very same building. It consisted of the leadership of provincial autonomy in seven of Austria's provinces. The Land-Chairmen of Lower Austria, Styria, the Tyrol, Carinthia, Salzburg, and Vorarlberg, as well as the members of each of these provinces' executive boards, the *Landesausschuss*, assembled in Vienna to coordinate policy among the primarily German-speaking provinces and, more importantly, to bring the crownlands into the discussion on the future German-Austrian Republic.[3] By late October 1918, the administrative authority and the centripetal power exercised by the imperial authorities in Vienna had largely melted away. But more than this, as Wilhelm Brauneder rightly notes, this conference of *Landesausschüsse* showed a remarkable resurgence of provincial authority and politics after four-and-a-half years of extreme centralism. None of Cisleithania's provincial diets had been allowed to meet during the war, but the crownland councils had been allowed to continue to operate in their administrative function as the executive board of the diets. In reality, however, their ability to function as independent policy-making bodies, functions that they had rigorously defended and expanded in peacetime, had been crushed by the centralizing policies of war administration.[4]

The result of this meeting with the provincial representatives, consisting of the members of the crownland councils, was the law of 14 November 1918, "regarding the transfer of state authority in the provinces."[5] In a basic sense, the law abolished the dual-track administrative system by eliminating the position of imperial governor and turning over his jurisdiction, as well as all the state officials who answered to him, to the provincial diets and their chairmen (the *Landeshauptmann*).[6] The social democrat Karl Seitz, the President of the National Assembly as well as a member of the Lower Austrian Provincial Council (*Landesrat*), noted that these laws were for the time being "provisional." He also gave this label to the legislative successors to the *Reichsrat* and the provincial diets, which for the moment carried the titles of the National and Provincial Assemblies.[7] But Seitz also recognized the opportunity of the moment—in the transfer of administrative and executive powers from *Reich* to republic, new rules and norms could be written and new chains of command could be erected. The moment (with the emperor increasingly powerless to impose his will upon state institutions) was ripe for the parties not only to take control of the reins of the state, but also to crown themselves the masters of the bureaucracy. Such a masterstroke was part of the "successive construction" of the constitutional norms and regulations that would become part of the new republic; this reflected the general consensus to expand the jurisdiction of democratically-elected institutions.[8] However, this was more than progressive democratization; it also reflected the deep-seated animus of regional politicians and the party leadership of the provinces to Vienna and its central administration. The latter institution was particularly saddled—somewhat unfairly—with the responsibility of wartime deprivations and by its association with the military administrative authorities during the First World War.[9]

The Provisional National Assembly took up the issue of the "transfer of state authority in the provinces" during its third session, on 12 November 1918. The chancellor of the new republic, Karl Renner, remarked that the law introduced a democratic administration in the provinces. To Renner, it was clear that an administrative reform in the provinces must accompany the institution of democratic elections. The new republican state would abolish the curial suffrage system—which persisted in the provinces even after universal male suffrage was instituted in 1907 for *Reichsrat* elections—in favor of a truly democratic suffrage law, a "universal, equal, direct and secret right to vote for all citizens without regard to gender."[10] Such a suffrage law was to apply not only to the elections of the new parliament, but to the provincial assemblies as well. In this context, with the future provincial assemblies elected by universal suffrage, it was "in the spirit of democracy ... that the officialdom which administers a province be integrated and incorporated under the provincially-elected representatives of the people." Not only would the two separate lines of administrative authority—the imperial-state and autonomous-provincial bureaucracies—be combined, it was in this same "spirit of democracy" that the "democratically configured representatives of the provinces elect from their midst the governments of the provinces and that these governments become the head of the administration."[11]

But, this process too, went unfulfilled in the early years of the republic. The law of 14 November had itself left much to be determined. It was understood, according to State Councilor (the new title for cabinet minister) Jodok Fink, that this law was a stop-gap measure until the National Assembly created a constitution and otherwise established a more permanent state system. In the early years of the republic, the door was left open to reestablish a type of central control of the administration in the crownlands. The law of 14 November did not combine the two separate bureaucracies (the formerly-imperial state and autonomous-provincial) in the provinces into one body, but maintained them as separate institutions.[12] Indeed, the law stipulated that the responsibilities of the former imperial bureaucrats and the former autonomous officials would remain the same; that is, the separate lines of command would continue to exist—but now former imperial officials in the provinces would answer to the Land-chairmen and, thus, the provincial assembly, while the provincial officials reported to the provincial executive board (the *Landesausschuss*).[13]

In essence, then, former imperial officials were able—at least provisionally—to maintain their distinct status. These vestiges of imperial prestige helped to forestall a massive bureaucratic resistance to the new republic. But it was clear that the provincialization of the state bureaucracy was not a welcome event within its ranks. Protests and angry letters from state officials to the government would follow, as the former imperial officials came further and further under the control of provincial party rule.

The questions of state organization and political jurisdiction (centralism and federalism) as well as state control and local autonomy thus carried over from *Reich* to republic. Many of these administrative questions, especially regarding the chain of command for the Austrian administration and the concomitant questions about how centralized or how federalist the new republic should be, were not settled either by the creation of the republic or by promulgation of the 1920 Constitution.[14] Rather, such issues lingered at least until the First Constitutional Revision of 1925—a revision that followed, both logically and chronologically, Austria's financial restructuring and the League's financial bailout.

In addition to taking on the former imperial structures, constitutional framework, and legal norms of the monarchy, the Austrian Republic that emerged in 1918 immediately took on the legions of imperial officials who staffed Vienna's central offices, the imperial governors' offices at the provincial level, and the district prefectures at the local level. The three presidents of the State Council of the German-Austrian Republic met with the last minister president of imperial Austria, Heinrich Lammasch, on 31 October 1918 (almost two weeks before Kaiser Karl abdicated and the republic was proclaimed). In what signaled the changing of the guard and the passing of monarchy to republic, Lammasch gave his assent to the "complete transfer of the administration" from the Austrian Empire to the German-Austrian government.[15] The law of 12 November 1918 (StGBl. Nr. 5), followed this gentlemen's agreement; it abolished the special laws and privileges of the emperor and the imperial house in one article and released the imperial bureaucracy from their oath of loyalty to the emperor in the next.[16] These steps paved the way to the imperial bureaucracy's wholesale incorporation into the administration of the republic. The bureaucrats themselves, however, had no legal right to automatic employment with the Austrian successor state. Moreover, the new Austrian state did not saddle itself with any legal obligation to carry over the officials' employment. Nonetheless, this is what happened.[17]

That the new republic tacitly acquired the central offices and personnel of a multinational empire is an example of what makes the story of Austria's bureaucracy an inherently Austrian story. It is an obvious question that one must ask, aided of course by hindsight, as to why the small successor state would take tens of thousands of officials into its ranks. Why did the German-Austrian state not take advantage of the fall of the Monarchy to rebuild a new, smaller, cheaper bureaucracy? Why did it not choose to free itself of the financial burdens of employing legions of civil servants? Furthermore, when one finally considers these questions in light of the wish of the leading social democrats, especially President Karl Seitz and State Chancellor Karl Renner, to place all the institutions of government under some form of democratic authority, why would the state take on the civil service wholesale—without picking and choosing those civil servants who were not arch-conservative or monarchist?

The answer to this question lay not only in the need for the new state to maintain the administrative expertise of many of the Monarchy's high and mid-level officials; it lay furthermore in the traditional patronage relationship between the state and its civil servants that Karl Renner, the new head of the government in 1918, hoped and, indeed, fully expected to take over as well. When State Chancellor Renner addressed the bureaucrats of the central offices of the new German-Austrian Republic in November 1918, he admitted that bureaucrats and public servants were also enduring the hardship of postwar hunger and inflation. Renner also recognized that many officials had to live with the daily anxiety of an unknown future: Would Austria's many officials be able to hold onto their jobs and earn a steady, middle-class salary? Renner gave his assurances that even though "German-Austria will be a poor state and will not be able to afford a larger bureaucratic apparatus" there would be every effort given "to take up all the German public servants and employees into the new state."[18] Renner hoped to harness both the expertise and the ethos of the imperial civil service to the new, small republic. Such hopes soon would be met by the harsh financial realities of post-war Europe.

In a very real sense then, Austria's transition from a group of crownlands that comprised the core of a multinational empire, to a rump republic of leftover provinces, is not the only story of the post-war. And, might I add, if the story one wants to tell is about state-building, or "forging a republic," this transition is, in itself, hardly a momentous one. Rather, state-building as regards the Austrian Republic was much more about dismantling the empire than building a state from wholly new cloth. The new state inherited not only the former imperial capital, Vienna, but much of its contents: its personnel, their expertise, their ideologies and mentalities of statecraft and policy-making. Importantly, the republic would also inherit the debates and questions which dominated constitutional scholars and administrative reformers in the empire: questions which focused on the relationship of center to periphery, of the *Länder* to the whole state.

The state financial crisis would shape how the institutions and people of the monarchy would be incorporated into the republic. However, Austria's path through the financial crisis was channeled in a very real sense through the mentalities of statecraft, bureaucratic governance, and party politics that the rump state had inherited from the empire. As we will see, the financial crisis was the catalyst that ended almost 200 years of central administration in the provinces. In this rather expansive chronological perspective, in the early 1920s Austria would bring the long-term presence of enlightened absolutism, and the sinews of power that connected Vienna to the provinces, to an end.

Financial crisis and reconstruction

The republic that the Treaty of Saint-Germain had delimited was small. A third of its 6.5 million citizens resided in the capital, Vienna. The new boundaries that had been erected as a result of the Paris Peace Treaties had separated the Austrian lands and the capital Vienna from its former trade lines, overturning what prosperity the large customs union that was the Habsburg Monarchy had created. Sir James Arthur Salter, the head of the economic and financial section of the League of Nations, would write in 1924 that the new borders of Central Europe had been especially cruel to Austria, separating its "urban populations from the food, without which they could not live, and the main industries from their raw materials and from their markets."[19] Thus, it is important to consider that while Austria's politicians were able, between 1918 and 1920, to create the constitutional and administrative edifice of a republic, the hardships and deprivation of war continued well into the 1920s. Salter noted that "Austria lived—but pitifully and precariously. She froze in winter, and a large part of her population was hungry throughout the year. Her middle class was almost destroyed [...]. The mortality was high and, among children, terrible."[20]

By February of 1922, Austria had seen numerous interventions of foreign credits and loans, as well as shipments of food supplies and outright charity on the part of the Allies. But these injections of foreign currency into the Austrian system only managed to keep the state afloat and the people fed, if inadequately clothed and heated, for brief periods of time. Firstly, Austria was unable to cover its budget—its projected budget exceeded its income by startling amounts. For the fiscal year July 1920-June 1921, parliament approved a revised operating budget of 70.6 billion Austrian crowns in March 1921; for the same fiscal year, the Austrian Finance Ministry projected that federal income would total less than 30 billion crowns, leaving more than half of the budget uncovered.[21] At the same time, the *Neue Freie Presse* published an article on its front page that addressed the viability of Austrian statehood. The article concluded that "Austria cannot be helped except through a serious relief operation that addresses the fundamental problems" and not simply one that simply solves the problems of the moment.[22]

But such a fundamental action did not come yet. The budget passed by parliament the next year exhibited more of the same, with 40 percent of the projected federal budget for the calendar year 1922 uncovered by state revenue.[23] Austria would again receive foreign credit to cover its budgets, but the charity upon which Austria had relied to keep the government running and to buy food and coal on the international market for its citizens had all but dried up.[24] Moreover, inflation threatened to starve the laboring and middle classes alike. Price rises had essentially been a part of Austrian domestic life throughout the war—doubling every year between 1914 and 1921.[25] By the end of 1921, however, hyperinflation had set in. Governmental expenses that were not covered by foreign credits—including expensive social welfare programs and food subventions for unemployed veterans and the working class poor—were increasingly covered by Austrian crowns from the printing press. In the first eight months of 1922, the number of Austrian crowns in circulation would balloon from 174 billion to over 1 trillion.[26] The cost of food rose exponentially and while Austrian manufacturers were able to dump their products on the international market at cut-rate prices, the financial solvency of Austria and its ability to secure any more financial aid were both in jeopardy.

Moreover, Austria's assets in 1922 were already all held as collateral against future war reparations, the foreign loans it already received, as well as occupation costs and other payments it owed to the various successor states of the Habsburg Empire. At the economic summit which was held in Genoa in April 1922, the Austrian federal chancellor, Johannes Schober, had failed to convince the Allies unanimously to lift their right of distraint from all the liens that they held against Austria's assets. Austria had nothing left to secure new loans—especially any long-term loans it would need to right its household and balance the government's budget.[27] It was under such circumstances that Johannes Schobers' "government of experts" fell in May 1922 and a new chancellor, Ignaz Seipel, would assume the reins of state in the worsening financial crisis.[28] Seipel spent the next few months striving to open the spigot of foreign aid again. The Pan-German and Christian Social governmental coalition initially embarked on a strategy to make Austria appear more financially capable of taking on new loans. The first tactic was comprised of a domestic financial plan, which Seipel's finance minister, August Ségur, presented to parliament in June 1922. It consisted of a series of laws which would have raised revenue through new taxes and imposed spending cuts on the government. Additionally, Ségur intended to finally stop using the printing press to print new money.[29] Such austerity measures failed by August 1922, when foreign-controlled banks baulked over the fine print: They sought financial guarantees from the Allies before they would consent to a new, independent bank of issue.[30]

When this did not work, Seipel played on the fears and ambitions of the Allies and Austria's neighbors in order to bring them back to the negotiation table. Seipel's second tactic was to turn to the international community for aid. In order to do this, however, Seipel's government emphasized Austria's desperation—not for international sympathy, but to fan fears of Austria's collapse. Over the summer months of 1922, after the failure of Seipel's domestic financial plan, Austria's delegation in London worked to secure a large foreign loan of £15 million. The argument that Seipel's government began to strenuously put forth however, was one that emphasized the precariousness of Austria's government and economic situation. If the Austrian crown would lose all of its value, Austria would not be able to import the foodstuffs necessary to feed its people or the coal necessary to keep its people warm. Food riots, anarchy, or worse, Bolshevism, would be the next step. The Austrian army, still in the firm hands of the Social Democrats, could not be counted upon to restore order; the government would collapse, and Austria would either be partitioned among its neighbors or fall completely into the hands of Italy or Germany. In any event, failure to help Austria—an artificial state that the Allied Powers had created—would result in a humanitarian disaster and possibly a war in Central Europe over Austria's dismemberment.[31]

By mid-August, such argumentation had failed to sway Lloyd George's government, though George did promise to raise the issue of a major foreign loan to Austria at the next meeting of the Allied Conference—to be held that very afternoon. The Allied governments, though, were likewise reticent to come to Austria's aid yet again. They referred the Austrian matter to the League of Nations, saying in their note that they would not come to Austria's aid "unless the League were able to propose a programme of reconstruction containing definite guarantees that further subscriptions would produce substantial improvement, and not be thrown away like those made in the past."[32]

Despite this major setback, the matter of Austrian reconstruction became a matter of prestige for the League and its supporters. In the meantime, Seipel had embarked on an international appeal of his own. He had traveled to Italy, Czechoslovakia, and Germany to discuss possible courses of action under which Austria could find a "Central European solution" to Austria's dire economic problems. The discussions included topics that, in the minds of League members, would have upset the balance of power in Central Europe. Thus, by entertaining Austria's dissolution and possible falling to Italy or Germany, Seipel simultaneously appealed to the political and humanitarian necessity of propping up an independent Austria through financial help.[33] In the meantime, the financial situation in

Austria continued to deteriorate. Austria's economic collapse was imminent and, thanks to Seipel, well-known. Under such circumstances, Seipel took a train to Geneva to address the general assembly of the League of Nations, which had just reconvened.

Seipel's address to the General Assembly of the League of Nations, on 6 September 1922, appealed to its membership to help Austria, not only for the sake of charity, but above all to secure its own legitimacy as an international organization that must follow its mission to insure peace. If the League failed to act, Austria would likewise fail:

> This would mean a hole would be ripped through the middle of the European map; it would mean the creation of a vacuum in the middle of Europe, a vacuum with a monstrous suction that would pull in [Austria's] neighbors and would disrupt the balance of power among them that had only been established with great skill.[34]

Seipel's appeal had the desired effect; on the next day the League established an "Austria Committee"—the *Sous-Comité de l'Autriche*—to discuss a future league action in Austria. [35]

A month later, on 4 October 1922, the League of Nations had worked out three protocols which were signed by representatives of Great Britain, France, Italy, Czechoslovakia and Austria.[36] These Protocols laid down the conditions through which Austria would receive a loan of 650 million gold crowns, 520 million of which were to help Austria cover its budget deficit in two years. The loan thus was to provide the Austrian government the time and the means to enact serious financial and governmental reforms. The state monopolies on tobacco and tariffs were put up by the government as security for the loan.[37]

The protocols each addressed different aspects of Austria's political and financial situation. Protocol I quashed any hopes among German Nationalists or Social Democrats for a German Anschluss. Protocol II set up the loan, how it was to be used, and the supervisory function of the League's members in the administration of the loan itself. The third and last Protocol spelled the most change for the structure of the Austrian Republic itself; moreover, it was the hardest for Seipel to sell to the Nationalrat, Austria's parliament.

Protocol III required Austria's legislature to approve and the government subsequently to undertake a series of reforms that would "enable [her] to re-establish a permanent equilibrium of her budget within two years" (§ 2). To do this, the Protocol saw the establishment of the office of "Commissioner General" to oversee Austria's financial reconstruction. Over the next three-and-a-half years, the Commissioner-General, who was stationed in Vienna, would file forty-two monthly reports to the League.[38] The Commissioner-General would also serve as a supervisor to the Austrian government in matters that related to the "execution of the reform programme."[39]

The reform program was necessary to provide Austria with a lasting balanced budget and a stable currency. In financial policy, this meant following a deflationary program and giving the right of note to an independent bank of issue defined by the League.[40] As far as balancing the budget, however, Austria's government promised to undertake radical internal reforms, reforms that were first brought to light in the "Rebuilding Law" of 27 November 1922.[41] The law projected, among new taxes and price increases for the federal railways, a significant reduction in the number of state employees and what was termed "administrative reform and austerity measures."

In addition to reducing the number of ministries and instituting measures to reduce paperwork, the government called for the reduction of public employees by about one-third; that is, by 100,000 state officials and employees of the federal railways.[42] In reality, however, the Austrian government stopped short of cutting 100,000 civil servants—but not by much. The League of Nations reported that "reduction" figures by December 1925 included some 96,613 public employees. These included 22,946 from the Central Administration; 21,062 from the State Monopolies; 39,783 from the Federal Railways; and 11,184 from the *Südbahn*.[43] Reduction measures had followed mechanical guidelines; civil servants who had reached the age of fifty-four but had not yet spent thirty years in the service were nevertheless to be automatically cut.[44]

In many ways, Seipel's financial reconstruction plan was more than successful. Sir Arthur Salter could report in *Foreign Affairs* in 1924 that Austria would not even need the full amount of the loan to cover its deficit.[45] But the collateral damage of the reconstruction plan—a not unforeseen one—was the major blow to the ethos of the bureaucracy. Instead of winning new republicans among the bureaucrats, Seipel's government had taken away their job security and thus their identification with the republic. By the time of the Great Depression in the late 1920s, the government had seen the immediate effects of reducing expenditure by laying off its employees and officials. After the official end of the "reduction" program in 1925, the government would pare down the bureaucracy even more. Its supposed low-point in 1925 of 208,500 employees would sink to 169,000 by 1933.

In essence, Seipel's response to the financial crisis and the Geneva Financial Reconstruction of Austria were never solely budgetary matters but also opportunities for Seipel and the Christian Socials to intervene in long-standing constitutional issues that the republic had inherited from the Monarchy. Victor Kienböck, Seipel's minister of finance, hinted that the imperial government's increasing interest in business regulation in the nineteenth and early twentieth centuries had led to the problem of an unsustainable number of civil servants—a number which had only increased during the Monarchy's increasing intervention into industry during the war.[46] It was left to the republic and Seipel's government to dismantle the imperial bureaucratic apparatus and the remnants of the central, regulatory state.

The *Beamtenabbau*, the cashiering of legions of civil servants, eliminated many jobs in the Federal Railways and the State Monopolies to be sure; but among the *Hoheitsverwaltung*—the administrative and ministerial bureaucracy—it eliminated almost 20 percent of Interior Ministry officials, more than half of the officials in Ministry of Social Affairs, and almost one-third of officials in the Ministry for Transportation and Trade.[47] But more than just dismantling the structures and personnel of an interventionist bureaucracy and the regulatory state, Seipel's Financial Reconstruction Plan cleared the path to both a significant administrative reform as well as a major constitutional revision in 1925.

While administrative reform sought to meet the reduced bureaucratic apparatus with a work reduction, the constitutional reform of 30 July 1925 reorganized the relationship between the federal government and the provinces. It ended Austria's long-standing dual-track administrative organization, which it had inherited from the Empire, by turning over all the federal offices at the provincial and district levels to the provincial governments. This was essentially a strike at the relationship between the central state and the bureaucracy; a relationship that the social democrat Karl Renner had hoped would directly carry over from *Reich* to republic. Instead, the bureaucracy that might have united the small republic was provincialized and handed over to the direct supervision of the Christian Social politicians outside of Vienna.

In the early 1920s, Ignaz Seipel was the one major political figure who sincerely believed in the viability of the Austrian Republic and the need to solidify its independence. The loan he helped to secure from the League of Nations, as well as the financial reform program which his government implemented, was intended to anchor Austria's viability in the international system and in its own financial solvency. At the same time, however, Seipel used Austria's financial reconstruction to resolve, once and for all, the debates regarding Austria's administrative system. But in downsizing the bureaucracy, Seipel also brought about its complete provincialization and—at least outside of Vienna's central offices—its dependence on provincial politicians and elected officials. By dismantling the imperial bureaucracy, Seipel thought he was building the foundations for a viable republic. But he had altered and reduced an important and once powerful component in Austria's political structure: the bureaucracy. In eliminating the ability of the bureaucracy to make policy independent of parliament and the political parties, Seipel made Austria financially secure, but all the more dependent on democracy, elected officials, and parliamentary government. These institutions would not prove themselves as active participants in a healthy political system until after the Second World War.

Notes

* I wish to thank the Austrian Cultural Forum, for generous travel support to present an early draft of this article at the 2009 German Studies Association Conference in Arlington, VA. In addition, thanks go to Carole Fink for her insightful comments and encouragement, as well as Günter Bischof and my fellow panelists for their helpful criticism. Finally, I wish to thank my colleagues in the Russian and East European Studies reading group and the Nanovic Institute for European Studies at the University of Notre Dame.

1. For information on the series of relief efforts and their negotiations between Austria and the Allies, see above all, Peter Edwin Schmidt, "The Relief of Austria, 1919-1922," PhD. diss., Case Western Reserve University, 1977.

2. For a contemporary analysis, which presents the League of Nation's bailout of the Austrian government as a success story for the League, see above all the official report written by the head of the economic and financial section of the League, Sir Arthur Salter, "General Survey," in *The Financial Reconstruction of Austria: General Survey and Principal Documents* (Geneva: Imp. Kundig, 1926), 9-85.

3. *Reichspost*, 23 Oct. 1918. See also Wilhelm Brauneder, *Deutsch-Österreich 1918: Die Republik entsteht* (Vienna: Amalthea, 2000), 64-68.

4. Brauneder, *Deutsch-Österreich 1918*, 65-66.

5. *Gesetz vom 14. November 1918, betreffend die Übernahme der Staatsgewalt in den Ländern*, StGBl. Nr. 24/ 1918.

6. An explanation of the Habsburg Monarchy's unique dual-track administrative system, in which two separate administrations (each with their own distinct bureaucracies) administered social welfare and the business of government at the provincial and local levels, can be found in Josef Redlich, *Austrian War Government*, Economic and Social History of the World War vol. 6 (New Haven: Yale University Press, 1929), 14-16.

7. See the minutes of 5 November 1918, *Stenographisches Protokoll der provisorischen niederösterreichischen Landesversammlung*, 9-11, quoted in Georg Schmitz, "Demokratisierung und Landesverfassung in Niederösterreich," in *Studien zur Zeitgeschichte der österreichischen Länder I. Demokratisierung und Verfassung in den Ländern 1918-1920*, ed. Alfred Ableitinger (St. Pölten: Verlag Niederösterreichisches Pressehaus, 1983), 164.

8. Theo Öhlinger, "Die Entstehung des Bundesstaates und ihre juristische Bedeutung," in *60*

Jahre Bundesverfassung, ed. Eberhard Zwinck, Schriftenreihe des Landespressebüros Salzburg (Salzburg: Landespressebüro, 1980), 42.

9. Josef Redlich, *Austrian War Government*, 100-06. See also, John W. Boyer, *Culture and Political Crisis in Vienna: Christian Socialism in Power, 1897-1918* (Chicago: University of Chicago Press, 1995), 370.

10. Article 9 of the *Beschluß der Provisiorischen Nationalversammlung für Deutschösterreich vom 30. Okotber 1918 über die grundlegenden Einrichtungen der Staatsgewalt*, StGBl. Nr 1.

11. *Stenographisches Protokoll der provisorischen Nationalversammlung für Deutschösterreich*, [Herafter SPpNV] 3. Sitzung (12 November 1918), 76.

12. See Fink's speech in SPpNV, 4. Sitzung (14 November 1918), 109.

13. Moreover, article 10 of this law (StGBl. Nr. 24/ 1918) reads "Until the completion of an administrative reform no change will enter into the existing employment status or compensation; officials of the formerly autonomous provincial administration will hold the title of 'Officials of the Land-Council' [*Beamte des Landesrates*] and officials of the former imperial governor's office will hold the title 'officials of the provincial government' [*Beamte der Landesregierung*]."

14. For the constitutional history of the creation of the republic and the Austrian Federal Constitution of 1920, see above all Brauneder, *Deutsch-Österreich 1918*, 70-75; Paul Brian Silverman, "Law and Economics in Interwar Vienna: Kelsen, Mises, and the Regeneration of Austrian Liberalism," PhD. diss., University of Chicago, 1984: ii, 660-76.

15. Gottfried Köfner, "Eine oder wieviele Revolutionen? Das Verhältnis zwischen Staat und Ländern in Deutschösterreich im Oktober und November 1918," *Jahrbuch für Zeitgeschichte 2* (1979): 138.

16. *Gesetz vom 12. November 1918 über die Staats- und Regierungsform von Deutschösterreich*, (StGBl. 5/ 1918), articles 5 and 6.

17. Herta Hafner, "Der sozio-ökonomische Wandel der österreichischen Staatsangestellten," PhD. diss., University of Vienna, 1990: 217-18.

18. *Der Staatsbeamte*, Nr. 491, 1 Dec. 1918, 70.

19. Arthur Salter, "The Reconstruction of Austria," *Foreign Affairs 2* (Jun. 1924): 631.

20. Ibid.

21. BGBl. Nr. 162, *Bundesfinanzgesetz vom 17. März 1921 für das Verwaltungsjahr 1920/21*.

22. "Die Frage der Lebensfähigkeit von Oesterreich," *NFP*, Nr. 20318, 22 March 1921 (Morgenblatt), 1.

23. The federal budget for the calendar year 1922 was set at 347.5 billion crowns. The projected state income for the same period was nearly 210 billion crowns. In other words, the budget proposed 137,770,399,300 K—nearly 138 billion crowns—in uncovered expenses. See the BGBl. Nr. 726/1921, *Bundesfinanzgesetz vom 21. Dezember 1921 für das Jahr 1922*; and Nr. 727/1921, *Verordnung, betreffend Grundsätze für die Führung des Bundeshaushaltes vom 1. Jänner bis 31. Dezember 1922*.

24. Salter reports that a monetary intervention in February of 1922 by Great Britain (£2,250,00); France (55 million Fr.); Italy (70 million IL); and Czechoslovakia (500 million Kr) prevented a complete financial collapse in the first half of 1922. But, in reality, only the British actually fulfilled their pledge. Compare Salter, "General Survey," 13-14; and Victor Kienböck, *Das österreichische Sanierungswerk*, vol. 85, Finanz- und volkswirtschaftliche Zeitfragen (Stuttgart: F. Enke, 1925), 19-20.

25. Roman Sandgruber, *Ökonomie und Politik: Österreichische Wirtschaftsgeschichte vom*

Mittealalter bis zur Gegenwart, Österreichische Geschichte (Vienna: Ueberreuter, 1995), 354-59.

26. Ibid., 355.

27. Carole Fink, *The Genoa Conference: European Diplomacy, 1921-1922* (Chapel Hill: University of North Carolina Press, 1984), 239-41.

28. For the fall of Schober's government see Rainer Hubert, *Schober: "Arbeitermörder" und "Hort der Republik": Biographie eines Gestrigen* (Vienna: Böhlau, 1990), 148-53. For the rise of the Seipel government, see Klemens von Klemperer, *Ignaz Seipel: Christian Statesman in a Time of Crisis* (Princeton: Princeton University Press, 1972), 163-74.

29. See NFP, 22 June 1922 (Morgenblatt), 1-2.

30. See John C. Swanson, *The Remnants of the Habsburg Monarchy: The Shaping of Modern Austria and Hungary, 1918-1922*, East European monographs no. 568 (Boulder: East European Monographs, 2001), 298. See also Klemperer, *Ignaz Seipel*, 184.

31. For Austria's appeals to the Allied Powers and especially Great Britain in the summer of 1922, see especially Kienböck, *Das österreichische Sanierungswerk*, 21-22; Schmidt, "Relief of Austria," 430-59.

32. Lloyd George to George Frankenstein, London, 15 August 1922, British Foreign Office 371/7339/c11517/74, quoted in Schmidt, "Relief of Austria," 459, 469.

33. For a detailed history of Seipel's "great trip" see especially, Klemperer, *Ignaz Seipel*, 186-97.

34. Large parts of Seipel's speech to the General Assembly of the League of Nations are reprinted in Friedrich Rennhofer, *Ignaz Seipel: Mensch und Staatsmann. Eine biographische Dokumentation* (Vienna: Böhlau, 1978), 310-11. This quote is taken from 310. The full text of Seipel's speech is in Josef Gessl, *Seipels Reden in Österreich und anderwärts: Eine Auswahl zu seinem 50. Geburtstage* (Vienna: Heros, 1926), 25 ff.

35. Gottlieb Ladner, *Seipel als Überwinder der Staatskrise vom Sommer 1922: Zur Geschichte der Entstehung der Genfer Protokolle vom 4. Oktober 1922*, vol. 1, Publikationen des Österreichischen Instituts für Zeitgeschichte (Vienna: Stiasny, 1964), 120.

36. The three "Geneva Protocols" are reprinted in League of Nations, *The Financial Reconstruction of Austria: General Survey and Documents*, Publications of the League of Nations, II. Economic and Financial (Geneva: Imp. Kundig, 1926), 137-50.

37. Lajos Kerekes, *Von St. Germain bis Genf: Österreich und seine Nachbarn, 1918-1922* (Budapest: Akad. Kiadó / Vienna: Böhlau, 1979).

38. League of Nations, Commissioner General for Austria, *Financial Reconstruction of Austria: Report by the Commissioner-General of Austria*, Geneva, 1923-1926. 42 vols.

39. See Salter, "General Survey," 25.

40. Salter, "The Reconstruction of Austria," 634.

41. *Budesgesetz vom 27. November über die zur Aufrichtung der Staats- und Volkswirtschaft der Republik Österreich zu treffenenden Maßnahmen*, BGBl. Nr. 843/ 1922.

42. For the figure of 100,000 civil servants see Waltraud Heindl, "Bürokratie und Beamte," in *Handbuch des politischen Systems Österreichs: Erste Republik, 1918-1933*, ed. Emmerich Tálos et al. (Vienna: Manz, 1995), 98; Kerekes, *Von St. Germain bis Genf*, 380. Kerekes actually lists the downsizing action as intending to cut 100,000 tenured civil servants; 61,000 public employees; 23,000 attendants [*Bedienstete*]; and 11,240 employees of the Federal Railways. Kerekes' figures essentially double Heindl's; though I have not been able to as of yet corroborate either figure among the archival records.

43. *The Financial Reconstruction of Austria: General Survey and Documents*, 122-23.

44. Heindl, "Bürokratie und Beamte," 100.

45. Salter, "The Reconstruction of Austria," 637. Salter was careful, however, to emphasize that the government needed to continue with the reduction of expenditure.

46. Kienböck, *Das österreichische Sanierungswerk*, 47-48.

47. See the table, "Personalabbau in der Zeit von 1. Oktober 1922 bis 14. März 1925," in ibid., 55.

II. COSTS OF WAR: SOCIAL/MENTAL/CULTURAL LEGACIES

Demographic Transitions Accelerated: Abortion, Body Politics, and the End of Supra-Regional Labor Immigration in Post-War Austria

Andreas Weigl

The Legacy of War

Not only did the end of the First World War mark the collapse of the old order within Europe. The beginning of the "short 20th century" (1918-89) was also accompanied by dramatic demographic changes. The shrinking of the Republic of German-Austria (*Deutschösterreich*), as the Republic of Austria was initially called, to the geographic and, in connection with this development, the demographic dimension of a small state was probably the most noticeable feature for the Austrian public. Even if the victorious powers had agreed to the extensive territorial claims of the young republic, which—the exception, of course, being the area which would later become the Burgenland—they did not, it would still only have consisted of a third of the population of the former Austrian half of the old empire.[1] Issuing two laws on 22 November 1918,[2] the State Council had laid claims to a territory which consisted of a population of 10.2 million or 10.4 million, including the linguistic enclaves of Brünn/Brno, Iglau/Jihlava and Olmütz/Olomouc, according to the last pre-war census.[3] In actual fact, the territorial remainder of what was now called Austria was left with a populace of barely 6.5 million. In the period between 1913 and 1919 it had lost about 350,000 of its population.[4] This was another aspect which caused the young republic to be one of the greater losers as a result of the outcome of the war. The demographic losses during the decade of the war were exceeded percentage-wise only by Yugoslavia and Poland.[5] Of the 1.46 million fallen soldiers of Austria-Hungary, who were either killed in battle or died in captivity, around 180,000 to 190,000 came from the area which is today known as the Republic of Austria.[6] It was especially those areas along the south front that were affected by the losses, namely the later provinces of Carinthia and Styria, but also those of Salzburg and Vorarlberg.[7]

An even greater number of other war victims may also be added to these losses. According to statistics from the year 1927, about 110,000 war-wounded veterans suffering from a loss of earning capacity of at least 15 percent were living in Austria. This number must have been substantially higher immediately after the war when one considers that the same number of applications were filed in 1923 in Vienna and Lower Austria alone.[8] The war also left behind many thousands of women who had been widowed and children who had been left orphaned. Two-thirds of them had to support themselves on meagre welfare provisions or on support provided by the military, according to a survey undertaken in Vienna on 1 July 1918 which can also be seen as representative for the rest of the country. Therefore it is hardly surprising that a third of those questioned in this survey defined themselves as "sick"—the survey itself having been undertaken before the influenza pandemic of 1918/1919.[9] Towards the end of the war, as hospital reports confirm, the term "sick" largely referred to states of exhaustion and malnutrition, as well as the physical conditions which resulted from these, such as open tuberculosis, pyelonephritis, colitis and oedemas.[10] According to contemporary statistical calculations, around 60,000 civilians fell victim to the war-inflicted excess mortality.[11] This was intensified and prolongated by the influenza pandemic—which cannot be explained as a direct result of the war—that reached Austria in the late summer of 1918 and probably afflicted more than half of the Austrian population.[12] The death toll of the influenza was set at 20,646 in 1918/19, but considering the drastic increase in the cause of death given as "pneumonia" the number must probably be set more correctly at 30,000 to 40,000.[13] The age group between fifteen and thirty and as the population of the open and mountainous countryside were affected way over proportion. The reasons for this over-proportionality, as have been correctly suggested, lay in the insufficient immunization of the first group: the previous influenza epidemic having taken place in 1889/90. For the second group the reason may be found in (pulmonary-)tuberculosis, which was widely spread in the urban and industrialized parts of the country, acting as a "great killer" and standing in direct competition with the influenza virus.[14]

If the demographic trends of the pre-war decade had continued, Austria (not counting the Burgenland) could have accounted for a population increase of about 950,000 or fifteen percent in the first census rather than the figure that was actually evaluated.[15] The largest hypothetical loss fell upon infants and men in the conscription age group. According to contemporary calculations, birth loss due to the war amounted to about 300,000.[16] A comparison of male cohorts of conscription age in the years 1910 and 1920 shows a loss of about 290,000 men, although about a third of this number was caused by post-war emigration.

Fig. 1: Population change by age group and sex 1910-1920[17]

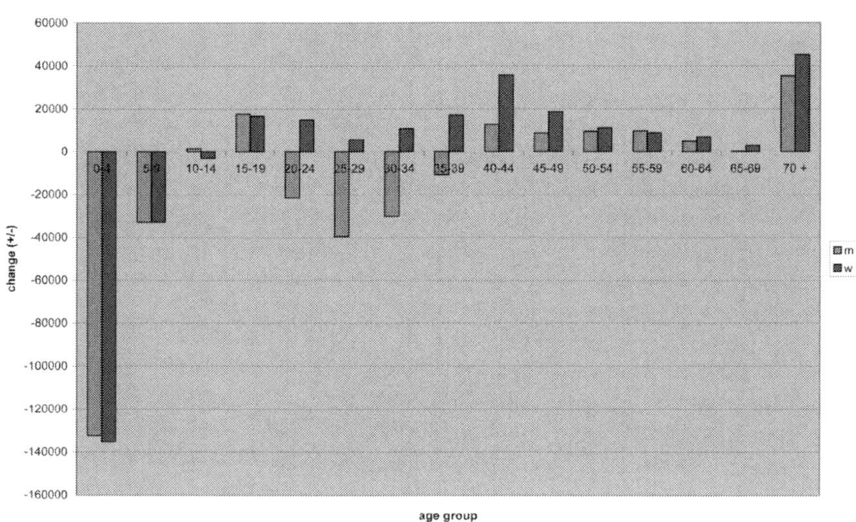

The main effect of this emigration was to be found in Vienna, although it also had an effect in the Burgenland and Vorarlberg. However, in the provinces it was not so noticeable.[18] The most prominent group among these emigrants were the Viennese Czechs. In total around 145,000 Czechs and 5,000 Slovakians left Austria.[19]

This emigration was met by a current flow of those returning from other parts of the Monarchy and the mainly Jewish refugees, leading to a positive net migration at a pre-war level in 1920 and 1921.[20] Although a large part of the refugees had already returned to their homes towards the end of the war, there were still about 20,000 Jewish war refugees under state care in Austria, almost all of them in Vienna. They were joined by "pogrom refugees," who lacked recognition as such. They had fled in the face of anti-

Jewish excesses during the Polish-Ukrainian battles, the Polish-Soviet War and the terror of the Council Regime (*Räterepublik*) in Hungary.[21] These war and post-war refugees accounted for a perceptible increase in the Jewish portion of the population. This was at least the case in Vienna. In total the Jewish migration balance during 1910-23 was +39,000.[22] This, of course, also takes into account the immigration and emigration of 1911-13, which may have amounted to a positive balance of perhaps +10,000 according to the trend of 1900-10.[23] Therefore the total number of war-refugees remaining in Vienna must have been about 30,000. This also corresponded approximately with the general growth of the Jewish population in Austria, as the number of the Jewish population was neither significant in the rest of Austria, nor did it undergo much change, as is best shown by the examples of the Burgenland and Carinthia.[24]

Medium-term, Austria lost 114,000 inhabitants within its new borders (i.e. today's borders) during the period between 1910-23. It was only in the case of Vienna that immigration failed to compensate for emigration by a long way. All the other provinces were able to compensate their loss within just a few years of the post-war period.[25] Reasons for this lay on the one hand in the characteristic post-war baby boom, and on the other hand in the immigration of German-speaking people from all parts of the former Monarchy which set in towards the end of the war.[26] It is difficult to grasp the extent of this immigration movement by quantitative means, but there is some indirect evidence. For example: On 1 December 1918 there were 27,918 non-Jewish refugees in state care in German-Austria[27]—no doubt a minority within these migrants. In contrast to the former state employees who came from all parts of the Monarchy, other prominent migratory groups came from German-speaking border regions of the Danube Monarchy's successor states. By estimate, around 30,000 people immigrated from Lower Styria and Carniola. Around 10,000 South Tyroleans added to this number. Nothing is known of the number of German-speaking Bohemians (*Deutschböhmen*), but it must surely have been significant.[28] In total, during the period of 1920-23 101,000 inhabitants of successor states—primarily Old Austrians (*Altösterreicher*)—opted for Austrian citizenship. Between 1920 and 1936 a further 120,000—some of whom had, of course, already been living within the territory of the later republic before the outbreak of war—assumed Austrian citizenship without opting for it.[29] As the calculated net migration for the years 1910-23 shows, the Old Austrian immigrants migrated in over-proportional numbers to Lower and Upper Austria, as well as Styria.[30] The immigration of these groups was also responsible for the slightly positive net migration for 1910-23 within the new borders.[31]

After the migratory movement of the immediate post-war phase had calmed down, temporary work migration dominated the situation. This migration was surely quite significant,[32] although immigration and emigration are likely to have more or less kept in balance. The reasons for the net migration figures becoming negative between 1923-34[33] may be sought in the overseas migration that took place.

The option of migrating to the USA gained in importance in the late years of the Danube Monarchy in the case of permanent and temporary migration, even though oversee migration failed to reach the degree of internal migration at the dawn of WWI.[34] After all, Austria-Hungary had at this time become the most important country of origin for U.S. immigrants.[35] However, the provinces of the young republic hardly played a role here, be it for one exception.[36] This exception was the Burgenland—then still western Hungary—where a continuous emigration had been taking place since the 1870s.[37] All in all, the number of inhabitants of the Burgenland who emigrated to the USA from the middle of the 19th century to the dawn of WWI may be estimated at about 30,000. However, an estimated fifth of these returned home.[38] The flow of emigrants from western Hungary came to a halt at the outbreak of WWI, leading to a build-up of "emigrant reserves" which was discharged in 1922-23.[39] A fifth of the population of the district of Güssing, in the especially backward and under-developed southern Burgenland, emigrated overseas during the interwar period.[40] Alongside this overseas emigration from the Burgenland, emigration from Vienna and some industrial areas played a certain role in the years after WWI. Overall, however, migration overseas remained within easy to survey limitation because the receiving countries were primarily in need of skilled agriculture workers, which the Austrian labour market was not able to supply.[41] Between 1919-37 approximately 80,000 Austrians officially migrated overseas. Destinations of choice were the USA, as well as Brazil and Argentina. A comparatively smaller number of illegal immigrants may be added to this number.[42]

Emigration from Austria to other European countries cannot be sufficiently quantified, in contrast to the well-documented overseas migration. According to the countries of birth surveyed in the national censuses of the 1930s, the long-term migration balance with Switzerland and also to a certain extent with Germany was negative.[43] It is hard to tell how far the interwar period contributed to this. Since the end of WWI labour migration could primarily be encountered in the form of strictly regulated "guest work" due to a visa and national job market policy. It fluctuated annually and reached its height during hyperinflation. During this time, a large number of Austrians were at work in mining in the north of France but also in Lower Lusatia. There was another modest peak in the number of labour migration during the favourable economic boom in the second half of the 1920s. Labourers travelled to Germany, but also to France.[44]

The major fluctuations in migratory movement did not, of course, relate to long distance migration. It was the breaking apart of the common market that acted as the most essential factor. The labour market of Vienna, together with its surrounding industrial areas, was hardly able to supply labour migrants from the successor states with enough work. A change in direction of migration currents, especially to Czechoslovakia, was hindered by language barriers and the protectionist labour market policies of the neighbouring states.[45] But it was the establishment of the so-called "respectable working class family" stemming directly from living circumstances too that led to a shift in migratory behaviour. The modern "nomadism" of the pre-war years came to an end. A migration transition in favour of a strongly reduced mobility was well underway in Central Europe.[46] What remained was a prominent internal migration from the adjacent eastern provinces to Vienna which had not changed much in dimension since the pre-war decades.[47]

An "Overpopulated" New State?

That the young Republic of Austria was "overpopulated" was not up for discussion among Austrian demographers—a view which was also shared by the political powers.[48] In 1919 there was even a "migration office" (*Wanderungsamt*) installed in the chancellor's office (*Bundeskanzleramt*), advising those who were willing to leave on migrating overseas. Emigration was obviously welcome as a "population buffer." At the same time, as had been the case before the war, experts who were associated with the moderately right-wing conservative movement (*bürgerliches Lager*)—in a somewhat contradictory manner—complained about birth decrease and strictly rejecting Neomalthusian agitation.[49]

The characterization of Austria as overpopulated may seem strange from today's perspective. However, it did have its contemporary logic. During the war Austria had started to become gradually cut off from its most important "granaries," especially Hungary. By the end of the war it had completely lost these resources.[50] The effects of the "hunger blockade" by the Entente—which was not lifted until early 1919—incapacitated efforts to substitute the missing grain supplies through other carbohydrates such as rice.[51] With the breakdown of agricultural production and organizational shortcomings which exacerbated the situation, this led to a supply disaster with regard to all supplies towards the end of WWI and during the post-war period. It was only with the help of compensational contracts with neighbouring states and Allied support that it was possible to prevent a severe famine. Structural problems also stood in the way of a sufficient supply of food, even outside Vienna, for a few years.[52] Even in the mid-1920s the harvest—for example, in Tyrol and Salzburg—remained far behind the pre-war level.[53] Austria had to rely on substantial food imports that burdened its trade balance throughout the whole interwar period.[54]

For growing children especially, food deprivation was the cause of lasting development deficits and connected illnesses.[55] This was brought to the attention of a global audience by the 1919 movie *Das Kinderelend in Wien* ("The Misery of Children in Vienna") in as dramatically a way as possible.[56] Pertinent research on Viennese apprentices and Tyrolean school pupils proved the most distinctive anthropometric deficits in teenagers.[57] According to the results of test rows conducted between 1918 and 1920, fifteen-year-olds showed an average underweight of ten kilograms compared to the pre-war situation.[58] The average body size of Viennese children during the post-war period was reduced to the dimensions of their late 18th century contemporaries.[59] Surveys conducted on more than 400,000 children in 1920-21 showed that 75 to 80 percent of them were underweight in every province except for Lower Austria. The situation was even worse in Salzburg and Carinthia, especially in the regional capitals there. In early 1921, 55 to 58 percent of infants in the city of Salzburg showed signs of rickets.[60] Up to 1922 there was no real improvement in the nutritional condition of Austrian children.[61] Only afterwards did the supply situation improve substantially. Even then the long-term effects were shocking. A quarter of the Viennese school children were still undernourished in the mid-1920s.[62] But it was not only the nutritional situation which affected the "lost generation." There were not enough clothes, shoes or hygiene products. As late as 1928, 40 percent of Carinthian children were, for example, considered to be "totally neglected."[63] The school reformer Otto Glöckel spoke of a "seriously damaged generation already in the making."[64]

The impact of the war would have been even worse, had it not been for foreign help in the form of loans for 26.7 million £[65] and campaigns for child aid. Between 1919 and 1921, about one-third of Austrian children were housed and supplied for by foster parents, especially in Switzerland and the Netherlands.[66] For those remaining in Austria, the American Relief Administration provided meal distribution for children, at least in the urban-industrial centres of each province.[67] Alongside other similar activities this helped to improve the nutritional situation of the children.[68]

Fig. 2[69]

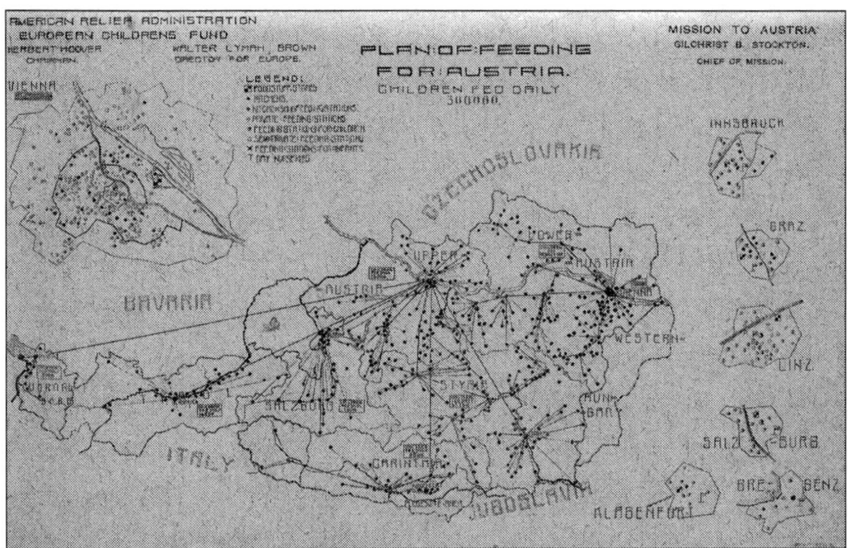

With regard to the population of school-age children between six and thirteen years of age, in 1920 more than 70 percent of Viennese children, more than a third of those from Salzburg and somewhere between a fifth and a sixth of school children from the other provinces—with the exception of the Burgenland, which was not yet under Austrian administration after the war—were supplied with a warm lunch on a daily basis. The number of portions served was increased even more the following year.[70] Taking into account the fortunate supply situation of the rural areas, the supply situation came relatively close to a full provision with food. In Vienna, the local municipal administration stepped into the succession of the American action from 1922 onwards. The measures were gradually reduced, the reduction of necessity, of course, being a reason for this.[71]

The famine, which worsened throughout the course of the war, and the declining harvests also hit hard on the adult population, both civilian and military.[72] Adults showed a weight loss of ten to twenty kilograms after WWI.[73] The situation in Vienna was the worst of all, its population having to survive on an official ration of 1,271 kcal during the spring and summer of 1919. As even the Allied nutrition-controller stated, survival was impossible without goods from the black market.[74] The situation was not much better outside Vienna, and it got worse during the immediate post-war period[75]—with lasting effects on the people's health (*Volksgesundheit*). Even during the mid-1920s the director of a sanatorium for lung diseases in Vorarlberg, referring to the local female population, expected that the long-term effects of malnutrition and physical exhaustion would be the cause for higher morbidity "even years from now."[76] The consequences of the war were so dramatic that experts who sympathized with eugenic ideas such as those of Julius Tandler and Heinrich Reichel painted a bleak picture of the dysgenic effects of the war. The fittest had died, the rest were alive![77] But they were wrong in their assumptions. It was mostly the chronically ill who made up the growing number of deaths among the civilian population (including prisoners of war) up to 1918.[78] In the years 1912-14, 25 percent of TBC patients died within a year, and in 1919 this had risen to 59 percent.[79] Still the largest pandemic of the 20th century, the Spanish Influenza of 1918-19 claimed many lives, particularly among young adults. However, it was not the war itself that caused the flue to spread. Neither warring nor neutral countries were spared by the pandemic.[80]

The Acceleration of Epidemiologic Transition

It was one of the paradoxes of the First World War that it brought forward the implementation of a public health program and welfare system which ultimately led to a considerable rise in life expectancy. In Great Britain and France this implementation had already occurred to some extent during the War. In Austria, on the other hand, it did not happen until the interwar period. This also explains the time lag in the cutback of total mortality.[81]

The discourse on this subject was led within the "Austrian Society for Population Politics and Social Welfare" (*Österreichische Gesellschaft für Bevölkerungspolitik und Fürsorgewesen*), which had been established in 1917. During the interwar period it was much agreed that critical improvements of the "people's health" could first and foremost be achieved through measures to confront the following problems: infant mortality, (pulmonary-)tuberculosis, especially in infants and adolescents, as well as venereal diseases.[82] Although the latter hardly played a role in the mortality rate, they were ever-present in public discussion.[83]

Contrary to total mortality, infant mortality had not risen dramatically, especially in comparison with the very high rate on an international level. The war had just interrupted the downward trend which had already been the case for a fairly long time. In 1919 the level of the last pre-war years had already been clearly undercut.[84] After that, a strongly accelerated cutback set in. Had the infant mortality rate[85] sunk annually by an average 1.3 percent between 1871-1919, from 1920-39 it was 3.7 percent.[86] During the war a massive rise in infant mortality was averted by the comparatively quite favourable neonatal mortality rate within the first month after birth. The post-war decrease in mortality from the second to twelfth month after birth turned out to be a bit heavier.

Fig. 3: Infant mortality in Austria 1913-1929 (1)[87]

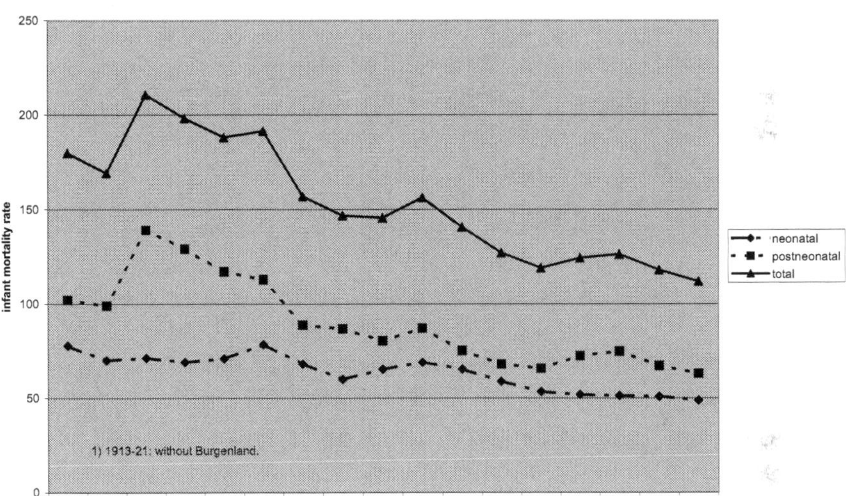

The favourable trend of neonatal mortality during and after the war was clearly a result of a higher practice of breast-feeding, at least in Vienna, which can be shown by the decrease in gastro-internal disorders of infants born in wedlock. In Vienna almost 90 percent of infants were breast-fed for more than half a year.[88] Considering the general milk shortage and the strong decline in birth rates[89] one can assume a more common breast-feeding practice, which is indirectly proven by the surprisingly constant death rate[90] of gastro-internal illnesses in view of the worsening living circumstances.[91] Medicalization via hospitalization played a substantial role for the following decrease in early mortality. This was at least the case in Vienna, where in-hospital births reached a proportion of 80 to 90 percent. The positive effects of this medicalization are mirrored in the mortality rate of Viennese infants during the second to fourth week after birth undercutting that of London in the early 1930s.[92] On the other hand, anthropometric examinations raise the assumption that the considerably improved nutritional situation of mothers, which did not take place until the mid 1920s, was not very relevant for the decrease in mortality during the first days of existence at first. The negative effects of the war and the post-war period on the nutritional situation of mothers were obviously also of little importance for early mortality.[93]

The massive decrease in post-neonatal mortality in the 1920s is linked to the major improvements within the basic conditions of infant care. The effects of health care policies—including legal protection for working mothers—as well as the gradual improvement of the hygienic situation, especially housing conditions in the cities, made the high level of infant mortality go down continuously on a wide level, embracing all social layers.[94]

There was however little change in the regional and social patterns of infant mortality though. Backward rural areas, such as the peripheral parts of the Waldviertel, had the highest rates, whereas regions with a high level of industrialization and a high density of health care facilities were able to improve their position.[95] As a case study from the late 1920s shows, it was essentially the cultural factors—lack of breast-feeding due to hardly any leave from work in the field after giving birth as well as unhygienic circumstances—that led to higher infant mortality in rural areas. In contrast to the situation in Vienna, social factors played mere background roles.[96]

However, the mortality decrease after the war was by no means limited to infants. Immediately after the war—delayed by the undersupplied city of Vienna as well as Styria and its large industrial areas—crude death rates, although these only serve as a rough indicator, decreased.[97] In 1921 they fell below the pre-war level.[98] The rapidity of the decrease which then set in was breathtaking. In just a few post-war years mortality sank by 75 to 84 percent in comparison with the average rates of the years 1918-20 and 1922-24.

Fig. 4: Age specific mortality rates 1918/20 and 1922/24[99]

Age group	1918/20	1922/24	changes in %
0-4	199.5	45.0	-77,4
5-29	22.7	3.7	-83,9
30-49	36.9	7.5	-79,6
50-69	105.9	25.9	-75,6
70 +	465.2	115.8	-75,1

The backdrop of age specific death rates in Austria until the mid-1920s was quite significant, even in comparison with the pre-war situation: about 40 percent for newborns and infants, and around 20 to 25 percent for adolescents and grown-ups up to about the age of fifty. For people over that age it was, however, merely 10 to 15 percent.[100]

In Vienna, life expectancy at birth rose by an incredible 12.8 years for the male population and 12.5 years for the female population from 1918-20 to 1921-23. After reaching the twentieth year of one's life, the gain was eight years for males and, what is more, fifteen for women. When comparing death rates by causes of death around 1910 and 1923, age-standardized, about two-thirds of the mortality decrease may be accounted for by the reduction in infectious diseases, respiratory illness and typical infantile causes of death.[101] Considering the age-specific death rates for the whole of Austria, one can assume that the epidemiologic transition was quite similar in the other parts of the country.

From 1915 onwards the already high tuberculosis mortality had begun to distance itself from that of many other European states. The mortality rate per 10,000 population rose from 25.6 in 1914 to 43.2 in 1917 and still lay at over 30 in 1919.[102] There were, however, regional disparities. In Vienna, tuberculosis mortality was three times higher than that in New York,[103] whereas it only reached its height in the first pre-war year in the industrial districts, while the rural areas were already pursuing the pre-war downwards trend during, as well as straight after, the war.[104] At the beginning of the 1920s, a drastic and continual decrease in TBC-mortality throughout all parts of the country set in.[105] In Vienna, especially, it plummeted from its initially high level from 1920 onwards.[106]

The reasons for the decrease in mortality during the immediate post-war years defy clear identification. A sinking virulence can be detected, showing itself in a decrease of rapid courses of TBC-illness, which had largely increased during the war.[107] This change was also apparent in the strongly regressive percentage of children with TBC in Vienna that went down by 50 percent from 1910 to 1923.[108] The part which the influenza pandemic of 1918-1920 played in this context cannot be underestimated. In all likelihood one can assume that the Spanish Flu did not only rocket the cases of death by pneumonia as a secondary effect of the illness, but also led to a re-surfacing of slumbering tuberculosis infections.[109] Seeing as the at-risk population for both tuberculosis and flu were practically the same group, the influenza pandemic diminished the at-risk population for tuberculosis, which promoted a reduction of tuberculosis mortality in the early 1920s.[110]

The obvious improvement in the hygiene situation presented another mortality-reducing factor mid-term, especially in the cities. The generous communal building scheme of the Vienna City Council played a special role in all of this.[111] But social building schemes played a much less important role outside Vienna. This, of course, means that the improvement of hygienic standards can only partially explain the sinking of tuberculosis mortality. However, as can be seen in contemporary surveys by the TBC welfare offices, there was a noticeable improvement in housing conditions around the welfare offices catchment areas. For example, while 30 percent of TBC-infected patients did not have their own beds in 1925, this was the case for no less than 10 percent in 1937.[112]

The impact of preventive medical facilities on tuberculosis mortality was limited. There were approximately 80,000 people under the care of TBC welfare offices in 1925, followed by 140,000 in 1930 and 190,000 in 1937. The provision of the population with such offices had a wide span—from 100 percent in Vienna to zero in Vorarlberg. [113] The height of TBC-mortality in areas with TBC welfare offices did not correlate distinctly with the proportion of people for whom they cared. The distribution of lung examinations did play a larger role though. In principal there was a high correlation between regional TBC mortality and the general level of mortality. This was still the case, even though tuberculosis mortality only contributed around 8 percent to the total mortality in 1937.[114]

As far as the trend of the total mortality rate went, the effects of the medicalizating mainstream that began with the newborn and infants and also influenced the parental generation as a result was not to be underestimated in the long run. Without doubt this comprehensive system of child aid as it was instigated in Red Vienna[115] had a considerable medium-term impact as well: as a role model function for the rest of the country, although similar measures there were prone to different ideological justifications.

The acceleration of epidemiologic transition due to unfavourable economic circumstances in interwar-Austria shows how little it is possible to draw conclusions for welfare from the development of the gross domestic product (GDP). The decrease in mortality by European comparison was astounding. In the year before the outbreak of WWI, life expectancy had still been quite low. In 1910 male newborns had a life expectancy of an average 43.5 years while females could expect 46.8 years. At the beginning of the 1930s life expectancy at birth was 54.5 years for the male population and 58.5 years for the female.[116] The catching-up process which set in from the beginning of the 1920s led to a 50 percent reduction of differential mortality compared to countries such as Sweden which were advanced economically as well as with regard to their social policies. Nevertheless, the deficit was still significant in the 1930s.[117]

Austria: The Core of the "Quiet Revolution"[118] in Interwar Europe

Birth decline held a certain place within population policy discussions, alongside the fight against infant mortality, tuberculosis and syphilis, although it was not a large subject for the public itself.[119] This was quite astounding, seeing as sinking fertility was not really far behind decreasing mortality. After the dramatic cutback in fertility after the war, a brief baby boom, which was characteristic for post-war times, set in. But even in this period by European comparison the marital fertility level was already low in Austria. By this time, it was only undercut by the traditionally low fertility level in France.[120] From then onward, however, fertility rates—following the pre-war trend—sank continually and with increasing pace.[121] The general fertility rate[122] had gone down annually by an average 2 percent from 1910-23. After that it was, however, more than 3 percent.[123] In the early 1930s the fertility rate in Austria had reached the lowest level in the whole of Europe, lying even below that of Germany. For each woman there were now about 1.6 children (total fertility rate[124]). Net reproduction had dropped down to two-thirds of the level necessary for total reproduction, corresponding roughly with the level of the late 20th century.[125] The capital of Vienna could be seen as the world "capital of infertility" (*unfruchtbarste Großstadt*), a title which had already been coined by the German demographer Friedrich Burgdörfer, who was closely affiliated to National Socialism towards the end of the 1920s.[126] As a matter of fact, with the net reproduction rate[127] being a fourth of what was necessary for reproduction, it had reached a historic low.[128]

The fertility decline after the war was one of marital fertility. Illegitimate fertility, which had turned out to be over-proportional during the war, stayed quite constant, sinking only after the Great Depression.

Fig. 5: Live births in Austria (1) per 1,000 women (age 15-44) by legitimacy 1908/13-1937[129]

Year	Birth rate for Married Women	Birth Rate for Unmarried Women	Share of illegitimate fertility
1908/13	204.7	43.8	21.4
1919	144.5	24.9	17.2
1920	175.8	31.5	17.9
1921	184.0	29.2	15.9
1922	181.1	29.8	16.5
1923	174.6	29.4	16.8
1924	163.8	31.0	18.9
1925	152.9	31.4	20.5
1926	140.1	31.0	22.1
1927	126.9	31.0	24.4
1928	122.4	31.8	26.0
1929	161.1	31.2	19.4
1930	113.7	32.9	28.9
1931	106.8	31.4	29.4
1932	101.5	30.9	30.4
1933	95.6	28.8	30.1
1934	90.1	27.9	31.0
1935	88.2	26.1	29.6
1936	88.6	25.2	28.4
1937	87.4	24.1	27.6
1) 1908/13: Alpine provinces without Carniola (Krain)			

In Austria, the number of children per marriage undertaken before, during and after the war sank continually. This was the case referring to marriages with children, as well as the total number of marriages. In Vienna, the marital fertility level fell from the 31.4 percent of the maximum marital fertility value (measured by the fertility of the Hutterites) in 1910 to 8.6 percent in 1931. This was only half as much as the already very low marital fertility level of 15.2 percent in Berlin in 1933—and only a third of that of London.[130] Taking Vienna as an example, it becomes clear that the shift in generative behaviour reached all socially relevant groups, even though the differential fertility stayed constant. Around about a year after the Anschluss, the number of children from working class marriages concluded in the early 1920s was about a third to a quarter higher than that of civil servants, employees and freelancers.[131] One can assume class specific fertility differentials in the other parts of the country as well, showing up as differences in the number of children from metropolitan cities, small and medium-sized towns and from the countryside. The corresponding chart also shows the range of the generative shift, which embraced the population of the small villages as well as that of the larger cities and towns.

Fig. 6: Number of children of parents at first marriage in 1934[132]

Year of first marriage	total	communes with ... population (in 1,000)				
		0 - 1,999	2,000 - 9,999	10,000 - 99,999	100,000 - 199,999	Vienna
	children per marriage					
1903 and before	2.6	3.2	2.8	2.1	1.8	2.0
1904-1913	2.4	3.2	2.6	2.0	1.8	1.6
1914-1918	2.1	2.9	2.3	1.9	1.6	1.4
1919-1923	1.9	2.6	2.0	1.5	1.3	1.1

Year of first marriage	total	communes with ... population (in 1,000)				
		0 - 1,999	2,000 - 9,999	10,000 - 99,999	100,000 - 199,999	Vienna
	children per marriage (marriages with children only)					
1903 and before	3.2	3.7	3.4	2.7	2.5	2.5
1904-1913	2.9	3.6	3.2	2.4	2.4	2.1
1914-1918	2.6	3.4	2.8	2.1	2.1	1.9
1919-1923	2.4	3.0	2.5	1.8	1.8	1.6

The obtainment of "basic commodities" was obviously the motivation behind such a complete universal shift in marital fertility, reaching from the big cities to the smallest town—especially under crisis-laden economic and revolutionary social conditions which were characterized by a questioning of existing social hierarchies. Due to the de-institutionalization of the old order that followed the war, biographic opportunity costs rose, encouraging a surge in individualization. Not without good reason was the trend towards contraception within the younger generation, which had already been proclaimed by experts during the immediate post-war years, brought into connection with a shift in consumer preferences and individualist tendencies within society.[133] For the working class milieu, this was shown by the establishment of the "respectable working class family" with its core and nuclear family structures. At its beginning stood a post-war marriage-boom that was also increased by a simplification in marriage procedures.[134] Subsequently a social legislation ensuring higher predictability of work relations and a social residential building scheme—guaranteeing a considerable availability of comparatively modernly outfitted social flats, at least in Vienna—facilitated a swift spreading of this family model within the working class.[135] At the center of the "respectable working class family" stood a type of "New Woman," ideologically elevated in Red Vienna, which distinguished itself amongst other things in a strong degree of biographical self-determination.[136] Demographically, this was evident in a deliberate limitation of family size.

It is obvious through which means birth control was carried out, but putting these into proportion is difficult. In Vienna, and probably in other large cities as well, abortion was the prevalent method to avoid unwanted births. This becomes clear amongst other things from the fact that the number of pregnancies of those women that had had an abortion and visited a hospital due to a "miscarriage" during the first year of the war did not go down, unlike the number of women who were hospitalized because of a normal birth. So when women conceived more often than usual for their social class, they chose abortion. The average number of "miscarriages" of married women lay at 1.5 to 1.8 in 1914.[137] What was now changing after the war, was that the decision for an abortion showed no connection to the number of children already born.[138] Therefore abortions definitely rose in relation to births, and it is very probable that it also rose in absolute numbers. As early as 1920 a social-democratic women's conference stressed in a resolution that tens of thousands of women "very likely secretly freed themselves from budding life" during the war and post-war periods.[139] There is clear statistical evidence that this was no overstatement. During 1920-24 around 20 percent of Viennese women admitted to having had a miscarriage during their life; in 1907, it was a mere 8 percent.[140] According to the results of abortions treated in Austrian hospitals at the beginning of the 1930s, the quota for married women in Vienna, which was better documented than in the other provinces, was 50 percent.[141] Of course the hospital statistics chronicle only a small portion of actual abortions, yet they still show that this "abortion epidemic"[142] was not a purely metropolitan phenomenon.

It is still plain that interwar Vienna especially was neither lacking the necessary mechanical or chemical abortion aids nor the doctors, midwives and other helpers willing to carry out an abortion. Furthermore, the mortality risk of an abortion sank substantially, unlike general maternal mortality. In the late 1920s in Vienna it was about 1 percent for "miscarriages," whereas it had still been 3.4 percent in 1919.[143]

The abortion devices distributed by the "preventative aid industry" (*Schutzmittelindustrie*) in mass since the early 20th century were used more and more often by midwives or pregnant women themselves.[144] Abortionists primarily used rubber catheters, which were easily available at rubber goods stores or from door-to-door salesmen. The insertion of these soft rubber catheters into the uterus usually led to contractions of the womb, causing the abortion. According to criminal procedure files, this was the most common method of abortion without medical assistance. Obturators were also used, as were so-called "mother injections," which were elongated by extensions.[145] A midwife estimated during the 1930s that around a quarter to a half of these procedures were undertaken by midwives[146] who still played a considerable role, especially outside Vienna. In the mid 1920s their distribution in the Burgenland, Carinthia, Tyrol and Vorarlberg was twice as high as that in Vienna, reaching a scale of about 3.5 to 4 midwives per 1,000 women in the age group of 14 to 55.[147] Doctors, on the other hand, frequently carried out procedures such as diletation and curettage (D- and C-method). The knowledge of these relatively non-hazardous procedures circulated, so that they presumably in time became the most important abortion method.[148]

The fertility decrease of the interwar period did not, however, stem from an "abortion revolution." Abortions were often just a last resort after contraceptive practices, contemporarily referred to as "preventive intercourse," had failed. These practices also spread rapidly. At least in Vienna this may have contributed to the fact that the absolute number of abortions did not significantly change before or after the war. According to calculations made by a Viennese doctor, based upon the anamnesis of women who had had an abortion inside Viennese hospitals, there were around 71 births and 18 to 23.5 abortions per 1,000 women of child-bearing age in 1912-13. In 1922 it was 55.5 births and 18 to 25.5 abortions. According to these figures, the birth decrease in Vienna after the war is supposed to have resulted from the large circulation of contraceptive methods.[149] This must have been a too optimistic estimate, even for Vienna. There is no doubt however that knowledge of contraception grew wider after the war. The "sexual educators" managed to reach a larger part of the proletarian youth mainly through print media. One can read, for example, in a prominent magazine for young workers from the year 1926: "Almost all young people know about preventatives for unwanted reproduction these days."[150] Such knowledge even found larger distribution in rural Catholic surroundings. A brochure from the early 1930s, for example, which has survived in the parish archives of the small community of Schiltern in Lower Austria, explained the Knaus-Ogino method to parishioners.[151] Nevertheless, one can still assume a strongly pronounced city-country divide with regard to knowledge of modern contraceptive methods.[152] Likewise, there were class-specific differences. Coitus interruptus was presumably the most important contraceptive method within the working class even in the interwar period.[153] The circulation of rubber condoms had also risen considerably due to the war. The usage of occlusive pessaries played an increasing role,[154] mainly however within the middle- and upper-class. Through the activities of the "Confederation against Enforced Motherhood" (*Bund gegen den Mutterschaftszwang*), who ran "help desks for the protection of women" (*Frauenschutzberatungsstellen*) in a number of Austrian cities and financed the adjustment of pessaries by doctors for destitute women, the accessability of these methods was also improved for those who were not so well-off.[155]

Illegitimacy: Stable Patterns, Changing Attitudes

In contrast to the conditions in Vienna, where the proportion of married persons made a long-term upward leap from the time of the Monarchy up to the mid-1930s,[156] and the industrial districts, social transformation went particularly hand in hand with illegitimacy within the rural regions. The Austrian Alpine provinces had already shown by far the highest illegitimacy rates in Europe and a high percentage of unmarried women before the war. None of this changed during the interwar period.[157] Nearly every fifth woman stayed unmarried until the end of her child-bearing age.[158] However, from the mid-1920s onward, there was another noticeable rise in illegitimacy. Soon more than one in four babies was born out of wedlock.[159] The high level of illegitimacy had, however, little influence on the fertility decrease. Birth rates for unmarried women[160] stayed constant until the early 1930s. Only after that time did they start to sink postponedly. However, even at the beginning of the 1930s they merely reached a third of the level of marriage fertility.[161]

The distinctive regional pattern of illegitimacy distribution remained. In its traditional core zones the share of illegitimate live births climbed up to 40 percent in some parts. These core zones were the mountainous parts of Upper Styria, the Carinthian districts of St. Veit/Glan and Klagenfurt

Land, Wolfsberg, Völkermarkt and Spital an der Drau and the peripheral Salzburg districts of Zell am See, St. Johann and Tamsweg.[162] In some Carinthian parishes the percentages reached about 75 to 80 percent.[163] These were regions with a low education level, larger farm estates that were passed on in their entirety to the oldest son (*Majorat*), and a large number of farmhands that consisted to a high degree of the farmer's younger siblings. Farmers' daughters, for example, made up about a quarter of all unmarried mothers in Carinthia. Again, against the background of the change of agrarian structure, their labour capacity and that of their adolescent children gained more importance within farmers' considerations, which favoured older patterns of delayed marriage.[164]

To a certain extent the drastic decrease in fertility in Austria during the interwar period reflected the extreme economic, social and mental situations in which the population found itself. The baby boom after the Anschluss would later show that the "mental modernization" did not go as far as the fertility rates had suggested in the mid-1930s. At the same time it would not be correct to think that the legacy of social transformation after WWI had been submerged by the follow-up births and the pronatalistic population policy measures for the "Aryan" populace. The birth rate of the Ostmark during the time of 1939-41 corresponded with the level of the mid-1920s, but lay notably behind the pre-war level. This was especially the case for the number of live births per woman aged 15 to 44 years old (general fertility rate) in Vienna.[165] The divorce rates also make room for the assumption of an altered attitude towards marriage and family. Before the war they were below European average. After the war they were the highest in the whole of Europe. They were to retain and top this high level in the following decades.[166]

Notes

1. K.k. Statistische Zentralkommission, *Statistische Rückblicke aus Österreich der XIV. Tagung des internationalen Statistischen Institutes* (Vienna, 1913), 2.

2. *Staatsgesetzblatt für den Staat Deutschösterreich 40, 41/1918*. See Hanns Haas, "Im Widerstreit der Selbstbestimmungsansprüche: Vom Habsburgerstaat zur Tschechoslowakei – die Deutschen in den böhmischen Ländern 1918 bis 1919," in *Der Erste Weltkrieg und die Beziehungen zwischen Tschechen, Slowaken und Deutschen*, ed. Hans Mommsen et al., Veröffentlichungen der Deutsch-Tschechischen und Deutsch-Slowakischen Historikerkommission 5 (Essen: Klartext, 2001), 181-82, 186-87.

3. *Karte von Deutschösterreich und der Nationen in den Grenzlandschaften: Mit einer statistischen Übersicht über die Flächengröße und Bevölkerung Deutschösterreichs und der gesetzlichen Bestimmungen über sein Staatsgebiet*, Flugblätter für Deutschösterreichs Recht 12 (Vienna: Alfred Hölder, 1919).

4. Franz Rothenbacher, *The European Population 1850-1945* (Houndmills: Palgrave, 2002),

102.

5. Dudley Kirk, *Europe's Population in the Interwar Years* (Geneva: League of Nations, 1946), 22.

6. Rüdiger Overmans, "Kriegsverluste," in *Enzyklopädie Erster Weltkrieg*, ed. Gerhard Hirschfeld et al. (Paderborn: Ferdinand Schöningh, 2009), 664-65; Wilhelm Winkler, "Die Bevölkerungslage Österreichs," in *Bericht über die wirtschaftlichen Schwierigkeiten Österreichs* (Vienna: Redaktionskomitee der Wirtschaftskommission, 1931), 43; "Totenverluste des zweiten Weltkrieges," *Statistische Nachrichten NF 10* (1955): 146-47.

7. Wilhelm Winkler, *Die Totenverluste der öst.-ung. Monarchie nach Nationalitäten* (Vienna: L.W. Seidl & Sohn, 1919), 6.

8. Verena Pawlowski and Harald Wendelin, "Die Verwaltung des Leides: Kriegsbeschädigtenversorgung in Niederösterreich," in *Niederösterreich im 20. Jahrhundert 2*, ed. Peter Melichar et al. (Vienna: Böhlau, 2008), 525-26.

9. "Ergebnisse der Zählung der Kriegshinterbliebenen in Wien," *Blätter für das Wohlfahrts- und Armenwesen der Stadt Wien 17* (1918): 277-84.

10. Sigrid Augeneder, *Arbeiterinnen im Ersten Weltkrieg: Lebens- und Arbeitsbedingungen proletarischer Frauen in Österreich*, Materialien zur Arbeiterbewegung 46 (Vienna: Europaverlag, 1987), 150.

11. Winkler, "Die Bevölkerungslage Österreichs," 43.

12. Siegfried Rosenfeld, *Die Grippeepidemie des Jahres 1918 in Österreich* (Vienna: Franz Deuticke, 1921), 54.

13. Ibid., 11; Bundesamt für Statistik, ed., *Die Bewegung der Bevölkerung in den Jahren 1914 bis 1921*, Beiträge zur Statistik der Republik Österreich 8 (Vienna: Österreichische Staatsdruckerei, 1923), 93.

14. Rosenfeld, *Die Grippeepidemie des Jahres 1918 in Österreich*, 15, 38-47.

15. Karl Helly, "Statistik der Gesundheitsverhältnisse der Bevölkerung der Republik Österreich in und nach dem Kriege," in *Volksgesundheit im Krieg 1*, ed. Clemens Pirquet (Vienna and New Haven: Hölder-Pichler-Tempsky and Yale Univesity Press, 1926), 17.

16. Wilhelm Hecke, *Der Geburtenrückgang und seine Folgen*, Veröffentlichungen des Volksgesundheitsamtes im Bundesministerium für soziale Verwaltung 20 (Leipzig: Franz Deuticke, 1923), 8.

17. Own calculations based on Statistik Austria, *Demographisches Jahrbuch 2006* (Vienna: Verlag Österreich, 2007), 319; Johann Ladstätter, "Die Veränderung der Altersstruktur in Österreich seit 1869," in *Geschichte und Ergebnisse der zentralen amtlichen Statistik in Österreich 1829-1979*, ed. Österreichisches Statistisches Zentralamt, Beiträge zur österreichischen Statistik 550 (Vienna: M. Salzer, 1979), 468-69; Statistische Zentralkommission, ed., *Ergebnisse der außerordentlichen Volkszählung vom 31. Jänner 1920: Endgültige Ergebnisse samt Nachtragszählungen* (Vienna: Österreichische Staatsdruckerei, 1921), 6-7; Bundesamt für Statistik, *Vorläufige Ergebnisse der Volkszählung vom 7. März 1923* (Vienna: Österreichische Staatsdruckerei, 1923), 8; Bundesamt für Statistik, ed., *Statistisches Handbuch für die Republik Österreich 9* (Vienna: Karl Gerolds Sohn, 1928), 6. Age structure of Burgenland estimated on the basis of the Austrian Census 1923 and the Hungarian Census 1920.

18. Statistik Austria, *Demographisches Jahrbuch 2006*, 352.

19. Karl Brousek, *Wien und seine Tschechen: Integration und Assimilation einer Minderheit im 20. Jahrhundert*, Schriftenreihe des Österreichischen Ost- und Südosteuropa-Instituts 7 (Munich: R. Oldenbourg, 1980), 34; Iva Heroldová, "Remigration," in *Die Wiener Tschechen 1945-2005:*

Zur Geschichte einer Volksgruppe 1, ed. Helena Basler et al. (Vienna and Prague: Tschechisches kulturhistorisches Institut and Koniasch Latin Press, 2006), 32.

20. Rothenbacher, *The European Population 1850-1945*, 102.

21. Beatrix Hoffmann-Holter, *"Abreisendmachung": Jüdische Kriegsflüchtlinge in Wien 1914 bis 1923* (Vienna: Böhlau, 1995), 283; Walter Mentzel, "Weltkriegsflüchtlinge in Cisleithanien 1914-1918," in *Asylland wider Willen: Flüchtlinge in Österreich im europäischen Kontext seit 1914*, ed. Gernot Heiss and Oliver Rathkolb, Veröffentlichungen des Ludwig-Boltzmann-Institutes für Geschichte und Gesellschaft 25 (Vienna: J&V Edition Wien Dachs Verlag, 1995), 38-39; David Rechter, *The Jews of Vienna and the First World War* (London: The Littman Library of Jewish Civilization, 2001), 82-83.

22. Own calculation (taking into account denomination conversion within the timeframe) on the basis of *Statistisches Jahrbuch der Stadt Wien für das Jahr 1914* (Vienna: Gerlach & Wiedling, 1918), 62, 77; "Wien im Großdeutschen Reich: Eine statistische Untersuchung über die Lage Wiens nach der Wiedereingliederung der Ostmark in das Deutsche Reich," ed. NSDAP-Gau-Wien-Organisationsamt, Gemeindeverwaltung des Reichsgaues Wien, in Gerhard Botz, *Wien vom Anschluß zum Krieg: Nationalsozialistische Machtübernahme und politisch-soziale Umgestaltung am Beispiel der Stadt Wien 1938/39* (Vienna: Jugend & Volk, 1978), 615; Leo Goldhammer, *Die Juden Wiens: Eine statistische Studie* (Vienna: R. Löwit, 1927), 9, 19, 22.

23. Own calculation on the basis of Andreas Weigl, *Demographischer Wandel und Modernisierung in Wien*, Kommentare zum Historischen Atlas von Wien 1 (Vienna: Pichler, 2000), 393.

24. Bundesamt für Statistik, *Die Ergebnisse der Volkszählung vom 22. März 1934: Bundesstaat, Textheft*, Statistik des Bundesstaates Österreich 1 (Vienna: Österreichische Staatsdruckerei, 1935), 50.

25. Ernst Bruckmüller, "Sozialstruktur und Sozialpolitik," in *Österreich 1918-1938: Geschichte der Ersten Republik*, ed. Erika Weinzierl and Kurt Skalnik (Graz: Styria, 1983), 383-84.

26. Arnold Suppan, *Jugoslawien und Österreich 1918-1938: Bilaterale Außenpolitik im europäischen Umfeld*, Veröffentlichungen des Österreichischen Ost- und Südosteuropa-Instituts 14 (Munich: Oldenbourg, 1996), 30.

27. Own calculation on the basis of Hoffmann-Holter, *"Abreisendmachung"*, 283.

28. Egon Lendl, "100 Jahre Einwanderung nach Österreich," in *Geographischer Jahresbericht aus Österreich 28, 1959-1960* (Vienna: Geographisches Institut der Universität Wien, 1961), 63-64.

29. Ibid., 62-64; Heimold Helczmanovszki, "Die Entwicklung der Bevölkerung Österreichs in den letzten hundert Jahren nach den wichtigsten demographischen Komponenten," in *Beiträge zur Bevölkerungs- und Sozialgeschichte Österreichs: Nebst einem Überblick über die Entwicklung der Bevölkerungs- und Sozialstatistik*, ed. Heimold Helczmanovszki (Vienna: Verlag für Geschichte und Politik, 1973), 139.

30. Bruckmüller, "Sozialstruktur und Sozialpolitik," 384; Statistik Austria, *Statistisches Jahrbuch Österreichs 2008* (Vienna: Verlag Österreich, 2007), 41.

31. Statistik Austria, *Demographisches Jahrbuch 2006*, 352.

32. Jürgen Illigasch, "Migration aus und nach Österreich in der Zwischenkriegszeit: Bemerkungen zum Forschungsstand," *Zeitgeschichte 26* (Jan./Feb. 1999): 18-21.

33. Statistik Austria, *Demographisches Jahrbuch 2006*, 352.

34. Annemarie Steidl et al., "Relations among Internal, Continental, and Transatlantic Migration in Late Imperial Austria," *Social Science History 31* (Spring 2007): 61-92; Heinz Fassmann, "Emigration, Immigration and Internal Migration in the Austro-Hungarian Monarchy, 1910," in *Roots of the Transplanted 1*, ed. Dirk Hoerder and Inge Blank (New York: Columbia University

Press, 1994), 275-76.

35. Hans Chmelar, "Exportgut Mensch: Höhepunkte der österreichischen Auswanderung bis 1914," in ... *nach Amerika: Burgenländische Forschungen*, Sonderband 9 (Eisenstadt: Amt der burgenländischen Landesregierung, 1992), 76-77; Michael John, "Push and Pull Factors for Overseas Migrants from Austria-Hungary in the 19th and 20th Centuries," in *Austrian Immigration to Canada: Selected Essays*, ed. Franz A. J. Szabo (Ottawa: Carleton University Press, 1996), 59.

36. Annemarie Steidl, "Ein ewiges Hin und Her: Kontinentale, transatlantische und lokale Migrationsrouten in der Spätphase der Habsburgermonarchie," in *Historische Migrationsforschung*, ed. Sigrid Wadauer, Österreichische Zeitschrift für Geschichtswissenschaften 19 (Innsbruck: Studienverlag, 2008), 22-23; Franz von Meinzingen, "Die Wanderbewegung auf Grund der Gebürtigkeitsdaten der Volkszählung vom 31. Dezember 1900," *Statistische Monatsschrift*, new series 8 (Vienna: Alfred Hölder, 1903): 161.

37. Walter Dujmovits, "Die Amerikawanderung der Burgenländer," in ... *nach Amerika*, 106-08.

38. Traude Horvath, "... I bin Amerikaner ... oba fühlen tua i wia ein Österreicher: Burgenländische Auswanderung nach 1945," in *Auswanderungen aus Österreich: Von der Mitte des 19. Jahrhunderts bis zur Gegenwart*, ed. Traude Horvath and Gerda Neyer (Vienna: Böhlau, 1996), 549.

39. Michael John, "Arbeitslosigkeit und Auswanderung in Österreich 1919-1937," in *Auswanderungen aus Österreich*, 86-89; Rothenbacher, *The European Population 1850-1945*, 102.

40. Dujmovits, "Die Amerikawanderung der Burgenländer," 110.

41. Dieter Stiefel, *Arbeitslosigkeit: Soziale, politische und wirtschaftliche Auswirkungen – am Beispiel Österreichs 1918-1938*, Schriften zur Sozial- und Wirtschaftsgeschichte 31 (Berlin: Duncker & Humblot, 1979), 112.

42. John, "Arbeitslosigkeit und Auswanderung in Österreich," 86-91; Illigasch, "Migration aus und nach Österreich in der Zwischenkriegszeit," 8-9.

43. Kirk, *Europe's Population in the Interwar Years*, 282-83.

44. Stiefel, *Arbeitslosigkeit*, 115-17; John, "Arbeitslosigkeit und Auswanderung in Österreich," 90-91; Jochen Oltmer, *Migration und Politik in der Weimarer Republik* (Göttingen: Vandenhoeck & Ruprecht, 2005), 344, 408, 410, 427; Felix Butschek, *Der österreichische Arbeitsmarkt – von der Industrialisierung bis zur Gegenwart* (Stuttgart: Gustav Fischer, 1992), 101; Illigasch, "Migration aus und nach Österreich in der Zwischenkriegszeit," 10.

45. Eugene Sensenig, "Reichsfremde, Staatsfremde und Drittausländer: Immigration und Einwanderungspolitik in Österreich," in *Das Ausland im Inland: Zur Geschichte der Ausländerbeschäftigung und Ausländerintegration in Österreich: Fremde, Zwangsarbeiter, Gastarbeiter und Flüchtlinge*, Unpublished research report, Linz University, 537, footnote 535.

46. Steve Hochstadt, *Mobility and Modernity: Migration in Germany 1820-1989* (Ann Arbor: University of Michigan Press, 1999), 217-54.

47. Michael John, "Mosaik oder Schmelztiegel? Bemerkungen zu Migration, Multikulturalität und Assimilation im Zeitalter Kaiser Franz Josephs," *Beiträge zur historischen Sozialkunde 21/2* (1991): 42; Weigl, *Demographischer Wandel und Modernisierung in Wien*, 128-129.

48. Hecke, *Der Geburtenrückgang und seine Folgen*, 6.

49. Gudrun Exner et al., *Bevölkerungswissenschaft in Österreich in der Zwischenkriegszeit (1918-1938): Personen, Institutionen, Diskurse*, Schriften des Instituts für Demographie der Österreichischen Akademie der Wissenschaften 18 (Vienna: Böhlau, 2004), 251-69, 289.

50. Hans Loewenfeld-Ruß, *Im Kampf gegen den Hunger: Aus den Erinnerungen des Staatsekretärs*

für Volksernährung 1918-1920, ed. Isabella Ackerl, Studien zur österreichischen Zeitgeschichte 6 (Vienna: Verlag für Geschichte und Politik, 1986).

51. Reinhard Sieder, "Behind the lines: Working-class family life in wartime Vienna," in *The Upheaval of War: Familiy, Work and Welfare in Europe, 1914-1918*, ed. Richard Wall and Jay Winter (Cambridge: Cambridge University Press, 1988), 111-12, 125.

52. Ingrid Böhler and Norbert Schnetzer, "Hunger im Ländle: Das lange Ende des Ersten Weltkrieges in Vorarlberg 1918-1920/21," *Zeitgeschichte 26* (Mar./Apr. 1999): 71-89.

53. Gerhard Prassnigger, "Hunger in Tirol," in *Tirol und der Erste Weltkrieg*, ed. Klaus Eisterer and Rolf Steininger, Innsbrucker Forschungen zur Zeitgeschichte 12 (Innsbruck: Studienverlag, 1995), 190; Gottfried Köfner, *Hunger, Not und Korruption: Der Übergang Österreichs von der Monarchie zur Republik am Beispiel Salzburgs: Eine sozial- und wirtschaftswissenschaftliche Studie* (Salzburg: Wolfgang Neugebauer, 1980), 287-89.

54. Jürgen Nautz, *Die österreichische Handelspolitik der Nachkriegszeit 1918 bis 1923: Die Handelsvertragsbeziehungen zu den Nachfolgestaaten*, Studien zu Politik und Verwaltung 44 (Vienna: Böhlau, 1994), 67-69.

55. Clemens Pirquet, "Ernährungszustand der Kinder in Österreich während des Krieges und der Nachkriegszeit," in *Volksgesundheit im Krieg 1*, 152-53.

56. Maureen Healy, *Vienna and the Fall of the Habsburg Empire: Total War and Everyday Life in World War I* (Cambridge: Cambridge University Press, 2004), 255-57.

57. Pirquet, "Ernährungszustand der Kinder in Österreich," 174-75; Ernst Mayerhofer, "Medizinische Studie über die Amerikanische Kinderhilfsaktion in Österreich," in *Mitteilungen des Generalkommissariates der Amerikanischen Kinderhilfsaktion No. 2-5* (Aug. 1920), 16; E. Kleinsasser, "Studie über die Ernährungs- und Wachstumsverhältnisse der Tiroler Schuljugend," in *Mitteilungen des Generalkommissariates No. 29-32* (Jan. 1921).

58. Pirquet, "Ernährungszustand der Kinder in Österreich," 154-55; Helly, "Statistik der Gesundheitsverhältnisse der Bevölkerung," 45; Elisabeth Dietrich-Daum, *Die "Wiener Krankheit": Eine Sozialgeschichte der Tuberkulose in Österreich*, Sozial- und wirtschaftshistorische Studien 32 (Vienna and Munich: Verlag für Geschichte und Politik and R. Oldenbourg, 2007), 245.

59. John Komlos, "Comments on the Economic Performance of the First Austria Republic," in *Economic Development in the Habsburg Monarchy and in the Sucessor States*, ed. idem. (Boulder: Columbia University Press, 1990), 298.

60. Pirquet, "Ernährungszustand der Kinder in Österreich," 161-69; Helly, "Statistik der Gesundheitsverhältnisse der Bevölkerung," 46; Dietrich-Daum, *Die "Wiener Krankheit"*, 242-43.

61. Clemens Pirquet, "Schülerspeisung als Teil der allgemeinen Ernährungsfürsorge," in *Volksgesundheit im Krieg 1*, 297-300; Elisabeth Dietrich, "Der andere Tod: Seuchen, Volkskrankheiten und Gesundheitswesen im Ersten Weltkrieg," in *Tirol und der Erste Weltkrieg*, 265.

62. Andreas Weigl, "Vom Versorgungsfall zur Zielgruppe: Konsumverhalten Wiener Kinder und Jugendlicher zwischen Kinderausspeisung und Markenfetischismus," in *Geschichte des Konsums*, ed. Rolf Walter, Viertljahrschrift für Sozial- und Wirtschaftsgeschichte Beiheft 175 (Stuttgart: Franz Steiner, 2004), 227-28.

63. Dietrich-Daum, *Die "Wiener Krankheit"*, 263.

64. Healy, *Vienna and the Fall of the Habsburg Empire*, 250.

65. J. van Walré de Bordes, *The Austrian Crown: Its Depreciation and Stabilization* (London: P.S. King & Son, 1924), 8.

66. Healy, *Vienna and the Fall of the Habsburg Empire*, 255; Renate Schreiber, "Großmacht der Menschenliebe – schwedische Kinderhilfe nach dem Ersten Weltkrieg," *Wiener Geschichtsblätter 64/3* (2009): 56-82; Oscar Bosshardt, *Die Schweizer Hilfsaktion für die hungernde Stadt Wien: Ihre Geschichte und Entwicklung auf schweizerischem und internationalem Boden, sowie ihre wirtschaftliche, politische und ethische Bedeutung* (Bern: A. Francke, 1921).

67. Franz Adlgasser, *American Individualism Abroad: Herbert Hoover, die American Relief Administration und Österreich, 1919-1923*, Dissertationen der Universität Salzburg 41 (Vienna: Verband der wissenschaftlichen Gesellschaften Österreichs, 1993).

68. Friedrich Reischl, "Die ausländische Kinderhilfe in Wien," in *Volksgesundheit im Krieg 1*, 363-428; Pirquet, "Schülerspeisung als Teil der allgemeinen Ernährungsfürsorge"; Dietrich-Daum, *Die "Wiener Krankheit"*, 244.

69. American Relief Administration European Children's Fund (ARA), "List of Child Feeding Stations in Austria," in *Mitteilungen des Generalkommissariates No. 18-26* (Dec. 1920), 107.

70. Own calculations based on ARA, ibid., 106; Bundesamt für Statistik, ed., *Statistisches Handbuch für die Republik Österreich 2* (Vienna: Karl Gerolds Sohn, 1921), 13.

71. Weigl, "Vom Versorgungsfall zur Zielgruppe," 231-32.

72. Dietrich, "Der andere Tod," 265-66; Hans Hautmann, "Hunger ist ein schlechter Koch: Die Ernährungslage der österreichischen Arbeiter im Ersten Weltkrieg," in *Bewegung und Klasse: Studien zur österreichischen Arbeitergeschichte: 10 Jahre Ludwig Boltzmann Institut für Geschichte der Arbeiterbewegung*, ed. Gerhard Botz et al. (Vienna: Europaverlag, 1978), 661-81; Marion Breiter, "Hinter der Front: Zur Versorgungslage der Zivilbevölkerung im Wien des Ersten Weltkriegs," in *Jahrbuch des Vereins für Geschichte der Stadt Wien 50* (1994), 229-67.

73. Dietrich-Daum, *Die "Wiener Krankheit"*, 260.

74. Eduar März, *Österreichische Bankpolitik in der Zeit der großen Wende 1913-1923: Am Beispiel der Creditanstalt für Handel und Gewerbe* (Munich: R. Oldenbourg, 1981), 297.

75. Köfner, *Hunger, Not und Korruption*, 248-54.

76. Böhler and Schnetzer, "Hunger im Ländle," 83.

77. Exner, *Bevölkerungswissenschaft in Österreich in der Zwischenkriegszeit*, 307-09.

78. Bundesamt für Statistik, ed., *Die Bewegung der Bevölkerung in den Jahren 1914 bis 1921*, 25, 93.

79. Sigismund Peller, "Krieg und Tuberkulose," in *Handbuch der sozialen Hygiene und Gesundheitsfürsorge*, vol. 3, ed. A. Gottstein et al. (Berlin: Julius Springer, 1926), 201; Dietrich-Daum, Die *"Wiener Krankheit"*, 237.

80. John M. Barry, *The Great Influenza: The Story of the Deadliest Pandemic in Historys* (London: Penguin, 2005), 398.

81. Jay Winter, "Some paradoxes of the First World War," in *The Upheaval of War*, 9-42.

82. Exner, *Bevölkerungswissenschaft in Österreich in der Zwischenkriegszeit*, 204-07.

83. Dietrich, "Der andere Tod," 266-69.

84. Statistik Austria, *Demographisches Jahrbuch 2006*, 55.

85. The number of deaths of infants under age 1 per 1,000 live births in a given year.

86. Christian Köck et al., *Risiko "Säuglingstod": Plädoyer für eine gesundheitspolitische Reform*, Schriften des Instituts für Demographie der österreichischen Akademie der Wissenschaften 8 (Vienna: Franz Deuticke, 1988), 32.

87. Bundesamt für Statistik, ed., *Statistisches Handbuch für die Republik Österreich 8* (Vienna: Karl Gerolds Sohn, 1927), 32; idem., ed., *Statistisches Handbuch für die Republik Österreich 9*, 18; Österreichisches Statistisches Zentralamt, *Demographisches Jahrbuch Österreichs 1986*, Beiträge zur Österreichischen Statistik 873 (Vienna: Österreichische Staatsdruckerei, 1988), 149; Ernst Führth, "Säuglings-Frühsterblichkeit in Österreich," *Archiv für Kinderheilkunde 112* (1937): 159.

88. Leopold Moll, "Vier Jahre ärtzliche Fürsorgearbeit in der Kriegspatenschaft nebst kurzen Bemerkungen zu meinem Vorschlage der Mutterräte," *Wiener klinische Wochenschrift 32* (1919): 10.

89. The number of live births per 1,000 population in a given year.

90. The number of deaths per 1,000 population in a given year.

91. Helly, "Statistik der Gesundheitsverhältnisse der Bevölkerung," 24.

92. Weigl, *Demographischer Wandel und Modernisierung in Wien*, 221, 255; Sigismund Peller, *Der Geburtstod (Mutter und Kind)* (Leipzig: Franz Deuticke, 1936), 14.

93. W. Peter Ward, "Birth Weight and Standards of Living in Vienna, 1865-1930," *Jounal of Interdisciplinary History 19* (1988): 222-25.

94. Köck et al., *Risiko "Säuglingstod"*, 36.

95. Andreas Weigl, "Ein mißlungener demographischer Zwischenspurt: Zur demographischen Entwicklung des Waldviertels von der frühen Neuzeit bis zur Gegenwart," in *Wirtschaftsgeschichte des Waldviertels*, ed. Herbert Knittler, Schriftenreihe des Waldviertler Heimatbundes 47 (Horn: Waldviertler Heimatbund, 2006), 451, 473.

96. E. Nobel and S. Rosenfeld, *Ursachen und Bekämpfung der Säuglingssterblichkeit in Österreich: Ergebnisse der von der Hygienesektion des Völkerbundes veranstalteten Enquete*, Sonderbeilage der Mitteilungen des Volksgesundheitsamtes (Vienna: Verlag des Volksgesundheitsamtes, 1930), 40.

97. The number of deaths per 1,000 population in a given year.

98. Rothenbacher, *The European Population 1850-1945*, 103; Statistik Austria, *Demographisches Jahrbuch 2006*, 55.

99. Own calculation on the basis of Bundesamt für Statistik, *Die Bewegung der Bevölkerung in den Jahren 1914 bis 1921*, 60, 126; Statistische Zentralkommission, ed., *Ergebnisse der außerordentlichen Volkszählung vom 31. Jänner 1920*, 6-8; Bundesamt für Statistik, ed., *Statistisches Handbuch für die Republik Österreich 8*, 9, 32.

100. Own calculation on the basis of Wilhelm Winkler, *Grundriß der Statistik II: Gesellschaftsstatistik* (Vienna: Manzsche Verlags- und Universitätsbuchhandlung sec. edition, 1948), 90.

101. Own calculation on the basis of Weigl, *Demographischer Wandel und Modernisierung in Wien*, 165, 182.

102. Peller, "Krieg und Tuberkulose," 201; Dietrich-Daum, *Die "Wiener Krankheit"*, 234, 265.

103. Weigl, *Demographischer Wandel und Modernisierung in Wien*, 244.

104. Helly, "Statistik der Gesundheitsverhältnisse der Bevölkerung," 32-37.

105. Dietrich-Daum, *Die "Wiener Krankheit"*, 265.

106. Alfred Götzl, "Die Tuberkulosefürsorge in Wien 1919 bis 1929," Sonderdruck aus *Blätter für das Wohlfahrtswesen 30* (1930): No. 283, 7.

107. Dietrich-Daum, *Die "Wiener Krankheit"*, 266-69.

108. E. Junker and H. Klima, "Die Entwicklung der Kindertuberkulose in Österreich," in Reprint of *Mitteilungen der Österreichischen Sanitätsverwaltung 81/12* (1980), 1.

109. Siegfried Rosenfeld, *Die Änderungen der Tuberkulosehäufigkeit Österreichs durch den Krieg*, Veröffentlichungen des Volksgesundheitsamtes im Staatsamte für soziale Verwaltung 11 (Vienna: Franz Deuticke, 1920), 73-74.

110. Wilfried Witte, *Tollkirschen und Quarantäne: Die Geschichte der Spanischen Grippe* (Berlin: Wagenbach, 2008), 42.

111. Helmut Gruber, *Red Vienna: Experiment in Working-Class Culture 1919-1934* (New York: Oxford University Press, 1991), 46-65.

112. Dietrich-Daum, *Die "Wiener Krankheit"*, 264.

113. Ibid., 273.

114. Own calculation on the basis of L. Haider and R. Lukesch, "Die Tätigkeit der Tuberkulosefürsorgestellen in Österreich im Jahre 1937," in Supplement to *Mitteilungen der Unterabteilung Gesundheitswesen im Ministerium für innere und kulturelle Angelegenheiten* (Vienna: Julius Springer, [1938]), Tabelle XIII.

115. Gruber, *Red Vienna*, 66.

116. Statistik Austria, *Demographisches Jahrbuch 2006*, 225.

117. Rothenbacher, *The European Population 1850-1945*, 82-83, 104.

118. John R. Gillis et al., "The Quiet Revolution," in *The European Experience of Declining Fertility, 1850-1970: The Quiet Revolution*, ed. idem. (Cambridge, MA: Blackwell, 1992), 1-9.

119. Exner, *Bevölkerungswissenschaft in Österreich in der Zwischenkriegszeit*, 268.

120. Winkler, *Grundriß der Statistik II*, 85.

121. Statistik Austria, *Demographisches Jahrbuch 2006*, 55-56.

122. The number of live births per 1,000 women ages 15-44 in a given year.

123. Own calculation on the basis of Statistik Austria, *Demographisches Jahrbuch 2006*, 55, 319; Ladstätter, "Die Veränderung der Altersstruktur in Österreich," 469.

124. The average number of children that would be born alive to a woman during her lifetime if she were to pass through her childbearing years conforming to the age-specific fertility rates of a given year.

125. Kirk, *Europe's Population in the Interwar Years*, 263-77; Winkler, *Grundriß der Statistik II*, 85.

126. Friedrich Burgdörfer, *Der Geburtenrückgang und seine Bekämpfung: Die Lebensfrage des deutschen Volkes*, Veröffentlichungen auf dem Gebiet der Medizinalverwaltung 28/2 (Berlin: R. Schötz, 1929), 59.

127. The average number of daughters that would be born to a woman if she passed through her lifetime conforming to the age-specific fertility rates of a given year, including the risk to die before the end of the childbearing years.

128. Jean-Claude Chesnai, *The Demographic Transition: Stages, Patterns, and Economic Implications: A Longitudinal Study of Sixty-Seven Countries Covering the Period 1720-1984* (Oxford: Clarendon Press, 1992), 124.

129. K.k. Statistische Zentralkommission, *Bewegung der Bevölkerung Österreichs im Jahre 1913*, Österreichische Statistik new series 14 (Vienna: Karl Gerold's Sohn, 1918), 44; Rothenbacher, *The European Population 1850-1945*, 102.

130. Weigl, *Demographischer Wandel und Modernisierung in Wien*, 296.

131. Andreas Weigl, "'Unbegrenzte Großstadt' oder 'Stadt ohne Nachwuchs'? Zur demographischen Entwicklung Wiens im 20. Jahrhundert," in *Wien im 20. Jahrhundert: Wirtschaft,*

Bevölkerung, Konsum, Franz X. Eder et al., Querschnitte 12 (Innsbruck: Studienverlag, 2003), 166, 196.

132. Own calculations based on Bundesamt für Statistik, *Die Ergebnisse der österreichischen Volkszählung vom 22. März 1934: Bundesstaat, Tabellenheft*, Statistik des Bundesstaates Österreich 2 (Vienna: Österreichische Staatsdruckerei, 1935), 400-01.

133. Hecke, *Der Geburtenrückgang und seine Folgen*, 11; Exner, *Bevölkerungswissenschaft in Österreich in der Zwischenkriegszeit*, 258-59.

134. Andreas Weigl, "Katholische Bastionen: Die konfessionellen Verhältnisse vom Vorabend des Ersten Weltkriegs bis in die frühen 1920er Jahre," in *... der Rest ist Österreich: Das Werden der Ersten Republik*, vol. 1, ed. Helmut Konrad and Wolfgang Maderthaner (Vienna: Carl Gerold's Sohn, 2008), 385.

135. Josef Ehmer, "The Making of the 'Modern Familiy' in Vienna 1780-1930," in *Vienna – Budapest: Studies in Urban History*, ed. Vera Bácskai, History & Society in Central Europe 1 (Budapest: Hajnal István Kör, 1991), 7-27.

136. Gruber, *Red Vienna*, 147-54.

137. Sigismund Peller, "Offizielle Abortusstatistik und klinische Kontrollergebnisse (Der Abortus in Wien)," *Wiener klinische Wochenschrift* (1919): 172.

138. Sigismund Peller, *Fehlgeburt und Bevölkerungsfrage*, Hippokrates-Bücher für Ärzte 5 (Stuttgart: Hippokrates-Verlag, 1930), 117.

139. Karin Lehner, *Verpönte Eingriffe: Sozialdemokratische Reformbestrebungen zu den Abtreibungsbestimmungen in der Zwischenkriegszeit* (Vienna: Picus, 1989), 100.

140. Edward Shorter, *Der weibliche Körper als Schicksal: Zur Sozialgeschichte der Frau*, [A History of Women's Bodies, trans. Hainer Kober] sec.ed. (Munich: Piper, 1987), 223.

141. Ernst Brezina and Valerie Reuterer, "Über die Fehlgeburten in Österreich nach den Berichten der Krankenanstalten für die Jahre 1929 bis 1932," in *Mitteilungen des Volksgesundheitsamtes* (1933), 101.

142. James Woycke, *Birth Control in Germany 1871-1933* (London: Routledge, 1988), 167-68.

143. Peller, *Der Geburtstod*, 92-93.

144. J. Robert Wegs, *Growing Up Working Class: Continuity and Change Among Viennese Youth, 1890-1938* (University Park: The Pennsylvania Press, 1989), 59.

145. Lehner, *Verpönte Eingriffe*, 181, 187-88.

146. Albert Niedermayer, *Zur sozialen Hygiene von Schwangerschaft, Geburt und Wochenbett: Ein Beitrag zur Frage des Arbeitsschutzes der Frau*, Wiener Beiträge zur Hygiene 1 (Vienna: Wilhelm Maudrich, 1949), 183-84.

147. Own calculations based on Bundesamt für Statistik, ed., *Statistisches Handbuch für die Republik Österreich 6* (Vienna: Karl Gerolds Sohn, 1925), 11, 33.

148. Peller, *Fehlgeburt und Bevölkerungsfrage*, 150-51; Shorter, *Der weibliche Körper als Schicksal*, 236.

149. Peller, *Fehlgeburt und Bevölkerungsfrage*, 179-84.

150. Gerta Morberger, "Mädel von heute – zur Ehe!" *Der jugendliche Arbeiter 29* (June 1926), in *Sozialismus und persönliche Lebensgestaltung: Texte aus der Zwischenkriegszeit* (Vienna: Junius, 1981), 86.

151. Ulrike Gstettner and Philipp Wagner, "Verhütung in den Dreißigerjahren," in *Virus:*

Beiträge zur Sozialgeschichte der Medizin 1 (Vienna: Verein zur Sozialgeschichte der Medizin, 1999), 75-76.

152. Peller, *Fehlgeburt und Bevölkerungsfrage*, 96.

153. Gruber, *Red Vienna*, 176.

154. Peller, *Fehlgeburt und Bevölkerungsfrage*, 97, 125.

155. Lehner, *Verpönte Eingriffe*, 38-39.

156. Ehmer, "The Making of the 'Modern Familiy' in Vienna," 11.

157. Rothenbacher, *The European Population 1850-1945*, 86; Wilhelm Hecke, "Die Unehelichen in Österreich," in *Mitteilungen der Österreichischen Gesellschaft für Bevölkerungspolitik und Fürsorgewesen 9* (Vienna: Helene Löhr, 1930), 3-4.

158. Without the Burgenland. Own calculations based on k.k. Statistische Zentralkommission, *Die Ergebnisse der Volkszählung vom 31. Dezember 1910 in den im Reichsrate vertretenen Königreichen und Ländern: Die Alters- und Familienstandsgliederung und Aufenthaltsdauer*, Österreichische Statistik NF 1/3 (Vienna: Karl Gerold's Sohn, 1914), 2, 4, 6, 8, 10, 12, 22, 24; Bundesamt für Statistik, *Die Ergebnisse der österreichischen Volkszählung vom 22. März 1934*, Statistik des Bundestaates Österreich 2-10 (Vienna: Österreichische Staatsdruckerei, 1935), Wien, 6; Niederösterreich, 72; Oberösterreich, 26; Salzburg, 10; Steiermark, 44; Kärnten, 14; Tirol, 16; Vorarlberg, 7.

159. Alois Haslinger, "Uneheliche Geburten in Österreich: Historische und regionale Muster," in *Demographische Informationen 1982* (Vienna: Institut für Demographie, Österreichische Akademie der Wissenschaften, 1982), 21; Wilhelm Hecke, *Statistik der Unehelichen in Österreich* (Vienna: Julius Springer, 1935), 2.

160. The number of live births per 1,000 unmarried women ages 15-44 in a given year.

161. Rothenbacher, *The European Population 1850-1945*, 102; Ansley J. Coale and Roy Treadway, "A Summary of the Changing Distribution of Overall Fertility, Marital Fertility, and the Proportion Married in the Provinces of Europe," in *The Decline of Fertility in Europe: The Revised Proceedings of a Conference on the Princeton European Fertility Project*, ed. Ansley J. Coale and Susan Cotts Watkins (Princeton: Princeton University Press, 1986), 80-81.

162. Haslinger, "Uneheliche Geburten in Österreich," 6, 22-23.

163. H. Simchen, "Statistische Beiträge zum Problem der Unehelichkeit," in *Mitteilungen des Volksgesundheitsamtes* (1925), 234.

164. Hecke, "Die Unehelichen in Österreich," 11-12; Haslinger, "Uneheliche Geburten in Österreich," 9-10.

165. Statistik Austria, *Demographisches Jahrbuch 2006*, 55-56; Weigl, *Demographischer Wandel und Modernisierung in Wien*, 280.

166. Rothenbacher, *The European Population 1850-1945*, 87, 103; Statistik Austria, *Demographisches Jahrbuch 2006*, 55-56.

Government Care of War Widows and Disabled Veterans after World War I

Verena Pawlowsky/Harald Wendelin

World War I has repeatedly been described in terms of significance. The "Great War" and "the great seminal catastrophe of this century"[1] are well-known expressions used to meet the scale and totality of this exceptional war waged at the beginning of the twentieth century.[2] Not only did this war involve more states in warfare than any other had done, it was new also with regard to the destructive weapons coming into operation, with regard to the masses of soldiers sent to the battlefields and, of course, with regard to the great numbers of victims. As for the Habsburg Monarchy, due to compulsory military service—introduced in 1868—about 7.8 million men were torn away from their families and civilian occupations to serve as soldiers. Thousands were wounded or infected by illness, and 1.5 million of them were killed. And so, one of the consequences of World War I—besides the collapse of empires and the emerging of new political concepts, besides ruined economies and huge unemployment—was the creation of masses of individually affected war victims—either men, bringing with them some physical handicap, or women, finding themselves deprived of their husbands after the war. Disabled veterans and war widows are the focus of the following remarks.[3] They were the visible relics of destruction the post-war society had to cope with and were used by different political factions to underline their respective claims and ideologies. Thus, they were both: a group actually in need of support within a society in which a new social policy was getting under way, and a symbol and screen for projections at the same time.

Four percent, or 260,000 men and women, of the Austrian post-war population were estimated to have fallen victim to the war.[4] Both the size and composition of this group were constantly changing: As many of the war-disabled died within the first post-war months, widows and orphans grew in number. Others would file their applications for compensation only long after returning home from war or captivity. In principle, the recognition of a person as a war victim was conditional upon meeting certain requirements specified by the law. What is unquestioned today, and in fact is practised in research literature, is to capture disabled veterans and war widows by the single term "war victims," was not possible during World War I nor immediately thereafter. The convention of referring to both categories as "war victims" is a rather recent one; before the mid-twenties it was not common to use the term in this sense, and—as Karin Hausen has pointed out with respect to Germany—it became fully accepted only in the late twenties. During the immediate post-war period the term "victim" seemed to be reserved to the soldiers who died in the war.[5] It was the same in Austria, where the collective term occurred in the records concerning the assistance for disabled veterans very rarely before 1920. It was only gradually that those responsible came to make use of this word, and the first association of disabled veterans and war widows to use the new expression in its name was established in 1924.[6] The associations set up immediately after the armistice in November 1918 had still made a sharp distinction between the two groups, using the older expressions "war-disabled persons" (*Kriegsbeschädigte*) and "war invalids" (*Kriegsinvalide*) to denote the disabled veterans, and "war widows" and "surviving dependents" (*Kriegshinterbliebene*), respectively, to refer to the wives (and children) of those killed in the war.[7] At that time the two groups had not yet been "combined into a single clientele of welfare."[8] But obviously a change took place, and some years later it was no longer necessary to draw a sharp line between the two groups. According to the special Austrian legislation enacted in 1919, they were brought together to form a single group of beneficiaries. What holds true for the disabled veterans—namely that they, as Michael Geyer wrote, were only partly a product of the war, but they were as well a product of legislation and of experts' understanding of the concept of health[9]—also applies to the war widows. The emerging group was heterogeneous with regard to its members, but homogenous with regard to their members' claims and the addressee of these claims: the state. This development is mirrored by the linguistic usage.

The construction of the group of war victims was not without influence on its members' self-perception as the existence of the disabled veterans' movements, along with the large associations of those affected, shows. Since

Wounded Austrian soldiers await their transport home on the Isonzo front. (Photo courtesy of Picture Archives of the Austrian National Library)

the beginning of the interwar period, disabled veterans and war widows had been considered—also by themselves—as a closely related group. "War victim," the term used to refer to them as a whole, was—and still is—a practicable, but rather imprecise term. Notably it obscures the fact that hierarchies between the male and the female members of the group remained in place, the latter never being able to enforce their claims by themselves. And the heroic status within society—even if it lost its significance in the course of time (although this will always remain a problematic theme in a state that has lost the war)—would, in the first place, be conferred upon the disabled veterans.

So what is aimed at here is to go back to the time when disabled veterans and war widows were still organised in two distinct groups and to analyse both the allowance system established during the war and the new system put into practice by the democratic government after the war by looking at the recipients of benefits as the disabled on the one hand, and as surviving dependents on the other.[10] Studying the development and the fundamental principles of the allowance systems reveals different sorts of interdependencies and shows how the seemingly homogeneous group of the war victims was being formed. But it particularly shows how a new relationship between the state and the citizen was being brought about —a relationship that differed depending on whether it involved a male or a female individual. A glance at the history of war victims' associations in the second part of this article will provide an idea of how war widows were integrated into these organisations and add a few aspects to the earlier described changes in the perception of war victims.

The Pension System: Fundamental Principles and Realisation in Practice

"Compensation will be provided only for the economic consequences of war disability, not for the wounds as such or the pain suffered nor for any actual trouble or the like. It is not the physical damage but the decrease in function that will be subject to compensation."[11] This is how in 1920 Alfred Deutsch, by profession a physician at the Vienna *Invalidenamt* (Office for the Disabled), described the ruling principle of the *Invalidenentschädigungsgesetz* (IEG, Law on the Compensation of the War-Disabled).[12] The IEG had been devised to govern the provision of assistance for disabled veterans and war widows and was brought into force in April 1919.

Deutsch had been entrusted by the Ministry of Public Health (*Staatsamt für Volksgesundheit*) to develop a manual standardising the examination and the reporting on disabled veterans. The quotation indeed puts in a nutshell what the Austrian system of assistance for disabled veterans was about: The law was not interested in the damage but in the economic consequences thereof. It was not the (however objective) bodily damage but the "functional loss" that was subject to medical judgement as well as to compensation. The contemporary acronym used to describe this object of compensation was "MdE." These three letters stand for "reduction of earning capacity" (*Minderung der Erwerbsfähigkeit*). The MdE—expressed as a percentage—was the central parameter used to determine the actual size of the financial compensation disabled veterans were entitled to after World War I. In order to get compensation a MdE of at least 15 percent was required; a MdE of 75 percent and more entitled the disabled veteran to the highest pension (*Vollrente*).

The *Invalidenentschädigungsgesetz* also included a regulation of pensions to which war widows were entitled. Women whose men were killed in the war and women whose men died as consequence of their war-inflicted disabilities after the war were both regarded as war widows. Their pension could amount up to 50 percent of their husband's *Vollrente*, but only in case they had to take care of children or were at an advanced age and no longer capable of earning their living by their own. As concerned the provision of benefits to war widows, the *Invalidenentschädigungsgesetz* adopted a totally novel—and remarkably progressive from today's perspective—approach: For the first time in the history of Austrian social legislation, marriage and cohabitation were treated equally with regard to entitlement to compensation. For a woman to be eligible for compensation it was thus irrelevant whether her relationship with a disabled veteran was one of marriage or whether it was based upon a domestic partnership[13] as long as it was a care relationship. Assuming that many couples had put off marriage or refrained from it altogether in view of the war, the legislator was anxious not to discriminate women who had become "widows" living in a non-marital union.[14] On the other hand, in case of remarriage a widow would lose her pension and thus her status. In order to be further granted a pension a war widow had to get married to a disabled veteran. Clearly, this regulation aimed at mitigating the law's potential marriage-inhibiting effects and, at the same time, at enhancing the disabled ex-servicemen's chances of getting married.

Back to the disabled veterans: The use of expressions like "economic consequences" and "functional loss" already indicates that it was not the wounded soldier whose compensation was supposed to be managed. It was the active member of civil society, the gainfully employed citizen who was to be paid damages. This kind of assistance for disabled veterans did not typically aim at granting any symbolic reward by emphasising military or even heroic aspects.[15]

One could suppose that this commitment was the visible expression of the young Austrian democracy's negative attitude towards soldierly virtues in 1919. However, it was not made under the impression of the just finished war; in fact it had been prepared much earlier, namely at the beginning of 1915, i.e. during the war. At that time it was becoming obvious that the numbers of wounded soldiers would go beyond anything one could imagine. The war the Austrian-Hungarian Monarchy had entered in 1914 was the first one that took place under the condition of compulsory military service.[16] At that time there was no idea how this fact would overtax the existing welfare system. A leading official at the Ministry for Social Affairs, recounting the beginning of the war, had to admit that the state was totally unprepared in respect of providing assistance to the disabled veterans.[17] As all other belligerents, the Austro-Hungarian Monarchy had no working arrangement to take care of the enormous number of wounded soldiers the war had produced right at the beginning.

The system that was in force when the war started was based on the *Militärversorgungsgesetz* (Military Provision Law) of 1875.[18] Even at the time of its origin this law did not satisfy the new conditions, and it proved completely insufficient with regard to the common soldiers. More or less a pension law for professional soldiers, it did not reflect the fact that compulsory military service had been imposed in Austria only seven years before, in 1868.[19]

With the war being under way, it soon became apparent that one of the law's most fatal flaws was that it took into account only military categories such as term of service and rank as a calculation basis for disability pensions and also that it defined disability solely in military terms. According to the *Militärversorgungsgesetz*, an invalid soldier was a (militarily) worthless, in the literal sense of the word, soldier, indeed. For soldiers who served less then ten years—and this applied to the majority of those liable for military service—the law of 1875 provided pensions only if they had become unfit for military service and in addition had lost 100 percent of their civil earning capacity. Yet in many cases there was an obvious discrepancy between the loss of military capacity and a complete loss of earning capacity. Having become unfit for service did not necessarily imply being totally incapable of pursuing gainful employment. Hence, at the beginning of the war, many wounded ex-soldiers had to leave the army without any provision as they, although virtually unfit for military service, were not regarded as to a 100 percent physically incapacitated.

It was this discrepancy that eventually prompted the creation of the system as described by Adolf Deutsch, the prehistory of which dated back to the beginning of the war. When at the beginning of 1915 the government came to realise the problem, it started to change the care system for the wounded soldiers so as to account for the fact that through the introduction of compulsory military service the state had become obliged to take care of those who had become victims in fulfilling their duty. In view of the large numbers of disabled veterans, it soon became obvious that the state would never be able to pay pensions that would ensure their livelihoods. So on the one hand the budget could not cope with the problem, but on the other hand no one challenged the fundamental duty of the state to provide for the ex-servicemen. As the government was not able to bring up a new law replacing the *Militärversorgungsgesetz* of 1875, the whole system developed during the war was based on makeshift solutions.[20] First of all, there was the problem to provide benefits for the surviving dependents of deceased soldiers. So at the beginning of the war the government adopted the

Alimony Law (*Unterhaltsbeitragsgesetz*)[21] of 1912 to supply them with an allowance paid by the state. Originally, this law was created for the affiliates of reservists who had been conscripted. Three decrees (of 1915, 1916 and 1917[22]) expanded the original benefits envisaged by this law to the circle of the surviving dependents of the deceased soldiers and the affiliates of the disabled veterans.

The beginning of a new approach adopted by the state in regard of the disabled veterans themselves was marked by a decree published by the Ministry of War in January 1915.[23] This decree obliged the commissions that had to judge whether a soldier was unfit and therefore had to leave the army—they were named *Superarbitrierungskommissionen*—not only to decide whether or not a soldier was to be considered having lost his civilian earning capacity, but also to express as a percentage the amount of the reduction of earning capacity. Since then disabled veterans were granted pensions not only in case they had lost 100 percent of their earning capacity. They now had to show at least a 20 percent reduction of earning capacity in order to be entitled to a pension. Benefits were composed of an (unvarying for privates) disability pension pursuant to the military provision law and a state allowance the amount of which depended on the degree of decrease in the "ability to pursue gainful employment."

Thus, already the beginning of 1915 marked a point at which the principles the system of provision for the war-disabled had hitherto complied with underwent fundamental changes. All of a sudden, compensation no longer came as a more or less symbolic gesture of the "gratitude of the fatherland" for the ex-servicemen's commitment. Now a much more precise, translatable into a percentage, element was brought into focus in addition to the "gratitude of the fatherland," by which it was to be ensured that those who had suffered from the war would be able to maintain their livelihoods in a civilian society: the remaining capacity of pursuing a profession or making one's living, respectively.

To be sure, the idea to measure the degree of decrease in earning capacity and to provide for an adequate compensation was not an invention of the military; rather, it was rooted in the accident insurance that had been in effect in Austria since 1888. Even the term "reduction of earning capacity" was adopted from the accident insurance. Accordingly, from 1915 onward damage inflicted to the body and life by the war was treated in the same manner as were industrial casualties.[24]

As for its theoretical underpinning, this development was built upon the assumption of the state and the citizen being responsible for each other. One might speak of a "triangle of duties." The first two corners of this triangle seem to be obvious: While the first one is constituted by compulsory military service, the second is represented by the state's obligation to take care of those who were wounded or disabled during military service. The third corner of this triangle was to transfer the ex-soldiers into gainfully employed civilians.

As far as we know this "triangle of duties" was first illustrated in 1915 by Gustav Marchet, a former Austrian minister and expert in social legislation.[25] According to his conception, the duty of military service imposed upon male citizens entailed an obligation to care on part of the state, which it would assume by providing assistance to the war-disabled. However, yet another duty added to the two others on the part of male citizens, namely the "duty to work." Compliance with this duty was interpreted such that only that part of the working ability whose loss was traceable to the war should be subject to compensation by the state, wheras it was left to the citizen, upon fulfilling his duty to serve and resuming his life as a civilian, to employ the remainder of the ability to work. The rationale put forward, among others, in order to justify this duty to work was to prevent the emergence of a so-called *"Fürsorgeproletariat"* (care-dependant proletariat).

The principle validity of this triangle of duties made up of the duty of military service, the duty of care and the duty to work in governing the relationship between the state and the male citizen remained unquestioned even after the war had ended; in fact, it informed the system of provision for the war-disabled throughout the First Republic and beyond. Not even the disabled veterans' interest pressure group, which after 1918 had gained quite some power, did ever make the slightest attempt at achieving full state provision for every single disabled veteran to justly reward them for their sacrifices. Certainly, however, this also meant giving their consent to the most delicate part of the mutual commitment, i.e. the duty to work.

The most tangible evidence of implementation of this set of duties implicitly accorded between the state and the (for the most part) male citizens was the *Invalidenentschädigungsgesetz* put into effect in April 1919, which covered all claims of the war-disabled, and also of the surviving dependents of deceased servicemen. As for the scope of benefits envisaged, it did not differ so much from the medley of interim measures that had been passed already during the war. What was essential was that this act eventually brought together in a *single* body of law all claims war victims were conceded; moreover, it brought about both the unification of procedures upon which the recognition of claims was conditioned and their compliance with constitutional principles.

There was yet another key point to the *Invalidenentschädigungsgesetz*, notably its attempt to implement the described compensation principle in an utmost consistent manner. This became manifest in the provision that the respective pension rates—apart from the reduction of earning capacity—was derived from factors such as former income or the beneficiary's educational attainment. Within a range between a minimum and a maximum pension level, the amount of pension directly reflected the beneficiary's social status. In short, what was attempted by this law was to meet the claims for compensation of the poor and the rich alike since, after all, both were equally liable to military service.[26] In this sense, the *Invalidenentschädigungsgesetz* might indeed be considered the first Austrian social law to convey an idea as to how social justice was conceived of from a state perspective and also of the notion of social justice the Social Democrats and the Christian Socials—who at that time formed a joint government—could agree upon. It was in particular Social-Democrat functionaries who accordingly considered the *Invalidenentschädigungsgesetz* as a forerunner of the general social insurance, the implementation of which, as we know, was yet to come.

Taking a look at how the new law was performing in practice, one will at once realise that it did not work at all. Once launched, the system collapsed within a couple of days, notably in Vienna, where about half of all Austrian war victims were living. Neither was the bureaucratic apparatus, which was only under construction, able to cope with the host of applications, nor did the applicants themselves meet the high demands required by the procedure, more often than not failing even to produce all documents necessary to prove their entitlements. Early in 1920, the competent bodies were confronted with somewhat more than 100,000 applications for disability pensions alone, i.e. excluding applications for pensions by surviving dependents. The *Invalidenentschädigungskommission* of Vienna and Lower Austria had received about 70,000 applications from which by that time—almost one year after the law had been enacted—less than one percent had been processed. As a matter of fact, years were to pass before—about 1923—the authorities managed to cope with the proceeding of applications.

No less than the bureaucratic collapse did the massive loss in the crown's purchasing power at the beginning of the 1920s come to bear on society. Although governments made regular attempts at compensating for the ever-rising inflation by granting so-called price-increase allowances that were added to the pensions, these compensations were not to become effective unless the currency stabilised as a result of the monetary rehabilitation agreed upon in Geneva in the autumn 1922. The *Zentralverband der österreichischen Kriegsbeschädigten*, the main representative of the war-disabled, initially having welcomed the law (to the formulation of which it had been instrumental), in view of these problems started fierce attacks on some of its provisions. By the middle of 1922 it had eventually pushed through a total reform of the law that deprived it of much of its original quality; under the pressure of budget consolidation the character of the law was bound to change, as well.

Thus, the pension pattern based upon educational attainment or former income, respectively, was replaced upon the association's explicit request by a so-called unified pension which depended solely on the degree of the decrease in earning capacity and did not take into account the beneficiary's social background.[27] Moreover, instead of increasing in line with the decrease in earning capacity, pensions now would rise significantly disproportionately. As a consequence, low-level pensions came to be degraded to a symbolic gesture. Given the lack of funds, so it was argued, the most pressing needs would have to be served first, and this affected those of the war-disabled who had lost most of their earning capacity. Thus, as a result of the massive economic and administrative problems a compensation law enacted in 1919 was retransformed into a provision law, with the focus shifting from granting compensation to ensuring a certain subsistence level.

Despite all these practical shortcomings, the notion of the wounded hero retained a certain implicit significance also in the First Republic. For how else could it be explained that the less severely wounded ex-servicemen were granted a pension, albeit of only symbolic value, instead of being denied their claims altogether? And even when two years later—in 1924—pension payments to the less severely wounded were terminated,[28] this was done not without making a one-off payment to those concerned, nor were they deprived of their status of war-disabled. Thus, although the provision for the war-disabled quite obviously needs some symbolism, the *Invalidenentschädigungsgesetz* remained entirely true, in programmatic terms, to the concept of the wage-earning citizen. It was this very feature of the provision for the war-disabled that made it so essential for the development of the social security system.[29] As for the war widows, however, they had a secondary status within this concept; not being a party to the triangle of duties, their entitlement was invariably a derived one. Their right to a war-widow pension ensued solely from having lost their husbands (or partners) in or as a consequence of the war. It was death as the ultimate form of war-inflicted damage that would entitle them to compensation. Taking on the role of the defunct breadwinner, the state thereby established a provision model which conferred universal validity to the model of the bourgeois family that had been in place already in the monarchy. The family—conceived of as a supply unit—formed an unit also with regard to these disbursements. That the pensions actually paid—in particular the reduced women's pensions—were by far too low to grant a living is another story.[30]

The Disabled Veterans' Movement: Formation and Orientation

"[...] when there was war, I gave many performances for our wounded, the war heroes, who have since then been seen fit to be deprived of their honorary titles and who today are supposed to be called nothing but war victims. They have remained war heroes for me, though."[31] These were the words of Maria Jeritza, an internationally acclaimed singer of the Vienna State Opera, that appeared in a 1929 Vienna newspaper. It was the *Reichsbund der Kriegsopfer Österreichs* that had readily placed them—under the heading "Words of a Woman Many an Austrian Should Take to Heart"—in its organ to underpin its own view and to launch an attack on its rival organisation, the *Zentralverband der österreichischen Kriegsbeschädigten*, whom it accused—as it used to any "red subversive(s)" in general—of "smashing all war heroes to a mass of humans."[32]

Thus giving an account of how her artistic skills were instrumentalised for patriotic ends, the singer postulates—through the concept pair "war hero/war victim"—a dichotomy between the active hero and the passive victim. However, these attributions were not so much opposed as they were actually related to each other, accompanying the war-disabled throughout the First Republic both as concerns the latter's status within society and their self-perception or, more exactly, the image they sought to create of themselves. It is therefore not without irony that an association whose policies were largely based on playing against each other the hero and the victim had named itself *Reichsbund der Kriegsopfer Österreichs*. As has been noted at the outset, this denomination is to some extent attributable to the association's relatively late founding date, which is why the *Reichsbund* had not been involved in the drawing up of the *Invalidenentschädigungsgesetz*. Representing the conservative strand within the entirety of Austrian war victims associations, its members were in the minority, though. The greatest part of the war-disabled were organised under the umbrella of the older—and much larger—*Zentralverband*.

Unlike in the German Empire and France,[33] in the Habsburg Monarchy no serious attempts were made to found associations of disabled veterans during the war. But as soon as fighting was stopped the organisation of the disabled veterans was tackled with full force. The first association was established in Vienna. Called *Verein der Kriegsinvaliden*, it directed first claims on behalf of the disabled veterans to the *Staatsrat* on 3 November, the day of the armistice between Austria-Hungary, the Entente and Italy.[34] But only a few days later this forerunner had become obsolete, when on 11 November, on the eve of the proclamation of the republic, the *Zentralverband der deutschösterreichischen Kriegsbeschädigten* was founded.[35] This association soon took over the central position within the rapidly growing movement of the disabled and, until 1934, remained by far the biggest and most influential organisation. By 1922, the *Zentralverband* counted up to 200,000 members,[36] representing 90 percent of all Austrian war victims at that time. The disabled veterans got a powerful lobby, an Austrian-wide operating organisation with numerous branches on provincial and local level, with independent examining doctors, lawyers, advice centres and its impressive own press.[37] "Never before had there been a movement like this; not having any model to work from, we had to build up everything from the scratch,"[38] as one euphoric statement, recalling the beginning of the organisation, ran. No government—neither the coalition government at the beginning nor the later conservative governments—could ignore the demands articulated by the disabled veterans' lobby. And although the *Zentralverband* did not stand outside the left- and right-wing dichotomy of the Austrian interwar period, but found itself in closeness with Social Democracy and developed itself—especially in the late 1920s and early 1930s—in constant rivalry to the conservative *Reichsbund*, it was the *Zentralverband* that always represented the majority of the Austrian war victims. Other small organisations of war victims always existed but remained unimportant.

For the single member the help of the organisation became essential to assert his or her entitlement to pensions. The growing complexity of procedures made it necessary for the majority of disabled veterans and war widows to make use of a competent advocate. As a consequence, communication between war victims and the state more and more passed into the hands of the organisation. Even the authorities were pleased to have an association opposite because it was—especially in the first restless months of the Austrian Republic—much more comfortable to negotiate with an acknowledged representative than to argue with an unpredictable mass of dissatisfied ex-soldiers. The attempt to integrate the disabled veterans also found expression in the *Invalidenentschädigungsgesetz* of April 1919 that explicitly stated the disabled veterans' right of participation in decision-making. So the *Zentralverband* grew into an important player in the fields of politics.[39]

As a consequence, the "organised disabled veteran" became standard.

But he was not alone; by his side there were the war widows who occupied, as female comrades, their own place within the organisation. It was only during the first months of existence that there were no war widows included in the disabled veterans' associations. Recalling the first big meetings in Vienna on the occasion of the tenth anniversary of the organisation, the secretary of the *Zentralverband* guiltily wrote, "Unfortunately I have to admit that by then we had not got that far so as to remember the widows and orphans too. That's why there were no women included."[40] But this was soon going to change when, with some delay, widows started to be included in the movement, as well. Usually it was the associations themselves that started wooing the surviving dependents in the spring of 1919, when they realised that the inclusion of this group, which, after all, also belonged to those entitled to benefits under the *Invalidenentschädigungsgesetz*, memberships would be pushed up at one stroke. None of the organisations was willing to let slip the opportunity to represent widows and orphans and leave this potential to one of the competitors. Eventually, women accounted for one third of the *Zentralverband*'s members, and by 1924, when the *Reichsbund der Kriegsopfer Österreichs* was set up, the inclusion of both war-disabled and war widows had already become an established practice. The decision to include women and thus, to abandon their male-bonding character, "turning civilian" in a much more comprehensive sense than their programmes did envisage anyway, was to shape the Austrian associations' image for many years to come.[41] Notably, this image—and this held true in particular for the *Zentralverband*—was that of an interest group pursuing *purely* social-political aims that had nothing in common with a traditional soldiers' organisation for which the social question would have been just *one among others*. Accordingly, the *Zentralverband* kept a clear distance from pure veterans, excluding them from membership. The fact that the *Invalidenentschädigungsgesetz* provided pensions for disabled veterans as well as for war widows (and war orphans) had far-reaching consequences on the forming and also the identity of this group of recipients of social security. This is underlined by the history of the war victims associations, too.

With the distance from the war growing, the group of war victims shrunk in both size and significance. If providing for them might have been an exigency at the beginning of the post-war period, from a long-term perspective this was an ephemeral problem that sooner or later was going to resolve itself. And this was yet another issue the war victims associations had to handle. For, sooner than the issue of provision for the war victims could be resolved biologically, a change took place in the attitudes towards the war-disabled on the part of the "sound." The war-disabled were a permanent and visible reminder of the past war in which Austria, after all, had been defeated. Visible signs of that defeat, the war-disabled would arouse a feeling of disturbance—in fact have their wounded and maimed bodies been repeatedly addressed as symbols of a destroyed masculinity.[42] What is more, owing to the fact that care measures considerably strained the central budget, the war-disabled came increasingly to be seen as a superfluous burden during the First Republic. Yet this attitude would not, as a rule, become manifest—the symbolism associated with this group was great enough to make it untouchable, if not sacrosanct.

Because the war-disabled served as a screen for projections of the most heterogeneous kinds, one might only speculate as to any common identity. We may, however, get some idea on this theme by taking a look at the powerful interest groups. These were indeed seeking to create certain "images of the disabled," distinct from the status of victims and carrying a positive connotation. The identification patterns the associations offered their disabled members were not only to assert their positive self-image, they were also intended to have a unifying function. And while the Christian-social *Reichsbund*, as shows the above passage, was indeed able to assign the war-disabled an unambiguous and well-known role—that of the "war hero" and the "defender of the fatherland"[43]—which would, in addition, exalt the image of the war-disabled, things are more complex with regard to the *Zentralverband*'s attitude. This organisation needed to convey an "image of the disabled veteran" more complex. Although it also had to reference the war in order to legitimise its claims, its interpretation of events could by no means be positive. Therefore, the *Zentralverband* would refer to the war only in order to radically distance itself from any militarism and heroism. Both the war-disabled and the dependent survivors of those killed were conceived of as victims indeed—namely of a war that had been incited by the Habsburgs. Yet, instead of coping with their status as victims, they were supposed, motivated through their war experiences, to embark on the fight for the right thing by actively taking part in the building of the young republic and a peaceful society. The counter-image of the war hero was thus that of the pacifist-minded war-disabled.[44] And although the latter also stood out from the rest of society (just as the war hero), the image he embodied was by far less common. The *Zentralverband* therefore had to struggle all the more to consolidate this construct: Witness the host of articles in its newspaper seeking to educate its members in a pacifist spirit and to commit them to this image.

In the course of years, and especially under Maximilian Brandeisz, the chairman of the huge Vienna regional organisation, who since the end of 1930 had also held the position of *Bundesrat* (member of the Federal Assembly) and in 1932 was elected president of the CIAMAC,[45] the 1926-established Geneva-based International Confederation of Disabled Veterans, the pacifist attitude adopted by the *Zentralverband* became all the stronger. In contrast to the Christian-social *Reichsbund*, which did not have any misgivings about getting involved with comrade associations and not even shied away from jointly promenading—dressed in full military regalia—along the Vienna *Ring* Boulevard, the *Zentralverband* rejected anything that might lend itself to glorification of the war. It took a critical attitude towards bravery medals, war commemoration medals, but also war memorials; it urged people not to buy war toys and to join peace demonstrations; it organised special trips to Bratislava for people to watch *All Quiet on the Western Front*—the film adapted from Remarque's novel—and filled its newspapers with peace addresses by the former enemies.

While one can only speculate as to the impressions of such an image of the disabled, it is without doubt that the *Zentralverband*'s main undertaking—the reintegration of the war-disabled into the post-war society—proved successful. The association thus lived up to its role as a mediator between the state and the war victims. Undeniable discontent on the part of war victims notwithstanding, major confrontations could be avoided. What is more, the war victims did never pose any threat to the state.[46]

It was only when the *Ständestaat* (Corporate State) was proclaimed that both associations came to an end. While the *Zentralverband* was liquidated already in the wake of the incidents of February 1934, and after the dismissal of its management was incorporated into the *Österreichische Kriegsopferverband* led by Emil Fey, the *Reichsbund* was terminated in 1936 when the *Einheitsverband der Kriegsopfer Österreichs* was set up. This association, based on compulsory membership, existed through 1938 whereupon it was incorporated into the National-socialist *Kriegsopferversorgung* (NSKOV). With the annexation of Austria, the system of war victims assistance was also replaced by that effective in the German Reich, which already at the beginning of 1933 resumed a positive attitude towards heroism, military tokens and symbolic gestures.[47] This ultimately put an end to the efforts of the *Zentralverband* to bring war victims together in a single interest group oriented towards social-political aims.

Conclusion

In summary it can be said that the enormous toll World War I had taken in terms of disabled veterans and surviving dependents of deceased servicemen brought about a revolution in the provision for this group of war victims. It has repeatedly been noted that in this respect the war may be attributed a social-political "thrust effect."[48] This was especially true for Austria, where already in April 1919—earlier than in any other country—a law regulating the provision for war victims, the *Invalidenentschädigungsgesetz*, was elaborated and enacted. This law was a modern social and compensation law and—along with the unemployment insurance introduced somewhat earlier[49]—one of the first laws to establish a direct link between beneficiaries and the state. And although such a link had been in place since 1868—with the introduction of general conscription, which is why it first applied to the male citizen—it became manifest and effective only during World War I. Rather than the wounded soldier no longer able to perform his (military) duty, the IEG addressed the wage-earning citizen who, in exercising his military duty, had sustained a decrease in his wage-earning capacity as a civilian. Therefore, what state indemnity aimed at in the first place was to provide compensation for that loss and, then, to ensure the affected individual's reintegration into civilian employability. A most differentiated social law in its original version of 1919 claiming to cover the needs of the whole society, the *Invalidenentschädigungsgesetz*, however, ultimately proved a failure owing to these high ambitions, the inadequate implementation as well as hyperinflation emerging soon after the war. As a consequence of this failure, the act underwent reform in 1922 as a result of which its character changed substantially and its original quality was largely lost. Thus, what once had been a compensation law turned into one that solely sought to provide for the subsistence for those who had been extremely severely wounded.

Since many of the World War I servicemen had families, it was only logical that in case of the family breadwinner's incapacitation the state would provide for the dependents. It did so by administering the provision of widows (and orphans) under the same law by which disabled veterans' entitlements were being governed. This way, disabled veterans and war widows during the First Republic merged into a group of welfare recipients which in the course of time came to be referred to as war victims.

The policies pursued by the powerful war victims' lobbies, which emerged in Austria only after the war was over, were likewise characterised by their representing through the same associations both disabled men and widowed women. The organisational degree being extremely high among Austrian war victims, joint representation of both war widows and the war-disabled entailed that war victims associations regarded themselves primarily as social-political interest groups strongly differing from military veteran and comradeship associations. These associations became major service institutions for their members and took an active role in the law-making process. The by far mightiest association was the *Zentralverband der österreichischen Kriegsbeschädigten*. Affiliated with the Social Democrats under the First Republic, it sought to create an image of the disabled that would be positively connoted yet keep a distance from anything associated with the military for its members to identify themselves with. Not only did the association serve as the war victims' organ, as a negotiating partner accepted by governments and a mediator between the state and the war victims, but also as a major communicator of a self-image that was to form the war victims into one group and to promote their coherence. Avowedly pacifist, the *Zentralverband* scrupulously avoided justifying war victims' claims on the grounds of military heroism—although like its counterpart, the conservative *Reichsbund der Kriegsopfer Österreichs*, it had also to build its policies on its members' war experiences. Its monopoly within disabled veterans' movements notwithstanding, the harsh reality by which the First Republic was characterised placed a permanent need upon the *Zentralverband* to defend its creed against alternative conservative concepts. Apart from the question as to the acceptance of its pacifist stance on the part of its members, it has to be acknowledged that one the *Zentralverband*'s central achievements was the reintegration of former combatants in the (admittedly agitated) post-war society. That there was relatively little time left for the reintegration to stabilise was due to the political developments of 1934 and 1938.

Notes

1. George F. Kennan, *The Decline of Bismarck's European Order: Franco-Russian Relations, 1875–1890* (Princeton: Princeton University Press, 1979), 3.

2. John Keegan, *Der erste Weltkrieg: Eine europäische Tragödie*, 2nd ed. (Reinbek: Kindler, 2000); Gerhard Hirschfeld et al., eds., *Enzyklopädie Erster Weltkrieg* (Paderborn: Schöningh, 2003).

3. The authors are preparing a book on this topic; their project was funded by Austrian Science Fund (FWF), project leader was Bertrand Perz (University of Vienna/Department of Contemporary History). Articles already published are for example: Verena Pawlowsky and Harald Wendelin, "Die Verwaltung des Leides: Kriegsbeschädigtenversorgung in Niederösterreich," in *Niederösterreich im 20. Jahrhundert*, vol. 2, *Wirtschaft*, ed. Peter Melichar et al. (Vienna: Böhlau, 2008), 507-36; Verena Pawlowsky and Harald Wendelin, "Kriegsopfer und Sozialstaat: Österreich nach dem Ersten Weltkrieg," in *Die Weltkriege als symbolische Bezugspunkte: Polen, die Tschechoslowakei und Deutschland nach dem Ersten und Zweiten Weltkrieg*, ed. Natali Stegmann

(Prague: Masarykův ùstav a Archiv AV ČR, 2009), 127-46.

4. War orphans are included in this figure. Trusted data were not available until 1927. As per that date, the numbers of war-disabled and surviving dependents of those killed were calculated to be 116,000 and 147,000, respectively, i.e. totaling the aforementioned 263,000. Prior to that the state had to rely upon estimates; given the fact that it took years to process the entirety of applications for compensation under the *Invalidenentschädigungsgesetz* of 1919, however, only the amount of those already settled could be stated.

5. Karin Hausen, "Die Sorge der Nation für ihre 'Kriegsopfer': Ein Bereich der Geschlechterpolitik während der Weimarer Republik," in *Von der Arbeiterbewegung zum modernen Sozialstaat: Festschrift für Gerhard A. Ritter zum 65. Geburtstag*, ed. Jürgen Kocka (Munich: Saur, 1994), 724-25.

6. That is, the conservative *Reichsbund der Kriegsopfer Österreichs*.

7. The biggest association was called *Zentralverband der deutschösterreichischen Kriegsbeschädigten*. When it started to place the emphasis on the war widows it was renamed into *Zentralverband der Landesorganisationen der Kriegsinvaliden und Kriegerhinterbliebenen Österreichs* in September 1920.

8. "*zu einer einzigen Fürsorgeklientel zusammengefaßt*": Hausen, "Die Sorge der Nation für ihre 'Kriegsopfer,'" 725.

9. "*Der anerkannte Invalide war nur zum Teil ein Produkt des Krieges. Er war ebenso ein Produkt der Gesetzgebung und der Vorstellung von Experten über die Gesundheit des Einzelnen und der Gesellschaft.*": Michael Geyer, "Ein Vorbote des Wohlfahrtsstaates: Die Kriegsopferversorgung in Frankreich, Deutschland und Großbritannien nach dem Ersten Weltkrieg," in *Die Organisierung des Friedens: Demobilmachung 1918–1920*, ed. Wolfgang J. Mommsen (Göttingen: Vandenhoeck & Ruprecht, 1983), 233-34.

10. Most of the existing studies on the theme lay their focus mainly on the disabled veterans and not on details of the legal framework in which the care for them was organized: Deborah Cohen, *The War Come Home: Disabled Veterans in Britain and Germany, 1914–1939* (Berkeley: University of California Press, 2001); David A. Gerber, *Disabled Veterans in History* (Ann Arbor: University of Michigan Press, 2000); Stephen R. Ward, ed., *The War Generation: Veterans of the First World War* (Port Washington: Kennikat Press, 1975); Robert Weldon Whalen, *Bitter Wounds: German Victims of the Great War, 1914–1939* (Ithaca: Cornell University Press, 1984).

11. "*Entschädigt werden nur die wirtschaftlichen Folgen der Kriegsbeschädigung, nicht die Verwundung an sich oder erlittene Schmerzen, nicht Beschwerden an sich oder dergleichen. Nicht die anatomische Schädigung, sondern der funktionelle Ausfall wird entschädigt.*": Adolf Deutsch, *Anleitung zur Feststellung der Erwerbseinbusse bei Kriegsbeschädigten*, 3rd ed. (Vienna: Staatsamt für Volksgesundheit, 1920), 8.

12. StGBl 1919/245, *Gesetz über die staatliche Entschädigung der Kriegs-Invaliden, -Witwen und -Waisen* (*Invalidenentschädigungsgesetz*).

13. StGBl 1919/245, § 20f. A woman was recognised as the decedent's common-law spouse if they had been living together in a common household for a minimum of one year. In this respect, the IEG eventually served as the model for the Pension Insurance Law for Salaried Employees (StGBl 1920/370) as amended in August 1920.

14. This was made explicit in an explanatory statement concerning the respective government bill: *Stenographische Protokolle der konstituierenden Nationalversammlung der Republik Österreich* (Vienna, 1919), Beilage 114.

15. This was one of the main differences between the Austrian and for example the French way of treating the war victims, see Antoine Prost, *In the Wake of War: Les Anciens Combattants and French Society, 1914–1939* (Oxford: Berg, 1992).

16. Christa Hämmerle, "Die k. (u.) k. Armee als 'Schule des Volkes'? Zur Geschichte der Allgemeinen Wehrpflicht in der multinationalen Habsburgermonarchie (1866–1914/18)," in *Der Bürger als Soldat: Die Militarisierung europäischer Gesellschaften im langen 19. Jahrhundert: Ein internationaler Vergleich*, ed. Christian Jansen (Essen: Klartext, 2004), 175-213.

17. Otto v. Gasteiger, head of department 2 (*Kriegsbeschädigtenfürsorge*) of the Ministry of Social Affairs, ÖStA/AdR 03, BMfsV KB-F, box 1356, 1244/1918.

18. RGBl 1875/158, *Gesetz betreffend die Militärversorgung des k.k. Heeres, der k.k. Kriegsmarine und der k.k. Landwehr.*

19. RGBl 1868/151, *Wehrgesetz.*

20. The main reason for the government's failure was the fact that everything that concerned the army had to be mutually agreed with the Hungarian part of the monarchy. Although the two governments negotiated a new law they did not come to a settlement before 1918, and this was too late to enforce the law in the Austrian part of the monarchy.

21. RGBl 1912/237, *Gesetz betreffend den Unterhaltsbeitrag für die Angehörigen von Mobilisierten.*

22. RGBl 1915/161, RGBl 1916/135; RGBl 1917/139.

23. *Erlass des Kriegsministeriums*, 22 January 1915, quoted in ÖStA/AdR 03, BMfsV KB-F, box 1359, 7950/1918.

24. See Paul Dittrich, *Praktische Anleitung zur Begutachtung der häufigsten Unfallschäden der Arbeiter* (Vienna: Braumüller, 1901); Siegfried Kraus, *Über das Berufsschicksal Unfallverletzter: Mit einem Zusatz über die Lage der Kriegsinvaliden* (Stuttgart: Cotta'sche Buchhandlung Nachf., 1915).

25. Gustav Marchet, *Die Versorgung der Kriegsinvaliden und ihrer Hinterbliebenen* (Warnsdorf i. B.: Strache, 1915), 27ff.

26. See Geyer, "Ein Vorbote des Wohlfahrtsstaates," 228-29.

27. BGBl 1922/430, *VII. Novelle zum Invalidenentschädigungsgesetz.*

28. BGBl 1924/256, *VIII. Novelle zum Invalidenentschädigungsgesetz.*

29. It was Skocpol who has emphasized that it was not the Social Security Act of 1935, but the assistance for disabled veterans and their relatives that stood at the beginning of the United States' social security system, see Theda Skocpol, *Protecting Soldiers and Mothers: The Political Origins of Social Policy in the United States* (Cambridge, MA: Belknap Press, 1995).

30. To the situation of women and their derived entitlement see Susan Pedersen, "Gender, welfare and citizenship in Britain during the Great War," *The American historical Review 95* (Oct. 1990): 983-1006; Susan Pedersen, *Family, Dependence, and the Origins of the Welfare State: Britain and France, 1914–1945* (Cambridge: Cambridge University Press, 1993).

31. Quoted in *Österreichs Kriegsopfer. Zentralblatt des Reichsbundes der Kriegsopfer Österreichs 5* (no. 4, 1929): 3-4.

32. Ibid.

33. The first associations of disabled veterans were founded in the German Empire already in 1917: *Bund* (later: *Reichsbund*) *der Kriegsbeschädigten und ehemaligen Kriegsteilnehmer*, from 1919 on: *Reichsbund der Kriegsbeschädigten, Kriegsteilnehmer und Kriegshinterbliebenen*, the *Bund erblindeter Krieger* even in 1916, see Whalen, *Bitter Wounds*, 120-21; James M. Diehl, "The Organization of German Veterans 1917–1919," *Archiv für Sozialgeschichte 11* (1971): 139-84. In France the formation of loose clubs was noticed in 1915 and in 1916, see Prost, *In the Wake of War*, 30.

34. *Verein der Kriegsinvaliden*, 5 November 1918, ÖStA/AdR 03 BMfsV KB-F, box 1364,

572/1918.

35. *Der Invalide. Offizielles Organ des Zentralverbandes der deutschösterreichischen Kriegsbeschädigten,* 15 Jan. 1919, 1.

36. ÖStA/AdR 03 BMfsV KB-F, box 1395, 5098/1922.

37. *Der Invalide,* 1918-1934. Naming the journal "the invalid" can be read as reference to the military background.

38. *"(N)iemals zuvor hat es eine derartige Bewegung gegeben und ohne Vorbild musste alles aus dem Nichts geschaffen werden.":* "Den Delegierten des Verbandstages zum Gruß!," *Der Invalide,* 30 Nov. 1925, 1.

39. See to this special aspect Ke-chin Hsia, "A Partnership of the Weak: War Victims and the State in the Early First Austrian Republic," in this volume; Emmerich Tálos and Bernhard Kittel, "Roots of Austro-Corporatism: Institutional Preconditions and Coorporation Before and After 1945," in *Austro-Corporatism: Past – Present – Future,* ed. Günter Bischof and Anton Pelinka, Contemporary Austrian Studies 4 (New Brunswick, NJ: Transaction, 1996), 21-52, especially 23-32.

40. *"Leider muß ich gestehen, dass wir damals noch nicht so weit waren, auch der Witwen und Waisen zu gedenken. Deshalb keine Frau dabei.":* Rupert Kainradl, "Wie wir die Ortsgruppe Wien gründeten," *Der Invalide,* Nov. 1928, 14, 16.

41. On the "civilizing"-aspect see Maureen Healy, "Civilizing the Soldier in Postwar Austria," in *Gender and War in Twentieth-Century Eastern Europe,* ed. Nancy M. Wingfield and Maria Bucur (Bloomington: Indiana University Press, 2006), 47-69.

42. See, besides a lot of articles the book of Sabine Kienitz, *Beschädigte Helden: Kriegsinvalidität und Körperbilder 1914–1923* (Paderborn: Schöningh, 2008); Joanna Bourke, *Dismembering the Male: Men's Bodies, Britain and the Great War* (Chicago: Reaktion Books, 1996); Eva Horn, "Die Mobilmachung der Körper," *Transit. Europäische Revue 16* (1998): 92-107; Heather R. Perry, "Brave Old World: Recycling der Kriegskrüppel während des Ersten Weltkrieges," in *Artifizielle Körper – Lebendige Technik: Technische Modellierungen des Körpers in historischer Perspektive,* ed. Barbara Orland (Zurich: Chronos, 2005), 147-58.

43. On the topic of the hero vs. victim see eg., René Schilling, "*Kriegshelden*": *Deutungsmuster heroischer Männlichkeit in Deutschland 1813–1945* (Paderborn: Schöningh, 2002); Dietrich Schubert, "Das 'harte Mal' der Waffen oder Die Darstellung der Kriegsopfer: Aspekte der Visualisierung der Gefallenen nach 1918," in *Mo(nu)mente: Formen und Funktionen ephemerer Denkmäler,* ed. Michael Diers (Berlin: Akademie, 1993), 137-52.

44. For Germany see Christian Weiß, "'Soldaten des Friedens': Die pazifistischen Veteranen und Kriegsopfer des 'Reichsbundes' und ihre Kontakte zu den französischen anciens combattants 1919–1933," in *Politische Kulturgeschichte der Zwischenkriegszeit 1918–1939,* ed. Wolfgang Hardtwig (Göttingen: Vandenhoeck & Ruprecht, 2005), 183-204.

45. Conférence internationale des associations de victimes de la guerre (mutilés, veuves, orphelins et ascendants) et anciens combatants.

46. Analyzing the German model of the care system for disabled veterans Deborah Cohen comes to a totally different result. In her opinion the German care system with its bureaucratic approach to the disabled veterans was in a way responsible for the radicalisation of the disabled veterans during the Weimar Republic: Cohen, *The War Come Home*; see also Deborah Cohen, "The War's Returns: Disabled Veterans in Britain and Germany, 1914–1939," in *The Shadows of Total War: Europe, East Asia, and the United States, 1919–1939,* ed. Roger Chickering and Stig Förster (Washington, D.C.: German Historical Institute, 2003), 113-28.

47. See Whalen, *Bitter Wounds*; Rainer Hudemann, "Kriegsopferpolitik nach den beiden

Weltkriegen," in *Staatliche, städtische, betriebliche und kirchliche Sozialpolitik vom Mittelalter bis zur Gegenwart*, ed. Hans Pohl (Stuttgart: Steiner, 1991), 269-94.

48. "*Schubwirkung*": Hudemann, "Kriegsopferpolitik nach den beiden Weltkriegen," 270.

49. StGBl 1918/20, *Vollzugsanweisung des Deutschösterreichischen Staatsrates betreffend die Unterstützung der Arbeitslosen.*

A Partnership of the Weak: War Victims and the State in the Early First Austrian Republic

Ke-chin Hsia

This essay examines one specific aspect of what actually was happening in immediate post-WWI Austria: How did war victims, a group of people most directly and adversely affected by the war's destructive power, interact with the new republican state? Understood by contemporaries to consist mainly of disabled veterans, widows and orphans, war victims were especially vulnerable—economically and physically—in postwar Austrian society. Lacking viable work abilities and opportunities in a broken economy, and identifying the origins of their suffering in previous acts of state, the future of war victims was to a large extent linked to the decisions and even the fate of the new Republic, which was experiencing its own difficult search for firm footings in the wake of the war and imperial collapse. This particular facet of state-civil society relationship presents an opportunity to explore the understudied question of how the First Republic tackled the complex issue of the war victim welfare within the larger context of its coping with the war's overwhelming domestic consequences.[1] More broadly, examining this renegotiation of state-civil society relationship without presupposing the predominance of party politics also sheds more light on the nature of the Austrian Revolution of 1918, as well as its implications for the long-term, post-imperial political development.

The focus of this essay is what I call a "partnership of the weak" in the new political space opened up by wartime upheaval and the revolutionary environment.[2] The interaction between state officials and war victims created this generally cooperative partnership under which the two sides dealt with pressing problems of physical and political survival, often as the state (and other public agencies) worked with, made concessions to, or even deputized organized war victims at the latter's urging or under serious pressure from them.

Emerging from both the events on the ground (*faits accomplis*) and a conscious strategy on the part of some officials, the partnership worked for both the new republican state (and its functionaries) and for war victims. The former needed to establish legitimacy quickly, and sought wider support among the citizenry by identifying and courting relatively receptive and symbolically significant constituencies; the latter wanted the state to provide both emergency and long-term care as well as a share of decision-making power in shaping their own future. Mutually beneficial, this partnership was somewhat formalized institutionally, and played a significant role in the political stabilization of postwar, post-revolution Austria.

Before surveying the workings and assessing the implications of this partnership, I discuss the context in which this partnership emerged and flourished. Specifically, I want to argue that the weakness of the state, or more broadly the weakness of the public authority in general in postwar Austria, compelled the authorities to acquiesce to or even approve of certain informal ways of "getting things done" on the one hand, and the inclination of war victims—though not unconditionally—to accept and work with the new Austrian Republic. Without this specific context, the relationship between the state and war victims could not have developed in such a manner.[3]

The Austrian Public Authority at a Moment of Weakness, and a Tale from Bruck an der Leitha

Near the end of the First World War, there were many indications that the Austrian state was in a deep crisis: famine in urban centers (especially Vienna),[4] the large-scale and spontaneous strikes and radicalization of Austrian workers since early 1918, the much-hated military justice system and the army's control of key necessities and industrial resources at the expenses of all others,[5] and the political class's constant scheming and secret maneuvering behind the scene.[6] The failure of the state to fulfill its part of the tacit wartime bargain with society—maintaining a basic standard of living and a stable social and moral order—led to the state's loss of credibility, as convincingly argued by Maureen Healy. This problem was no doubt aggravated by the crumbling credibility of conventional male authority figures in wartime Vienna, since, as Healy points out, those who actually manned the state administration, tenured (*pragmatisiert*) or tenure-eligible bureaucrats of all sorts, were mostly men who either did not serve on the battlefront at all, or had returned from active front service and thus did not match the profile of new martial conceptions of masculinity. They could be a liability, rather than an asset, to the imperiled state when the emperor himself was trapped as a paternalistic symbol and not able to respond sufficiently to the demands of *his* people in times of need.[7]

The imperial government was aware of the de-legitimizing process at work, and certain reforms were introduced. But the depth of the crisis made it doubtful whether institutional adjustments in the area of welfare politics, particularly the establishment of the new Ministries of Social Welfare and National Health at the end of 1917, could salvage the state's legitimacy. The relatively quiet end of the monarchy and the rather smooth transition of power in October and November 1918 could therefore be seen as a sign that the crisis had reached a high point and few wanted to fight the tide. Before Emperor Karl renounced his participation in state affairs on 11 November, the imperial bureaucracy that swore loyalty to the Habsburg monarchs had been working for or with the revolutionary government of Austria for more than two weeks,[8] and there were few instances of conflict of conscience or even principled early retirement after the end of the monarchy.[9] Even people who in their daily work embodied the falling imperial state also welcomed some kind of way out.

However, this relatively easy transition did not mean smooth sailing for the new Republic. The chaos on the street in the months after October 1918 and the persistent subsistence crisis reminded us that with many difficulties outside of their control, the state and its officials did not restore their credibility and efficacy by quickly becoming the instruments of the democratic Republic. Finding a new constitutional basis for state power or replacing government leaders did not suffice. Facing the overwhelming weight of material shortages, social and economic displacement, political uncertainty, and a very active and aggressive civil society, the state seemed to lose its paternalistic-interventionist instinct, orientation and confidence. In the sphere of welfare provision which, as mentioned earlier, was a key to the wartime de-legitimizing of the monarchy,[10] the public authorities at different levels remained generally reactive, rather than proactive, if they did take action. It may be the case that when there were more urgent and fundamental political issues, such as conflicts over borders and constitutional rule-making, social welfare initiatives took lower priorities (some notable exceptions did exist, like the eight-hour workday legislation championed by the Social Democrats). But knowing how basic provisions and welfare measures could determine the fate of a regime, officials tacitly acknowledged their moment of weakness by being responsive to new social forces.

The emergence of the war victim organization in then-border town Bruck an der Leitha was a case in point. In December 1918, some Bruck an der Leitha disabled veterans organized themselves as the local branch of the largest national war victim's organization *Zentralverband der deutschösterreichischen Kriegsbeschädigten* (hereafter the *Zentralverband*) in a rather "flat" (*sic*) meeting with an agitation expert from the *Zentralverband* Viennese headquarters attending.[11] Like any start-up interest group, the local branch needed money immediately, but its parent organization in Vienna was itself in need of funds. Bruck an der Leitha branch leaders thus turned to the local public first. With only five days' preparation, they hosted a successful New Year's Eve fundraiser that yielded 4,000K net proceeds. This successful fundraiser clearly contradicted the common perception and rhetoric among many war victims that the society-at-large was cold and indifferent to war victims' plight.[12]

Notwithstanding the "flat" first meeting, disabled returning soldiers flooded the local branch soon afterwards. Contrary to what military and other state authorities had promised, the local branch alleged that almost all the returning disabled soldiers in Bruck an der Leitha were not informed about what kind of public care provisions or post-demobilization assistance they were entitled to. Many of them were simply released, or even pushed out, from Hungarian military hospitals after the collapse of the monarchy.[13] The local branch found itself, not without satisfaction, becoming *the* clearinghouse for helpful and sometimes life-saving information. But that also resulted in an urgent need to find furnished offices to handle the rapidly increasing traffic. This time the mayor of Bruck an der Leitha stepped up and offered space and furniture. The new republican armed forces, the *Volkswehr*, also chipped in.[14]

With money raised and an office at its disposal, the local branch's leaders went to serious work. They partnered with the local Soldiers' Council (*Soldatenrat*) to procure food for immediate distribution. At the same time, the local branch hired a full-time employee who was also a disabled veteran, "of course paid with our organization's own resources," to meet the need of the increasing numbers of those seeking help. No matter how much the local branch wanted to show its independence and abilities, it did not shy away from boasting that it received subsidies from a central state-funded *Land* agency to pay for the office supplies.[15] This was not a coincidence: Talking about this good working relationship with the authorities was a way to show connections, resourcefulness, and legitimacy that could appeal to potential members and persuade those who were not war victims to work with them. Having favorable contacts with the authorities, moreover, was only the local branch's the first step in creating a niche for itself. It wanted more.

The local branch took a very proactive approach to help "undocumented" returning disabled soldiers who, with no proper identification papers (thanks to the chaotic dissolution of the monarchy), were ineligible for any public assistance, not even a set of proper civilian clothes long promised by the military. It first negotiated with the military office responsible for distributing civilian clothes to demobilized soldiers and arranged to have the "undocumented" disabled soldiers examined by the district state doctor (*Bezirksarzt*). More importantly, the local branch issued authentication papers to go with temporary certificates of disability from the district state doctor. The two documents together made the "undocumented" disabled soldiers deserving citizens again and thereby entitled to public assistance. This initiative, as the local branch claimed, helped more than 500 soldiers secure shoes, clothes, and underwear on 4 February 1919, with the said military office setting up shop in a local beer hall for a fair-like event.[16] The local branch not only scored a major success by calling attention to a serious problem, but also took the initiative and forced the authorities to endorse its solution. It stepped in not only as an advocate for its members, but also as an intermediary with screening power to determine individuals' access to public resources. More striking was the fact that the civilian and military authorities in question were willing to concede that power to the self-appointed advocate/screener.

In the meantime, the local branch began a new offensive on the political front. Wanting "to represent the interest of war victims" more forcefully, the local branch's leaders decided to have a political voice of their own and to participate directly in the municipal administration. They informed the mayor that they wanted three representatives from the local branch, and three from the local Soldiers' Council, to be added to the Bruck an der Leitha city council as regular members. The mayor balked at such a bold power grab.[17] His less-than-enthusiastic attitude was not a surprise, given the fact that soldiers' and workers' council movement (the *Rätebewegung*, a kind of Soviet movement inspired by the example of their Russian counterparts) was growing in power and influence and did not hide its aspiration to seize public power from the established authorities.[18] Some Soldiers and Workers' Councils actually did take on administrative functions with the accompanying coercive power that was supposed to be the preserve of central state or *Land* authorities.[19] Giving in to the local branch's extralegal demand would be more than a small alteration of the local balance of power. It carried a great risk in acquiescing to the first step of a possible revolutionary takeover.

However, the local branch in Bruck an der Leitha had a powerful ally in the state administration. After its leadership appealed to the district government (*Bezirkshauptmannschaft*), the latter agreed with the organized war victims' rationale for special representation in the local government, and intervened on their behalf. The district government pressured the mayor to accept a compromise allowing one representative each from the local *Zentralverband* branch and the local Soldiers' Council to join the city council.[20] The local branch thereby transformed itself into a semi-political, semi-official force with direct participation in the local administration, and this leap had the official blessing from the state administration. Being endorsed by the state authorities had an immediate positive effect: People were now more willing to respond positively to the local branch's requests. Other communities in the Bruck an der Leitha district contributed money to the local branch, and the local movie theater promised to do a monthly screening for the benefit of the local branch.[21]

After pulling off this feat, the local branch's leaders started working on their next goal: abolishing the local Invalid Office (*Invalidenamt*),[22] and transferring the office's power, such as "purchasing office supplies and paying the salaries of bureaucrats working there," to the local branch. In other words, they wanted to run official war victim services themselves. To this end they had two meetings with Dr. Franz Fahringer, the top administrator of Lower Austrian Land Commission for the Care of Homecoming Soldiers (*Landeskommission zur Fürsorge für heimkehrende Krieger*), the Land agency delegated and funded by the central government to take care of both healthy and disabled veterans' welfare once they were no longer under military jurisdiction. In Fahringer they found a sympathetic official who stated that he wanted the "Invalid Office to become a permanent agency uniting all related public efforts under its roof...[by becoming] more or less the mother of war victims [*sic*]."[23] The negotiations, with some help from the *Zentralverband* headquarters in Vienna, essentially achieved what the local branch had desired: The state would cover the operating costs of the local branch's own invalid service office and pay the salaries of its essential full-time staff of three. The state would, in addition, pick up the additional 200K per-month compensation to the district state doctor who was now providing regular clinical care for ill war victims at the behest of the local branch. It would also bankroll the local branch's project to open a second service office in Schwechat with two more employees. Without explicitly agreeing to let the local branch take over the official Invalid Office, the Land Commission basically accepted the main points of the local branch proposal.[24] A local interest group's own service office, in the end, more or less supplanted the official one, but remained beyond the direct control of the official administrative system or its chain of command. This also meant that war victim activists in Bruck an der Leitha represented not only their own interests, but also functioned as the state's contract workers addressing those same interests.

Throughout this local organization's success story, the initiative was taken by organized war victims. All the benefits and material gains for war victims were solely the local branch's doing, the source seems to suggest. The once-proud, paternalistic, and interventionist state bureaucracy as well as the local elite who used to run community politics were only reacting on the margin at this critical moment. Given the public-relations nature of the source, the heroic narrative of the local branch's achievements in *Der Invalide* should be read with a grain of salt. But it would not be a stretch to conclude that though the authorities had the most important resource—money—in hand, they were unable either to come up with their own measures to help the growing war victim population in the first place, or to effectively resist the pressure from the local interest group. Bureaucratic inertia or "turf" concerns may have played a role in official inaction or pliability. But when the Land Commission responded rather obligingly without much of a fight, it was clear that the once-dominant state apparatus and its *Länder* counterparts/deputies lacked a sense of orientation, an adequate grasp of the situation on the ground, or even a practical vision in the chaotic immediate postwar months.[25] The state authorities were ready to accommodate, even sacrifice formal power and legally-established authority to keep situations from further deteriorating, as anything for the survival of the Republic and the political class that ran it would be worth considering.

This tale from Bruck an der Leitha shows that the state's crisis of authority during 1917-1918 did not end with the Revolution of 1918 and the proclamation of the Republic. The monarchy as such was de-legitimated long before it collapsed, and the authority and credibility of its administrative apparatus, along with the imperial or even *Länder* bureaucracies that once upheld it, were severely damaged before the Republic could inherit them.

Furthermore, the rapidly growing war victim movement did not spare the new Austrian Republic of its outspoken criticisms,[26] for activists often held a somewhat contradictory view regarding the question of whether there was a legal and constitutional continuity between the new state and the old. In some instances, they argued that the post-revolutionary state inherited the debts, both moral and material, the imperial state owed to them; to careful observers, it was basically the same old state with only a different name and a new leadership team, even when many of their contemporaries emphatically denied such continuity.[27] On the other hand, they also professed their faith in the Republic as a new beginning, and expected that it could, and should, do things differently because it was a people's state, a democracy, and a better moral entity.[28] This convenient inconsistency not only gave organized war victims more room for rhetorical and tactical maneuvering, but also put the new Republic on the defensive from the very beginning. And on the defensive it was. The accommodating attitude among many state officials (both new leaders and old bureaucrats) facing war victims' activism, or even aggressiveness, suggested that the power balance between state and society was undergoing a renegotiation. In the first months of 1919, the scales seemed to be tilting toward society. Facing a rather aggressive and sometimes volatile population, the state was a relatively weak player in the postwar political arena.

The Bruck an der Leitha case also reveals a trend that became prevalent in the early years of the Republic: war victim interest groups cooperating with the public authorities in designing and operating welfare systems for themselves. The third section of this paper will return to this point. I will first discuss the state-centered mentality of war victims, which to a large extent explained why war victims, with both potential and opportunity to become radicals, were predisposed to accept the current state and willing, or even actively seeking, to work with it.

The "State-Friendly" War Victims

War victims composed approximately five to eight percent of the Austrian population in 1919,[29] but they enjoyed disproportionate attention from the state. One main reason for that was the focus of war victims' successful mobilization and organization. Despite their confusing and sometimes conflicting language, they had only one clear goal from the very beginning: making the state pay what war victims considered they were owed. War victims also talked about the duty of the fatherland to express its gratitude. But presenting themselves as the "first creditors,"[30] they were actually talking about what the state should do for them not just as tokens of gratitude, but as moral and even contractual obligations.[31]

War victims' state-centered mentality and practices were conscious choices. The justification for their many demands centered on the imperial state's war-making. The burden could be shared by many, but ultimately it was the state that was to be held responsible, because "[it] believed it could be the ruler of Central Europe within a short period of time.…believed it was called upon to punish entire peoples [*ganze Völker*] for a crime committed by two murderers, though the same state itself had committed enough crimes to atone for."[32] An example of this line of thinking can be found in the letter of a provincial widow, Mitzi Schwarz. Initially she complained about the general indifference to the plight of widows, but she left no doubt who had to make up for it:

> It is the same everywhere for widows. We are defenseless, and are treated as the dregs of society [*Auswurf der Menschheit*].…And the Father State [*sic*] is not conscious of its duty. It forgets us poor creatures who were ruined by it. But now our patience runs out—even widows have a right to live.…We want to remind the state of its duties, because things cannot go on like this anymore.[33]

It was the state's fault that one became a widow, a disabled person or an orphan, and people had the right to be compensated for by the state.

The state-centered mentality of war victims can be illustrated by another example: the meaning of "self-help" in the war victim movement. In spite of the emphasis on the individual's own effort, what war victim activists meant by "creating their own future" was not self-reliance as commonly understood. Self-help in this context meant taking matter into one's own hand and aggressively and proactively asserting one's rights, forcing the state to acknowledge these rights with all necessary means, and then using state provisions to lead an independent (at least economically) life.[34] This not only showed a state-centered thinking, but also discursively assumed the continued existence of the state that waged the war—if the state that wronged them had been dismantled, there was no one to be held responsible.

War victims' state-centered conception of "self-help" was inseparably linked with their leaders' unfavorable view of charity. To them, charity would interfere, if not defeat, the argument put forth in support of their claims on public resources. Their argument against receiving charity was based on the belief that the sacrifices of war victims must be honored and compensated in a solemn, appropriate, and just manner—accountability was the core issue. Charity, on the other hand, was tantamount to opening an escape route for those who should be responsible, according to a more radical activist.[35] From the very beginning the *Zentralverband*, the largest and in 1919 the only state-recognized national war victim's organization,[36] consistently condemned begging and reliance on charity. Its leaders pointed out that it was not only an issue of dignity, but a basic question of what state and society should do for those who suffered the most in their names. So they preferred state programs and a legislated public welfare system as a more neutral, egalitarian, and collective way to provide care that symbolized the participation of the whole society.[37] However, it must be added that this anti-charity position did not prevent war victim organizations from receiving donations or acting as an intermediary between generous benefactors and needy war victims.[38]

Focusing almost exclusively on the state also had another purpose: The state should step in where civil society had failed. Ignoring other reasons, such as economic dislocation and social unrest, that forced the society-at-large to partially withdraw from its previous active participation in providing for war victims, war victim groups complained about the "short memory" or ingratitude of the Austrian society.[39] Being exploited and then deserted was a sentiment that permeated the war victim movement's public rhetoric. The state thus became the last-resort option for war victims seeking systematic and long-term care provision. The substantial contribution civil society made to war victim welfare during the war and, to a much smaller but not negligible degree, after the war, was lost in the disappointed and angry rhetoric. Similar to post-WWI Germany, perception was more powerful in shaping attitude and action for a group of people who experienced the war's devastation directly.[40]

War victims' state-centered mentality was in part based on their conception of the state as a moral entity. According to this conception, the state had inherent responsibilities to ensure and cultivate the general welfare of all its citizens. War victim activists' ideas and expectations of the state were therefore more or less in line with the enlightened-interventionist tradition of Austrian state administration: The state had inherent responsibilities to safeguard a just order as well as to promote social improvements and economic prosperity. The individual's economic productivity and psychological well-being fell into the state's purview in this understanding,[41] especially when the damage or hindrance to physical and psychological well-being and independence were traceable to the state's own decisions and actions.

This conception can be better teased out from war victims' demand for privileged treatment vis-à-vis other disabled persons. War victims insisted that their sacrifices and losses were different. It was not enough to treat them similarly to those industrial victims with similar disabilities because "the majority of other disabled or ill persons are victims of their jobs. We, on the other hand, are not, but are *the victims of a violence that deprived us of our freedom of action and forced us to go to war; a violence, if it was still existing today, against which usual channels of asserting our claims to compensation would not be available*" (emphasis original). The civil code and its principles provided the legal basis for workers who were injured or disabled on the job to seek compensation. But from the perspective of war victims, there was no comparable legal basis or precedent for their situation.[42] Based on this reasoning, war victims disagreed with leading state officials, including Minister of Social Administration and Social Democrat Ferdinand Hanusch, who believed that "war-victim care on the whole should fall into the categories and already-existing welfare system for the handicapped and the injured."[43] They argued instead that there should be a dedicated public welfare system for them: "[W]e war victims [were] justified in demanding to be treated as a totally special group in social life."[44] The state's duty to take care of them should have a very different significance, and hence a separate system to embody it.

From the war victims' point of view, the state abused its coercive power and forced common people to go to war. Being disabled or widowed was therefore not their fault, and particularly not a result of their free choice. Contrary to the view shared by a host of their contemporaries (and some of today's historians) that soldiers fighting in World War I were laboring for an industrialized warfare in a manner much like industrial workers,[45] war victims did not see themselves as workers in an industry that produced industrialized violence and mass death.[46] They believed that their relationship to the state was not comparable to an employer-employee one, and their disabilities or losses were different from private ownership being infringed by another entity of legal or natural personality.

Instead, war victim activists argued that a person who served the state and suffered damage or service-related losses in war should be seen either as a victim of the state's exploitation and coercion (being forced to fight the war) or as unfortunate servants of a higher and collective cause (defending the fatherland and the homeland), or both. If war victims were the victims of the state's abuse, then as an ethical being the state had an existential need to make reparations to justify itself.[47] If war victims were unfortunate public servants, then the state, as an ethical being, must represent the community as a whole to support these who sacrificed for a higher, collective cause.[48] Either way, the argument as well as its assumptions put forth by war victims amounted to a demand that the state's care provision for war victims was a necessary act of redemption.

This conception also allowed war victim activists to overlook, or downplay, the problematic issue of constitutional continuity between the monarchy and the Republic. If the Republic was a total break from the monarchy, a new beginning so to speak, then what kind of guilt did it have vis-à-vis war victims? To what extent did it still owe to them in an existential way? Most leading political and legal minds of the day did not subscribe to the view that the Republic was *a*, not to mention *the*, legal successor to the monarchy, and hence did not inherit responsibilities and obligations incurred by the war-making monarchical state; the Republic was a new state in international law by virtue of the revolution from which it emerged.[49] This posed a potential problem for war victims, as their argument for preferential treatment from the state would be significantly weakened if the Republic had no inherent responsibility to redeem itself. They would become just another needy constituency competing for limited public resources.

But by invoking the state's inherent duty to people's well-being, to uphold rights, and to affirm justice, some war victim activists could make the same strong demands on the state even when the latter was not necessarily the same entity that sent them to suffer. In one unusual instance, and specifically when the Viennese leaders of the *Zentralverband* presented their first comprehensive demands to the state authorities in November 1918, they acknowledged that the Republic was trying to salvage what could be salvaged from the ruins of its imperial predecessor, "the old system 'Austria' that muddled through from time immemorial with its red-tapism (*bürokratische Zopfe*) and the notorious Article 14." Therefore on the war victim issues, "German-Austria and its current state administration is the creditor's committee of the failed former state entity (*Staatsgebilde*), and we war invalids…are its first creditors whose demands should be met with full power immediately."[50] The new Republic in this interpretation was construed as the executive body of the suffering people, and by definition had the duty to faithfully carry out its mandate—taking care of war victims to the same extent, if not more, as the failed predecessor would have to do to really redeem itself. War victims took advantage of the more expansive understanding of the state to make their case, and it helped them even when the authorities did not agree with their rationales or their views were not consistent all the time.

This moral conception of the state, moreover, entailed a strong and competent administration staffed by impartial professionals. In the Austrian political tradition, the state and *Länder* bureaucracies provided this professional and experienced staff. War victims did complain about mistreatment in the hands of bureaucrats, and correctly recognized the retaining of the same bureaucracies by the Republic despite the revolution.[51] However, they did not seek a structural revamp or a wholesale purge of the bureaucracy. Any discussion on new forms of executive power or administration was missing in the mainstream war victim movement. The *Zentralverband*, which represented almost all organized war victims at this point and was recognized officially as the main organization for all war victims,[52] concentrated on forcing the existing state and its bureaucracy to respond to its demands. It never raised the issue of radically reforming the bureaucracy, let alone the state itself. All it wanted was a more "caring" and responsive state which catered to war victims' needs, and the bureaucracy acting in a "modern spirit"—polite and efficient—which treated citizens with respect.[53]

More fundamentally, the long list of time-sensitive demands war victims made was premised on the continued functioning of the state apparatus.[54] The continued existence of the current situation was both a necessity and a given for the majority of war victims. If the state and its bureaucracy were to be constituted anew, and henceforth to have a thorough break with the past, war victims' arguments would lose the punch—it would be more difficult to hold a whole new organization accountable for what was not its doing. Some war victim activists were rather ambiguous or conflicted about whether the Republic was really that new, as we have seen earlier. But in the end they invariably returned to the theme of state's responsibility to those whose lives were negatively affected by its action.[55] Otherwise, all the talk about responsibility and duty would themselves need new justifications, and arguments for state welfare provision based on fault and reparation would be irrelevant.

The continuation of the existent state administration and it personnel was therefore discursively assumed in much of the rhetoric and demands of war victims. On a more practical level, if war victims wanted their demands to be answered satisfactorily, they also had to have a competent state as an active counterpart in their brand of interest group politics. More often than not, they sought to co-opt the state rather than dismantle it. To further undermine it would be self-defeating.

Overwhelmed state functionaries were confused and lacked resolve or authority they once enjoyed. But the majority of war victims still believed in the Austrian state and the ability and responsibility of civil servants to work for them. The very confusion, if not paralysis, of state functionaries actually created many openings to directly and effectively influence them by people who rarely had such access before the war. Despite threats implying working with radical movements (the Communists, for example), war victims did not seriously contemplate a world without a paternalistic state staffed by those experienced bureaucrats.[56] In the realm of social welfare, they even expected the state's ability to foster, organize, coordinate, and guide civil society and its private initiatives.[57] What they wanted from the state was what we can call a new citizen-oriented service ethos. As long as the state administration showed its willingness to reciprocate this rather friendly disposition and the belief in state's omnipotence, it had a constituency in favor of its survival. And in practice, the weak state and organized war victims did cooperate in a "partnership of the weak."

The Partnership of the Weak

The parliamentary democratic experiment did not automatically guarantee a free pass for the Republic and its state administration in the eyes of its demanding citizens.[58] To gain legitimacy, the Republic had to function properly and satisfy them in some way. Facing a rather aggressive population, the republican state urgently needed to take concrete actions to show its efficacy, and thereby regain trust and credibility. One obvious option was to address an issue where the previous regime's failure and the Republic's commitment could most easily be contrasted, especially when the issue had been raised with increasing political pressure and thus relevant to the Republic's own survival. In a February 1919 public meeting of Viennese war victims, Deputy Interior Minister and Social Democrat Otto Glöckel said as much to the gathered crowd: "[A]s the monarchy has placed the burden of sacrifice, especially surrendering health, on your shoulders, the free Republic will see to it that your sacrifices will be made up for to the fullest extent, and it will make sure that these sacrifices will not be in vain."[59]

War victims were, in contrast, a group who seized the initiative at the right moment. With some enterprising leaders armed with organizational talents, "the poorest of the poor" (their favorite public self-description) turned disadvantages and disability into a huge advantage—phrasing state welfare as moral imperative when the state was seeking a supportive constituency. These weaker members of society became quite aggressive when they made their claims, usually in words, sometimes with deeds, but seldom with violence.[60] Their leaders deftly used a mixture of moral arguments, appeals to sympathy (though they insisted their cause had nothing to do with sympathy—it was supposed to be a purely duty-and-right issue), and threats of radicalization (such as supporting the Communist cause, for example)[61] to force their agenda on the state while, to some extent, elbowing out other competitors to claim a larger share of public resources.[62]

The moral claims of these weaker members of society met no strong public challenge. Criticism was usually based on the perception of comparative deprivation, or the possible over-burdening of state finances in certain war victim welfare practices, but not from the premise that war victims should not be given long-term public aid and certain degree of power over its administration.[63] Thanks in part to this advantageous position in the discursive realm, war victims could achieve extensive co-determination power that warranted the name of "partnership" with the state.

For example, a *Zentralverband* leader publicly and quite indignantly talked about the potential use of violence to boycott or overturn the hated Military Invalid Superarbitration Commission (*Superarbitrierungskommission*) procedure after war victims discovered that the commission members who decided their degree of disability, and hence the amount of their pensions (under the old military pension regulations), were the same people who "overzealously" sent them to war in the first place.[64] They especially resented the presence and influence of Ministry of Finance representatives, whom they believed were determined to pay war victims as little as possible.[65] Not long after this public threat, the procedures and the composition of the commissions were changed under the agreement reached between organized war victims and the authorities. From mid-February 1919 representatives and doctors sent by the war victim organization sat on all Military Invalid Arbitration Commissions with an equal number of state appointees, and participated in determining the degree of individual's loss of earning power, which was the most important factor in calculating the benefits awarded to each disabled veteran or their dependents. War victim representatives even enjoyed tie-breaking power in commission voting.[66] The state also invited *Zentralverband* representatives to participate in the inter-ministerial commission on war victim affairs. Through this commission the *Zentralverband* gained formal entry into the decision-making process, and participated in the drafting of the Invalid Compensation Law of 1919 (*Invalidenentschädigungsgesetz*, IEG), the future cornerstone of war victim welfare system, before the draft law was forwarded to the Constituent National Assembly.[67]

In light of the successes war victims had with welfare legislations and many other issues, these "weaker members" of society successfully made good use of their physical weakness to become symbolically and materially powerful. But their success depended to a large extent on both the weakness and the willingness of the state in the immediate postwar period. Beyond the immediate and strong political motive to placate (potentially) volatile constituencies, some state leaders also believed that the Republic's viability was tied to its citizens being given the opportunity to contribute with all their creative and working power—their economic independence in addition to political freedom.[68] Ferdinand Hanusch, the first Social Minister of the Republic, argued that "to hire war-disabled employees [was] not only a result of humane considerations for broken livelihoods, but a social obligation, because the society would lose all their productive power—their capabilities may be reduced but still [were] serviceable and able to contribute."[69] War victims deserved special attention, he seemed to say, because they possessed some left-over productivity that was needed, and not necessarily because of those moral concerns war victims represented.

Hanusch's rationale for state welfare intervention focused on harnessing war victims' economic productivity, which could lead to the economic independence war victims long desired. But it was directed more towards strengthening and consolidating the Republic as the ultimate end and equated war victims with other disabled workers. Hanusch did not take up organized war victims' arguments about why they should get the state's extra care. His rationale was geared more toward the future, while war victims' more moral arguments put an emphasis on the past. No wonder Hanusch was criticized early on by war victim leaders for this position, for it was potentially detrimental to war victims' claim to special status.[70]

But the underlying principle of Hanusch's thinking neither contravened nor veered far from the aforementioned enlightened-interventionist tradition, and it echoed war victims' belief in the state's intrinsic responsibilities in cultivating and ensuring the welfare of its citizens. Preserving war victims' productive power was just the state doing what was expected. Hanusch's was a language war victims understood and shared, as we have discussed in the previous section. The state and its leaders may have had different reasons from those of war victims when entering into a partnership. Some of them were obviously politically self-interested, while others drew the ire of war victim leaders. But under the revolutionary circumstances and with strong democratic aspirations, the two sides still had enough common ground, both on matters of principle and of material interest, to work with each other. The same policy measure could be argued for in many different ways.

Still, "the partnership of the weak" had to work for both partners and brought in concrete results so that it could emerge in the first place and be maintained. In the aforementioned Bruck an der Leitha story, the state (through district government), *Land*, and local authorities responded favorably, even to the degree of willing to relinquish some of their power, to the local war victims organization to prevent any trouble. On the national level, the central state was also eager to have war victims, organized as a single block, on its side. Strengthening the organized war victims, if they became an ally or at least remained a friendly neutral, was helping the state itself.

When Hanusch sent his ministry's 1919-1920 fiscal year war victim welfare expenditure estimates to the Finance Ministry, he added an unusual item to the budget: subsidies to war victim organizations totaling 300,000K. The subsidies were to help war victim organizations covering their general costs and would come with no prescribed uses. Comparing to the amount that would be needed to pay for inflation-adjusted pensions under the IEG, 351.21 million K, it was only a small amount. But apparently Hanusch felt the need to justify this specific item. He pointed out to the Finance Ministry that the state welfare provision had to be complemented by the work of war victim organizations; otherwise it would lose orientation and focus. Moreover, "[o]nly with the support of the will of the greatest majority of invalids will it be possible to effectively counter the unjustified wishes of individuals and representatives of small groups. The existence of a strong organization is more important, as individual invalids are all too easily exploited by unsatisfactory elements with political agitation....[and become a burden for society and the state]."[71] It was not an exaggeration to say that a strong and well-organized war victim movement was more a help than a threat to some officials at this specific moment. The state-centered and moderate attitude of mainstream war victims certainly contributed significantly to this political calculation.

Sponsoring the war victim movement was not a brand-new policy, however. The Ministry of Social Administration began to subsidize the *Zentralverband* (with an immediate payment of 10,000K) and its periodical *Der Invalide* in November 1918 upon the request from war victim leaders.[72] State officials publicly urged disabled war veterans to join the *Zentralverband* to make it strong, explaining that the *Zentralverband* could help war victims receive public assistance in a more timely fashion and protect individuals from perishing.[73] Indeed the state was willing to subsidize the *Zentralverband* for these purposes almost from the beginning. On 4 January, 1919, the *Zentralverband* requested an immediate subsidy of 60,000 to 80,000K, so that it could hand out cash to needy war victims who came to the organization for help. Within a week the Social Ministry approved a subsidy of 50,000K, which was paid through an intermediary bank before 13 January.[74] During the 24 March, 1919, meeting of the aforementioned inter-ministerial commission, the Social Ministry even authorized a same-day 5,000K subsidy after *Zentralverband* representatives asked for funds to facilitate its upcoming national conference that would discuss the draft IEG.[75] When several much smaller splinter war victim organizations emerged around or after the passage of IEG in mid-1919, Hanusch and Interior Ministry officials personally intervened and tried to broker a compromise that would lead to the re-creation of a united and all-inclusive war victim interest group.[76] The state desperately needed to attract this natural constituency to solidify itself, and from the very beginning it was willing to do so by making significant concessions.

Cooperating with war victims through their organization brought an added advantage to the state: It became a major way to reconnect with this segment of citizens after wartime alienation, distrust, and revolutionary confusion. Beyond gestures of goodwill, the state had to find ways to interact with this alienated, but also relatively friendly, group of citizens/clients. Before it set out to relate to and court war victims, the state had to know who and where they were. But obviously the state had no reliable answer for either of these two questions,[77] and it implicitly admitted this serious problem. On 23 April, 1919, the Ministry of Social Administration wrote to the *Zentralverband* (signed by Hanusch), "[the ministry]...believes that a fair distribution of the aid would be best carried out by the organized invalids themselves..."[78] Therefore, before war victims actually began to receive new IEG pensions, for which they could only apply after the law went into effect on 1 July, 1919, the state deputized the *Zentralverband* to perform the task of administering a massive 2 million K stopgap project of distributing emergency aid to war victims (*Lebensmittelaktion* of 1919).

In the process of implementing this program, many war victims were mobilized, registered, and organized with the incentive of receiving packages of food, paid for by the state and administered through "their own people" in the *Zentralverband*. The state, on the other hand, got a chance to know this potentially significant constituency, which could number well above 300,000 (including orphans and other categories of dependents),[79] because it did closely monitor the *Zentralverband*'s actions and required the latter to submit detailed reports about the processes and results of the *Lebensmittelaktion* of 1919. Deputizing state power thus prepared war victims for future state welfare measures without overtly giving the state's power away. A few telling numbers can reinforce this point: During the first installment of the *Lebensmittelaktion* in May 1919, 20,263 people received assistance in Vienna, which translated into nearly 17,000 members who were participating in the project.[80] The second installment followed immediately. This time the number of *Zentralverband* members receiving packages jumped to 40,000 in just one month,[81] which translated into another 20,000-plus constituents—and potential supporters of the new

Republic—being identified and becoming beneficiaries of the state (and the *Zentralverband*, of course).

Through the enabling agent of the *Zentralverband*, the state could re-establish a semi-direct connection to individual war victims in a positive way. This was because the state was delivering goods and services, most importantly in the form of foodstuffs in times of need. The *Lebensmittelaktion* also worked symbolically among the general population, as this program could substantiate the claim of crucial differences that distinguished the new Republic—a "social" one—from the previous regime. Having a comparatively moderate war victim organization to carry out the program also helped to cover the state's left flank when radicals from the far Left were a significant threat, as people would flock to join the *Zentralverband* instead of turning to radicals.

The "partnership of the weak" also ensured the status of war victims as privileged wards of the state, giving them a better position to compete for public resources. This satisfied one of their core demands: the power to control their own fate in an uncertain world. On the policy and administrative side, war victim representatives already sat on almost all committees and commissions that dealt with invalid affairs, and they actively participated in the meetings of the inter-ministerial commission for war victim affairs, which was instrumental in all important war victim-related government policies and legislations.[82] By pressuring the authorities and being part of the decision-making process, moreover, the *Zentralverband* made sure that its members would be considered for existing or soon-to-be created positions in state welfare agencies before others.[83] They even successfully put some of their leaders on state payrolls, arguing that as resident interest group representatives in certain government offices, they had assisted officials by offering advice to war victims coming for information or help and thus contributing to the discharge of official functions.[84]

In sum, letting organized war victims to share some power was the state's productive way to "buy" support from a group that was politically significant. In a passionate plea to Linz war victims for their continued support for the Republic, a Social Democrat parliamentarian emphasized that in spite of deep fiscal crisis, the passage of the IEG in itself was a proof that the state would fulfill "one of its primary duties"—the compensation of war victims.[85] Making concessions to organized war victims was simultaneously a partial solution to the pressing subsistence crisis (for some), a symbolic exercise to (re)gain legitimacy and hence popular support with the electorate, and a political move to fend off looming competing appeals from those who envisioned a very different politico-social order. It was telling, then, that after pointing out inadequacies and unfulfilled promises, a war victim leader fumed in late 1919: "during the time of Communism the *Zentralverband* was an important prop for the government....This government would not have survived had the *Zentralverband* declared itself communist. We thought we could take in the thanks of the government (*den Dank der Regierung werden einheimsen können*)."[86] Now that the threat from the Communists receded, some wondered if the state would honor all its promises.

In the end, the general effect of this partnership was that even when the state could not fulfill all war victims' demands, war victim groups expressed a kind of half-reluctant acceptance of what they could gain from the partnership. A war victim leader even thought that many war victims were too accommodating and too uncritical of what the state authorities had offered.[87] The success of the "partnership of the weak" had allowed some early practices, such as client participation in welfare administration, to become operative principles in the long-term welfare system. Even after the Republic's high politics entered into a new phase that was not conducive to participatory or partnership practices, some vestiges of the old partnership arrangements, such as the composition of the board of the War Victim Fund under the Ministry of Social Administration,[88] were still present, though the more extensive partnership itself was not renewed in a substantial way after 1920.

Conclusion

A relatively peaceful unfolding of events marked the Austrian Revolution of 1918. But a seemingly smooth transition from monarchy to Republic was a mixed blessing. It held out the promises of liberal democracy without shedding much blood or causing more suffering, but it also lacked a clear, dramatic, and sweeping departure from the past that would have made it easier to convince the population that there was a substantial (and beneficial, of course) difference between the old regime and the new. In addition to facing significant material difficulties that continued or even worsened since the last years of the war, the republican state was working under the same persistent authority crisis that had greatly undermined the monarchy.

On the other hand, the wartime experience on the homefront and various forms of political mobilization since 1917 had not only opened up a much larger political space, but also schooled and encouraged the general population to take advantage of that space in a more aggressive way.

Previously existed only as an administrative or legal category on the fringe of political consciousness, war victims spontaneously and quickly materialized into a significant social group. Seeking to defend their interests and assert their rights in a time of uncertainties, members from that group further organized themselves into a formidable social movement. The second section of this essay points out that the mainstream war victims were mostly moderate, "state-friendly" and predisposed to the Republic. This provided a necessary precondition for the close cooperation between war victims and public authorities on different levels.

When the credibility and coercive ability of the state were in short supply in the early Republic, Austrian war victims capitalized on the opportunity. In the cases of Bruck an der Leitha and the Viennese *Lebensmittelaktion*, they became a kind of contractor running the state's welfare functions for their own benefit. Clients of public welfare became agents of state. State authorities resigned themselves to a more reactive or supervisory role, while war victims obtained state resources and the authority to distribute these resources on their own terms. In the process, they also established some legitimacy in further participating in policy-making process and sharing administrative power with state authorities.

The partnership of the weak, though declined after a political normalization process set in over the course from late 1919 through 1920, contributed significantly to that same stabilization of the post-revolution Austrian politics. The majority of war victims aligned themselves firmly with the new democratic Republic. The Communists' deliberate efforts in 1919 to recruit them did not succeed, even when war victims were very visible in two attempted putsches in spring 1919.[89] Though in July 1919 the Vienna Police President, Johannes Schober, singled out war victims along with the unemployed and returning soldiers as especially susceptible to Communist agitation,[90] leading war victim activists from the *Zentralverband*, on their part, advocated a moderate, sober, and practical approach to secure their interests. They came out hard against what they saw as dangerous, irresponsible, and immoral Communist actions.[91] They chose to blame local communities or district officials for what they considered mismanagement or suspicious decisions at the expense of war victims, accusing those officials engaging in treasonous behavior by favoring privileged bigwigs; but they spared the Republic per se and its central administration when the radical Left's recruiting efforts went into high gear.[92] Later, in a tone more of mourning than of anger or disgust, they put the blame on the victorious Powers for the demoralizing peace settlements of St. Germain, but not on the Republic or its democratic government that accepted them. They preached solidarity and hard work on the part of war victims ("rallying to the organization!")—despite obvious disappointment and frustration—in facing the upcoming difficulties the peace settlements would bring about.[93]

This moderate approach was ultimately effective in terms of political stabilization; the majority of war victims did not follow the radicals. They complained and they threatened to withdraw their support repeatedly. But ultimately they remained loyal to the Republic and its parliamentary-democratic government. The discontent and frustration against the new welfare system, which was built in a short period of time thanks largely to their activism, did not explode into mass disillusion. War victims almost ascetically and heroically accepted what they could get from it. By forging a partnership with the state, they became stakeholders in the new system. Rocking the boat too much was not a real option for them.

On a different level, the partnership of the weak also signaled a long-term development in the Austrian political culture. The collapse of the Habsburg Monarchy was not only the end of a dynastic multinational political entity, but also a realignment of social-political forces. The creation of institutions for a liberal democratic state, despite ups and downs in the following three decades, has been argued as one of the most important of the Austrian Revolution's long-lasting achievements.[94] If we take a closer look at how the state confronted some of the consequences of the First World War, there were other new signs in the political culture anticipating Austrian political development in the next several decades; that is, both formal and informal cooperation between the state and interest groups to meet various challenges to political and social stability.[95] In other words, the case of war victim politics foreshadowed a state-interest group collaborative model in crisis prevention and management that became the norm later.

The phenomenon of partnership between organized war victims and the state highlighted the importance of the "intermediaries," powerful interest groups, as a stabilizing mechanism in immediate postwar Austria. Even if the institutionalization and formalization of the "partnership of the weak" under discussion was partial and limited,[96] it shared the same basic spirit with the parallel establishment, systemization, or strengthening of occupational-industrial "chambers" and other early "social partnership" arrangements.[97] This suggests that the newly democratizing Austrian state's "way to do business" was not necessarily directly with its citizens, but with socio-economic interest groups.[98] This also suggests that in the wake of the Revolution of 1918, the Austrian state was willing to reinforce civil society, especially in assisting and taking advantage of the already ongoing organizational build-up, integration and centralization, as a price worth paying to regain control of the situation. Given the fact that there were social groups ready to play the part, this intermediary-heavy political culture ensured that the "long shadow of the state" would persist in spite of the state's obvious moment of weakness, aggressive socio-political forces, and a democratic revolution.[99]

The tendency to favor organized social and economic interests in politics paid early dividends by keeping war victims from radicalizing in the first years of the Republic. With intervening trials and errors, this modus operandi went on to play an even more significant role in Austria's next postwar era after 1945.

Notes

1. Scholarly research on this topic is still at the beginning stage. An overview in English can be found in Verena Pawlowsky and Harald Wendelin, "Government Care of War Widows and Disabled Veterans after World War I" in this volume. Barbara Hoffmann's *Kriegsblinde in Österreich* (Graz: Verein zur Förderung der Forschung von Folgen nach Konflikten und Kriegen, 2006) has a narrow focus on the ca. 300 "war-blinded persons." Maureen Healy's insightful essay, "Civilizing the Soldier in Postwar Austria," in *Gender and War in Twentieth-Century Eastern Europe*, ed. Nancy M. Wingfield and Maria Bucur (Bloomington: Indiana University Press, 2006), 47-69, includes disabled veterans in discussing the wider issue of the integration (or the lack thereof) of former soldiers in the early First Republic. I am completing a dissertation entitled "The Scar of War: War Victims and Politics in Interwar Austria" that will discuss war victim politics in its various aspects within the larger postwar context.

I would like to thank Margarete Grandner, Jeremy King, Heather Perry, Aviel Roshwald, Iryna Vushko, Tara Zahra, and members of the Modern Russian and European History Workshop at the University of Chicago for commenting on parts or earlier versions of this essay.

2. Gabriella Hauch touches on this new political space from the vantage point of women's political participation in "Welche Welt? Welche Politik? Zum Geschlecht in Revolte, Rätebewegung, Parteien und Parlament," in *Das Werden der Ersten Republik: ... der Rest ist Österreich*, Vol. 1, ed. Helmut Konrad and Wolfgang Maderthaner (Vienna: Carl Gerold's Sohn, 2008), 317-26.

3. A note of clarification: in this essay "the state" refers generally to the central state (and its administrative apparatus) in Vienna and its subordinate agencies in the *Länder*, such as district governments (*Bezirkshauptmannschaften*). War victims, however, did not always make clear distinctions between the central state administration and those of the *Länder*; at least in some cases, by "state" they meant all public authorities that were part of a particular political order. It is therefore difficult to maintain a perfectly consistent and immaculate usage of the term "the state" in this essay.

4. Maureen Healy, *Vienna and the Fall of the Habsburg Empire: Total War and Everyday Life in World War I* (Cambridge: Cambridge University Press, 2004), esp. ch. 1.

5. On internal unrests and growing problems of troop reliability, see the classic Richard G. Plaschka et al., *Innere Front: Militärassistenz, Widerstand und Umsturz in der Donaumonarchie 1918* (Munich: R. Oldenbourg, 1974); on the draconian military justice applied to civilians, see Oswald Überegger, *Der andere Krieg: Die Tiroler Militärgerichtsbarkeit im Ersten Weltkrieg* (Innsbruck: Wagner, 2002) and the latest discussion in Jonathan Gumz, *The Resurrection and Collapse of Empire in Habsburg Serbia, 1914-1918* (Cambridge: Cambridge University Press,

2009), 105-41; on the military leadership's domination of wartime administration, see Joseph Redlich, *Österreichische Regierung und Verwaltung im Weltkrieg* (Vienna and New Haven: Hölder-Pichler-Tempsky and Yale University Press, 1925), esp. 113-56; on the military's hoarding of foodstuffs at the expense of the homefront, see Gumz, *The Resurrection and Collapse of Empire in Habsburg Serbia*, 176-92.

6. John W. Boyer, *Culture and Political Crisis in Vienna: Christian Socialism in Power, 1887-1918* (Chicago: University of Chicago Press, 1995), ch. 7.

7. Healy, *Vienna and the Fall of the Habsburg Empire*, ch. 6 on the dangerous implications of changing (and changed) conceptions of authority for homefront men and imperial paternalism.

8. Österreichisches Staatsarchiv (hereafter abbreviated as ÖStA), Archiv der Republik (hereafter abbreviated as AdR), Bundeskanzleramt (hereafter abbreviated as BKA), Staatsratsprotokolle and Kabinettsratsprotokolle, esp. October to December 1918, passim. I did not find serious discussion on the reliability of the existing bureaucracy.

9. On career bureaucrats' willingness to work for the new order, see Walter Goldinger, "Verwaltung und Bürokratie," in *Österreich 1918-1938: Geschichte der Ersten Republik*, Vol. 1, ed. Erika Weinzierl and Kurt Skalnik (Graz: Styria, 1983), 195-96.

10. In addition to the cited Healy work on the state's failure to deliver its part of the wartime bargain (see especially "Conclusion" in *Vienna and the Fall of the Habsburg Empire*), I also show in my upcoming dissertation's Chapter 1 that through successive prewar legislations and wartime systematic build-up, the Cisleithanian state had practically made an issue of political legitimacy out of its performance on welfare provision for the dependents of mobilized soldiers and war victims.

11. "Aus den Ortsgruppen: Tätigkeitsbericht der Ortsgruppe Bruck an der Leitha," in *Der Invalide* 2.5, 1 Mar. 1919, 5-6. The most important sources for organized war victims' activities and opinions in the early years were the *Zentralverband*'s biweekly newspaper *Der Invalide* and documents scattered in ÖStA AdR Bundesministerium für soziale Verwaltung (hereafter abbreviated as BMfsV), Kriegsbeschädigtenfürsorge (hereafter abbreviated as KBF).

12. For example, Karl Burger, "Der Invalide," *Der Invalide* 1.1, Nov. 1918, 1; Dr. H. H., "Neujahr, wir und die Gesellschaft," *Der Invalide* 2.1, 1 Jan. 1919, 1; K. Sch., "Der Kriegsbeschädigte Arbeiter," *Der Invalide* 2.4, 15 Feb. 1919, 4. Mitzi Schwarz, "Witwenlos," *Der Invalide* 2.14, 15 Jul. 1919, 2-3. Another counter-example was Archduke Salvator's 10,000K donation to Amstetten's organized war victims, Karl Grundei, "Meine Urlaubsreise," *Der Invalide* 2.16, 15 Aug. 1919, 6.

13. On emergency measures to make up for this big hole, see for example ÖStA AdR BMfsV KBF Karton (hereafter abbreviated as K) 1360 10878/1918; on the alleged Hungarian nonchalance, "Aus den Ortsgruppen: Tätigkeitsbericht der Ortsgruppe Bruck an der Leitha," 5.

14. "Aus den Ortsgruppen: Tätigkeitsbericht der Ortsgruppe Bruck an der Leitha," 5. Local authorities offering space to organized war victims was not unusual. For example, the *Zentralverband*'s Vienna 12th District Local Branch was housed in the 12th district's Magistratisches Bezirksamt building on Schönbrunnerstraße 259, "Aus den Ortsgruppen: Wien XII," *Der Invalide* 2.23, 1 Dec. 1919, 5.

15. "Aus den Ortsgruppen: Tätigkeitsbericht der Ortsgruppe Bruck an der Leitha," 5.

16. Ibid.

17. Ibid.

18. Hans Hautmann, *Geschichte der Rätebewegung in Österreich, 1918-1924* (Vienna: Europaverlag, 1987).

19. Alfred Ableitinger, "Grundlegung der Verfassung," in *Österreich 1918-1938*, Vol. 1, 161.

20. "Aus den Ortsgruppen: Tätigkeitsbericht der Ortsgruppe Bruck an der Leitha," 5.

21. Ibid., 6.

22. Invalid Offices were planned and set up by imperial government in 1918 as part of the effort to build a comprehensive war victim welfare system. Every district (*politischer Bezirk*), or in exceptional cases, several districts together, should have one Invalid Office under the control of Land Commission for the Care of Homecoming Soldiers. They constituted a department within each district government. See ÖStA AdR BMfsV KBF K1359 6544/1918.

23. "Aus den Ortsgruppen: Tätigkeitsbericht der Ortsgruppe Bruck an der Leitha," 5-6.

24. Ibid.

25. See also John W. Boyer's short discussion on the "sense of shock and trauma" among some officials during the immediate postwar months in "Silent War and Bitter Peace: The Revolution of 1918 in Austria," *Austrian History Yearbook 34* (2003): 3-4.

26. I discuss the spontaneous, and in most cases non-partisan rise of war victim movement more fully in the Chapter 2 of my dissertation. For contemporary reports, see for example, "Versammlung im Verbandsheim," *Der Invalide* 1.2, Dec. 1918, 2-3; A. v. Sch. "Der Zentralverband der deutschösterreichischen Kriegsbeschädigten: Werden, Aufgabe und Organisation," *Der Invalide* 2.1, 1 Jan. 1919, 2-3; "Der Ausschuß und seine bisherige Tätigkeit," *Der Invalide* 2.2, 15 Jan. 1919, 1-3. On the mobilization of widows following the passage of *Invalid Compensation Law* in April 1919, see, for example, "Aus den Ortsgruppen: Wien XVI," *Der Invalide* 2.11, 1 Jun. 1919, 3; and "Aus den Ortsgruppen: Generalversammlung der Ortsgruppe und Bezirksstelle Gmunden," *Der Invalide* 2.12, 15 Jun. 1919, 6.

27. Hans Kelsen, one of the architects of the Constitution of 1920, had emphasized the constitutional dissociation and discontinuity of the Republic from the monarchy in his "Die Verfassung Deutschösterreichs," *Jahrbuch des öffentlichen Rechtes der Gegenwart 9* (1920): 247-49. This view was made official in Article 1 of the *Gesetz vom 21. Oktober 1919 über die Staatsform* (Staatsgesetzblatt 1919/Nr. 484): "Deutschösterreich ... ist eine demokratische Republik unter dem Namen 'Republik Österreich.' *Die Republik Österreich übernimmt jedoch—unbeschadet der im Staatsvertrage von St. Germain auferlegten Verpflichtungen—keinerlei Rechtsnachfolge nach dem ehemaligen Staate Österreich* [my emphasis], das ist den 'im Rechtsrate vertretenen Königreichen und Ländern.'"

28. See, for example, Hunold, "Volk in Not!" *Der Invalide* 2.11, 1 Jun. 1919, 1.

29. The early estimate put the total number of war victims at around 300,000. See K. Sch. "Der Kriegsbeschädigte Arbeiter," 3-4. The first postwar official population count was 6,067,430 as of 31 January 1920, according to *Statistisches Handbuch für die Republik Österreich 1* (1920): 8. The government's high estimate of *Invalid Compensation Law of 1919* beneficiaries were 100,000 disabled veterans, 80,000 children of disabled veterans, 125,000 widows, and 225,000 orphans, which meant that more than 8 percent of the total population could be qualified clients, ÖStA AdR BMfsV KBF K1366 12415/1919. See Chap. 2 of my dissertation for a more detailed discussion on the size of the war victim population.

30. "Denkschrift der Foderungen der Kriegsbeschädigten," *Der Invalide* 1.1, Nov. 1918, 3.

31. Burger, "Der Invalide," 1-2.

32. A. K. "Einige Worte an die Kameraden," *Der Invalide* 1.2, 15 Dec. 1918, 1.

33. Schwarz, "Witwenlos," 2-3.

34. From the seasoned war victim organizer Weißsteiner's talk in a Hietzing local branch meeting, "Aus den Ortsgruppen," *Der Invalide* 2.15, 1 Aug. 1919, 8.

35. "Beschlagnahme oder Besteuerung der Kriegsgewinne?" *Der Invalide* 2.19, 1 Oct. 1919, 1-2.

36. ÖStA AdR BMfsV KBFK1364 4580/1918, K1366 13136/1919, K1367 21310/1919.

37. Dr. H. H., "Neujahr, wir und die Gesellschaft," 1-2. The Tyrolean war victim organization declined local *Volkswehr*'s offer to host a ball for their benefit on the ground that "[w]e ... totally do not agree with the basic idea behind this kind of charity events, because our position is that we are not a beggars' association, and we want our demands to have a solid legal grounding," "Aus den Ortsgruppen: Landes-Vollversammlung des Vereines der 'Kriegsinvaliden Deutsch-Tirols,'" *Der Invalide* 2.6, 15 Mar. 1919, 5. On organized war victims' opposition to begging, see "Die Kriegsbeschädigten und der Straßenbettel," *Der Invalide* 2.19, 1 Oct. 1919, 4.

38. For example, "Ein Tag in der Schutzstelle für Kriegerwitwen und -Waisen," *Der Invalide* 2.19, 1 Oct. 1919, 2-3. For *Zentralverband*'s charity broker role (connecting help-seekers with potential benefactors), see the example in Die Schutzstelle für Kriegerwitwen und -Waisen, "Beschäftigungsraum für Kriegerwaisen," *Der Invalide* 2.19, 1 Oct. 1919, 3.

39. The complaint of being forgotten or simply ignored after the war was over was copious, especially in the *Der Invalide* coverage on local war victim organization meetings. For more articulate complaints, see for example Dr. H. H., "Neujahr, wir und die Gesellschaft," 1-2.

40. Richard Bessel, *Germany after the First World War* (Oxford: Clarendon, 1993), 251-53, 263-84.

41. A. v. Sch. "Der Zentralverband der deutschösterreichischen Kriegsbeschädigten," 2-3.

42. Dr. H. H., "Neujahr, wir und die Gesellschaft," 1.

43. Ibid. More on Hanusch's thinking in the next section.

44. Ibid.

45. See, for example, Eric J. Leed's discussion in his *No Man's Land: Combat and Identity in World War I* (Cambridge: Cambridge University Press, 1979), esp. 73-97, 120-23.

46. K. Sch., "Die Superarbitrierungskommissionen und wir Invaliden," *Der Invalide* 2.3, 1 Feb. 1919, 5-6.

47. Hunold, "Volk in Not!" 1.

48. For example, "Aus den Ortsgruppen: Wien III," *Der Invalide* 2.19, 1 Oct. 1919, 8; Walter Rentmesiter, "Zur Invalidenfrage," *Der Invalide* 2.24, 15 Dec. 1919, 1-2.

49. See note 27, and Boyer, "Silent War and Bitter Peace," 3.

50. "Denkschrift der Forderungen der Kriegbeschädigten," 3.

51. For example, B... "Die Pensionliquidatur," *Der Invalide* 2.16, 15 Aug. 1919, 9-10; "Ein Tag in der Schutzstelle für Kriegerwitwen und -Waisen," 2-3.

52. The *Zentralverband* claimed it had 170,000 members in A. v. Sch., "Der Zentralverband der deutschösterreichischen Kriegsbeschädigten," 2-3. The state authorities had a lower estimate at 100,000 in October 1919, after the fracturing of the *Zentralverband*. See ÖStA AdR BMfsV KBF K1368 29149/1919. The *Zentralverband*'s status of being the only war victim organization that enjoyed partnership co-determination rights ended in 1920. See, for example, ÖStA AdR BMfsV KBF K1370 63/1920.

53. Robert B..., "Zeit ist Geld," *Der Invalide* 2.13, 1 Jul. 1919, 3-4.

54. See for example, the 22-point demand in "Denkschrift der Forderungen der Kriegsbeschädigten," 3-4.

55. For example, Hunold, "Volk in Not!" 1.

56. Vague threats: Oberleutnant H. Kauders, "Aufklärungen über die 'Zuwendung an

Kriegsbeschädigte,'" *Der Invalide* 2.2, 15 Jan. 1919, 5; more concrete: "Aus den Ortsgruppen: Wien, Protokoll der Sitzung des Landesverbandes Niederösterreich...," *Der Invalide* 2.24, 15 Dec. 1919, 4-6.

57. A. v. Sch., "Der Zentralverband der deutschösterreichischen Kriegsbeschädigten," 4.

58. Polizeidirektion Wien to Staatsamt für Inneres, 17 November 1919, ÖStA AdR BKA/allgem. Inneres 22 K4860 42409/1919.

59. "Aus den Ortsgruppen: Generalversammlung der Ortsgruppe Wien am 9. Februar 1919," 7.

60. On war victims' demonstrations, see, for example, ÖStA AdR BKA/allgem-Inneres 15/3 K2435 2104/1919, and AdR BKA/allgem. Inneres 22 K5099 18369/1920 incident in Linz.

61. The head of the *Zentralverband* made a public threat in the presence of several high-level government officials in a large rally of Viennese war victims, "Aus den Ortsgruppen: Generalversammlung der Ortsgruppe Wien am 9. Februar 1919," *Der Invalide* 2.4, 15 Feb. 1919, 6. A strong barrage of threats forced ministerial officials to adopt a conciliatory and at times pleading tone in another big rally, "Aus den Ortsgruppen: Wien, Protokoll der Sitzung des Landesverbandes Niederösterreich...," 4-6.

62. According to a *Zentralverband* representative, one-sixth of the annual national budget for the 1919-1920 fiscal year would be devoted to war victim welfare-related expenses, "Aus den Ortsgruppen: Generalversammlung der Ortsgruppe und Bezirksstelle Gmunden," 6-7. An example of successfully forcing their way onto other interest groups' turf, see H... "Kleine Mitteilungen: Trafikantenversammlung," *Der Invalide* 2.12, 15 Jun. 1919, 4. See also ÖStA AdR BKA/allgem. Inneres 22 K5067 23892/1919 and 25248/1919 on occupying spaces that were already designated for other uses.

63. About possible over-burdening state finances by certain welfare practices, see Finance Ministry's criticisms in ÖStA AdR BMfsV KBF K1367 22894/1919. Tobacconists' Association fought hard to prevent its members' concessions from being revoked to make way for war victim applicants. See Burger, "Trafiken!" *Der Invalide* 2.4, 15 Feb. 1919, 2. There was detectable opposition from the business circles against the proposed compulsory hiring quota reserved for disabled veterans. See, for example, Karl Grundei, "Ein Jahr!" *Der Invalide* 2.22, 15 Nov. 1919, 3.

64. K. Sch., "Die Superarbitrierungskommissionen und wir Invaliden," 5-6.

65. Ibid., 5. In fact, as the Republic reactivated Military Invalid Superarbitration Commissions after 19 November 1918, two non-military members were added to each commission. ÖStA AdR BMfsV KBF K1364 1290/1918.

66. Dr. Hollitscher, "Vollzugsanweisung des Deutschösterreichischen Staatsrates vom 12. Februar, betreffend Abänderungen und Ergänzungen der Superarbitrierungsvorschriften," *Der Invalid*e 2.6, 15 Mar. 1919, 1-2. Before the said public warning, reform in this matter had been discussed by state officials. See ÖStA AdR BMfsV KBF K1365 593/1919, 1469/1919. The public warning was obviously a strategy to pressure the authorities to move immediately.

67. Representatives from the *Zentralverband* were present in both the 30 December 1918 preparatory meeting and the first official meeting on 10 January 1919. They enjoyed voting power in the commission deliberation process. ÖStA AdR BMfsV KBF K1364 4580/1918, K1365 988/1919, K1367 7603/1919.

68. For example, Ferdinand Hanusch, "Ein Geleitwort," in Ludwig Brügel, *Soziale Gesetzgebung in Österreich von 1848 bis 1918* (Vienna: Franz Deuticke, 1919), viii.

69. "Entlassung von Kriegsbeschädigten Staatsangestellten: Staatssekretär Hanusch an den Zentralverband der deutschösterreichischen Kriegsbeschädigten am 30. Jänner 1919," *Der Invalide* 2.4, 15 Feb. 1919, 5.

70. Dr. H. H., "Neujahr, wir und die Gesellschaft," 1.

71. ÖStA AdR BMfsV KBF K1366 12415/1919.

72. "Der Ausschuß und seine bisherige Tätigkeit," 3. The money to subsidize the publication of *Der Invalide* came originally from the Economic Ministry. *Der Invalide*'s circulation did grow substantially from 3,000 copies per issue at its inception to 50,000 copies per issue near the end of 1919, see Die Redaktion, "Das erste Jahr unserer Zeitung," *Der Invalide* 2.22, 15 Nov. 1919, 1.

73. For example, Dr. A. Deutsch, Arzt des Invalidenamtes Wien, "Merkblatt für Invalide: Zur Wiederrinführung ins Erwerbsleben," *Der Invalide* 2.3, 1 Feb. 1919, 1-3; and Deputy Interior Minister Otto Glöckel's speech at the 9 Febrauary 1919 Viennese war victim rally, "Aus den Ortsgruppen: Generalversammlung der Ortsgruppe Wien am 9. Februar 1919," 7.

74. ÖStA AdR BMfsV KBF K1365 672/1919, 1245/1919.

75. ÖStA AdR BMfsV KBF K1365 8533/1919.

76. "Die Invalidenbewegung," *Der Invalide* 2.15, 1 Aug. 1919, 4.

77. There was no official or precise statistic in this regard at the beginning of the First Republic. This had much to do with the imperial nature of the military data collecting and the rapid and chaotic dissolution of the monarchy. See also ÖStA AdR BMfsV KBF K1367 21094/1919, in which the Social Ministry and the National Statistics Office discussed the need to collect relevant data in the wake of IEG's taking effect.

78. ÖStA AdR BMfsV KBF K1366 11174/1919.

79. On the planning and implementation of *Lebensmittelaktion*, see ÖStA AdR BMfsV KBF K1366 10675/1919 and K1554 folders on *Lebensmittelaktion*. For this project, 2 million K were made available to the *Zentralverband*.

80. "Unsere Lebensmittelaktion," *Der Invalide* 2.12, 15 Jun. 1919, 3. A few small organizations (with membership smaller than 1,000) or institutions received assistance through the *Zentralverband*, too.

81. "Aus den Ortsgruppen: Ortsgruppe Wien XVII. Protokoll," *Der Invalide* 2.18, 15 Sep. 1919, 8.

82. For organized war victims' participation in other official committees, see, for example, the composition of subcommittees of the Upper Austrian *Invalidenentschädigungskommission* in ÖStA AdR BMfsV KBF K1367 21114/1919.

83. "Der Ausschuß und seine bisherige Tätigkeit," 2; J. Vietoris, "Bericht über die Tätigkeit des Staatsangestelltenausschusses bis 15. März 1919," *Der Invalide* 2.8, 15 Apr. 1919, 5. To organized war victims, war victim welfare administration being staffed by their own was a top priority. See, for example, the *Zentralverband*'s intervention in Invalid Office personnel issues in Upper Styria on 4 March 1919, ÖStA AdR BMfsV KBF K1365 6081/1919.

84. See, for example, the Styrian case in ÖStA AdR BMfsV KBF K1366 18098/1919.

85. "Aus den Ortsgruppen: Erster Verbandstag des Landesverbandes Oberösterreichs," *Der Invalide* 2.12, 15 Jun. 1919, 6.

86. "Aus den Ortsgruppen: Wien, Protokoll der Sitzung des Landesverbandes Niederösterreich…," 5.

87. "Aus den Ortsgruppen: Ortsgruppe Pottendorf," *Der Invalide* 2.17, 1 Sep. 1919, 8-9. According to this account, the *Zentralverband* representative Weißsteiner pointed out that many war victims thought "the government had tried to fulfill its duties towards widows and orphans as much as possible, or at least good enough to offer them the minimum of what people had been promised during the national election campaigns."

88. Paul Nikola, *Zehn Jahre Kriegsgeschädigtenfond: Auf Anregung des Präsidenten des Kriegsgeschädigtenfonds Dr. Josef Resch, Bundesminister für soziale Verwaltung* (Vienna: Kriegsgeschädigtenfond, 1930), 7-9. Of the 36 board members, only 12 were sent by war victim organizations. The norm for similar institutions before mid-1920s was half of the seats going to organized war victims.

89. About Communists' recruitment efforts during the first half of 1919, see ÖStA AdR BKA/allgem. Inneres 15/3 K2435 14577/1919, 14856/1919, 16820/1919, 19044/1919, 21102/1919, 25243/1919; AdR BKA/allgem. Inneres 22 K5066 7417/1919, 13456/1919. Karl Grundei reported that Communist agitators were mobilizing disabled veterans against the IEG in sanatoriums in "Meine Urlaubsreise," 7. About war victims' presence in the putsches, see Gerhard Botz, *Gewalt in der Politik: Attentate, Zusammenstöße, Putschversuche, Unruhen in Österreich, 1918-1934* (Munich: Wilhelm Fink, 1976), 45-70. Of the ca. 3,000 demonstrators on 17 April, there were around 800 disabled veterans and homecoming soldiers.

90. Polizeidirektion Wien to Staatsamt für Inneres, "Ungarische Gesandtschaft; Einflussnahme auf die Gestaltung der innerpolitischen Situation in Deutschösterreich," ÖStA AdR BKA/allgem. Inneres 22 K4860 23886/1919.

91. Der Zentralverband, "Unser I. Verbandstag," *Der Invalide* 2.9, 1 May 1919, 2; "Generalversammlung der Ortsgruppe und Bezirksstelle Gmunden," 6. Perhaps a sign of success, the *Zentralverband* had to defend its own cooperative approach. It criticized the radical Left for using war victims only as means to ulterior ends. See Hunold, "Invalide als Mittel zum Zweck," *Der Invalide* 2.10, 15 May 1919, 1-2.

92. See, for example, the case of Waidhofen a.d. Ybbs in Karl Burger, "Keine Lebensmittel für Kriegsbeschädigte, aber Ueberfluß für Kriegsgewinner und Preistreiber," *Der Invalide* 2.13, 1 Jul. 1919, 1-2. Burger's account portrayed organized war victims in alliance with the republican state against the alliance between community leaders (and district administrators) and the alleged war profiteers.

93. "Deutschösterreichs Tod," *Der Invalide* 2.15, 1 Aug. 1919, 1.

94. Boyer, "Silent War and Bitter Peace," 52-56.

95. On the Austrian brand of corporatism, see, for example, Günter Bischof and Anton Pelinka, eds., *Austro-Corporatism: Past, Present, Future* (New Brunswick, N.J.: Transaction, 1996) and Peter J. Katzenstein, *Corporatism and Change: Austria, Switzerland, and the Politics of Industry* (Ithaca: Cornell University Press, 1986).

96. Some contemplated the possibility of "Invalids' Council" following the model of Soldiers' and Workers' Councils. But it was not supported by the majority organized war victims. See the police report on a 6 May 1919 Viennese rally, ÖStA AdR BKA/allgem. Inneres 15/3 K2435 16820/1919. The idea of a straight "Invalid Chamber" was also raised in 1919, but the Social Ministry shot it down for potential incursions on state jurisdiction, ÖStA AdR BMfsV KBF K1367 27672/1919.

97. For social partnership attempts in early First Republic, see Peter G. Fischer, "Ansätze zu Sozialpartnerschaft am Beginn der Ersten Republik: Das Paritätische Industriekomitee und die Industriekonferenzen," in *Österreich November 1918: Die Entstehung der Ersten Republik*, Protokoll des Symposiums in Wien am 24. und 25. Oktober 1978 (Vienna: Verlag für Geschichte und Politik, 1986), 124-40. On the "deep history" of social partnership, see Gerald Stourzh and Margarete Grandner, eds., *Historische Wurzeln der Sozialpartnerschaft* (Munich: R. Oldenbourg, 1986).

98. On intetest group politics during the First Republic, see Emmerich Tálos, "Interessenvermittlung und partikularistische Interessenpolitik in der Ersten Republik," in *Handbuch des politischen Systems Österreichs: Erste Republik, 1918-1933*, ed. idem. et al. (Vienna:

Manz, 1995), esp. 376-82, 385-89.

99. I borrow the terms from Ernst Hanisch, *Der lange Schatten des Staates: Österreichische Gesellschaftsgeschichte im 20. Jahrhundert, 1890-1990* (Vienna: Carl Ueberreuter, 1994), esp. 15-16.

Memory-Landscapes of the First World War: The Southwestern Front in Present-Day Italy, Austria and Slovenia

Gunda Barth-Scalmani[1]

For men living at the beginning of the twenty-first century, the First World War dates back nearly hundred years. Thus it belongs to a past time no eye witness can any longer describe. Traces of memories of those who lived through the First World War and survived are fading in the memories of families, as this war has already been over some three to four generations. The experiences of grandparents cannot be directly told to grandchildren any more: That means that the perspective of women as well as men as they personally experienced war with its gender-different roles, expectations and challenges does not exist any more in the realms of oral history. They might be known to their descendants from the inscriptions on family gravestones, and men might be commemorated in the local war memorials—often combined with those lost in the Second World War—existing in nearly every Alpine village.

Private commemoration for a dead soldier (© G. Barth-Scalmani 2006).

In German as well as in international historiography, the First World War was for a very long time, and still is to some extent, an event that predominantly took place on the western front.[2]

The eastern as well as the southern fronts are paid less attention, namely that against Serbia after Austrian troops crossed borders on the 11 August 1914 and that against Italy after the kingdom had declared war on 23 May 1915. Various reasons can be found for this: The "new military history"—evolving from the English-speaking scientific discourse—concentrated for a long time primarily on the western front;[3] the western world had a blind spot after the Second World War for nearly everything that was locked in the "east" until the end of the Cold War 1989/91;[4] the lack of interest of Soviet historiography for a war of tsarist Russia, thus the eastern front was no item of scholarly interest. Furthermore, there was the trap of national master narratives that had been shaped in many former warring states according to their relevant political and often ideological breaks after 1918, after 1945/47 or even as recently as after 1989/91.[5]

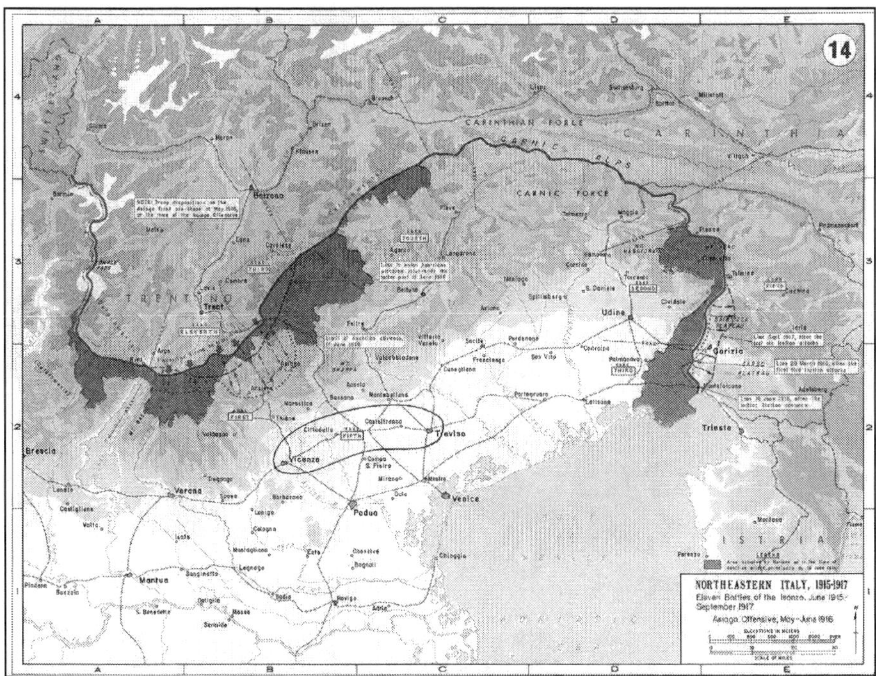

Italian front (Courtesy of Wikimedia commons)

In order to make clear the referential frame of my arguments, I want to emphasize that the term *southwestern front* includes all theaters of war that pinned down the Austrian armed forces following Italy's entry into war and shaped the experiences of civilians in these areas and their hinterland.

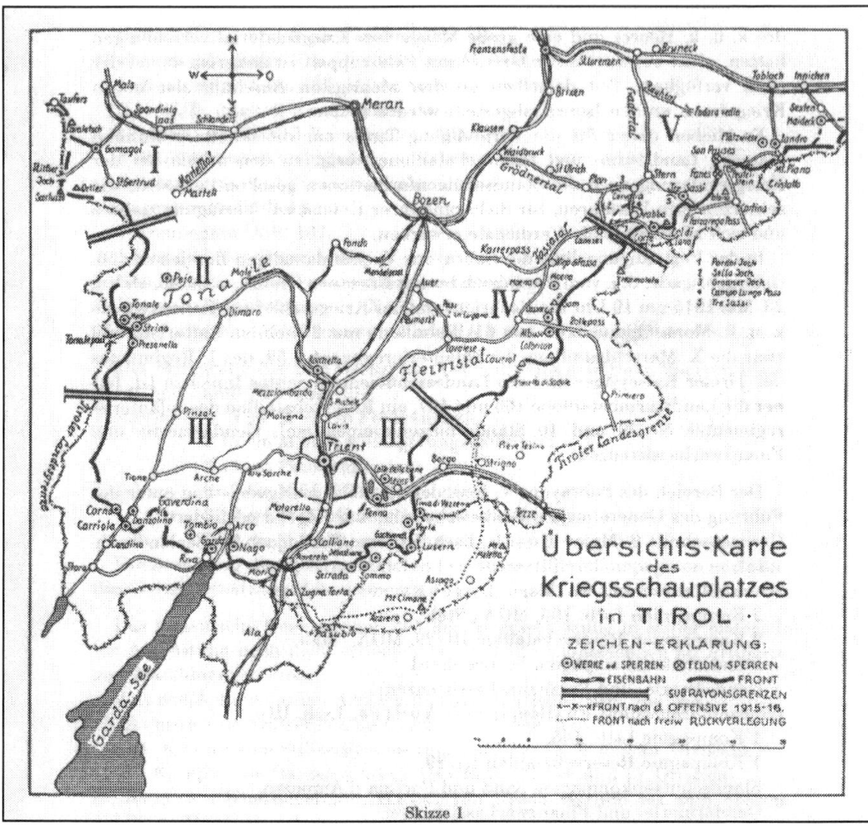

Dolomite front (© Viktor Schemfil)

The front line between the Austro-Hungarian monarchy and the kingdom of Italy extended in the Alpine mountain range (from the Ortler group in the west via the Adamello and the Dolomites, the Carnian and Julian Alps to the mountain ranges on both sides of the upper Isonzo valley in the east ending in the carst plateau near Triest/Trieste/Trst) and stretched over 600 km/400 miles. As in the western front topographical names echo the specific way of fighting: The term “war in the Dolomites” stands for static warfare in high alpine areas just as “Isonzo” has become a synonym for battles of materiel in the limestone terrain of the carst.[6]

Traces of World War I have not dissappeared; they even surface quite unexpectedly in various contexts. Some examples from regional memory-landscapes may illustrate this:

In 2003 in South-Tyrol at Innichen in the Pustertal, a franciscan monk organized the local sharp shooters corps *Hofmark Innichen* to excavate

War cemetery *Burg* at Innichen shortly after the renovation 2004. S. Volgger and M. Bichler, *Der Soldatenfriedhof "Burg" in Innichen* (Innichen: published by the authors, 2006), 13, fig. 2.

a cemetery that had been built during the war but had been overgrown after 1945. The military cemetery *Burg* was developed into an atmospheric monument in scenic surrounding with a newly constructed chapel bearing the names of all who had been buried there and listing their places of origin, thus giving the informed observer an idea that men from all corners of the former Habsburg monarchy died here fighting Italy.[7] The reconstruction initiative gains another meaning when it is related to a clearly political monument: East of the village on a distinctive turn of the national road an ossuary is situated. With monuments like this in different sizes and shapes, Italian Fascism institutionalized its memory of the war along the border of the territories acquired according to the London Treaty of 1915 and as a result of the peace treaty of St. Germain. But no fighting had taken place where these monuments stand; their origins have a different reason. Numerous cemeteries had been built during the war near the front line on both sides because of sanitary necessities and Christian piety. They could not all be maintained properly after the war—many of them were difficult to reach—so a lot of them had to be ceded. Large-scale excavations took place, and the fascist authorities superimposed these organizational necessities by shaping public memory according to their beliefs: The mortal remains of Italian soldiers as well as those of soldiers of the Imperial and Royal army originating in South Tyrol were stored in the very same charnel-houses. So Austrian soldiers killed in action were used to uphold the message of fascism/ Risorgimento. The construction of the "Italian" ossarium in the 1920s was related to the then still-existing war cemetery from the Austrian era, just as its reconstruction in 2003 was related to the by then nearly 70-year-old ossuary. Unintentionally or, more probably considered in the context of present day South Tyrol[8], intentionally, the monuments are related to each other, as both of them are monuments of belated interpretations of past events. According to the context of the (re-) construction, they are charged with current meaning.

The "seminal catastrophe" of the 20th century" (George Kennan) left traces in the ecosystem. The public mind became aware of this when evidence of positional warfare in high alpine conditions came to light due to the global warming of the glaciers. Quite spectacular was the recovery of three soldiers (probably *Kaiserschützen*) in summer 2004 in the Ortler group. In an unusually hot summer they were found by mountaineers, who were specialized in tracing evidence of conflicts in high alpine areas. Regional media followed the developments, and the question of the nationality of the soldiers became a controversial issue.[9] In the fall they were buried at Pejo (Trentino Province) in the presence of Italian and Austrian escorts of honour.[10] Afficionados of war technology were moved by the surfacing of a barely used Skoda cannon that had to be lifted from the glacier by a helicopter. This Skoda heavy artillery survived the war in excellent shape, something rather unique for specialists to see. The canon will be one of the highlights at the new museum dedicated to the "white war" (*guerra bianca*) in Temu (province of Lombardy).[11]

The ecological consequences of a war (still called *grande guerra*, or "great war") that is fading in public memory are less spectacular but more far-reaching for both nature and the economy. Economic damage can be illustrated by looking at a combat sector at the Carnic frontline (between the present federal Austrian province Carinthia and the northeast Italian region Carnia). The combat zone Kleiner Pal (1867m), an area of approximately 1500 ha, has been managed agriculturally by the same family for some generations. About 100 ha of the forest area were devastated by artillery fire, such that the trees that have grown since do not provide economically viable timber. Timber logs from other parts of the forest have to be checked first by the metal detector of the modern saw machine. They sort out those logs containing shell splinters, shrapnel or projectiles to prevent damage to the automatized equipment. Every spring, barbed wire surfaces from lightly covered alpine pastures, causing serious damage to the cattle and injuries to udders of the cows. Cattle, horses and sheep become trapped in the trenches and communication lines, which have just a smooth surface of earth. Since the European Union has been financially supporting the mowing of alpine pastures—something that had not been done for decades because it demanded hard physical labor—accidents happen frequently: Men using modern heavy mowing equipment break into trenches and rotten substructures. Barbed wire and other iron fragments among the brushwood injure the scrotum of roebuck and deer, lead to abnormalities of the antlers, and thus reduce the number of hunting trophies. So World War I is causing economic disadvantages nearly hundred years after it took place, reducing the profits in agriculture, forestry and hunting.[12] Strangely enough, the long-lasting contamination of earth by the gas used in the Isonzo valley in the areas of Flitsch/Bovec and Tolmein/Tolmin in October 1917 (a mixture of phosgene and diphenylchloroarsine) is ignored, possibly because that region is working hard at becoming recognized as an area of soft summer tourism (fishing, water sports, hiking etc.).

Traces of modern warfare techniques used nearly hundred years ago are still imprinted on the territory and have become indelible parts of memory-landscapes.

"Lieux de Mémoire": From the National to the Regional Level

With his *lieux de mémoire* concept, Pierre Nora[13] triggered a debate fifteen years ago that affected nearly all historiographies of western societies. Studying the places and monuments that had become crucial for national histories, some of which literally enshrine the nation in specific moments of its development, it became clear that the nation-state itself and the teleological historiographies were constructions. Places of remembrance are not only important on a larger, national level, but they also exist on smaller scales or in pre-national historic areas; there too they are made, they develop and fade or acquire new meanings. National and regional historiographies have osmotic bonds and often follow similar patterns, but in times of de-nationalization of historiography, the national grip on regional histories is loosened somewhat.[14]

In the patterns of traditional national history, the First World War was an event connected with the last phase of Italy as an emerging nation-state and of the Habsburgs' declining multinational state. Dealing with the heritage of World War I in the eastern Alps beyond the claims of national histories means understanding regional histories as a concave mirror of pre-national European history.[15]

I aim to show that the memory of the First World War, which left similar traces in the eastern Alps, in its topographical landscapes as well as in the mental landscapes of people living there, is a useful way to present a shared intertwined, entangled history of the Great War. First I shall present the background to the national and regional historiography on World War I, then I shall deal with some museums and initiatives illustrating the change of approach and conclude with some arguments about the role of World War I memories in regional European history.

The Political Contexts of Memory Landscapes in the Area of the Southwestern Front

To understand the distortions of historical national and regional memory one has to bear certain facts in mind. The implosion of the Austro-Hungarian monarchy in November 1918, the proclamation of so called nation-states entirely or partly on its former territory and the rules and regulations of the Paris peace treaties of 1919 entirely changed the political landscape of central and eastern Europe. The Republic of Austria had to accept the cession of South Tyrol and the *Kanaltal*[16] to Italy as well as some southern areas of the former crownlands Carinthia and Styria to the newly proclaimed Yugoslav monarchy of the Serbs, Croats and Slovenes (SHS). Already in the first six months of 1919 in Styria and Carinthia, quickly formed local militias fended off newly formed troops of the SHS-monarchy that tried to occupy the southern parts of these lands. In Carinthia, a referendum was held 10 October 1920, and even in ethnically mixed districts roughly 70 percent of the Slovenes voted to stay with Austria. The kingdom of Italy, after 1922 a fascist state, was granted according to the London Protocol the central Alpine range (*Brennergrenze*) as the new border with Austria: Predominantly German districts in South Tyrol and the predominantly Italian southern parts of the historic Province of Tyrol were ceded, plus in the northeast bend of the Alpine range the Isonzo valley, the Istrian peninsula and the port of Fiume (Rijeka) including the islands offshore.

For German-speaking Austrians as well as for Slovenes, the cession of these territories—populated partly by monoethnical, partly ethnically mixed populations—was perceived as traumatic loss and likewise coined interwar historic cultures among Austrians as well as Slovenes. The republic of Austria and the SHS-monarchy were living with that feeling of territorial loss. The German and Slovene population in the ceded areas were living in a state that gave them the status of acquired provinces whose representatives had been shaped with the ideas of the Italian Risorgimento and behaved in the fascist context as culturally superior to them. What happened in South Tyrol and in the Isonzo valley are parallel procedures, which differ only in number of persons affected, not in the actions performed. One has the impression that the South Tyrol of today has to be reminded of this comparability, because considering their own past with the injustice of the Paris treaties of 1947, their own trauma receives a unique value.[17] From an Italian point of view, the territorial gains were perceived as a logical continuation of the Risorgimento wars and, respectively, their closing. That is the reason for the construction of memorials transcending the mere commemoration of dead soldiers as a moral act to become a national obligation. The one in Pocol above Cortina[18] or in Sv. Anton in Kobarid/Karfreit/Caporetto[19] and the numerous charnel houses in the newly acquired territories were charged with ideological meaning in the 1920s and 1930s. Very often the *Duce* Benito Mussolini inaugurated them personally.[20]

This national Italian interpretation obviously did not work with the German-speaking South Tyrolians after 1918/1922. Furthermore, it did not match the experiences of the majority of the Italians in the southern districts of historic Tyrol (corresponding approximately to present-day Trentino Province) and the Slovenes of the Isonzo valley. Between 1914 and 1918, men from these areas had served in the Austro-Hungarian army, had died or been captured as Habsburg soldiers. As former wartime enemies, their personal experiences after 1922 did not fit in with the new Italian master interpretation of the past war. From a contemporary point of view, they had finished the war on the "wrong" side. Being losers and members of a national minority in a new nation-state that was not their own, they quickly disposed of their experiences of war—not to forget in economically difficult times—in private silence.[21]

It was not before Italian historiography raised contradictions to the long-lasting impact of fascist views on the *grande guerra* on a national level, that the public debate started as to whether inhabitants of Trentino or of the eastern parts of Friuli and Venezia-Giulia have a different, namely a non-national Italian history of World War I. These counterparts to the then still-existing main narrative became audible in regional historiography in the late 1970s and 1980s. Something similar had happened in peripheral regions of the Italian nation-state on other topics, though. In the northeastern parts of Italy, in Friuli and Venezia-Giulia the concept of the nation-state had already suffered its first cracks in the late 1970s. Predominantly for domestic, political and economic reasons civil groups uttered their unrest with the central government by revealing their past under Habsburg rule: *Civiltà mitteleuropea* became the slogan to reject the applied modes of centralism and to express distinct differences with other parts of Italy and their history. These movements were primarily cultural and did not become a political factor like the various *Lega* movements in the Lombardy of the 1990s.

In the SHS-monarchy of the interwar period with its unsolved territorial questions with Mussolini's Italy and the growing inner tensions between Serbs on one hand and Croats and Slovenes on the other, the discussion of World War I was of minor significance. But here again Slovenes and Croats as members of the former cis- and transleithanian parts of the Habsburg monarchy had been on the "wrong," the Serbs on the "right" side, when the war had ended. After the Second World War, in the Yugoslavia of Josip Broz Tito, which tried to propagate a supranational (i.e. Yugoslavian) identity, the commitment to single pre-national ethnic groups was not a top priority; the topic was disguised under the aspect of more urgent problems. With the implosion of Yugoslavia in 1991 and the creation of new national states, Slovene historiography opened a new page: regional history turned national.[22]

Patterns of Regional Historiography Relating to the First World War

Nearly all European historiographies display a specific pattern when dealing with World War I.[23] Referring to Austria it can be schematized as follows:[24] In the interwar period, voluminous official publications were produced, which are labeled as general staff or officers' historiography, referring to the sources primarily used or the background of their authors.[25] Besides that, a growing number of memoirs of war veterans of all ranks were printed, publications which partly justified what had happened, partly tried to give meaning to the experiences in retrospect.[26] All of them integrated and harmonized the varying front and war experiences in a general store of remembrance everybody could agree with. In spite of (or because of) growing economic difficulties in the 1920s, there was a growing market of memoir literature. War veterans did not publish diaries or written remarks from the war days, though; they wrote about war with the knowledge of its outcome and under the conditions of the 1920s and the early 1930s, and thus already interpreted the war in specific ways. That holds true for all postwar societies.[27] Furthermore the German-speaking orbit was dominated by the war guilt matter. Male roles, for instance, which had been damaged by the war, received a retrospective interpretation and re-evaluation.[28] With regard to ego-documents, one should recall that documents from the Hungarian or Bosnian-Herzegovinian area that deal with the war in the Dolomites or in the Isonzo area probably do exist, might even be published, but their views on the war in the Alps are not known at all in earlier or current Austrian historiography.

After the Second World War, the First World War nearly disappeared from Austrian historiography, especially in the university sphere. The Fischer controversy in the 1960s in the Federal Republic of Germany caused hardly a ripple.[29] The fifty-year commemoration of the foundation of the republic in 1968 shifted the dissolution of the Austro-Hungarian monarchy and consequently the war more into the focus of historians. In connection with the change of paradigms from political history to social history, the emphasis shifted from diplomatic and military history to the situation of the civil society, especially to the situation of the workers, the breakdown of solidarity and the social revolutionization in the last year of the war.[30] Since the late 1980s and from the 1990s onward the impulses of the emerging new military history inspired research on World War I in Austria, too, and enlarged the topics and the methods toward history of everyday life, history of mentality and women's history.[31] The latest approach came with cultural history. This increase of topics, focusing on civilian as well as on military aspects of past war experiences, was partly caused by the wars in the Balkan area in the 1990s. All of a sudden, war had returned to peoples' own front doors. With regard to university teaching and research, one can conclude that the First World War is still not a prominent topic in Austria in comparison with other nations. Third-party fund projects do exist,[32] but they are not connected nationwide, let alone internationally. One might speculate whether the one-hundred anniversary of the great European war will change that situation.

Tyrolean regional historiography is a mirror of the national pattern. But it does occupy a specific situation among other Austrian regional historiographies. Due to the loss of South Tyrol, the context with World War I remained more at the core of research activities.

That started already after the war by former regular officers who covered events of the Dolomite front like Cletus Pichler[33] or Viktor Schemfil. Their works can be classified as regional officers' historiography. In 1926, Schemfil published a traditional regimental history[34] and continued with monographic studies about main combat areas of the Dolomites.[35] They were even translated into Italian, and most of his publications are still in print. Apart from that there are less extensive publications of war veterans. Older publications are mostly written by commanders and transport their point of view.[36] In the past twenty years, the ego-documents by war veterans lacking significant military rank were printed. They already had written about their experiences during the fighting in notebooks and started to review these at the end of their lives, or else they remembered the time of war in old age and felt the need to pass this on. The gap between writing and being printed was bridged by the growing interest for the war of the ordinary men in the street.[37] The books by Heinz von Lichem[38] had and still have a lasting impact on the way war is perceived in the Tyrol of today, probably because of their inumerable photos and simple descriptions. Although he was an academically trained historian, his oeuvre, which is based on the quotations of sources without documentary evidence of origins and his subjective verdicts, does not meet the requirements of academic history. But it still is popular among general readers.

At the university of Innsbruck in 1991/92, academic research on the war received a major impulse by the joint organization of the department for contemporary history and the local archive for a series of lectures on "Tyrol and the First World War." The publication offers clear evidence that the research interest on the local level had shifted from apologetic war history to new approaches.[39] For Richard Schober, [40] then director of the archive, it was the trigger for a series of books entirely dedicated to issues of war in the Tyrol, which extends now by eight volumes. [41] Apart from such proof of modern regional historiography, the First World War has since then become a focal topic in teaching. The courses were and still are mostly related to excursions[42], to confront academic research and analysis with reflection on the location of theaters of war, the hinterland and the traces that still exist or are made visible again.[43] As a result, many students concentrated for their thesis or dissertation on war-related topics using documentary sources and not just published literature.[44]

It is certainly not by chance that in the Tyrol of today cooperation between historians of the historic area of Tyrol, especially from the Trentino, has started to develop. In 2001 a bilateral convention took place in Cortina d'Ampezzo under the heading *Ein Krieg—zwei Schützengräben / una trincea chiamata Dolomite* (Same War—Two Trenches) with subsequent publications in both languages.[45] The Innsbruck university department of history was one of the organizers of that meeting. The latter was also related to the development of the open-air museums at the Lagazuoi and the Cinque Torri which were under construction by then. In spring of 2005 historians from the Tyrol and South Tyrol and the sophisticated bilateral South-Tyrolean periodical *Geschichte und Region/Storia e regione*[46] organized an international meeting at *Bolzano Der Erste Weltkrieg im Alpenraum: Erfahrung, Deutung, Erinnerung* (The First World War in the Alps: Experience, Interpretation, Memory).[47] Apart from a new interpretation of the Italian *Intervento* it concentrated on the specifics of war in the Alps, on the interdependency of military actions and hinterland experiences.

A description of Tyrolean historiography would be incomplete without referring to the Italian publications of the Trentino (the predominantly Italian-speaking part of historic Old-Tyrol).[48] Although Trento does have a university, the main impulses originate from two institutions. The impact of their commitment extended beyond the province and received national attention: the Italian war museum, *Museo Storico Italiano della Guerra*, in Rovereto[49] and the archive for popular ego-documents (*archivio della scrittura populare*)[50] affiliated with the museum of Trento. The museum in Rovereto, still being a predominantly private institution and therefore not charged with national responsibilities, organizes very carefully curated exhibitions, and the museum as well as the archive publish extensively.[51] Thus they have always been on the avant-garde of Italian historiography and have strongly contributed to it.[52] The apology of war which originated in the tradition of Risorgimento and fascism was challenged—not coincidentally from the 1970s onward in some publications contesting the myth of the Great War.[53] Many proceedings in the 1970s and 1980s picked out the mobilization of civil society towards war as central theme.[54] Research on the hinterland during war time coincided with a re-evaluation of warfare.[55] In this new orientation of Italian research on the Great War, the publications from the Trentino area with their emphasis on the experiences of soldiers and civilians alike have to be seen. They focused on ordinary men and women who in prewar times had lived in multiple patterns of loyalty—if one looks to the historic space without a nationally moulded view. Due to the war, one single mental orientation was accentuated and tightened.[56] In some families some men had crossed the border to serve in the Royal Italian army, whereas their kinsmen served in the Austrian army. The population in the mountainous countryside was said to be loyal to the Habsburg *Kaiser* whereas townsfolk, being better educated, were attracted to Italian nationalism. Many representatives of Austrian military commands and of the central administration in Vienna were already suspicious about the non-German-speaking minorities along the borderline, which was aggravated during the war. By reason of that mistrust and of military necessities, inhabitants in the border areas that became combat zones were forced to emigrate into the hinterland in a very short time. Measures taken against politically unreliable persons were applied to many ordinary civilians as well. These traumatic experiences—for example, being transported overnight into camps in Bohemia or Austria without knowing what would follow, living under miserable circumstances for years to come in these camps—caused or accented anti-Austrian feelings and subsequently Italian national self awareness.[57] The fate of these war refugees, the so-called *profughi*, was and still is a central topic for both regional and national Italian war historiography.[58] After the war, when their homeland had become part of Italy, these people were confronted with the approach being *austriacanti* (emotionally related with Austria). The fact that the realignment of Italian historiography from the 1970s onward happened to some degree in the geographic periphery of the Italian nation-state is probably no coincidence and has a lot to do with the discontinuities of domestic politics in Italy in the last three decades.

The specific framework of recent Slovene war historiography has already been mentioned earlier, referring to the political developments. The First World War is not a central topic of Slovene historiography, and the publications that do exist are hardly noticed in Austria, except when translated into German[59] or when arriving in a roundabout way via English or Italian translations.[60] Attempts have been made to perceive history in the border triangle of Austria, Slovenia, Italy not along the narratives of the nation-states, but as common Carnic, Isontinic or Friulan regional history.[61] A conference dedicated to the First World War at the beginning of Slovene statehood had the title "Isonzo Protocols" because the name of the river Isonzo/Soča or of the limestone plateau Karst/Carso will be linked forever with enormous human losses in the German as well as in the Italian and in the Slovene memory culture.[62]

Is There a New View on the Traces of War in the Landscapes of the Southwestern Theater of War?

Students who participated in the University of Innsbruck History Department's first excursion to the Dolomite front in 1997 reported that their knowledge about the First World War was shadowed by the knowledge they had gained in school about the Second World War and National Socialism. Many of them were familiar with frontline areas from their skiing, hiking or climbing experiences without knowing that, years before, a static combat had taken place there. The relics of war that could be seen during summertime could obviously no longer be "decoded." Reading landscapes, like a historic manuscript that can be deciphered, was one of the goals of the excursion.[63] Even the inhabitants of the Alpine war areas had lost the knowledge of the traces of history in their areas after 1919. In the late 1990s, those who could remember the war were already very old. Those who as children had collected scrap-iron and nonferrous metals with their parents in the economically difficult times of the interwar period, the *recuperanti*, did still live and know about it. Among them were many who had kept unique items and thus formed collections of war-related objects.[64] The innumerable private war collections in the Alpine range, from Lombardy, Trentino, Belluno, Veneto, Friuli to the Isonzo/Soča valley, have not yet been registered or compared. They are very similar, looking like serial sequences of the same: all kind of weapons (or parts of them), soldiers' equipments (uniforms, clothes, shoes, cooking ware, razor sets), personal objects (cards, prayer book) that have been found in the debris of rocks, in melting ice or snow. Their presentation is untouched by refined ideas of didactics in museology, sometimes characterized by the sheer joy of finding objects or competing with other collectors. But that artless approach should not deceive us that these collections manifest the effort to remember the war in a specific area. The three soldiers who were surfaced out of the ice in 2004 in the Ortler massif were not found by chance, but by local mountaineers who had been searching for war objects for years. Eighty years after the Italian *intervento*, in the summer of 1995 in the Trentino Dolomites, many local initiatives organized small exhibitions in villages to illustrate the life of the civilian inhabitants during the war, how men had been called to arms to fight for the *Kaiser* in 1914 far away in the east, how soldiers had defended their home area against the Italians just a year later in 1915.[65] The exhibitions met unexpected interest by locals and tourists alike. For the first time objects of private collections and items of family histories were exhibited. In retrospect, 1995 can be considered the start of a new interest of locals in the history of their living space, an interest that was no longer burdened by the political pressure of postwar Italy. The work of professional historians and locals interested in the past merged, and the nation-state faded as framework of historical reference.

When the nation-state Italy was proclaimed in the newly acquired territories after the war the first museums had been founded. In Rovereto and Gorizia (Görz) they were carried de jure by private societies[66] and supported by the Risorgimento ideas and the growing climate of fascism. The location in Rovereto (Trentino) and Gorizia (Venezia Giulia) were no coincidence as these were areas the Risorgimento ideas had wanted to "redeem." From the beginning, private collectors were asked to contribute their items. These museums had a double message: They proclaimed the idea of the Italian nation-state and commemorated war in a specific way, whereas the local, smaller exhibitions recorded war without the national-Italian message. In the new republic of Austria, no museums dedicated to the war were founded. War veterans, however, contributed to regimental museums that had already existed before the war, although very often in smaller scales. Such was the case with the Rainer regiment in Salzburg or the Kaiserjäger in Innsbruck.[67] The idea to present and commemorate war in a museum originated straight from the war years, as recent research has shown.[68] Reproduction of trenches and pictures of war in the alpine areas—which the middle-class visitors knew as sophisticated summer resorts—was meant to motivate the support of the civilian population without confronting them with the human suffering of real war actions.

The idea to show the imprint of war on landscapes did not arise before the 1970s. The idea mostly derived from private initiatives, outside academe, associating with locals. The development was and still is the same nearly everywhere: The idea of using existing mountain trails to propagate the memory of the First World War leads to the creation of open-air museums at scenic or thematically motivated points. The next step is the foundation of museum buildings in order to expose the objects found in setting the trails or already existing in private collections. These developments in the Alpine range have precursors and respectively comparable initiatives in France, Belgium and Germany.[69] The *Dolomitenfreunde* (friends of the Dolomites) are a good example for that pattern.

In 1973 Walther Schaumann (1923-2004), at the time an active member of the Austrian federal army[70], founded together with likeminded men from Italy the *Dolomitenfreunde* society.[71] As a boy, Schaumann had already hiked the sectors along the Carnic range at where his father had been stationed during the war. The society's slogan was that trails that separated the frontline should connect people today ("*Wege, die einst Fronten trennten, sollen uns heute verbinden*")—their name "trails of peace" in German and Italian wording (*Friedenswege – Le vie della Pace*), their aim to repair decayed front trails with the help of volunteers and to connect them with the existing mountain trails.[72] By the end of the 1970s the first section of trails was completed; by the 1980s hikers could wander along the Dolomite front on marked trails from the Ortler in the West down to the Pasubio in the south and the Kreuzberg near Sexten (Passo Croce near Sesto) in the east.[73] The opening of the trails and partly the reconstruction of military posts was supported by Italian societies commemorating the war. At the summit of the Monte Piano an open-air museum was set up 1977-1982, by reconstructing front lines, excavating trenches, and setting up hay-wire circuits and barbed wire fences in front of the trenches, thus leading the interested visitor from the Italian to the Austrian front. Information panels in both languages, even printed publications,[74] deepened the picture of living and fighting in high Alpine areas. At that time the local tourist boards did not yet grasp the chance to promote these private initiatives beyond their traditional target groups. It was still the time of bipolarity in world politics. Italy was a member of NATO—and as we know today heavily armed on its northeastern borders. The pattern of the first activities of the *Dolomitenfreunde* demonstrates that the idea of open-air museums along the trails or even museums down in the valley developed quite automatically from the increasing reconstruction work.

In 1983, Schaumann moved the activities of the *Dolomitenfreunde* to Carinthia. The Carnic mountain range was the only area where front lines of the war were situated in present-day Austria. At the same time, the Alpine associations were setting up a network of long-distance hiking trails. In collaboration with the new Carnic hiking trail,[75] the *Dolomitenfreunde* started excavations in the front areas of the Kleiner Pal near the Plöckenpass (Monte Croce Carnico, 1357 m) in the community of Kötschach-Mauthen. With the courtesy of the owner and the support of the volunteers' network, Schaumann established hiking trails with the help of other local initiatives and the Austrian Federal Army, which shipped in every summer. Reconstruction work still is underway, so the open-air museum is enlarged every year.[76] The implosion of the Eastern bloc in 1989/91 brought further help in the form of voluntary support from the so-called successor states of the monarchy, e.g. the Czech Republic, Slovakia, Hungary and Poland. Thanks to the annual excavation, many civilian and military objects were collected. When the community Kötschach-Mauthen built a new city hall, quite unexpectedly space for a museum was offered. Schaumann grasped the chance, and in 1992, the museum *1915-1918: Vom Ortler bis zur Adria* opened. It aims to demonstrate the futility of war using the experiences of ordinary soldiers and civilians in the area of the Southwestern front on both sides. It intends to appeal to peace based on the assumption that conflicts cannot be solved with bellicose means.[77] This museum near the Italian border was, and still is, the only museum in Austria that is entirely dedicated to the memory of World War I.[78] It receives financial support from the public authorities, but the museum is still a private enterprise run by the *Dolomitenfreunde*. They alone are responsible for the concept of the museum.

From the beginning, all explications have been displayed in German as well as in Italian. The presentation depicts the steps toward war in both countries laterally reversed and focuses on war that is experienced by both sides in the same pattern. On an area of approximately 600 square meters, visitors are confronted with the political and diplomatic causes of the war, the development of the war, war technology, the everyday life of soldiers, and the exposure of soldiers to the power of nature (avalanches, freezing temperatures, scarcity of water during summer). Propaganda and human losses are illustrated by objects, written documents, pictures, models of specific areas and reconstructed shelters or field telephone posts. The retreat from any national perspective, the appeal for peace and the emphasis on the daily life of the soldiers on both sides and the hierarchical differences between ordinary soldiers and officers (bottles, biscuits, cans) was the new approach at the time of the opening.

Schaumann, who was responsible for that concept, may have been influenced by his own experiences during the Second World War. He developed the program without any real contact to professional historians, who at that time were not yet affected by the new military history in Austria. In 1993 the museum received the Austrian Museum Prize, in 1994 it was selected candidate for the European Prize and in 1996 it received the status of cultural asset according to the the Hague Convention. From a current point of view, nearly twenty years after the opening, the exhibition seems to challenge the concentration of visitors with a plethora of written information, too many showcases in small rooms and countless objects.[79] The exhibition may not meet the didactic demands of fashionable museum studies, which in its turn depends very much on changing trends. But the visitor's response is not thus harmed, the museum's *Dolomitenfreunde* are quite satisfied with the number of visitors. It was not the first intention, but it has become a cornerstone of regional tourist programs in the meantime, especially on days when outdoor activities are prevented by bad weather.[80] The combination of history in scenic surroundings and intellectual immersion in the museum's focus became a tourist attraction even before the notion of cultural tourism.

Private initiatives had founded a museum as early as 1990 in Kobarid (Karfreit/Caporetto), Slovenia, at the historic palace of Mašera.[81] It aimed to present the local history of the Soča valley, of the village and of the Isonzo frontline from 1915 to 1917.[82] A main part was focused—according to contemporary notion at the time—on the "breakthrough" at Flitsch-Tolmein, the "miracle of Karfreit,"[83] and the "defeat" of Caporetto. The subject of the museum is a past war and a current antiwar topic. Here, too, the ordinary soldiers without regard to their national background are the focal point. The foundation of the museum is clearly linked with the decay of Yugoslavia and the creation of the Slovene state in 1991. The bulk of the museum's items are derived from private collections, which existed previously.

As its counterpart in Carinthia, the First World War museum at Kobarid was also nominated for the European Prize Museum of the year in 1993. The very same year it was granted the museum prize of the Council of Europe, having already in 1992 received the Valvasor-Prize, the highest national award for museums in Slovenia. Kobarid has some more square meters at its disposal than its Carinthian counterpart. Next to the general concept (introduction to the outbreak of war, supported by a film, situation in the area, a white room covering combat in the war, the hinterland, positional war and death), it deals with a general concentration on human suffering. The didactics of the displays (informational texts in four languages, numerous objects in showcases, reconstructions of caverns) in the two museums are very similar.

The success of the Slovene museum has to be understood against the background of the presentations in the Yugoslav era with their inherent heroic pathos. When Slovenia became independent, many collectors who had previously stored their items privately saw the chance to show what had earlier not complied with the dominating Yugoslav master narrative. That explains why within a very short period smaller museums also came into existence in the same area.[84] When the stifling atmosphere of Yugoslavia lifted, Slovene identity emerged, including interest in and knowledge of its own history. That explains all the initiatives being undertaken within a very short time. Along the Isonzo line during the 1990s several open-air museums came into existence in Bovec/Flitsch (Čelo: high positions over the basin of Bovec, Ravelnik: the foremost Austrian line north of Flitsch), Kobarid[85] (Kolovrat, Matajur) and Tolmin/Tolmein (Mrzli vrh, Javorca).[86] Together with the Austrian Black-Cross organization, war cemeteries that had been neglected for a very long time were restored,[87] like the one in Log pod Mangartom in the upper Koritnica valley, likewise chapels[88] and other small monuments dating from the war. Based on grants by the European Union in 2000, the republic of Slovenia founded *Fondacija Poti Miru v Posočju/Stiftung Wege des Friedens im Sočatal.*[89] Within ten years they were supposed to link all local initiatives and to connect them with similar Italian and Slovene undertakings. The future aim is a transnational theme park memory about the cultural heritage of the war. Every point of interest for the visitor, from the Predil pass in the north down the valley as far as Tolmin, was branded with a distinct logo between summer 2006 and summer 2007: "Peace trail Soča valley" (a pigeon with POT MIRU). Everyone interested can obtain a map[90] with information on all points. Compared with the initiatives in Carinthia, the Slovene project is more related to tourism in the Soča valley. The area has structural economic deficits—for a long time it had been an area of emigration—and is in a peripheral position of the new republic. Apart from the natural advantages for summer tourism (wild water activities, fishing, hiking, climbing) and winter tourism (skiing), the remnants of the First World War have been

Austrian war cemetery in Log pod Mangartom in the upper Koritnica valley (SLO), part of the "Peace trail Soča valley" (© G. Barth-Scalmani 2006).

acknowledged as a basis for cultural tourism. Slovenia is actively promoting it because it is thus inscribing its history into a greater common Central European framework and further alienating itself from the Yugoslav past.

Down the lower Soča valley, on the Karst plateau, the local collections and museums in Italy and Slovenia have been connected organizationally in recent years. Hikers or bicycle riders find information panels along the marked trails.[91]

It was dedicated amateurs and historians who started to concern themselves with the heritage of the First World War in Carinthia and Slovenia, and professional promoters of tourism afterwards realized how they could make use of it to add cultural assets to their array of products. Two examples from the Dolomite area may illustrate that the initiative to do something with the war relics can also be stimulated by the tourism industry.

By the end of the 1990s, some owners of cablecars and chairlifts and dedicated amateur historians initiated an Interreg II-project[92] in Cortina d'Ampezzo (now province Belluno, until 1918 a district of historic Tyrol), supported by the European Union, to set up an open-air museum in the areas of Lagazuoi (2752m) and Cinque Torri (2137m). This sector of the front was one of the focal points as it offered a breakthrough into the Pustertal/val Pusteria and consequently into the center of Austria. There Italy and Austria-Hungary faced each other for more than thirty months in a high Alpine environment: Mountains were tunneled through, peaks blown up, and both sides struggled in the rocks in summer and wintertime. Col di Lana (2452m), branded Col di Sangue by the Italians, is a name that evokes endless human misery. On one hand the cablecars of today were not charged to full capacity in summer, and on the other hand the scenic road—opened in 1909 as an Imperial road[93]—is a travel destination that attracts a lot of vehicles and motorbikes in summertime. The majority of these travelers are not the mountaineer type of tourist. To make them stay longer in the area, programs without the attraction of hard sports were needed. Projects in cultural tourism seemed the right answer.

Historically interested persons met in the Comitato Cengia Martini Lagazuoi since 1996/1997, and finally Stefano Illing set up an Interreg II-project. Apart from the existing technical prerequisites (roads, funiculars), this sector of the Dolomite front was considered a focal point to illustrate the changes of European history in a burning glass: the heart of the Dolomites, where German, Ladin and Italian settlements had overlapped for centuries, had been claimed by the growing German and Italian national movements of the nineteenth century as autochthonic settling area and as a sacred borderline to be defended against the other. Furthermore the evidence of war on the landscape is still seen today (mountains tunneled through like swiss cheese, debris of blasted peaks). Strategically, the area is one of the spots from which the Italian Supreme Command wanted to profit the topographical setting and enforce a breakthrough to the Pustertal/Val Pusteria with its important train line from South Tyrol to Carinthia and Vienna.

In spite of vast losses in attacking (and, respectively, in the Austrian force defending) the sector,[94] the Italians were not successful; on the contrary, it resulted in static warfare under high Alpine conditions. During the combat cable cars came to that area to conquer the heights for use by men and material; after the war this modern technology was adopted and became the main infrastructure of modern winter tourism. In 2000 the project set up an open air museum on the Lagazuoi (2752m). Both sides had assessed the rock on different altitudes and fought each other from different shelves. Inside the rock, they built galleries for shelter and to shell the adversary. The gallery today links both sides, so the visitor can walk within the rock from the peak 600m down to the pass. In the Cinque Torri museum, the Italian Second Line, one can visit communications lines, pickets, shelters against heavy artillery, and medical support zones. Static warfare in Alpine altitudes was high-tech warfare, using floodlights and the latest equipment. Information panels and audio guides[95] refer to documents of individuals who served in the area and thus add a human touch to events hard to grasp. Access to both open-air museums is by cablecars from the Falzarego Pass (2105m). Booklets in Italian, German and English and DVDs complete the service for the visitors.[96] In bad weather conditions, a museum nearby at the Valparola-pass displays the history, based on a private collection of *recuperanti*; the location itself is unique. An old Austrian fortress already outdated in 1914 and destroyed by artillery fire in 1915, has been restored. The museum designs completed the project in the summer of 2008 by integrating the Hexenstein/Sasso di Stria (2477m), opposite Lagazuoi. Due to its strategic position as a point of observation, the Austrians had it tunneled on all sides. In 1973, Schauman had already made some improvements to the trails there. More than thirty-five years later it was the last stage in the construction of a huge open-air museum.[97]

In administrative terms the complex is now situated in the Province of Belluno (regione Veneto). Due to the political changes that took place after 1918 the war theaters by the majority are beyond the territory of the current South Tyrol. Sexten (Sesto) is the only village in German-speaking South-Tyrol whose inhabitants had to be evacuated within a very short time because of their closeness to the frontline. Here the owners of funicular enterprises launched an approach to set up an open-air museum; some years earlier a similar attempt by different proponents had failed. In 2005, some "citizens of Sexten" formed the society *Bellum Aquilarum/Krieg der Adler* (war of eagles)—ONLUS "to restore the traces of the First World War, to prevent them from being forgotten and to save them for coming generations, the country and all the people of Europe…as a monument against war and its consequences."[98] The project includes the realization of an open-air museum at the Rotwand (1900m, climbing trails/*vie ferrate* until 2900m), the restoration of the fortresses Mitterberg and Haideck and, in the long run, the installation of a documentary center in Sexten. After the first presentation of the project for the community, response and support were unexpectedly high in contrast to earlier attempts. Donations of privately conserved objects were offered, such as a children's push chair that once had contained all the belongings a family had taken with them and had been maintained afterwards as a special item of family's history through all political changes and inheritances. The amount of items offered resulted in the idea to set up an exhibition all at once. In February 2007, *1914-1918: Erster Weltkrieg. Karl und Kaspar auf der Rotwand* (First World War. Karl and Kaspar at the Rotwand) opened. The two curators, Brigitte Strauss and Sigrid Wisthaler, two graduates from Innsbruck University, took the diaries of two men from the area as a red ribbon to illustrate the war from the perspectives of low-ranking individuals.

During summer 2005, the federation of the South Tyrolean sharp shooters corps had organized a traveling exhibition about the war in general and specifically in the area. Listing all the activities that were maintained in the neighbouring areas, they concluded negatively: "Only **South Tyrol** has **not yet** obtained an adequate **site** by which to remember the Tyrolean front 1915 to 1918!/Nur **Südtirol** besitzt noch **keinen** entsprechenden **Ort** der Erinnerung an die Tiroler Front von 1915 bis 1918!" [original accentuation].[99] This lamentation of the sharp shooters federation in South Tyrol probably was not aware of the initiative that had already taken momentum in Sexten.

1995 had seen local commemoration initiatives in the Italian-speaking Trentino. It lasted a decade longer before the First World War had become a topic in South Tyrol in 2005. Though still a big trauma, the cover of silence is being lifted finally and at the very same time it is historized.

Clearly the local tourism industry experts realized the importance of the remnants of the war and the potential of commemorating the local consequences of war as a European tragedy. Cultural tourism became a further attraction to compliment winter and summer tourism.

But if tourism experts and experts in history (professionals or respectable amateurs) do not collaborate, initiatives quickly may lose their serious common ground. Two examples illustrate this point. The tourist board Friuli Venezia Giulia has published an elaborate 24-page booklet entitled "Sceneries of the Great War."[100] The text is without any specific references to the war between 1915 and 1918. Either one assumes that everybody knows about it, or if it is left void, anyone might add his own idea. Who was fighting against whom and why remains unclear. Risorgimento-inspired, nation-state master narratives have vanished without being replaced by multi-layered or translational approaches. Strikingly, the only name mentioned is that of one Erich Rommel.[101] The brochure has a lot of photos of men of the twenty-first century in newly tailored uniforms of soldiers and Red Cross nurses ninety years back. It seems a sort of historical reenactment, but what might be its intention? There are more pictures with "Austrian" than with "Italian" soldiers. Clearly, it was an Italian historical society that has created it. Is there a link to the *civiltá Mitteleuropea* movement that emerged some thirty years ago in Friuli, finding support in the local population because of its identification with the Central European, Habsburgian past and the hidden anti-Rome orientation? Does it display multiple identities of people living in areas which, due to their mixed ethnic composition, had never fit into the scheme of nation-states? The "Living history movement" has reached the First World War, whatever the reasons of the participants may be. They are present in Cortina d'Ampezzo as well as in Friuli.[102] The professional (Central European) historian might not be entirely able to cope with this. But one has to respect the fact that for all participants, it does add meaning and identification.

Reasons for Mooring the First World War in the Regional Functional Memory

In the opening decade of the twenty-first century, nearly all areas of former war theaters in the Alps have launched cultural initiatives. They vary in depth and extent in reviving and commemorating the war. If one recalls the handling of the artifacts in the memory-landscapes, the pattern of development is threefold: reconstruction of trails, open-air museums, and museums. The framework has changed drastically within the last thirty-five years. In 2001, Italy was the only country to have already passed a bill to safeguard the preservation of the war theater landscapes.[103] That even includes a financial commitment by the state. The former alpine war zones of Italy, Austria and Slovenia are situated in comparable biogeographic and cultural zones, far from industrialized urban areas. They have felt the consequences of the economic changes of the last decades: the structural change with displacement of industrial plants and a decrease of population in these peripheral areas, increasing mobility, and the impact of globalization. This has resulted in a growing importance of (summer and winter) tourism to guarantee the viability of these areas. Regional policy of the European Union is promoting the cooperation of similar areas beyond national borders. Between 2000 and 2006, various local and regional initiatives have concentrated on the cultural heritage of the war and have made use of Interreg-III programs. But drastic differences do exist in calling on the supranational instruments. Italy and to some extent the recent EU member country Slovenia have acquired considerable expertise in utilizing these EU programs. Austrian regions oddly rarely play a leading role.

World War I has entered the realm of the tourism industry. The "seminal catastrophe" of the twentieth century is among the topics which are displayed by cultural tourism. Three generations have passed. It has become an event distant enough in the past for people to no longer resort to personal resentments. Without the fast-changing paradigms in the field of history, the legal or economic framework to broach the issue of the First World War would have been without consequences. Following the disappearance of the national master narratives, the military, economic and civil consequences of this war in the peripheral areas (periphery itself being a construction of the center) became a topic. Interpretations of past events from the perspective of the nation-state had met with criticism. Professional and amateur historians in the peripheral regions respected such narrow nationalistic approaches. Despite the changes of the cultural landscape and the growing usage of natural high Alpine landscapes, the material far-reaching impact of the war could be seen still fifty years (the *Dolomitenfreunde* initiative) or eighty years after the event (project Grande Guerra in Cortina d'Ampezzo). Moving men, women and children alike to the limits of what they could bear physically and mentally and the effects on civil society have become paramount foci. These interests on war in the heart of Europe shifted the historical interest from scholars to a larger public.[104]

Using the terminology of the culture of remembrance, one might say that war is being integrated into the functional memory of the landscapes of the Southwestern front. The functional memory selects a choice from the vastly growing diffuse accumulation of historic and scholarly pieces of information, which "is recordable for living memory, and is setting a tool for identification and supplies orientation."[105] The mountainous landscapes on the peripheries of nation-states with their war theaters and their differently developed tourist structures have peeled off the *only mandatory*, i.e. the *national* interpretation of the Great War. A variety of institutions whose backgrounds and aims may hardly be balanced constitute the numerous actors, which will finally set up the polyphonic memories in the alpine landscapes of the Great War Theater 1915–1918.

Notes

1. I would like to thank Adrienne Huter for her help with the English text.

2. Even the desirable encyclopedia Gerhard Hirschfeld et al., eds., *Erster Weltkrieg*, 2nd ed. (Paderborn: Schöningh, 2004), includes the keywords "*Westfront*" and "*Ostfront*". The latter is covered only from a German point of view. The combat events are reduced to geographic keywords "Galizien," (Bukowina missing), "Serbien," "Isonzo," "Südtirol."

3. Thomas Kühne and Benjamin Ziemann, "Militärgeschichte in der Erweiterung: Konjunkturen, Interpretationen, Konzepte," in *Was ist Militärgeschichte?*, ed. idem., Krieg in der Geschichte 6 (Paderborn: Schöningh, 2006), 9-46.

4. An early exemption is Norman Stone, *The Eastern Front 1914-1917* (London: Hodder and Stoughton, 1975). One of the first German publications including contributions of "eastern European" scholars Gerhard Paul Gross, ed., *Die vergessene Front – Der Osten 1914-1915*, Zeitalter der Weltkriege 1 (Paderborn: Schöningh, 2006).

5. See for the term Konrad H. Jarausch and Martin Sabrow, "'Meistererzählung' – Zur Karriere eines Begriffs," in *Die historische Meistererzählung: Deutungslinien der deutschen Nationalgeschichte nach 1945*, ed. idem. (Göttingen: Vandenhoeck & Ruprecht, 2002), 9-32.

6. Wolfgang Etschmann, "Die Südwestfront 1915-1918," in *Tirol und der Erste Weltkrieg*, ed. Klaus Eisterer and Rolf Steininger, Innsbrucker Forschungen zur Zeitgeschichte 12 (Innsbruck: Studienverlag, 1995), 27-60.

7. Siegfried Volgger and Martin Bichler, *Der Soldatenfriedhof "Burg" in Innichen* (Innichen: published by the authors, 2006); idem., *Namenbuch des Soldatenfriedhof "Burg" in Innichen* (Innichen: published by the authors, 2007).

8. The inumerable monuments of the fascist period rouse anger among the German population still today.

9. Cover of the Austrian political periodical *Profil*, "Die Toten im Eis," 30 Aug. 2004; see also <http://www.profil.at/nw1/gen/slideshows/slide.php?show=profil/cover/2004/&template=&nopop=1&aut=mr&top=&next=1&ref=noref&ftemplate=&kid=560&noad=0&nonavctrl=0&pos=35> (17 Dec. 2009).

10. A television film by Verena Gruber and Peter Paul Kainrath which was produced in 2005 in South Tyrol, *Weltkrieg – Kriegswelt: Kriegsalltag in Tirol 1914-1918*, starts with the burial of these three soldiers. They probably had been Italian speaking Tyroleans.

11. This is the intention of John Ceruti, of the Museo della Guerra Bianca in Adamello 1915 to 1918, in a lecture to participants of an excursion of the Department of History of the University of Innsbruck in September 2005. The building of the new museum is already completed, but the community does not open it. See <http://www.museoguerrabianca.it/index.php?option=com_content&task=view&id=19&Itemid=48> (18. Dec. 2009).

12. Information by mountain guide Sepp Brandstätter (Würmlach, Carinthia) and the proprietor (Kötschach-Mauthen, Carinthia) in September 2007.

13. Pierre Nora, *Rethinking France: Lieux de mémoire*, 4 vols. (Chicago: University of Chicago Press, 1999-2010).

14. In German two terms, *Landes-* and *Regionalgeschichte* coexist. To insiders they are not synonyms, but competing research traditions and concepts. See Ernst Hinrich, "Landes- und Regionalgeschichte," in *Geschichte: Ein Grundkurs*, ed. Hans-Jürgen Goertz (Reinbek: Rowohlt, 1998), 539-56.

15. See for Austria, Arno Strohmeyer, "'Österreichische' Geschichte der Neuzeit als multiperspektivische Raumgeschichte: Ein Versuch," in *Was heißt "österreichische" Geschichte? Probleme, Perspektiven und Räume der Neuzeitforschung*, ed. Arno Strohmeyer and Martin Scheutz, Wiener Schriften zur Geschichte der Neuzeit 6 (Innsbruck: Studienverlag, 2008), 167-97.

16. In Friulano Val Cjanâl, Italian Val Canale, Slovene Kanalska dolina, is a march through valley stretching 23 km in the border triangle of Austria, Slovenia and Italy with the historic center Tarvis/Tarvisio.

17. The ethnic policy applied by Italian fascism in South Tyrol and in the Isonzo valley after 1922 was very similar in enforcing homogenous nationals (school and culture politics). This has not yet been compared.

18. See view under <http://static.panoramio.com/photos/original/26390546.jpg> (18. Dec. 2009).

19. See view under <http://static.panoramio.com/photos/original/3300790.jpg> (18. Dec. 2009).

20. See Patrizia Marchesoni, ed., *Monumenti delle grande guerra: Progetti e realizzazioni in Trentino 1916-1935* (Trento: Museo Storico in Trento, 1998).

21. In 1969 Klaus Gatterer (1924-1984), a famous Austrian journalist dedicated a chapter of his autobiography to this silence, *Schöne Welt, böse Leut: Eine Kindheit in Südtirol* (Vienna: Folio, 2005).

22. See recently a German publication, Peter Štich et al., *Slowenische Geschichte: Gesellschaft – Politik – Kultur* (Graz: Leykam, 2008).

23. Gerd Krumeich and Gerhard Hirschfeld, "Die Geschichtsschreibung zum Ersten Weltkrieg," in *Erster Weltkrieg*, 304-15.

24. For still the best see Oswald Überegger, "Vom militärgeschichtlichen Paradigma zur 'Kulturgeschichte des Krieges'?," in *Zwischen Nation und Region: Weltkriegsforschung im internationalen Vergleich: Ergebnisse und Perspektiven*, ed. Oswald Überegger, Tirol im Ersten Weltkrieg: Politik, Wirtschaft und Gesellschaft 4 (Innsbruck: Wagner, 2004), 63-122.

25. Bundesministerium für Heerwesen und Kriegsarchiv, ed., *Österreich-Ungarns letzter Krieg, 1914-1918*, 7 vols. (Vienna: Verlag der Militärwissenschaftichen Mitteilungen, 1930-1938).

26. A few examples: Franz Conrad von Hötzendorf, *Aus meiner Dienstzeit 1906-1918*, 6 vols. (Vienna: Rikola Verlag, 1921-1926); Heinrich von Schullern, *Erinnerungen eines Feldarztes aus dem Weltkrieg* (Hall in Tyrol: Union Verlag, 1934).

27. See Jay Winter and Antoine Prost, *The Great War in History* (Cambridge: Cambridge University Press, 2005), esp. ch. 4.

28. The oeuvre of Fritz Weber, who had experienced war on fortresses in the Dolomites an in the Carso, and published a lot, was analyzed by by Christa Hämmerle, "'Es ist immer der Mann, der den Kampf entscheidet, und nicht die Waffe': Die Männlichkeit des k.u.k. Gebirgskriegers in der soldatischen Erinnerungskultur," in *Der Erste Weltkrieg im Alpenraum: Erfahrung, Deutung, Erinnerung; La Grande Guerra nell'arco alpino: Esperienze e memoria*, ed. Hermann Kuprian and Oswald Überegger, Veröffentlichungen des Südtiroler Landesarchivs 23 (Innsbruck: Wagner, 2006), 35-60.

29. An exception is Fritz Fellner's comment to the paper of Fritz Fischer at the XII. International

Meeting of Historians, in *XIIe Congrès International des Science Historiques 1965*, vol. 5, Actes (Horn: 1967), 746-48.

30. In retrospect it is striking to observe that Austrian Eastern European historians backed this topic, see Richard Plaschka et al., *Innere Front: Militärassistenz, Umsturz und Widerstand in der Donaumonarchie 1918*, 2 vols. (Vienna: Verlag für Geschichte und Politik, 1974).

31. See Christa Hämmerle, "Von den Geschlechtern der Kriege und des Militärs," in *Was ist Militärgeschichte?*, 229-62; Gunda Barth-Scalmani, "Le donne austriace durante la Prima Guerra Mondiale nella storiografia austriaca," in *Donne in guerra 1915-1918*, ed. Paola Antolini et al., Judicaria Summa Laganensis 12 (Rovereto: Centro Studi Judicaria, 2007), 31-46.

32. The Austrian Science foundation FWF is currently listing four war-related projects: P 20307 "Der Erste Weltkrieg im kollektiven Gedächtnis" (Werner Suppanz); P 22233 "Kinderschutzbewegung in Österreich" (Elisabeth Malleier); P 21505 "Besatzung der Ukraine durch Mittelmächte" (Stephan Karner); P 20189 "Österreichische Pressefotografie" (Anton Holzer).

33. Cletus Pichler, *Der Krieg in Tirol 1915/1916* (Innsbruck 1924).

34. Viktor Schemfil, *Das k.u.k. 3. Regiment der Tiroler Kaiserjäger im Weltkriege 1914 - 1918* (Bregenz: Teutsch, 1926).

35. Viktor Schemfil, *Col di Lana: Genaue Geschichte der Kämpfe 1915-1917 um den heißestumstrittenen Berg der Dolomiten, verfasst aufgrund österreichischer Truppenakten und authentischer reichsdeutscher Berichte sowie italienischer kriegsgeschichtlicher Werke* (Bregenz: Teutsch, 1935); idem, *Die Pasubio-Kämpfe 1916 – 1918: Genaue Geschichte des Ringens um einen wichtigsten Stützpfeiler der Tiroler Verteidigungsfront, verfasst aufgrund österreichischer Feldakten und italienischer kriegsgeschichtlicher Werke* (Bregenz: Teutsch, 1936); idem., *Die Kämpfe im Drei Zinnen-Gebiet* (Innsbruck: Wagner, 1955); idem., *Die Kämpfe am Kreuzberg in Sexten 1915-1917* (Innsbruck: Wagner, 1957); idem., *Die Kämpfe am Monte Piano und im Cristallo-Gebiet 1915-1917* (Innsbruck: Wagner, 1984).

36. Anton Tschurtschentahler, *Col di Lana 1916: Erinnerungen des letzten Verteidigers* (Innsbruck: Wagner, 1957). An example for a foreign view is Paul Niehans, *Fünfzehn Monate im Kampfgebiet der Dolomiten: Erlebnisse eines Schweizer Arztes* (Bern: Wyss, 1918).

37. Fridolin Tschugmell, *"Während der Messe sangen die Granaten": Kriegstagebuch 1915-1918* (Schaan: Alpenland Verlag, 2004); Gerhard Oberkofler, "Das Tagebuch von Hauptmann Hugo Huslig im 2. Tiroler Kaiserjäger-Regiment (29. Juli 1914 bis 25. November 1914)," *Tiroler Heimat: Jahrbuch für Geschichte und Volkskunde 53* (1989): 67-103; Alois Schreiber, *Vier Jahre als Infanterist im 1. Weltkrieg: Tagebuch von Josef Schreiber* (Freiberg: published by the author, 1998); Matthias Ladurner-Parthanes, *Kriegstagebuch eines Kaiserjägers* (Bozen: Athesia, 1996).

38. Heinz Lichem, *Rommel 1917: Der Wüstenfuchs als Gebirgssoldat* (Munich 1975); idem., *Spielhahnstoß und Edelweiß: Friedens- und Kriegsgeschichte der Tiroler Hochgebirgstruppe "Die Kaiserschützen" von ihren Anfängen bis 1918* (Kottgeisering 1977); idem., *Der Einsame Krieg: Erste Gesamtdokumentation des Gebirgskrieges 1915-1918 von den Julischen Alpen bis zum Stilfser Joch*, 8th ed. (Bozen: Athesia, 2002; Italian ed. 1996); idem., *Der Tiroler Hochgebirgskrieg im Luftbild* (Berwang: Steiger, 1985); idem., *Krieg in den Alpen*, 3 vols. (Augsburg 1993; Italian ed. 1991-1995).

39. Eisterer and Steininger, eds., *Tirol und der Erste Weltkrieg*, with contributions focusing on Tyrol about the myth and reality about the *Standschützen* (Christoph von Hartungen), about the people's mood and experiences during the war (Hans Heiss), about hunger and starvation (G. Prassnigger), about the Dolomite war in the movies (Helmut Alexander), and about refugees, evacuation and social welfare (Hermann Kuprian).

40. See Richard Schober, "Die neueren Forschungen über den Ersten Weltkrieg im Rahmen des EU-Interreg-III-Projektes (Österreich-Italien) am Tiroler Landesarchiv: Ein projektbezogener Überblick," in *Zwischen Nation und Region*, 135-45.

41. Gerd Pircher, *Militär, Verwaltung und Politik in Tirol im Ersten Weltkrieg*, Tirol im Ersten Weltkrieg 1 (Innsbruck: Wagner, 1995); Matthias Rettenwander, *Stilles Heldentum? Wirtschafts- und Sozialgeschichte Tirols im Ersten Weltkrieg*, Tirol im Ersten Weltkrieg 2 (Innsbruck: Wagner, 1997); Oswald Überegger, *Der andere Krieg: Die Tiroler Militärgerichtsbarkeit im Ersten Weltkrieg*, Tirol im Ersten Weltkrieg 3 (Innsbruck: Wagner, 2002); idem., ed., *Zwischen Nation und Region*; Matthias Rettenwander, *Der Krieg als Seelsorge: Katholische Kirche und Volksfrömmigkeit in Tirol im Ersten Weltkrieg*, Tirol im Ersten Weltkrieg 5 (Innsbruck: Wagner, 2006); Oswald Überegger, *Heimatfronten: Dokumente zur Erfahrungsgeschichte der Tiroler Kriegsgesellschaft im Ersten Weltkrieg*, Tirol im Ersten Weltkrieg 6,1 und 6,2 (Innsbruck: Wagner, 2006); Werner Auer, *Kriegskinder: Schule und Bildung in Tirol im Ersten Weltkrieg*, Tirol im Ersten Weltkrieg 7 (Innsbruck: Wagner, 2008).

42. 1997: Der Gebirgskrieg: Front und Hinterland; 2001: Gebirgskrieg in den Dolomiten: Der Raum Cortina d'Ampezzo; 2004: Galizien und Bukowina: Auf den Spuren der Kaiserjäger; 2005: Gebirgskrieg – Spurensuche und Erinnerungskultur zum Ersten Weltkrieg im Trentino: Trient-Rovereto-Folgaria-Lardaro-Tonale; 2007: Erster Weltkrieg: Karnien – Isonzo – Karst; 2009: Civilian and military war experiences in the Dolomites. See Gunda Barth-Scalmani and Hermann Kuprian, "Der erste Weltkrieg in den Bergen: Familiäre Erinnerungsspuren – Didaktische Annäherung – Bilaterale Forschungskooperation," *L'Homme. Zeitschrift für feministische Geschichtswissenschaft 12* (2001): 154-59.

43. Brigitte Mazohl-Wallnig and Kurt Scharr, "Der Forschungsschwerpunkt Erster Weltkrieg der Abteilung für Österreichische Geschichte am Institut für Geschichte der Universität Innsbruck," in *Zwischen Nation und Region*, 125-34. For the surplus value added by these excursions for professional activities see Gunda Barth-Salmani, "Kulturtourismus: Herausforderung für Geschichtsabsolventen," *Der Schlern. Monatszeitschrift für Südtiroler Landeskunde 78* (Dec. 2004): 75-80.

44. Some were presented at a conference and extracts published in *Der Schlern. Monatszeitschrift für Südtiroler Landeskunde 78* (Dec. 2004).

45. Emilio Franzina, ed., *Una Trincea chiamata Dolomiti* (Udine: Paolo Gaspari, 2003); and Brigitte Mazohl et al., eds., *Ein Krieg – Zwei Schützengräben: Österreich – Italien und der Erste Weltkrieg in den Dolomiten 1915-1918* (Bozen: Athesia, 2005).

46. Special issue "Region in Waffen," ed. Oswald Überegger and Camillo Zadra, *Geschichte und Region/Storia e regione 14* (2/2005).

47. Überegger and Kuprian, eds., *Der Erste Weltkrieg im Alpenraum*.

48. Present Trentino includes the Italian speaking parts of the historic county Tyrol (the district of Cortina d'Ampezzo being a part of the Veneto region). Some refer to it with the old term of "Welschtirol," others dismiss the term, arguing it transports still a sublime pejorative viewpoint.

49. <http://www.museodellaguerra.it> (19 Dec. 2009); partly also in English.

50. Quinto Antonelli, "Das Archiv für populare Selbstzeugnisse und die neue sozial- und mentalitätshistorische Geschichtsschreibung über den Ersten Weltkrieg," in *Zwischen Nation und Region*, 153-62. See also <http://www.museostorico.tn.it/asp/default.htm> (19 Dec. 2009).

51. Some examples are Girolamo Borella et al., *Chiedo notizie o di vita o di morte: Lettere a don Giovanni Rossi capellano militare della Grande Guerra*, Memorie 9 (Rovereto: Museo Storico Italiano della Guerra, 2004); Damiano Chiesa, *Diario e lettere 1914-1916*, Memorie 10 (Rovereto: Museo Storico Italiano della Guerra, 2006); Gian Luigi Fait, ed., *Sui campi della Galizia 1914-*

1917, 2nd ed. (Rovereto: Museo Storico Italiano della Guerra, 2004); for more see <http://www.museodellaguerra.it/3_book_01.htm> (19 Dec. 2009); Quinto Antonelli and Donatella Segata, eds., *Kriegsnotizen: la Grande Guerra nei diari austriaci*, testi 14 (Trento: Museo storico in Trento), <http://www.museostorico.tn.it/asp/default.htm> (19 Dec. 2009).

52. Diego Leoni and Camillo Zadra, eds., *La Grande Guerra: Esperienza memoria immagine* (Bologna: il Mulino, 1986). Recently published in German: Giovanna Procacci, *Die italienische Forschung über den Ersten Weltkrieg*, in *Zwischen Nation und Region*, 33-62.

53. See Mario Isnenghi, *Il Mito della Grande Guerra*, 6th ed. (Bologna: Mulino, 2007); Enzo Forcella and Alberto Monticone, *Plotone d'esecuzione: Processi della prima guerra mondiale*, 1st ed. 1968, reprint (Bari: Laterza, 1998).

54. See Giovanna Procacci, *Dalla rassegnazione alle rivolte: Mentalità e comportamenti populare nella grande guerra* (Rome: Bulzoni, 1999).

55. Mario Isnenghi and Giorgio Rochat, *La Grande guerra 1914-1918* (Florence: Scandicci, 2000).

56. The peasantry loyal to the emperor and catholic vs. the liberal, higher educated townsfolk moved by Italian nationalism. See Luciana Palla, *Fra realtà e mito: La Grande Guerra nelle valli ladine* (Milan: Ngeli, 1991); Fabio Todero, *Morire per la Patria: I Voluntari del "Litorale austriaco" nella Grande Guerra* (Udine: Gaspari, 2005); Roberto Todero, *Dalla Galizia all'Isonzo: Storia e storie soldati Triestini nella Grande Guerra* (Udine: Gaspari, 2006); P. Dogliano et al., *La scelta della patria: Giovanni voluntari nella grande Guerra* (Rovereto: Museo Storico Italiano della Guerra, 2006). A comparative research of men with Austrian or Hungarian citizenship who served as war volunteers in armies of co-national states (i.e. Rumanians of the Bukowina in the Rumanian army) has not yet been made. The most prominent Trentino war veterans in Italian service were the former member of the Austrian *Reichsrat* and Tyrolian *Landtag* (diet) Cesare Battisti (1875-1916), Damiano Chiesa (1894-1916), and Fabio Filzi (1884-1916), who having been captured by the Austrian army, were sentenced to death by an Austrian court martial.

57. See Hermann Kuprian, "'Entheimatungen': Flucht und Vertreibung in der Habsburgermonarchie während des Ersten Weltkriegs und ihre Konsequenzen," in *Der Erste Weltkrieg im Alpenraum*, 289-308; Walter Mentzel, "Kriegsflüchtlinge in Cisleithanien im Ersten Weltkrieg," PhD. diss., University of Vienna, 1997. The various refugee camps in Styria, Upper Austria or Bohemia have been studied by historians of the regions they came from. See Diego Leoni and Camillo Zadra, eds., *La città di legno: Profughi trentini in Austria* (Trento: Temi, 1981).

58. See Bruna Bianchi, ed., *La violenza contro la polulazione civile nella Grande Guerra: Deportati, profughi, internati* (Milan: Unicopli, 2006).

59. Best known in German are the books by a historical amateur Vasja Klavora, *Blaukreuz: Die Isonzofront: Flitsch/Bovec 1915-1917* (Klagenfurt: Hermagoras, 1993); idem., *Schritte im Nebel: Die Isonzofront Karfreit/Kobarid – Tolmein/Tolmin* (Klagenfurt: Hermagoras, 1996); idem., *Monte San Gabriele: Die Isonzofront* (Klagenfurt: Hermagoras, 1998); idem., *Die Karstfront* (Klagenfurt: Hermagoras, 2008); and Marko Simić, *Die Schlachten am Isonzo: 888 Tage Krieg im Karst* (Graz: Stocker, 2003; reprint Klagenfurt: Hermagoras, 2006; Slovene original in 1996); idem., *Auf den Spuren der Isonzofront* (Graz: Stocker, 1999; reprint Klagenfurt: Hermagoras, 2004; Slovene original in 1996); idem., *Utrbi pod Rombonom* (Ljubljana: Rombon, 2005).

60. See for the population of the Isonzo area Petra Svoljšak, "La populazione civile nella zona di guerra," in *Grande Guerra e populazione civile*, ed. Camillo Pavan (Treviso: Pavan, 1997), 241-66. On refugees, Drago Sedmak, "Profughi nelle 'citta di legno,'" in ibid., 265-98.

61. See Andreas Moritsch, ed., *Alpen – Adria: Zur Geschichte einer Region* (Klagenfurt: Hermagoras, 2001).

62. MartaVerginella, "Der Erste Weltkrieg und die Slovenen," in *Alpen – Adria*, 417-21. With a larger perspective on the Isonzo area see Andreas Moritsch, *Isonzo-Protokolle* (Klagenfurt: Hermagoras, 1994). The contributions of a conference given by the Austrian Science and Research Liason Office ASO in Ljubljana/Laibach, which took place in 2005 in Bovec/Flitsch, focusing on "Die Isonzofront 1915-1915: Kultur des Erinnerns," unfortunately has not yet been published <http://www.aso.zsi.at/sl/veranstaltung/707.html> (20 Dec. 2009).

63. To understand war as an extreme form of change of cultural landscapes, see B. Alavi and G. Henke-Bockschatz, "Mit Schülern Kulturlandschaften lesen," *Geschichte in Wissenschaft und Unterricht* 57 (5/2006): 300-09.

64. I.e. the collection of the Lancedelli family in Cortina d'Ampezzo, has been on public view for a few years in the former Austrian fortress Tre Sassi at the Valparola Pass, "Museo della Grande Guerra a Cortina d'Ampezzo," <http://www.lagrandeguerra.net/ggmtresassi.html> (18 Dec. 2009).

65. I.e. at Pieve di Livinalongo/Buchenstein. See Luciana Palla, *Vicende di guerra sulle Dolomiti (1914-1918): Soldati e populazione nella zone del Fronte del Col di Lana* (Seren del Grappa: DBS stampa, 1995).

66. Rovereto 1919 first drafts, 1921 opening; Gorizia: 1924 Museo della redenzione, 1938 new name: Museo della Guerra e della Redenzione; See Antonio Sema and Lucio Fabi, *Guida al Museo della Grande Guerra* (Gorizia: published by the museum, 2002).

67. *Katalog zum Museum der Tiroler Kaiserjäger, der Andreas Hofer Galerie und des Tiroler Ehrenbuches, mit Erläuterungen der Gedenkstätten auf dem Berg Isel* (Innsbruck without publisher and year); *Museumsführer Rainer-Museum auf der Festung Hohensalzburg* (Salzburg without publisher and year).

68. Brigitte Strauss is currently working on a PhD about war museums in Austria and Italy in the interwar period.

69. Camillo Zadra, "Der 'Große Krieg' und seine Spuren im Trentino: Historisches Bewusstsein und Erhaltungsmaßnahmen," in *Zwischen Nation und Region*, 147-53.

70. Ideas about war museums might have been transferred by professional officers and their networks.

71. The first president of the *Dolomitenfreunde* until 1977 was Ludwig Jedlicka, by then the nestor of Austrian contemporary historians; this supported the seriousness of Schaumann's attempts. See *Fünfundzwanzig Jahre Friedenswege, Jahresbericht Dolomitenfreunde 1997*, <http://www.dolomitenfreunde.at/index_d.htm> (18 Dec. 2009).

72. See in his autobiography Walther Schaumann, *Unterwegs zwischen Krieg und Frieden* (Klagenfurt: Hermagoras, 2006). The motto chosen reflects that it had been motivated by the violent conflicts that took place in the 1960s by Germans of South Tyrol against Italian state institutions.

73. Based on his experiences, Schaumann published special guide books for tourists in both languages. See Walther Schaumann, *Schauplätze des Gebirgskrieges* (Bassano del Grappa: Tassotti, 1972-1978). Several editions cover the Austro-Italian front from the Ortler to Carinthia. They are very helpful for planning excursions and reflect the authors' interest for war technology, the broader historic framework is missing. In the meantime his books found many follow-ups.

74. Walther Schaumann, *Monte Piano: Landschaft und Geschichte: Das Freilichtmuseum 1915-1917* (Bassano del Grappa 1986, 3rd ed. 1995).

75. <http://www.karnische-alpen.com> (18 Dec. 2009). See Gabriele and Walther Schaumann, *Unterwegs vom Pustertal zum Plöckenpass: Auf den Spuren der Karnischen Front 1915-1917* (Klagenfurt: Hermagoras, 2003).

76. Walther and Gabriele Schaumann, *Führer durch das Freilichtmuseum am Plöckenpass und seine Zugangswege*, 2nd ed. (Klagenfurt: Hermagoras, 2005); idem., *Unterwegs vom Plöckenpass zum Kanaltal: Das Freilichtmuseum 1915-1917* (Klagenfurt: Hermagoras, 2004).

77. Walther Schaumann, *Die Südwestfront in ausgewählten Texten und historischen Bildern aus dem Museum der Dolomitenfreunde in Kötschach-Mauthen* (Vienna 1993), <http://www.dolomitenfreunde.at/index_d.htm> (26 Aug. 2008).

78. The *Heeresgeschichtliche Museum* (<http://www.hgm.or.at>), Vienna, financed by the Republic of Austria, has dedicated some rooms of its permanent exhibitions to the First World War.

79. Unpublished evaluation of questionnaires of participants of the excursion in September 2007.

80. In the last ten years, on average, 15,000 visitors every year, mid-May to mid-October.

81. According to the information in the travel guide by Friedrich Köthe and Daniela Schetar, *Slowenien mit Triest*, 3rd ed. (Bielefeld 2006), 204. The homepage of the museum does not give any background information on the foundation of the museum.

82. <http://www.kobariski-muzej.si> (28 Aug. 2008).

83. Wording following the title of the book by a then leading commander Alfred Krauss, *Das Wunder von Karfreit im besonderen der Durchbruch von Flitsch und die Bezwingung des Tagliamento* (Munich: Lehmann, 1926).

84. In the former fortress Flitscher Klause (Kluže north of Bovec). Simič, *Spuren der Isonzofront*, 30, regreted in 1996 that the fortress was without reasonable function, but in 2005 a museum based on private collections was already in existence.

85. See <http://www.lto-sotocje.si/pdf/Kobariska_zgodovinska_pot_DEU.pdf> (19 Dec. 2009).

86. A first presentation in the net by 2007, <http://www.potimiruvposocju.si/_de/index.php?lang=de&page=muzejinaprostem> (19 Dec. 2009), since 2008 also in German (besides Slovene, English and Italian).

87. For example at Log pod Mangartom, with information panel (in three languages) at the entrance to the railroad gallery to Cave del Predil/Raibl (Italy) in Kanaltal/Canale di ferro south of Tarvis.

88. For example the Holy Saint Chapel (Heiliggeist/Sv.duh) in Javorca (<http://www.lto-sotocje.si/deutsch/znamenitosti_javorca.asp>, 18 Dec. 2009), a wooden construction built in 1916 by the 3rd k.u.k. *Gebirgsbrigade* in art deco style. It is a good example of a specific culture of remembrance: in the interwar time, situated on Italian territory then, Italians looked after it, in the 1960s and 1980s local initiatives cared for it. After damages by a heavy earthquake in 1998, the Slovene state had it renovated completely in 2004/05. In 2007 it was declared a European cultural monument. Its relevance is also reflected by the fact that the website of the foundation *Poti miru v Posočju* does show its picture and elements of the side altar are used for the frame of other pages of that site. See in English <http://www.potimiruvposocju.si/_en/index.php?lang=en&page=predstavitev> (19 Dec. 2009).

89. Ibid.

90. Topical map *Pot Miru/The Walk of Peace/Weg des Friedens/Il Sentiero della pace/ Sočka Fronta/ The Isonzo Front/Die Isonzofront/Il fronte Isontino* (Kobarid 2007), in four languages with comments can be obtained for free by the tourist information board. A map with scale 1:50,0000, *Die Isonzofront vom Rombon bis Mengore: Historisch-touristische Landkarte*, 2nd ed. (Kobarid 2006), indicates the front line in a mat of trails. Additional a booklet *Weg des Friedens: Führer der Isonzofront im oberen Sočatal* (without year). Both media are in all four languages.

91. See Lucio Fabi, *Sul Carso della Grande Guerra: Storia, itinerari, monumenti, musei* (Udine: Paolo Gaspari, 2005); Information about various activities: <http://www.prolocofoglianoredipuglia.it/index.php?idcategoria=3> (19 Dec. 2009).

92. Interreg programs intend to stimulate the cooperation on the regional level beyond national borders. The European Union pays 50 percent of the project, the participating regions the other half.

93. Opening 1909, a year after the 60 year anniversary of Franz Joseph's reign, as "Imperial road". Due to reconstruction work on existing roads or trails it made possible to ride in an automobile from Toblach (1241m) in the Pustertal via Cortina d'Ampezzo (1237m) to the Falzarego Pass (2105m), via Buchenstein/Pieve di Livinalongo (1475m) to the Pordoi Pass (2239m), via the val di Fassatal to the Karrerpass/Paso di Costalungo(1745m) and the Karrersee/Carezza al lago to Bozen/Bolzano (266m). See Theodor Chrisostomannos, *Die neue Dolomitenstrasse* (Vienna: Reisser, 1913).

94. One can assume that more men have been killed by the force of nature (avalanches, freeze) than by combat activities.

95. Prepared in collaboration with the universities of Innsbruck and Venice, see Brigitte Mazohl-Wallnig and Kurt Scharr, "Der Forschungsschwerpunkt Erster Weltkrieg," 127-28.

96. *Die senkrechte Front 1914-1917: Der Erste Weltkrieg von Cortina d'Ampezzo bis zum Kleinen Lagazuoi*, *Montagne Armate*, video tapes and DVDs without year (2003/04). A map of trails *Dolomitenfront/Fronte Dolomtico italo-austriaco 1915/17*, German and Italian edition (Innsbruck: Kompass, 2004) has been out of print very quickly.

97. <http://www.dolomiti.org/ita/cortina/laga5torri/storia/introGuerra.html> (19 Dec. 2009); <http://www.grandeguerra.dolomiti.org/default.html> (19 Dec. 2009). The first site is more connected with tourist activities. The sites are also published in German and English. See Stefan Illing and Isabelle Brandauer, *Der Erste Weltkrieg auf dem Sasso di Stria: Illustrierter Führer der Kriegstellungen mit historischen Zeugnissen* (Cortina d'Ampezzo: published by the authors, 2008).

98. <http://www.bellumaquilarum.it> (19 Dec. 2009).

99. *Der Erste Weltkrieg 1914-1918: Die Tiroler Front 1915-1918*, Die große Ausstellung zum Krieg in den heimatlichen Bergen (Südtiroler Schützenbund, 2005).

100. Italian and German version online, Italian version of the tourist brochure "Sceneries of the Great War," <http://www.turismofriuliveneziagiulia.it/areadownload/pdf_ing/Scenaries_of_the_Great_War.pdf> (19 Dec. 2009).

101. His military rank from the Second World War (!) is mentioned without referring to his position in 1917.

102. See for the activities of an initiative in Redipuglia, only in Italian: <http://www.prolocofoglianoredipuglia.it/index.php?idcategoria=3&idsezione=19> (19 Dec. 2009).

103. See Daniele Ravenna and Giuseppe Severini, *Il Patrimonio Storico della Grande Guerra: Commento alla legge 7 marzo 2001, n. 78*, 2nd ed. (Udine: Paolo Gaspari, 2002). Online <http://www.earmi.it/diritto/leggi/prguerra.htm> (19 Dec. 2009).

104. See Fortunato Turrini, "Die Auseinandersetzung von Schülern mit einem Krieg der Ur-(Großväter)," in *Pejo 1914-1918: La guerra sulla porta*, ed. idem. (Pejo: Comune di Pejo, 1998).

105. Aleida Assmann, "Das kulturelle Gedächtnis zwischen Archiv und Kanon," in *Speicher des Gedächtnisses: Bibliotheken, Mussen, Archive*, vol. 2, *Die Erfindung des Ursprungs, Die Systematisierung der Zeit*, ed. Moritz Csáky and Peter Stachel (Vienna: Passagen, 2001), 22.

Pan-Germanism after Empire: Austrian "Germandom" at Home and Abroad

Julie Thorpe

In June 1937, the Benedictine historian and professor at the University of Graz, Hugo Hantsch, addressed dignitaries of the government and Catholic Church on the occasion of the St Boniface Day celebrations in Vienna. Hantsch was also chairman of the Austrian Association for Germandom Work Abroad (*Österreichischer Verband für volksdeutsche Auslandsarbeit*), which had been founded in 1934 by the Austrofascist state's Fatherland Front to foster relations with German minorities outside of Austria. In his opening remarks, Hantsch noted that this was the second Boniface Day he had organized under the umbrella of the ÖVVA and he explained why he had chosen to appropriate the legacy of Boniface for the work of "Germandom" abroad. Firstly, the very existence of the *Auslandsdeutsche* was due to the missionary work of St. Boniface, who had woken the German lands from "a slumbering Christendom"; secondly, because if the ÖVVA and its supporters did not continue Boniface's mission to the German-speakers abroad, if they did not see to it that their coreligionists continued to say German prayers, sing German hymns, and hear German sermons, then these people would be lost to the German nation.[1]

The humble pleasure Hantsch took in linking this First Apostle to the Germans to Austria's mission to preserve and advance German Christianity in Europe suited the political and religious climate in Austria during the 1930s. We will see in this chapter how religion and nation were twinned together not only during the years of Austrofascism in the 1930s, but also during the first years of the Austrian republic.[2] Reviving "all-German" themes of belief and action were important ways of commemorating the destruction of the German nation after the First World War. By rebuilding Austria's German Christian heritage through its political and religious institutions, Austrian leaders helped to politicise and popularise the memory of a pan-German identity in the aftermath of empire. Germans abroad and Germans at home were all members of this pan-German community in the political and religious imagination of interwar Austria.

Pan-Germanism was thus not an ideology of fringe dwellers, but the preferred cultural and political framework for constructing an Austrian national identity. It was broad enough to encompass, at various times, liberals, German-nationalists, Catholics, socialists and Nazis, but it was also specific to particular events that it could represent social needs and concerns on different occasions. My definition of pan-Germanism, therefore, is also broader than the conventional Anglophone usage of the term and my evidence reflects that breadth of analysis by selection of examples typically not associated with a pan-German movement in Austria. This article demonstrates that to subscribe to pan-Germanism in Austria one had only to subscribe to the notion that Austria belonged to the German nation and was itself a German state.

"Pan-Germans" and Pan-Germanism

> Pan-Germanism in its original and most comprehensive sense meant no more than the general desire to promote the political and cultural unity of all Germans wherever they lived, and to make all Germans realise that to work for this unity was their highest mission .... [It] repudiated the entire conventional political spectrum and the ethical, humanitarian, and religious principles that underlay the conventional political camps of both the Left and the Right.... It was, in short, a movement that aimed at replacing the politics of consensus with the politics of extremism.[3]

Andrew Whiteside's study of pan-Germanism's origins and fluctuating fortunes over the course of half a century prior to World War One is striking for what it reveals about the absence of a pan-German movement in Austria. Divided by class, regional, ethnic, religious and generational loyalties, Whiteside's "Pan-Germans" were neither a camp nor a movement. His definition of pan-Germanism as a belief or "desire" for German unity and a common mission is much more useful in assessing the breadth of pan-Germanism in Austria both before and after 1918. It might also be understood as an identity matrix in which various camps, movements and parties followed their own political and cultural agendas at the same time that they had to orientate their multiple paths within the same national framework.

Traditional histories of pan-Germanism, however, including Whiteside's, emphasize only one path of radical nationalists from Georg von Schönerer's "All-German" liberals in the late nineteenth century to Heinrich von Srbik's interwar "pan-German" (*gesamtdeutsche*) school of historiography that gave intellectual credence to National Socialism's Thousand Year Empire. Schönerer's "all-German" solution, which gained popular support amongst university fraternities, was to dismember Austria-Hungary and join Austria with the German Reich through a constitutional alliance.[4] Later he moved away from strictly political solutions to champion racial legislation against Jews, eventually losing all but a handful of supporters amongst former radical fraternity members. As a former student radical nationalist in Vienna, Srbik had shunned Schönerer's populist brand of nationalist activism but rejected none of the political goals of the "Schönerianer" movement. Although he preferred to think in terms of idealist rather than political solutions, Srbik firmly believed that political unity of the German nation was the natural course of German history since the days of the Holy Roman Empire.[5]

The linear connection between Schönerer and Srbik—or more commonly Schönerer and Hitler—in most accounts of pan-Germanism in Austria has led to a narrow definition of "pan-Germans" as a fringe political group outside the mainstream Christian Social and Social Democratic parties.[6] Following this definition, historians of interwar fascism in Austria have subscribed to the teleological view that the Nazis were the twentieth-century heirs of the Schönerianer.[7] The argument that pan-Germans were fringe dwellers on the political landscape may appear warranted when we compare the fortunes of German-nationalist parties with the "cradle to grave" parties of Catholics and socialists. Unlike the mass followings gained by the Christian Social and Social Democratic parties towards the end of the 1880s, electoral success for German nationalists remained elusive due to their factionalism and regional disunity, and they concentrated their energies instead on local activism in schools, municipal councils and the press to win support at the ballot box.

Yet when we consider that each of the major parties in interwar Austria—the Greater Germans, the Christian Socials and the Social Democrats—all used the term "pan-German" to describe the national identification of Austrian Germans with other Germans in Central Europe, and the special identity of Austria as a German state, historians may need to look beyond the ballot box to explain how pan-Germanism formed the contours of Austria's national identity and allowed "being German" to govern other political, social, cultural, regional and spiritual forms of identity.[8] The following sections will trace these forms of identification with pan-Germanism as a national identity that articulated Austria's mission both within and beyond its borders.

Germandom at Home: Rebuilding Austria's German heritage

In the wake of military defeat and imperial collapse, Austria's German-speaking political parties expressed their pan-Germanism in political terms of unity with the German republic. The SDAP was initially the leading advocate of Anschluss while German-nationalists, wary of socialism, and the Christian Social Party, fearing another *Kulturkampf* against Catholics, distanced themselves from union with Germany. The SDAP's chief architect and spokesperson of the Anschluss idea was Otto Bauer, who succeeded Viktor Adler as party leader in 1918 and was Austria's foreign minister from 1918-1919. Bauer's main forum prior to the party's ban in 1934 was the socialist journal *Der Kampf*, in which he continued to promote Austro-German unity on economic and political grounds. The party's 1926 Linz Programme advocated Anschluss "by peaceful means," and the party only abandoned this goal in October 1933, ten months after Hitler had come to power in Germany. Throughout his exile in Czechoslovakia, and briefly in Paris, between 1934 and 1938, Bauer wrote for the journal of the underground Social Democrats, *Der sozialistische Kampf*. In April 1938, he cautioned his readers not to resist the political union between Austria and Germany because, he believed, the eventual defeat of Nazism would ultimately bring about the "pan-German (*gesamtdeutsche*) revolution" first espoused by Marx in 1848. Not all workers shared these pan-German sentiments and the left wing of the party did not support Anschluss, but the party leadership defended its position until 1943, in contrast to their socialist counterparts in non-German states who fought for national independence under fascist regimes.[9]

For his part Bauer never retracted his position that Austrians were simply a tribe (*Stamm*) within the German nation.[10] Karl Renner, who famously voted "yes" in a plebiscite on Anschluss with Germany in April 1938, declared that Austrians and Germans were "one tribe [*Stamm*] and one community of destiny."[11] The statements of Bauer and Renner in the particular contexts in which they were made do not stand on their own as evidence for broad pan-German sympathies amongst Austria's working population, but aside from their political content these statements do express the universal dimensions of pan-Germanism that were broadly held and articulated repeatedly in the interwar years. The belief that Austria was part of a wider German nation—whether as a separate tribe within that nation or of one common tribe and community—remained undisputed before 1938 and even by war's end. Perhaps the German nation had suffered a political and moral defeat, but none doubted that Germans shared a unity that went beyond political borders.

Commitment to a universal idea of pan-Germanism did not waver amongst Austria's Christian Social leaders either during the interwar years despite their initial divisions on the issues of Anschluss and republicanism. Backed by a predominantly agrarian sector that had been drained by the wartime economy, the party's republican wing tended to support Anschluss for economic reasons, while anti-republican groups with economic interests in the Habsburg successor states advocated a Danubian Federation.[12] These divisions were far from clear-cut, however, and views on Austro-German relations shifted throughout the interwar years. The official Christian Social programme of November 1926 stated the party's commitment to the right of self-determination for Germans and its task of "cultivating German ways" and combating Jewish influence in intellectual and economic spheres.[13] During the 1930s, the Christian Socials adopted a more explicit German-nationalist position in a calculated effort to attract young right-wing Catholics to the party and prevent them from joining the National Socialist party. Richard Schmitz's 1932 commentary to the 1926 party programme with its references to cultural German unity and Austrian "*völkisch*" character was a deliberate strategy of wedge politics aimed at marginalizing the Nazis by narrowing the terms of pan-Germanism to cultural identity rather than ethnicity.[14] Yet the party's anti-Semitism, couched in cultural, economic and religious arguments, was not averse to ethnic arguments about quotas on Jews in universities and in the professions, and party leaders considered legislation for an Aryan paragraph well before the Nazis took to the streets and printing presses to demand similar restrictions.[15]

Outside of party politics, other visions of pan-German unity drew on religious themes of a common humanity to preserve the spiritual mission of the German people in Europe. One did not even have to be a practising Catholic to uphold this mission, though it certainly helped to have the archbishop on one's side. Salzburg's archbishop, Ignatius Rieder, championed a religious renewal movement in the interwar period that included plans to establish both a German Catholic university and an international festival in Salzburg. The idea for a German Catholic university had its roots in the 1848 Catholic associational movement in Germany and Austria, but the Austro-Prussian War and dissolution of the German Confederation had halted plans for such a university, and Rieder wanted to revive the idea in the aftermath of military defeat in 1918.[16] Along similar lines to renew the spiritual and intellectual life of German-speakers in Europe, Rieder also lent his support to the founders of the Salzburg Festival, Hugo von Hofmannsthal and Max Reinhardt. Hofmannstahl consulted with Rieder in 1922 for final approval of his manuscript for *Das Salzburger grosse Welttheater* (The Salzburg Great World Theatre) in return for permission to stage the play in Salzburg's Baroque Church, and Rieder defended Reinhardt against frequent anti-Semitic attacks from Salzburg's Nazi organs.[17] For their part the Festival's founders also wanted to promote German art and culture in Salzburg: Hofmannstahl described Salzburg as the historic heart of the Bavarian-Austrian tribal lands, whose "instinctively German" folk ethos was the antithesis of Vienna's "alien" intelligentsia and obsession with novelty, while Reinhardt envisaged the Festival's "home-grown" German art as "the master of the house who chooses to extend the hand of friendship to guests."[18] Through their mission to preserve religious belief, German universalism and cosmopolitanism, the Festival organisers and patrons invoked an Austrian pan-German identity as a counterpoint to Nazism specifically, and to Protestant Prussian German identity more generally.[19]

Rieder was also patron of another cause to commemorate German Christendom's triumph over the unholy warriors from the Orient. On the occasion of the All-German Catholic Congress held in Vienna in September 1933, Rieder wrote the foreword for a book entitled *Catholic Faith and the German National Character in Austria*, produced by the National German Working Group of Austrian Catholics and published in Salzburg, in which he described 1933 as a "holy year for Germans" because it commemorated the 250th anniversary of the victory over the Turks in 1683.[20] Congress organizers were also commemorating two other events that year: the 500th anniversary of the completion of the tower of St. Stephens Cathedral in 1433 and the 80th anniversary of the first Catholic Congress held in Vienna in 1853. In addition, the pope had declared 1933 a "holy year" to commemorate the year of Christ's death and resurrection in the Church's calendar.[21] Pius XI sent a papal legate to attend the commemorative events in Vienna, but the papal declaration of a "holy year"was also interpreted by Austria's leaders as licence for a holy war against the enemies of "German Christian" Austria. Dollfuss's famous speech on 11 September in Vienna's racecourse in which he spoke of Austria's defeat in 1683 over the "hordes from the East" and called for a "Christian-German spirit of renewal" that would again repel the newest threat from "the East" was an attack on socialists, communists and Jews, including Jewish refugees from Nazi Germany.[22]

But whatever Rieder understood by a "holy year for Germans," he did not share Dollfuss's belligerence in linking wars of old with new. Indeed, while a few of the Austrian bishops did attend Dollfuss's speech, Rieder was notably absent, as was Cardinal Innitzer.[23] While Austria's politicians hoped to gain political mileage from the celebrations on the world Catholic stage, Austrian church leaders were hoping for a different kind of result: minds, bodies and souls actively participating in a pan-German mission throughout Europe. In March 1933, Cardinal Theodor Innitzer spoke about this mission in the lead up to the Catholic Congress. Touching on the subject of "blood and homeland" as the nation's source of renewal, Innitzer said that "it would be a misfortune for the happy future development of the German people" if the Catholic Church and its teaching stood opposed to this idea. "No, the Catholic Church knows exactly what indescribably great and ideal values lie in blood and homeland, in the unity of culture and tradition, in the unity of language and faith, in a common millennial history ...and the best national struggles have always had people who fought as true sons both of their Church and of their national faith."[24] The Nazi organ, *Deutsch-Österreichische Tageszeitung*, headlined Innitzer's comments two days later declaring that the cardinal's speech was a "recognition of the National Socialist work in rebuilding Central Europe" and that Innitzer had shown himself to be the true leader of the German church "who refuses to deny those forces rooted in blood and soil simply in order to remain the sinecure of a certain party, but seeks instead to ignite the power of faith in the awakening of those forces."[25]

Here we can begin to trace the multiple meanings that pan-Germanism held for its diverse proponents in Austria. While Innitzer spoke of the Catholic Church and its place in building the German nation, the Nazi organ spoke of a "German church" whose task it was to join forces with the national movement of "blood and soil." Interestingly, Innitzer did not use the term "soil" (*Boden*) to denote a common territory, but referred to "homeland" (*Heimat*) as a spiritual, historical and cultural place of belonging. Nor did he expound on his reference to blood in either the racial sense of German blood, or the redemptive sense of Christ's blood. Furthermore, whereas Innitzer likened the efforts to rebuild Germandom to all great national struggles that had involved Catholic patriots previously, the Nazi organ promoted only National Socialism's mission in Central Europe.

Innitzer chose not to mention "blood and homeland" in his welcome to Catholic pilgrims in Vienna in September, three months after the Nazi Party and its organs were banned in Austria. Instead he emphasized the dual loyalties of German Catholics to the Roman Catholic Church, "the mother of all nations," and to the German nation, which was manifest in their God-given identity as "people of the centre" (*Volk der Mitte*) between Eastern mysticism and Western humanism. Vienna and Austria were the "holy hearth" of this centre, and only when Catholic Vienna was again restored to its purpose and place as the imperial chamber of the whole German nation would Christendom be able to gain new strength and vitality in its centre. This imperative was not a matter of politics, Innitzer said, but of faith.[26] He did not refer to Austria's ties with Germany, nor did he mention the absence of the 36,000 German pilgrims who had registered for the congress but were prevented from attending after the German government imposed a 1000-Mark tariff on all travelers to Austria in May 1933.[27] Innitzer was personally saddened by the absence of the Germans and Cardinal Faulhaber, who was to have been the papal legate, but on this occasion he chose not to enter into the political domain.[28]

The absence of the German pilgrims at what was supposed to be an "All-German" Congress did not mar the proceedings for the delegates who did attend. Along with the 100,000 Austrian delegates, more than 30,000 pilgrims came from Czechoslovakia, Poland, Hungary, Switzerland and Italy, exceeding organizers' expectations that the Congress would be a celebration of things pan-European as well as pan-German.[29] The opening procession and reception for the papal delegate, Cardinal La Fontaine, in which pilgrims marched from St. Stephen's Cathedral in their "tribes" and "lands" to pay homage before the cross in square in front of the Karlskirche, was as much baroque Catholic spectacle as it was demonstration of national loyalties.[30] What was on display, above all, was the unity of Christendom in the "holy hearth" of Catholic Vienna: Led by the German "tribes and lands," this celebration embodied what Innitzer had meant by the German nation at the centre of Christendom.

The next section of this chapter shows Innitzer again promoting German Christianity alongside other proponents of a pan-German mission to reclaim German minorities outside of Austria for the German nation. Where he had come short of condemning "blood and soil" ideas in 1933 but instead had integrated these within a larger religious vision of tradition, culture, history, language, faith and patriotism, he spoke openly in 1937 against the persecution of German Catholics by an "un-Christian" regime. His religious commitment to the German nation remained intact as he spoke of the suffering of the whole German people when one part was afflicted, but he also spoke of a broader commitment to claim Germans and non-German minorities as part of an imperial mission to spread German Christianity abroad.

Germandom Abroad: Activists and Missionaries for German Austria

The Austrofascist government's chief organ for its work amongst German minorities outside Austria, the Austrian Association of Germandom Work Abroad (ÖVVA), was founded in April 1934 by the former Christian Social education minister, Emmerich Czermak; another former Christian Social politician and co-editor of the *Reichspost*, Heinrich Mataja; as well as Hugo Hantsch, who took over the leadership of the ÖVVA in January 1936 and was appointed advisor to the federal leadership of the Fatherland Front on all national matters. These men believed that by establishing an organization to serve the interests of German-speaking minorities abroad and continue the work of Germanizing Austria's own minorities, and by bringing this organization under the authority of the Fatherland Front, they could foil the attempt of National Socialists to gain a stronghold in provincial German-nationalist associations and redirect the activism of these groups towards the Austrian state rather than Nazi Germany.[31] One of these groups, the *Südmark* schools' association in Carinthia, which had led a campaign during the 1920s to shut down private Slovenian schools and remove Slovenian priests from their teaching posts, had been receiving funds from the German foreign office to build German schools and kindergartens in Slovenian-speaking towns.[32] Wanting to ensure that the Germanized inhabitants of Carinthia would be claimed for Austria not Germany, the ÖVVA invited leaders of the *Südmark* association to sit on its leadership in exchange for ÖVVA leaders to be represented on the leadership of the *Südmark* association.

In addition to rivalry with local nationalist groups, the ÖVVA also had to contend with *Auslandsdeutsche* organizations in Germany, in particular those with links to German-speaking Catholics in Czechoslovakia. The leader of the Reich Union for Catholic Germans Abroad wrote to Czermak in June 1934 demanding the ÖVVA's dissolution. The two men eventually reached a mutual understanding, but the hostility from the German side did not deter Austrian authorities from inviting children from Czechoslovakia for the Fatherland Front's children's summer holiday programme that year. The original idea of the *Kinderferienwerk* programme was to provide malnourished children from poor rural and working class families in Austria with a time of rest, outdoor activities and a nutritious diet, but the invitation was also extended to children abroad after 1933. Only seven came in 1934, but the following year 102 spent the summer in Austria, the majority from Czechoslovakia, and some from Yugoslavia as well.[33] In its efforts to make children from bilingual areas in neighbouring countries into German-speaking Austrians, and so prevent them becoming Czechs, Slovenes or Reich Germans, the *Kinderferienwerk* was a variation on the earlier *Kinderaustausche* in Bohemia and Moravia. Czech activists in the empire had originally sought to discourage these private exchanges of children in rural areas, but after 1918 they invented their own state-sponsored programmes in the interwar period with invitations extended abroad to children of Czech-speaking families in Vienna to spend a summer in Czechoslovakia.[34] In laying claim to German-speaking minorities outside of Austria, the ÖVVA was one of many state-sponsored initiatives throughout post-Habsburg Central Europe that sought to define a national community across state borders.

To carry out its mission abroad, the ÖVVA recruited members of the Austrofascist youth organization, the Austrian *Jungvolk* (ÖJV), supplying their leaders with teaching manuals so they in turn could recruit volunteers to collect money and books to donate to German-speaking minorities. The first major fundraising initiative of the ÖJV in June 1937 raised more than 20,000 Schillings for the work of the ÖVVA.[35] The ÖVVA also joined forces with the Lower Austrian farmers' league to invite a group of farmers from Hungary for a short visit in January 1937, and in October that year a whole class of young farming apprentices were invited to take part in a course on national education in Graz. Even the Vienna Boys' Choir were recruited as youth ambassadors of Austrian Germandom, touring abroad alongside the "Waltharia" university choral society, which held concerts as well as lectures in German-speaking areas of Hungary and Czechoslovakia.[36]

To be sure, these activities were not on the scale of the borderland "pilgrimages" in interwar Germany, where youth groups, women's leagues and academics were recruited by state-sponsored agencies to keep alive memories of Germany's lost borderland in the East, and were later incorporated wholesale into Nazi agencies in 1933 to continue the work abroad.[37] But in spite of the relatively late mobilization of youth and women's groups in Austria, ÖVVA leaders wasted no time getting the ÖJV on board as well as recruiting a women's auxiliary committee in Vienna and appointing a woman as deputy advisor under Hantsch to the federal leadership of the Fatherland Front.[38] That women were excluded from all public offices other than in the women's section of the Fatherland Front makes this achievement all the more remarkable and indicates that there were many women in the Austrofascist state who saw their service to the state not just in terms of motherhood and in the broader cultural and social function of motherhood in state- and Church-sponsored maternal and child welfare initiatives, but also in the realm of "Germandom" work. The success of this initiative also shows that the Austrofascist state had little trouble mobilizing followers behind its goal of Germanizing the borderlands, thanks to its ingenious idea to co-opt activists who had already cut their teeth on the borderlands of the empire.

The ÖVVA also founded its own press agency, the Austrian Correspondence for Germandom Work (ÖKVDA), to file stories from the front lines of the organization's work abroad.[39] These reports resembled articles in the German-nationalist press on the lack of schools for German-speakers in Slovenia and the "Czechification" of towns with a German-speaking population.[40] The work was often described as a mission field to which the faithful should give donations, if not their labour. An article in May 1937 reported that German Catholics outside the borders of Austria and Germany were forced to attend protestant churches because they could not attend mass in their mother tongue and called on readers to donate German prayer books, catechisms, Catholic newspapers and Bibles to these stranded believers. "Work in this mission field is Catholic work and German work, a service to the faith and the Church and a service to the German people at the same time." One only had to look to the "shining" example of the Holy Father himself, who had ministered to German Catholics in their mother tongue in Milan during the Great War.[41] Here the analogy to the mission field was embodied in the man who became Pius XI in 1922, whose papacy was marked by a call to lay missionary activism. The work of Germandom abroad required missionaries who, like soldiers, would be sent by their families and fellow believers in the cause to achieve victories for the nation. In making both a religious and national claim on the *Auslandsdeutsche*, the ÖVVA was able to represent a broad church of activists whose common goal was to extend the boundaries of the pan-German community to include German minorities outside of Austria. In this sense, both spiritual and secular visions of pan-Germanism converged in the dual religious and national claims to Germandom abroad.

If we return to the Boniface Day celebrations in June 1937, we can see how these multiple pan-German visions were able to be accommodated within the institutional structures of the ÖVVA, the Fatherland Front and the Catholic Church. Among the dignitaries who attended the festivities were Cardinal Innitzer; the Education Minister, Hans Perntner, as the official representative of Chancellor Schuschnigg (who had had to cancel his attendance at the last minute); and leaders of the Fatherland Front, including Hantsch. As we have already seen, Hantsch's opening remarks linked the apostolic legacy of Boniface to the work of the ÖVVA. Perntner also drew on this legacy as he praised the ÖVVA for continuing the "old and established tradition of the pioneering cultural work of the *Ostmarkdeutschtum*" and called on St Boniface to bless "this German cultural work...for our fatherland Austria."[42]

As saintly blessings were being invoked on behalf of the work of the Fatherland Front and the ÖVVA, it was left to the invited speaker, Leonhard Steinwender, canon of Mattsee monastery in Salzburg, to explain the meaning of Boniface's legacy for the German nation. In his speech Steinwender spoke about the eighth-century "Apostle to the Germans" who had united the German nation by converting the German tribes to Christianity and thereby "opened the door to world history for the German nation" to play a leading role in Western Christendom. But Boniface Day was more than just a day of commemoration, Steinwender cautioned; it was also a call to renounce those who had made idols out of the German nation instead of following the laws of the "eternal God" and to reclaim Boniface's legacy so that the German nation would not be consigned to a spiritual "desert" like the Africa of St Augustine, or descend into chaos like the Orient of the saints Chrysostom and Jerome. Echoing Innitzer's earlier call to reclaim their role as "people of the centre," Steinwender warned that if the German nation fell, all of Christendom would fall with it.[43]

Steinwender was referring primarily to the persecution of German clergy and Catholic associational life in Nazi Germany although he also mentioned the "satanic wave of anti-Christ Bolshevism" in his address.[44] But as we have seen in the cooperation between leaders of the *Südmark* association and the ÖVVA, the relationship between "Germandom" work and National Socialism was far more ambivalent than Steinwender believed. Steinwender was well known in Fatherland Front circles as editor of Salzburg's Catholic newspaper he had officially been made a functionary of the state on his appointment in 1934 as director of the Fatherland Front propaganda office and editor of Salzburg's official Front publication, *Die Front in Salzburg*.[45] But on this occasion, Steinwender's views went beyond the official propaganda of "Germandom" work to warn the German people of the danger of making idols out of human leaders. He ended his remarkable speech with a call to the German people to follow "a leader so noble, so courageous, so gloriously good ... Christ the King, the Son of God and Man, with his cross of redemption and his promise: Have faith, I have overcome the world!"[46]

If Steinwender strayed slightly from the official message of Germandom work abroad, Cardinal Innitzer was also somewhat distracted by the events in Germany on the occasion of St Boniface Day. When it came time for Innitzer to address the gathering, the cardinal did not dwell on Boniface's legacy but instead focused on the work of the ÖVVA in providing succour to the German people abroad at a time when the Church was under attack in Germany. "It is a bishop's duty of conscience, above all, that he also speak up regarding these regrettable events." He went on to express on behalf of Austria and "in the interests of the German people" his deep remorse over the treatment of the German clergy and the battle against Christianity that was without precedent in history.[47] Unlike his earlier refrain from political comment during the All-German Catholic Congress, Innitzer's public expression of grief over the events in Germany at the Boniface Day celebrations prompted the Austrian bishops' conference to issue a statement later that year expressing solidarity with the German clergy.[48]

Innitzer's choice to comment directly on Nazi Germany's treatment of clergy on this occasion was all the more remarkable for his failure to link the work of the ÖVVA with its goal of reaching out to the German minority in Czechoslovakia. Innitzer himself was of Sudeten German background, but he chose not to mention his heritage or the Sudeten Germans other than to recognize their part of a larger "splintered" German whole.[49] Indeed, the previous year the cardinal had been the guest of honour of Vienna's Czech community when he attended the opening of the new Komenský middle school in Vienna's third district, evidence at least that in his public office he made no distinction between assisting German-speakers in Czechoslovakia and Czech-speakers in Austria.[50] Celebrating the achievements of Austria's Czech-speakers at a time when Perntner's education ministry was writing them out of school textbooks was not exactly what the ÖVVA understood by "German cultural work."

This is not to say that the Austrian Church and its leading representatives did not see their mission also in terms of "Germandom" work. After 1938 Innitzer was shunned by Western Catholic leaders for his "yes" vote in the April plebiscite following the Anschluss and for signing letters to Nazi authorities with "Heil Hitler." But there was little difference between the Innitzer before and after 1938: Both under the Austrofascist and Nazi regimes the cardinal intervened in politics only where the interests of lay Catholics were concerned, even if he misjudged the political implications of his actions.[51] Within the Church as outside it, multiple versions of pan-Germanism could be accommodated so long as the Austrofascist state continued to promote a "German Christian" identity. The ÖVVA was one of the most successful programmes of the Fatherland Front precisely because it drew on the breadth and depth of pan-Germanism in the new Austria. Having made its pact with *Südmark* leaders and other German-nationalist activists the organization was able to assemble a wealth of experience on Austria's linguistic frontiers that contributed to its astonishing success and diversity of activities across state borders.

In the end, however, the ÖVVA mirrored the larger fate of the Austrian state. The organization's determined push into Czechoslovakia, initially motivated by rivalry with Reich organizations, gave way to cooperation with Nazi Germans just as it had already done with their sympathizers in Austria. In December 1937, the German ambassador in Prague wrote to the German Foreign Office reporting on the ÖVVA and the reactions of Sudeten German groups and Sudeten German Party (SdP) leaders to the Austrian manoeuvres. According to the ambassador, leaders of the Sudeten German *Turnverein* and SdP leaders had been invited by leaders of the Fatherland Front's *Jungvolk* to a retreat in the Tyrolean mountains in early 1938 to discuss cooperation between the Sudeten German and Austrian organizations, including a proposal to establish a central agency for *Auslandsdeutsche* that would work alongside similar agencies in Berlin and Stuttgart, and a number of cultural initiatives, such as a press agreement between the ÖKVDA and Sudeten German press agencies.[52] Plans were also discussed for a combined programme of concerts, exhibitions, and the joint participation of Austrian and Sudeten German *Turnvereine* at the German *Turnfest* in Breslau. The German ambassador assured the Foreign Office that the SdP representatives had declined these offers because the party's leader, Konrad Henlein, by that point had turned to Nazi Germany for assistance.[53] But this appears to have been wishful thinking on the ambassador's part. It is not clear at all what Henlein's intentions were during 1937 and he may well have seen the ÖVVA's push into Czechoslovakia as an opportunity to build alliances with Austrian "Germandom" groups against a Czech nationalist onslaught against his party and Sudeten German associational life.[54] What is clear from the Austrian side is that the cooperation between state youth groups, German-nationalist groups like the *Turnvereine*, the Fatherland Front's highest dignitaries in the ÖVVA, and a broad spectrum of its supporters in the Church, the press, women's groups and cultural associations, were all working towards the Germanization of the Austrian state and the German nation beyond its borders.

The aftermath of war and imperial collapse left Austrians searching for meaning in their identity as German-speakers in Europe. While politicians sought to harness their political and social programmes to the national question of Austria's relationship with Weimar Germany, and later with the Nazi state, a host of other interest groups also asserted their visions of pan-German identity. Whether a school for Slovenian-speakers should be built in a Carinthian town; what kind of festival programme would best capture the spirit of a universal German culture; how a celebration of faith could save the soul of the nation: These were all questions that occupied the self-proclaimed "guardians of the nation" in interwar Austria.[55] Furthermore, they were also questions that went beyond the borders of Austria. How to reclaim the lost German "lands and tribes" was a cause that united activists and missionaries alike.

Religion had a role to play in this quest to build Germandom at the centre of Christendom. The Catholic Church was an important part of the Austrian landscape in the interwar period as it sought to reclaim its power and visibility of the baroque era. But the Church's mission, like the work of Germandom itself, also extended beyond Austria's borders as it refashioned its apostolic heritage for a new era of nationalist activism. Thus while Germandom at home was imbued with religious underpinnings of a spiritual homeland in the Catholic lands and heritage of Austria, Germandom abroad embraced both the secular and the spiritual to recover the lost German lands of the empire. Along with politicians, activists, poets, directors and artists, the pilgrim Church also saw its work in terms of striving for unity, common purpose and mission of all Germans in Europe. Far from being a fringe radical movement, pan-Germanism was the unifying creed of all Austrians before 1938.

Notes

1. Österreichische Staatsarchiv (ÖStA)/Archiv der Republik (AdR), Bundeskanzleramt (BKA)/Heimatdienst (HD), Carton 10, Österreichische Korrespondenz für volksdeutsche Arbeit (ÖKVDA), 19 June 1937.

2. It is beyond the scope of this article to address the debate on whether the Dollfuss/ Schuschnigg state was "authoritarian" or "fascist" or "Austrofascist." For further discussion of this term, see Tim Kirk, "Fascism and Austrofascism," in *The Dollfuss/Schuschnigg Era in Austria: A Reassessment*, ed. Günter Bischof et al. (New Brunswick, NJ: Transaction, 2003). See also the contributions in *Austrofaschismus: Politik - Ökonomie - Kultur 1933-1938*, 5th rev. ed., ed. Emmerich Tálos and Wolfgang Neugebauer (Vienna: Lit, 2005).

3. Andrew G. Whiteside, *The Socialism of Fools: Georg Ritter von Schönerer and Austrian Pan-Germanism* (Berkeley: University of California Press, 1975), 1-3.

4. Ibid., 91-92. The so-called Linz solution in 1882 called for the union of the German hereditary lands of Cisleithania with Bohemia and Moravia and the exclusion of Galicia and Dalmatia in this alliance.

5. Ibid., 143. On Srbik's life and historical idealism, see Paul R. Sweet, "The Historical Writing of Heinrich von Srbik," *History and Theory 9* (Feb. 1970): 37-58.

6. For example, Andrew Whiteside sees pan-Germans as the representatives of a German-nationalist camp in the Austro-Hungarian Empire. See Andrew G. Whiteside, "The Germans as an Integrative Force in Imperial Austria: the Dilemma of Dominance," *Austrian History Yearbook 3* (Jan. 1967): 157-200. For this usage, see also Carl E. Schorske, "Politics in a New Key: An Austrian Triptych," *Journal of Modern History 39* (Dec. 1967): 343-86; Roger Fletcher, "Karl Leuthner's Greater Germany: The Pre-1914 Pan-Germanism of an Austrian Socialist," *Canadian Review of Studies in Nationalism 9* (Spring 1982): 57-79; Kurt Tweraser, "Carl Beurle and the Triumph of German Nationalism in Austria," *German Studies Review 4* (Oct. 1981): 403-26; Robert S. Wistrich, *Hitler and the Holocaust* (New York: Modern Library, 2001), 35. William T. Bluhm refers to pan-Germanism in connection with Schönerer, the Social Democrats and the National Socialists, which is typical of the ambiguity of this term in historiography. See William T. Bluhm, *Building an Austrian Nation: The Political Integration of a Western State* (New Haven: Yale University Press, 1973), 12-45.

7. This teleology has also entered into most comparative studies of fascism. See, for example, Robert Paxton, *Anatomy of Fascism* (New York: Vintage, 2004). For a rebuttal of the claim that the Nazis were the offspring of Schönerer's followers, see Robert Hoffmann, "Gab es ein 'Schönerianisches Milieu'? Versuch einer Kollektivbiographie von Mitgliedern des 'Vereins der Salzburger Studenten in Wien,'" in *Bürgertum in der Habsburgermonarchie*, vol. 1, ed. Ernst Bruckmüller et al. (Vienna: Böhlau, 1990), 275-98.

8. With a few exceptions, Austrian historians have glossed over the question of pan-German identity in the interwar period. Anton Staudinger and Michael Steinberg have offered most insight into the pan-German idea within Austrofascist ideology, but still neither gives a useful definition of pan-Germanism. See Anton Staudinger, "Austrofaschistische 'Österreich'-Ideologie," in *Austrofaschismus*, 28-52; and Michael Steinberg, *The Meaning of the Salzburg Festival: Austria as Theatre and Ideology, 1890-1938* (Ithaca: Cornell University Press, 1990).

9. "Das 'Linzer Programm' der Sozialdemokratischen Arbeiterpartei Österreichs, 1926," in *Die Grundsatzprogramme der österreichischen Parteien: Dokumente und Analyse*, ed. Albert Kadan and Anton Pelinka (St. Pölten: Niederösterreichisches Pressehaus, 1979), 93; Hanns Haas, "Staats- und Landesbewusstsein in der Ersten Republik," in *Handbuch des politischen Systems Österreichs: Erste Republik 1918-1933*, ed. Emmerich Tálos et al. (Vienna: Manz, 1995), 482. The Austrian Socialists' active resistance against National Socialism gained impetus after the 1943 Moscow Declaration, which stated Allied intentions to create an independent Austrian state. Alfred D. Low, "Otto Bauer, Austro-Marxism, and the Anschluss Movement 1918-1938," *Canadian Review of Studies in Nationalism 6* (Spring 1979), 56.

10. Bauer's description of Austria as a German tribe appeared in an article in *Der sozialistische Kampf* in June 1938, shortly before his death. See Susanne Frölich-Steffen, *Die österreichische Identität im Wandel* (Vienna: Braumüller, 2003), 47.

11. Bluhm, *Building an Austrian Nation*, 25, 30. Renner stated this in his address to the Provisional National Assembly of German-Austria in 1918.

12. Andreas Lüer, "Nationalismus in Christlichsozialen Programmen 1918-1933," *Zeitgeschichte 14* (Jul./Aug. 1987), 150.

13. Ibid., 156-59; "Das Programm der Christlichsozialen Partei, 1926," in *Die Grundsatzprogramme der österreichischen Parteien*, 116.

14. Lüer, "Nationalismus in Christlichsozialen Programmen," 160-62. For example, Schmitz disparaged the National Socialist idea of race by claiming that the true "national" idea embraced the mind, body and spirit of the people, whereas the "*völkisch*" idea in National Socialism devalued the people by emphasising only their ethnicity, race and natural history.

15. Bruce Pauley, *From Prejudice to Persecution: A History of Austrian Anti-Semitism* (Chapel Hill:

University of North Carolina Press, 1992), 80-82.

16. Steinberg, *The Meaning of the Salzburg Festival*, 130-31.

17. Ibid., 72-74. Harald Waitzbauer, "'San die Juden scho' furt?': Salzburg, die Festspiele und das jüdische Publikum," in *Der Geschmack der Vergänglichkeit*, ed. Robert Kriechbaumer (Vienna: Böhlau, 2002), 256.

18. Kenneth Segar, "Austria in the Thirties: Reality and Exemplum," in *Austria in the Thirties: Culture and Politics*, ed. Kenneth Segar and John Warren (Riverside: Ariadne, 1991). Steinberg, *The Meaning of the Salzburg Festival*, 48.

19. This is Steinberg's central thesis in *The Meaning of the Salzburg Festival.* He also makes a crucial and much under-recognised point that the Austrofascist state's attempt to define Austrian identity against Nazism was thwarted by the state's own manufacturing of a pan-German identity.

20. Staudinger, "Austrofaschistische 'Österreich'-Ideologie," 31-33.

21. Peter Hofrichter, "Die österreichischen Katholikentage des 20. Jahrhunderts (bis 1933)," PhD. diss., University of Vienna, 1966, 148-49.

22. Ernst Hanisch, "Der Politische Katholizismus als ideologischer Träger des 'Austrofaschismus,'" in *Austrofaschismus*, 76-77. The speech at the Trabrennplatz on 11 September was not part of the official Congress programme, but rather, the first official rally of the Fatherland Front timed to coincide with the final events of the Congress. That Dollfuss was hoping to attract delegates to the rally is evidenced by the fact that he gave virtually the same speech in his welcome to Congress delegates in the Vienna Stadium two days earlier on 9 September. Hofrichter, "Die österreichischen Katholikentage," 166-68.

23. Hofrichter, "Die österreichischen Katholikentage," 168.

24. Viktor Reimann, *Innitzer: Kardinal zwischen Hitler und Rom* (Vienna: Amalthea, 1988), 65-66.

25. Ibid.

26. See Cardinal Innitzer's preface to the official guidebook for pilgrims, *Festführer zum Allgemeinen Deutschen Katholikentag in Wien, 7-12. September 1933* (Vienna: Verlag des Allgemeinen Deutschen Katholikentages Wien, 1933), 15-17.

27. Hofrichter, "Die österreichischen Katholikentage," 159-62. The 1000-Mark tariff was applied after the Austrian government expelled Germany's Justice Minister Hans Frank, who had urged opposition to Dollfuss on Austrian radio. See also C. Earl Edmondson, *The Heimwehr and Austrian Politics, 1918-1936* (Athens, GA: University of Georgia Press, 1978), 190.

28. Reimann, *Innitzer*, 55, 63-64. On earlier occasions Innitzer had spoken out more directly against Nazi attempts to foil the "All-German" Congress, declaring in June 1933 to those who wished to harm "our Austrian pan-German Catholic Congress, I say: no return!" Hofrichter, "Die österreichischen Katholikentage," 160.

29. Hofrichter, "Die österreichischen Katholikentage," 164, 182.

30. Ibid., 170-71.

31. Irmgard Bärnthaler, "Geschichte und Organisation der Vaterländische Front: Ein Beitrag zum Verständnis totalitärer Organisation," PhD. diss., University of Vienna, 1964, 265-68.

32. Hanns Haas and Karl Stuhlpfarrer, *Österreich und seine Slowenen* (Vienna: Löcker & Wögenstein, 1977), 42; Erwin Steinböck, "Kärnten," in *Österreich 1918-1938: Geschichte der Ersten Republik*, vol. 2, ed. Erika Weinzierl and Kurt Skalnik (Graz: Styria, 1983), 810-13; Thomas M. Barker, *The Slovene Minority of Carinthia* (Boulder: Columbia University Press, 1984), 181-89.

33. Bärnthaler, "Geschichte und Organisation der Vaterländischen Front," 261.

34. On the *Kinderaustausche* in Bohemia and Moravia, see Tara Zahra, *Kidnapped Souls: National Indifference and the Battle for Children in the Bohemian Lands, 1900-1948* (Ithaca: Cornell University Press, 2008).

35. ÖStA/AdR, BKA/HD, Carton 10, ÖKVDA, 24 April 1937 and 19 June 1937. See also Bärnthaler, "Geschichte und Organisation der Vaterländischen Front," 269.

36. Bärnthaler, "Geschichte und Organisation der Vaterländischen Front," 268-69.

37. See Elizabeth Harvey, "Pilgrimages to the 'Bleeding Border': Gender and Rituals of Nationalist Protest in Germany, 1919-39," *Women's History Review 9* (June 2000): 201-29; idem., *Women and the Nazi East: Agents and Witnesses of Germanization* (New Haven: Yale University Press, 2003). There are many studies of the German "*Ostforscher*," notably Michael Burleigh, *Germany Turns Eastward: A Study of Ostforschung in the Third Reich* (Cambridge: Cambridge University Press, 1988).

38. Bärnthaler, "Geschichte und Organisation der Vaterländischen Front," 268.

39. Ibid., 267-68. The ÖKVDA began publication in November 1935 and was edited by Josef Tzöbl.

40. ÖStA/AdR, BKA/HD, Carton 10, ÖKVDA, 20 March 1937 on Germans in Slovenia, for example, and 24 April 1937 on municipal plans to build a Czech commerce academy and teachers' college in Iglau.

41. Ibid., 8 May 1937.

42. Ibid., 19 June 1937.

43. Ibid.

44. Ibid.

45. Ernst Hanisch, "Die Salzburger Presse in der Ersten Republik," *Mitteilungen der Gesellschaft für Salzburger Landeskunde 128* (1988): 359-60; Michael Schmolke, "Das Salzburger Medienwesen," in *Geschichte Salzburgs: Stadt und Land*, ed. Heinz Dopsch and Hans Spatzenegger (Salzburg: Universitätsverlag Anton Pustet, 1991), 1980.

46. ÖStA/AdR, BKA/HD, Carton 10, ÖKVDA, 19 June 1937.

47. Ibid.

48. Reimann, *Innitzer*, 90.

49. Ibid.

50. On the opening of the new school see Karl M. Brousek, *Wien und seine Tschechen: Integration und Assimilation einer Minderheit im 20. Jahrhundert* (Munich: Oldenbourg, 1980), 48.

51. See Reimann, *Innitzer*. Innitzer intervened on behalf of Austrian Nazis imprisoned in Wöllersdorf in 1934 and again in 1935 when a request came from families of the prisoners to send Christmas parcels to their loved ones. He also defended the young priests and members of the Catholic "*Neubund*" when Rome sought an official explanation for the numbers of Nazis in the organization.

52. Bärnthaler, "Geschichte und Organisation der Vaterländischen Front," 269-70. The Austrian propaganda bureau already had on file all the publications of the *Volksdeutsche Presse- und Informationsdienst* and the *Sudetendeutsche Presse-Briefe*, the press agency of the SdP. See ÖStA/AdR, BKA/HD, Carton 11.

53. Ibid.

54. Henlein had already sought out Hungary, Italy, Sweden, Britain and even the League of Nations as allies in the cause of the Sudeten minority and his political alliances remained flexible right up until the end of 1937, as Mark Cornwall has recently shown. Even Henlein's famous letter to Hitler in November 1937 asking him to invade Czechoslovakia (before Hitler had even annexed Austria) does not indicate that Henlein saw Nazi Germany as the only chance for the Sudeten Germans, but simply that this was another one of Henlein's "manoeuvres." See Mark Cornwall, "'A Leap into Ice-Cold Water': The Manoeuvres of the Henlein Movement in Czechoslovakia, 1933-1938," in *Czechoslovakia in a Nationalist and Fascist Europe 1918-1948*, ed. Mark Cornwall and R.J.W. Evans (Oxford: Oxford University Press, 2007), 123-42.

55. Pieter M. Judson, *Guardians of the Nation: Activists on the Language Frontiers of Imperial Austria* (Cambridge, MA: Harvard University Press, 2006).

Sudeten Germans in Austria after the First World War[1]

Johannes Koll

Introduction

For Austria, the end of the First World War did not just mean the end of the Habsburg monarchy and the transformation of the political system into a republican democracy. The defeat of the Central Powers in 1918 also involved the loss of territories and their respective populations that for centuries had belonged to an empire of which Vienna had been the administrative center. Not more than 6.5 out of ten million German-speaking people of the defunct Habsburg Empire lived within the boundaries of the new Austrian Republic. The strong economic, cultural and political ties which, prior to 1918, had connected Austria's territory with Hungary and many of the Habsburg Crown lands were now severed.[2] The newly established multinational state of Czechoslovakia was patronized by the former Entente and during the interwar period protected against German and Austrian territorial claims. It was especially the French government that at all costs wanted to extinguish and avoid every precondition that might lead to the realization of the political concept of *Mitteleuropa* (Central Europe) by which the Central Powers during the First World War had tried to build up a political order in Europe dominated by Germany and Austria.[3]

Both politically and culturally, during the whole interwar period the Austrian–Czech and the German–Czech relationships were full of tension. On the Czech as well as on the Austrian and German sides, public debates about the fate of the German-speaking parts of the former Lands of the

Crown of Saint Wenceslaus (Bohemia, Moravia, and Austrian Silesia) were essentially guided by nationalist points of view. Compared with the Imperial era, after 1918 on each side nationalist rhetoric increased substantially and dominated public debate.[4] Czechs on the one hand and Austrians and Germans on the other continually disputed whether the Sudetenland should belong to Czechoslovakia or Austria respectively Germany. Both sides found the national affiliation of the German-speaking areas along the language frontier and in the linguistic enclaves of Brno/Brünn, Jihlava/Iglau and Olomouc/Olmütz highly controversial. The situation deteriorated further after Hitler seized power in Germany in January 1933.[5] In order to destabilize the multicultural Czechoslovakian Republic, German National Socialists did not just urge the Slovaks to declare independence, but above all they fostered secessionist movements of the German-speaking population in Czechoslovakia. The *Sudetendeutsche Heimatfront*, founded in October 1933 by Konrad Henlein, felt encouraged to act as political representative for these so-called Sudeten Germans. Having changed its name to the *Sudetendeutsche Partei* in 1935, this organization revealed more readiness to cooperate with the National Socialist regime in Berlin than ever before.[6] Following the radicalization of German foreign policy, which was marked by the reintroduction of military conscription (1935), the remilitarization of the Rhineland (1936) and the incorporation of Austria into the Third Reich (*Anschluss Österreichs*) in March 1938, the government in Prague saw itself compelled to sign the Munich Agreement on 30 September 1938. By this the German-speaking area of Czechoslovakia was incorporated into the Greater German Reich. For many Austrians, Germans and Sudeten Germans, uniting the Sudetenland with Germany could be interpreted as the re-establishment of a historical state which had its roots in Imperial times. For others, the Munich Agreement formed an overdue correction of the peace treaties of Saint-Germain and Versailles (a "sweet revenge for the humiliations of 1918," as Mark Mazower puts it)[7] or a logical consequence of the fundamentally racist ideology of National Socialism. According to this interpretation, the German-speaking people of Austria, Germany and the Sudetenland formed one nation, which had the right to live together in one state. Hitler took no more than another half year to destroy the rest of Czechoslovakia: In March 1939 the German Wehrmacht entered the country. The administrative institution of the *Reichsprotektorat Böhmen und Mähren* could well supersede the Czechoslovakian Republic, which had been destroyed gradually and systematically by the Third Reich in the preceding months. A further step in the unleashing of the Second World War had been taken.[8]

It is self-evident that the outcome of the First World War did have immediate consequences for the German-speaking burghers of the former Habsburg Crown lands of Bohemia, Moravia and the Austrian part of Silesia. The history of the Sudeten Germans in Czechoslovakia, as well as the history of Austrian–Czech and German–Czech relationships, between 1918 and 1939, has been dealt with in plenty of publications. Several books and articles reflect the historical interpretations of those organizations which claimed and still nowadays claim to represent the interests of displaced persons. In addition, for scholarly research, the history of the Sudeten Germans in Czechoslovakia, and Austrian–Czech and German–Czech relationships in the twentieth century have been interesting and fruitful topics.[9] However, the role Sudeten Germans have played in Austria during the interwar period has hardly been scrutinized by serious historiography. The purpose of this article is to analyze the constitutional status their former homelands held for the First Austrian Republic; to outline the implications the evolution of the designations of the Sudetenland and the Sudeten Germans had for the history of their political image, particularly their self-image, and to give an answer to questions about the impact of the Sudeten Germans on the Austrian Republic and the corporative state which has been shaped since 1933 by the Austrian Chancellors Engelbert Dollfuss and Kurt Schuschnigg via societal associations and publications.

Constitutional aspects

From the outset it was clear to both the victorious and vanquished powers that after the end of hostilities the vast extent of the Austrian-Hungarian dual monarchy could not be maintained. In Austria, during the first months of the interwar period the constitutional organs of the embryonic republic concentrated on remaining in possession of all those areas in which German was the prevailing or even exclusively used vernacular language. In this sense, the German-Austrian Privy Council (*Deutschösterreichischer Staatsrat*) and its departments (*Staatsämter*) which since 31 October 1918 had executive power in place of the Imperial government, felt responsible not only for Austria but also for the Sudeten Germans. For example, the Department for Justice installed courts in towns situated in former Bohemia and Moravia; the local and the financial administration of these areas was organized in a manner consonant with the regulations in force in Austria; and the inspection of schools, as well as social law issues concerning Sudeten Germans, were implemented by the German-Austrian government in Vienna. Also the legislative organ of the new republic claimed the Sudetenland for Austria: On 22 November 1918 the Provisional National Assembly, which since 21 October functioned as the parliament of the German-speaking parts of the former Habsburg Empire, passed a law stating unequivocally: "The German-Austrian Republic exerts territorial sovereignty over the complete realm of the Germans in the kingdoms and lands represented hitherto in the *Reichsrat*." In this context among others the Sudetenland and the German linguistic enclaves of Brno, Jihlava and Olomouc were explicitly enumerated.[10] On the same day, the Provisional National Assembly underlined in a public declaration that the German-speaking population of all these areas living now under the rule of foreign countries would be considered as belonging to the sovereignty of the German-Austrian Republic "until their political and national rights will be guaranteed by constitutional and international law"; so long as—according to the public declaration of 22 November 1918—the inhabitants of these areas had the right to be represented in the Provisional National Assembly in Vienna and were subjected to the laws and authorities of the German-Austrian Republic. The same was said about German minorities in Hungary and the Germans living in linguistic enclaves of this recently independent country: they too "belong to the national sphere of interest of the German-Austrian state," because for the Provisional National Assembly, they were part of "the indestructible national community" (*unzerstörbare Volksgemeinschaft*) and of "the century-old imperial community" (*mehrhundertjährige Reichsgemeinschaft*).[11] It seemed to be a consequence of this point of view that the German-Austrian government dispatched delegates from the Sudetenland to the peace negotiations at Saint-Germain.[12]

By claiming the German-speaking areas of former Bohemia, Moravia and Austrian Silesia for Austria, the German-Austrian government and parliament could base themselves on the political representatives of the Sudetenland. They too favored secession from the newly created Czechoslovakian nation state and full integration into the German Austrian Republic. In this sense, the German Bohemian delegates declared one day after the founding of the Czechoslovakian Republic (28 October 1918), that their homeland would be a "province with original rights (*eigenberechtigte Provinz*) of the German-Austrian state" which ought to be united as soon as possible with Germany.[13] To underline the intention of the Sudeten Germans to attach themselves to Austria, a German Bohemian provincial government was formed consisting of middle-class parties and Social Democrats. Under its prime ministers, Rafael Pacher and especially Rudolf Lodgman von Auen, this *Landesregierung* took over the executive function in Liberec/Reichenberg. When units of the Czechoslovakian army started to occupy this area in November 1918, the hardly established provincial government, however, lost power and moved to Vienna. From here the members of the German-Bohemian government continued to propagate the unification of their homeland with Austria or Germany up to its dissolution at the end of September 1919.[14] Also, other parts of the Sudetenland declared their Anschluss to Austria in autumn 1918.[15]

In reality the defeated Austria did not have the political and military capacity to stand up substantially for the integration of the Sudeten German areas into its territory or to enforce an annexation of them. In Austria as well as in the Sudetenland the idea that the Sudeten Germans should belong to Austria was again and again formulated in 1918–19 on the basis of historical, cultural and statistical arguments as a matter of course. The juridical dimension, furthermore, is reflected by the electoral law to the Constitutional National Assembly passed by the Provisional National Assembly on 18 December 1918. Under it the German-speaking areas of former Bohemia, Moravia and Silesia basically constituted elements of the German-Austrian Republic.[16] As in the case of Styria, Carinthia and South-Tyrol, the occupation of the Sudetenland by military force and the fact that the populations of these areas finally were hindered from participation in the election were regarded as acts of "unlawful violence"[17] and contrary to the right of national self-determination proclaimed solemnly by the American president Woodrow Wilson on 8 January 1918 in his famous Fourteen Points.

The pan-German dreams, which in 1918–19 had formed some kind of official doctrine in Austria, ended abruptly when the Treaty of Saint-Germain revoked the constitutional basis and doomed the country to a small state which was economically barely viable. In its article 88, the peace treaty forbade the fusion of Germany and Austria, and from now on there could be no doubt that the whole of the Sudetenland irrevocably belonged to the Czechoslovakian Republic. On 21 October 1919, the National Assembly had to conform to the new circumstances: A law determining the form of government obliged the members of the Austrian parliament to transform the "German-Austrian Republic" into the "Austrian Republic" (*Republik Österreich*),[18] thus giving up the ethnically based pretense of representing all German-speaking people of the former Habsburg monarchy. Consequently, the constitution which the National Assembly adopted on 1 December 1920 did not mention the Sudetenland at all.[19]

Sudeten Germans and Sudetenland: Conceptual Aspects

The varying designations of the territory and the people reveal the way in which each country and its population was perceived by contemporaries at home and abroad. This is true not only with regard to Austria, but also concerning those German-speaking areas which Czechoslovakia was granted by the Treaty of Saint-Germain.

Before, during and immediately after the First World War, the traditional terms "German Bohemia," "German Moravia" and "Austrian Silesia" were most commonly used. They reflected the particularistically fragmented heritage of the dethroned Habsburg monarchy. Although the corresponding administrative entities had been abolished in 1919, the expressions survived for several years as linguistic relics of a perished era and of a vanished political history. In the course of the interwar period, however, an important semantic shift took place: Instead of enumerating the diverse parts of the German-speaking area of Czechoslovakia, the singular "Sudetenland" was employed more and more from the early 1920s onwards. This term—derived from the geographical name of the mountain range Sudety/Sudeten—was not only convenient for denominating the political reality shaped by the peace treaties of 1919. It also aptly stressed the coherence among the German-speaking population of Czechoslovakia and created or reinforced a collective identity among them. At the same time the singular expression "Sudetenland" was designed to distance the "Sudeten Germans" from Czech-speaking people.[20] Significantly, with regard to the German-speaking people living in the former Lands of the Crown of Saint Wenceslaus, there was no phrase like "Sudeten Austrians"; instead they were called (and called themselves) "Sudeten Germans." Apart from expressing togetherness among the German-speaking people of former Bohemia, Moravia and Silesia and distinctiveness from the Czech-speaking people, the pretense of a national connection with Germans and Austrians could be achieved subtly by increasingly—and eventually exclusively—referring to "Sudeten Germans." In this way, the history of the designation evidences the abandonment of particularistic notions derived from outlived administrative entities and the simultaneous ethnicizing of a political (self-)image. Some kind of compromise between the traditional particularistic designations and the singular form of "Sudetenland" was the notion of "Sudetenländer" which amalgamated unity and variety. This plural form, however, faded away at the latest in the 1930s. The National Socialist propaganda used solely the singular word "Sudetenland."

Societal aspects

As shown above, the Provisional and later the Constitutional National Assembly demonstrated clearly that in Austria, it was common sense to feel responsible for Austrians and Sudeten Germans alike. From the political right to the left the vision of national coherence of all those for whom German was the vernacular language has been taken for granted. Although in many fields of public debate there were significant differences between the political camps after the First World War (for example over the legitimacy and economic necessity of socialization or the relationship between state and church), with regard to the cultural and ethnic togetherness of all German-speaking people there was some kind of consensus above party lines: irredentism was shared by Social Democrats as well as by Catholics and the *Großdeutsche Volkspartei*, which demonstrated Greater German objectives by its very designation.[21] Ultimately, the pan-German irredentism implied the desire to regain the Sudetenland as well as the longing for a political union between Germany and Austria via a constitutionally procured Anschluss. From an ethnic point of view, shared by the majority of the contemporaries of the interwar period, both aspects were related indissolubly to each other. "Most 'Austrians' in 1918–19 did not want an independent Austrian Republic. They regarded 'German Austria' as a stepping stone to integration into the larger German Republic. The inclusion of the more than two million Germans in northern Bohemia in 'German Austria' in 1918–19 only made sense if 'German Austria' joined Germany, and the newly elected constituent national assembly openly declared on 12 March 1919 that 'German Austria is a part of the German Republic.' The Allies, particularly France, would have none of it."[22]

Generally speaking, the question of the unification of Austria and Germany attracted more attention in public discourse and in the activities of associations than the integration of the Sudeten German areas into Austria, Germany or a united German-Austrian state. For most Austrians the Anschluss was undoubtedly of greater political and economic relevance than the fate of the Sudeten Germans. Nevertheless both aspects stemmed from the same ideological source: the belief in the cultural and ethnic togetherness of all German-speaking people essentially merged the question of Anschluss with the Austrian respectively German claims on the Sudetenland. Their interconnection caused dissatisfaction with the political order in Europe sanctioned by the Treaties of Saint-Germain and Versailles. It was this dissatisfaction which was expressed during the interwar period by a multitude of organizations and in plenty of publications.

Whereas from 1919 onwards constitutional law in Austria had to attune to the new reality, within the society and among leading political figures irredentism endured. Several Austrian organizations dedicated themselves to agitating in favor of the Anschluss. One of the most influential and widespread associations in this respect was the Austrian-German People's League (*Österreichisch-Deutscher Volksbund*), founded in June 1925; according to its periodical *Der Anschluß*, the League counted no fewer than 1.8 million members in 1931.[23] Like similar organizations, the *Volksbund* continually criticized the interdiction of a political union of all German-speaking countries and the loss of territories and inhabitants caused by the peace treaties of 1919. In publications, demonstrations or at solemn events its members made innumerable efforts to emphasize that, contrary to other nations, the German-speaking people were hindered from living together in a nation state. During an official reception, on 18 July 1929, for example, the Austrian-German People's League and leading Austrian politicians used the presence of American and German journalists in Vienna during a German Press Tour to sensitize the American public to the question of Anschluss.[24] Also, the nationalistic and irredentist German School's Association Südmark (*Deutscher Schulverein Südmark*) contributed to the spread of a revanchist atmosphere. Among its publications were booklets on *Germandom in Czechoslovakia* and caustic critiques of the supposedly anti-German politics of Czech parties or associations in Austria.[25] In the course of the 1930s, even those Greater German associations like the *Österreichisch-Deutscher Volksbund*, which in the beginning had been composed above party lines, clearly diverted to right-wing radicalism. But it cannot be ignored that, in the first years following the end of the First World War, Social Democrats, liberals and Catholic conservatives alike partook in organizations which pleaded for the political unification of all German-speaking people. In several Austrian towns and villages, there also existed associations that functioned as particular interest groups for the Sudeten Germans. Although—in contrast to the time after the Second World War—there was no mass exodus from the Sudetenland during the interwar period, there was a substantial number of Sudeten Germans living in Austria. Many of them played an active role in the political, economic and cultural evolution of the First Austrian Republic (1919–1933) or the corporative state (1933–1938). Among those who had been born or who had grown up in one of the former Crown lands of Bohemia, Moravia or Austrian Silesia were Social Democrats such as Karl Renner, Julius Tandler, Adolf Schärf, and Ferdinand Hanusch; Catholics or members of the Christian Social Party such as the archbishop of Vienna, Cardinal Theodor

Innitzer, Emmerich Czermak, Rudolf Ramek and Ernst Streeruwitz; National Socialists such as the lawyer Arthur Seyß-Inquart, the medico Hugo Jury or the writers Karl Hans Strobl, Robert Hohlbaum and Bruno Brehm; scientists such as Sigmund Freud and Joseph A. Schumpeter; and artists such as the opera singer Leo Slezak. For most Sudeten Germans living in Austria, the complaint about the loss of their homeland constituted an often recurring element of political discourse up to the Munich Agreement.

To a considerable extent, Sudeten German associations contributed to maintaining contacts among them. Such organizations had been partly founded under Habsburg rule, but others were new foundations after 1918. Their statutes explicitly emphasized their non-party character thus, at least theoretically, allowing accession to all the ideological camps of Austrian society. In most cases, however, membership was confined to German-speaking people. It is worth noting that it was not the command of the German language as such that was decisive, but rather an ethnic dimension of lineage. The Society of Germans from the linguistic enclave of Jihlava in Vienna (*Verein der Deutschen der Iglauer Sprachinsel in Wien*), for example, admitted as ordinary members only "Germans of Aryan parentage";[26] in this way, Jews or Slavs were excluded from membership as a matter of principle. For most such organizations, pan-Germanism embraced an anti-Semitic and an anti-Slavic attitude.

The ethnic and revisionist dimension of Sudeten German associations is revealed clearly in the statutes of the League of German Bohemians in Austria. According to its first article, the objective of the *Bund der Deutschböhmen in Österreich* was "to strengthen and enhance the mental and the economic level of Germandom (*Deutschtum*) in Bohemia, to secure the territories in which German is spoken (*deutscher Sprachboden*) and to awaken and to keep alive the ethnic conscience (*das völkische Bewusstsein*) in all groups of the German people."[27] In other words: The League of German Bohemians in Austria publicly appealed for a commitment that referred to a region and a population outside of the frontiers of the Austrian Republic. And it is indicative of the attitude of the authorities in Austrian towns and provinces that the establishment of the *Bund der Deutschböhmen in Österreich* or of other Sudeten German associations had been approved by the appropriate office—as far as is known—without any serious difficulties. Whereas the federal government officially had to confine its policy strictly within the realm of the Austrian Republic after signing the Treaty of Saint-Germain in 1919, local and provincial authorities continued to legitimize, throughout the interwar period, openly irredentist associations and student fraternities like the *Verein deutscher Studenten aus Nordmähren*, the *Deutsch-*

akademische Verbindung 'Ostschlesier' and the *Verein Deutscher Studenten aus Schlesien in Wien 'Oppavia.'*[28]

In an almost paradigmatic way, the Friendly Society for German Bohemia and the Sudeten areas formulated the revisionist objectives of Sudeten German associations in Austria. The statutes of the *Hilfsverein für Deutschböhmen und die Sudetenländer*, approved by the government of the province Lower Austria on 1 February 1919, proclaimed: "The purpose of the association lies in uniting German compatriots (*Heimatsgenossen*) originating from German Bohemia, the Bohemian Forest, North and South Moravia, Western and Eastern Silesia without any difference of sex, class and political attitude in order to sustain and to practice common love for the home country (*gemeinsame Heimatsliebe*) and to foster the compatriots culturally, both at home and abroad. But the association also accepts as members Germans of all tribes (*Deutsche jeder Stammeszugehörigkeit*) who are interested in the lot of German Bohemia and the Sudetenland." These objectives were to be achieved mainly by relief for needy compatriots, by informing authorities of the specific interests of the Sudeten Germans, by influencing the all-German public (*gesamtdeutsche Öffentlichkeit*) in favor of the culture of their homelands, and finally by integration into a general organization for the welfare of all Germans living in border regions or in foreign countries (*Grenz- und Auslandsdeutsche*).[29]

Obviously the propaganda of the Friendly Society was quite successful: Even in its founding year, the association counted 11,000 members.[30] In order to accentuate its position within the debate on the political future of Austria, Germany and the Sudetenland, in January 1920 the *Hilfsverein für Deutschböhmen und die Sudetenländer* published a leaflet which in a dramatic style cautioned against a new war if 80 million Germans in Central Europe were further hindered from uniting as a common and independent nation by the victorious powers of the First World War. "What peace in Central Europe may look like in future decades, for political, national, economic and strategic reasons a subjugated German Bohemia, Sudetenland and South Moravia will become the lever for a potentially decisive war (*Entscheidungskrieg*) regarding the existence or the non-existence of Germandom (*Sein oder Nichtsein des Deutschtums*) in Europe. The firm maintenance of the national character of these areas will depend on the stubborn determination of each German believing in a future of his people." In this sense the Friendly Society regarded itself as a national association acting essentially above party lines: "The feeling of national togetherness shall suppress class hatred and activities which give preference to personal advantages at the expense of national honor and national future.

The social position of the compatriot (*Volksgenosse*), his commitment to a political party and a religious belief do not refer to his obligation of honor (*Ehrenpflicht*) to make sacrifices for the right of national self-determination and the independence of the home country."[31]

The Czechoslovakian government observed the activities of the Friendly Society and similar Sudeten German associations with much suspicion. On 10 May 1921, its foreign mission in Vienna informed the Austrian State Department that the *Hilfsverein* tended to destroy "the amicable relationship" between the inhabitants of the two states. According to the government in Prague, the Friendly Society represented "a genuine organization of combat against the Czechoslovakian Republic and its existence." In a "most insistent and systematic manner" the *Hilfsverein für Deutschböhmen und die Sudetenländer* "prepares and executes assaults on Czechoslovakia and all its institutions, and for that purpose it tries to seduce the mass of the indigenous Austrian population." At the end of its note, the Czech foreign mission posed the rhetorical question of "how far it might be advantageous to the Federal Republic of Austria to tolerate within its boundaries an irredentist movement which is directed against the Czechoslovakian state."[32] No matter if the diplomatic intervention of the Czech government had any practical consequences—the mere existence and the dramatic tone of the note reveal the tensions caused by Sudeten German associations like the *Hilfsverein für Deutschböhmen und die Sudetenländer* in the politically and economically unstable interwar period.

For the Sudeten German associations in Austria, the situation fundamentally changed with the Anschluss of Austria to the Third Reich. After March 1938, most of them were compulsorily dissolved, and all of their funds were confiscated by the office of the *Stillhaltekommissar für Verbände und Organisationen*, Albert Hoffmann, whose task it was to liquidate all non-National Socialist organizations. Some Sudeten German organizations like the Austrian associations of German-speaking students from Northern Bohemia or from Silesia were integrated by the *Stillhaltekommissar* into existing National Socialist organizations—in this case into the National Socialist Students' Federation (*N.S. Deutscher Studentenbund*).[33] By dissolving the Sudeten German associations, in compliance with its policy of *Gleichschaltung*, the political leadership in Berlin wanted the Sudeten Germans to conform to the patterns of National Socialism without having the chance to play a distinctive part within German society. From now on it was the German government that claimed to represent Sudeten German interests vis à vis the Czech government. So in the end, Hitler managed to achieve international acceptance of the annexation of the Sudetenland via the Munich Agreement by the brutally deployed weight of the political prestige of his regime. In paving the way to the Munich Conference of September 1938 and to the further subversion of the Czechoslovakian Republic, up to the erection of the *Reichsprotektorat Böhmen und Mähren* in March 1939, Sudeten Germans like Arthur Seyß-Inquart obviously played a decisive role behind the scenes and in German propaganda policy.[34]

Aspects of the public discussions

The fact that in the late 1930s it was the Greater German Reich, which by diplomatic, political and military force effected the annexation of the Sudetenland to Germany, should not lead to the conclusion that the desire to integrate the Sudeten Germans into either Austria or Germany or a unified German-Austrian state was monopolized by the political right during the interwar period. Of course, for the racial ideology of National Socialism, the axiom of togetherness of all German-speaking people was out of question. And from time to time, National Socialists stressed that the origin of their party lay in the Sudetenland. Thus one of the founders of the *Deutsche Nationalsozialistische Arbeiterpartei*, which in 1918 emerged from the pan-German *Deutsche Arbeiterpartei* (founded in 1904) proudly stated in 1923: "The cradle of the German National Socialist movement stood in the Sudetenland of former Austria."[35] Finally, even before the *Nationalsozialistische Deutsche Arbeiterpartei* (NSDAP) rose to power in Germany in 1933, National Socialists from Germany, Austria and the Sudetenland were repeatedly searching for cooperation, without ever attaining a coherent organizational structure.[36]

Nevertheless it is important to note that well into the 1930s the belief in national togetherness of Austrians and Sudeten Germans was in no way the preserve of the extreme right. On the contrary, the wide-ranging participation in public discussions on the future of the Sudetenland after the First World War shows that in all parts of the political spectrum in Austria, the Sudeten Germans were regarded as an integral part of the German national community on linguistic, cultural, and partly racial grounds. In this sense it cannot be dismissed as a mere legal formality when all Sudeten German associations in Austria emphasized in their statutes that their objectives were above party lines. Equally in this sense, the repeatedly mentioned *Hilfsverein für Deutschböhmen und die Sudetenländer* published a leaflet with the significant title "Sudeten Germany! A battle cry and exhortation to all Germans." Though written in 1928 by a rightist author, this and similar publications were intended to appeal to all German-speaking people regardless of political affiliation.[37]

In the public discussions, many Austrian politicians, journalists and scientists gave the impression that they were not just speaking on behalf of Austrians, but also in the name of the Sudeten Germans when claiming the Sudetenland and its inhabitants for Austria. In this sense Rudolf Laun, at that time professor of administrative law at the University of Vienna, was convinced "that an overwhelming majority of all Germans in Bohemia, Moravia and Silesia will forever repudiate the union with the Czechoslovakian state and consider the unification with the grand German nation under constitutional law as the primary objective, despite all the economic lures and all the threats and violent measures."[38] In a leaflet published in the months before the signing of the Treaty of Saint-Germain and certainly designed to influence the peace negotiations in Paris, Laun reminded the victorious powers of Wilson's principle of national self-determination, and he hoped that with regard to the Sudeten Germans the Western democracies would strive for a solution in accordance with demographic reality.

Aside from Laun, many other intellectuals living in Austria invoked historical aspects and demographic factors to contest the affiliation of the Sudeten Germans to Czechoslovakia and to underline Austrian and/or German claims on the Sudetenland during the interwar period by demanding respect for national self-determination. Thus the well-known statistician Wilhelm Winkler imputed to "the Czechs" the intention "to transform German Bohemia and the Sudetenland into colonies of the Czech state." In a contribution to a book edited in 1919 by Lodgman von Auen on German Bohemia for the German publishing house Ullstein, Winkler opposed the hope that sooner or later "the sorely tested German Bohemian people" would reach the desired unification with the German-speaking mother country to the ongoing "Czechification of German Bohemia (*Tschechisierung Böhmens*)."[39] In the same book, the Viennese medievalist Alfons Dopsch gave an overview on the history of the Germans in Bohemia. He came to the conclusion: "History doesn't entitle the Czechs to impede the free national development of the Germans in Bohemia. These Germans were not just the first to take possession of the country; again and again they were also active as pioneers of material and mental culture. Supporting them has lead to the flourishing of the country, repressing them has entailed general decline."[40] Finally, the economist Friedrich Wieser, during the Imperial era Secretary of Trade in Austria and after the war president of the *Hilfsverein für Deutschböhmen und die Sudetenländer*,[41] sketched two options for the German-speaking population of former Bohemia: Because of their numerical strength, they would be able to form a state on their own according to the right of national self-determination. But they also ought to be allowed to join German Austria and then to join Germany together with German Austria. Like the other contributors to Lodgman von Auen's book, Wieser based his argument on demography and history as well. From both he drew juridical conclusions: "The historical development has shaped two nationally conscious and politically organized peoples in Bohemia, two nations, and law has to align itself to this underlying fact (*rechtserzeugende Tatsache*) (…)."[42]

In the cited writings, as well as in many other irredentist publications, reference to the demographic situation in the Sudetenland and its history was used to claim the principle of national self-determination for the Sudeten Germans, which, in turn, was interpreted as an essential element of democracy: If the Allied Powers really wanted to guarantee democracy as they repeatedly proclaimed, following the call of president Wilson, they had to grant national self-determination to the German-speaking people, including the Sudeten Germans, as for any other people in Europe. In particular before the signing of the peace treaties, Wilson's Fourteen Points were explicitly invoked time and again. But also after September 1919, Austrian intellectuals accused the victorious powers of the First World War of depriving the German-speaking population of the principle of national self-determination. In 1931 the Austrian-German People's League published a memorandum containing quotations from speeches or articles in which politicians and journalists of the former Entente powers had criticized the injustice and economic burden that the Treaty of Saint-Germain constituted for Austria. The author Stefan Hofer posed the rhetorical question: "In the light of this, should one be surprised that in Austria the peace treaty has generated the sentiment of violation which by inflaming protests has turned the conscience of the world (*Weltgewissen*) against the breach of promise?"[43]

Finally, for Austrian Social Democrats, the national question was not a new item. Discussing the relationship between different nationalities in the multi-national Habsburg Empire had had a long tradition in the *Sozialdemokratische Arbeiterpartei* (SDAP). For its members, spokesmen and sympathizers, however, the collapse of the monarchy in 1918 brought about a change of policy: Up to the First World War, the Austrian Social Democrats had advocated the transformation of the Habsburg Empire into a democratic confederation of German-speaking and non-German nationalities.[44] With the dissolution of the Empire at the end of the war and the proclamation of independent states, the SDAP and her main ideologues, Otto Bauer and Karl Renner, started to emphasize the claim of national togetherness of all German-speaking people. This claim was expressed clearly in a memorandum which Bauer launched on 25 December 1918. As Secretary of State for Foreign Affairs in the Austrian government, Bauer delineated the territory of the Austrian state in such a way that all German-speaking areas of the former Habsburg Empire were part of the German Austrian Republic—including the Sudetenland and South Tyrol.[45] Among Austrian Social Democrats it was above all Karl Renner who, along with Bauer, repeatedly underlined the togetherness of Austrians, Germans and Sudeten Germans. Having being born in 1870 in the Moravian village Dolní Dunajovice/Untertannowitz, Renner had clear-cut feelings of solidarity with the German-speaking inhabitants of the Sudetenland, cut off as they were from their virtual fatherland by the outcome of the First World War. Therefore, personally and politically, it was certainly bitter for him that as leader of the Austrian delegation at the peace negotiations in 1919, he had to sign the Treaty of Saint-Germain which signaled the formal surrender of the Sudeten German areas to the Czechoslovakian Republic. Nevertheless, as a publicist and prominent Social democratic politician, Renner continued to advocate a unification of all German-speaking people, because for him, Austria did not constitute a viable nation-state: "We are not a nation, we never have been and we never will be able to become a nation!"[46] In this respect he represented a mindset that was widespread among Austrian Social Democrats during the interwar period. Contrary to others in the party, the attachment to the notion of the existence of a Greater German nation, however, drove Renner so far that in 1938 he did not just welcome the National Socialist Anschluss of Austria to the Third Reich but also the incorporation of the Sudeten German areas into the Greater German Reich. In an unpublished work on the foundation of the German-Austrian Republic, the Anschluss and the Sudeten Germans (*Die Gründung der Republik Deutsch-Österreich, der Anschluß und die Sudetendeutschen*), Renner celebrated the incorporation of the Sudetenland into the Greater German Reich as an achievement of a policy most Austrians had pursued for two decades. Instead of unmasking the political and diplomatic extortion that the Munich Agreement actually constituted, he stressed the fact that the affiliation of the Sudeten Germans and their homeland to the growing National Socialist empire was accomplished without significant bloodshed and at the same time with the approval of those powers that since the end of the First World War had done everything to prevent the political unification of all German-speaking people in one state. The subtitle "Documents of a struggle for justice" (*Dokumente eines Kampfes ums Recht*) suggested that according to Renner the Munich Agreement in every respect had to be considered highly justified.[47] Whereas most Austrian Social Democrats had abandoned the claim for the political unification of the German-speaking people after Hitler had risen to power in Germany in 1933, the former chancellor of state and minister Karl Renner in 1938 fully and disastrously accepted the politics of the NSDAP in this field as the fulfillment of Pan-German hopes nourished for twenty years.

Final remarks

In no way was the Sudetenland considered a fatherland lost in Austria after the end of the First World War. Via associations and publications, many Austrians kept alive the memory of the Sudeten Germans who in the Imperial era had been associated with Austria as part of the Lands of the Crown of Saint Wenceslaus. Although for juridical and political reasons the Austrian government was unable to patronize officially and effectively the German-speaking population of former Bohemia, Moravia and Silesia after 1918, within Austrian society the preoccupation with the Sudeten Germans was quite intensive during the interwar period. In line with an ethnically based definition or perception of the German-speaking people, the desired affiliation of the Sudetenland with Austria was interwoven with the wider problem of a political unification of Austria and Germany. Procuring the *Anschluss Österreichs*, as well as incorporating the Sudetenland into Germany in 1938, was reserved for the aggressive politics of the Third Reich. Not a few Sudeten Germans actively contributed to the integration of their homeland into the Greater German Reich. On the other hand, one should not lose sight of the fact that in individual cases Sudeten Germans have participated in the resistance to the thoroughly inhuman National Socialist regime. One of them is Roman Karl Scholz, acting as order priest in the collegiate church Klosterneuburg (nearby Vienna). Born in 1912 in Sumperk/Mährisch-Schönberg, Scholz changed from supporter of National Socialism to resistance fighter and rigorously rejected the criminal atrocities committed by the Greater German Reich in the name of the German people. On account of his hostility towards National Socialism, Scholz was imprisoned for four years before being sentenced to death by the notorious People's Court (*Volksgerichtshof*) and hanged on 10 May 1944.[48]

The expulsion of the Sudeten Germans from Czechoslovakia after the Second World War on the basis of the Beneš-decrees did not lead to a peaceful settlement. On the contrary, after 1945, the expulsion and expropriation of the Sudeten Germans made sure that their fate and their history remained on the political agenda in the Federal Republic of Germany and the Second Austrian Republic alike. The bilateral relationships of Austria and Germany with Czechoslovakia were far from being better in the postwar period than they had been in the interwar period. For the future, the common political and legal framework of the European Union affords the opportunity to look for generally acceptable and durable solutions.

Notes

1. I am grateful to the Netherlands Institute for Advanced Study in the Humanities and Social Sciences (Wassenaar) for providing me with the opportunity, as a Fellow-in-Residence, to complete this paper. Furthermore I am grateful to Sylvia Jones for editing the text.

2. Ernst Hanisch, *Der lange Schatten des Staates: Österreichische Gesellschaftsgeschichte im 20. Jahrhundert* (Vienna: Ueberreuter, 1994), 271.

3. For discussions about the concept of "Central Europe" see Richard G. Plaschka et al., eds., *Mitteleuropa-Konzeptionen in der ersten Hälfte des 20. Jahrhunderts* (Vienna: Verlag der Österreichischen Akademie der Wissenschaften, 1995) and Jürgen Elvert, *Mitteleuropa! Deutsche Pläne zur europäischen Neuordnung (1918–1945)* (Stuttgart: Franz Steiner, 1999).

4. See Mark Cornwall, "The Struggle on the Czech–German Language Border, 1880–1940," *The English Historical Review 109* (1994): 914-51. See also Catherine Albrecht, "Economic Nationalism in the Sudetenland, 1918-1938," in *Czechoslovakia in a Nationalist and Fascist Europe, 1918-1948*, ed. Mark Cornwall and R.J.W. Evans (Oxford: Oxford University Press, 2007), 89-108. For the Imperial era see Pieter M. Judson, *Guardians of the Nation: Activists on the Language Frontiers of Imperial Austria* (Cambridge, MA: Harvard University Press, 2006).

5. See Ronald M. Smelser, *The Sudeten Problem, 1933–1938: "Volkstumspolitik" and the Formulation of Nazi Foreign Policy* (Middletown: Wesleyan University Press, 1975) and Ralf Gebel, *"Heim ins Reich!" Konrad Henlein und der Reichsgau Sudetenland (1938–1945)*, 2nd ed. (Munich: R. Oldenbourg, 2000).

6. Mark Cornwall, "'A Leap into Ice Cold Water': The Manoeuvres of the Henlein Movement in Czechoslovakia, 1933-1938," in *Czechoslovakia*, 123-142.

7. Mark Mazower, *Hitler's Empire: Nazi Rule in Occupied Europe* (London: Allen Lane, 2008), 55.

8. For the gradual demolition of the Czechoslovakian Republic by the Third Reich see ibid., 54-63.

9. The literature is discussed in Christiane Brenner et al., eds., *Geschichtsschreibung zu den böhmischen Ländern im 20. Jahrhundert: Wissenschaftstraditionen – Institutionen – Diskurse* (Munich: R. Oldenbourg, 2006).

10. *Staatsgesetzblatt für den Staat Deutschösterreich*, 28 November 1918, StGBl. 40/1918; see also StGBl. 4/1919. All the laws mentioned and decrees promulgated in the *Staatsgesetzblatt* are available via *ALEX – Historische Rechts- und Gesetzestexte Online* of the Austrian National Library: <http://alex.onb.ac.at/alex.htm>. The *Reichsrat* mentioned was the parliament of the Austrian part (*Cisleithania*) of the Austrian-Hungarian double monarchy for the period 1867–1918.

11. StGBl. 41/1918.

12. Lorenz Mikoletzky, "Saint-Germain und Karl Renner: Eine Republik wird 'diktiert,'" in …

der Rest ist Österreich: Das Werden der Ersten Republik, vol. 1, ed. Helmut Konrad and Wolfgang Maderthaner (Vienna: Carl Gerold's Sohn, 2008), 180.

13. Julia Schmid, "'Deutschböhmen' als Konstrukt deutscher Nationalisten in Österreich und dem Deutschen Reich," *Bohemia 48* (2008): 479.

14. Susanne Maurer-Horn, "Die Landesregierung für Deutschböhmen und das Selbstbestimmungsrecht 1918/19," *Bohemia 38* (1997): 44-45, 37. In several towns of the Sudetenland, Austria, Germany and Switzerland, the German-Bohemian government erected offices for making propaganda in favor of an Anschluss of the Sudetenland to Austria and/or Germany. See Hans Hanns, "Die deutschböhmische Frage 1918–1919 und das österreichisch-tschechoslowakische Verhältnis," *Bohemia 13* (1972): 375-77, 380-83.

15. Schmid, "'Deutschböhmen,'" 479; Walter Reichel, "Tschechoslowakei–Österreich: Grenzziehung 1918/1919," in ... *der Rest ist Österreich*, 165ff.; Paul Molisch, *Die sudetendeutsche Freiheitsbewegung in den Jahren 1918–1919* (Vienna: Wilhelm Braumüller, 1932), ch. II.

16. See StGBl. 115/1918 and StGBl. 47/1919.

17. StGBl. 175/1919. See also Maurer-Horn, "Die Landesregierung für Deutschböhmen," 53.

18. StGBl. 484/1919.

19. The *Bundes-Verfassungsgesetz* of 1 December 1920 is published in the *Staatsgesetzblatt für die Republik Österreich*, StGBl. 450/1920, and available online on ALEX.

20. Hans Lemberg, "Von den Deutschböhmen zu den Sudetendeutschen: Der Beitrag von Geschichtswissenschaften und Geschichtspolitik," in *Geschichtsschreibung zu den böhmischen Ländern*, 95-107 and Cornelia Znoy, "Die Vertreibung der Sudetendeutschen nach Österreich 1945/46 unter besonderer Berücksichtigung der Bundesländer Wien und Niederösterreich," Diplomarbeit, University of Vienna, 1995: 9; this unpublished diploma thesis can be downloaded via <http://www.sudeten.at/de/dokumente/pdf/znoy.pdf> (18 April 2010).

21. See Rolf Steininger, "12 November 1918 – 12 March 1938: The Road to the Anschluß," in *Austria in the Twentieth Century*, ed. idem. et al. (New Brunswick, NJ: Transaction, 2002), 85-114.

22. Steven Beller, *A Concise History of Austria* (Cambridge: Cambridge University Press, 2006), 200. See also Rolf Steininger, *Austria, Germany and the Cold War: From the "Anschluss" to the State Treaty, 1938–1955* (New York: Berghahn, 2008), ch. I: "1918–1938: The Road to the 'Anschluss.'"

23. *Der Anschluß*, 2 March 1931, 1.

24. See invitation card, Parteiarchive – Großdeutsche Volkspartei/46/Völkische Verbände, Österreichisches Staatsarchiv, Archiv der Republik, Vienna.

25. See Wilhelm Maschke, *Das Deutschtum in der Tschechoslowakei* (Graz: Verlag der Alpenland Buchhandlung, 1925) and Günther Berka, *Die tschechische Irredenta in Deutschösterreich* (Graz: Verlag der Alpenland Buchhandlung, 1928). Both publications appeared in the series of the *Deutscher Schulverein Südmark.*

26. § 5 of the statutes of the *Verein der Deutschen der Iglauer Sprachinsel in Wien* dating from 1 June 1919, Gelöschte Vereine A32/1954/1921, Wiener Stadt- und Landesarchiv (WStLA), Vienna. Originally this association had been founded in 1911.

27. Gelöschte Vereine A32/7594/1928, WStLA. The statutes of the *Bund der Deutschböhmen in Österreich* are undated.

28. Gelöschte Vereine A32/9558/1937, A32/5362/1924 and A32/6291/1921, WStLA.

29. Statutes of the *Hilfsverein für Deutschböhmen und die Sudetenländer*, cited from the printed edition from January 1920, in Gelöschte Vereine A32/301/1921, WStLA; the following facts also rest on this archive collection: In 1925 the *Hilfsverein* changed its name to *Sudetendeutscher*

Heimatbund. In 1929 it added the designation *Kreis Deutschösterreich* thus stressing its cultural and ethnic aspirations. Just seven years later the association changed its name to *Sudetendeutscher Heimatbund, Kreis Österreich*. When the Anschluss had been carried out, the last change of name took place: As in the Greater German Reich, "Austria" was transformed to *Ostmark*, and the *Sudetendeutsche Heimatbund* replaced its designation *Kreis Österreich* by *Kreis Ostmark* in 1938. After Czechoslovakia had been destroyed and replaced by the National Socialist *Reichsprotektorat*, at its general meeting of 21 June 1939 the *Sudetendeutsche Heimatbund* declared "unanimously" and "deliberately" its dissolution, "because the objectives have been reached in accordance with its statutes" (Letter to the police department of Vienna, 4 July 1939). Before its self-liquidation, the association comprised the following branches: *Böhmerwaldgau, Deutschböhmen, Sudetenland, Südmährerbund* and *Allgemeiner Zweigverein* in Vienna.

30. Police Department of Vienna to the Government of Lower Austria, 8 September 1919, Gelöschte Vereine A32/301/1921, WStLA.

31. *Merkblatt für unsere deutschböhmischen und sudetenländischen Heimatsgenossen* of the *Hilfsverein für Deutschböhmen und die Sudetenländer*, January 1920, ibid.

32. Gelöschte Vereine A32/301/1921, WStLA.

33. See Gelöschte Vereine A32/9558/1937, WStLA (*Verein deutscher Studenten aus Nordböhmen*) and A32/6291/1921, WStLA (*Verein Deutscher Studenten aus Schlesien in Wien 'Oppavia'*), in both cases letters by the *Stillhaltekommissar* of 24 August 1938.

34. See Henry Delfiner, *Vienna broadcasts to Slovakia 1938–1939: A case study in subversion* (New York: Columbia University Press, 1974). See also David Schriffl, *Die Rolle Wiens im Prozess der Staatswerdung der Slowakei 1938/39* (Frankfurt: P. Lang, 2004).

35. Cited from Rudolf Jung's *Der nationale Sozialismus – Träger der deutschen Zukunft* (1923) as quoted in Eva Hahn, "Über Rudolf Jung und vergessene sudetendeutsche Vorläufer und Mitstreiter Hitlers," in *Hundert Jahre sudetendeutsche Geschichte: Eine völkische Bewegung in drei Staaten*, ed. Hans Henning Hahn (Frankfurt: P. Lang, 2007), 103.

36. See Hahn, "Über Rudolf Jung," 96.

37. [Alois Ciller], *Sudetendeutschland! Ein Kampf- und Mahnruf an alle Deutschen* (Vienna: Emmerich Auer, 1928).

38. Rudolf Laun, *Die tschechoslowakischen Ansprüche auf deutsches Land*, 2nd ed. (Vienna: Alfred Hölder, 1919), 23-24. Laun's leaflet appeared as number four of the *Flugblätter für Deutschösterreichs Recht* [Leaflets for the rights of German-Austria]. All together, thirty-nine numbers of this series, which was edited by the German-Bohemian provincial government, have been published; see Maurer-Horn, "Die Landesregierung für Deutschböhmen," 45 (fn. 45), 50-51 (fn. 77). Laun also had published a French translation of his leaflet in 1919, possibly in an effort to influence the peace negotiations in the French capital. On Laun, who somewhat later participated in the Austrian delegation to the peace negotiations at Saint-Germain, see the article by Georg Stadtmüller in *Neue Deutsche Biographie*, vol. 13 (Berlin: Duncker & Humblot, 1982), 715-17.

39. Wilhelm Winkler, "Deutschböhmens Wirtschaftskraft," in *Deutschböhmen*, ed. Rudolf Lodgman [von Auen] (Berlin: Ullstein & Co., 1919), 110, 129, 131. On Winkler see Alexander Pinwinkler, *Wilhelm Winkler (1884–1984) – eine Biographie: Zur Geschichte der Statistik und Demographie in Österreich und Deutschland* (Berlin: Duncker & Humblot, 2003). In his own contribution to the book *Deutschböhmen*, the editor Lodgman von Auen blamed the Czech people (*Tschechenvolke*) for exerting an "autocratic foreign domination" over the German-speaking people in the Czechoslovakian Republic ("Das alte und das neue Österreich," in *Deutschböhmen*, 15).

40. Alfons Dopsch, "Die historische Stellung der Deutschen in Böhmen," in *Deutschböhmen*, 49.

41. Maurer-Horn, "Die Landesregierung für Deutschböhmen," 48-49, fn. 65.

42. Friedrich Wieser, "Deutschböhmens Selbstbestimmungsrecht," in *Deutschböhmen*, 261-62.

43. Stefan Hofer, *Die Anschlußfrage in der internationalen Presse* (Vienna: Deutsche Einheit, 1931), 6. Concerning its campaign against the Peace Treaty of Saint-Germain, the "Austrian-German People's League" can be compared with the *Deutscher Fichte-Bund* founded in the 1920s: this German association likewise was eager to publish contributions by foreign critics on the peace treaties of 1919; see Dietrich Orlow, *The Lure of Fascism in Western Europe: German Nazis, Dutch and French Fascists, 1933–1939* (New York: Palgrave Macmillan, 2009), 22-23.

44. Hans Mommsen, *Die Sozialdemokratie und die Nationalitätenfrage im habsburgischen Vielvölkerstaat*, vol. 1, *Das Ringen um die supranationale Integration des zisleithanischen Arbeiterbewegung (1867–1907)* (Vienna: Europa-Verlag, 1963).

45. See Ernst Hanisch, "Im Zeichen von Otto Bauer: Deutschösterreichs Außenpolitik in den Jahren 1918 bis 1919," in *... der Rest ist Österreich*, 212. South Tyrol had to be ceded by Austria to Italy after the First World War.

46. Karl Renner, "Was soll aus Österreich werden?," in *Der Anschluß*, 15 Feb. 1930, 2. See Siegfried Nasko, "Ein 'deutschösterreichischer' Staatsmann? Karl Renners Haltung zur Anschlußidee 1918–1938," in *Ungleiche Partner? Österreich und Deutschland in ihrer gegenseitigen Wahrnehmung: Historische Analysen und Vergleiche aus dem 19. und 20. Jahrhundert*, ed. Michael Gehler et al. (Stuttgart: Franz Steiner, 1996), 399-424. Nasko underlines that, notwithstanding his numerous public statements, in his foreign politics Renner did not initiate concrete measures for an Anschluss. On the whole, making politics suit the changing circumstances seems to have been more important to Renner than the pursuit of a consistent policy (ibid., 408, 413).

47. See Nasko, "Ein 'deutschösterreichischer' Staatsmann?," 421-22.

48. Wolfgang Neugebauer, *Der österreichische Widerstand 1938–1945* (Vienna: Steinbauer, 2008), 133-34.

Consensus vs. Control: The Politics of Culture in Interwar Austria, a Reassessment (with special emphasis on literature and the theatre)[1]

Robert Pyrah

The non-Nazi aspects of the literary, artistic and cultural scene of interwar Austria, with an inevitable bias towards Vienna and Salzburg, have received plentiful and renewed attention in scholarship in recent years.[2] Amid the various facets under scrutiny, particular comment has been reserved for the "politics" of Austrian culture.[3] This is broadly defined in two ways: how literary or artistic forms either *per se*, or else through their institutional framing (e.g. production and dissemination), have reflected or sought actively to promote different ideological agendas during the period. Book publishing,[4] cabaret and so-called "Kleinkunst" forms,[5] and the theatre have all been examined,[6] with more recent work emerging on dance and the cinema.[7] This essay looks primarily at developments in the mainstream spoken theatre, construed as a highly public artform of especially high discursive status in interwar Austria, with a measurable institutional function through its promotion, sponsorship and reception. There are obvious overlaps with wider literary developments and concerns during the period, both inherent to text and context, and these will be discussed as relevant.

This essay will not, however, deal with works that thematize political events between 1918-38 written some years after the fact.[8] Of primary concern is the canon of work as construed *during* the period, rather than subsequently. This important distinction, which is stressed by Wendelin

Schmidt-Dengler, a pre-eminent Austrian literary scholar, is sometimes missed in discussions of 1918-38 that prefer to stress either discursive "continuities" with the Habsburg era, or else the achievements of writers more palatable to the tastemakers of today.[9] Works trading in Habsburg nostalgia are certainly relevant, and a boom on the stage (in drama and operetta particularly) and in literature was marked, but not until the late 1920s. An emphasis on Habsburg themes, retroactively, appears to fit better the agendas of Austrian historiography until around the early 1990s, coloured as it was by the notion of being Hitler's first prey, which subsequently came to be known as the "victim myth."[10] More common at the time were works trading in post-naturalist social criticism, and increasingly by the 1930s, an interest in *völkisch* motifs. Against this background, the likes of currently celebrated authors Robert Musil (1880-1942) and Jura Soyfer (1912-39) were marginal at best.[11] Leaving aside questions of relative literary merit, their satirical viewpoint and political credentials are certainly more attractive today than the likes of Friedrich Schreyvogl (1899-1976), Max Mell (1882-1971) or Anton Wildgans (1881-1932), who have been forgotten by the canon but were heavily promoted and successful authors and dramatists at the time.[12]

Literary and cultural scholarship has taken cues from the mass of excellent research into Austria's political situation during the interwar period, which tends to stress the implacable opposition between the mainstream ideologies of the Social Democrats on the Left, and the Christian Socials on the Right.[13] These parties occupied physically different spheres of influence, the former concentrated in the working class citadels of so-called "Red Vienna," the latter ruling all national government coalitions and mainly representing the provinces. Counterparts to this division are therefore traced in cultural life. For instance, through organisations known as Kunststellen that until 1933 were organised along party (although also professional) lines, and distributed cut-price theatre tickets to their members;[14] not to mention the various smaller cultural associations such as the *Arbeiterbüchereien* in Vienna, authors' associations, and publications like the Kunststelle organs of the mainstream Left and Right respectively, *Kunst und Volk* and *Der Kunstgarten*. Certain literary forms at face value further reinforce these political divisions, such as the play *Lenin* by Ernst Fischer (1899-1972), intended for a new Social Democrat canon that failed to emerge—this is, of course, notwithstanding the problematics of classifying individual works where a clear ideological motive is not inscribed or else immediately visible. Indeed, an ambivalence has again been linked to political developments, most notably concerning authors, works and linked institutions in the 1930s, like the Bund deutscher Schriftsteller Österreichs, that traded in *völkisch* discourse, imagery and motifs. Klaus Amann in particular has documented how these so-called "Brückenbauer" (bridge-builders), which included Mell and Schreyvogl, were able to exploit overlaps between the Austrian state's insistence on a German cultural basis and Nazi ideology, and thus helped smooth the intellectual and cultural transition to Nazism in 1938.[15] This is not to say, however, that Austrian cultural life of the period is not increasingly being appreciated on its own terms, as set against the state's retroactively known political failures.[16]

The present essay intends to build on this existing scholarship by drawing attention to selected facets of cultural life that do not correspond with the political category of monolithic and mutually antagonistic ideologies. I will cite examples that illustrate mitigating forms of consensus in the cultural sphere across parties on the one hand; and on the other, of challenges from *within* camps to their official or predominant ideological determinism. The bias of my examples reflects a longstanding research interest in the Vienna Burgtheater, which clearly exempts this essay from claims to complete coverage of the period, let alone Austria as a whole. But seen in tandem with other developments in literary and cultural life both discussed elsewhere and sketched below, I suggest that this case study offers a useful crucible for examining both these cross-party and, to borrow Anton Pelinka's phrase, "system-internal" (*systemimmanente*) factors.[17] By the late 1920s, the Burgtheater had transformed from the epithetical "first German stage" to a "national theatre for Austria" to which Left and Right had access through their Kunststellen;[18] meanwhile its status as both a "national" theatre controlled by the incumbent Christian Social Minister of Education, but one that was situated right in the heart of "Red Vienna," offers a further symbolic aspect to the study of Austrian culture as ideologically divided.[19] To be sure, further research needs to be carried out on cultural life in the provinces; however, the basic geopolitical paradigm of Left/Right in interwar Austria, as Charlie Jeffery affirms in his study of Social Democracy, necessarily pivots on Vienna, due to the sheer concentration of that party's energies there.[20]

I: Literary Background: The Inconsistent Mapping of Themes to Political Ideology, 1918-1934

In this section, I'd like to discuss briefly three salient literary themes and their inconsistent relationship to the political categories of interwar Austria. These concern the notion of "Heimat"; the status of Catholic interests; and thematizations of history.[21] At face value, each appears to map onto right-of-centre political inclinations, but the Left was able to accommodate to each, to varying degrees, with particular consequences.

"Heimat" refers to the local place more narrowly, or else the "homeland" more abstractly, and as such is geographically as well as ideologically flexible. As I have shown elsewhere, the notion may imply a sense of belonging to the German nation or people ("Volk"), when taken in maximalist terms, but also to the separate Austrian state.[22] Heinz Wassermann summarized this slippage in referring to contemporary Austrian school textbooks' use of the term as follows: "Wenn Volk, dann deutsches Volk, wenn Heimat, dann Österreich" ["If we say Volk, this means the German Volk, if Heimat, then it refers to Austria"].[23] This ambivalent discourse is one that clearly lent itself to those seeking to justify Anschluss with Germany after 1934, but also to the majority of Austrians before that date who defined their identity as culturally German: This included the Social Democrats, who famously also sought Anschluss as an official party policy, and rejected Catholic definitions of Austrian separatism, until Hitler's rise to power. A literary and historical basis was provided by Josef Nadler's influential "Stamm" [tribe]-based theory of the Germanic peoples which again allowed the interpreter to interpret flexibly whether this implied belonging to a common state, or merely a shared culture.[24]

The promotion and enjoyment of "Heimat" literature until 1933-34 therefore represents a shared aspect of culture that cuts across political divisions. At face value it does not seem to fit with Socialist concerns, since it represents a conservative pattern of response to the modern world from a provincial (often rural) perspective, the changes wrought by industrialization in the late nineteenth and early twentieth centuries, and questions of regional and national identity. But the mode also contained aspects of social criticism, cognate with those in Naturalism, notwithstanding its reactionary aspect.[25] The main Austrian representatives of this broadly defined category include among the dialect poets the Styrian Michael Hainisch (1858-1940), Austria's president between 1920 and 1928, and the novelists Peter Rosegger (1843-1918), Maria Grengg (1889-1963), Karl Heinrich Waggerl (1897-1973) and Rudolf Hans Bartsch (1873-1952).[26] It was consequently promoted by the Left as a more palatable alternative to German bourgeois realism;[27] and its overwhelming popularity across social groups is reflected by sales figures and by borrowing statistics from Workers' Libraries in Vienna established by the Social Democrats.[28]

The form later came to be associated with Nazism through the programmatic *Heimatkust* of Adolf Bartels (1862-1945), who coined the term, which preserves the mythical and religious associations with the "homeland" but collapses its regional associations a narrowly racial, German-nationalist conception of *Volk* [the people].[29] In the Austrian context, Heimat writing is also associated with political calls to rebalance attention from the outsized former Imperial capital of Vienna to the rural provinces. This contrast between the "decadent, urban" and (tacitly or otherwise) "Jewish, cosmopolitan" city versus the "authentic, rural" provinces clearly maps onto the geopolitical division of Austria in the period, and was codified into literary stereotypes. The best-known example is the deliberate juxtaposition of Arthur Schnitzler (1862-1931), the urbane chronicler of Vienna's fin-de-siècle bourgeoise, with Tyrolean doctor and playwright Karl Schönherr (1867-1943) in the contemporary work edited by Nagl, Zeidler and Castle, the *Deutsch-Österreichische Literaturgeschichte*.[30] The contrast is deliberate and emblematic, pitching Vienna against the autochthonic province represented by Schönherr's dramas with such emblematic titles as *Erde* [*Earth*] (1908) and *Glaube und Heimat* [*Belief and Homeland*] (1910). This transposition of the city/country divide from literature into politics arguably represents the culmination of the call by Rosegger for a re-orientation of the cultural agenda away from a perceived metropolitan bias in his piece "Die Entdeckung der Provinz" ["Discovering the Provinces"], published in 1899 in the liberal weekly edited by Hermann Bahr, *Die Zeit*;[31] one that was matched by contemporary publicists such as Max Pirker (1886-1931), a friend of Hugo von Hofmannsthal (1874-1929), in such pamphlets as *Die Zukunft der österreichischen Alpenländer* (1919) [*The Future of Austria's Alpine Provinces*].[32] This conquest of the city by provincial forces would be invoked frequently, including by composer Ernst Krenek during the period of the Austrian fascist-inspired state from 1934-38.[33]

However, these neat political categories obscure more fluid realities. Schönherr was by no means purely concerned with narrowly rural themes, especially in later work; and his writing was evidently acceptable to Left as well as Right, as his continued success through all regimes from 1900-1938 and beyond arguably shows.[34] Pivotal to this acceptance by the Left is the concern with "Volk" which these and other works in the Heimat mode reveal. Although as demonstrated, the term is ambiguous, *a priori* it fulfils the Left's mission to provide art for and of the people, regardless of whether they belong to a narrowly defined urban working class. The views of the most influential cultural politician on the Left make this clear: David Josef Bach (1874-1947), cultural editor of the *Arbeiterzeitung* and leader of the party Kunststelle. Recent research on his legacy has revealed him to be a consensus politician who actively promoted "traditional" cultural forms rather than a specifically left-wing canon, stemming from his Wagnerian view of all true art, regardless of intent, as being perforce "revolutionary."[35] This view allowed him for instance to promote church music in his 1905 Workers' Symphony Concerts, despite the party's vociferous anticlericalism, as well as to foster personal contacts with such Catholic cultural stalwarts as Richard von Kralik (1852-1934).[36] He also stresses a practical *Volkstümlichkeit* [relating to the people] over an abstract notion of ideological purity, writing in *Kunst und Volk* in June 1929:

> Ein sozialistisches Kulturprogramm, das seine Wirkung auch auf das Theater ausdehnen muß, fordert zwar nicht ein sozialistisches Theater in dem Sinne, als ob nur sozialistische Stücke gespielt werden dürften, wohl aber fordert es wie auf jedem anderen Gebiet der Kunst auch hier den Zusammenhang mit dem Leben, ohne darum dem älteren künstlerischen Gut entsagen zu wollen.[37]
>
> [A Socialist cultural programme that must also extend its influence onto the theatre does not demand a Socialist theatre in the sense that only Socialist plays may be staged but here too it does demand—as in all other spheres of art—a connection to real life, without wishing for the sake of that to renounce the older artistic material.]

That these views were not shared by many in his party, occasioning internal criticism for promoting reactionary forms, is moot in this context, and has been well documented elsewhere. More important are the overlaps with the cultural policies of the political Right resulting from Bach's policy, which defy the neat mapping of political divisions onto literary and cultural categories in interwar Austria. A further example is worth mentioning briefly, the promotion of the morality play *Jedermann* [*Everyman*] by Hugo von Hofmannsthal (1874-1929), which again contradicts the geographical and literary map of Austrian politics. The play opened the Salzburg Festival each year from its inception in 1920, an event conceived explicitly as the celebration of an Austrian identity defined in Catholicizing terms by its founders, Hofmannsthal, Richard Strauss (1864-1949) and the theatre impresario Max Reinhardt (1873-1943).[38] Notwithstanding, the first half of Hofmannsthal's 1912 essay "Das alte Spiel von Jedermann" ["The Old Everyman Play"] was reproduced in *Kunst und Volk* in 1929—unattributed, and described merely as "Einleitung" ["Introduction"]—when *Jedermann* was staged at the Deutsches Volkstheater in Vienna, October 1929, as a memorial to Hofmannsthal, who had died in July.[39]

This is not to say, of course, that all cultural forms readily pleased Bach, and by 1928 he had begun to identify a tendency in Austrian culture, particularly at the state-run Burgtheater, to favour forms of drama that were clearly more flattering to Right-wing political agendas than his own. The performance of Max Mell's play, *Das Nachfolge-Christi-Spiel* [*The Play of the Imitation of Christ*, 1927] occasioned a 1928 *Arbeiterzeitung* article emblematically titled "Kunst oder Tendenz?" ["Art or political tendentiousness?"] that demanded parity for left-wing forms.[40] Meanwhile, by 1930, historical dramas dealing with themes from Austria's specifically Habsburg past were dominating repertoires not only at the Vienna Burgtheater, but across a range of stages in the capital. This trend mirrors the broader literary *Zeitgeist* which Schmidt-Dengler has called a "Bedürfnis nach Geschichte" ["need for history"].[41] In the theatre, the trend includes works by such now-forgotten authors as Hanns Sassmann (1882-1944), whose "Austrian Trilogy" of plays about Austria's reactionary post-Napoleonic years, *Metternich*, *Haus Rothschild* and *1848*, were big hits at the Burgtheater from 1929-1932. These use historical settings to suggest unflattering parallels with the present and express a "pro-Austrian" reactionary political agenda in increasingly explicit terms—a fact borne out by Sassmann's other published statements.[42] But historical drama again shows the difficulty of tracking ideological programmes along cultural lines. Clearly such works caused Bach discomfort, as emerges in an unpublished letter from 1931 to Franz Schneiderhan, the general director of the state theatres, where Bach makes the point that "legitimist comedies" are unpalatable to his constituents.[43] (Bach also amplifies his point from the *Arbeiterzeitung* quoted above that the concerns of the Left ought also to have fair representation.) However, in his published reviews he fails or declines to identify a programme behind historicizing works, preferring to focus on their inconsistencies. This position arguably reflects the variegated range of agendas the works represent. Analysis by Aspetsberger and others has shown some to be highly politicized, for example the bestselling novels by Mirko Jelusich (1886-1969), *Cäsar* [*Caesar*] (1929) and *Cromwell* (1933), with the latter supposedly described by the author himself as "eine kaum noch getarnte Hitler-Biographie" ["a scarcely disguised biography of Hitler"].[44] Authors of this type include Karl Heinz Strobl (1877-1946), Bruno Brehm (1892-1974) and Josef Wenter (1880-1947).[45] Other works are more apolitically nostalgic, as for instance in the now-celebrated writing by Joseph Roth (1894-1939) and Stefan Zweig (1881-1942); others still use history more functionally for pomp and pageantry as in popular operettas like *Sissy* by Ernst and Hubert Marischka (1893-1963; 1882-1959). Elsewhere historical settings are little more than the background to universal psychological conflicts first and foremost, as in *Juarez und Maximilian* (1924) by Franz Werfel (1890-1945), staged at the Theater in der Josefstadt in 1925, migrating to the Burgtheater in 1929. A new wave of home-grown films trading in nostalgic themes also reflects a spectrum of positions.[46]

However, despite the retroactive association with right-wing politics, seen from the perspective of the period and the response of the Left, these broad literary trends and their reception add nuance to the political stereotype of two camps divided implacably along strict ideological lines, at least in the realm of culture.

II: Institutional Factors for Overlap, 1918-1934

In tandem with these literary factors, I'd like to consider briefly some of the institutional respects in which culture (especially in the theatre) did not reflect monolithic political divisions. The first has already been mentioned, namely the Kunststellen, which although organised along party and professional lines, ultimately helped open up the traditional temples of elite culture (the Vienna Opera and Burgtheater) to wider constituencies than before 1918. The other effect was that, differences in emphasis apart, the two largest bodies—those affiliated with the Social Democrats on the Left, and the Christian Socials on the Right—ultimately served to foster an embryonic sense of a shared culture by giving access to similar forms to their constituents. Admittedly this was a somewhat one-sided process: It centres on Vienna rather than the provinces, and hinges on Bach's views quoted above, which allow for the promotion of "bourgeois" cultural forms on account of their transformative power, in a Wagnerian understanding of art.

In his survey of Austro-Marxism in literature, Alfred Pfoser concludes of Bach and his colleagues:

> Die politische Entzweiung der deutschen sozialistischen Kunst und Literatur wollte man nicht gelten lassen, korrespondierend zum politischen Bereich neigte man zu einer integrierenden Position, die einen Traditionalismus mit politisch und künstlerisch avancierten Bestrebungen unter einen Hut bringen wollte.[47]
>
> [They did not wish to acknowledge the political division of German Socialist art and literature, and corresponding to the political sphere they tended toward an integrating position that sought to bring a traditionalism with politically and artistically advanced endeavours under one umbrella.]

Performance records for the Social Democratic Kunststelle reflect this statement. While they show support for authors of a socially critical tendency that did not readily endear them to the Right, such as Georg Büchner, Hans Kaltneker and Ferdinand Bruckner, established theatrical "classics" such as Hauptmann, Shakespeare, Goethe and Schiller were heavily promoted, and made up the majority of the tickets sold.[48] Additionally, Bach's agenda was based on a notion of "Volksbildung" ["popular education"] that, despite its differing ideological content, overlaps with the promotion both of German classics and literary forms associated with *Heimat*, particularly the *Volksstück*, pursued by the Christian Socials and the Christian camp through the "Kunststelle für Christliche Volksbildung."[49] This in turn overlaps with calls from across the political spectrum recorded by Margret Dietrich until 1933 to make the Burgtheater an instrument of popular education *tout court*.[50]

Such commonalities even struck Hans Brečka (1885-1954), Bach's opposite number as cultural critic at the Christian Social daily *Reichspost* and president of the party-affiliated Kunststelle. Not a man given to conciliatory statements on cultural matters in his reviews, he nevertheless notes that the ideological differences between Left and Right did not stop them from a shared promotion of the classics:

> Ursprünglich war ein Zusammenarbeiten dieser beiden, scheinbar dem gleichen Ziele zugewendeten Gruppen geplant, doch zeigte sich bald, daß bei der Programmbildung, bei der Wahl der aufzuführenden Stücke allzuhäufig die Verschiedenheit der Weltanschauungen in Erscheinung treten müsse, wenngleich eine ansehnliche Reihe von Bühnenwerken, vor allem natürlich die Dichtungen der Klassiker, von beiden Kunststellen [...] in gleicher Weise gewünscht wurden.[51]

> [It was originally planned that these two groups (the Social Democratic and Christian Social Kunststellen), which apparently pursued the same goal, would collaborate but it soon became evident that in putting together a repertoire and choosing plays for performance the differences in world view would all too often become apparent, despite the fact that a considerable number of works for the stage, above all of course the Classics, were desired equally by both Kunststellen.]

A further conciliatory gesture came in private correspondence between Bach and Hermann Bahr (1863-1934), that famous Catholic convert and propagator of trends. Bach works hard in a 1922 letter to counter literary stereotypes associated with Socialism and insists, perhaps too protestingly, that the workers are hostile to modern drama dealing with revolution and war ("Einen wahren Horror empfinden die Arbeiter bei den sogenannten Revolutionsstücken. Sie sind ihnen ebenso zuwider wie alle Kriegsstücke, gleichgiltig welcher Tendenz."[52] ["The workers genuinely feel horrified by so-called revolutionary dramas. They loathe them just as much as all war dramas, of whatever political complexion."]). Instead Bach suggests the Volksstück form is his priority, albeit in a different form than originally encountered in Viennese theatre criticism of the 1830s and 40s referring to works by Ludwig Anzengruber (1839-1889), Ferdinand Raimund (1790-1836) and Johann Nestroy (1801-1862). Here, as he explains, Bach means high art by Goethe and Grillparzer made accessible to the masses. He goes on to blame theatre directors for hindering this programme by inflicting their private aesthetic sensibilities on audiences ("Ich brauche Ihnen nicht erst auseinanderzusetzen, daß das sogenannte Theater der Intellekuellen in Wahrheit das Ende des Theaters bedeutet."[53] ["I do not need to explain to you that the so-called theatre of intellectuals in reality means the end of theatre itself."]).

These factors of course do not fully contradict the political narrative of Left and Right at ideological loggerheads during the period. Indeed, the implacable rhetorical opposition continued in the fora of the two sides' respective dailies, with cultural reviews offering sometimes starkly different interpretations of the quality, worthiness or political agenda of particular literary works or dramatic performances.[54] And there were some significant divergences in their programmes. One noteworthy case concerns the promotion of a 1932 revival of Schnitzler's play *Der junge Medardus* [*Young Medardus*, 1910] at the Burgtheater,[55] a play that fits Bach's definition of a modern "Volksstück" for its concern with real lives and modern social problems,[56] but which came under tendentious attack for "cheap pacifism" from the successful historical dramatist Hanns Sassmann writing in the *Neues Wiener Journal*.[57] The play was dropped from the repertoire after just four performances. However, Bach's efforts do at least suggest nascent moves towards consensus politics in the cultural sphere, and aspects of genuine overlap and interaction between the rival camps, beneath the official party positions of class warfare and implacable opposition.

A further mitigating factor is the spectrum of divergent positions on the Right, which at face value is masked by a shared concern with the cultural place and expression of Catholicism. Again, "literary Catholicism" in its various forms encompasses a strikingly diverse range of authors and concerns, from the more doctrinaire Kralik, through the later Nazi sympathizers Mell and Schreyvogl, to a number of authors with Jewish extraction interested in the more symbolic than liturgical dimensions of Catholicism, as the projection of an "Austrian idea." Foremost among this last group were Franz Werfel, mentioned above; a number of his plays were staged successfully at the Burgtheater in the period. His biography encompasses a flirtation with Expressionist forms and left-wing politics around 1919, then a move toward a pro-Austrian position, to the point of personal friendship with Austrian Chancellor Schuschnigg (1897-1977).[58] His ambiguous relationship with Catholicism has also received plentiful coverage in the secondary literature, with novels such as *Barbara oder die Frömmigkeit* (1929) and the Burgtheater drama *Paulus unter den Juden* (thirty-five performances in a four-year run between 4 May 1927 and 23 September 1931) leading to speculations of a conversion.[59] However, the play was received coolly by Brečka in the Catholic Reichspost, reserving praise for the Burgtheater production rather than the author or work.[60] And this coolness from the party-affiliated circle was emblematic of a wider suspicion of Jewish elements promoting "Catholic culture."

In the case of the Salzburg Festival, this suspicion spilled over into open hostility from some quarters. As Michael Steinberg and others have analysed, the Festival sought to enact and codify a new Austrian identity through ritual performance; however both its poet laureate (Hofmannsthal) and star director (Reinhardt) were at least partly of Jewish extraction and anti-Semitism tinged some of the attacks on the project.[61] The staging of Hofmannsthal's more doctrinaire play *Das Salzburger große Welttheater*, written especially for the Festival and put on inside the Kollegienkirche itself in 1922, was deemed sacrilegious[62] (incidentally, it also marked the tipping point at which Bach no longer supported the author's work).[63] Further attacks came from Karl Kraus in his famous article "Vom großen Welttheaterschwindel" ["On the Great World Theatre Swindle"], the culmination of a series of attacks on Reinhardt and Hofmannsthal in the 1920s for a range of perceived hypocrisies.[64] These attacks focused on the Festival's uneasy fusion of Joseph Nadler's ethnic theories of indigenous art with a deliberate cosmopolitanism that in practice often excluded those it was supposed to represent through high ticket prices.[65] Indeed, Kraus went so far as to cite the "Great World Theatre Swindle" as his reason for leaving the Catholic Church. But more importantly, such attacks on this attempt to give an institutional framework to a "Catholicizing" vision of Austria ultimately reveal the degree of differences of opinion and fissure within the cultural spectrum of the Right. Again, the cultural sphere proves a contradictory barometer of much more neatly defined political categories.

III: The "Corporate State," 1934-38: Internal Tensions

The brief Civil War, culminating in the suppression of Social Democracy, its press and cultural institutions in 1934, would appear to have resolved the issue of ambiguous tensions between political fractions.[66] The story of how such institutions came under the control of the single-party, fascist-inspired Austrian "corporate State," including the creation of authors' groups and a single "Österreichische Kunststelle" has received plentiful coverage elsewhere.[67] So, meanwhile, has their gradual subversion by covert Nazi sympathisers, who exploited the weakness of the state's insistence on a Germanic basis to Austrian culture in its separatist, patriotic ideology.[68]

In his study of literary resistance and opposition to the cultural policies of the fascist-inspired Austrian Corporate State of 1934-38, Horst Jarka, using Anton Pelinka's term, focuses on what he calls "systemimmanente" ["system-internal"] factors. These are tensions from within the system that work against the appearance of a unified, harmonious and consistently applied set of cultural policies. Examples include the government publication *Der Christliche Ständestaat*, which included some surprisingly critical voices, in particular that of composer Ernst Krenek, whose controversial "Jazz-Opera" *Jonny spielt auf* [*Jonny strikes up*] had excited Nazi protests on its performance in Vienna in 1928.[69] Jarka also mentions cabaret forms, poetry, and government-sanctioned initiatives of a leftist stripe. The first was the Österreichische Arbeiterschriftstellerverband [Austrian Authors' Association], which counted forty members in its two-year existence. The second was the "people's university" in the largely working class Viennese suburb of Ottakring, the Volksheim, whose deputy vice-chancellor Viktor Matejka (1901-1993) combined Catholic with left-leaning sympathies. A performance of working class drama *Hiob* at the institution in 1936, an adaptation of a work by Walter Bauer, is cited to demonstrate the potential for subversive elements: It was read by the *Reichspost* as arousing Marxist sympathies and led to Matejka's sacking.[70] As Jarka underlines, these factors mitigate the split picture of a cultural scene administered around a pro-Austrian, Catholic-inspired ideology on the one hand, or else covert Nazism on the other.

Similarly, my work on the Burgtheater focused on elements either in drama or the institutional set-up of the theatre that run counter to such monolithic views of cultural output, notwithstanding the reintroduction of official censorship and tighter controls over productions also at the private theatres in Vienna.[71] In this context, three productions are of particular note. The Burgtheater production of *Kaiser Joseph II.* by Rudolf Henz in 1937 needed what Brečka called "Eine Art von besonderer Legitimation" ["a particular kind of legitimation"] to avoid controversy[72]—namely, the author's spotless credentials as a loyalist to the regime. The problem lay with the play's central confrontation between the Pope and the reforming Emperor, which led to its performance before a "censorship committee" convened by Burgtheater director Hermann Röbbeling before the premiere.[73] The danger of the play being seen as an attack on the clergy was underscored by the reaction of Nazi reviewers on the pre-premiere press night,[74] prompting reviewers from the government side to work hard to resolve any tensions. Thus Brečka again refers to Henz's background:

> Es kann nicht ausbleiben, daß bei einer ernsten Diskussion des Verhältnisses dieses Herrschers zur Kirche gewisse Anschauungen zur Sprache kommen müssen, deren Formulierung heikel ist und nur von einem Dichter gewagt werden kann, dessen religiöse Gesinnung und Überzeugung außer Zweifel ausgesetzt ist [*sic*].[75]
>
> [It cannot be avoided that in a serious discussion about the relationship between this ruler and the Church certain views must be spoken, whose formulation is sensitive and can only be ventured by an author whose religious beliefs and convictions are beyond doubt.]

These credentials appear to have been amply borne out elsewhere in the play, with discussions about the necessity for a strong state to resist external threats reflecting clearly the concerns of 1937, in words that could be taken verbatim from Austria's contemporary rulers.[76]

Another play that provided less than ideal fodder for the patriotic concerns of Austria's rulers before 1938 was *Kaiser Karl V.* by Felix Braun (1885-1973). As with *Kaiser Joseph II.*, the plot deals episodically with the life of a great leader figure in Austrian history, and ends with the ruler reflecting on his failings at the play's close. But Braun's play focuses resolutely on the psychology of the ruler and his personal tragedy, avoiding contemporary parallels, a fact noticed by reviewers.[77] Brečka, who criticizes the play for lacking theatrical effectiveness, again works hard to make the drama fit the Procrustean bed of "Austrofascist" concerns, here on the flimsy grounds that this was a play written by an Austrian, and staged at the Burgtheater:

> Über alle diese Bedenken hinweg wird uns die achtunggebietende Dichtung eines Österreichers vom Burgtheater durch eine wahrhaft grandiose Aufführung nahe gebracht.[78]
>
> [Despite all these concerns, we are brought closer to the awe-inspiring literary work of an Austrian from the Burgtheater through a truly magnificent production.]

A final production of note was that of *Ein treuer Diener seines Herrn* (1830) by Franz Grillparzer (1791-1872), which premiered at the Theater in der Josefstadt on 6 December 1935 (twenty-six performances in total). Edda Fuhrich has noted that the theatre's director in the period, Ernst Lothar (1890-1974), was particularly concerned with balancing artistic standards and humanitarian concerns with flattering the regime,[79] and this high-profile production, given quasi-official status through the presence of clergy and government figures and pushed hard by the Kunststelle, appears to have been no exception.[80] At face value, the drama appears ideally suited to the government line, thematizing loyal service to an absent ruler against all odds. However, Lothar changed the ending of the play, reversing the inward focus of the original to become a powerful statement of the human responsibility that rulers explicitly carry. The final lines of the play after "Laß dir den Menschen Mensch sein" ["Let man retain his humanity"] to "Da tat ein alter Mann, was er vermochte / I nu! Ein treuer Diener seines Herrn" ["An old man did what he could / Me! A loyal servant of his master"][81] are completely rewritten to read as follows:

> Lass Deine *Untertanen* Menschen sein,
> *Als Menschen achte sie!*
> Richt auf die Schwachen, halt im Zaun die Starken.
> Das Gute tu und tu es rasch und gern.
> *Sei ein getreuer Herr erst Deinen Dienern,*
> *Dann sind sie treue Diener ihres Herrn!* [82] [emphasis added]
>
> [Let your *subordinates* be humans,
> *And respect them as such!*
> Focus on the weak, keep the strong in check.
> Do good and do it quickly and willingly.
> *Be first a loyal servant of your servants,*
> *Then you are a loyal servant of your master!*]

As in Henz's case, Lothar's impeccable patriotic credentials (he had produced two other Grillparzer dramas with more explicitly "pro-Austrian" motifs)[83] helped guarantee the play's performance. It may also have been the case that its message flattered the regime's own sense of justice and legitimacy, attested often enough by other sources: for instance, its self-perceived mildness in dealing with anti-Semitism and censorship, rejecting Nazi methods on the grounds of being too harsh and therefore "unösterreichisch" ["un-Austrian"].[84] That a humanitarian message apparently questioning the nature of rule could have been communicated at all, however, further modifies the view of Austrian culture in 1934-38 as monolithically determined by the twin forces of covert Nazism or a narrowly defined, state-sponsored patriotism.

The symbolic significance of the Burgtheater in particular within the patriotic cultural rhetoric of the "Corporate State" was confirmed by the 1934 edition of a book by Rudolph Lothar,[85] with a foreword by then-Minister of Education Schuschnigg, which claims it had reached an evolutionary end-point as "unser Nationaltheater" ["our national theatre"]. His claim depends on the idea that the Burgtheater is at the representative centre of Austria's new cultural mission: "Österreichs geistige Größe, Österreichs nationales Bewußtsein ist in seine [the Burgtheater's] Hand gegeben." ["Austria's spiritual greatness, Austria's national consciousness is facilitated by (the Burgtheater)."].[86] And yet, the situation behind the scenes at this state-run cultural institution, no less than in the wranglings that took place in authors' associations described by commentators, also modifies the picture of tight control from the top down.[87]

A key source of tension was the official appointment of Friedrich Schreyvogl, historical dramatist and covert Nazi sympathiser, to the role of artistic secretary in 1933 at the theatre. This added to the already complicated bureaucratic layers of command between the artistic director, the general director of the state theatre administration, and the incumbent minister of justice, a structure that previous directors had long bemoaned. In practice it tied the hands of the director and created scope for personal point-scoring. Schreyvogl had held this new role covertly since 1929, acting as unofficial censor of productions through reports on the suitability of plays for performance, using both aesthetic and political criteria.[88] But after 1933, he used it to attack director Röbbeling for a series of reasons: for the decision to stage Braun's drama *Kaiser Karl V.*;[89] for being primarily concerned with theatrical effect;[90] and for not supporting enough Austrian authors[91]—a statement not confirmed by production statistics. Brečka, who remained as *Reichspost* critic and leader of the newly nationalised Kunststelle, further complicated matters by being a fan of neither man. He criticised the German Röbbeling for his failure to understand local specifics,[92] and complained of having to do too much work for the travelling theatre of the provinces [*Länderbühne*] which Schreyvogl nominally led, but neglected.[93]

Cited in brief form here for reasons of space, these features of the cultural sphere appear to be minor squabbles between individuals working towards a nominally similar goal. However, taken together with the other known disruptions to the supposedly unified façade of cultural life described, they do help modify the picture of tightly controlled organisation suggested by the state's fascist inspiration.

Conclusion

This essay has not sought to revolutionise our picture of Austrian culture of the interwar years, nor to provide a complete picture of its many facets: literary, institutional, social. Instead what I have attempted to do is sketch a number of factors that disrupt the notion of politics and culture as mutually mapable categories, something that commentators often take for granted in the understandable rush to delineate the mutual ideological antagonisms of Left and Right.

The efforts of Bach before 1934; the ambivalence of cultural forms promoted by both Left and Right at the time, however they were later construed; and features of institutional life after 1934 all suggest more complex sub-phenomena that defy categorisation into neat political or ideological categories. The recent recognition of Austria's cultural complexity in the interwar years beyond its divided ideologies is the first step in this direction: Reconnecting this discussion to the politics of the period in a less linear way, as I have tried to outline here, is the next.

Notes

1. Parts of this article appeared in different form in my book *The Burgtheater and Austrian Identity* (London: Legenda, 2007). I would like to thank the publisher for his permission, and John Warren for his comments on a draft version of this article. Any errors and omissions are mine. This article was researched during a British higher education councils'-funded CEELBAS fellowship held at Oxford University, and my thanks are acknowledged.

2. Edited volumes: Franz Kadrnoska, ed., *Aufbruch und Untergang: Österreichische Kultur zwischen 1918 und 1938* (Vienna: Europa, 1981); Deborah Holmes and Lisa Silverman, eds., *Interwar Vienna: Between Culture and Modernity* (Rochester: Camden Huse, 2009); Ritchie Robertson and Katrin Kohl, eds., *A History of Austrian Literature, 1918-2000* (London: Camden House, 2006); Ritchie Robertson and Judith Beniston, eds., *Catholicism in Austrian Culture*, Austrian Studies 10 (Edinburgh: Edinburgh University Press, 1999). Surveys: Wendelin Schmidt-Dengler, *Ohne Nostalgie: Zur österreichischen Literatur der Zwischenkriegszeit*, Literaturgeschichte in Studien und Quellen 7 (Vienna: Böhlau, 2002); Margret Dietrich, ed., *Das Burgtheater und sein Publikum*, 2 vols. (Vienna: Österreichische Akademie der Wissenschaften, 1976). Various works on "Red Vienna," including Judith Beniston and Robert Vilain, eds., *Culture and Politics in Red Vienna, Austrian Studies 14* (Oct. 2006); Helmut Gruber, *Red Vienna: Experiment in Working-Class Culture, 1919-1934* (Oxford: Oxford University Press, 1991).

3. C. E. Williams, *The Broken Eagle: The Politics of Austrian Literature from Empire to Anschluss* (London: Elek, 1974); Friedbert Aspetsberger, ed., *Staat und Gesellschaft in der modernen österreichischen Literatur* (Vienna: Österreichischer Bundesverlag, 1977); Michael P. Steinberg, *Austria as Theater and Ideology: The Meaning of the Salzburg Festival*, 2nd ed. (Ithaca: Cornell University Press, 2000); Claudio Magris, *Der habsburgische Mythos in der modernen österreichischen Literatur*, trans. Madeleine von Pásztory and Renate Lunzer, 2nd German ed. (Vienna: Zsolnay, 2000), originally published in Italian in 1963 under the title *Il mito absburgico nella letteratura austriaca moderna* (Turin: Einaudi, 1963). This is especially true of works dealing with "Red Vienna"

or else developments in the 1930s: Alfred Pfoser, *Literatur und Austromarxismus* (Vienna: Löcker, 1980); Klaus Amann, *Die Dichter und die Politik: Essays zur österreichischen Literatur nach 1918* (Vienna: Falter/Deuticke, 1992); Jürgen Doll, *Theater im Roten Wien: Vom sozialdemokratischen Agitprop zum dialektischen Theater Jura Soyfers* (Vienna: Böhlau, 1997).

4. Articles by Murray G. Hall, including "Buchhandel und Verlag der dreißiger Jahre im Spiegel von Innen- und Außenpolitik," in *Österreichische Literatur der dreißiger Jahre: Ideologische Verhältnisse, institutionelle Voraussetzungen, Fallstudien*, ed. Klaus Amann and Albert Berger (Vienna: Böhlau, 1985).

5. Janet Stewart, "Popular Culture in Austria: Cabaret and Film, 1918-45," in *A History of Austrian Literature*, 87-106; Hilde Haider-Pregler, "Die große Zeit der Wiener Kleinkunst: Positionen der Unterhaltungskultur von der Jahrhundertwende bis zum Zweiten Weltkrieg," in *Kringel, Schlingel, Borgia: Materialien zu Peter Hammerschlag*, ed. Monika Kriegler-Griensteidl and Volker Kaukoreit (Vienna: Turia & Kant, 1997), 113-54.

6. Individual aspects are well covered but broad surveys are mostly lacking except for Margret Dietrich's work cited above (note 2); my own attempt (note 1, which includes a review of the literature, 1-7); and the works of Prof. W.E. Yates: *Schnitzler, Hofmannsthal and the Austrian Theatre* (New Haven: Yale University Press, 1992); idem., *Theatre in Vienna: A Critical History, 1776-1995* (Cambridge: Cambridge University Press, 1996); and as editor with Allyson Fiddler and John Warren, *From Perinet to Jelinek: Viennese Theatre in its Political and Intellectual Context*, British and Irish Studies in German Language and Literature 28 (Bern: Peter Lang, 2001). The useful volume edited by Hilde Haider-Pregler and Beate Reiterer covers the thirties only: *Verspielte Zeit: Österreichisches Theater der dreißiger Jahre* (Vienna: Picus, 1997); and Birgit Peter's recent survey acknowledges the research gap but is rather brief: "Between Tradition and a Longing for the Modern: Theatre in Interwar Vienna," in *Interwar Vienna*, 161-74.

7. Andrea Amort, "Free Dance in Interwar Vienna," in *Interwar Vienna*, 117-42; Robert Dassanowski, *Austrian Cinema: A History* (Jefferson: McFarland, 2005).

8. See Andrew Barker, "The Politics of Austrian Literature, 1927-56," in *A History of Austrian Literature*, 107-26.

9. Wendelin Schmidt-Dengler, "Das langsame Verschwinden des Anton Wildgans aus der Literaturgeschichte," in *Die einen raus – die anderen rein: Kanon und Literatur: Vorstellungen zu einer Literaturgeschichte Österreichs*, ed. idem. et al. (Berlin: Erich Schmidt, 1994), 71-84.

10. Anton Pelinka and Erika Weinzierl, eds., *Das große Tabu: Österreichs Umgang mit seiner Vergangenheit* (Vienna: Österreichische Staatsdruckerei, 1987); Peter Utgard, *Remembering and Forgetting Nazism: Education, National Identity, and the Victim Myth in Postwar Austria* (New York: Berghahn, 2003).

11. For a brief discussion of the context surrounding Soyfer's canonisation and the status of ongoing myths in Austrian culture, see the essays on Austria in Diana Mishkova and Marius Turda, eds., *Discourses Of Collective Identity In Central And Southeast Europe*, vol. IV, *Anti-Modernism: Radical Revisions of Collective Identity* (Budapest: Central European University Press – in press).

12. Schmidt-Dengler, "Das langsame Verschwinden des Anton Wildgans aus der Literaturgeschichte"; Karl Müller, "Christlich-deutsches Abendland – goldenes Wienertum: Zum dramatischen Schaffen Max Mells und Friedrich Schreyvogls," in *Zeit der Befreiung: Wiener Theater nach 1945*, ed. Hilde Haider-Pregler and Peter Roessler (Vienna: Picus, 1998), 256-99.

13. See for example: Anton Pelinka, *Zur österreichischen Identität* (Vienna: Ueberreuter, 1990), 17; Ernst Hanisch, *Der lange Schatten des Staates: Österreichische Geschichte 1890-1990*, ed. Herwig Wolfram (Vienna: Ueberreuter, 1994), 324-36.

14. Judith Beniston, "Cultural Politics in the First Republic: Hans Brečka and the 'Kunststelle für Christliche Volksbildung,'" in *Catholicism and Austrian Culture*, 101-18;

15. Klaus Amann, "Die Brückenbauer: Zur 'Österreich'-Ideologie der völkisch-nationalen Autoren in den dreißiger Jahren," in *Österreichische Literatur der dreißiger Jahre*, 60-78.

16. Holmes and Silverman, *Interwar Vienna*, 1-6.

17. Quoted by Horst Jarka, "Opposition zur ständestaatlichen Litearturpolitik und literarischer Widerstand," in *Österreichische Literatur der dreißiger Jahre*, 14.

18. By neglecting their role in her book on alterations to stage manuscripts, Susanne Fröhlich wrongly asserts that workers were denied access to such higher cultural institutions as the Burgtheater until after 1933: *Strichfassungen und Regiebücher: Kulturpolitik 1888-1938 und Klassikerinszenierungen am Wiener Burg- und Volkstheater*, ed. Bertrand Michael Buchmann, Beiträge zur neueren Geschichte Österreichs 4 (Frankfurt: Peter Lang, 1996), 15. For an assertion of the Burgtheater's evolution into an Austrian national theatre, see the "official" publication by Rudolph Lothar with a foreword from then-Education Minister Schuschnigg: *Das Wiener Burgtheater: Ein Wahrzeichen österreichischer Kunst und Kultur* (Vienna: Augartenverlag Stephan Szabo, 1934).

19. Pyrah, "The 'Enemy Within'? The Social Democratic Kunststelle and the State Theatres in Red Vienna," *Austrian Studies 14* (Oct. 2006): 143-44.

20. *Social Democracy in the Austrian Provinces, 1918-34: Beyond Red Vienna* (London: Leicester University Press, 1995). Note the conclusion he draws in the Preface, that lack of a provincial backbone effectively destroyed Austrian Social Democracy (viii).

21. This is a summary of the broader discussion in *The Burgtheater and Austrian Identity*.

22. On debates about the character of the new state see: Hanisch, *Der lange Schatten des Staates*, 265. For an expansion of the "Heimat" theme in Austrian political and theatre life in the period, see Pyrah, *The Burgtheater and Austrian Identity*, chs. 1-2.

23. Heinz P. Wassermann, "Lehrpläne und nationale Identität: Ein österreichisches Kaleidoskop," *Sterz 92* (3/2003): 14-17.

24. Josef Nadler, *Literaturgeschichte der deutschen Stämme und Landschaften*, 4 vols., published in serial form from 1918, 3rd ed. (Regensburg: Habbel, 1928-32). See also Amann, "Die Brückenbauer," 65.

25. Pfoser, *Literatur und Austromarxismus*, 164-65. See also Konstanze Fliedl, "Künstliche Konkurrenzen: Schnitzler und Schönherr," in *Metropole und Provinz in der österreichischen Literatur des 19. und 20. Jahrhunderts*, ed. Arno Dusini and Karl Wagner (Vienna: ZIRKULAR/Literaturhaus, 1994), 119.

26. See: Walter Zettl, "Literatur aus Österreich von der Ersten zur Zweiten Republik," in *Geschichte der Literatur in Österreich von den Anfängen bis zur Gegenwart*, VII: *Das 20. Jahrhundert*, ed. Herbert Zeman (Graz: Akademische Druck- und Verlagsanstalt, 1999), 92-98. On Waggerl, see also: Friedbert Aspetsberger, "Literatur und Politik in den dreißiger Jahren: Josef Wenter und Karl H. Waggerl," in *Österreichische Literatur seit den 20er Jahren*, ed. Friedbert Aspetsberger (Vienna: Österreichischer Bundesverlag, 1979), 5-26.

27. Zettl, "Literatur aus Österreich von der Ersten zur zweiten Republik," 98.

28. Donald Ray Richards, *The German Bestseller in the 20th Century: A Complete Bibliography and Analysis 1915-1940* (Bern: Lang, 1968), quoted in: Amann, *Der Anschluß österreichischer Schriftsteller an das Dritte Reich: Institutionelle und bewußtseinsgeschichtliche Aspekte* (Frankfurt: Athenäum, 1988), 66.

29. On the distinctions between "Volk" and "Nation," see: Reinhart Koselleck, "'Nation' als

vorstaatlicher, 'Volk' als politischer Begriff: Normierungsversuche," in *Geschichtliche Grundbegriffe: Historisches Lexikon zur politisch-sozialen Sprache in Deutschland*, ed. Otto Brunner et al., 7 vols. (Stuttgart: Klett-Cotta, 1992), vol. VII, 385-89, 396-97.

30. Friedrich Kainz, "Jung-Österreich und Jung-Wien: Arthur Schnitzler und Karl Schönherr," in *Deutsch-Österreichische Literaturgeschichte*, vol. IV, *1890-1918* (ed. Eduard Castle), ed. Johann Nagl et al., 4 vols. (Vienna: Carl Fromme, 1899-1937).

31. *Die Zeit*, 234, 25 March 1899, 184. Quoted in *Geschichte der Literatur in Österreich*, vol. VII, 93.

32. Max Pirker, *Die Zukunft der österreichischen Alpenländer* (Vienna: Amalthea, 1919).

33. "Zwischen 'Blubo' und 'Asphalt,'" in *Der Christliche Ständestaat*, June 1936, 520. For a schematic treatment of the metropolitan/province divide, see also Ernst Hanisch, *Der lange Schatten des Staates: Österreichische Gesellschaftsgeschichte im 20. Jahrhundert* (Vienna: Ueberreuter, 1994), 324-33. On "anti-modernism" in Austrian literature: Karl Müller, *Zäsuren ohne Folgen: Das lange Leben der literarischen Antimoderne Österreichs seit den 30er Jahren* (Salzburg: Otto Müller, 1990).

34. Pyrah, *The Burgtheater and Austrian Identity*, ch. 2, 35-49; Judith Beniston, "Drama in Austria, 1918-45," in *A History of Austrian Literature*, 29-30.

35. Doll, *Theater im Roten Wien*, 26-30. Conference: *David Josef Bach and Austrian Culture between the Wars* at the Austrian Cultural Forum and the Institute of Germanic Studies, London, 12-13 Feb. 2003. Some of the papers appear in *Austrian Studies 14*: *Culture and Politics in Red Vienna* (Oct. 2006). Also: Pfoser, *Literatur und Austromarxismus*, 59.

36. Henriette Kotlan-Werner, *Kunst und Volk: David Josef Bach 1847-1947* (Vienna: Europa, 1977).

37. Bach, "Rechenschaftsbericht für 1928," *Kunst und Volk 3* (June 1929): 285-86. See also Bach's letter to Hermann Bahr: 17 July 1922. Österreichisches Theatermuseum, Handschriftensammlung: Bahr-Nachlass. Correspondence.

38. The programme of the festival has been thoroughly analysed by Steinberg in *Austria as Theater and Ideology*.

39. Anon [=Hugo von Hofmannsthal], "Einleitung zu Jedermann," *Kunst und Volk 4* (1929-30): 132-33.

40. "Schon dieses eine Beispiel zeigt uns, daß die Tendenzen unserer Zeit auch ihren Eingang auf die Bühne finden müssen. [...] Es mögen in diesem einen Fall die scheinbar katholisierenden Tendenzen gewesen sein, [... Aber D]as Burgtheater würde sich heute sozialistischen Tendenzen wahrscheinlich verschließen, obwohl sie doch unsere Zeit aufs schärfste mitbestimmen." [This example alone shows us that contemporary trends must also find their way onto the stage. It may in this case have been the apparently Catholicizing tendencies [... But] the Burgtheater would probably close itself off to Socialist tendencies, even though they play a major role in shaping our times.]. D[avid Josef] B[ach], "Kunst oder Tendenz: Das Nachfolge Christi-Spiel im Burgtheater," *Arbeiterzeitung*, 28 Jan. 1928, 3.

41. "Bedürfnis nach Geschichte," in *Aufbruch und Untergang*, 393-404.

42. In his journalism, and systematically in *Das Reich der Träumer: Eine Kulturgeschichte Österreichs vom Urzustand bis zur Republik* (Berlin: Verlag für Kulturpolitik, 1932).

43. "Die Burgtheatervorstellungen erfreuen sich immer geringer[er] Beliebtheit. Bei der Gestaltung des Spielplanes wird es immer schwieriger, ein für unsere Mitglieder passendes Stück zu finden. Wir können diesen weder legitimistische Komödien versetzen, noch sogenannte klassische Vorstellungen, die kaum noch die studierende Jugend interessieren dürfen." [The

performances at the Burgtheater are becoming less popular all the time. In formulating the programme it is getting increasingly difficult to find a play that suits our members. We can't flog these legitimist comedies, nor can flog the so-called classical performances which must scarcely interest the young who are still in education.] D[avid] J[osef] Bach to the *Generalintendanz der Österr. Bundestheater*, 19 Oct. 1931. Source: Austrian State Archives, Archiv der Republik, Österreichischer Bundestheaterverband, 2588/6/1931.

44. Quoted by Schmidt-Dengler in *Ohne Nostalgie*, 95.

45. Friedbert Aspetsberger, "Metaphysische Grimassen: Zum biographischen Roman der Zwischenkriegszeit," in *Österreichische Literatur der dreißiger Jahre*, 247-76.

46. Robert Dassanowski, "Finis Austriae, vivat Austria: The Re/Vision of 1918 in Austrian Film," in *Österreich 1918 und die Folgen*, ed. Karl Müller and Hans Wagener (Vienna: Böhlau, 2009), 179-96.

47. Pfoser, *Literatur und Austromarxismus*, 64

48. Ibid.

49. See also: Judith Beniston, *Welttheater: Hofmannsthal, Richard von Kralik and the Revival of Catholic Drama in Austria, 1890-1934* (Leeds: Maney, 1998), 169-70.

50. "Burgtheater und Öffentlichkeit in der Ersten Republik," in *Das Burgtheater und sein Publikum*, ed. Dietrich, I, 479-707, esp. 514-15, 519.

51. B. [Hans Brečka], "Die Wiener Kunststellen," *Der Kunstgarten 3* (1924-25), 202-03.

52. David Josef Bach to Hermann Bahr, 17 July 1922. Österreichisches Theatermuseum, Handschriftensammlung (ÖTM HS): Bahr-Nachlass. Correspondence (ordered alphabetically by author).

53. Ibid.

54. For examples, see Pyrah, *The Burgtheater and Austrian Identity*, 93-95, 142-43, 146-48.

55. First staged at the *Burgtheater* in 1910 (premiere: 24 Nov.) in a run of eighty-eight performances up to 23 Dec. 1927. New version: 6 and 27 May 1932.

56. D[avid Josef] Bach, "Volksstück und Theaterstück," *Arbeiterzeitung*, 15 Sept. 1932, 5.

57. "Er war es schon lange vor der Mobilisierung, wo es vis-à-vis dem Burgtheater noch Burggendarmen gab. Wie leicht haben es dagegen die dramatisierenden Pazifisten nach Saint-Germain unter dem Schutz der gesamten Wiener Linkspresse. Und wie billig machen sie davon Gebrauch." [And it [=the play] was [anti-war] long before mobilization, when there were still armed officers in front of the Burgtheater. What an easy time in comparison the dramatizing pacifists have had since Saint-Germain under the protection of Vienna's entire Left-wing press. And how cheaply they have exploited it.] Hanns Sassmann, "Burgtheater: Neueinstudierung: Arthur Schnitzlers *Der junge Medardus*," *Neues Wiener Journal*, 7 May 1932. Press cutting extracted from: Österreichisches Theatermuseum, Handschriftensammlung. Bahr-Nachlaß (Box 20), page number not given.

58. Franz Joachim Eggers, *"Ich bin ein Katholik mit jüdischem Gehirn" – Modernitätskritik und Religion bei Joseph Roth und Franz Werfel* (Frankfurt: Lang, 1996), esp. 173-74; Peter Stephan Jungk, *Franz Werfel: Eine Lebensgeschichte* (Berlin: Fischer, 1987), esp. 75, 167-68, 193.

59. Werfel's own couching of a broader sense of moral dislocation after WWI in religious, quasi-Catholicising terms is expressed in his newspaper article, "Krise des Dramas," *Neue Freie Presse*, 24 Dec. 1922, 33-34. Discussed in Pyrah, *The Burgtheater and Austrian Identity*, 89. Contemporary speculation on Werfel's conversion: [Anon.], "Franz Werfel und das Judentum," *Neues Wiener Journal*, 5 Nov. 1929, 7.

60. [Hans] B[rečka], "Burgtheater: Paulus unter den Juden," *Reichspost*, 5 May 1927, 1-2.

61. For a summary, see: Günter Fellner, *Antisemitismus in Salzburg, 1918-1938* (Vienna: Geyer, 1979), 101-04. Publicist Max Pirker also made a spirited rebuttal of this claim in his pamphlet *Die Salzburger Festspiele* (Zürich: Amalthea, 1921): "Ungeist ist endlich der zähe Kampf, den gewisse Kreise gegen den Salzburger Festspielgedanken führen. [...] Man verhält sich ablehnend, wittert fremde Einflüsse, nicht ganz autochthonen Geist" [the demon is ultimately the tenacious battle that certain circles are waging against the idea of the Salzburg Festival. [...] They reject it, detect the whiff of foreign influences, and a not wholly autochthonic spirit], 9.

62. Steinberg, "Jewish Identity and Intellectuality in Fin-de-Siècle Austria: Suggestions for a Historical Discourse," *New German Critique 43* (1988): 5.

63. D[avid Josef] B[ach], "Kunst und Wissen: Theater der Kirche," *Arbeiterzeitung*, 22 Nov. 1931, 3.

64. *Die Fackel*, ed. Karl Kraus (Munich 1968-76). Nov. 1921, No. 601-07, 3-4. Quoted in: Edda Fuhrich and Gisela Prossnitz, *Die Salzburger Festspiele: Ihre Geschichte in Daten, Zeitzeugnissen und Bildern*, 2 vols. (Salzburg: Residenz, 1990), vol. I, 41-42.

65. *Schnitzler, Hofmannsthal and the Austrian Theatre*, 216-17.

66. Wolfgang Neugebauer, "Die Folgen des Februar 1934: Die österreichische Arbeiterbewegung in der Illegalität," in *Der 12. Februar 1934: Ursachen, Fakten, Folgen*, ed. Erich Fröschl and Helge Zoitl (Vienna: Wiener Volksbuchhandlung, 1984), 367-81.

67. Hans Mommsen, "Theorie und Praxis des österreichischen Ständestaates 1934 bis 1938," in *Das geistige Leben Wiens in der Zwischenkriegszeit*, ed. Norbert Leser (Vienna: Österreichischer Bundesverlag, 1981), 174-92; Alfred Pfoser and Gerhard Renner, "'Ein Toter führt uns an!' Anmerkungen zur kulturellen Situation im Austrofaschismus," in *"Austrofaschismus": Beiträge über Politik, Ökonomie und Kultur 1934-1938*, ed. Emmerich Talos and Wolfgang Neugebauer, 4th ed. (Vienna: Verlag für Gesellschaftskritik, 1988), 223-46; Horst Jarka, "Zur Literatur- und Theaterpolitik im 'Ständestaat,'" in *Aufbruch und Untergang*, 502-03; Anton Staudinger, "Abwehr des Nationalsozialismus durch Konkurrenz? Zur Kulturpolitik im Austrofaschismus," in *100 Jahre Volkstheater*, ed. Evelyn Schreiner (Vienna: Jugend und Volk, 1989), 34-87. Christian Dunzinger, "Staatliche Eingriffe in das Theater von 1934-1938 als Teil austrofaschistischer Kulturpolitik," master's thesis, University of Vienna, 1995, esp. 60-73. See also: Rainer Schubert, "Das vaterländische-Frontwerk 'Neues Leben': Ein Beitrag zur Geschichte der Kulturpolitik der Vaterländischen Front," PhD. diss., University of Vienna, 1978, 31; Edda Fuhrich, "'Schauen Sie sich doch in Wien um! Was ist von dieser Theaterstadt übriggeblieben?' Zur Situation der großen Privattheater," in *Verspielte Zeit*, 111-14.

68. See Amann's publications: *Der Anschluß österreichischer Schriftsteller an das Dritte Reich*; "Die Brückenbauer," 60-78; Gerhard Renner, "'Hitler-Eid für österreichische Schriftsteller?' Über österreichische Schriftstellerorganisationen der dreißiger Jahre," in *Österreichische Literatur der dreißiger Jahre*, 150-63; and two works by Friedbert Aspetsberger, "Übergänge: Zur Kulturpolitik des Ständestaates am Beispiel des Dichters Josef Wenter," in *Aufbruch und Untergang*, 561-77; *Literarisches Leben im Austrofaschismus: Der Staatspreis*, vol. 2, ed. Friedbert Aspetsberger et al. (Königstein: Hain, 1980).

69. Horst Jarka, "Opposition zur ständestaatlichen Literaturpolitik," in *Österreichische Literatur*, 14-19.

70. Ibid., 22-23.

71. The *Kunststelle*'s contracts with private theatres stated they could refuse to perform works on several grounds: "mit religiösen, sittlichen, politischen oder allgemein literarischen Argumenten. Die Beurteilung des Stückes liegt im freien Ermessen der Österreichischen Kunststelle." [on

religious, moral, political or general literary grounds. Judging a play is at the free discretion of the Österreichische Kunststelle.] Source: Austrian State Archives, Archiv der Republik, Parteiarchive: Vaterländische Front, Box 38. See also: Fuhrich, "Zur Situation der großen Privattheater," 112.

72. [Hans] B[rečka], "Kaiser Josef II in der Burg: Erstaufführung des Schauspieles von Rudolf Henz," *Reichspost*, 9 Apr. 1937, 2-3

73. John Warren, "Austrian Theatre and the Corporate State," in *Austria in the Thirties*, ed. Kenneth Segar and Warren (Riverside: Ariadne, 1991), 286.

74. Rudolf Henz, *Fügung und Widerstand* (Graz: Stiasny, 1963), 208.

75. B[rečka], "Kaiser Josef II in der Burg". See also Ernst Decsey, "Feuilleton. Burgtheater. Kaiser Josef II in fünf Akten von Rudolf Henz," *NWT*, 9 Apr. 1937, 3.

76. Pyrah, *The Burgtheater and Austrian Identity*, 198-99.

77. Professor Dr. Joseph Gregor, "Kaiser Karl der Fünfte im Burgtheater: Tragödie von Felix Braun," *Neues Wiener Journal*, 3 May 1936, 26.

78. Brečka, "Kaiser Karl der Fünfte: Drama von Felix Braun (Erstaufführung im Burgtheater)," *Reichspost*, 3 May 1936, 13.

79. Edda Fuhrich-Leisler, "The Theater in der Josefstadt under Ernst Lothar," in *Austria in the Thirties*, 221-22.

80. *Mitteilungsblätter der Österreichischen Kunststelle (MBÖKS) 27*, 15 Nov. 1933; *MBÖKS 29*, 15 Dec. 1935.

81. Franz Grillparzer, *Sämtliche Werke*, ed. Peter Frank and Karl Pörnbacher, 4 vols. (Munich: Hanser, 1960), I: *Gedichte, Epigramme, Dramen I*, 1085-1166 (1166). Abbreviated: *SW I*.

82. Stage manuscript from the *Archiv des Theaters in der Josefstadt*, p. 130. The original lines in full read: "Laß dir den Menschen Mensch sein, und den Diener / Acht als ein Spargut für die Zeit der Not. / Gedenk als Mann der Zeit, da du ein Kind / Und hilflos lagst in eines Mörders Armen. / Wie da der Aufruhr an die Pforten pochte, / Und jeder Rat und jede Hilfe fern; / da tat ein alter Mann – wa er vermochte. / I nu! Ein treuer Diener seines Herrn." [Let Man be Man, and the servant / See to as a something to save for times of need. / As a man think of the time when you were a child / And lay helpless in the arms of a murderer. / When pandemonium raged at the gates / With help and support beyond reach; / there, an old man did what he could. / Me! His master's loyal servant.] In: *SW I*, 1166.

83. Hilde Haider-Pregler, "König Ottokars Glück und Ende – ein 'Nationales Festspiel' für Österreichs 'Nationaltheater'? Die Burgtheater-Inszenierungen von Grillparzers Trauerspiel im 20. Jahrhundert," in *Stichwort Grillparzer*, ed. Haider-Pregler and Evelyn Deutsch-Schreiner (Vienna: Böhlau, 1994), 195-222.

84. "Gleichschaltung wird als unösterreichisch abgelehnt. [...] Unsere Förderung lassen wir [...] nur den Werken zukommen, die wir als positiv christlich ansprechen können, die also Achtung vor den Lehren des Christentums (Ethik, Ordnung), Achtung vor dem wahren Deutschtum und daher der österreichischen Idee und Achtung vor der neuen Volksgemeinschaft bezeugen." [The Nazi policy of] *Gleichschaltung* is rejected as un-Austrian. [...] We only give our support to works which we can describe as Christian in the positive sense, which thus testify to respect for the teachings of Christianity (ethics, order), respect for real Germanness and therefore for the Austrian idea, and respect for the new national community] – *Kulturdienst*, 1, June 1935, published at irregular intervals by the cultural department (*Kulturreferat*) of the Fatherland Front. Source: Austrian State Archives, Archiv der Republik, Parteiarchive/Vaterländische Front Box 38.

85. *Das Wiener Burgtheater: Ein Wahrzeichen österreichischer Kunst und Kultur* (Vienna: Augartenverlag, 1934).

86. Ibid., 522.

87. Klaus Amann, *Der Anschluß österreichischer Schriftsteller an das Dritte Reich*, 152-63. Mell was its first President. More details of the group's genesis and its contacts with the *Reichschrifttumskammer* in Nazi Germany are given by Gerald Tuma: "Friedrich Schreyvogl: Vom Ständestaatpoeten zu einem NS-Apologeten," master's thesis, University of Vienna, 1996, 5, 60-63.

88. Pyrah, *The Burgtheater and Austrian Identity*, 163-67.

89. Schreyvogl, "Gutachten: Betreff: Karl V [*sic*]". Source: Austrian State Archives, Archiv der Republik Österreichischer Bundestheaterverband, 1663/1936.

90. Ibid., 143/1938, dated 31 Jan. 1938, addressed "an die Bundestheaterverwaltung".

91. Ibid., 2139/2/1936. "[Gutachten] Betr.: Die Komödie in 3 Akten Der Nationalheld von Hans Naderer und Heinrich Rienössl," dated 2 June 1936.

92. Letter to Hans Naderer about the play *Lueger*, 15 Aug. 1934. Österreischisches Literaturarchiv, Nachlass Brečka: 10/90, Gruppe 2.2.1.

93. Addressee unknown ["Lieber Freund"], dated 5 Oct. 1936. Source: Austrian State Archives, Archiv der Republik, Parteiarchive/Vaterländische Front, Box 38.

Jewish Education in Interwar Vienna: Cooperation, Compromise and Conflict Between the Austrian State and the Viennese Jewish Community

Sara O.M. Yanovsky

Introduction

With nearly 200,000 Jews, Vienna had one of the largest urban Jewries in pre-holocaust Europe, managed by a powerful communal organization, the *Israelitische Kultusgemeinde* (IKG).[1] The IKG had been officially recognized as the representative body of Viennese Jews since 1852. In response to particular challenges it faced, including in the inter-war period, the IKG formulated policies and strategies, weighed alternatives and set priorities in order to organize communal Jewish life in the city.

The realm of Jewish education was one of the key functions undertaken by the IKG—in contrast with some other major urban Jewries on the Continent, where Jewish education was reserved to the private sphere. In Austria, religious education was by law a public, communal function, regulated by the Imperial Law of 25 May 1868,[2] which reserved the paramount control and supervision to the state, but at the same time made the Church and other religious associations, in the case of the Jewish community the IKG, directly responsible for organizing religious education for children under their authority. This not only compelled the IKG to organize religious instruction for Jewish children in the public sphere, but also made close cooperation with state authorities inevitable. Jewish communal leaders entered into a direct exchange with state authorities in the shaping of religious instruction for Jewish children, but on a wider scale in shaping the sphere in which Jewish children were educated in a largely non-Jewish surrounding.

Life in a major metropolitan city posed numerous challenges for Jews in the late nineteenth and early twentieth century. On the one hand, the city, and in particular the metropolis, often offered Jews new economic, cultural, and social opportunities that provincial Jews did not have. On the other hand, city life was potentially a corrosive solvent of traditional Jewish culture, language, religion and identity. Both these trends, accelerated assimilation and enhanced resources, were also reflected in Jewish education in the capital. On the one hand, in inter-war Vienna, the large majority of Jewish children attended non-Jewish schools. On the other hand, in addition to Bible schools, Hebrew schools and even Jewish primary schools, Vienna had a Jewish secondary school, an undertaking that was only possible in a large community. The Viennese Jewish community clearly had unprecedented resources, but was also burdened by an unprecedented range of problems. Particular challenges of the inter war-period included the outcome of World War I, such as human losses and a financial crisis, rising anti-Semitism and the definition of a Jewish identity in an atmosphere of advanced integration into Austrian society, which itself was forced to deal with the effects of World War I and a re-definition of Austrian identity.

This essay aims to assess how the leaders of the IKG balanced their interests in the management of Jewish education, and therefore their expectations in terms of fostering a certain type of Jewish identity, with state laws and policies. Educational strategies formulated within urban settings both enabled and constrained integration into larger society. Education provides a perspective that helps to gain a better grasp of Jewish society in the metropolis, the decision-making and the often conflicting ideologies within the Jewish community as well as between the Jewish community and Austrian state authorities.

Prior research has focused on ideological, cultural, and social-demographic issues. Rarely if ever have historians considered communal functions on a citywide scale, such as education, as a venue for determining larger issues. Looking at the decisions made on Jewish education by community leaders and the way they dealt with challenges on a state level, sheds new light on the role that communal governance played in responding to challenges Jews, and in particular Jewish education, faced during the inter-war period.

The state was generally represented either by the Ministry of Education or in the particular case of Vienna by the Lower Austrian Education authority, the municipality of Vienna and particularly the Vienna School Board.

The main questions this essay aims to answer are: What were the visions of the Jewish community leaders concerning Jewish education, and how did these fit those of state authorities and state-schools? How did the IKG and state authorities cooperate in order to make their visions into reality? When did cooperation between state authorities and the Jewish community turn into compromise or even conflict? In what way did state laws and policies influence the strategy of the IKG in responding to one of the key challenges facing Jews in the modern era, namely the transmission of Jewish identity via Jewish education to future generations?

Decision Making in the IKG

The IKG in Vienna had an executive committee and several permanent commissions, one of the main ones (Sektion II) responsible for educational issues. The commission, whose members were generally members of the IKG's executive committee, met from the 1860s until 1937 several times a year in order to discuss matters concerning Jewish education and make decisions in this respect.[3] When crucial decisions had to be made on educational matters, the issues were discussed by the executive committee in addition to the school commission. The main responsibilities of the school commission included the organization of religious instruction at public, non-Jewish schools or accumulative stations, so-called *Sammelstationen* for children, who did not have religious classes at their school. It was responsible for the curriculum including textbooks and time tables, as well as the employment and allocation of teachers and inspectors, in cooperation with state authorities. This cooperation was regulated by state law, which required on the one hand the agreement of the respective religious authority before any teacher for religious instruction could be employed at a school and on the other hand the authorization of state authorities before any textbook could be used in class.[4] The state law also gave religious authorities permission to establish private schools and courses. The IKG, in addition to public religious classes, ran Bible schools, organized weekly or bi-monthly youth services at Viennese synagogues in cooperation with the teachers and cantors as well as lectures with slide shows for children who had dropped out of school. It also granted financial aid to a large number of societies that ran their own educational institutions including Bible schools, Hebrew classes and youth organizations, a Jewish primary school and a Jewish secondary School. In 1935 the IKG opened its own Jewish primary school.

Conversion, Intermarriage and the Denomination of Children

Cases of conversion and intermarriage during the interwar period created situations in which the denomination of children became unclear. In several cases, state authorities, the IKG and parents were involved in a decision-making process, which determined whether children were officially to be considered Christian, Jewish or undenominational and therefore attend religious instruction of a certain type.

The law of interdenomination regulated the denomination of children born of mixed marriages as well as of children whose parents converted.[5] In case of mixed marriages girls were to follow the religion of their mother, boys the religion of their father, unless the parents decided otherwise through a contract. Children born out of wedlock followed the religion of their mother, and if none of the above was relevant, the legal guardian decided the denomination. Generally, the denomination of a child could not be changed until he or she reached the age of fourteen and was therefore regarded as mature enough to choose his or her own denomination. The parents, however, were allowed to change the denomination of children through a contract, if the children had not yet reached the age of seven. In the case of conversion of one or both parents to another religion, the children followed the conversion of the parents as long as they were under the age of seven. Parents as well as religious authorities were responsible for the adherence of these laws and had the right to turn to state authorities if these were violated. This law therefore set clear guidelines which had to be adhered to and directly controlled, amongst others by the IKG. However, it also left room for disputes, primarily when it came to children aged seven to fourteen or when parents did not convert to another religion, but decided to become undenominational.

The IKG, with strict adherence to this state law, used it as a tool to keep children from leaving the IKG and its sphere of influence. State regulation had given the IKG an important opportunity of influence through compulsory Jewish education for those who were members of the community. It should be stated at this point that the efficiency of religious instruction at public schools was not taken for granted and the option of abolishing religious education at public schools was debated in Austria at the beginning of the interwar period, a step, which would have enlarged the separation between the state and the Church and would have further decreased the Church's influence on public schools. Proponents of the abolition of religious instruction were concerned about the contradictions between science and religious teachings. From the Jewish point of view, as the IKG school inspector Prof. Dr. Heinrich Redisch pointed out in an article he published in 1919 in the monthly Jewish teachers' magazine *Freie Jüdische Lehrerstimme*, the contradiction between science and religion was less problematic, as it could be explained logically. The years passed since the history of the creation, for instance, could be explained with the mythological character of numbers in religious texts and did therefore not necessarily contradict science. In any case, as he wrote, "Jews will not be able to influence the solution of the debated question, our religious instruction shares the destiny of the Catholic and Protestant. If the Christian religious instruction will be abolished, so the Jewish of course will fall too."[6] But Christian religious instruction did not fall and, as elaborated later, gained significant importance in the 1930s. Therefore also Jewish religious instruction at public schools stayed on, and although orthodox Jewish circles repeatedly criticized the inefficiency of two lessons a week, usually not at a satisfactory level, public religious instruction still gave the IKG a basis to gather Jewish children and to recruit them for further activities in Jewish circles such as the very well frequented youth services.

It was therefore seen as worthwhile to make efforts to keep Jewish children IKG members in the following cases:

On 31 March 1921 Thomas Luzian August Brunner's Jewish father, Heinrich Brunner, and his undenominational mother, Irene Brunner, notified the Viennese district magistrate in the nineteenth district that they were planning to raise their nearly seven-year old child according to the religion of the mother, who had just left the Jewish religion and IKG the day before to become undenominational and was planning to convert to the Evangelical (Lutheran) religion. The child had been raised Jewish up to that point. After being informed of the parents' decision by the magistrate, the IKG objected, claiming that the marriage of the parents was not a mixed one as the mothers' changed status to undenominational was not regarded a conversion and therefore the parents were not allowed to change the denomination of the child. It is not clear how the case ended, but the Federal Chancellery was asked by the Ministry of Education to make the final decision on the case and four years later, after the mother had already converted to the Evangelical religion, it was still being discussed, as correspondence between the Chancellery and the Ministry of Education shows.[7] The age of the child, being over seven years by that time, probably complicated the issue further. The IKG clearly made efforts to keep Thomas Luzian August Brunner a member of the Jewish community after the mother had left. It might also be worthwhile to note that the parents had decided to change the denomination of the child shortly before his seventh birthday, possibly being aware that after the age of seven they would not have been allowed to do so.

In another case in 1922, Elsa and Dr. Siegfried Brecher, both Jewish, agreed after their divorce that their two children should be raised Roman Catholic. The mother stated her plan to convert to the Roman Catholic religion, too. At that point both children were under seven years old. When the IKG received notification of the planned conversion of the children, it objected to the district magistrate of the thirteenth district stating that converting the children was against the law because both parents were Jewish and there was no case of a mixed marriage, which would have been covered by the law of interdenomination. Therefore the parents were not allowed to convert their children. The district magistrate decided that the children were to be considered Jewish. However, by that time, the children had already converted with their mother, after the older son had celebrated his seventh birthday. Documents of the Ministry of Education show that following the conversion, the state authorities brought up the question whether the decision of the district magistrate could still be adhered to, as it might not be in the interest of the children to force them to grow up as Jewish children in the Catholic household of their mother.[8] Again, it is not clear how this case ended, but it repeatedly shows that with the help of state law, or of loopholes in the state law, the IKG made efforts to prevent children from leaving the Jewish community and therefore ensure a minimal Jewish education through religious instruction classes at public schools.

A third case is a good example of a dispute on the denomination of a child without direct involvement of the IKG, when in 1923 the Jewish mother Olga Haas (born Janowitz) and the Roman Catholic father Eugen Haas, wanted to register their newborn daughter Hilde as undenominational. The Viennese magistrate decided that according to the law the girl had to be registered at the IKG. This particular case turned out to be more complicated because the parents were, although living in Vienna, citizens of Czechoslovakia, where the law of interdenomination had been slightly changed in 1920. When the parents appealed against the decision of the Viennese magistrate, the case reached higher instances such as the Chancellery and the Ministry of Education, where it was discussed further.[9]

It is interesting to note that the disputes on children's denomination generally did not appear to be directly between the state authorities and the Jewish community, but rather between the Jewish community and the parents, while state authorities got involved for legal reasons; or, as the last case shows, directly between state authorities and parents. The state authorities apparently adhered to the law in disputes with parents and if they believed the law required it, ordered them to register their children as Jewish even without the IKG being involved directly. The law of interdenomination, which applied to all recognized religions, ensured that Jews were treated equally by law and the IKG was treated equally to other religious authorities. In 1935, the Federal Court of Justice decided that all children, whose parents belonged to a denomination at the time of their child's birth and only later became undenominational and stayed undenominational until the child had reached the age of seven, had to attend religious education in the religion their parents had belonged to at the time of the child's birth.[10] The state had thus narrowed the loophole in the law significantly when it came to children of undenominational parents. More children hence had to attend religious classes, including Jewish religious classes, than before.

To take the issue one step further, without state legislation, the law as well as the enforcement of the law, the Jewish community would not have been able to proceed legally against parents' decisions to take their children out of the IKG. Although it restricted their authority in many cases for the sake of freedom of religion of the parents, the IKG learned to use the law and the loopholes in the law to prevent children from leaving the Jewish community.

Similarly, cooperation between the state and the Jewish community seemed to have worked quite well when it came to children's attendance of religious instruction classes, as the following letter from the Vienna School Board to the IKG concerning an intervention of the IKG president in the year 1928 shows: "Concerning the intervention of the president of the IKG on 9 February 1928...I am honored to disclose in the name of the Vienna School Board, that it surely cannot be put into doubt, that parents...are obliged to make their children participate in the obligatory religious instruction and that inefficiently excused absence from this instruction represents an unexcused absence from school. The Vienna Schools Board will therefore turn its attention to the compliance of this statutory obligation."[11] In this case too, only the state had the authority to make the attendance of religious education obligatory. Without state law, the Jewish community could hardly have made religious classes anything more than voluntary.

Religious Exercises and Customs in Public Schools

Some aspects of public schooling contradicted Jewish religious laws and customs. To find compromises in issues such as prayer in school, head covering and keeping the laws of the Sabbath, the IKG and state authorities were in continuous correspondence.

Religious Exercises

The so-called *Glöckel-Erlass*, passed in 1919 by Social Democrat politician Otto Glöckel, abolished the obligation to participate in religious exercises such as religious services.[12] During a revision of these voluntary religious exercises at public schools in 1922, the religious authorities, including the Catholic Church, the Protestant Church and the IKG representatives, were asked by the Vienna School Board to hand in their proposals for religious exercises for the children under their authority, which those would attend in addition to the regular religious instruction. The exercises for Jewish children were the regular youth services at several Viennese synagogues, which were announced by the Vienna School Board. Christian children also attended religious services as part of their religious exercises, but the archiepiscopal representatives also requested a confessional prayer before and after daily instruction at schools. The Vienna School Board denied this request because of the "objections by other religious associations" and explained further that a "celebration of a confessional prayer by the teacher in the presence of all the children who attend the class, including children of other confessions, is perceived by these as a disregard of their religious sentiment."[13] Further, the Vienna School Board argued that a confessional prayer before and after regular instruction contradicted the inter-confessional character of primary schools. The Vienna School Board had no objection to confessional prayers during religious instruction classes.

The year before, in 1921, the school commission of the Jewish community had asked their inspector Professor Heinrich Redisch to intervene at the Vienna School Board after the Christian parents association of the nineteenth district in Vienna had decided to introduce prayer before and after classes. Following this, the commission decided to send a letter to the Vienna School Board, stating that in consideration for the upcoming revision of religious exercises, the executive committee of the IKG was objecting against the fact that Jewish students were forced to participate in religious exercises with other confessions.[14] The decision of the Vienna School Board in 1922 against such exercises did not solve this issue for long. In April 1933 Minister of Education Anton Rintelen in the Engelbert Dollfuss government abolished the Glöckel order and religious exercises once again became obligatory.[15] In November that year the archiepiscopal representatives ordered all Roman Catholic children in public and private primary schools to say the following prayer, asking the Holy Spirit for assistance in learning:

Heiliger Geist, komm zu verbreiten
Über uns dein Gnadenlicht,
Dass wir immer weiter schreiten
In Erlernung unserer Pflicht!
Mache uns zum Lernen Lust,
Hilf, dass wir in unserer Brust
Das Erlernte wohl behalten
Und im Guten nicht erkalten.[16]

Additionally the children were ordered to say the prayer "Our Father who art in heaven" with the Angelic Salutation and make the sign of the cross before and after prayer while saying, "In the name of the Father and the Son and the Holy Spirit." In classes in which Catholic pupils were the minority it was enough to say the prayer "*Heiliger Geist, komm zu verbreiten*" at the beginning of instruction and at the end say the following prayer, this time asking the Father to bless the knowledge learned in the lesson:

Vater, segne diese Lehren,
Die du durch des Lehrers Mund
Deinen Kindern machtest kund,
Uns zum Heil und dir zu Ehren.
Präge sie durch deinen Geist
Tief ins Herz, dass wir im Leben
Stets zu handeln uns bestreben
So, wie dein Gebot uns heisst.[17]

The executive committee of the IKG was asked by the Vienna School Board to comment on the order for Catholic children.[18] The IKG argued against confessional prayers at Viennese primary schools, promoting in the interest of all pupils and for educational reasons an unconfessional prayer. In case that the confessional prayer would be implemented, the IKG requested that in schools where Jewish children were the majority, the words "Holy Spirit" would be replaced by "Holy God." The IKG did not object to Jewish children staying in class during the Catholic school prayer.[19]

As the cases of Christian Prayer services make quite clear, all official parties involved showed more or less preparedness to compromise. The Catholic Church did not request Catholic children in classes, where they were the minority, to cite all the prayers generally required, the state authorities asked the Jewish community representatives to comment on the planned implementation of Catholic prayer during class, and although the IKG representatives were clearly not supporting confessional prayer, they were ready to accept it as long as Jewish children did not directly participate in it, or alternatively they allowed Jewish children to participate if it was rephrased to become unconfessional or confessionally neutral. The question whether the respective bodies compromised out of respect and belief that it was the right step in a multi-cultural state or rather out of lack of choice in the given time and situation, needs to be looked into further. What can be argued quite certainly, however, is that the Austrian school system was becoming increasingly confessional by the 1930s and the level of confrontation had just not yet reached the point, at which it would be recognizable on an official level, as it would soon become.

The Sabbath at Public Schools

The Sabbath was another potentially confrontational case in public schools, but quite peacefully handled by state authorities and the IKG. A decree of the ministry of education in 1876 ordered schools to be considerate of the Israelite commandment to refrain from writing, drawing and handiwork on the Sabbath when organizing class schedules and ruled that any direct or indirect force to transgress this commandment should be refrained from.[20] This decree was still valid in the 1930s. That does not, however, mean that it was always adhered to. The Lower Austrian Education authority confirmed that Jewish orthodox organizations had complained to the IKG and the Vienna School Board, claiming that Jewish children were forced to write on Saturdays.[21] The Vienna School Board was always ready to confirm the validity of the decree, but while in 1911 k.k. Governor of Lower Austria Richard von Bienerth-Schmerling reminded all secondary school headmasters and district representatives to ensure consideration of the Sabbath[22], in 1930 the Vienna School Board declined to do so, claiming that there was no need to, as class schedules were considerate of the Sabbath.[23] But also among Jewish representatives, apart from orthodox circles, the observance of the Sabbath was generally not seen as a pressing issue. Just as the majority of Viennese Jewry was not religiously observant and many parents did not mind if their children wrote on the Sabbath,[24] the IKG did not invest a lot of effort in publicly objecting to apparent infringements of the Sabbath at schools. On the contrary, although the Sabbath is considered strictly religiously speaking no less important than other Jewish holidays, the IKG did not request it to be one of the days, on which Jewish children should be exempt from school, as it did with other major holidays.[25] The IKG, and even most other orthodox organizations, saw it as self-evident, that Jewish children would have to attend public schools on Saturdays and accepted the compromise that they would not write, strictly religious organizations pressing for the implementation of this decree somewhat stronger than the IKG itself.

Head Covering

Another decree, of which schools had to be reminded, concerned the head covering of Jewish boys during religious instruction. In 1921, a teacher for Jewish religious instruction handed in a petition to the state education authority in the name of the teachers at the federal secondary school in the second district of Vienna requesting a uniform decision concerning the head covering of Jewish boys during religious education classes.[26] According to the petition, this issue had caused quite a bit of confusion as in 1906 the IKG had ordered to let boys wear a head covering during religious instruction if their parents wished so, and a year later the Lower Austrian Education authority had apparently decided that boys should not be allowed to wear a head covering. However, in 1911, the state education authority again referred to the order of the Jewish community to let students wear a head covering during religious classes if their parents wanted them to do so. Some teachers therefore introduced the obligation to wear a head covering during their class, but in other classes the teachers themselves apparently did not wear a head covering and the order lead to a split between the more or less religious pupils as well as to disciplinary problems, as the teacher states in his letter to the state authorities: "Apart from the fact, that exceptional regulations seriously endanger the discipline—they say that in schools, where individual pupils are allowed to cover themselves, they hide each other's caps to fool around—it can impossibly be the aim of the decree to make room for ambivalence in class through two different customs, nor even less to position the religious education teacher behind individual religiously devoted pupils."

The letter shows that teachers for religious instruction did not always wear a head covering, an interesting fact keeping in mind that the Jewish community was at least partly responsible for choosing teachers. Teachers teaching Jewish religion at public schools therefore did not necessarily have to be religiously observant according to all aspects of orthodox Jewish law. This tendency seems to be consistent with the fact that writing on the Sabbath was not a major concern of the IKG. There are two possible explanations for such a tendency. Either the Jewish community was trying to avoid confrontations with the schools and state authorities, or individual adherence to religious law was not seen important enough to interfere. Quite possibly it was not seen by the Jewish leaders, many of whom were not religiously observant themselves, as a public issue or the responsibility of the IKG.

The cases above repeatedly show that although there were several issues which could have caused friction in IKG-state relations, it usually did not require too much effort to reach compromises in matters concerning religious customs, at least on the official level. Jewish Orthodox associations might not have agreed with all official IKG policies, but they did have their own private primary school, which was closed on the Sabbath and received substantial grants from the IKG on a regular basis.

The Parallel Class Crisis, the Jewish Primary School and the Road to Segregation

As minimal as confrontation between the state authorities and the IKG on school matters had been until the mid-1930s, at least on an official level, the friction enlarged after the implementation of the new Austrian Constitution in May 1934.[27] The Constitution incorporated the third Concordat, concluded by the Federal Chancellor E. Dollfuss on 5 July 1933, which granted the Church major influence, particularly in school matters.[28] Amongst others it increased religious instruction for Catholic children and prepared the grounds for a confessional Catholic school system with Catholic state schools.

The *Parallelklassenverordnung*

On 18 September 1934, the IKG received notification of an order published three days earlier by the Vienna School Board under the title "parallel class division of pupils at secondary schools and teacher training institutions," which stated that on 4 July 1934 the Ministry of Education had ordered for school-practical reasons that parallel classes were to be organized in a way that united non-Catholic pupils in one class and separated them from the Catholic class.[29] The leaders of the IKG were outraged, as nobody had consulted with them on the matter. By the time they received notification, the order was already in place. However, it was not entirely unexpected. Rumors on the plans had prompted leaders of the IKG to turn to the Ministry of Education in June. Nevertheless, the IKG had been left out of the decision-making about the division of parallel classes and realized in September that the order was already being implemented. In addition, the IKG learned, without any official notification, that as a result of the parallel class order children were also being separated in primary schools, not just secondary schools, and in many cases the implementation of the order went further, when children were separated according to confessions within one class even where there was no need for a parallel class considering the number of pupils.[30] Jewish children were forced to switch schools in order to attend non-Catholic classes; separate specifically Jewish classes were created at some schools and Christian classes at other schools. Jeanette Weiss, headmaster of a school in the second Viennese district in the *Kleine Pfarrgasse*, was forced into retirement after all Jewish children had been sent to attend another school in the *Kleine Sperlgasse*.[31] Furthermore, in the *Sophien-Gymnasium*, the headmaster had been removed from his position for belonging to the Social Democratic Party and the new headmaster, who had been dismissed from another school for National Socialist engagements, was put in his place to manage the school, where half of the pupils were Jewish.[32]

IKG president Dr. Desider Friedmann pointed out that the implementation of the parallel class order did not conform with §36-38 of the 1905 School and Education decree, according to which children were to be admitted to the school responsible for the area they were living in and therefore should not be forced to attend schools further away only because they were Jewish.[33] Furthermore, Friedmann underlined that the IKG had not received any explanations concerning reasons for the order from state authorities. The community leaders clearly refused to accept the official claim that classes were divided for school practical-reasons as Jewish community leaders had been willing to solve any technical problems connected to religious instruction classes had they been contacted. Any practical problem seemed to them proportionately minor considering the disadvantages of the class divisions, which, as Friedmann noted in an open plenary session of the IKG executive committee, would "cause and strengthen feelings of inferiority among Jewish youth" and therefore the IKG could "not agree to a spatial segregation of our children from the children of other confessions."[34] Friedmann continued: "I think that I do not have to elaborate why certain sensitivity exists specifically in current times among Jewish circles. You will agree that from such a spatial distancing a transition to discrimination can be found very easily." His speech clearly reflected the already very tense and increasingly anti-Semitic atmosphere in Austrian society.

In 1898 a very similar decree had also caused a lot of unease among IKG representatives, who then complained about a planned confessional division to the Minister of Education Count Artur Bylandt-Rheidt, and after an examination of the case it was decided that pupils were only allowed to be separated according to confessions if the technical difficulties concerning the class schedule of religious instruction could not be solved otherwise.[35] In general, therefore, the 1898 order had not been implemented.

In 1934, on the other hand, exaggerated implementation of the order had already begun before the IKG was even notified. While using the same means of protest as in 1898, appealing to state authorities that the order was illegal, IKG leaders did realize that this time the opponent was more than a decree, namely a changing tendency in Austria's political sphere. In his speech at the IKG plenary session, where the parallel class order was discussed, Dr. Leopold Plaschkes, member of the executive committee, outlined: "What is happening here is to be valued as a collapse of a tendency, the liberal tendency, which unites Christian and Jewish children in order to decrease anti-Semitism."[36] Liberal tendencies had not succeeded in combating anti-Semitism and the Ministry of Education was accused of enforcing it further with an order that was conceived as a humiliation and insult, not just by the IKG, but by many Jewish parents who had turned to the IKG for help. Plaschkes admitted that no laws had been passed directly to discriminate against Jews, but an administrative practice of public authorities, which excluded Jews from certain professions and economic circles, this time had resulted in Jewish children having to leave schools, switch schools and being herded in Jewish classes, causing the IKG to be up in arms against the parallel class order.

The Jewish Primary School

At the same time as confessional classes in public schools caused strong sentiments and opposition, the majority of the IKG, with the backing of many parents, was planning the establishment of its own Jewish primary school. Critics within the IKG, such as representatives of the non-Zionist *Union Österreichischer Juden* represented by Dr. Jakob Ornstein, believed that the establishment of a Jewish school contradicted the fight against confessional division at public schools, as it was just another type of segregation.[37] However, to most IKG representatives, confessional classes at public schools were an entirely different matter than confessional schools. While Catholic children were separated from Jewish children in public schools with the aim to provide them a better Catholic education, the separated Jewish children on the other hand did not receive better Jewish education in public schools. The only difference was a sense of being separated. In his speech at the IKG plenary session, executive committee member Oberbaurat Ing. Robert Stricker clarified that the Jews wanted "no *Judenklassen*, no Jewish Ghetto, but a Jewish schooling system with absolute equal status, included into the framework of the state, with Jewish influence and not as a private matter of the Jews, but a Jewish school system, which is cared for in a material and moral way by the state just as the other school system. We demand a religious-national education of the youth without Ghetto and without restriction."[38] Executive committee member Dr. Jakob Ehrlich spoke along the same lines to point out that fighting against confessional separation at public schools and establishing a Jewish primary school did not contradict each other: "If Jews unite in freedom to advance Jewish aims, then such a union, which was formed out of free choice, to advance valuable aims, will be able to respect itself and will also find the respect of the non-Jewish world. But when a separation is implemented against our will, which possibly serves a foreign interest, but definitely not ours, then the memory of Jewish Ghettos of the past will be called up."[39]

In November 1934, the school commission of the IKG discussed the option to file a petition with state authorities concerning the establishment and financing of Jewish primary schools. The majority of IKG leaders believed that the state was responsible for financing Jewish schools. In March 1935, the school commission discussed sending a petition to the state authorities to make clear that "not the IKG, but actually the state would be obliged to establish Jewish schools."[40] Furthermore, "if the state makes its school system German-Christian, then the Jews also want their own school system. But the state also has the obligation to care for the Jewish school."

Not all members of the commission agreed whether to approach the state, and therefore no decision was made at that plenary session whether to turn to the state for financial support. Apart from the *Union Österreichischer Juden*, also some Orthodox circles opposed the establishment of an IKG-managed primary school. They believed such a school would not put enough emphasis on religious values, but instead would focus on Zionist ideology, conforming to the ideals of the leading party of the community. Articles published during the debates about the parallel class order in the Orthodox

Jewish newspaper *Jüdische Presse* express not only sharp criticism of the planned IKG primary school, which was seen as irreligious and at the same time a competitor for the Orthodox Talmud Torah primary school, but also support for the confessional classes at public schools.[41] While the IKG leadership fought against the parallel class order, some orthodox circles saw in it, just like state authorities, a first step towards creating more religiously observant confessional schools. State authorities were aware of inner-Jewish conflicts, and at several occasions the IKG leadership corresponded with Austrian politicians to convince them that their views and demands represented the large majority of Viennese Jewry and not those of the *Jüdische Presse*, whose publications on the matter they saw as damaging to Jewry in general.[42]

Despite the debates on the Jewish primary school, the IKG opened the gates of its new primary school in September 1935, and the Austrian state school inspector and district school inspector for the second Viennese district came to congratulate the IKG in the name of the Viennese mayor and the president of the Vienna School Board. [43]

Towards Complete Segregation

When in January 1938 count Georg Thurn-Valsassina, leader of the *Vaterländische Front*'s youth division, suggested to organize Jewish youth in a separate subdivision because of differences in religious education, the IKG officially welcomed the step, while the *Union Österreichischer Juden* strongly opposed it as anti-Semitic segregation.[44] In the same month, the *Jüdische Presse* published in a small notification the details of an upcoming ban on Jewish religious education at public schools, introduced by the Ministry of Education. Such a move would have changed the IKG's education policy in the extreme, as their main activity had been focused on exactly those classes. However, the IKG leadership did not have a lot of time to contemplate about that matter, because less than two months later Austria was annexed to the German Reich. Shortly thereafter, the Nuremberg race laws were introduced in the Ostmark, resulting in a complete segregation of Jewish children into Jewish schools or accumulative classes, at times several age-groups in one class. Children had to walk long, dangerous ways to their new schools, and the number of Jewish children allowed to attend secondary education in Jewish schools was significantly restricted. Jewish schools later served as accumulative stations for Jews before they were deported. By 1942, Jewish children did not attend schools. Most of them had either fled or were deported. When there were hardly any Jews left in Vienna, previously Jewish schools were again used for Christian children.[45]

Conclusion

Jewish education during the interwar period was strongly connected to state policies and laws concerning religious instruction in general for all churches and religious organizations. Not only did the Jewish community take on Jewish education as one of its main responsibilities because state law required this, but the state also enforced the attendance of religious instruction. Furthermore, although the law of interdenomination was set up to enhance the freedom of religion, its restrictions also served as a tool to prevent conversions of Jewish children by their parents. When in line with the law, the Austrian state authorities cooperated fully with the IKG and ordered parents to leave their children in the IKG to receive Jewish religious instruction, even if they themselves had left the Jewish religion. Without state law and cooperation with state authorities in enforcing this law, the IKG could not have set up a compulsory public system for religious instruction and a large number of Jewish children would not have received any religious education.

Not only did state policies guarantee that all Jewish children received Jewish religious instruction, but it also ensured the right of Jewish children to keep basic laws of the Sabbath by not having to write, draw or do handiwork on Saturdays. Jewish boys were generally allowed to wear a head covering at religious instruction classes. When it came to compulsory prayers in class for Catholic children, state authorities consulted with the IKG to find the most acceptable solution for classes attended also by Jewish children. The IKG, on its side, did not make big efforts to enforce the Sabbath laws or the head covering at public schools. Although they did not promote confessional prayer in class, they had no objections to Jewish children staying in class while Christians were praying according to their customs.

The Jewish values and identity the IKG leadership wanted to convey to the Jewish children was not necessarily a religious one. They themselves were mostly not religiously observant apart from an orthodox minority, which had its own orthodox primary schools and other educational institutions. The emphasis of the official IKG leadership was put on culture, history, language and customs in order to participate in services at the synagogues. This tendency was in line the aim to be considered equal, with equal rights to other confessions. The curriculum was quite universal, with a Jewish emphasis, but based on values the non-Jewish society could identify with.

The aim was to stay Jewish, but in a way which was very similar to any other confession. In practice this worked quite well as long as Austrian state policy regarded education an interconfessional matter.

From the mid-1930s, however, after the implementation of the third Concordat and the new Constitution, this approach changed drastically, Austria became increasingly confessional, education increasingly Catholic. When Jewish children were to be separated from Catholic children, the Jewish community leaders changed their approach to the state as the state had changed its approach to them. Cooperation and compromise had turned into conflict. The values of universality and equality the Jewish community wanted their children to grow up in vanished. In the light of rising tension and anti-Semitism, the IKG also turned to a further segregation of choice and established its own primary school, while still hoping that state policies causing segregation in public schools could be overturned. The question of segregation and integration around the state policy of separation at public schools and the Jewish primary school also caused a lot of inner-Jewish tension between orthodox, Zionist and non-Zionist parties. There remained not much time, however to engage in discussions and solution-searching as the annexation to the German Reich brought about a new policy of total segregation and finally the abolishment of any kind of public education for Jewish children in Vienna.

Notes

* This research project and the publishing of its findings were made possible by the generous support of the Center for Austrian Studies at the European Forum at the Hebrew University. It is part of a doctoral dissertation "Facing the Challenge of Jewish Education in the Metropolis – A Comparative Study of the Jewish Communal Organizations of Budapest and Vienna, from 1867 until World War II," conducted under the supervision of Michael K. Silber. The author continues her research at Scholion – Interdisciplinary Research Center in Jewish Studies at the Hebrew University and is supported by the Leo Baeck Fellowship Program of the Studienstiftung des deutschen Volkes.

1. On the Jews of Vienna see Marsha Rozenblit, *Die Juden Wiens, 1867-1914: Assimilation und Identität* (Vienna: Böhlau, 1989); Robert Wistrich, *Die Juden Wiens im Zeitalter Kaiser Franz Josephs* (Vienna: Böhlau, 1999).

2. *Reichs-Gesetz-Blatt für das Kaiserthum Oesterreich*, Jahrgang 1868, <http://anno.onb.ac.at/cgi-content/anno-plus?apm=0&aid=rgb&datum=18680004&seite=00000097&zoom=2> (24 Jan. 2010).

3. Protocol books of the IKG's school commission meetings (Sektion II), Central Archives for the History of the Jewish People Jerusalem (hereon CAHJP).

4. *Reichs-Gesetz-Blatt für das Kaiserthum Oesterreich*, Jahrgang 1868.

5. Ibid., <http://anno.onb.ac.at/cgi-content/anno-plus?apm=0&aid=rgb&datum=18680004&zoom=2&seite=00000099&x=18&y=7 >(24 Jan. 2010).

6. *Freie Jüdische Lehrerstimme*, 15 Nov. 1919.

7. Federal Chancellery to Federal Ministry of Education, 13 February 1925; Federal Chancellery Z1.149314/9/1921; Österreichisches Staatsarchiv, Vienna, 52 D8 Neuer Kultus, Isr. Kultus.

8. Federal Ministry of Education, 25 Oct. 1922, 2934; 3 Dec. 1923, 3096; 17 Jan. 1924, 1538; Österreichisches Staatsarchiv, Vienna, 52 D8 Neuer Kultus, Isr. Kultus.

9. Federal Ministry of Education, 22 Jul. 1924, 25 Jul. 1924, Z.88.158-24.18210; 30 Sep. 1924, Z.18210-17/Kultus; 4 Nov. 1924, Z12Z129; 18210; 23 Jan. 1925, 2201-IZ; Federal Ministry of Foreign Affairs, 7 Jan. 1925, Z 124.250-24, Österreichisches Staatsarchiv, Vienna, 52 D8 Neuer Kultus, Isr. Kultus.

10. IKG, 23 Apr. 1936, IKG Z.1660 ex 1936, A/W 1562, CAHJP.

11. Stadtschulrat für Wien to IKG, 21 June 1928, A/W 1518.8, CAHJP.

12. Glöckel-Erlass, <http://de.wikipedia.org/wiki/Glöckel-Erlass>.

13. Stadtschulrat für Wien, 24 Jul. 1922, A/W 1555, CAHJP.

14. Protocol books of the IKG's school commission meetings (Sektion II), A/W 1518.8, CAHJP.

15. Glöckel-Erlass.

16. Stadtschulrat für Wien to IKG, 18 October 1933; Stadtschulrat für Wien Z1.I-6723/33; copy in the protocol books of the IKG plenary meetings A/W 71.20, CAHJP.

17. Ibid.

18. Ibid.

19. IKG to Stadtschulrat für Wien, Z.7361 ex 1933; protocol books of the IKG plenary meetings A/W 71.20, CAHJP.

20. K.k. Ministry of Education, 31 Jan. 1876, Z1208; referred to in letter from K.k. Niederösterreichischer Landesschulrat to headmasters of all secondary schools and all district school inspectors, 14 Nov. 1911, A/W 1556, CAHJP.

21. K.k. Niederösterreichischer Landesschulrat to headmasters of all secondary schools and all district school inspectors, 14 Nov. 1911, A/W 1556, CAHJP.

22. Ibid.

23. Stadtschulrat für Wien to IKG, 30 April 1930; protocol books of the IKG plenary meetings A/W 71.20, CAHJP.

24. *Jüdische Presse*, 28 Jun. 1935.

25. Bezirksschulrat, 22 Nov. 1891, A/W 1556, CAHJP.

26. Teachers at the federal school of the second district of Vienna to Landesschulrat, 1921; protocol books of the IKG's school commission meetings (Sektion II), A/W 1518.8, CAHJP.

27. *Verordnung der Bundesregierung vom 24. April 1934 über die Verfassung des Bundesstaates Österreich*, B.G.Bl. 1934 I. Nr. 239, <http://www.verfassungen.de/at/oesterreich34.htm>.

28. *Concordat between the Holy See and the Republic of Austria of 5 July 1933*, Article 6, <http://www.concordatwatch.eu/showtopic.php?org_id=921&kb_header_id=1811>.

29. Speech by IKG president Dr. Desider Friedmann, including attached copies of relevant documents, 26 September 1934; protocol books of the IKG plenary meetings A/W 71.20, CAHJP.

30. *Neue Freie Presse*, 25 Sept. 1934.

31. IKG, 27 Sept. 1934, A/W 1528, CAHJP.

32. IKG, 26 Sept 1934, A/W 1528, CAHJP.

33. *Verordnung des Ministeriums für Kultus und Unterricht vom 29. September 1905*, <http://alex.onb.ac.at/cgi-content/anno-plus?apm=0&aid=rgb&datum=19050004&seite=00000406&zoom=2>.

34. Dr. Desider Friedmann at the IKG plenary session, 26 September 1934; protocol books of the IKG plenary meetings A/W 71.20, CAHJP.

35. Ibid.

36. Dr. Leopold Plaschkes at the IKG plenary session, 26 September 1934; protocol books of the IKG plenary meetings A/W 71.20, CAHJP.

37. Dr. Jakob Ornstein at the IKG plenary session, 26 September 1934; protocol books of the IKG plenary meetings A/W 71.20, CAHJP.

38. Oberbaurat Ing. Robert Stricker at the IKG plenary session, 26 September 1934; protocol books of the IKG plenary meetings A/W 71.20, CAHJP.

39. Dr. Jakob Ehrlich at the IKG plenary session, 26 September 1934; protocol books of the IKG plenary meetings A/W 71.20, CAHJP.

40. IKG, protocol book of school commission, March 1935, Sektion II, A/W 1518.8, CAHJP.

41. *Jüdische Presse*, 14 Sep. 1934, 5 Oct. 1934, 12 Oct. 1934.

42. IKG to the Federal government, ministry of education and mayor of Vienna, 8 Oct. 1934 Z.7219 ex 1934, A/W 1528; note of a meeting of the IKG executive committee with State Secretary Dr. Pernter, 27 Sep. 1934, A/W 1528; IKG to Adass Jisroel, A/W 1528, CAHJP.

43. Report of IKG on the inauguration of the Jewish primary school, 25 Sep. 1935, A/W1652.6, CAHJP.

44. *Jüdische Wochenschrift*, 4 Feb. 1938.

45. Hedwig Millan, "Jüdische Schüler an den Wiener Pflichtschulen vom März 1938 bis 1942," <www.david.juden.at/kulturzeitschrift/70-75/73-millian.htm>.

III. HABSBURG SUCCESSOR STATES: ECONOMIC LEGACIES

Under Pressure to Adapt: Corporate Business and the New Order in Post-1918 Central Europe

Andreas Resch

Comparative studies on economic development between the two world wars reveal that Central and Eastern European national economies achieved quite impressive growth rates but "fell short of their potential."[1] The aim of this paper is to illustrate the difficulties and opportunities for big banks and industrial firms in Austria, Czechoslovakia, and Hungary during the first decade after the Great War. In the aftermath of World War I corporate business in Central and Eastern Europe had to adapt to manifold economic and political challenges. Section 1 briefly recapitulates some immediate economic consequences of the war; in two subsequent chapters, developments of selected banks and industry firms are portrayed, and Section 4 concludes.

1. The Immediate Economic and Political Consequences of World War I for Corporate Business in Central and Eastern Europe

The central powers had not ended the Great War in 1918 until they were forced to capitulate due to a complete depletion of all kinds of resources. During 1917 the general supply position in the Habsburg monarchy deteriorated from a general shortage of food, coal, and ammunition to an acute need for any kinds of military goods at the front lines and widespread famine in the interior.[2] The goods most urgently needed were food and coal.

This situation intensified national conflicts within the dual monarchy. Hungary was no more able to supply sufficient amounts of foodstuffs for the industrial regions in Austria, and on a regional level communities began to obstruct deliveries to other parts of the empire because of local food shortages and nationalist sentiments. Furthermore, lack of coal for railway transports and poor maintenance of the railway system aggravated the supply problems. As a consequence, conflicts related with food shortage accelerated the dissolution of the monarchy and the entire area developed from a net exporter to a net importer of food.[3]

After 1918, supply was made even more difficult by thousands of kilometers of new national borders, by territorial conflicts among the successor states, and by the introduction of new national currencies. While democratic forces remained in power in Austria and Czechoslovakia, Hungary experienced a phase of communist rule in 1919, followed by white terror and the consolidation of Horthy's regime from 1920 on.[4]

On an international level the Paris peace treaties provided the legal foundation for the new successor states.

Agrarian production recovered quite sluggishly, due to exhaustion during the war and institutional uncertainties with respect to further developments.[5] In Czechoslovakia, on the one hand land reform produced an increase of "dwarf holdings" which were not able to invest in modern production methods. On the other hand, 2,291 "residual estates" with an average size of 100 hectares remained. As a consequence, last traces of feudalism vanished and the agricultural bourgeoisie was strengthened.[6]

Austria's agrarian sector was dominated by small and medium farms. The peasants gained strong influence in the political process. Due to modest job opportunities in the other economic sectors, drift to the cities came to a halt and the farmers could rely on cheap labor. In some cases, rural employment even was subsidized by unemployment funds.[7] As a consequence, productivity and investments remained low.

In Hungary, first Kun's rule hampered investments into the post-war reconstruction of the agrarian sector, and from 1920 on the Bethlen era brought a "sham agrarian reform"[8] which slightly increased the share of small holdings and stabilized the role of traditional rural elites. Economics of the big estates continued to be based on extensive production of wheat, cheap labor, and low rates of investments.

In the given setting, mechanization of the agrarian sector made little progress in most of the successor states and yields remained low.[9] In Austria and Hungary, harvest per acre hardly exceeded levels of pre-modern times.[10]

Since Hungary had the highest relative share of agrarian production, her national economy was affected the most by the detrimental effects of weak agrarian modernization on overall welfare and economic growth.

Due to experiences of war economy and economic nationalism, foreign trade policy was determined by tendencies towards import substitution. Until the early 1920s, trade was restricted to direct compensation. This meant that for each delivery a quid pro quo had to be found. Around the mid 1920s a regime of trade agreements with most favored nations' clauses followed. Successful lobbying of agrarian and industrial groups in line with politics of economic nationalism provided for an increased level of tariffs compared to the pre-war tariff structures.

Table 1: Tariff levels in 1913, 1927 and 1931 in Central and Eastern Europe (ad valorem tariffs in percent)

	Food			Semi-manufactured goods		
	1913	1927	1931	1913	1927	1931
Austria	29.1*	16.5	59.5	20.0*	15.2	20.7
Bulgaria	24.7	79.0	133.0	24.2	49.5	65.0
Czechoslovakia	29.1*	36.3	84.0	20.0*	21.7	29.5
Hungary	29.1*	31.5	60.0	20.0*	26.5	32.5
Poland	69.4**	72.0	110.0	63.5**	33.2	40.0

	Industrial goods		
	1913	1927	1931
Austria	19.3*	21.0	27.7
Bulgaria	19.5	75.0	90.0
Czechoslovakia	19.3*	35.8	36.5
Hungary	19.3*	31.8	42.6
Poland	85.0**	55.6	52.0

* Austria-Hungary
** Russia

Source: H. Liepman, *Tariff Levels and the Economic Unity of Europe* (London, 1938) quoted after Z. Drabek, "Foreign Trade Performance and Policy," in *The Economic History of Eastern Europe 1919-1975*, vol. I, ed. M. C. Kaser and E. A. Radice (Oxford: Clarendon Press, 1985), 476.

The table illustrates the massive increase of tariff levels for all categories of goods. Markets for food as well as for semi-manufactured and industrial goods were separated by increasing tariff walls.[11]

It is plausible to assume that the import barriers in the given situation provided for a certain degree of import substitution and improved trade balances to the disadvantage of more expensive investment and consumer goods. In a more dynamic view, this hampered real investment, growth of productivity and modernization.

Furthermore, newly founded and enlarged successor states, such as Czechoslovakia, Poland, Yugoslavia or Romania emphasized national economic development by measures of "nostrification" of corporate business within their territories to underpin their newly gained economic independence from Vienna and Budapest. Public authorities exerted substantial pressure on local branches of firms that had become multinational due to the division of the old empire, to be transferred into national companies and to hire management boards of domestic nationality.[12]

Since the Bohemian lands had been the most industrialized area before the war while most head offices of large companies had been in Vienna, Czechoslovakia became the most important stage for this kind of economic nationalism. Until 1928 more than 230 firms had to undergo a Czechoslovak "nostrification" procedure.[13]

In many cases yet, conversions of local branches into separate firms allowed to attract fresh capital provided by investors located in the national states and in Western countries (France, United Kingdom etc.).[14]

As a consequence of the supply problems and food shortage mentioned above most of the successor states got into massive foreign indebtedness. Austria had the highest import demand, which was the main reason for enormous public deficits and hyperinflation. In the autumn of 1922 the currency was stabilized at one fourteen thousandth of the pre-war level, and in 1924/1925 the Austrian Schilling was introduced as new currency, one pre-war gold crown equaling 1.44 Schilling.[15]

At the same time, Hungary missed the opportunity to benefit from the conditions of an international supplier market for agrarian goods since domestic production suffered from upheavals and instabilities until 1921. As a consequence, this country too suffered from financial disorder and hyperinflation. After the national currency was stabilized in 1924 the pengő was introduced at a value of 1.16 new currency units to the pre-war gold crown.[16] Both countries had to agree to a reconstruction scheme developed by the League of Nations and received internationally guaranteed stabilization loans. As a consequence, domestic financial policy was gradually subordinated to international control and the newly established central banks had to pursue a policy of tight money and high interest levels.

Czechoslovakia found herself in a somewhat better position, due to comparably productive domestic agrarian structures and strong export industries. Industrial and mining exports provided for an active balance of trade.[17] The monetary authorities succeeded already in 1922/1923 in stabilizing the Czech crown (Kč) at a rate of 6.84 Kč to the gold crown.

The domestic capital market was strong enough to allow Czechoslovakia to support the stabilization schemes of Austria and Hungary.

In all three countries stabilization was followed by recession and a restrictive monetary policy, which increased interest rates.[18] The stabilization crisis occurred in Czechoslovakia in 1922/23, and in Austria and Hungary in 1924/25.

2. The Banking Sector in Czechoslovakia, Hungary and Austria after World War I

Since the late nineteenth century, the Central and Eastern European capital market was dominated by strong Viennese bank and industry groups. In the aftermath of World War I old monetary institutions broke down while turbulences of the currencies and subsequent stabilization allowed for many kinds of speculative business dealings. In this atmosphere, new banks mushroomed and existing banking houses increased their staff. After stabilization a massive banking crises followed, in Czechoslovakia from 1922 onward, and in Austria and Hungary during the years 1924 and 1925.[19]

The number of banks in Austria first increased from 180 in 1919 to 358 in 1923 and subsequently decreased to 192 in 1927.[20] In Hungary, the number of banks went down from 680 in 1924 to 572 in 1927, and the number of Czechoslovak joint stock banks dropped from 279 in 1920 to 120 in 1928.[21]

During the banking crisis in Austria, numerous failing banks merged, frequently leading to bigger but weakened banks, which were overstaffed and dragged along dubious claims. Ben Bernanke and Harold James have commented on this process as follows: "Austria is probably the most extreme case of nagging banking problems being repeatedly 'papered over.'"[22]

The big Austrian universal banks were severely affected by the loss of most of their equity due to the vicissitudes of a war economy, and inflation. In spite of their weakened position, universal banks like the Oesterreichische Creditanstalt für Handel und Gewerbe or the Niederösterreichische Escompte-Gesellschaft tried to defend at least a part of their former economic position in Central and Eastern Europe. They continued to finance industrial groups in post-war Austria and aimed at maintaining financial relations to customers in regions which had become foreign due to the newly drawn national borders.

Two Viennese institutes, Länderbank and Anglo-Austrian Bank, became French- and British-owned firms respectively and in general, foreign stock-holders gained weight. For example, the share held by foreign proprietors in Vienna's largest bank, the Creditanstalt, rose from 3.9 percent in 1913 to more than twenty percent in 1923.[23]

The most important "newly foreign" market was Czechoslovakia, because Viennese banks had played a decisive role as capital market institutions for industries in the Bohemian countries.

Two Austrian banks, Niederösterreichische Escompte-Gesellschaft and Creditanstalt, merged their branches and businesses in Czechoslovakia into the Böhmische Escomptebank und Creditanstalt (BEBCA). The biggest Czech bank, Živnostenská banka, acquired the largest share of BEBCA, and the two Viennese players became minority shareholders. Other Viennese banks converted their branches into autonomous bank firms, whereby Czech and Western investors purchased majority shares.[24]

The ambitions of the Viennese banks were hampered by great difficulties. They had to bear high costs for financing their activities on Western monetary markets due to impaired creditworthiness, and they suffered of reduced efficiency due to labor hoarding after the inflation era. Supply of reasonable domestic financial means was restricted, since saving rates remained low after inflation had destroyed all saving deposits, and the central bank was committed to a policy of high bank rates.[25]

As a consequence, loans of the Viennese banks came with high interest, and long-term loans were backed by short-term money from Western money markets which caused increasing structural tensions within the entire Austrian banking system.

Among the big Viennese banks, the Allgemeine österreichische Boden-Credit-Anstalt found herself in the most difficult situation. Before the war, this company had held some profitable industrial investments, but mortgage loans had been the main business. Due to inflation this sector broke down completely after the war. The management tried to overcome the crisis by an aggressive expansion of the industrial business. This ambitious strategy together with her structural inability to provide loans at reasonable interest rates was an obstacle to acquire best-rated customers of undoubted creditworthiness. Losses due to defaults of debtors and immobilized investments mounted during the second half of the 1920s. The Boden-Credit-Anstalt crashed in 1929 and was taken over by the Creditanstalt.[26]

Beyond the level of individual firms, a statistical survey on the ten biggest Viennese banks of the year 1913 illustrates the decline of Vienna as a financial centre.

–

Table 2: Big Austrian banks and savings banks 1913-1928

	1913*	1913*	1925**	1928***	1928
	Million crowns	Million schilling			as % of 1913
Equity	1233.3	1775.9	306.0	376.8	21.2
Creditors	4822.8	6944.9	1953.2	3005.8	43.3
Balance	6183.1	8903.6	2317.2	3455.8	38.8
Debtors	4277.0	6158.9	2051.9	2408.1	39.1
Stocks, shares, and bonds	526.4	758.0	291.5	345.1	45.5
Profits	104.8	150.9	27.6	33.2	22.0
Austrian savings banks	0.0				
Savings deposits	2963.2	4267.0	501.3	932.2	21.8

* 1913 Creditanstalt, Boden-Credit-Anstalt, Bankverein, Niederösterreichische Escompte-Gesellschaft, Mercurbank, Länderbank, Unionbank, Verkehrsbank, Anglobank, Depositenbank.
** 1925 Same as 1913 except Anglobank and Depositenbank due to banking crisis, Austrian branch of Länderbank
*** 1928 Same as 1925 except Unionbank and Verkehrsbank due to banking crisis.
Sources: Calculated after Walther Federn, *Die österreichischen Banken: 10 Jahre Nachfolgestaaten* (Vienna 1928), 56-57 and Compass Österreich, 1928 and 1930.

In 1928, all reference numbers of the biggest Viennese banks only amounted to 20 to 40 percent of the respective figures in 1913. Equity and profitability had suffered most.

Commercial and savings banks in Hungary experienced decay similar to their Austrian counterparts. In this country as well, most of bank's equity and saving deposits were annihilated during hyperinflation.

The most influential player before and after the war was the Hungarian General Creditbank (Magyar Általános Hitelbank), which had traditional ties to the Rothschild Family and the Viennese Creditanstalt.[27] This universal bank held shares of several smaller Hungarian banks and industrial firms. After the war Austrian (and German) banking connections were weakened and replaced to a high degree by French, British and American influence. In 1920 a French capital group led by Union Européenne Industrielle et Financière of Paris acquired substantial shares, and in 1926 again a group of foreign banks participated in an increase of the banks' joint stock capital.[28]

The Hungarian General Creditbank financed numerous firms in the fields of industry, transport and agrarian production and acted as a trading house for agrarian and industrial goods. The entire Hungarian banking sector was massively affected by hyperinflation until 1924, and the domestic capital and money market remained dependent of foreign finance. Together with their Western shareholders the banks were able to organize a massive inflow of foreign loans. The peak of the balance of payment deficit was reached in 1928. The Hungarian economy got into highest foreign indebtedness per capita of all Central and Eastern European states.[29]

Statistical data on the entire banking sector show a picture similar to the Austrian development.

Table 3: Hungarian banks and savings banks 1913-1928* (in million pengő)

	1913	1925	1928	1928 as % of 1913
Equity	1007.39	234.05	356.290	35.4
Creditors	1551.40	294.53	1650.42**	70.1**
Deposits	801.90	26.98	/	
Balance	6225.16	613.12	2491.300	40.0
Bills	934.12	66.67	693.278	74.2
Debtors	3952.60	270.65	1228.030	31.1
Stocks and bonds	735.81	92.05	144.430	19.6
Profits	82.24	9.03	37.620	45.7

* Members of Takarékpenztárak és bankok egyesülete (Union of savings banks and banks). Comparison between 1913 and post-war years is somewhat distorted because of losses of territories. But most relevant banks were within "Trianon-Hungary".

** Deposits included

Source: Compass Ungarn (Vienna: Compassverlag), div. years.

In 1928, equity and total balance of the banks and savings banks had not recovered to more than 40 percent of the pre-war level, savings deposits having been destroyed by the hyperinflation.

In general, in most Central and Eastern European countries during the 1920s interest rates for loans remained at a high level of 15 to 30 percent as a consequence of scarce domestic savings, high bank rates and expensive "Western" finance.[30] This meant that the real interest rate even for best debtors hardly declined to less than 10 percent. No doubt, excessive cost of capital supply was an important reason for low levels of investment in the respective countries. In Austria, during the years from 1924 to 1928, gross investment as a share of gross national product always remained in a range between 6 and 9.2 percent, while it had been some 13 percent in 1913.[31] In Hungary around 1928, gross fixed capital formation rose to more than 13 percent of the net national product, thanks to substantial capital imports. Yet around 40 percent of the means invested were directed into the housing sector, while only a small share was utilized for investments enhancing productivity.[32] Actual investments in agriculture, manufacturing and communications probably remained at an even lower level than in Austria.

In Czechoslovakia, capital market and banking developed in a somewhat different manner, thanks to the stronger economic starting point of this national economy after the war. The only Czech bank which had already before 1918 grown to a size comparable to the big Viennese universal banks was the Živnostenská banka. After 1918 this company exploited its closeness to national political authorities and became the most powerful financial institution.

In general, after the war Czech banks gained weight due to the fact that Vienna failed to provide for loans in Czechoslovak currency, so that domestic firms had to seek loans from domestic suppliers. Furthermore, due to the "nostrification" procedures a group of banks with Czechoslovak majority shareholders and minority partners from Austria and Western states emerged, which were capable as well to play an important role in the Czechoslovak market for loans and participation capital. The most important commercial bank with mixed ownership was the above mentioned BEBCA.

Thanks to higher savings rates and close cooperation with the savings banks, all of the Czechoslovak commercial banks were able to mobilize abundant domestic financial sources for the modernisation of successful industrial branches at lower interest rates than in most other Central and Eastern European countries.[33]

For Czechoslovakia, data from 1913 for the entire banking sector, which allow comparison with the post-war situation, are not available. But the figures of the biggest single Bohemian bank, Živnostenská banka, can be taken as an indicator for the successful development of Czechoslovak banking, compared to Vienna.

Table 4: Živnostenská banka 1912-1928

	1912	1912	1925	1928	1928 as % of 1913
	Million gold crowns	Million Kč	Million Kč	Million Kč	
Equity	80.00	547.2	304.3	574.8	105.1
Creditors	130.47	892.4	2436.7	2792.1	313.0
Deposits	107.89	737.9	1636.1	1838.0	249.1
Balance	386.75	2645.4	4597.9	5296.8	200.2
Bills	123.92	847.5	856.7	693.1	81.8
Mortgage credits	28.74	196.6	30.6	41.8	21.3
Debtors	100.55	687.8	2666.3	3041.1	442.2
Stocks and bonds	41.22	281.9	370.9	610.3	216.5
Profits	28.74	47.7	39.0	40.5	84.9

Source: Compass Čechoslovakei, 1914, 1928 and 1930.

Between 1912 and 1928, the leading Czechoslovak bank was able to increase most of the relevant reference numbers by factors between two and four, while the leverage was increased due to markedly enhanced business activities and reasonable financial resources.

To give a more representative overview of Czechoslovak banking after 1918, the following table displays data for all joint stock banks after 1918 and the development of saving deposits in the entire banking sector.

Table 5: Czechoslovak banks and development of deposits in the entire banking sector (values in million Kč)

	1920	1925	1928
Czechoslovak joint stock banks			
No. of banks in consideration	279	164	120
Share capital	1637.9	2271.7	2209.3
Creditors	14740.8	15336.9	19182.3
Deposits	3626.5	9132.4	11177.3
Bills	1737.1	3176.4	4827.8*
Debtors	13863.3	19561.3	21687.2*
Profits	220.4	271.1	306.0
Savings deposits**			
No. of banks, saving banks and credit cooperatives in consideration	6180	6262	6484
Deposits	18720.5	45388.7	58342.8

*for 1928 only the total sum of debtors and bills is known for joint stock banks in Slovakia and Karpathorussia. This sum is divided into the two categories by the respective percentages of 1927.
**at commercial banks, saving banks, and credit co-operatives except associations of credit co-operatives which made up for some 4 percent of all sums on saving deposits.
Source: Calculated after Compass Čechoslovakia 1931, 246-247.

The collective data for the banking sector reveal a certain process of concentration and a strong increase of savings deposits. The strength of national capital formation provided domestic finance at reasonable costs and allowed for an active capital balance during the 1920s. As a consequence, in contrast to all other Central and Eastern European states, in Czechoslovakia foreign shares in corporate business and credits decreased during the post-war years while investment rates were sustained on a high level. In 1928 more than 15 percent of the gross national product was used for gross fixed asset formation.[34]

3. Adaptive Strategies of Industrial Firms

Not only commercial banks, but also their main customers, i. e. industrial firms, had to adapt to the changed conditions after 1918. The emergence of separate successor states, need for capital supply and access to markets in a dramatically changed setting required drastic organizational responses.

As examples for corporate business in the industrial sphere, leading firms of the mining and steel sector, three mechanical engineering companies and finally the Mautner textile group are portrayed.

3.1 Coal and Steel

In all of the three states considered here, domestic production of iron and steel was an important input sector for construction and mechanical engineering. The following tables give an impression of the relative sizes of coal and iron production.

Table 6: Production of hard coal before and after World War I in 1000 tons*

	1913	1928
Czechoslovakia	14570	15170
Poland	/	40518
Germany	173896	150876
USA	516060	516632

* post-war territories
Source: Compass Čechoslovakei 1931, 723.

Table 7: Production of iron and steel before and after World War I in 1000 tons*

	1913		1928	
	Iron	Steel	Iron	Steel
Czechoslovakia	1200	1450	1569	1972
Austria	607	890	458	636
Hungary	190	443	287	486
Germany	10912	12186	11804	14517
USA	31462	31812	38766	52369
World	73000	70000	82241	102655

* post war territories
Source: Compass Čechoslovakei 1931, 725.

Of the three national economies in consideration here, Czechoslovakia was the foremost producer of coal and iron. Steel production in 1928 increased by more than a third compared to 1913 and amounted to some fourteen percent of German output. Hungary also achieved a slightly increased steel output, while Austrian production remained nearly thirty percent below the last pre-war year.

These figures quite well characterize the entire development of metallurgy and mechanical engineering in the three countries.

In Czechoslovakia, steel production was dominated by the Vítkovice Mining and Foundry Works, the Mining and Metallurgic Company, and the Prague Iron Company. In 1921/22, "the big Three" founded a national iron cartel, which ran a central sales organisation. During the 1920s, the cartel controlled more than 80 percent of Czechoslovak iron production. In 1926 the respective industrial groups from Germany, France and other Western European states formed an international steel cartel, which was joined by Czechoslovakia, Austria and Hungary in 1927.[35]

Before and after the war the Mining and Metallurgic Company developed more dynamically than any other corporation of this industry in the entire area of the former monarchy.[36] That is why this company is portrayed here in some more detail.

The firm was founded in 1905 by the Boden-Credit-Anstalt to run the works of Archduke Friedrich von Habsburg in Těšín. Most of the works were situated in Třinec on the disputed so-called plebiscite territory in Těšín. The coal mines were located in the region around Ostrava-Karviná, a sheet rolling mill in Karlova Huť.

The valuation of the shares and the ability to continue production were harmed by political tensions with respect to the new borderlines between Poland and Czechoslovakia. Furthermore, worker's strikes due to attempts at socialisation of the former Archduke's works and national conflicts between Polish and Czech workers endangered production.[37] In this situation the French metallurgy combine Schneider et Cie., Creusot acquired a majority share of the firm from the Boden-Credit-Anstalt and the former archduke. The Živnostenská banka became a major shareholder as well. Consequently, influential business and government circles of Western Europe favoured a settlement of the territorial conflict conducive for the Mining and Metallurgy Company. In July 1920, Těšín was divided in a way that the valuable coal-fields (hard coal) and iron and steel works of the Company remained on Czechoslovak territory. Only the iron foundry, situated in Wegierska Górka, lay on the Polish side of the border.[38]

In accordance with the Czechoslovak "nostrification" legislation in 1920 the head office of the company was transferred from Vienna to Brno.

The financial and political commitment of the new shareholders allowed continuing production with minor disturbances. Thanks to favourable terms of trade for coal during the immediate post-war years, the company came out of this era in a sound economic condition. During the following years, the Mining and Metallurgy Company was able to modernize her coal mines and metallurgical sites, and to expand production. Above all, Třinec became a highly productive steel work. Furthermore, the company bought other firms, cartel quotas and realised joint investment projects together with other companies. For example, in 1922 and 1923 the Mining and Metallurgy Company acquired together with the Vítkovice Works cartel quotas of two firms in Slovakia that had been run by the Hungarian Rimamurány Iron Works Ltd. and built a huge power plant. In 1928 the Company began to construct a modern sheet rolling mill in Karlova huť in cooperation with the Rotava-Nýdek Iron Works. The Mining and Metallurgy Company also participated in an international network of iron trading firms that had been built up by the Czechoslovak metallurgy industry and held shares of the Czechoslovak Oder Shipping Co.[39]

Table 8: Output of the Mining and Metallurgy Company 1913 to 1928 (in 1000 tons)

	Coal	Coke	Iron	Ingots	Rolled material
1913	1975.4	669.5	169.1	163.1	135.1
1920	2032.0	533.0	126.0	112.7	80.0
1928	3381.0	958.4	392.4	404.9	348.5

Source: Compass Čechoslovakei 1925, 575, and 1931, 744.

Thanks to internal and external growth output of coal rose by more than 70 percent between 1913 and 1928 while iron and steel production more than doubled. Due to the company's mining output far exceeding its own needs, the iron and steel business was complemented by market sales of coal and coke.[40]

In accordance with the growth of the company, joint stock capital was increased several times. In 1920, when Schneider acquired a substantial share, capital rose from 45 to 76 million crowns. During the subsequent years capital was increased to 100 Million Kč, to allow for further investments. In 1928 a newly issued balance sheet, which took into account the effects of the post-war inflation, was presented, which stated a share capital of 250 Million Kč.

In spite of political tensions with respect to new national borders, the Mining and Metallurgy Company remained very productive during the immediate post-war years—above all thanks to its own coal resources—and it had been able to build upon this strong starting position a successful development throughout the entire 1920s. For example, in 1928 the company paid out a dividend of 30 percent of the nominal share capital.

In Hungary, the Rimamurány-Salgó-Tarján Ironworks Joint Stock Company (Rima) dominated the market for iron and steel. The company had been founded in 1881 by Länderbank and Wiener Bankverein. Among the company's subsidiary firms were the Hornád Iron Works Ltd. and the Union steel plate factory, both located in Slovakia.

The entire group had developed successfully until 1914 under the favourable economic conditions, provided by moderate tariff protection and the Austro-Hungarian iron cartel.[41]

After the war, production was threatened by the drawing up of a new border between Czechoslovakia and Hungary. Most of the production centres were situated in the border-zone. Finally, the borderline was drawn in a way the company could well cope with. Most of the relevant production centres remained located on the Hungarian side. Disturbances did not end before the final definition of the borderline in the Trianon treaty and the conclusion of an agreement between the governments of Hungary and Czechoslovakia in 1922 that allowed for the continuation of the production process across the new national border.

Iron production was concentrated in Ozd, where Rima ran four blast furnaces, productive steel works and rolling mills. Other works for finished goods were situated in Nádasd (sheets) and Salgótarján (rolling mills, forges and foundry). Furthermore the company owned several mines for brown coal in Hungary. Due to an intergovernmental agreement of 1922 Rima also was able to utilize several quarrying and mining sites for ore and limestone in Slovakia.[42]

The Hornád Iron Works Ltd. and Union steel plate factory, which were located in Slovakia, turned out not to be viable in the face of the strong established iron works in the Czech lands. Rima shut them down and sold their cartel quotas to the Vítkovice works and the Mining and Metallurgic Co.[43]

During the inflation years, Rima repeatedly increased its joint stock capital. In 1922, the old majority owners issued 5120 preferential shares with increased voting rights to secure their majority in the board when they offered numerous fresh shares to the public during the subsequent years. All in all, share capital was raised from 40 million crowns in 1912 to 392 millions in 1925. During this year an American financial group led by F. J. Lisman & Co. acquired 100.000 newly issued shares (5 % of total share capital) and placed a mortgage based loan on the American market.[44] After these capital measures and the stabilization of the Hungarian currency the company was able to present a new balance sheet in July 1925 which revealed a nominal share capital of 19.6 million pengő and a total balance of 67.9 million pengő.[45]

In 1926, Rima together with the Austrian Alpine Montan Steel Corporation and the Czechoslovak iron industry joined the international steel cartel. The stability of the cartel agreement effectively was enhanced by substantial tariffs on iron and steel imports. Besides negotiated cartel-imports, Rima enjoyed a monopolistic position, as she was the only producer of raw iron and delivered some 70 percent of Hungarian steel output.

Sales heavily depended on public investment, construction and the mechanical engineering industry in Hungary. Rima benefited from the fact that gross investment in Hungary until the late 1920s was enhanced by an inflow of foreign capital. In 1928 this financial source markedly decreased as a first indicator of the Great Depression to come.

Thanks to the American loan and increasing profits during the entire 1920s the company was capable of continuous investment in modernisation and enlargement of the plants. In 1927 Rima bought two additional subsidies (Rudabánya ore mine and Kuritány coal mine).

Production developed as follows:

Table 9: Production of the Rimamurány-Salgó-Tarján Ironworks Ltd. (in 1000 tons)

	Iron ore	Raw iron	Steel	Coal
1913/14	482.1	235.1	238.0	408.2
1919/20	58.8	4.7	25.7	217.7
1927/28	520.8	232.5	308.0	560.8

Source: *Die Bilanzen*, 13 Dec. 1924, 81 and 10 Nov. 1928, 61.

In 1919/1920, iron production nearly came to a complete halt and steel production remained at some 10 percent of the pre-war level. Only extraction of coal was continued at a somewhat higher scale, thanks to the fact that most of the mines were located on Hungarian ground. Until 1928, most of the reference numbers surpassed pre-war levels. Above all, coal production was raised by 40 percent, which allowed for a certain import substitution. Steel production as well surpassed the pre-war level by 30 percent.

Until 1929 the company could achieve substantial annual profits, and dividends rose from 12 percent of the nominal joint stock capital in 1926/27 and 1927/28 to 14 percent in 1928/29.[46] Obviously, to a certain degree the rest of the Hungarian economy had to pay for it by prices for iron and steel above the level on international markets.

In interwar-Austria the Oesterreichisch Alpine Montangesellschaft (Alpine Montan Steel Corporation) was by far the most important coal and steel company. She produced nearly 100 percent of Austrian iron ore and raw iron, around 70 percent of the entire steel production, and some 30 percent of the entire Austrian brown coal output.[47]

The company had been founded in 1881 by the French Bontoux group, which broke down in 1882, and in 1897 the Prague Iron Company and the Bohemian Coal and Steel Company acquired about 50 percent of the share.

Before the war, the production program had been coordinated between Alpine and the two Bohemian sister companies. Under the market conditions, which from 1903 on were determined by the Austrian steel cartel, Alpine developed as a quite profitable company and invested in modern production technology. During the war, however, productivity deteriorated because production means were worn out and maintenance was deficient.[48]

After the war, no other company was hit harder by the Central European coal shortage than Alpine. In autumn 1918 the works had to be closed down completely, and during the year 1919 phases of depressed production were interrupted by phases of complete standstill. During the first post-war years, difficulties due to coal shortage were aggravated by social tensions, worker strikes and discussions about the socialisation of heavy industry. Indebtedness in hard currency rose dramatically, and the decline of valuation of the stock progressed even faster than the inflation of the Austrian currency.[49] Alpine joint stock capital became a highly speculative asset.

In 1919, the Italian Fiat group purchased a determining share to secure steel deliveries for her mechanical engineering works. It turned out however, that Fiat had underrated the difficulties to ensure sufficient coal and coke supply and the production output remained on a disappointingly low level. As a consequence the Italians sold their shares, and in 1921 the German Stinnes Group became new majority shareholder of the Alpine. Hugo Stinnes was head of the Rheinelbe-Union, a combine of leading German coal and steel producers. They commanded over rich coal supply but had lost some important ore deposits due to the new western borders of the Reich. That explains why the German investors were above all interested in Austria's highest-yield iron ore deposit (Erzberg), which for the largest part belonged to Alpine.[50]

After the death of Stinnes in 1923, his entire industrial group ran into acute financial difficulties. In a further process of concentration which lasted until 1926, Stinnes' steel properties became part of the newly founded Vereinigte Stahlwerke (United Steelworks Ltd.). The Alpine remained a minor subsidiary company of this German steel giant.

During the immediate post-war years, repeated slackening of production together with inflation led to increasing indebtedness of the Alpine group. Joint stock capital was increased repeatedly and new outside financing had to be found. In the speculative atmosphere during the inflation and post-inflation years, those deals often were accompanied by financial scandals. For example, the sale of shares to the Fiat group, which was organised by the Austrian financial investor Camillo Castiglioni, was said to be a disloyal manoeuvre against plans of the Austrian government for socialisation of the steel producer.

When in 1923 joint stock capital was raised from 300 to 600 million crowns, this transaction was carried out in a way which allowed an insider group around Castiglioni and Niederösterreichische Escompte-Gesellschaft to buy substantial new shares at modest prices and reap enormous profits, while the other shareholders were excluded from this opportunity for private profits.[51] In general, all the deals with Alpine shares were carried out in a way characteristically for the kind of crony financial market, which prevailed in Central and Eastern Europe after the war.

After the final increase of share capital in 1926 a balance sheet in the new Austrian currency was drawn up. While in 1912 total joint stock capital had been 72 million crowns (103.7 million schilling) and total balance had amounted to 122.7 million crowns (176.7 million schilling), the respective sums in 1926 were 60 million and 148.3 million schilling.[52]

When in 1921 the Stinnes group acquired the Alpine majority, the Germans had promised to supply 600,000 tons of coal from the Ruhr per year to provide for undisturbed production. These deliveries though, were repeatedly interrupted. First, in 1919 coal from the Ruhr was not allowed to be forwarded to Austria because of French reparations claims, and in early 1923 once again deliveries ended due to the French Ruhr occupation. In this year the Alpine managers tried to secure another source for hard coal by buying a substantial share of the Bismarck hut in Poland. After coal deliveries started again, a few months of enhanced sales followed because of the dramatic decline of German iron production.[53]

The German proprietors also were unable in supplying sufficient capital. In 1922/23, Alpine got close to bankruptcy because of loans that fell due in British pounds and Czech crowns. The German shareholders were not able to relieve the financial strain, since they themselves suffered of notorious capital shortage.[54] In this situation the company was bailed out by new loans provided by the Niederösterreichische Escompte-Gesellschaft. In 1924 again the Escompte-Gesellschaft helped to substitute expensive short-term bank credits by a substantial loan, issued on "Western" capital markets. In a manner similar to the banks's organizing a loan for the Hungarian Rima, she was able to see to it that the American banking houses F.J. Lisman & Co., A.M. Lampert & Co. and Morgan, Livermore & Co. issued an investment bill of a total amount of 5 million dollars at an interest rate of 7 percent. Due to sales below the nominal value and the fees of the involved banking houses, Alpine realized 27.4 million schilling, while the nominal volume of the loan was 35.53 million schilling. In spite of this cost burden, the loan came at a better price than Austrian bank loans.[55]

In 1926, indebtedness could be slightly reduced by selling the Bismarck shares and a coal field that the company owned in Poremba (Czechoslovakia). On the other hand, Alpine purchased a majority share of Graz-Köflacher Railway and Mining Company, which owned several brown coal deposits to increase coal production within Austria.

Thanks to the American loan and increasing sales, Alpine could renew the worn out and obsolete means of production. Already in 1922, productivity of iron ore extraction had been markedly enhanced by the construction of an elevator on the "Erzberg." Before this facility was available, the workers had a one hour's walk to the ore deposits. After the elevator was put in operation, two working hours per labourer and per day were saved.

During the 1920s, ore and coal production was modernized. Among others, improved production machineries and newly invented dehydration facilities were installed to enhance the amount and quality of coal and ore extracted. Modernisation of the furnaces and steelworks was oriented towards increased energy efficiency.[56]

The Alpine also tried to enhance profitability by participating in agreements to organise the iron and steel markets. A domestic Austrian iron cartel was revived in 1924. In the same year Alpine entered into an agreement with the Czechoslovak producers, which regulated the approaches to the respective domestic markets and export trade in Central and Eastern Europe. An agreement with the Hungarian Rima works followed suit, and as mentioned above, in January 1927 the three Central European producers became members of the International Steel Cartel.[57]

Obviously, the steel processing industries were adversely affected by the monopolistic position of the iron producers, which in turn in the long run would have reduced the sales of steel. To provide at least for gradual relief, the Austrian steel producers granted to the steel consuming industries an agreement which paid out partial refunds of the price differentials between Austrian and international steel prices in the case that goods made of steel were exported.[58] With no doubt, this measure gradually improved the situation of the exporting mechanical engineering industry in Austria, but this effect was partially set off by the costs of additional bureaucratic measures.

All in all, modernization of the plants and institutional developments allowed only for a moderate recovery of the Austrian coal and steel production after 1918.

Table 10: Production of the Oesterreichisch Alpine Montangesellschaft 1912-1928 (in 1000 tons)

	Coal	Ore	Raw iron	Steel (ingots)	Rolled material
1912	1206.8*	1874.4	583.5	504.1	321.2
1919	640.7	244.3	59.4	115.2	70.6
1928	1072.2	1913.1	458.3	451.3	279.6

*Mines in Austria and Orlová (Czech lands).
Sources: Compass 1914, vol. 2, 358, Compass Österreich 1931, 661.

After a near breakdown of production in 1919, a slow and volatile recovery followed. All in all, the different categories of products achieved different growth rates. Due to large investments into the coal mines on Austrian territory, Alpine increased the domestic output of brown coal to a level similar to the total output of mines she had owned in the Alpine and Czech lands before the war.[59] Obviously, the company has pursued this strategy in spite of higher production costs in Austria to decrease the dependence of coal imports. Since other Austrian coal producers behaved in the same manner, total domestic brown coal output rose from to 2.5 million tons in 1912 to 3.3 million tons in 1928.[60] But the Austrian industry remained dependent of imported hard coal which was essential for most of the metallurgical processes.

The ore deposits owned by the Alpine had been a main reason why Stinnes purchased a majority share. In fact, the new owners were able to raise output slightly beyond the pre-war level, and the process of roasting the ore was made much more efficient thanks to a newly invented dehydrating process.

Output of metallurgical products (crude iron, steel, and rolled material) yet remained significantly below the level of 1912.

The number of employees fell from more than 17,000 in 1917 to some 13,000 in 1919 and reached again a maximum of more than 17,000 in 1922. Thereafter, the workforce was reduced to some 13,000 persons in 1926/27 due to investments in increased productivity and did not recover to more than 14,000 during the most productive years 1928 and 1929.[61]

In terms of dividends and profitability, Alpine was not a successful investment for the German owners. After dividends were completely cancelled from 1924 to 1927, the years 1928 and 1929 brought modest payments of 4 percent of the nominal joint stock capital. Thereafter, dividends were cancelled again due to the ongoing economic crisis. In most of the years, profits were near to zero, only in 1928 and 1929 they rose to modest 2.5 million schilling. For comparison, in 1912 profit had amounted to some 24 million crowns (34 million schilling).[62]

3.2 Selected Mechanical Engineering Companies

As examples for companies depending on steel as input factor, Skoda (Czechoslovakia) and the two Hofherr-Schrantz-Clayton-Shuttleworth companies for agricultural machines that were situated in Hungary and Austria, are portrayed.

The Skoda joint stock company was founded in 1899 by the Creditanstalt and Bohemian Escomptebank to reorganize the works for armament and machinery of Emil Skoda. The following years saw massive investments, and from 1906 on, the Skoda works were sufficiently strengthened to pay out dividends. In 1914 the corporation acquired a dominating share of a powerful competitor named United Machine Factories Ltd., and during the war, the capacities of the entire group were massively expanded for war production.[63]

After the war, Skoda got under acute financial pressure due to indebtedness at her banks, urgent needs to convert war production to output for the peace economy and voluminous claims on the former Habsburg state that could not be brought in.[64]

In October 1919 politicians and business personalities from Czechoslovakia and France arranged that the French group of Schneider et Cie., Creusot became majority shareholder of Skoda. In accordance with the "nostrification" law, the central offices were transferred from Vienna to Plzen, and the German-speaking board members were substituted by Czech and French citizens.[65] In 1923, Skoda managed to obtain a loan of one million pound sterling at an interest rate of 8 percent, which was issued by the British and Allied Investment Corp. at a price of 92 percent. In 1925 and 1926 new loans at even better conditions were placed, which allowed for a conversion of the older loan and for substantial investments and acquisitions.

Between 1921 and 1925, several companies were merged with Skoda, among them the United Machine Factories (1921), a coal mine in Nýřany (1923), the Iron and Steel Joint Stock Company in Hrádek (1924) and the most successful Czechoslovak car factory Laurin & Clement (1925). Furthermore, Skoda acquired a shipyard at the river Danube (1924), two works for electrical engineering (1927 and 1928) and substantial shares of the Federal Arms Factory in Brno (1924), a factory for electric cables (1925), the Joint Stock Company for the Construction of Machines and Bridges in Adamsthal (1928) and the Joint Stock Company for Road Construction (1929).[66] The company ran an international network of sales subsidiaries and several producing subsidiaries in Central and Eastern Europe.[67]

Table 11 illustrates the development of joint stock capital, equity, and balance from 1912 to 1928.

Table 11: Joint stock capital, equity and balance of the Skoda joint stock company 1912 to 1928

	Currency	Joint stock capital	Equity	Balance
1912	Mill. gold crowns	35.0	47.95	100.78
1912	Mill. Kč	239.4	327.98	689.33
1922	Mill. Kč	194.0	229.88	1702.86
1928	Mill. Kč	200.0	751.55	2266.71

Source: Compass, div. years.

A comparison of the post-war years to the pre-war balance in gold crowns reveals that between 1912 and 1928 equity grew by the factor 2.2 and total balance by the factor 3.3. Thanks to the availability of reasonable loan capital, the process of rapid internal and external growth after the war has increased the leverage.

In the late 1920s, the company employed some 30,000 workers and white collar workers. The most important production centres in Czechoslovakia were Plzen (cast steel, rolling stock, arms, and ammunition), Plzeň-Doudlevce (machines, bridges), Hradec Králové (machines, boilers), Prague (machines, foundry, and boilers), Hrádek (Martin steelworks, etc.), Komarno (shipyard), Brno (electro technical engineering) and Mladá Boleslav (cars). All in all, Skoda was the leading company in mechanical engineering and above all, the Peace Treaties left the firm as the only important manufacturer of armaments in Central and Eastern Europe.[68]

Decisions concerning investments and the production program were determined by the French shareholder, which meant that seeking for profitability had to fit in with the higher strategies of the entire Schneider combine.[69] For some product lines like cars it must have been a certain disadvantage to be situated in a small domestic market. For cars most successor states charged tariff rates around 40 percent, which impeded exports and worked against cost reductions by economies of scale. As a consequence, producers in small markets suffered from massive cost disadvantages compared to manufacturers situated in big domestic markets like the United States, France, or Germany.[70] This problem was even more severe for Austrian car manufacturers like Steyr-Works Ltd. In spite of difficulties due to the fragmentation of Central and Eastern European markets, the Skoda group could be run quite profitably, thanks to its modernisation of the production facilities and access to reasonable financial resources. From 1922 to 1929 each year a dividend of more than 10 percent of the nominal joint stock capital was paid out. In 1929 and 1930 the dividend rose to 28.125 percent. While payments had to be suspended from 1931 to 1933, the company thereafter profited from the international armament boom before World War II and dividends again increased from 9 percent in 1934 to 22.5 percent in 1938.[71]

In Budapest and Vienna, before the war, the families of Hofherr and Schrantz founded works for the production of agricultural machinery. In close cooperation with the Boden-Credit-Anstalt in 1908, the factories were converted into two separate joint stock companies. The corporations were firmly linked together by common owners of blocks of shares, common board members and the dominating influence of the Escompte-Gesellschaft.

In 1911/1912 the Hofherr firms acquired the factories of Clayton & Shuttleworth, a British manufacturer of agricultural machinery, in Austria and Hungary. They were renamed into Hofherr-Schrantz-Clayton Shuttleworth Ltd., Budapest and Hofherr-Schrantz-Clayton Shuttleworth

Factory for Agrarian Machinery Ltd., Vienna. The purchase price pending was scheduled to be paid during the following years, but payments were suspended during the war.[72] Around 1913, the Austrian Hofherr works employed some 2,000 workers and the Hungarian sister company had some 1,400 personnel. Compared to Skoda, this was not a very impressive scale, but the size of the companies was above the average of the Austrian and Hungarian mechanical engineering sector, which was dominated by medium-sized firms.

During the first post-war years both Hofherr companies faced similar economic problems, while during the second half of the decade they experienced very different developments. In 1919 the existence of both firms was threatened by acute declines in sales and hard currency debts from pre-war times. The claims of Clayton & Shuttleworth amounted to 160,000 pound sterling, and the Länderbank had granted reimburse loans of 2 million French francs. In 1920 the claims were settled by an increase of the joint stock capital and by handing over substantial blocks of shares to the creditors.[73]

After the war, business was impaired by a multitude of trade restrictions, malfunctions of the transport system and substantial increase in tariffs and freight rates. Eventually, from the beginning of the 1920s, accelerated currency depreciation provided for a kind of export premium and both Hofherr firms managed to move into the profit zone again, yet at a reduced level of business activities.

At the same time, indebtedness with banks increased and expensive interest payments consumed an increasing share of gross earnings. In the course of the inflation years, further increases of capital followed. As a consequence, the shares of the British partners were watered down and business contacts came to an end. In Vienna, several increases of joint stock capital were managed by a syndicate led by the Escompte-Gesellschaft. In Budapest, the Hungarian General Creditbank won out in a competition for a dominating share of the Hofherr corporation against the National Banking Corporation Ltd. and decided to continue cooperative relations with the Austrian sister company. The two manufacturers continued an accord with respect to sales markets. Each firm exclusively served the domestic market, and Vienna delivered to Czechoslovakia, Poland and Romania while the Hungarian company exported to Greece, other Balkan countries and Turkey. Exports to Italy were shared among the two companies.[74]

Since Hungary still was an agrarian economy and investment activities gradually recovered during the second half of the 1920s, Hofherr in Budapest was able to make 80 percent of her turnover on the domestic market, while exports mainly contributed to increasing capacity utilization and reducing average costs.

The Austrian Hofherr corporation however had to effect 50 to 70 percent of her sales in foreign countries, which were shielded by increasing tariff rates. To secure these foreign markets, an expensive structure of sales agencies in Czechoslovakia, Poland and other countries had to be maintained. The subsidiaries in Romania were sequestrated after the war, and the Czech subsidy was converted into a separate joint stock company with domestic production in 1928 to avoid tariff problems and to comply with the "nostrification" legislation. During the years from 1927 to 1929 losses of foreign sales were gradually offset by deliveries to Soviet Russia, which were made possible by export loan guarantees granted by the city council of Vienna.[75] The sales to Russia and other export deliveries required to allow increasing periods for payment, which in turn raised the indebtedness of the company.

As a consequence of the export barriers, capacity utilization in Vienna always remained at a low level (between 50 and 60 percent), which impeded economies of scale and kept costs on a high level. Furthermore, the works had to produce a big multitude of different types of machines due to the different requirements of foreign markets, which as well increased costs. In spite of increases of the joint stock capital, the amount of bank loans increased. Peaks of indebtedness were reached each year in spring due to the fact that both of the companies had to continue production during the entire business year while the season for sales was limited to the period from April to August. Since the corporations were too small to directly approach "Western" finance they remained in complete dependence of expensive domestic bank loans. Interest payments continued to absorb a large quantity of gross earnings and means for investments remained scarce.

Due to this demanding business environment, the Viennese factory had to reduce the number of workers from 2000 before the war to around 1400.

Table 12: Turnover and profits of Hofherr, Schrantz, Clayton, Shuttleworth Ltd., Vienna

	Turnover (million schilling)	Profits (1000 schilling)
1925	17.0	395
1926	17.0	-218
1927	13.5*	-20
1928	16.0	56
1929	17.5	59

*Decision to found subsidiary firm in Czechoslovakia
Source: *Die Bilanzen*, 1 Feb. 1930, 193-94.

All in all, the turnover of Hofherr Vienna showed a stagnant development between 1925 and 1929. The years 1927 and 1928 saw a first setback due to the separation of the Czechoslovak subsidy and beginning financial problems of foreign customers. Profitability was negative in two out of five years documented here and remained low in the other periods. From 1930 on, agrarian investments broke down and the Austrian Hofherr company practically was bankrupt from 1931 on.[76]

The Hungarian Hofherr company found herself in a better economic position since around 80 percent of the sales were realized on the domestic market, which was protected by substantial tariff rates. Domestic sales were shared with only two relevant competitors, the First Hungarian Factory for Agrarian Machinery Ltd. and the works of the Hungarian Federal Railways. Only in the market for tractors did competition of American suppliers have to be met.[77]

Until the late 1920s steam-driven threshing machines amounted to some 60 percent of the sales. Modern machinery like tractors, irrigation plants, internal combustion engines and modern machines for mills gradually gained weight.

Due to good capacity exhaustion and profitable domestic sales the company was able to develop new products (e.g. tractors) and increase the number of workers employed to some 2,200 persons in 1927. Demand was fostered by a revival of the agrarian mortgage loan business after the stabilization of the Hungarian currency in 1924.[78]

Detrimental factors which affected the Hungarian company as well as the Austrian sister firm were increasing periods for payment and financial needs due to the seasonal nature of sales. But thanks to lower levels of wages and taxes, higher capacity utilisation and a protected domestic price level the Hungarian manufacturer was able to secure higher growth rates and profits.

Table 13: Turnover and profits of Hofherr, Schrantz, Clayton, Shuttleworth Ltd., Budapest 1926-1929

	Turnover (million pengő)	Profits (1000 pengő)
1926	11.1	606
1927	15.4	598
1928	21.5	814
1929	19.0	488

Source: *Die Bilanzen*, 18 Aug. 1925, 547; 12 July 1930, 471.

Between 1926 and 1928, nominal turnover increased by the factor 1.9 and profitability could be held at a stable level. In 1929 first signs of the impending economic crises appeared. Above all, domestic sales dropped by more than 50 percent, since capital imports from Western markets had gone down since 1928 and terms of trade for agrarian goods had deteriorated during the second half of the 1920s.[79]

When the Great Depression caused a breakdown of sales from 1930 onwards, Hofherr Budapest as well as her Austrian sister company got into massive troubles. But in contrast to the Viennese firm, the losses of Hofherr in Hungary never completely absorbed equity capital, and in 1934 the company was recapitalized by a supply of fresh joint stock capital at an extent of 2.4 million pengő, for which the Hungarian General Creditbank provided the underwriting.[80]

3.3 Mautner Textile Group

Before the war, the largest Austro-Hungarian producer in the field of textiles was the industrial group lead by Isidor Mautner. The combine was directed by the Oesterreichische Textilwerke AG, vormals Isaac Mautner & Sohn (Austrian Textile Works Ltd., formerly Isaac Mautner & Son). The firm, which had equity of 7.45 million crowns and a total balance of 27 million crowns in 1912, ran eight spinning and weaving mills in Austria, and had three subsidiary companies in Hungary and one subsidiary firm in Prussian Silesia. Furthermore, the Oesterreichische Textilwerke AG was a major shareholder of the Vereinigte Österreichische Textilindustrie AG (United Austrian Textile Industry Ltd.), which had come into existence in 1912 by a merger of 9 textile companies.[81]

During the war and post-war inflation Isidor Mautner, president of the company, continued a daring expansion strategy. Until the late 1920s the firm controlled 31 factories located in all the successor states of the monarchy, and employed nearly 9,000 workers.

Due to the Czechoslovak "nostrification" legislation, the central office was transferred from Vienna to Prague and the Živnostenská banka became the second bank Mautner cooperated with, besides the Boden-Credit-Anstalt. In Prague, the Textile Works Mautner Ltd. (Mautnerovy textilní závody) functioned as a holding company for the entire group. As a kind of sub-holding for the subsidiary firms in Hungary, Austria, Romania and Yugoslavia, the Vereenigde Textiel Maatschappijen Mautner (Rotterdam), was founded, in cooperation with the Bohemian Union Bank (Prague). Another aim of the Dutch holding was to acquire short term credits from western markets for the purchase of raw materials. The complex structure of the entire trust increased overhead costs substantially.

To enlarge factories in other successor states except Czechoslovakia was not from the start an implausible reaction to import substitution policies in the separated states and unbalanced national production structures. In Hungary, the given productive capacity was unable to meet more than a quarter of total domestic demand. Thanks to new investments and the relocation of formerly Czech and Austrian mills into Hungary, the textile industry grew rather quickly. The total number of cotton spindles increased from 33,000 in 1921 to 196,000 in 1929. This development was promoted by massive import tariffs.[82] Austria however, had "inherited" 25 percent of the cotton spinning capacities but only 9 percent of the weaving capacities of the old empire. As a consequence, during the following years the number of spindles was reduced from 1.17 million to 875,000, while the number of looms increased from 12,000 to 16,700.[83]

The Mautner companies tried to adapt to these developments. In Austria, the group invested in additional weaving capacities, while in Hungary spinning mills were expanded in relation to existing weaving mills. Yet in practice this strategy met with massive problems. In most cases it was difficult to find adequately trained workers for the new production sectors and the trust soon suffered acute indebtedness.

Thanks to the tangled structure of the international group of companies it was possible to cover up the financial difficulties in the balance sheet of the headquarter firm in Prague. Under the surface, financial problems already snowballed in the early 1920s. In 1922 share capital was raised from 24 million to 100 million Kč. Most of the new shares were taken over by Boden-Credit-Anstalt and Živnostenská banka in lieu of credit repayments. In 1925 President Mautner lost most of his personal fortune, when a bank he had founded in 1919[84] broke down. Subsequently, he resigned from the position as president.[85] His successor, Arthur Kuffler, tried to meet most urgent financial needs by taking out new loans, while means for investments to increase productivity remained scarce. Still, in 1928 the vice president of Živnostenská banka, Jaroslav Preiss, stated in an internal meeting that "relevant investments would have been necessary to modernise and economise the factories" of the Mautner group.[86] With respect to this difficult situation, increasing conflicts arose between Boden-Credit-Anstalt and Živnostenská banka. While the Viennese bank insisted that the Mautner group conceal the real situation (a strategy the Boden-Credit-Anstalt applied in her own case) and to take up further loans at high interest rates, Živnostenská pressed for a reduction of dividends to reduce demand for new loans and to use available means for necessary investments. The situation was made even worse by the fact that the Boden-

Credit-Anstalt had to charge high interest rates for the loans because of high internal costs, while Živnostenská banka worked more efficiently and had access to more reasonable financial resources. Until the late 1920s the Viennese bankers put through their strategy, which meant that Mautner built up a kind of pyramid of pretended profits and dividends financed by new loans. Finally, in 1929 Mautner and the Viennese bank collapsed. Since the failing Boden-Credit-Anstalt was taken over by the Creditanstalt, this bank also "inherited" the Mautner problems and the crash of the textile group turned out as one of the biggest loss makers in the early 1930s.

4. Conclusions

After the war corporate business in Central and Eastern Europe had to cope with acute needs for working capital and investments in worn out plants under the conditions of a radically changed business environment. Institutional impediments like political tensions connected with the foundation of new national states, the splitting of the former customs union of the Habsburg Empire, currency turbulences and new trade barriers made this task even more difficult.

Before and after the war, capital markets were dominated by leading banks, but in most countries the financial institutions worked less efficiently and had to rely on expensive finance from "Western" capital markets due to insufficient savings and tight monetary policy of the central banks. Above all, the position of the big Viennese banks was lastingly weakened. Due to the deficiencies of the banking sector, investment activities were burdened with an increased level of real interest for scarce credits.

Most industrial branches were dominated by small and medium-sized enterprises. While big firms with a sound financial status had the opportunity to directly approach foreign capital markets for cheaper finance, smaller companies remained in complete dependence of the domestic banks. As a consequence, the majority of companies had to cut back investment activities due to the high level of interest rates prevalent on national financial markets, which no doubt hampered total investments during the reconstruction years.

Only the Czechoslovak national economy enjoyed a slightly more favorable starting position than the other successor states, due to a comparatively productive agrarian sector, competitive export industries and lower foreign indebtedness.

Industrial corporations, which had been active within the borders of the old Empire, had to adapt to changed market structures, which were characterized by small national economic areas. Strategies that aimed at maintaining business activities in the entire area of Central and Eastern Europe required costly networks of national sales agencies. In many cases, local production centers were built instead of central factories to circumvent tariff barriers and national measures of protectionism. Expensive capital was tied up in hardly manageable entrepreneurial structures, and the splitting up of production made it difficult to exploit economies of scale. All those structural features caused additional cost burdens.

In the given institutional setting, from the perspective of individual firms or national branches, it was rational to lobby for increases of tariff protection to secure profitability. Furthermore, from the mid- 1920s on, national and international cartel organizations developed, which increased monopoly power of single, national industries. They could be operated even more effectively than before the war, thanks to the new national borders and trade restrictions.

As an overall effect of all the aspects mentioned, cost and price levels were increased. Big monopolistic producers—above all of basic goods like coal and steel—were able to shift their increased cost burdens to their customers. Doubtlessly, buyers of investment goods and consumer goods had to bear the brunt of the burden which on their part dampened demand for primary goods. All in all, the dynamics of economic development were impeded.

Clearly, on the macroeconomic level these structural features hampered productivity growth in agriculture and industry. Beyond that, sectoral shift from agriculture to more productive industrial production was impeded and import substitution policy provided for incentives to invest in branches with low marginal productivity, as production of coal in Austria and Hungary or agrarian production in Alpine regions.

In sum, the institutional settings of the post-war years created a social environment where conformist behavior of individual companies resulted in weak total growth. The Central and Eastern European countries found themselves in a kind of an institutional poverty trap which was the main reason why they fell short of their potential.

Notes

1. David F. Good, "The state and economic development in Central and Eastern Europe," in *Nation, State and the Economy in History*, ed. Alice Teichova and Herbert Matis (Cambridge: Cambridge University Press, 2003), 133-58; David F. Good and Tongshu Ma, "The economic growth of Central and Eastern Europe in comparative perspective, 1870-1989," *European Review of Economic History 3* (Aug. 1999): 103-37.

2. Gustav Gratz and Richard Schüller, *Der wirtschaftliche Zusammenbruch Österreich-Ungarns* (Vienna: Hölder-Pichler-Tempsky, 1930); Robert J. Wegs, *Die österreichische Kriegswirtschaft 1914-1918* (Vienna: Schendl, 1979); Zdeněk Jindra, "Der wirtschaftliche Zerfall Österreich-Ungarns," in *Österreich und die Tschechoslowakei 1918-1938*, ed. Alice Teichova and Herbert Matis (Vienna: Böhlau, 1996), 17-50.

3. Z. Drabek, "Foreign Trade Performance and Policy," in *The Economic History of Eastern Europe 1919-1975*, vol. I, ed. M. C. Kaser and E. A. Radice (Oxford: Clarendon Press, 1985), 386-89.

4. For the institutional development see the contribution of Peter Berger in this volume. For a concise overview of the political history in Czechoslovakia and Hungary see Joseph Rothschild, *East Central Europe between the Two World Wars* (Seattle: University of Washington Press, 1974).

5. I. T. Berend, "Agriculture," in *The Economic History of Eastern Europe 1919-1975*, vol. I, 148-209; Peter R. Berger, *Der Donauraum im wirtschaftlichen Umbruch nach dem Ersten Weltkrieg*, vol. 1 (Vienna: VWGÖ, 1982), 13-64.

6. Alice Teichova, *The Czechoslovak Economy 1918-1980* (London: Routledge, 1988) 24-28; Camillo Worliczek, "Die landwirtschaftliche Bodenreform der Tschechoslowakei," in *10 Jahre Nachfolgestaaten* (Vienna: Der Oesterreichische Volkswirt, 1928), 136-38.

7. Siegfried Strakosch, "Die Landwirtschaft Österreichs," in *10 Jahre Nachfolgestaaten*, 69.

8. Rothschild, *East Central Europe between the Two World Wars*, 158-60.

9. Joseph Badics, "Ungarische Landwirtschaft," in *10 Jahre Nachfolgestaaten*, 174-76; Ivan T. Berend and György Ránky, *The Hungarian Economy in the Twentieth Century* (London: Croom Helm, 1985), 54-55.

10. The low level of mechanization can be illustrated be the numerical relation of agrarian holdings to tractors. While in Hungary there were some 1.6 million holdings the total number of tractors in use only amounted to some 2,000 in 1926 and was raised to 6,000 until 1929. In Czechoslovakia in a similar manner, on a total of 1.6 million estates there were 2,294 tractors in use in February 1928. Berend, "Agriculture," 166. In the Austrian agrarian sector mechanization remained at an even lower level of development. As a consequence, human labor and draft animals remained the prevailing source of power. Roman Sandgruber, *Ökonomie und Politik* (Vienna: Ueberreuter, 1995), 369-70, 502; Roman Sandgruber, "Die Landwirtschaft in der Wirtschaft – Menschen, Maschinen, Märkte," in *Geschichte der österreichischen Land- und Forstwirtschaft im 20. Jahrhundert*, ed. Ernst Bruckmüller et al. (Vienna: Ueberreuter, 2002), 323-38.

11. Drabek, "Foreign Trade Performance and Policy," 408-13; Andreas Resch and Zdeněk Sládek, "Integrations- und Desintegrationstendenzen: Die Handelsbeziehunen 1921-1937," in *Österreich und die Tschechoslowakei 1918-1938*, 255-85.

12. Peter Eigner, "Nostrifikation und Bodenreform in den Nachfolgestaaten der Habsburgermonarchie – ein Vermögensentzug?," *Österreich in Geschichte und Literatur 45* (2001): 281-99; Vlastislav Lacina, "Kapitalumschichtungen in der Tschechoslowakei im Laufe der Nostrifizierung," in *Der Markt im Mitteleuropa der Zwischenkriegszeit*, ed. Alice Teichova et al. (Prague: Karls-University, 1997), 169-87.

13. Lacina, "Kapitalumschichtungen in der Tschechoslowakei im Laufe der Nostrifizierung," 164.

14. See Alice Teichova, *An Economic Background to Munich: International Business and Czechoslovakia 1918-1938* (London: Cambridge University Press, 1974), chs. 2 to 6.

15. Hans Kernbauer, "Zur Entwicklung des österreichischen Kapitalmarkts in der Zwischenkriegszeit," in *Der Markt im Mitteleuropa der Zwischenkriegszeit*, 98-104.

16. Berend and Ranky, *The Hungarian Economy in the Twentieth Century*, 30-55.

17. Drabek, "Foreign Trade Performance and Policy," 399, 424.

18. Agnes Pogany, "The Hungarian Financial Market Between the two World Wars," in *Der Markt im Mitteleuropa der Zwischenkriegszeit*, 125.

19. Fritz Weber, "Vor dem großen Krach: Die Krise des österreichischen Bankwesens in den zwanziger Jahren," Habilitationsschrift, University of Salzburg, 1991, 110-402; Dieter Stiefel, "Österreich," in *Europäische Bankengeschichte*, ed. Hans Pohl (Frankfurt: Knapp, 1993), 438-43.

20. Stiefel, "Österreich," 441.

21. Georg Kemény, "Ungarns Finanz- und Kreditwesen," in *10 Jahre Nachfolgestaaten*, 171-73; *Compass Čechoslovakei 1931* (Prague: Compassverlag, 1931), 246-47.

22. Ben Bernanke and Harold James, "The Gold Standard, Deflation, and Financial Crisis in the Great Depression: An International Comparison," NBER Working Paper No. 3488, Cambridge, MA, 1990, 26.

23. Hans Kernbauer and Fritz Weber, "Multinational banking in the Danube basin: The business strategy of the Viennese banks after the collapse of the Habsburg monarchy," in *Multinational enterprise in historical perspective*, ed. Alice Teichova et al. (Cambridge: Cambridge University Press, 1986), 185-99; Fritz Weber, "Große Hoffnungen und kleine Erfolge: Zur Vorgeschichte der österreichischen Finanzkrise von 1931," in *Bank Austria Creditanstalt: 150 Jahre österreichische Bankengeschichte im Zentrum Europas*, ed. Oliver Rathkolb et al. (Vienna: Zsolnay, 2005), 180-95.

24. Vlastislav Lacina, "Bankensystem und Industriefinanzierung in der Tschechoslowakischen Republik (1918-1931)," *Österreichische Zeitschrift für Geschichtswissenschaften 4* (1993): 542-47.

25. Stiefel, "Österreich"; Andreas Resch, "Wien – die wechselvolle Entwicklung eines Finanzplatzes in Zentraleuropa," *Bankhistorisches Archiv*, Beiheft 45: Europäische Finanzplätze im Wettbewerb (2006): 116.

26. P. L. Cottrell, "'Mushrooms and dinosaurs': Sieghart and the Boden-Credit-Anstalt during the 1920s," in *Universal Banking in the Twentieth Century*, ed. Alice Teichova et al. (Aldershot: Elgar, 1994), 155-77.

27. Ivan T. Berend, "Banking and the Hungarian Economy in the 20th Century," in *Bank Austria Creditanstalt: 150 Jahre österreichische Bankengeschichte im Zentrum Europas*, ed. Oliver Rathkolb et al. (Vienna: Zsolnay, 2005), 218.

28. Among the "western" consortium were the London banks Lazard Brothers Ltd., Industrial Finance & Investment Corporation Ltd., and Kleinwort Sons & Co., as well as International Acceptance Banc Inc. New York, Hallgarten & Co. New York and the German banks M. Warburg & Co. and Mendelsohn & Co. See Pogany, "The Hungarian Financial Market Between the two World Wars," 129.

29. More than 50 percent of this sum resulted from loans raised before 1924, among them foreign debt "inherited" from the imperial era. Ibid., 131-32.

30. Alice Teichova, "Interwar Capital markets in Central and Southeastern Europe," in *Der Markt im Mitteleuropa der Zwischenkriegszeit*, 88.

31. Andreas Resch, "Konjunkturelle Rahmenbedingungen, investitionshemmende Politik und Arbeitslosigkeit zwischen den Weltkriegen," in *Rationalisierung und Massenarbeitslosigkeit*, ed. Günther Chaloupek et al. (Graz: Leykam, 2009), 96; "Österreichs Volkseinkommen 1913 bis 1963," *Monatsberichte des Oesterreichischen Institutes für Konjunkturforschung*, 14. Sonderheft, Vienna, 1965, 41.

32. E. Lethbridge, "National Income and Product," in *The Economic History of Eastern Europe*

1919-1975, vol. I, 558.

33. Lacina, "Bankensystem und Industriefinanzierung in der Tschechoslowakischen Republik,", 542-50.

34. Lethbridge, "National Income and Product," 543.

35. Teichova, *An Economic Background to Munich*, 137-52; Andreas Resch, "Phases of competition policy in Europe," in *The European Economy in an American Mirror*, ed. Barry Eichengreen et al. (London: Routledge, 2008), 409.

36. *Die Bilanzen*, 5 Oct. 1929, 1.

37. *Die Bilanzen*, 3 July 1920, 155-56.

38. Teichova, *An Economic Background to Munich*, 101.

39. *Die Bilanzen*, 5 Oct. 1929, 1-2; *Compass Čechoslovakei 1931*, 740-45.

40. Teichova, *An Economic Background to Munich*, 107.

41. Andreas Resch, *Industriekartelle in Österreich vor dem Ersten Weltkrieg* (Berlin: Duncker & Humblot, 2002), 111-16.

42. *Compass Ungarn 1928*, 626-27.

43. *Die Bilanzen*, 13 Dec. 1924, 81.

44. Total volume of the loan was 3 million U.S. dollars, interest rate was 7 percent. The loan could be sold at a price of 88 percent of the nominal value.

45. *Die Bilanzen*, 11 Dec. 1926, 121.

46. *Compass Ungarn 1931*, 608.

47. Otto Hwaletz, *Die österreichische Montanindustrie im 19. und 20. Jahrhundert* (Vienna: Böhlau, 2001), 230-31.

48. Barbara Schleicher, *Heisses Eisen* (Frankfurt: Lang, 1999), 37-47.

49. Just at this time, the Prague Iron Company sold off her Alpine shares, which exerted additional pressure on the going rate. *Die Bilanzen*, 17 Apr. 1920, 109.

50. By the Germans the Erzberg could be used as a means of exerting pressure in negotiations concerning trade agreements and the formation of an international steel cartel, when ore producers in Saar and Lorraine wanted to re-negotiate trade relations with the German industry. Schleicher, *Heisses Eisen*, 88-92; Alfred Reckendrees, *Das "Stahltrust"-Projekt* (Munich: Beck, 2000), 122ff.; Charles S. Maier, *Recasting Bourgeois Europe* (Princeton: Princeton University Press, 1975), 387ff., 516ff.

51. *Die Bilanzen*, 24 Feb. 1923, 162 and 7 June 1924, 273-74.

52. *Compass 1914*, vol. 2, 359 and *Compass Österreich 1930*, 679.

53. Jens-Wilhelm Wessels, *Economic Policy and Microeconomic Performance in Inter-War Europe: The Case of Austria, 1918-1938* (Stuttgart: Steiner, 2007), 37.

54. *Die Bilanzen*, 24 Feb. 1923, 162.

55. Schleicher, *Heisses Eisen*, 184-85.

56. Wessels, *Economic Policy and Microeconomic Performance in Inter-War Europe*, 39, 172-74.

57. Founding members were the steel producers of Belgium, France, Germany, Luxemburg and Saar.

58. Andreas Resch, "Große Marktmacht in einer kleinen Volkswirtschaft: Die österreichischen

Kartelle in der Zwischenkriegszeit," in *Kartelle in Österreich*, ed. idem. (Vienna: Manz, 2003), 53-60.

59. Production in Orlová had amounted to some 150,000 tons of hard coal in 1910 and was to be increased to 300,000 tons during the following years. *Compass 1914*, vol. II, 356.

60. Karl Bachinger and Herbert Matis, "Strukturwandel und Entwicklungstendenzen der Montanwirtschaft 1918-1938," in *Österreichisches Montanwesen*, ed. Michael Mitterauer (Vienna: Verlag für Geschichte und Politik, 1974), 117, 128; Hwaletz, *Die österreichische Montanindustrie im 19. und 20. Jahrhundert*, 221.

61. Hwaletz, *Die österreichische Montanindustrie im 19. und 20. Jahrhundert*, 311-12.

62. *Compass Österreich*, div. years.

63. Resch, *Industriekartelle in Österreich vor dem Ersten Weltkrieg*, 222-28; Gerhard A. Stadler, "Die Rüstungsindustrien der Donaumonarchie und ihre Exporte nach Lateinamerika," PhD. diss., University of Vienna, 1985.

64. *Die Bilanzen*, 30 Oct. 1926, 52.

65. Teichova, *An Economic Background to Munich*, 195-217.

66. *Compass Čechoslovakei 1931*, 856-58.

67. See Teichova, *An Economic Background to Munich*, 200-01.

68. Arms factories in Hungary and Austria (e.g. Austrian Armaments Factory, Styria) had to quit this business due to the requirements of the peace treaties of St. Germain and Trianon. M. Hauner, "Military Budgets and the Armaments Industry," in *The Economic History of Eastern Europe 1919-1975*, vol. II, ed. M.C. Kaser and E.A. Radice (Oxford: Clarendon Press, 1986), 49-116.

69. "Among the bans imposed by the French concern on the Skoda-Works was an embargo on imports of certain raw materials and semi-finished goods from Germany, because the Paris head-office reserved deliveries of these for itself." Teichova, *An Economic Background to Munich*, 213-14.

70. Contemporary industrialists were very aware of this fact. See Georg Hanel, "Fragen der Kraftwagenindustrie," in *10 Jahre Nachfolgestaaten*, 61-62. For an analysis of the Austrian car manufacturer Steyr works Ltd. see Wessels, *Economic Policy and Microeconomic Performance in Inter-War Europe*, 68-70, 205-07, 349-52.

71. Hauner, "Military Budgets and the Armaments Industry," 54.

72. *Compass 1914*, vol. II, 474-75, 933.

73. The joint stock capital of the Austrian Hofherr company was raised from 45 to 60 million crowns and Clayton & Shuttleworth was let to have shares of a nominal value of 12.5 million crowns. In the same way the Hungarian company increased capital from 15.5 to 17.5 million crowns and transferred shares of a nominal value of 4 million crowns to the British creditor. *Die Bilanzen*, 29 Oct. 1921, 26.

74. *Die Bilanzen*, 25 May 1929, 382-83.

75. *Die Bilanzen*, 1 Feb. 1930, 193-94, and 12 July 1930, 470.

76. The company was put back on its feet by the banks in 1934 and taken over by the German manufacturer of agrarian machines Lanz after the "Anschluss" in 1938. Wessels, *Economic Policy and Microeconomic Performance in Inter-War Europe*, 330-31.

77. *Die Bilanzen*, 14 May 1927, 376-77.

78. Berend and Ránky, *The Hungarian Economy in the Twentieth Century*, 54.

79. *Die Bilanzen*, 12 July 1930, 471.

80. *Compass Ungarn 1935*, 489-90.

81. Resch, *Industriekartelle in Österreich vor dem Ersten Weltkrieg*, 134.

82. Berend and Ránky, *The Hungarian Economy in the Twentieth Century*, 56.

83. Johannes Jetschgo et al., *Österreichische Industriegeschichte 1848 bis 1955* (Vienna: Ueberreuter, 2004), 169.

84. *Neue Wiener Bankgesellschaft*.

85. *Die Bilanzen*, 2 Nov. 1929, 56.

86. Weber, "Vor dem großen Krach," 451.

Wealth, Poverty and Institutions in the Habsburg Empire's Successor States (1918-1929)

Peter Berger

Introduction

This paper addresses the political and institutional determinants of economic growth in post World War I East Central Europe. More precisely, it deals with the successor states of the defunct Austro-Hungarian Empire: Austria, Hungary, and Czechoslovakia, whose entire territory consisted of former Habsburg provinces, as well as Poland, Yugoslavia, and Romania who, as a consequence of the 1919 peace treaties, acquired large chunks of land previously governed by Vienna or Budapest. The focus of my analysis will be on Austria and Czechoslovakia, two countries with a relatively advanced level of industrialization, and Hungary as a predominantly agrarian state with some modern industry clustered mainly in the Budapest area.

As the Austrian economic historian Otto Hwaletz aptly remarked, the breakup of the Dual Monarchy and the subsequent redrawing of the political map of East Central Europe constituted a major experiment in "destroying the old, and creating the new."[1] In the eyes of most contemporary observers, the ultimate success or failure of that experiment was bound to depend on the quantity and quality of production factors available to each of the emerging new states of the region. With hindsight, the importance attributed in the 1920s to the resource endowment aspect appears as a logical consequence of wartime economic doctrine with its undue, if understandable, emphasis on autarchy. Economic nationalism remained high on the agenda during the Depression years and World War II, and so did the almost exclusive interest of economists, geographers and historians in the relative wealth of nations measured in millions of tons of coal, steel, or wheat, the number and equipment of factories, and the size and skills of the industrial workforce. In contrast, and to this date, no systematic effort was made to establish a link between interwar East Central Europe's fiscal, monetary, and economic performance and its levels of institutional and organizational development. The notion of "institutions" is used here in accordance with Douglass North, who defines them as a society's rules of the game—formal rules, informal norms and their enforcement characteristics. "Organizations" are defined by North as the players of the game. They operate on the economic, political or educational level, as firms, trade unions, political parties, legislatures, universities, schools, etc.[2]

Admittedly, an institutional approach to the comparative strengths and weaknesses of Austria-Hungary's interwar successor states poses a host of methodological and theoretical problems. Foremost among these problems is the near-total absence of empirical data, and of empirical studies, concerning post-World War I institutions in transition. What knowledge we possess of such critical institutional variables as the efficiency of national executives and bureaucracies, the technicalities of the policy making process, or the strength of civil society in interwar East Central Europe is contained, chiefly as dispersed anecdotal evidence, in the narratives of historians—who by the nature of things were at best marginally interested in institutions *per se*.[3]

While thus being forced to rely, overall, on weak evidence, the student of post-Habsburg institutional change must also be aware of the utter deceptiveness of some of the successor states' formal institutional arrangements. Those were often merely designed to impress foreign public opinion (including potential investors and officials of the League of Nations) by their seeming commitment to liberal constitutionalism and enlightened principles of social management while in fact concealing the pursuance by the ruling elites of extremely partisan class interests.[4]

This leads us to the next difficulty of a theoretical nature: Any attempt at explaining economic success with "good governance" presupposes an idea of what good governance is meant to be. The statements of economists and political scientists are far from unambiguous in this respect. Some scholars hold that political regimes based on democratic and free-market practice warrant positive economic growth, while others view economic controls and restricted personal freedom as prerequisites of high growth rates. In a relatively recent study dealing with interwar East Central Europe, David Good makes the point that "there seems to be no systematic relationship between the nature of political regimes in the region and their economic

The Viennese collect fire wood in the Vienna woods after the war to heat their apartments. (Photo courtesy of Picture Archives of the Austrian National Library, Vienna)

A Viennese lady scrounges for food in garbage piles. (Photo courtesy of Picture Archives of the Austrian National Library, Vienna)

performance."[5] However, he distinguishes between the intra-regional comparison of real growth rates (suggesting in his view that both democratic and autocratic regimes were capable of promoting economic growth), and an alternative approach juxtaposing actual growth figures with the *growth potential* of nations. Here, the underlying assumption is that low-income economies have the potential to outgrow competitors with a higher initial per capita income. If they fail to do so, responsibility rests with a flawed institutional setting.

In the following pages I will argue that the democratic and enlightened content of political and social institutions, if present, was of no small importance for the economic performance of East Central European states, at least during the 1920s. I will further argue that, in the case of the poorer countries of our sample, good governance was (or rather would have been) a prerequisite for utilizing the leverage on growth of a comparatively low initial income level. In the descriptive sections that follow I hope to arrive at an assessment of the quality of governance in each of the successor states. The focus here will be on four institutional variables: (1) the degree of political freedom as expressed in the constitutional division of power between legislative and executive, and in the uncompromised character of elections; (2) the susceptibility to corruption of the bureaucracy; (3) the amount of class, nationalistic or religious bias in foreign, economic and social policies; and, finally, (4) the capability of the educational system to promote skills employable for sustained economic development.

Before entering into the country-by-country analysis, some statistical evidence concerning the relative economic strength (and growth performance) of the successor states is presented in Tables 1-3. The choice of 1920 as a point of reference was dictated by convenience rather than historical logic: For no other year of the early post-war period do we possess a complete picture of East Central European income distribution. The reader should bear in mind, however, that in 1920, Poland was still at war with the Soviet Union, parts of Hungary suffered occupation by Yugoslav troops, and in Czechoslovakia a general strike following the political separation of Social Democrats and Communists threatened the stability of the republic.

Table 1: Six successor states of the Habsburg Monarchy, ranked according to their 1920 levels of per capita GDP (in 1990 international Geary-Khamis dollars, and relative to Czechoslovakia = 100)

	Per capita GDP in 1920	Position relative to Czechoslovakia
Austria	2.412	124.78
Czechoslovakia	1.933	100
Hungary	1.709	88.41
Yugoslavia	1.054	54.52
Romania	831	42.99
Poland	676	34.97

Source: OECD Development Centre, ed., *The World Economy*, vol. 2, *Historical Statistics* (OECD: Paris, 2006), 440, 478.

Table 2: Six successor states of the Habsburg Monarchy, ranked according to their 1929 levels of per capita GDP (in 1990 international Geary-Khamis dollars, and relative to Czechoslovakia = 100)

	Per capita GDP in 1929	Position relative to Czechoslovakia
Austria	3.699	121.54
Czechoslovakia	3.042	100
Hungary	2.476	81.39
Poland	2.117	69.59
Yugoslavia	1.364	44.83
Romania	1.152	37.86

Source: OECD Development Centre, ed., *The World Economy*, vol. 2, *Historical Statistics* (OECD: Paris, 2006), 440, 478.

Table 3: Changes in per capita GDP of six successor states of the Habsburg Monarchy, 1910, 1920, and 1929. (1990 international Geary-Khamis dollars)*

	1910	1920	Increase/ decrease 1910-20, in %	1929	Increase/ decrease 1920-29, in %
Austria	3017 (3290)	2429 (2412)	-19.5/-26.7	3722 (3699)	+53.2/+53.3
Czecho-slovakia	2495 (1991)	1935 (1933)	-22.4/-2.9	3046 (3042)	+57.4/+57.4
Hungary	2192 (2000)	1707 (1709)	-22.1/-14.6	2473 (2476)	+44.9/+44.9
Poland	1690 (1690)	678 (-)	-59.9	2120 (2117)	+212.7
Romania	1660 (1660)	828 (-)	-50.1	1153 (1152)	+139.3
Yugoslavia	1525 (1057)	1056 (1031)	-30.8/-2.45	1368 (1364)	+29.5/+30.6

*Good and Ma proxy measures of 1999. In brackets: A. Maddison estimates based on Good and Ma.

Source: OECD Development Centre, ed., *The World Economy*, vol. 2, *Historical Statistics* (OECD: Paris, 2006), 440, 478; David F. Good, "The State and Economic Development in

Central and Eastern Europe," in *Nation, State, and the Economy in History*, ed. Alice Teichová and Herbert Matis (Cambridge: Cambridge University Press, 2003), 138.

Institutions in the service of revisionism: the case of Hungary in the 1920s

Historical literature is unanimous in the judgment that Hungary belonged to the countries least successful in digesting the consequences of World War I.[6] Prior to 1918, the Lands of the Crown of Saint Stephen had been a multi-ethnic state in which the non-Magyar nationalities represented a numeric majority[7] exposed to strong pressures of linguistic and cultural Magyarization. Allegedly, the refusal by Hungary's ruling elite to grant the Slavs, Germans and Romanians cultural autonomy, let alone to enfranchise them, was grounded in the "threat" that these ethnic groups posed to the survival of the Magyar nation. In practice, the Magyars' supposed interests were just those of a small but politically powerful stratum composed of the feudal nobility, the lesser aristocracy or gentry holding a large portion of the country's administrative jobs, and the industrial-financial bourgeoisie in which the Jewish element played an important part. Entirely geared to the needs of this power triangle, the pre-war Hungarian constitutional system deserved to be called "isolated, narrow, and brittle" (Joseph Rothschild). It has been said that Hungary's annual GDP growth rate between 1870 and 1910, exceeding that of Austria by a margin of 1.45 to 1.25, to some extent justified her obsolete and partisan policy styles. But relatively rapid growth may as well have been due to an initial income level significantly lower than Austria's (1.180 vs. 1.891 Geary-Khamis dollars in 1870).[8]

In the wake of defeat and territorial dismemberment, the pendulum of Hungarian post-war politico-constitutional development swung from moderate left dominance to Soviet-style dictatorship, and back to an aristocratically tinted right-of-center regime. To begin with, Count Mihály Károlyi's revolution of October 1918 swept away the monarchy and the king alike, and turned Hungary into a federalist republic in which all adult citizens irrespective of their mother tongue were to have full voting rights. However, elections were postponed until after the signing of a peace treaty, and hence did not take place during Károlyi's brief tenure.[9] The socialist/trade unionist coalition backing his government failed to secure Allied support against territorial claims presented to Hungary by her northern, eastern, and southern neighbours. As a consequence of the obvious uselessness of appealing to Anglo-French generosity in setting the peace terms, Béla Kun of the splinter Communist party, who advocated a Soviet-

Russian alliance to regain Transylvania (from the Romanians), Vojvodina (from the Serbs) and Slovakia (from the Czechs), was to become head of a leftist coalition government and Hungary's strongman in March 1919. Kun, a Jew, ex-POW in Russia and eyewitness to the Bolshevik triumph in 1917, enjoyed the tacit support of conservative revisionist circles and, more important, the active backing of some of the old Habsburg army's most gifted officers. His government embarked on a course of military adventurism vis à vis Hungary's neighbours, coupled with an equally daring crusade in interior politics, implying expropriation of the large landowners (without, however, distributing the confiscated holdings to the land-hungry peasantry), and radical reforms of, inter alia, the educational system and family law.[10] In August 1919 Kun's Soviet regime was ousted after only 133 days in office by an intervention of Romania's armed forces. The seizure of Budapest by the Romanians prepared the ground for a "white" Hungarian counterrevolution led by prominent aristocratic figures such as Pál Teleki and Gyula Károlyi (cousin of Mihály Károlyi), but owing its extremely violent character to gentry officers like Gyula Gömbös, a devoted anti-Semite and Germanophile who in the early 1930s was to become Hungary's first fascist head of government.

While a number of semi-private officers' bands crossed Hungary from West to East, terrorizing real or suspected sympathizers of Kun's fallen regime (Jewish citizens being their preferred target), a new Hungarian National Army was formed under French patronage, its commander being Miklós (Nicholas) Horthy, a Protestant gentry nobleman from Eastern Hungary and former admiral of the Habsburg navy. Early in 1920, parliamentary elections produced a solid right-of-center majority, partly due to the fact that the Socialists withdrew their candidates from the ballot under semi-overt white pressure. Technically, the 1920 elections were the fairest ever held in interwar Hungary. A decree issued in November 1919 broadened the franchise to include a record 39.5 percent of the population, the voting age for both men and women being set at twenty-four years, and property (but not educational) qualifications being abolished. Soon after the ballot, the National Assembly proceeded to settle the constitutional issues of the country. The monarchy was reintroduced. But neither was a new king elected nor was the monarch-in-exile, Charles IV Habsburg, recalled to the throne. Instead, a compromise solution appeasing both "free electors" and "Habsburg legitimists" consisted in letting the Parliament appoint a caretaker regent to be vested with almost every constitutional prerogative of the Crown of Saint Stephen. On 1 March 1920 the regency was bestowed upon Miklós Horthy, who held his high office until the Germans forced him into abdication and imprisonment in October 1944.[11] Nine months after Horthy's installation, the National Assembly faced the ungrateful and traumatic task of ratifying the Trianon Peace Treaty, by which Hungary lost two-thirds of her pre-war area and more than half of her population (3 million ethnic Magyars and practically all the nationalities). From this point onward, passionate revisionism—and its alleged prerequisite, the concentration of power in the hands of the landowning (aristocratic) and big business (bourgeois) elites—became the alpha and omega of Hungarian political thought and action.

Hungary's pre-eminent politician of the 1920s was count István (Stephen) Bethlen, whom Horthy appointed premier in April 1921. A Calvinist magnate expelled from his native Transylvania by the occupying Romanians, and a talented power-broker, Bethlen quickly earned the respect of both radicals and conservatives within Hungary's ruling establishment, not least because of his views on democracy, which he considered an ineffective form of government for countries faced with external constraints or deeply rooted social problems.[12] Soon after Bethlen's assuming the premiership, he proceeded to dismantle the relatively liberal electoral law of 1920 by elevating the voting age for women to thirty years, and reverting to rigorous educational and residency requirements. Moreover, balloting was to remain secret only in Budapest and seven other autonomous cities, while everywhere else the casting of votes would henceforth be open. Since the Hungarian countryside was firmly controlled by a bureaucracy sympathetic to (and rewarded accordingly by) Bethlen's Government Party, the latter easily scored victory in every election between 1922 and 1935. In November 1926, Hungary's constitution was amended to reintroduce an Upper House of Parliament, acting as a mouthpiece of vested corporatist interests, but lacking substantial influence on legislation.[13]

No doubt the Bethlen regime accepted the challenge of modernizing the Hungarian economy, albeit for the sake of revisionism and not so much as a goal in itself. Moreover, economic development was supposed to leave the rigid Hungarian caste system intact, a condition precluding any meaningful attempt at social reform. The option of fighting rural poverty by means of a redistribution of estate holdings was not seriously taken into account, despite a limited land reform in 1920 affecting not more than one-ninth of the arable land.[14] To explain its soft stance vis-à-vis the big landed interests, the government, not entirely without justification, stressed the competitive export advantage of large-scale extensive wheat growing over more intensive medium-size farming. Magnates and the landowning gentry also profited from the inflationist policies deliberately chosen by Bethlen's advisers to rid the state of the costs of war and revolution. Estate mortgage debts could be paid off at a fraction of their previous value. As soon as inflation began to threaten its beneficiaries, it was halted in 1924 by a successful appeal to the League of Nations, which sponsored a Hungarian Reconstruction Loan. It threw the gates open for a stream of foreign short-term credit flowing into the country throughout the rest of the decade, saddling it, on the eve of the Great Depression, with the largest per capita foreign debt of Europe. Hungary's collaboration with, and partial dependence upon, international high finance brought grist to the mills of Hungarian anti-Semitism. In spite of Bethlen's own commonsense approach to the "Jewish question" (he honestly opposed institutionalized anti-Judaism as represented by the Numerus Clausus Act of 1920, barring Jews from higher education, and he repeatedly stressed the importance for his government to gain the confidence of Jewish business elites at home and abroad), Hungarian society at large remained throughout the interwar period deeply suspicious of its Jewish element. Proof of that suspicion can be found in the declining percentage of Jews in the ministries, the provincial administration, and the judiciary. Nowhere did it exceed 1.7 percent.[15] Reacting to their ubiquitous discrimination, urbanized, bourgeois Jews followed a course of backing the Bethlen regime economically, but otherwise staying aloof from it. Hungary's Jewish intellectuals overwhelmingly supported smaller democratic parties or the socialist labor movement.[16]

Concerning the position of the industrial workforce within Hungary's neo-corporatism of the 1920s, Bethlen and his advisers remained deliberately ambiguous. Being aware of the pivotal role industrial development had to play in the modernization of a semi-peripheral agrarian country, they could not reasonably ignore the legitimate interests of the working class. But their vivid memories of Mihály Károlyi's and Béla Kun's socialistic experiments cautioned them against the complete political emancipation of the left. The compromise solution consisted in granting the workers piecemeal social legislation together with a limited catalogue of political rights laid down in a formal pact dated December 1921 between Bethlen's government and the Social Democratic Party. The pact allowed Hungarian labor representatives to regain control of trade union property confiscated during the white counterrevolution, to participate in elections, to organize strikes, and to enjoy full freedom of speech and press. In return, the Socialists agreed to refrain from recruiting and mobilizing activities among agricultural workers, miners, the public service, and transportation personnel.[17]

Pacification of the industrial proletariat was one sine qua non of sustained economic growth, another being the spread of elementary and higher education so as to provide all sectors of the economy with the knowledgeable workforce required. In the case of post-Trianon Hungary, public investment into higher learning served an additional purpose, that of compensating for the country's loss of political and military weight by making it a first-rate cultural power.[18] Thus, economic need and nationalism worked together to reduce the Hungarian illiteracy level to a fraction of its pre-war status (5 percent of the industrial workforce and 15 percent of agricultural workers in 1930).[19] In contrast, the proportion of blue collar workers with a secondary school diploma remained insignificant throughout the interwar period (an overall 2.7 percent in 1930, only 1 percent in agriculture, but 10 percent in industry). An irresponsibly large number of graduates from secondary schools either found employment in the public sector or got transferred into an oversized university system[20] to study theology and law (40 percent), technology and economy (17 percent), or medicine and pharmacology (14 percent).[21] Alumni from the universities, reinforced by a stream of highly educated immigrants from severed ex-Hungarian territories such as Transylvania, added to a problem of "intellectual overpopulation" (Andrew C. Janos), which the Bethlen government tried to mitigate by once again inflating public administration. As a result of overstaffing and the strain on the state budget caused by bureaucratic hypertrophy, Hungarian civil servants tended to earn dramatically less than educated personnel in the professions or the business sector. Their discontent, greatly enhanced by the arrival of the Depression in East Central Europe, caused them to rally behind gentry right-wing radicalism and obscure racist ideologies which were to weaken and ultimately destroy both the Bethlen system and Horthy's rule.

Institutions in the grip of party politics: the case of Austria's First Republic, 1918-1933

If it is true that the Austrian half of the Habsburg Monarchy between 1867 and 1918 was no more democratic than its Hungarian counterpart, its politico-institutional culture still rested on very different foundations. In spite of the fact that elections to the provincial diets in all of the seventeen Austrian provinces were based on a curial system favoring the propertied and professional classes, representation in the central Parliament (Reichsrat) was more or less guaranteed for each relevant ethnic group living in Cisleithania—even before the introduction in 1907 of universal adult manhood suffrage.[22] Enfranchisement, no matter how limited, of Austria's non-Germanic nationalities was accompanied by a rise in their economic development and living standard to a level unattainable for Hungarians of non-Magyar extraction. In the words of David Good, "Cisleithanian" Austria was a weak state, her economic policies being less consequent than Hungary's due to the need to attain workable compromises between Germans, Czechs, and Poles. Growth per annum of Austrian GDP between 1870 and 1919, from an initial level somewhat higher than Hungary's, nonetheless almost reached Hungarian proportions maybe just because of this lack of "statism" in politics, indicating the prevalence of a relatively well developed civil society. As far as state intervention went, it was exercised by an honest and reliable officialdom playing the role of "modernizer from above."[23]

Universal male franchise in Austria after 1907 was counterbalanced by the monarch's right to keep governments in power against the intentions of a parliamentary majority, and by the governments' right to suspend Reichsrat sessions and to rule by emergency decrees.[24] In March 1914, just months preceding the outbreak of World War I, Parliament was dissolved for the last time under the Habsburgs by acting Prime Minister Count Karl Stürgkh. Sessions were not to be held again before October 1916. Two years from that date, with the Imperial Court's authority gone due to the lost War, and with both the Habsburg army and the civil service in disarray, the German-speaking deputies of the Reichstag's Lower Chamber (Socialists, Christian-Socials, and Pan-Germans) took the initiative in convening a Provisional National Assembly to proclaim "German Austria" a Democratic Republic, part of the neighboring Republic of Germany.

During the first interwar decade and until 1933, the pace and direction of republican Austria's institution building process were determined by four variables: the mutual relationship of the Socialist and Christian-Social mass parties; the relative strength of constitutional centralism as opposed to federalism (an issue closely connected with party politics); foreign diplomatic interference, first by the Paris peacemakers and then by the League of Nations; and, last not least, the varying influence upon public opinion exerted by the advocates of "Anschluss" (i.e. union with Germany).

In the view of the political scientist Anton Pelinka, the lifespan of Austria's First Republic (1918-1933) should be divided into three distinct stages of development of inter-party relations. He calls them the stages of concordant, competitive, and centrifugal democracy.[25] The generally democratic character of Austrian politics prior to 1933 is beyond doubt. Several attempted plots against the lawful order by local communists and their comrades of Hungarian and Bavarian origin (I refer the reader to Wolfgang Maderthaner's article in this volume) were nipped in the bud already before 1920. The rigging of election results, commonplace in Hungary, occurred in none of the Austrian national or provincial polls held until Chancellor Dollfuss' decision in 1933 to abandon the parliamentary road. Throughout the First Republic, the franchise remained universal (all adults, male and female, having the right to vote) and secret, and the principle of proportional representation applied.

The earliest all-Austrian elections were called in February 1919 to replace the Provisional National Assembly with a Constituent Chamber. The Socialists gained a relative majority, but their main opponents agreed to join them in an all-party coalition that lasted until the Pan-German party, unwilling to underwrite the paragraph of the Peace Treaty of Saint-Germain prohibitive of the Anschluss, withdrew their representatives from the Cabinet (September 1919).[26] The remaining thirteen months of Austrian concordant democracy were overshadowed by a widening ideological rift between the "red" and "black" partners in government[27], whose mutual antipathy was dampened only to enable a unanimous vote on the new Austrian constitution prepared by the eminent law professor Hans Kelsen.

This was, in the words of the historian Steven Beller, a rather progressive document despite the fact that Socialist principles had to be watered down considerably to reach a compromise acceptable to Austrian political Catholicism.[28] Kelsen's constitution devised Austria as a moderately centralized federal state, in which real political power rested with the party or parties controlling the "National Chamber" of Parliament (as opposed to the Federal Chamber, representing the provinces). The State Presidency's functions were largely decorative, its holder being elected by the deputies of both the National and Federal Chambers. Originally, constitutional federalism was strongly resented by the Austrian left, but supported by conservatives, since all Austrian provinces with the exception of Lower Austria/Vienna had a Christian-Social majority. But when Vienna was declared an autonomous province (1 January 1922), the Socialists learned to appreciate federalism as a means to insulate their proletarian stronghold from an increasingly hostile political climate.

As long as the left could make its influence strongly felt in Austrian government, social legislation—and institutions designed to promote social partnership—enjoyed top political priority. Together with the eight-hour workday and paid holidays, works councils were introduced in industry. Jobless persons were entitled to a dole. Briefly, de-privatization ("socialisation") of large enterprises was contemplated by a joint commission of experts from the red and black camps, but the project was silently discarded when in mid-1919, following the fall of Hungary's communist regime, Christian-Social resistance to it stiffened. Since post-war tax returns proved insufficient to warrant expensive social policies, Austria's financial authorities resorted to inflation. Like in Hungary, money depreciation also helped to solve the problem of state indebtedness and speeded up economic recovery (e.g. by giving exports a competitive edge on the world market). Austrian anti-Semitism, rampant since the arrival in 1914 of more than 100,000 Jewish refugees driven westward by Russian offensives into Austrian Galicia, received yet another boost from the miraculous wealth amassed within the shortest time by inflation profiteers of Jewish origin.[29] Inflation was halted with the financial assistance of the League of Nations when it ceased to fulfil its dual task of preserving social peace and the wealth of those who had skilfully exploited it (1922). Much to the chagrin of Austria's Pan-Germans, but also of the Socialists, the League loan was made conditional upon a renewed declaration of the government to defend Austrian independence—in other words to renounce union with Germany.[30]

The era of Austrian "competitive democracy" (1920-1927) was ushered in, according to Anton Pelinka, by elections held immediately after the passage through parliament of Kelsen's constitution. Cooperation between government and opposition did not, however, cease completely during this period of conservative political dominance. Proof can be found, inter alia, in the Socialists' de-facto support for the League of Nations loan, despite its obvious consequence of shifting the burden of economic reconstruction from the shoulders of the rich onto those of the average taxpayer. Without ever being popular among native opinion leaders and the political elites, the League's influence, while promoting administrative centralization and retrenchment[31], worked to stabilize Austria's political system and institutions. It could, however, neither prevent frequent Cabinet changes (meaning also rapid fluctuation in government personnel), nor the ever-more conspicuous militarization of Austrian political life. All in all, the First Republic counted twenty-four Cabinets with an average tenure of less than eight months. Since there were only coalition Cabinets, inter-party bickering was the most common reason for a government's premature fall. Less frequently, Cabinets resigned as a consequence of unbridgeable differences within the leadership of the Christian Social party, usually the one holding the Chancellor's office.[32] Fragmentation of Austrian socio-economic pressure groups matched the level of political polarisation. In the field of trade alone, more than 300 lobbying organisations, most of them connected with one or the other party of the bourgeois-peasant camp, catered to the needs of their respective clientele.[33]

The steady rise in importance of private armies acting as military backup for either the Socialists or the anti-Marxist forces set the stage for Austria's slow but steady transition from democracy to authoritarianism. In the contest for controlling the streets, right-wing militias such as the "Heimwehr" were decidedly more aggressive than their proletarian counterparts. The Heimwehr's success in suppressing a general strike, called by the Socialists in reaction to police violence against demonstrating workers (15 July 1927), marked a watershed in Austrian interwar history. Inaugurating what Pelinka calls the stage of centrifugal democracy, the "Justice Palace riots" triggered a massive assault of the right on the constitutional foundations of the First Republic. In December 1929 the Socialist party, under heavy political pressure and following protracted negotiations, reluctantly assented to changes in the 1920 constitution. These involved a substantial increase of the state president's power relative to parliament. A surprise offer at forming a black-and-red coalition government, made by the Christian Socials following disclosure of the Credit-Anstalt bank's dire straits in summer 1931, was somewhat myopically rebuffed by the Socialist leader, Otto Bauer. From this point onward, the Austrian left was locked in a hopeless struggle against the Great Depression undermining the morale of its constituency, and against a desperate ruling alliance of Catholics and Heimwehr trying to take the wind out of the sails of emergent Nazism by stepping up anti-Socialist policies. Austria's government under Chancellor Dollfuss (1932-34), despite a renewed appeal to the League of Nations for economic and financial assistance (which indeed arrived in 1933), was decidedly more corporatist than capitalist in outlook. Both its social and economic policies, but even more so its choice of killing Austrian political pluralism, testified to a deep-seated anti-modernist resentment[34], and hence failed to result in an improvement of the average citizen's living standard so as to neutralize the impact of Hitler's Anschluss propaganda.

To be sure, pan-German sentiment in Austria antedated the Nazi's siren songs and was deeply engrained in the minds of the better educated since the early stirrings of ethno-nationalism in the Habsburg Empire. Notably those institutions on which the functioning of a public administration depended were already prior to 1918 heavily imbued with feelings of German national superiority: secondary schools in the provincial towns, students' corporations, and the law and philosophy faculties of the Universities of Vienna and Graz, to name but a few. As long as the Habsburg state existed, its German-speaking elites found fulfilment in their self-imposed mission to "civilize" and develop the non-German peoples of the realm. With the advent of the republic, and the pressure exerted upon its bureaucracy first by inflation and later by the retrenchment program of the League of Nations, the higher echelons of the civil service either indulged in fruitless Habsburg nostalgia or pinned their hopes on Austrian union with Germany, still considered a first-rate power despite her defeat in the War. Societies for the promotion of the "Anschluss" mushroomed all over the country, some of them emulating the rituals and discreetness of freemasonry. Membership consisted of mostly younger men with an educated, upper middle-class background and political affiliations ranging from Pan-German to Catholic or even Socialist. Given the anti-Semitic tendency of organizations like the "Deutscher Klub" or "Österreichisch-Deutscher Volksbund," Jews as a rule did not join them. Among the Jewish financial and commercial bourgeoisie, heavily concentrated in Vienna, the idea of a "Danubian" confederation of successor states of the Habsburg Monarchy enjoyed far more support than the notion of Anschluss. But the majority of Austria's Jewish intelligentsia strongly identified with the achievements in the fields of public housing, health care, and educational reform of Socialist counterculture in Red Vienna.[35] The deadly blow dealt to East Central European business by the economic crisis of the 1930s, and the violent liquidation of Socialist rule in Vienna after the short Civil War (1934), foreshadowed both the end of Austrian Jewry and of Austrian independent statehood.

Institutions as a vehicle of national unity: the case of Czechoslovakia in the 1920s

In 1918/19 the Czechoslovak state was born, thanks to the diplomatic skills and perseverance of a small group of internationally renowned politicians like Tomáš G. Masaryk and Edvard Beneš, and the success of a national-democratic revolution[36] in Prague during the final days of the Habsburg Empire. Czechoslovakia came to include within her frontiers territories with vastly different political, administrative and economic traditions. Throughout the interwar period, the young state faced the challenge of integrating its component parts, inhabited by a large number of nationalities, into a coherent political unit. In a way, Czechoslovakia's problems resembled those of neighboring Poland, a patchwork of very unevenly developed former Russian, Prussian, and Austrian lands.[37] But while the Poles could claim that their provinces' common history from medieval times up to the eighteenth century, and a degree of national coherence provided by the presence everywhere of a strong Polish ethnic element, justified modern political union, this was not evidently so in the case of Czechoslovakia. True, Czechs could boast of their medieval and early modern statehood as much as the Poles could. But Slovakia and the Carpathian Ukraine (Ruthenia) had never belonged to the historic Kingdom of Bohemia. For a thousand years both had formed an integral part of Hungary. Also, the existence of a single Czechoslovak nation, stubbornly insisted upon by Masaryk and his colleagues to win Allied support at the Paris Peace Conference and defeat Hungary's "historic" claims on Slovakia, remained a contested issue among both Czechs and Slovaks throughout the 1920s and 1930s. It has been said that Czechoslovak territorial consolidation following World War I was a matter of luck and Allied tutelage[38] rather than being dictated by reason. Be that as it may: In the management of their state's internal and economic affairs the Czechoslovak leaders displayed remarkable capabilities, and it was certainly not due to luck that their country until 1938 enjoyed a higher degree of democracy and prosperity than any of the states surrounding it.

This is not to say that the process of building political institutions was entirely without drawbacks. When in October 1918 the Czech political parties represented in the now defunct Austrian Reichsrat convened a Provisional National Assembly, fifty-five out of 256 delegates were invited from Slovakia, but the German, Polish, Ukrainian, and Hungarian minorities abstained from cooperation or were not asked. Consequently they had no say in the negotiations for a new republican constitution, which was adopted on 29 February 1920.[39] It conferred legislative power on a Chamber of Deputies numbering 300 members, while the right to elect the state president (whose executive functions were considerable) fell to a National Assembly comprising both the Chamber and a 150-member Senate. Czechoslovakia was to have universal, direct, secret, and compulsory franchise, the voting age for the Senate being set somewhat higher than that for the Chamber. Real power rested with the parties, due to the fact that votes were cast for them and not for individual candidates. Parliamentary seats were distributed by the party machines according to "fixed lists" arranged prior to each election. This process guaranteed that MPs remained loyal to their own party's leadership, while both the large number of political groupings and proportional representation resulted in the country being governed by a series of coalitions.[40] In the early stages of the Republic these were dominated by liberal-conservatives ("Blacks"), later by socialists ("Reds"), and finally by agrarians ("Greens"). Furthermore, early coalitions had an "all-national" profile, meaning they did not include parties of non-Czech or non-Slovak ethnic affiliation.[41] In October 1926, the German Christian Social and Farmers' parties for the first time participated in a government, a move then considered to reflect the growing stability of Czechoslovakia's infant democracy.

A semi-constitutional arrangement enhancing the calculability of Czechoslovak political life, but of doubtful democratic value, was the so-called pětka. Convened for the first time in 1920 to facilitate communication between a non-party government of bureaucrats and the party apparatuses, it brought together the heads of the five most important Czech and Slovak parties (hence the name pětka, meaning committee of five) and the prime minister, for the purpose of exchanging information. Exercising its discreet and in the main beneficial influence upon all governments in office until the end of the first Czechoslovak Republic, the pětka nonetheless came under criticism for its side-stepping of parliamentary control and alleged susceptibility to corruption.

In contrast, the Czechoslovak civil service not only was spared corruption charges but also enjoyed a reputation of impeccable correctness and efficiency, largely due to the administrative experience gained by Czech citizens in the bureaucracy of Habsburg Austria.[42] Since the Slovaks and Ruthenes had been too much disenfranchised in pre-War Hungary to acquire similar skills, let alone to challenge Magyar domination of Slovakia's and the Carpatho-Ukraine's provincial administrations, the departure in 1918 of almost all Magyar officials required their replacement by native Czechs. This turned out to be a mixed blessing. Despite the Czech's honest efforts at expanding and modernizing the Slovak (and Ruthenian) educational system, including the launch in 1919 of a new Slovak university at Bratislava, and a Ukrainian one at Uzhorod-Ungvár), and despite their unquestionable merits in the promotion of social legislation, land reform, and an independent press, they were resented by many Slovaks and Ruthenes for their alleged paternalism and tactlessness.[43] Similarly, when the technical backwardness and lacking profitability of many Slovak industrial businesses made them fall victim to Czech competition (between 1918 and 1923 alone, more than 200 plants, stripped of their former protection by Hungarian customs tariffs, were closed down), the resulting unemployment brought grist to the mills of Slovakia's autonomist movement.

As in other East Central European countries, the immediate post-War years in Czechoslovakia were a period of social unrest caused by food shortages, lack of job opportunities in industry, and the hunger for land of tens of thousands of dwarfholders and agricultural labourers.[44] Governments led by Karel Kramář (of the National Democratic party) and Vlastimil Tusar, a Social Democrat in office since July 1919, enacted substantial pieces of social legislation and even contemplated nationalization of the mining and heavy industry sectors to contain far-left radicalism. Following the breakdown of Hungary's Soviet regime[45] and the final defeat of the Red Army in the Russo-Polish War of 1919-21, the threat of a Bolshevik takeover in Czechoslovakia subsided, and the pace of social reform slowed down considerably. (Similar developments occurred, as we have seen, in Austria about the same time.) However, three major achievements of the Czechoslovak reform period were to survive the political drift towards the right of the mid-1920s: currency stability, "nostrification" of industries owned by foreigners, and the confiscation of all landed property in excess of 150 hectares for the benefit of those who possessed either no land at all or too little for sustaining profitable production.

The ambitious monetary strategies of finance minister Alois Rašin—who in fact did not content himself with stabilizing the Czechoslovak Crown but allowed its exchange rate to rise to levels unwarranted by the state of the economy—made him become a highly controversial figure in domestic politics and, in the event, the only victim of political murder in the First Czechoslovak Republic. But even Rašin's opponents admitted that, by sparing his country the chaos of inflation rampant everywhere else in East Central Europe, he rendered it an invaluable service.[46] It is doubtful whether the authors of Czechoslovakia's nostrification laws did the same thing. Taking offence at the fact that not more than 20 to 25 percent of all industrial capital present in Czechoslovakia was in domestic hands, much of the rest being held by Viennese banks, the parliament in Prague issued an act requiring that joint stock companies operating on Czechoslovak soil be registered as domestic firms, that their boards of directors be staffed with Czechoslovak citizens (preferably of Czech or Slovak, but not of German or Polish nationality[47]), and that the majority of shares be owned by Czechoslovak instead of foreign financial institutions. Clearly, nostrification benefited a few large Prague banks, chiefly the Živnostenská banka, whose influence on Czechoslovak business grew at the expense of its Viennese counterparts.[48] But then, nostrification also triggered an avalanche of fake property transfers and partnership treaties to enable continued, albeit limited, Austrian and German interference in Czechoslovak business. The resulting increase in transaction costs cannot be measured accurately, but it is safe to assume that the money could have been used in more productive ways. Land reform, in contrast, was an almost universally accepted means to reduce social tension in the countryside, and to secure peasant loyalty towards the Republic. Admittedly, it sometimes served nationalist ends, as in the case of the expropriation of Hungarian magnates in Slovakia and of aristocratic German-Austrian landowners in Bohemia and Moravia, but in general the motive of promoting justice in the distribution of agricultural holdings prevailed. Profitability of the farms created or enlarged by land reform was not always guaranteed, however. Too many of the new proprietors fell into the categories of dwarf- or smallholders (one to five hectares). Also, land redistribution remained unfinished until 1938 when independent Czechoslovakia ceased to exist. This was due, inter alia, to the Agrarian party's decision to leave a number of confiscated plots in the custody of the "state office of land reform" which the party controlled, so as to utilize the proceeds of their later sale for political purposes.[49]

For Czechoslovakia, the Golden Twenties were more prosperous and lasted longer than in neighbouring Austria and Hungary. Ironically, the balanced occupational distribution of the country's population[50], being more modern in outlook than elsewhere in East Central Europe, exacerbated the effects of the Great Depression, which came to be felt for the first time in 1931. The drop in industrial exports reached dramatic proportions (33 percent between 1929 and 1933), and the independent farming sector, despite the government's readiness to resort to protectionist means, suffered from a severe fall in incomes (minus 40 percent between 1929 and 1937). Since the consumer industries that were hit hardest by the crisis were located in German-speaking areas, fresh oil was poured into the smouldering fire of earlier Sudeten German grievances. The organization of Czechoslovakia into four provinces, enacted in 1927, had destroyed German hopes for a majority in some of the twenty-four prefectures scheduled under an earlier plan for administrative reform. Rašin's policies of strengthening the Czech currency were abhorred because of their alleged deleterious impact on Sudeten German export business. The compulsory use of the Czech language in commercial documentation was resented in German business circles, which tended to ignore the generosity of Czechoslovak language law in all other respects. While in the late 1920s Sudeten German discontent showed little effect on the predominantly activist (i.e. co-operative) attitude of the German parties vis-à-vis the Czechoslovak government, matters changed when the strongest grouping opposed to activism, Konrad Henlein's "Sudetendeutsche Heimatfront" (SdHF), received financial backing from the Nazi rulers at Berlin. It is illustrative of the liberal political climate in the Czechoslovak Republic that President Masaryk, under pressure to ban the SdHF, preferred to side with the advocates of freedom of opinion. Thus, the Henlein party was allowed to destroy Czechoslovak democracy from inside.

Institutions and the clash of traditions: a brief survey of Poland, Romania, and Yugoslavia in the 1920s

Post-1918 politico-institutional unification in the three countries discussed in this section bore enough parallels to justify treatment under one heading. However, some analogies are more appropriate than others. While Poland shared with Romania and Yugoslavia the existence within the new boundaries of fairly developed and extremely backward provinces, another problem—that of reconciling different "state-nations" to the concept of national Unitarianism—was primarily one of Yugoslavia's Serbs (and reminiscent of the Czechoslovak situation). Romanians of the Regat, Bessarabia, Dobruja, and Transylvania no doubt formed one single nation, as did the Poles of Galicia, the Kongresówka and Kresy, and Poznania-Pomerania-Silesia. What separated Regateni Romanians from those in the annexed territories (and "Russian," "Austrian," and "Prussian" Poles from each other) were mutual pretensions and grievances[51] caused by their having been exposed, up to the end of World War I, to widely divergent cultural, administrative, religious and political regimes.

In the core states of Serbia and the Old Regat, which were to be enlarged by the addition of provinces of the defunct Habsburg Empire, that enlargement was seen as a just reward for high casualties suffered in the War, and ultimately of victory. Both Belgrade and Bucharest displayed a strong penchant for centralizing the administration of their new states, arguing that none of the recently "liberated" provinces possessed experience in self-rule, let alone the capability of defending itself militarily.[52] In contrast, politicians of the former Habsburg territories showed their determination to extract from their new rulers a maximum federalist content of politico-administrative reorganisation. In Croatia, a strong political current inspired by peasant radicalism squarely opposed the concept of one Yugoslav nation composed of three tribes, and insisted on the distinct national character of Croats, Slovenes, and Serbs. When it became clear that the Yugoslav "Saint Vitus Day" (Vidovdan) constitution of 28 June 1921 would deny the Croats acknowledgement as a separate nationality, peasant leader Stepan (Stephen) Radić proceeded to convene a Croat constituent assembly at Zagreb which proclaimed the "Neutral Peasant Republic of Croatia"—a symbolic move without any practical relevance, but a deliberate offence of Belgrade.[53]

On paper, the provisions of the Vidovdan Charter were impeccably democratic. Prior to King Alexander's coup d'état in 1929, legislative powers rested with the unicameral Parliament to be elected by universal, direct, and secret suffrage of males over twenty-one. Proportional representation of parties was secured and civil and religious freedom (theoretically) guaranteed. An administrative law of April 1922, however, organizing the country into thirty-three departments, was criticized everywhere except in Serbia for its exceedingly centralistic outlook. The dominance of ethnic Serbs in the military and the civil service gave rise to similar objections, the more so as Serbian officials often showed incompetence, brutality, and dishonesty.

The Romanian constitution, promulgated in 1923, was a far less enlightened document than Yugoslavia's, and despite frequent references to the French model at best pseudo-democratic. It declared Romania a centralized nation-state[54] and Romanian citizenship a prerequisite for owning land, the latter provision being dictated by xenophobia and anti-Semitism. Natural resources, oil chiefly among them, were declared state property. The right of association was severely restricted, to the disadvantage of industrial workers and farm hands. Parliament was at the mercy of the King who could dismiss it, or the government, or single ministers, at his own discretion. There was universal male suffrage, but election results were usually fabricated by the Interior ministry with the help of an exceedingly corrupt bureaucracy. Romania's 1923 Charter reflected the political dominance of the Liberal party, who between 1918 and 1928 ran most of the country's cabinets. The Liberals' power base was the Old Regat, where they could count on the support of banking, big business, and officialdom. King Ferdinand (1914-1927) was their man.

In new Poland, basic institutions of government owed their shape to suspicions of the political Right that Marshal Józef Piłsudski, the hero of the Russo-Polish War and former Socialist, aspired at presidential dictatorship. Hence, the constitutional powers of a bicameral Parliament were extended so as to reduce the presidency to an impotent organ. Cabinets and individual Cabinet ministers were to be responsible to the Lower House (Sejm) elected on the basis of universal male suffrage and proportional representation. The Polish charter of 17 March 1921 favored centralism over federalism (a result of the nationalistic and Germanophobic Right's control of the Constituent Assembly), and it failed to acknowledge the fact that the German, Ukrainian, Lithuanian, and Jewish national minorities were too numerous to warrant their full absorption into the Polish body politic—let alone their cultural assimilation.

During the early stages of Polish, Romanian, and Yugoslav statehood, inter-ethnic problems were exacerbated by debilitating regional variations of socio-economic development and a level of peasant poverty which made the threat of a Russian-inspired Bolshevik revolution seem very real. To immunize the peasants, all three states resorted to the means of land reform, but only in Romania and parts of Yugoslavia did the confiscation and redistribution measures affect a sizeable proportion of the agricultural area. In both states, the chief victims of expropriation were "foreign" estate holders (i.e. Germans, Magyars, Turks/Muslims, or Russians) whose surplus land got transferred into Romanian or South Slav hands. Conversely, the moderate character of Polish land reform can be explained by the fact that its extension would have harmed large Polish landowners and benefited members of the Byelorussian and Ukrainian minorities. Except for some regions in Yugoslavia, land reform nowhere diminished the pressures of rural overpopulation, low productivity, and backwardness.

This was due, in part at least, to the limited success of post-War industrialization policies. Theoretically, the territorial gains of the Balkan states and the resulting expansion of their home market favored the development of import-substituting industries.[55] Thus, Romania's Liberal governments of the 1920s imposed levies on agricultural exports to subsidize domestic infant industry which in turn was shielded from foreign competition by high tariff walls. But foreign direct investment was discouraged by prohibitive legislation limiting share ownership and the representation of foreign stockholders on industrial boards. (Instead, board membership was generously awarded to Liberal Party cronies and dispossessed landowners of the Romanian boyar class.) When in early 1929 the Liberals were forced out of power by the National Peasant Party advocating foreign investments and the abolition of export levies on farm produce, the about-face came too late to undo the harmful effects on industry of the incipient Great Depression.

Serbia's and Poland's industries entered the interwar period with the handicap of having suffered, between 1914 and 1918, extensive physical destruction. Post-war Yugoslavia offered the Serbs partial compensation in that a Serbian-dominated government could draw on the experience of Croatian banking and Slovenian industrial enterprises.[56] A generous endowment with coal, iron, timber, and minerals proved to be a mixed blessing, since it supported the heavily extractive character of Yugoslav industrialization. Not before the 1930s did the government at Belgrade invite foreign capitalists to develop both the industrial processing of local resources and the sector of light industry, notably textiles. Poland, in contrast, lacked the wealth in natural resources that Yugoslavia possessed, with the exception of coal and (as yet untapped) hydro-power. In the absence of a sufficiently strong internal market and unable to overcome the loss of traditional outlets in pre-War Russia, Germany, and Austria-Hungary, Polish industry remained ephemeral until serious efforts at state-guided industrialization were initiated at the time of Piłsudski's death in 1936, just three years before the Nazis' successful assault on Polish independence.

In all three countries discussed here, the failure of nascent industries to absorb rural overpopulation was matched by a superabundance of academically trained young people eager for jobs that an overwhelmingly agrarian society could not offer them. Interwar Yugoslavia alone produced an estimated 30,000 university graduates[57], two-thirds holding a degree in philosophy or law which made them suited almost exclusively for recruitment into politics or the already swollen (and underpaid) civil service. The enormous prestige enjoyed in the Balkan states by formal academic education vividly contrasted with the neglected state of primary schooling. As late as 1930, illiteracy in Yugoslavia hovered around 50 percent (Slovenia: 8 percent, Vojvodina: 23.3 percent, Croatia: 32.3 percent). In Romania, the national average of illiteracy above the age of seven stood at 43 percent (but only at 33 percent in formerly Hungarian Transylvania). Polish illiteracy was highest in the poorest provinces of Ukrainian and Byelorussian concentration (with peaks around 48 percent), but the national average in 1931 of illiteracy above the age of ten was only 23.1 percent.[58]

Given the numerous difficulties that confronted institutional integration in Poland, Yugoslavia, and Romania, the results achieved until the outbreak of the Depression were not negligible. Everywhere, new monetary regimes were introduced. In Romania and Yugoslavia, this amounted to the replacement by the Lei and the Dinar, respectively, of all currencies previously in circulation in former Habsburg or Russian provinces. However, the exchange rate set by Belgrade for converting Austro-Hungarian Crowns into Dinars failed to satisfy the Croatian public and thus exacerbated tension between Croats and Serbs. Poland substituted the Polish Mark for Austro-Hungarian, Russian, and German currencies. A brief but violent inflation was halted, in 1926, with the aid of foreign credits and the introduction of the Złoty. Yugoslavs and Romanians were spared the horrors of hyperinflation, but their currency stabilization schemes, too, hinged on foreign financial assistance. Fiscal and legal homogenization in Poland and the Balkan states proceeded at different speeds, Romania lagging far behind the rest. Romanian civil and commercial law were not applied in Transylvania before 1943.[59] Romania's record was similarly poor in the field of railroad network integration. The main lines of Transylvania and Bessarabia were geared to the pre-War Hungarian and Russian railway systems, and the Bessarabian lines were broad-gauged (like those in the formerly Russian segment of Poland). Lack of funds and government corruption prevented a reorientation of the railroad infrastructure so as to better connect the Regat with the annexed territories. Poland and Yugoslavia experienced difficulties of the same kind.

Without the debilitating effects on East Central Europe of the 1929 Wall Street Crash, the Polish, Yugoslav, and Romanian regimes might have succeeded in consolidating their limited social and economic achievements, even in expanding them. This is not to say that they would have tempered their authoritarian leanings. As early as 1926, Marshal Piłsudski staged a successful putsch against Polish parliament, transferring real power to an elite of technocrats which was able to score some results at the economic front as well as to professionalize the state bureaucracy and speed up political integration. In 1929, Serbia's Alexander Karađorđević followed suit with the abolition of the Vidovdan Constitution and introduction of Royal dictatorship, allegedly to secure unity of the Yugoslav state. In fact, the coup d'état played into the hands of the most radical elements of non-Serbian opposition. Joseph Rothschild argues that the appeal of (semi-)dictatorial government methods on East Central European political elites was reinforced after January 1933 by the Nazis' policies in Germany, rendering revisionism, ethnic prejudice, and especially anti-Semitism "psychologically respectable."[60] It is an irony that the "methods of the strong hand" advocated by the military-bureaucratic leaderships of Poland and the Balkan states in the end failed to save their countries from being overrun by German expansionism.

Conclusion

In the preceding narrative sections, I have briefly sketched out the process of institution building and institutional change in East Central Europe during the first interwar decade. Table 4, seen on the following page, is an attempt at translating the contents of my analysis into a ranking of states according to the quality of their politico-institutional framework. I have set out my requirements for good governance in the introduction to this paper. The difference between the previous checklist and Table 4 is in the inclusion in the latter of two indicators for political stability: frequency of Cabinet changes and of changes in Cabinet personnel.

Table 4: Democratic content of political institutions in six successor states of the Habsburg Monarchy, 1920-1929.

	Austria	Czechoslovakia	Hungary	Poland	Yugoslavia	Romania
Democratic distribution of legislative and executive powers	yes	yes	no	yes, until 1926	yes, until 1929	no
Election results fabricated	no	no	yes	yes, after 1926	no	yes
Frequent cabinet changes	yes	yes	no	yes, until 1926	yes	yes
Frequent changes of cabinet personnel	yes	no	no	yes, until 1926	yes	no
Class-biased politics	yes	no	yes	yes	yes	yes
Nationalistic bias in politics	no	yes	yes	yes	yes	yes
Political Anti-Semitism	yes	no	yes	yes	yes	yes
Functional higher education	yes	yes	no	no	no	no

The above results confirm that of all the states under scrutiny, Czechoslovakia seems to have been the most democratic and enlightened, in spite of frequent backroom dealing and logrolling connected with the pětka system and a tendency of the Czech bureaucracy to patronize the Slovaks and Ruthenes, albeit in a benevolent manner. At the same time, the

Czechoslovak economy of the 1920s, boasting the second-highest initial level of GDP per capita in the region, grew at a relatively fast pace (5.7 percent per annum), faster than that of Austria—whose per capita GDP in 1920 was roughly 25 percent higher than Czechoslovakia's (See tables 1 and 3). The reason for the growth differential between the two republics may have been in the relative poverty of the Slovak and Ruthene provinces of Czechoslovakia, providing her (in relation to her southern neighbor) with the leverage of backwardness. What suggests a more nuanced explanation, however, is the conspicuous slowdown in Austria's economic performance coincident with her transition from competitive to centrifugal democracy. Until 1927, the year of the Justice Palace riots, the Austrian economy outgrew its Czechoslovak counterpart. Afterwards the relationship was dramatically reversed.

Clearly, Hungary's neo-baroque political system of the Bethlen years (1921-1931) accounted for much of her disappointing economic performance in the first interwar decade. From a per capita GDP representing approximately 88 percent of Czechoslovakia's, the Hungarian economy grew at a modest average annual rate of 4.5 percent to finish roughly 18 percentage points behind the Czechoslovak GDP-level in 1929. Similarly, the Balkan states lost ground to Czechoslovakia during the 1920s, while Poland displayed an impressive energy in the catching-up race, partly due to her stunning initial backwardness, but maybe also as a consequence of Piłsudski's technocratic and semi-authoritarian style of government. The apparent contradiction lying in the economic success of both a near-model democracy (Czechoslovakia) and a pseudo-parliamentary regime (Poland) invites further research into the institutional causes of poverty and wealth.

Notes

1. Otto Hwaletz, *Der große Bruch* (Norderstedt: Books on Demand, 2008), 9.

2. See Douglass C. North's contribution to Claude Ménard and Mary M. Shirley, eds., *Handbook of New Institutional Economics* (Dordrecht: Springer, 2005), 21-30. Peer Vries uses a broader definition of institutions, regarding players, too, as belonging to the institutional realm, and emphasizing the role of the state as "super- and supra-institution." Peer Vries, *The Role of Culture and Institutions in Economic History: Can Economics be of any Help?*, <http://www.lse.ac.uk/collections/economicHistory/GEHN/GEHN-Workshops.htm>, see Konstanz 2004, 29.

3. This is not to belittle the achievement of a whole generation of Habsburg and East Central European historians who greatly contributed to our understanding of the region's interwar difficulties. One example of highly informative scholarship is Hugh Seton-Watson, "The Political System of Eastern Europe between the Wars," in *Man, State, and Society in East European History*, ed. Stephen Fischer-Galati (London: Pall Mall Press, 1970), 249-74.

4. Seton-Watson, "The Political System of Eastern Europe between the Wars," 273ff.

5. David F. Good, "The state and economic development in Central and Eastern Europe," in *Nation, State, and the Economy in History*, ed. Alice Teichova and Herbert Matis (Cambridge: Cambridge University Press, 2003), 152.

6. Joseph Held, "Notes to the Collapse of Hungarian Society between the Wars," in *Man, State, and Society in East European History*, 275-86.

7. 52 percent of the entire population, if Croatia-Slavonia is included in the Hungarian total. See Oscar Jászi, *The Dissolution of the Habsburg Monarchy* (Chicago: University of Chicago Press, 1961), 271ff.

8. Good, "The state and economic development in Central and Eastern Europe," 138, 143.

9. On Károlyi's controversial personality see George Barany, "From Fidelity to the Habsburgs to Loyalty to the Nation: The Changing Role of the Hungarian Aristocracy before 1848," *Austrian History Yearbook 23* (1992): 49.

10. Andrew C. Janos, *The Politics of Backwardness in Hungary, 1825-1945* (Princeton: Princeton University Press, 1982), 197.

11. Two attempts by King Charles IV to reclaim his throne by force, one early in 1921, the other in November of that year, were skillfully repelled by Horthy who feared international repercussions harmful to Hungary should Habsburg rule be restored.

12. Janos, *The Politics of Backwardness in Hungary*, 210.

13. Joseph Rothschild, *East Central Europe between the Two World Wars* (Seattle: University of Washington Press, 1974), 161-62.

14. Janos, *The Politics of Backwardness in Hungary*, 229.

15. Iván T. Berend and György Ránki, *Underdevelopment and Economic Growth: Studies in Hungarian Social and Economic History* (Budapest: Akadémiai Kiadó, 1979), 202.

16. Janos, *The Politics of Backwardness in Hungary*, 227.

17. Ibid., 235.

18. Peter F. Sugar, "The More It Changes, the More Hungarian Nationalism Remains the Same," *Austrian History Yearbook 31* (2000): 146.

19. Berend and Ránki, *Underdevelopment and Economic Growth*, 216.

20. Following defeat in World War I, Hungary opened new universities in Pécs and Szeged (to compensate for the loss of those of Bratislava and Cluj). Besides, there were universities at Budapest and Debrecen.

21. Berend and Ránki, *Underdevelopment and Economic Growth*, 217.

22. George Barany, "Political Culture in the Lands of the Former Habsburg Empire: Authoritarian and Parliamentary Traditions," *Austrian History Yearbook 29* (1998): pt. 1, 203.

23. See Waltraud Heindl, "Bureaucracy, Officials, and the State in the Austrian Monarchy: Stages of Change since the Eighteenth Century," *Austrian History Yearbook 37* (2006): 35-57.

24. Hermann J.W. Kuprian, "On the Threshold of the Twentieth Century: State and Society in Austria Before World War I," in *Austria in the Twentieth Century*, ed. Rolf Steininger et al. (New Brunswick, NJ: Transaction, 2002), 11-35.

25. Anton Pelinka, "Parlament," in *Handbuch des politischen Systems Österreichs: Erste Republik 1918-1933*, ed. Emmerich Tálos et al. (Vienna: Manz, 1995), 59-71.

26. Failure of the peace conference to reward Austria with German-populated territories she claimed (South Tyrol, Southern Bohemia, parts of Moravia, the Sudetenland, Carniola, and

Southern Styria) aroused some revisionist sentiment. More important, the Anschluss movement was able to bank on the peacemakers' obvious infringement of the Wilsonian principles of ethnic self-determination.

27. A bipartite government of Socialists and Christian Socials, led by the Socialist Karl Renner, stepped down in June 1920 following a relatively minor dispute over defence issues. Michael Mayr of the Christian Socials was then chosen to head Austria's last (all-party) "government of concordance," in office until elections could, for the first time, be held under the constitutional law of October 1920. Peter Berger, *Kurze Geschichte Österreichs im 20. Jahrhundert* (Vienna: Facultas, 2007), 75.

28. Steven Beller, *A Concise History of Austria* (Cambridge: Cambridge University Press, 2006), 205.

29. Niko Wahl, "Kaffeehäuser zu Bankfilialen: Ein kurzer Abriss der Wiener Spekulation," in *Das Werden der Ersten Republik,* Band II, ed. Helmut Konrad and Wolfgang Maderthaner (Vienna: Carl Gerold's Sohn, 2008), 49-66.

30. Peter Berger, "The League of Nations and Interwar Austria: Critical Assessment of a Partnership in Reconstruction," in *The Dollfuss/Schuschnigg Era in Austria: A Reassessment*, ed. Günter Bischof et al., Contemporary Austrian Studies 11 (New Brunswick, NJ: Transaction, 2003), 73-92.

31. The League-inspired reconstruction scheme called for the dismissal of 85,000 civil servants. Barbara Jelavich, *Modern Austria: Empire and Republic, 1815-1986* (Cambridge: Cambridge University Press, 1987), 175.

32. Wolfgang C. Müller et al., "Die Regierung," in *Handbuch des politischen Systems Österreichs: Erste Republik 1918-1933*, 72-89.

33. Peter Berger, "The Dynamics of Consultative Arrangements in 20th Century Europe: The Case of Austria (1945-2000)," in *Changing Liaisons: The Dynamics of Social Partnership in 20th Century West-European Democracies*, ed. Karel Davids et al. (Brussels: P.I.E. Lang, 2007), 140-41.

34. Gerhard Senft, *Im Vorfeld der Katastrophe: Die Wirtschaftspolitik des Ständestaates: Österreich 1934-1938* (Vienna: Braumüller, 2002), 243ff.

35. Paul Hofmann, *The Viennese: Splendor, Twilight, and Exile* (New York: Doubleday, 1988), 193ff.

36. Alice Teichová, *The Czechoslovak Economy, 1918-1980* (London: Routledge, 1988), 10.

37. Joni Lovenduski and Jean Woodall, *Politics and Society in Eastern Europe* (Basingstoke: Macmillan, 1987), 41.

38. This point is stressed by Johannes Koll in his contribution to the present volume.

39. For slightly more than a year an interim constitution written by a Social Democratic deputy of the Provisional Assembly was in force. See Victor S. Mamatey and Radomir Luža, eds., *Geschichte der Tschechoslowakischen Republik 1918-1948* (Vienna: Böhlau, 1980), 62.

40. Robert J. Crampton, *Eastern Europe in the Twentieth Century* (London: Routledge, 1995), 61.

41. Mamatey and Luža, eds., *Geschichte der Tschechoslowakischen Republik*, 144-45.

42. Lovenduski and Woodall, *Politics and Society in Eastern Europe*, 42.

43. Rothschild, *East Central Europe between the Two World Wars*, 120.

44. See Franz Adlgasser, "The Roots of Communist Containment: American Food Aid in Austria and Hungary after World War I," in *Austria in the Nineteen Fifties*, ed. Günter Bischof et

al., Contemporary Austrian Studies 3 (New Brunswick, NJ: Transaction, 1995), 171-88.

45. In June 1919, Béla Kun sent Hungarian troops into Slovakia to protect a short-lived Slovak Soviet Republic which was proclaimed in the city of Prešov. The Hungarians were forced to retreat within a fortnight. Crampton, *Eastern Europe in the Twentieth Century*, 58.

46. Historians agree today that the experience of monetary stability as opposed to inflationary turmoil in Germany and Austria was one of the factors that reconciled Czechoslovakia's German population, at least temporarily, with Prague's rule.

47. Vlastislav Lacina, "Kapitalumschichtungen in der Tschechoslowakei im Laufe der Nostrifizierung," in *Der Markt im Mitteleuropa der Zwischenkriegszeit*, ed. Alice Teichová et al. (Prague: Karls-University, 1997), 159-68.

48. Teichová, *The Czechoslovak Economy*, 68.

49. Mamatey and Luža, eds., *Geschichte der Tschechoslowakischen Republik*, 101.

50. In 1930, 34.7, 34.9, and 30.4 percent of the employed Czechoslovakian population worked in agriculture, industry and trades, and the services, respectively. Teichová, *The Czechoslovak Economy*, 9.

51. Rothschild, *East Central Europe between the Two World Wars*, 286.

52. This argument was of particular relevance in the case of Croatia, being under threat of losing its coastal areas to Italy.

53. Holm Sundhaussen, *Geschichte Serbiens, 19. – 21. Jahrhundert* (Vienna: Böhlau, 2007), 261.

54. Kurt Scharr and Rudolf Gräf, *Rumänien: Geschichte und Geographie* (Vienna: Böhlau, 2008), 63-64.

55. Iván T. Berend and György Ránki, "Polen, Ungarn, Rumänien, Bulgarien und Albanien 1914-1980," in *Europäische Wirtschafts- und Sozialgeschichte vom Ersten Weltkrieg bis zur Gegenwart*, ed. Wolfram Fischer (Stuttgart: Ernst Klett, 1987), 795.

56. John R. Lampe and Marvin R. Jackson, *Balkan Economic History, 1550-1950* (Bloomington: Indiana University Press, 1982), 432.

57. Sundhaussen, *Geschichte Serbiens, 19. – 21. Jahrhundert*, 278.

58. Rothschild, *East Central Europe between the Two World Wars*, 44, 285.

59. Scharr and Gräf, *Rumänien: Geschichte und Geographie*, 64.

60. Rothschild, *East Central Europe between the Two World Wars*, 21.

CODA: A TWENTIETH CENTURY FAMILY

The Lost and Saved: A Memoir of the Persecution of Jews in Vienna and Budapest

Peter Berger[*]

It is the year 2008. Edith H., daughter of the retired real estate agent Walter H., graduate of the Lycée Français in Vienna and managing director of a well-known international nonprofit company, enters a skiing hut in Carinthia. Sitting at the table of the small inn she notices a distant acquaintance of hers, a clerk whose bank occasionally donates money for charitable causes. The man cannot remember the woman who has just entered, but greets her in a friendly enough way and asks for her family name. "Oh, you must be a relative of the artist André H., the SAUJUDEN," he replies to Edith's introduction. Edith is completely taken aback. "It is true that my father is Jewish, but his name is Walter," she finally answers.

Walter H. is the youngest of the three sons of Andor (Aaron) H., who was born in Eger/Erlau in the Kingdom of Hungary in 1888. As a child, Andor undergoes a strict religious education; he wears ear locks and a skullcap, visits the temple regularly and is going to do so into his advanced age. On the collapse of the Habsburg monarchy, Andor is a young man of thirty and lives in Budapest. We do not know anything about his political beliefs. As a fairly affluent citizen of the capital, it is possible that he detested the revolutionary upheaval in post-war Hungary. It is equally possible that he sympathised with the communist soviet republic of Béla Kun, which, on account of its anti-feudal and, in certain respects, emancipatory programme was supported by many Jewish intellectuals. In

January 1920—the communist regime has long since been destroyed by the white terror—Andor H. emigrates to Vienna. He may have taken this step out of fear of the anti-Semitism raging in Horthy's Hungary. Whatever his motives, he does not arrive in Vienna as a poor man. The money he has brought to Austria is invested in the "Workers' Bank" located at the corner of Nussdorferstraße-Widerhofergasse.

Not far from there is the Colosseum Theatre, later a cinema and today a food discounter. In the café next to the theatre, Andor meets the love of his life, Fräulein Schlögl. Ida Schlögl's family may not be Mosaic—the quaint official euphemism that is used for Jewish in Austria—but her father and grandfather are well known Viennese builders whose company at times employs up to 4,000 people, and which is involved in huge projects like the restoration of the Karlskirche and the construction of the Palais Tedesco next to the Vienna State Opera. Andor and Ida get married in 1920. Their first son, Ernst, is born in January 1921, followed by Georg (1922) and Walter (1923). Baumeister Schlögl does not witness the birth of his two youngest grandchildren; he dies in the summer of 1920. Ida Schlögl's married bliss is relatively short. In the middle of the world economic crisis in the early 1930s, Ida, who in the meantime has converted to Judaism, meets a Slovenian student at Vienna University and becomes pregnant. In 1934, Andor draws the consequences of his wife's infidelity. He divorces her and from then on lives as a single parent in Schlagergasse, a parallel road to the Gürtel located in the ninth district. He makes a living for himself and his children by dealing in iron tools and timber. His most important business partner is the estate of the Princely House of Esterházy in Eisenstadt.

On the other side of the Gürtel is the beginning of the upper Währingerstraße, which leads out of town and is lined by numerous shops, many of which (an estimated fifty percent) are Jewish owned. There are many shops in Schlagergasse, too: a baker, a butcher, three grocers, three tailors, a handful of shoemakers. Not a single one of them is Jewish. Every day Andor H.'s sons walk past these shops on their way to school; the two elder ones, Ernst and Georg, to the grammar school in Schopenhauerstraße, Walter to secondary modern school. None of the children will finish school and do their "Matura" in Austria. Urged by his father, Ernst emigrates to the United States in 1937, aged sixteen. An uncle from his father's side of the family gives him a home there. For far-sighted people, it is obvious as early as 1937 that Austria's authoritarian Christian state will not be able to resist the expansionary tendencies of Nazi Germany. Ernst is lucky to hear about the Anschluss in Detroit where he has begun an apprenticeship as a watchmaker. In 1945 he will temporarily return to Europe as a soldier in the U.S. army and, being a German speaker, serve as an interpreter at the Nuremberg Trial. Ex-Reichsmarschall Hermann Göring is among the Nazi leaders whose statements Ernst H. translates for the court. When Göring talks to his fellow inmates without a prison guard present—as he is allowed to do from time to time—his conversations are recorded by hidden microphones and Ernst has to transcribe the taped conversations and translate them into English.

For Andor H. and his sons Georg and Walter, 13 March 1938 turns into a nightmare. The mob all over Vienna chases Jews out into the streets, submitting them to humiliating rituals like cleaning pavements with tooth brushes. Still, the H. family in the Schlagergasse is left alone. However, in Währingerstraße, outside the Gürtel, Jewish shops are stormed and looted. Unbeknown to the followers of the swastika, the fifteen-year-old Walter H. manages to photograph the excesses.

The photos still exist today. Georg, Andor's second eldest son, no longer goes to grammar school in 1938. He is doing an apprenticeship in mechanics at Neuhaus & Derflinger a medical technology company. One of the owners of the enterprise, Heinrich Neuhaus, is a doctor at the Rothschild hospital in Vienna. After the Anschluss, the Nazis deport him to Theresienstadt together with his wife and child, from where—luckily—all of them manage to escape the Holocaust. Later on, in the newly constituted Republic of Austria, Neuhaus's son will become one of the founders of the "Association of Jewish University Students" and will maintain a close friendship with Walter H. Georg H. leaves Neuhaus& Derflinger in spring 1938, when the company's name is changed to just "Derflinger." Jewish apprentices are not welcome. In the middle of November, after the so-called Reich Crystal Night, Georg manages to flee to Hungary—completely on his own and without a penny. A few days later, on 28 November 1938, Walter follows him. Andor remains alone in Schlagergasse, desperately trying to resist his neighbours' repeated attempts at "arianising" his flat and the adjoining office. When he hints at his imminent emigration, this works wonders. He is not being thrown out, but by February 1939, the month of Andor's departure, all his furniture, carpets and paintings have been carried away by unwelcome "guests."

At the end of February, father H. and his two sons celebrate a subdued reunion in Budapest. Of the five of Andor's brothers and sisters (we have encountered the brother in Detroit), one brother owns a metal factory in the Hungarian capital. This is where Georg and Walter find unpaid employment for the time being. None of them speaks more than a few words of Hungarian at that stage. Andor, on the other hand, neither benefits from his perfect language skills nor his Hungarian birth certificate: the Horthy regime considers him an unwelcome stateless Jew and puts the fifty-one-year-old into a troop of slave labourers, from which he luckily is dismissed after a relatively short time. Family H. is desperately trying to create a bourgeois existence for themselves. Father H. contacts Swedish, Danish, Czechoslovakian and German producers of iron goods, offering to work as their representative. His son Walter takes the letters to the post office, often very late at night after an exhausting workday in the factory. Slowly but surely this persistence bears fruit; a room in the Hs' flat, located in Szondi utca near the so-called "Heroes Square" in Budapest, is transformed into an import-export agency. However, it does not take long until the first problems occur with the German partners. Andor is informed that the Reichsbank refuses to transfer commissions to Jewish sales representatives. Company H. therefore employs a Christian frontman, the schoolteacher Ede Deák-Bardos, who figures as the "aryan" partner in the firm and the recipient of Andor's income from the German business. The sale of Swedish tools in Hungary, one of Andor's commercial ventures, later on turns out to be a safety anchor for him and his youngest son Walter. Hungarian Jews who either have relatives or business relations in Sweden—about 500 to 800 persons—in 1944 will be able to apply for a "protection passport" from the northern Kingdom, thus standing at least a chance of escaping deportation to the Nazi death camps.

It is one of the paradoxes of history that Hungary with its pronounced anti-Semitic tradition proves a more or less safe haven for native and immigrated Jews until Hitler occupies it in 1944. One of the reasons for the German invasion is what the powers in Berlin consider the "undecided" attitude of Magyar politicians towards the Jewish question. It is true that the Regent Horthy and his Prime Minister Miklós Kállay would like to get rid of the roughly 800,000 Jews who live in Trianon Hungary and its territories in Slovakia and Transylvania, which were annexed in 1940 with the help of German diplomats, but only "after the war," as they put it. Until then, the half-hearted anti-Jewish politics in Hungary concentrate on official harassments, like restricted admission for Jews at schools, universities and certain professions. In addition, Jews can at all times be recruited to do labour service (*munkaszolgálat*). In 1943, at the age of twenty-one, Georg H. is ordered to work in Szászrégen ("Reghin" in Romanian) in the Hungarian northeast Transylvania. It is there that he and his comrades hear of the German invasion in Budapest. From one moment to the next the situation of the Jews has become extremely precarious. Hundreds of them are arrested and interned in the first few days after the invasion, or marched towards the east, in the direction of the Russian front, as slave labourers. Walter H. is one of them. To begin with, his painful march takes him to "Upper Hungary"—as the territories, which in 1940 were regained from Slovakia, are referred to in the Magyar nationalist jargon—and later on to the east Hungarian industrial town of Miskolc, which is hit by the first allied bombs on 2 June 1944. Walter's gang of labourers clear the debris of collapsed houses, risk their lives removing a few unexploded bombs, and dig a mass grave for 200 victims of the air raid. Not a single one of the men who carry out these tasks is used to doing physical work. Most of the men in his work gang come from a music school in Budapest. In August 1944 they are ordered back to the capital. There, tens of thousands of Jews have been crowded into apartment blocks marked with yellow stars (*csillagosházak*), in order to facilitate their deportation. Among them is Andor H., Walter's father. The deportation of the Jews from the Hungarian provinces to the Nazi death camps is already in full swing, with the approval of the new Prime Minister, Döme Sztójay.

People in allied and neutral countries watch the fate of Hungarian Jews with pity and concern. Among those who actively help are the Wallenbergs, a Swedish industrial and financial dynasty. One member of the family, Raoul, born in 1912—his father, who is also called Raoul, was born in 1888, the same year as Andor H.—uses the connections of the Wallenberg clan to be sent to Budapest as First Secretary at the Swedish Embassy in 1944. Within a few weeks he manages to establish a highly efficient network of "Swedish Houses," which offers shelter and rudimentary medical care to numerous tormented Jews. It is also Wallenberg who issues the above mentioned "Protection Passports." In theory, only Jewish Hungarians who have personal or business ties with Sweden are entitled to these passports, but Wallenberg and his staff decide independently who is under Swedish protection and exceed the official limits of their powers by far. By September 1944, both Andor as well as Walter H. are in possession of Swedish passports. Thanks to this document, Walter, who after his return from Miskolc had been working in an armaments factory, is sent to a "Special Labour Camp" for foreigners, where conditions are relatively harmless. He spends his nights in the Swedish House Katona József utca 24. In the meantime, no Jews are deported from Hungary any more. Rumour has it that diplomatic pressure from Sweden and the Vatican has led Regent Miklós Horthy to dismiss Prime Minister Sztójay and persuade the Nazis to stop their murderous programme. However, on 15 October 1944, Horthy goes too far in Hitler's eyes.

He tries to get his country out of alliance with Germany and secretly puts out peace feelers to Moscow. What was meant to be a liberation move ends in a fiasco. Horthy is removed from power and forced into exile in Germany. After this, in late autumn 1944, the complete power in the Hungarian state falls into the hands of the fascist Arrow Cross movement of Ferenc Szálasi, a rabid Jew-hater.

Szálasi starts his reign by issuing a decree which forces all Jews in Budapest to move to a fenced-in ghetto that has been erected around the main synagogue in Dohány utca. In addition, the imposing temple building in Byzantine-moorish style, designed by Otto Wagner's teacher Ludwig von Förster, is turned into living quarters for several thousand interns in November 1944. Their guards have placed big wicker baskets along the walls, into which the prisoners have to throw all their valuables: watches, belt buckles, fountain pens, rings, all kinds of jewellery, and money. Sanitation consists of three toilets. Walter H. becomes a victim of the indescribable conditions in the Dohány utca synagogue. A patrol of Arrow Cross men has caught him in the street and ignored the Swedish Protection passport. The transportation of Jews into the Reich has started again. It is coordinated by Adolf Eichmann, who from March 1944 onward periodically stays in Hungary together with two German "Plenipotentiaries in Jewish Affairs," Edmund Veesenmayer and HSSPF (dem Höheren SS- und Polizeiführer) Otto Winkelmann. After the war, the latter will be jailed in Hungarian prisons for three years and appear at several Nazi trials. U.S. officer Ernst H., Walter's eldest brother, will be present when Winkelmann is handed over to Hungary at the end of 1945.

But this is premature. In November 1944 the Soviet army starts by occupying Debrecen, located 220 km east of Budapest. The advance of the Soviet army increases the pressure on the members of the Eichmann Special Task Force to bring their criminal work to an end. The last rail shipment of Hungarian Jews to Auschwitz will leave the train station (*Józsefvárosi pályaudvar*) on 28 November 1944. After this there will only be the so-called death marches, deportations by foot. Walter H. has to join the troop marching from the main synagogue to the train station. A photo that survives shows him, a miserable little bundle of clothes under his arm, on his way through an alley lined with plane trees. In the background a shop with the sign "Shoes" can be made out. And there is also another photo taken on the same day. This one shows Walter on the station platform, amongst a crowd of people who are about to board the freight train. A tall, slim man in civilian clothing is turning his face to the camera apparently about to shout something. It is Raoul Wallenberg, who has come hurrying in order to rescue the owners of "Swedish passports" from their certain

Jews on their way to the deportation train, November 1944. Walter H. is second from left. (Photo Private Collection)

death. Thus the moment in which Walter, so to speak, cocks a snook to death, is captured on celluloid by the twenty-one-year old Tamás (Tom) Veres, who later will have a photo studio in New York. Walter is taken back to Katona József utca on the evening of 28 November. Until the invasion of the victorious Red Army in the part of Budapest called Pest (15 January 1945), he lives there undisturbed. Only now and then is he "lent out" to the German army to help the soldiers with the loading of trucks.

In the meantime the company of slave labourers, to which Walter's younger brother Georg belongs, is fleeing from the approaching Soviets. The route from Transylvania to the west takes them south of Budapest not far from Lake Balaton. There twelve lads, among them Georg H., decide on a desperate move. Near Jásd in county Veszprém they manage to leave their convoy unnoticed by anyone and find shelter among the local farm population. One of the farmers, however, reports the refugees to the police. Georg and four of his comrades are taken prisoner and executed on 23 March 1945, less than two weeks before the end of hostilities on Hungarian territory and six weeks before the capitulation of Hitler's Germany.

For family H., the balance of two years' war and persecution is disastrous. It is true that Andor has escaped the Holocaust, but for the third time in his life he has to make a new start in his career, and this at the age of fifty-seven. He has lost one of his sons, one is wearing the uniform of the United States of America, and only his youngest son, Walter, aged twenty-two, is in a position and willing to help his father. Initially it looks as if fate is going to be kind to the Hs. Father and son are assigned a spacious flat by the Budapest town council, the former office of a German enterprise. There, father and son try to revive their pre-1944 business activities. They contact former partner companies, partly to represent them again in Hungary, partly to claim commissions which were not paid in 1943 and 1944. All these attempts are in vain, as in the case of the Sudeten German export agent Wilhelm Dreier, who under the Beneš-decrees was forced to leave Czechoslovakia and abandon his company. Now living in north Germany, he points out that he has nothing at all. Still, Andor manages to initiate some contracts to represent Scandinavian and German companies in Hungary.

In the meantime Hungary sees the gradual takeover of power by the Stalinists under the leadership of Mátyás Rákosi, who refers to himself as Stalin's best Hungarian pupil. Rákosi uses highly effective tactics to soften up his political rivals—in the first place against the Smallholders Party, which was far more successful in the first post-war elections of 1945, and also against the Farmers Party and the Social Democrats. All groups left of centre are coerced into joining forces with the Communist Party. The Right, spied on, denounced and terrorized by the police, is paralyzed. The fact that the country is occupied by the Soviet army and the ministry of the interior is run by one of Rákosi's men, helps the plans of the communists. Their influence on the coalition government of national unity is sufficient to first expropriate large landowners and then nationalize banks, mines and enterprises with more than 100 employees. In 1947 when America wants to include Hungary in the ERP-Programme, the Magyar government, seconded by the USSR, declines. Hungarian citizens' freedom to travel is restricted. Whoever is able to see the writing on the wall, knows that the country is moving toward a leftist dictatorship and a planned economy. Family H., too, are aware of it and are beginning to consider emigration. Andor has spent almost all the interwar years in Austria, and Walter was born in Vienna. It is not surprising, therefore, that both apply for Austrian citizenship. Still, the naturalization process drags on for five years, and only is started after the resistance of the "State Protection Office of the Ministry of the Interior" (AVH) has been overcome. Andor attempts to do this by sending a five-litre-jug of red wine (*Egri bikavér*) every fortnight to a high official of the ministry of the interior, Gyula Princz. He lives on Deák Square together with his two daughters and a son. The bribe turns out to be counter-productive. The tippling protector of the state is not interested in losing his wine supplier and leaves H.'s file unprocessed. Only when Princz together with his superior, the head of State Security, Gábor Péter, is arrested and found guilty in a show trial, are both Andor and Walter given the long-awaited emigration permit. They arrive in Vienna on 13 March 1954. At that time, Andor has barely a year to live. Walter, on the other hand, is going to marry, become a successful car dealer and buy a house in a nice district of Vienna (Pötzleinsdorf), where his daughter lives today. His half-brother Josef, born in 1935 of the second marriage of Ida Schlögl (with the Slovenian student, whom we encountered earlier), lives in Mödling near Vienna too. When the two brothers meet, they often joke about who of them is more Jewish: Walter with a Jewish father and a Christian mother, who shortly before she is about to give birth, waits to become Jewish, but is not Jewish yet? Or Josef, with a Christian father and the same mother, who now counts as Jewish? As perverse as it may sound: in the twentieth century, the age of extremes, the answer to these questions could be a matter of life and death...

This text is the edited write-up of an interview with Walter H., which was conducted on 23 January 2010 and lasted for about two hours. The memory of the interviewee, who I am extremely obliged to, was absolutely precise in every respect. No political or military event mentioned by him took place at a different time than the time indicated by him, and no names of places or people proved wrong when checked. I deliberately decided to do without footnotes in order to keep the narration flowing. In case some readers would have preferred to read about structures rather than persons, they might be prepared to indulge me when I remind them of the words of the great Frenchman (and Jew) Marc Bloch, who said, "The historian is like a cannibal: Where there is human flesh, he scents his prey."

* The author would like to express his gratitude to Dr. Liselotte Pope-Hoffmann, who translated this essay into English.

BOOK REVIEWS

Brigitte Hamann, *Hitlers Edeljude: Das Leben des Armenarztes Eduard Bloch* (Munich: Piper, 2008)

Evan B. Bukey

In this extraordinary book, Brigitte Hamann recounts the life and times of Hitler's Jewish childhood physician, Dr. Eduard Bloch (1872-1945). Relying on meticulous research in Austria, Germany, and the United States, the author provides insights into the ambiguous feelings of admiration and respect that characterized the relationship of the Jewish doctor and the Nazi dictator throughout their lives. Hamann not only sweeps away misconceptions about Hitler's youth, but in lucid, often gripping, prose provides a heartrending account of the disastrous, long-term impact of the collapse of the Habsburg Monarchy on Jewish life in interwar Austria.

Born in southern Bohemia, Eduard Bloch was the fifth child of poor but highly educated parents. Between 1891 and 1899 he studied medicine at the Charles University in Prague, where he carried a revolver to protect himself from roving bands of anti-Semitic students. After serving six months as a medical officer in Linz, Bloch chose to establish his practice in the Upper Austrian capital, a city he considered both tolerant and safe. Was this assessment sound? Prior to the Great War, Hamann reminds us, the provincial capital never succumbed to the ethnic struggles disrupting the Habsburg Monarchy. Compared with Prague and Vienna, local German Nationalist agitation was relatively moderate and directed primarily against the Czechs. Since the small number of Jews belonged to the educated bourgeoisie, they managed to live an equal but separate existence. Anti-

Jewish sentiment prevailed in Linz, as elsewhere in Austria, but while Roman Catholic parents forbade their children to play with Jewish classmates, they did not hesitate to frequent Jewish firms or to consult Jewish physicians. Under these conditions, Dr. Bloch's practice flourished from the outset. Patients, rich and poor, flocked to his clinic, holding him in the highest regard. Among them were the adolescent Adolf Hitler and his mother Klara.

On 18 January 1907, Bloch and Dr. Karl Urban operated on Klara Hitler for malignant breast cancer, apparently performing a partial mastectomy. Neither physician held out much hope for the patient, although it was not until mid-October that Bloch informed Adolf that his mother's days were numbered. To alleviate her suffering Bloch applied doses of idoform, an antibacterial palliative that, far from intensifying her agony – as subsequently charged by the "psycho-historian" Rudolf Binion – did provide some relief. Throughout two months of daily house calls, the doctor developed an unusual affection for the young Hitler, whom he later recalled as thoughtful, courteous, and well-mannered, though following his mother's death also the "saddest man I had ever seen." As for the grief-stricken son, he expressed "everlasting gratitude" both in person and in painted postcards to the sensitive physician he would subsequently protect as his "noble Jew."

Although Bloch never forgot Hitler, his brief encounter with the future murderer of the Jewish people constituted only a brief episode in a successful life. Married in 1902 to Lilli Kafka, the daughter of a prosperous distiller and delicatessen owner, Bloch and his family enjoyed a happy, prosperous existence until the outbreak of the Great War. The couple's only child, Trude, born in 1903, excelled in primary school, where she came to love the Lord's Prayer with a zeal that at age twenty would lead her to the baptismal font. In 1913, she enrolled in the female gymnasium under the aegis of Dr. Leopold Poetsch, a highly respected educator and public speaker who had inspired Hitler in the local Realschule. Far from being the fiery German Nationalist depicted in the historical literature, Poetsch emerges in Hamann's account as a moderate liberal entranced by Germanic sagas, but fiercely loyal to the Habsburg Monarchy. He was also a strong advocate of women's rights, encouraging his pupils to continue their education in order to pursue independent careers as fashion designers, teachers, and even physicians.

The assassination of Francis Ferdinand in faraway Sarajevo ushered in three decades of turmoil and violence that did not leave the Blochs, their Jewish coreligionists, or the Linz population itself untouched. While Bloch returned to service as a medical officer in the local garrison, severe shortages of fuel and food in Linz rapidly led to widespread hunger, disease and social discontent. Worse, the arrival of 20,000 impoverished Jewish refugees from Galicia inflamed anti-Semitic sentiment, partly because the refugees appeared as alien parasites, partly because they had to be housed and fed by the hard-pressed municipality. Nor did the wartime upsurge of Judeophobia abate after 1918. Military defeat, hunger, and despair only reinforced a general sense of fear and loathing of Jews that no longer exempted the acculturated residents of the Upper Austrian capital. Hamann concedes that a measure of civility persisted among Gentiles and Jews of the older generation, but that younger Jews were increasingly subjected to abuse in classrooms, playgrounds, and swimming pools. There were also occasional fist-fights and a gradual rise in boycotts of Jewish-owned firms. Dr. Bloch's practice continued to flourish, for example, but sales in his brother-in-law's once elegant delicatessen declined precipitously.

Hamann devotes considerable attention to the lugubrious history of the First Austrian Republic. While some readers may find her account slightly distracting, it is difficult to see how she could have proceeded otherwise, for example, in detailing how Otto Bauer's fiery speech of 26 November 1926 exacerbated the growing divisions of civic life in Linz as well as in Austria as a whole. Simultaneously, she deplores Chancellor Ignaz Seipel's harsh monetary policies, his veiled anti-Jewish pronouncements, and his support of the Heimwehr. Hamann is particularly adroit in revealing how the unsettled interwar era affected both Bloch's extended family and Linz's hard-pressed Jewish congregation. The Great Depression, for example, left the physician's patients unable to pay their bills and municipal councilors such as Dr. Hermann Schneeweis, subject to vicious anti-Semitic abuse by Linz's metastasizing Nazi movement. Nor did conditions improve under the Christian Corporative dictatorship, a regime that drove the embittered working class into the hands of the illegal NSDAP, promoted anti-Semitic publications, and denied hospital privileges to Jewish physicians. Indeed, Bloch's adolescent grandson, Georg Kren, never forgot the bullying of Catholic classmates he endured at the humanistic gymnasium.

When Hitler returned in triumph to Linz on the evening of 12 March 1938, Dr. Bloch observed the Fűhrer's motorcade from the window of his apartment on the Landstraβe with a mixture of pride, shock, and anxiety. Much has been made of the Jewish physician's conflicting feelings, but the very fact that he had kept two postcards received in 1908 surely reveals something about Hitler's magnetic charm long before his entry into politics. Furthermore, Bloch had learned from reliable sources that the

Fűhrer remembered him fondly as a "noble Jew." Citing Bruno Kreisky's ambivalent reaction to the Anschluss, Hamann speculates that Bloch's hopes of privileged treatment may also have been fueled by bitter resentment of the Christian Corporative regime. On 28 March, the Gestapo confiscated Bloch's treasured postcards, but thereafter treated him with kid gloves. His son-in-law, Dr. Franz Kren, was not so fortunate; in April local Nazis trashed his home in Urfahr and imprisoned him for three weeks. In September, however, official notice arrived, granting Bloch and his immediate family exemption from the Nuremberg Laws.

Hamann makes it unmistakably clear that for a brief spell, Bloch relished his status as a privileged Jew, seeking only to recover Hitler's youthful postcards. According to the physician's unpublished memoirs, upon which much of this work is based, he was treated with courtesy and respect by the Nazi authorities, even by Dr. Otto Rasch, the local SD chief, who in 1941would distinguish himself by orchestrating the mass murder of Ukrainian Jews at Babi Yar. Bloch was hardly oblivious to the persecution of his coreligionists in Linz: For nearly three years he and Lilli provided aid, comfort, and shelter to numerous relatives and members of the local congregation. Even so, Hamann suggests it was not until Kristallnacht that he fully grasped the scale of suffering described in her own grim account. Alarmed by Hitler's seizure of Prague, the elderly doctor worked with the Swedish mission in Vienna to arrange for his grandchildren to leave on a Kindertransport to Britain. Within a year they were followed by their parents, who made their way across the Atlantic on a troubled voyage by way of Genoa and an Algerian internment camp to New York. Finally, on 19 November 1940 Lilli and Eduard Bloch abandoned their home of thirty-eight years. Unlike other Jews, they had been allowed to retain their assets so long as they remained in the Greater German Reich. On 8 January 1941, however, they arrived in the Bronx virtually penniless.

The last years of Dr. Bloch's life were spent in a modest apartment, reading Hebrew scripture and watching cowboy movies at a nearby cinema. Although he never learned English, he created a sensation in March 1941 when Collier's Weekly published a long interview, "My Patient Hitler." Asked if the dictator had been an adolescent hooligan, Bloch responded: "This is simply not true. As a youth, he was quiet, well-mannered, and neatly dressed." Among those incensed by these words was the doctor's fifteen-year-old grandson, Georg Kren, who had arrived in America with his younger sister a few months earlier. Having personally experienced Nazi savagery in Linz, Vienna, and Berlin, Kren would go on to fight as a combat infantryman in Europe and later became a scholar of the Holocaust.

He never forgave his grandfather. What Kren failed to grasp, Hamann contends, is that Dr. Bloch simply could not acknowledge the eighteen-year-old Hitler had been anything other than a polite young man devoted to his mother. More likely, the elderly physician never managed to reconcile his own contradictory feelings and emotions.

What is one to make of all this? First, here is a richly textured portrait of Jewish life in a provincial Austrian city covering the first half of the twentieth century, one revealing that under the Dual Monarchy it was possible for middle-class Jews to prosper and win a measure of social acceptance similar to their coreligionists in the German Reich. At the same time, the provincial Catholic diocese promoted Judeophobia, stifled social contacts, and put up road blocks to intermarriage. Second, Hamann's canvas is so inclusive that one yearns for a family tree to keep track of Bloch's extended family and friends. In this respect, careful editing should have caught a number of small errors and mistakes, e.g. in 1918 the Central Powers dictated the Treaty of Brest-Litovsk to Soviet Russia, not to the Tsarist Empire (p. 400). Third, Hamann's excruciating account of the merciless wave of terror engulfing Upper Austrian Jews after 1938 recaptures something of their sense of anxiety and pain, partly because of its graphic prose, partly because of its focus on individuals. All that being said, some readers may put down this book still unconvinced that nothing "occurred at Linz" to transform the young Hitler into W.H. Auden's "psychopathic god." Wiser ones may take note of Francois de La Rochefoucauld's Maxim: "There are evil men in this world who would be less dangerous if they had not something good in them."

Richard Faber and Sigurd Paul Scheichl, eds., *Die geistige Welt des Friedrich Heer* (Vienna: Böhlau, 2008)

William Johnston

The intellectual powerhouse that was Friedrich Heer continues to confound interpreters. Historian, lay theologian, and intellectual provocateur, Heer defies compartmentalizing. Anti-Nazi (at least after 1945) and anti-Communist, as a publicist he advocated "humanistic" renewal in all spheres of public life, particularly in the Roman Catholic church, European universities, and Christian-Jewish relations. He denounced complacency, stagnation, and narrow-mindedness wherever he found it, except perhaps in himself. By serving as an intellectual gadfly toward every camp, he made it nearly impossible for readers to discern his own camp. In retrospect, he seems to have belonged to a camp of one member, and the self-deceptions unmasked in this book mean that some of its contributors rejoice that this self-fashioner has found no emulators.

From the start, Friedrich Heer cultivated an unclassifiability that has weakened his influence. His range of reference daunted colleagues in history, cultural criticism, and church politics; his proteus-like lability unsettled opponents who could not pin him down; and his roster of intellectual heroes grew unmanageably diverse. To take one example, in his thousand-page celebration of nineteenth-century thought, *Europa Mutter der Revolutionen* (1964), he extolled figures as irreconcilable as the Catholic conservatives Friedrich Schlegel and his protégé Joseph von Eichendorff at one extreme, the visionary idealist philosopher Friedrich Schelling and the lifelong provacateurs Bettina von Arnim and Heinrich Heine in the middle, and the theological revolutionaries Bruno Bauer and Ludwig Feuerbach at the other extreme. Heer's capacity to empathize with intellectual forbears knew no limits. In assessing contemporaries he showed a similar breadth of sympathy. He admired Leopold Figl and Bruno Kreisky, Reinhold Schneider and Cardinal König, Teilhard de Chardin and John XXIII, Elie Wiesel and Marshal Tito. How is one to interpret such a disparate, not to say incoherent range of homage?

In 2006 Richard Faber of Berlin and Sigurd Paul Scheichl of Innsbruck invited twelve colleagues to re-evaluate Heer's contributions on the occasion of the ninetieth anniversary of his birth. In this painstaking and often painful volume, many of the authors vie with Heer in virtuoso displays of learning and insight. Four of the essays examine relations between Heer's lay theology and his humanism, while six assess his contributions as a historian of Europe since 1100, and four weigh controversies about his stature. Heer the author of ten large "monographs" (pp. 108-109), Heer the polemicist, and Heer the self-inventor receive ample attention. Everyone interested in the development of history-writing in Austria since the 1930s will want to digest these assessments. Not least they offer a sophisticated introduction to many phases of Heer's historical argumentation, particularly concerning the period 1100 to 1600.

Friedrich Heer (1916-1983) flourished before post-modernity had asserted itself as a mode of intellectual self-awareness. His versatility, or if you prefer his volatility, or, as some would now argue, his irresponsibility, manifested itself in a world still riven by seemingly irreconcilable ideological divides. Moreover, during his lifetime it was still permissible to make sweeping pronouncements about European history in the manner of the universal historian Arnold Toynbee (1889-1975) or the philosophical anthropologist Arnold Gehlen (1904-1976) and to exalt past masters as models for the present. Until very late in Heer's career, scholars in the humanities had not yet adopted categories like "self-fashioning" or "self-positioning" to describe a colleague's maneuvering among options. As it happens, such categories fit Heer to perfection. Without the ballast of cultural theory to check his enthusiasm, Heer functioned as a self-proclaimed, if sometimes temporary, advocate of the most divergent figures, trends, and positions. By any measure he lacked self-critical probity, and his many-sidedness must seem to us post-moderns not only provocative, but irresponsible. One man's vision can seem another man's posturing. Delighting in his role as an intellectual irritant, Friedrich Heer needlessly offended potential allies and discredited many of his best insights by diluting them with nonsense. No one can admire all sides of Friedrich Heer's productivity, and the essays in this volume tackle with honesty the questions, "How much if any of Heer's legacy remains viable? How badly did his excesses undermine his credibility? What can be salvaged amid so much posturing?" Needless to say, the contributors reach no consensus, but they do lay the foundations for fresh assessment. To do so they cite an astonishingly wide range of parallel figures, and several like Jürgen Ebach and Anne Kwaschik fashion oxymorons to describe a historian who like the early German Romantic Novalis (1772-1801) saw himself as a utopian, a prophet, and even a seer.

Essay # 1 by Anton Pelinka abounds in anecdotes about fellow shapers of Heer's reputation. As an ambivalent admirer Pelinka sets the tone of re-appraisal by dividing Heer's roles as "*the* public intellectual" of Austria's Second Republic into three "personalities": Heer deployed an "integrating" personality (above all as a left-wing Catholic), a "polarizing" personality (above all as a critic of Dollfuss and Schuschnigg), and an "innovative" personality (above all as an elegist of the Holocaust) (pp. 12-15). Pelinka could have called Heer the chief "polarizing" intellectual of the period, and the article foresees the possibility of someone eventually writing an intellectual history of the period 1945-1980 anchored in Heer's many campaigns of subversion (p. 18). Needless to say, contributors to this book affirm that it is much too early to attempt such a synthesis. Instead the contributors tackle those aspects that interest them as specialists, and one's reaction to the essays will depend on whether one cares most about Catholic issues (Essays # 2-5, 8), historical methodology (# 6,9,11, 12), Austrian cultural politics (# 1, 10, 14), or the fate of European Humanism (# 4, 7, 11, 13).

It may be useful to classify some of the chapters according to which allies of Heer receive prominence. In two chapters Heer's Habilitationsschrift *Aufgang Europas* (Vienna, 1949) on the 12th-century church plays a major role. Bristling with quotations, the most useful essay for renewing acquaintance with Heer is probably # 4, Richard Faber, "Friedrich Heer's Path of Faith: From Humanistic Catholicism to Poetic Humanism." One of the very few articles to attempt an overall portrait, it deepens arguments that the author first presented in 2005 (p. 47, note 1). A master dialectician, Faber makes Novalis, "a poetic pan-humanist," play an uncanny role as well nigh a *Doppelgänger* of the poetic utopian Heer (pp. 55-64). One of the most learned and insightful articles is # 5, Jürgen Ebach, "Heer as Exegete of the Bible and Interpreter of its Reception." Focusing on the Old Testament, Ebach praises Heer's ability to place Bible interpreters in unexpectedly wide contexts (p. 72). For interpreting the historical methodology of the "methodically unmethodical" Heer (p. 84), the most innovative chapter (and also the second longest) is # 9, Helmut Kuzmics' piece on "Friedrich

Heer and Norbert Elias: Two Approaches to the Psychohistory of Central European States and Their Societies." Born nineteen years before Heer, the vastly more judicious Norbert Elias (1897-1990) outlived him by seven years. The two historians are discussed further below. The most sprightly chapter and one of the most original is # 11, Anne Kwaschik, "On the Use and Abuse of the Essay for Historians or the 'Daylight Mysticism' of Friedrich Heer." Here Robert Musil's "essayism" serves as a foil to Heer's "montages of associations and images" (p. 197), which all too often degenerate into a mere "carousel of associations" (p. 202). As Kwaschik shows, mastery of lateral thinking does not suffice to qualify Heer as a master essayist. In the most personal and second most painful chapter, # 13, Helmut Rumpler recounts his mounting disappointment with Heer as a mentor for historians of Austria, narrated through a series of encounters beginning in 1958. With mild contempt Rumpler refutes Heer's "Germanophobe" ideology that an "Austrian nation" (as distinct from the Habsburg dynastic realm) has existed since at least the 16th century (pp. 243-246).

The most scathing reappraisal, and by far the longest, is # 14, Adolf Gaisbauer's "'Images of Heer' or a 'Retraction' with its Consequences." As described below, Gaisbauer, author of a previous biography of Heer (1990), cannot conceal his bitterness as he dissects Heer's lies about alleged involvement in the anti-Nazi resistance as well as in Nazi military service. Several of the other authors single out the centrality of Hitler for Heer's development, most notably # 8, Justus H. Ulbricht, "Eliminative Confession: *Der Glaube des Adolf Hitler*: Notes on the *Wirkungsgeschichte* of an almost Forgotten Book." In a very subtle analysis of scholarship on pre-Nazi ideology Ulbricht seeks to "rehabilitate Heer's rehabilitative critique" of the religious dimensions of nationalism (p. 145) and laments that Heer's book of 1968 was not read more deeply at the time.

The intention to "rehabilitate Heer's rehabilitations" of various figures (Novalis, Friedrich Schlegel, Nietzsche) and ideologies (Humanism as a Third Force, Catholicism as a mainspring of Austrian culture, and philo-Semitism as a corrective to its opposite) may be said to underpin this entire book. These partial rehabilitations are, however, outweighed, both in persuasiveness and acerbity, by unmaskings of Heer's volatility, over-reaching, and self-disguise. One's previous image of Heer is not only complicated by this book, but unhinged. After a first or even a second reading one no longer knows what to think about this problematic figure.

The remainder of this review will concentrate on two essays, # 9, Helmut Kuzmics' exploration of previously unnoticed parallels between Heer and Norbert Elias, and # 14, Adolf Gaisbauer's denunciation of Heer's self-mythologizing, not to say delusions of grandeur. The first essay avoids issues of what we may call Heer's self-fashioning, while the other exposes them.

The Graz sociologist Helmut Kuzmics compares Heer's sprawling *Der Kampf um die österreichische Identität* (1981) with Elias's weighty late work *Studien über die Deutschen* (1989). He suggests that Heer provides rich material for applying Elias's categories from the "human sciences" to the "national habitus" of the Austrians. Together with Roland Axtmann, Kuzmics had developed this analysis in a work translated as *Authority, State and National Character: The Civilising Process in Austria and England, 1700-1900* [German edition, 2000] (Aldershot and Burlington VT: Ashgate, 2007). A compost of Austrian attitudes raked over by literary essayists provides the soil out of which a cultural sociologist like Kuzmics can pinpoint Austrian particularity using Elias's methodology. My book *Der österreichische Mensch. Kulturgeschichte der Eigenart Österreichs* (Wien: Böhlau, 2010) examines many other explorers of the Austrian habitus in a similar way. As I discovered, Heer himself cited only a narrow range of the twentieth-century essayists who had anticipated his various portraits of Austrianness. Friedrich Herr, the seemingly well-read portraitist of Austrian identity, overlooked dozens of major and minor predecessors of his endeavor. Here as in so many other spheres, he overestimated his own mastery.

Adolf Gaisbauer writes in a very different vein. Wisely his bombshell of an essay comes after the others, for its indictment of wilful mendacity can only undermine confidence and even interest in Heer's other achievements. As a disillusioned biographer, Gaisbauer confesses his bewilderment at his discovery of Heer's total fabrication of non-existent war-service on the Russian front. Frankly ashamed, the biographer retreats into factual indictments massively footnoted as a way to minimize more damaging conclusions about Heer's character. The reader too feels a sense of shame as one reads the summary of Heer's "liberties with the truth, compulsions, and gifts" on p. 270. Appendix 1 fills twenty-five pages with minute refutations of Heer's self-mythologizing about his wartime experiences. Not only did the Gestapo never threaten him, but he strove as late as mid-1944 to enter the service of the Nazi state as an archivist (p. 285). Appendix 2 requires a full three pages simply to list Heer's major "irreale" autobiographical details. Most damaging of all, Appendix 3 offers three case studies in Heer's delusions about his presumed capacity to penetrate the secrets of historical reality. Pages 305-312 examine Heer's mythomania concerning God's role in the Holocaust, a self-inflation that borders on pathology even when it reminds us of Novalis.

In disbelief the reader is reminded of Olivier Todd's biography, *Malraux a Life* (2005). André Malraux (1901-1976) too excelled as a fabricator of autobiography. Both these manipulators of their self-image possessed unusually vivid powers of recall, both fancied themselves as arbiters of institutional, not to say national fate, and both are now seen as having been overrated during their lifetimes. Yet even Malraux did not claim to expound God's motivation in permitting or unleashing mass murder, as Heer did in 1967 in *Gottes erste Liebe* (pp. 311-12). This reviewer shares Gaisbauer's near-paralysis at the spectacle of self-fashioning that tips over into self-delusion. One's bewilderment is all the greater because Heer did not need to cover up published support for the Nazis (like Paul de Man) or to conceal allegiance to ethnically rooted fascism (like Mircea Eliade) or to confess youthful blindness about Communism (like Arthur Koestler). As these parallels suggest, one might well ask to what extent a comparative study of autobiographical mendacity concerning the Nazi era may prove helpful. The task will require the combined gifts of an historian, a depth psychologist, and a cultural anthropologist. We await perhaps a new genre of comparative study of the great ideological Self-Fashioners of the twentieth century. Heer would seem to hold a unique place among them because he at different times was not only disowning but also fabricating a record of service in Hitler's armies. This sort of mythomania led eventually to purporting to read God's purposes into the Holocaust. In light of all this one can imagine how the Austrian novelist Walter Kappacher, an analyst of thwarted geniuses, might write a novel about how self-disguise may evolve into self-betrayal. In such a novel Heer the misguided seer might emerge as even more tragically conflicted than Gaisbauer suggests.

As one recoils from so much dissimulation, not to say moral decay, this book does answer the question of why Heer's work as a historian has exerted so little influence among professionals. The answer is not simply that demands for precision in conceptualisation and for expertise in the social sciences have increased since the 1970s. Rather it is, as half a dozen contributors argue, that Heer conflated the role of "prophet" or "exhorter" with that of restorer of faded reputations. He did not so much investigate the past as seek to celebrate favored portions of it. For him the study of intellectual history threw up a repertoire of potential models, mentors, and instigators to be emulated now. His view of the past was hortatory, nothing less than an updated version of what Nietzsche in the *Unzeitgemässe Betrachtungen* (1873-74) pilloried as "monumental" history. In a word, Friedrich Heer monumentalized his intellectual ancestors, and our anti-monumental age will not applaud his self-inflation, even when we might share some of his enthusiasms.

Moreover, even if one disregards subsequent changes of fashion in methodology, one can still doubt whether as an intellectual and as a lay theologian Friedrich Heer had the temperament that we now expect of a scholar. Never one to distance himself from partisanship, Heer identified himself unreservedly with certain audacious mentors (Erasmus, Novalis, Bettina von Arnim). He did not aspire at any time to write a phenomenology or a distanced classification of key concepts. In this neglect he is the antithesis of earlier Austrian thinkers like the philosopher Edmund Husserl, the essayist Rudolf Kassner, or the jurist Hans Kelsen. Their kind of self-distancing is more to our taste, and no one can expect that Heer's preference for partisanship, advocacy, and exhortation will ever again become acceptable, let alone fashionable in today's Europe. By a piquant irony, Heer now needs the kind of rehabilitation that he performed on so many others. In light of Gaisbauer's exposé, one wonders who can possibly provide it.

Although none of the essayists says so, one can surmise that Heer's more obvious deficiencies have already helped to discredit certain of his principal concerns. Lay theology, particularly among Roman Catholics, now seems passé, and the sweeping kind of intellectual history at which Heer excelled is no longer viable or expected. More regrettably, Heer's lifelong wrestling with discourse about Austrian cultural identity has not evoked the response it deserved. His last major book, *Der Kampf um die österreichische Identität* (1981), did not inspire any successors or rebutters, perhaps because its profusion of citations and whirligig of associations bewilders more than it clarifies. Heer's delight in overwhelming a reader with a torrent of quotations no longer suits our age of media-saturation. What we need is not more references or bolder asociations, but clearer structuring and firmer prioritizing.

For all his ardor and expostulation, Friedrich Heer lacked a talent for structuring a sustained argument, either within a single book or between books. Still worse, he did not plot his career astutely. Too seldom did he deepen his own pioneering efforts. In the Faber and Scheichl volume, the "intellectual world of Friedrich Heer" emerges as a many-faceted prism, as a variety-show of shifting intellectual commitments, and as a perpetual questing that found no resting place other than in pontification. Heer identified with previous questers, often young ones like Novalis and Hölderlin or perpetually youthful ones like Schelling and Bettina von Arnim, and he never ceased hunting for new and fascinating fellow questers. Heer did not admire thinkers who aged gracefully, nor did he emulate such colossi of perseverance as Leopold von Ranke or Theodor Mommsen. In contrast to the sage Norbert Elias, Friedrich Heer is not someone to guide a scholar toward a fruitful old age.

Access to this volume suffers through the lack of an index. If ever a volume of papers required one, this is it, if only to gauge what has been omitted. One would like to know, for example, how much discussion is accorded to friends of Heer like Wilfried Daim or Reinhold Schneider, but only the most attentive reading will disclose that Daim appears on page 16 as one who early on supplied his friend with ideas for interpreting Hitler as an Austrian, while Schneider appears to be missing altogether. These omissions suggest that entire facets of Heer have eluded our authors. In particular, Reinhold Schneider's stance as an internal émigré in post-1945 Germany suggests that a similar intransigence came to animate Friedrich Heer. After 1945 he defied propagandists of nation and church as he probably wished he had done during the Nazi-regime. An increasingly embattled Friedrich Heer never felt fully at home in the Austrian Second Republic or in the Roman Catholic Church. Indeed, some admirers might wish to apply to Heer the perpetual dissident what he said about his friend: "Reinhold Schneider lived as a man possessed. His life is greater than his work."[1] Sadly, in light of Gaisbauer's disclosures, some might want to rephrase this to read, "Friedrich Heer's lies about his life and his overestimate of his intellectual powers are greater than his work."

The essays in this volume form a crazy-quilt of interpretations, revisions, and new starts. Even more relentlessly than André Malraux, Heer opened his mind and spirit toward so many mentors and interlocutors in so many camps and of so many eras that it becomes impossible to grasp him as a whole person. Heer's vast productivity has protected him from scrutiny. As Novalis had urged, this Catholic progressive tried very late in the day to encompass in one career the entirety of European culture from 1100 to 1960. Heer's failure shows yet again that even Oswald Spengler (1880-1936) came too late to pull off this Gargantuan feat of intellectual digestion. Unlike the dour Spengler, Heer's lability and shape-shifting makes him an alluring target for post-modernist perspectivism. Each observer will see a different face of the prism, and any attempt like Richard Faber's to synthesise the faces through parallels to Early German Romantics will fall victim to Heer's mania for self-fashioning. He was a flawed giant – whether he stands as a giant of asking hard questions or as a giant of self-delusion or merely as a giant of free associating remains for each reader to decide. This painfully honest volume has made the task of assessing Friedrich Heer as historian, lay theologian, and polemicist more hazardous than ever. Perhaps like one of his favorite German gadflys, Bettina von Arnim, Heer wanted above all else to baffle posterity.

Notes

1. "Als ein Ergriffener hat Reinhold Schneider gelebt. Seine Existenz ist grösser als sein Werk." Friedrich Heer, "Reinhold Schneider (1903-1958)," [1974] in *Über Reinhold Schneider*, ed. Carsten Peter Thiede (Frankfurt: Suhrkamp, 1980), 153. The entire article (pp. 136-153) reads like a self-portrait of Heer, as does the verdict, "He died as he had lived: asking questions in mind and heart...a bundle of questions." ("Er [Schneider] stirbt, wie er gelebt hat: fragend, im Hirn, im Herzen...ein Bündel von Fragen." p. 153).

Bertrand Michael Buchmann, *Österreicher in der Deutschen Wehrmacht: Soldatenalltag im Zweiten Weltkrieg* (Vienna: Böhlau, 2009)

Michael S. Maier

More than sixty years after the collapse of the Third Reich and with the last surviving members of the war generation grown old, the question of Austria's involvement in World War II has by no means lost its explosive historical nature. On the contrary, events like the controversial annual war veterans commemoration at the Ulrichsberg in Carinthia ("*Ulrichsbergtreffen*") and the heated political debate surrounding the rehabilitation of Wehrmacht deserters in 2009 prove the need for an informed academic discourse regarding the role of those 1.3 million Austrians who served in the German armed forces from the time of the Anschluss in March 1938 until the end of the war.

The eroding of the state-official "victims doctrine" (*Opferdoktrin*)—the myth that all Austrians, including all Austrian soldiers in Hitler's army, had been a collective "victim" of National Socialist Germany—in the later 1980s and 1990s, together with the Wehrmacht exhibition (*Wehrmachtsausstellung*) about German war crimes in the mid-1990s, led to a long overdue reassessment of Austrian's Nazi past and opened the door for a new wave of military historians to reevaluate the complex history of Austrian World War II veterans.[1] Recently Richard Germann and Thomas Grischany completed studies on the Austrian element in the German Wehrmacht. Both draw a relatively homogeneous portrait of loyal and well-integrated generals, officers, and soldiers of Austrian origins who shared the attitudes of their Reich German comrades and identified themselves with the German cause. In other words, despite all the differences in mentality, regional identity, and military tradition, Austrians represented an integral part of the Nazi war machinery and served as mostly willing and able combatants in all theaters of World War II.[2]

Bertrand Michael Buchmann, an Austrian scholar with a focus on the Habsburg Monarchy, adds to this burgeoning field of Austrian World War II history. In his recently published monograph, written for a broader audience, Buchmann deals with the everyday life (*Alltagsgeschichte*) of Austrian soldiers in the Wehrmacht. He tries to capture their often very contradictory individual experiences and perceptions within the Nazi military system. Based on existing studies and autobiographical sources like war diaries, memoirs, military letters, plus a very small number of oral history interviews, he presents a military history "from below" and examines the military environment and mindset of Austrian World War II participants.

Unfortunately, for a number of reasons, Buchmann's book does not meet the expectations aroused by his introduction. First of all, the reader will miss a common thread; in fact, the study as a whole suffers from a lack of sharp focus and an arbitrary choice of topics, often without an explicit Austrian point of view. As a result, the 319 pages of the book are more reminiscent of a mosaic of sometimes rather banal episodes of military everyday life in World War II than a coherent historiography of Austrian Wehrmacht service. In 33 widely varying chapters (in terms of content and length) the author covers a vast range of issues, from the transfer of the Austrian *Bundesheer* into the Wehrmacht and the harsh living conditions on the frontlines to the political indoctrination of the German armed forces and the participation of Austrians in war crimes. But too often the topics are only addressed superficially, lacking the necessary analytical depth, or neglecting the Austrian context. Major historical questions such as the involvement of the Wehrmacht in the Holocaust, or the significance of comradeship for the fighting spirit in the Third Reich's army (which also may have been an important factor for the integration of the Austrian soldiers) are treated within a few pages, including no more than a handful of sources and bibliographical references. On the other hand, as an example for the inconsistency in the structure of Buchmann's analysis, he fills eight pages of his book—embedded between the chapters "Military Justice" and "Military Pastoral Care"—with a digression concerning Austrians serving in the Allied forces. Of course, one will never be able to grasp all the elements of Austria's complex military history within the Third Reich. But even in the key parts of the study the author circumnavigates the really pressing questions: How could so many Austrians have become such reliable and obedient soldiers in the German Wehrmacht? What were those men fighting for? How did the military service affect their identity and ideological mindset? What did these mean for their lives and the coping with their own past after the end of the war?

Furthermore, astonishingly for a book on World War II, the reader will not find a rendering of the major elements of Nazi warfare or even a word about the combat experiences of Austrian soldiers in the Wehrmacht. Alternatively, several chapters are devoted to more or less important questions of hygiene, the postal system, the tone in the Wehrmacht, and other comparable facets of military life. Thus we get, for instance, detailed background information on the outfit of a Wehrmacht soldier up to the number of his underwear, but on the other hand we hear nothing about the impact of war on the daily routine on the front. I do not want to deny the relevance of these issues brought up by the author for our understanding of the Wehrmacht. Nevertheless I want to take into consideration that the war itself represented the core of *all* war-related experiences in the life histories of the World War II generation and thus can hardly be ignored, especially in a study grounded on an everyday life approach.

What is even more problematic is Buchmann's almost non-existent methodological framework, in particular his uncritical use of the autobiographical sources, which leads in sum to a lack of scholarly distance and a Wehrmacht-friendly tendency in his book. Instead of scrutinizing the motives behind the genesis and essence of these ego documents (most of them published long after the war or already discussed in other studies), the author accepts them as irrefutable facts, devoid of almost any analysis or interpretation. In quotation after quotation, Buchmann echoes the memories and personal viewpoints of those former Austrian Wehrmacht soldiers and summarizes their perceptions. Subsequently, many of Buchmann's conclusions stand on shaky ground or remain unproven, as for instance in his claim that "the vast majority of the *Bundesheer* officers took the oath on Adolf Hitler, although they showed no sympathy for National Socialism" (p. 16). He also cites two contemporary witnesses who had visited the Jewish ghetto in Warsaw without becoming aware of the genocide, which leads him to the conclusion that the "the mass executions (of Jews) remained hidden for the average *Landser*" (p. 199).

Without a doubt, despite all the methodological shortcomings, Buchmann's book will find its readers among historically interested persons and scholars who are not familiar with this genuine Austrian chapter of World War II history. Though the author is able to provide a vivid, albeit very fragmentary, insight in particular aspects of the everyday life of Austrian soldiers during the war, the complexity of Austrian Wehrmacht service is unfortunately only scratched at the surface. Moreover, Buchmann fails to address the key issue of his work, as given in the title, namely the question of the Austrian component in Hitler's armed forces, and widely ignores to address the most important topics in Austria's intellectual process of coming to terms with its wartime past. Thus, it would be an important step for the advancement and promotion of research on the role of Austrians in the Wehrmacht as well as the public debate on the history of the Wehrmacht in Austria, if the more insightful dissertations from Germann and Grischany would be published.

Notes

1. See especially the series of contributions by Walter Manoschek and Hans Safrian on war crimes committed by Austrian Wehrmacht soldiers, for e.g., "Österreicher in der Wehrmacht," in *NS-Herrschaft in Österreich: Ein Handbuch*, ed. Emmerich Tálos et al. (Vienna: öbv and hpt, 2001), 123-58.

2. Richard Germann, "'Österreichische' Soldaten in Ost- und Südosteuropa 1941-1945: Deutsche Krieger—Nationalsozialistische Verbrecher—Österreichische Opfer?," PhD. diss., University of Vienna, 2006; Thomas R. Grischany, "The Austrians in the German *Wehrmacht*, 1938-45," PhD. diss., University of Chicago, 2007; see also the essays of these authors in Günter Bischof et al., eds., *New Perspectives on Austrians and World War II*, Contemporary Austrian Studies 17 (New Brunswick, NJ: Transaction, 2009).

Wolfgang Schüssel with Alexander Purger, *Offengelegt* (Salzburg: Ecowin, 2009)

Reinhard Heinisch

Wolfgang Schüssel's memoir of his time at the helm of the Austrian Conservative Party (ÖVP) is sure to disappoint. *Offengelegt* [lit.: *Laid out in the Open*] does very little of what the title tantalizingly suggests. The somewhat turgid prose reads more like an episodic transcription of a long interview. No great secrets are revealed, no scores are settled, and no major new insights are provided into the soul of Austria's arguably most successful and powerful political figure since Bruno Kreisky. In its rather simple style, the book takes us from event to event introducing us to Schüssel's actions and thoughts in third person, thereby presenting the former Chancellor not so much in a glowing light but as a straightforward and humble man. His passions are soccer, hiking, and the cello, writing amusing tales along with illustrating children's books, not to mention the crossword puzzles, skiing, and the headphone piano. Instead of important revelations, we are offered a nugget of detail here and a tidbit of new information there: Some of it is puzzling (Why was Schüssel spared the draft as a matter of "national interest"?); some is unexpected (Incredibly, Schüssel twice offered the Ministry of Women and Family Affairs to Austria's version of Oprah Winfrey, Vera Russwurm); and much is plain trivial ("Combining skiing and politics was a particular specialty of his!"). Schüssel appears as the idealized Austrian everyman with few conceits, but personifying the perfect combination of a classical education, unpretentious savvy, religious piety, personal charm and a love for the outdoors while being equally at home in the fine arts. He may be friends with the likes of Helmut Kohl or Mstislav Rostopowitch, Schüssel, above all, is a man of common sense and with a common touch: What, for instance, did he ominously whisper into President Bush's ear upon the latter's arrival in Vienna in 2006? No great secret but the humble request that the Schüssels be allowed to tour the famous "Air Force One."

Overall, Schüssel remains true to his reputation as Austria's taciturn politician ("der große Schweiger"), which he acquired by being famously reluctant to answer his critics and comment on crucial developments during his tenure in office. Motivated seemingly only by good intentions and policy goals that any sincere person would surely recognize as the best possible course under the circumstances, Schüssel comes across as a sort of Mr. Smith goes to Washington. Although having served in politics for 32 years prior to his chancellorship and despite 18 years in the government overall, the memoir presents the former chancellor as an accidental and reluctant political figure to whom concepts such as power, ambition, ideology, or partisanship seem completely alien. Reliant on the advice of his wife and daughter as well as a cadre of saintly confidants, Schüssel is time and again thrust into the limelight by reluctantly accepting position after position that he professes not to have expected, sought, or wanted: party leader, foreign minister and vice chancellor, and finally chancellor.

The image of Schüssel as the accidental politician is, of course, ironic in light of Schüssel's reputation as master tactician who managed to outwit or outlast his opponents both in Austrian and on the international stage. Having served in the corridors of power for that many decades, it appears unlikely that only the best intentions and hard work for the good cause have swept him willy-nilly along to find himself "under the shower in his house" when in 1995 the call to lead his party unexpectedly arrived. In this and several other episodes, *Offengelegt* presents a curiously deterministic account of politics in which developments unfold, things happen, and others act, while Schüssel, time and again, is forced to re-act based either on a sober analysis of the facts or his instincts and better judgment. More often than not, this turns out to be fortuitous for him, his party, and his government. Luck comes to those who look after it.

The austerity programs of the 1990s, the two pension reforms, the controversial purchase of 4th generation fighter planes, forming a government with the Freedom Party, pushing Austria toward NATO membership, and championing the EU membership of the nations of the Western Balkan while vetoing Turkey's entry are all presented as matter-of-fact decisions; inconceivable therefore that others might legitimately want to object to any of this on grounds of politics or principle. The memoir therefore implies that Schüssel's opponents were typically motivated by partisanship, ideology, or worse. Among this group, the memoir lists later President Heinz Fischer and especially the Social Democratic unions as examples of the dogmatic left who time and again acted behind the scenes to oppose even the most sensible economic reforms.

Also Schüssel's coalition partner, the FPÖ, appears caught up in ideology and personal ambition. He professes great surprise that a year into his chancellorship, the Freedom Party base was about to explode with Haider leading the charge. Had there not been great legislative progress? How, Schüssel marvels, could the Freedom Party become so unhinged by merely dropping below 20% in public support (from over 30% in opinion polls a year earlier)? The nature of his coalition partner unaccustomed to normal politics and affected by a string of bitter electoral defeats while being horrified by the plunging public support do not seem shake Schüssel's amazement. Adding insult to injury, it was his own party that benefited the most from the FPÖ's implosion. Little wonder therefore that Haider seeing his life's work ruined reacted with a vengeance. Schüssel claims to have been equally nonplussed when news of the sanctions by the other EU governments arrived. Once again there were unexpected phone calls – two by the Portuguese Foreign Minister and another by French President Jacques Chirac. As readers, we cannot help but marvel at Schüssel's bewilderment. How could such an internationally connected and politically experienced figure not have seen this coming? What had been his standing as foreign minister in the eyes of his international peers that nobody saw it fit to inform him in advance that something was up?

The book remains also curiously quiet about his own party's move to the right in the 1990s. As Schüssel offers little perspective on the ÖVP's increasingly neo-conservative agenda, especially in family and education policy, he does not have to tackle the uncomfortable question of whether the Conservatives' own political posture may have helped undermine the grand coalition. He appears not to see the contradiction between chiding the Social Democrats for their reluctance to embrace politically costly economic and social reforms and his making common cause with the very Freedom Party to whom the SPÖ was shedding voters, thanks to Haider's social populism.

Following Otto Habsburg's advice never to bear any grudge for more than a year, Schüssel finds it in himself to forgive his rivals and opponents; also those either in his own party, like President Thomas Klestil or on the international stage, like Jacques Chirac and Belgian Foreign Minister

Louis Michel. In general, Schüssel treats his political opponents more with reluctant sympathy than with scorn. Haider is described as conflicted and self-destructive soul. In a telling episode he is shown to apologize under tears to Vice Chancellor Riess-Passer for his relentless attacks against his party's own ministers in government while promising greater support only to do the opposite a few days later. Also the ÖVP leader's direct counterparts, the Chancellors Vranitzky and Klima, seem at the worst weak-willed and at best victims of their own party's left wing. Only in the cases of German Foreign Minister Joschka Fischer and SPÖ-leader Alfred Gusenbauer, Schüssel cannot help but reveal glimpses of considerable tactlessness on the part of the two.

When recounting his own blunders and setbacks such as making an unflattering comment about German Bundesbank President Hans Tietmeyer, or precipitously provoking unhelpful national elections in 1995, or his unexpected loss in 2006 to (of all people) Gusenbauer, Schüssel finds himself often the victim of circumstances. Occasionally, he admits to sensing a cause to have been probably lost (i.e. nominating Benita Ferrero-Waldner, thus a woman to be the conservative party's candidate for federal president) but defends sticking by the decision out of loyalty or principle. Loyalty is also the rationale offered for holding on to people long after they had became political liabilities, including the hapless Education Minister Elisabeth Gehrer and the glib Finance Minster Karl-Heinz Grasser, whose personal antics had become fodder for the media.

Overall, Schüssel's political world is a happy one. Important meetings take place in locales with funny names, such as the "Happy Biker," in which he awaits election returns. When the going gets tough, such as during the restitution negotiations for Nazi victims, Schüssel just orders pizza to brighten the mood of U.S. Deputy Foreign Minister Stuart Eizenstat. On other occasions he goes skiing with Putin, jogging with Bill Clinton, on bike tours with his cabinet, and hikes with Kofi Anan. In between all this, he finds time to attend operas, write amusing books, save Vienna's zoo, play the cello, and give President Bush advice on how to tone down a statement on Iran.

In the end, Wolfgang Schüssel remains an enigma. Was it all just as straightforward as he makes his term in office out to be? No Austrian politician has been more influential but faded so quickly from the public limelight and even the collective memory of his own party. He offers all but tiny glimpses of a growing internal resistance to his power and political agenda. As dissatisfying as *Offengelegt* may be for the political observer of Austrian politics, Wolfgang Schüssel certainly appears as one of the few politicians not to have been embittered and consumed by his long tenure in office. In fact, he seems to have enjoyed himself and never complains. Despite reaching political depths and heights that few Austrian politicians have ever experienced, he keeps a sense of perspective about it all and remains always an optimist. In this more than anything else, Wolfgang Schüssel represents a welcome departure from Austrian politics as usual. Ironically, in this the Austrian everyman appears so thoroughly un-Austrian.

Martin Strauß and Karl-Heinz Ströhle, eds., *Sanktionen—10 Jahre danach: Die Maßnahmen der Länder der Europäischen Union gegen die österreichische Regierung im Jahr 2000* (Innsbruck: Studienverlag, 2010)

Alexander Smith

It has been ten years now since the fourteen partner states of Austria in the European Union (EU-14) at the time implemented diplomatic measures against the newly formed Austrian government. The elections to the Nationalrat of 3 October 1999 brought Jörg Haider's right-wing populist Freedom Party (FPÖ) with 26.9 percent of the vote in second place. As it became apparent that Wolfgang Schüssel, chairman of the Christian-conservative People's Party (ÖVP), intended to build a coalition government with the FPÖ, Austria's fourteen EU partners sent an unprecedented warning to Vienna. On behalf of the EU-14, the Portuguese Presidency informed in a statement on 31 January 2000 both the President and the Chancellor of Austria that any participation of the FPÖ in the government would entail a joint reaction consisting primarily of a downgrading of bilateral diplomatic relations between the EU-14 and Austria. These warnings notwithstanding, on 4 February 2000 a new government, composed of the ÖVP and the FPÖ as equally strong partners, was inaugurated by a stony-faced President Thomas Klestil, who tried to avoid the FPÖ's participation until the very last. Albeit the ÖVP was only the third party in the Nationalrat, due to the coalition with the right-wing populists Schüssel managed to become Federal Chancellor instead of continuing the unloved "grand coalition" with the Social Democrats (SPÖ), where he would have played only the second fiddle. The following isolation of the Austrian government by the other EU member states represented, according to the editors of *Sanktionen—10 Jahre danach* (Sanctions—10 Years Later), the two visual artists Martin Strauß and Karl-Heinz Ströhle, the severest crisis in Austria's external relations since the beginning of the Second Republic.

Even though the EU-14 only imposed diplomatic measures exclusively targeting the ÖVP-FPÖ government, as rightly outlined in Michael Frank's essay, the latter succeeded through a propagandistic campaign in reframing the measures into "sanctions" against the whole country. The two parties called for a national *Schulterschluss* (closing of ranks) and managed to rally a big majority of the population and the media behind them (p. 25). Doron Rabinovici points out that even the liberal media dismissed the measures as an injustice against the whole country. He goes on writing that their rejection turned into a national consensus and any critique of the government was labeled, in the typical vocabulary of the right-wing populists, *Vernaderung* (an Austrian word for betrayal) or *Nestbeschmutzung* (fouling one's own nest) (p. 15). The government's success becomes evident by the fact that the term "sanctions" found its way into daily parlance. The measures were soon generally interpreted in Austria as an illegitimate and unfair attack by the EU on the whole country. In this general mood of victimhood, a serious debate about the causes of the measures of the EU-14 could not ensue.

Ten years later, the controversies over the "sanctions" have largely subsided. They are no matter of political discussion anymore and seem to have fallen into oblivion. The distance in time should allow for an objective reflection and analysis of the EU's measures, which have overshadowed Austrian and European politics for months. As stated by Strauß and Ströhle in the preface, the aim of their edited volume *Sanktionen* is to give an impetus to such a long overdue debate on the real causes and motives of the EU-14's harsh reaction.

According to the eleven essays written by renowned Austrian and German journalists, academics and writers, the main cause for the measures taken against the Austrian government is to be found in Austria's sloppy approach to its (Nazi) history[1]—this distinguishes it from other Western European countries—in general and the unique nature of the FPÖ in particular. Martin Strauß convincingly argues in a brilliant essay with the laconic subtitle "Austrian conditions and European standards" that the FPÖ's participation in the government of an EU member state, a party that has an ambivalent attitude toward Nazism, had to be completely unacceptable to the EU. The European Community was founded, after all, in the spirit of anti-Nazism (p. 36). The integration of the FPÖ into the government not only entailed the danger that high-ranking politicians of the EU-14 have to deal on an equal basis with the populist Haider and sit at the same table with him; it also implied that a right-wing extremist party would wield direct influence in the highest EU committees (pp. 33-34). Seen from such a perspective, the formation of government integrating the FPÖ was a "*Nötigung*" (coercion) of the EU.

Strauß furthermore criticizes the specific "Austrian conditions," characterized by the country's deficient coping with its past, the resulting political and societal tolerance of right-wing extremist ideas and parties and, as a consequence, a problematic political culture. In France and Germany—as outlined in Danny Leder's and Wolfgang Benz's contributions—the radical right-wing parties are isolated since the established parties refused any cooperation and preserved a *cordon sanitaire* around them. In Austria the ÖVP and the SPÖ do not have scruples to engage the FPÖ if deemed beneficial. The formation of a government with the FPÖ meant, according to Strauß, the imposition of these "Austrian conditions" on the EU and thus threatened to thwart the consistent and uncompromising stance of other EU governments toward right-wing populism. The governments of the EU-14 were not willing to give up their policy of isolating parties with extremist elements only because the Austrian Christian Conservatives have "surrendered all standards in this regard" (p. 38).

Even if there is some truth in this reasoning, the application of double standards by the EU cannot be disavowed. Its harsh rebuke of the ÖVP-FPÖ government was out of proportion when compared to its complete silence about Silvio Berlusconi's 1994 and 2001 governments with the neo-fascist *Alleanza Nazionale* and the racist *Lega Nord* in Italy.[2] The EU also remained silent after the recent problematic electoral success of the far-right and anti-Semitic Hungarian *Jobbik* party, which maintains the extremist neo-Nazi black-clad paramilitary organization.[3]

Rabinovici interprets the "sanctions" of the EU-14 as an expression of the common political approach in Europe to oppose right-wing extremism on principled grounds. In Austria, where this kind of extremism is handled in a sloppy and negligent manner, the EU's resolute reaction was incomprehensible (p. 18). It did not register with most Austrians that the FPÖ was considered a radical right-wing party and that Haider's outrageous statements, downplayed as mere "words" in Austria, were taken seriously in other European countries.[4] Rabinovici notes that Austria obviously did not develop those "Western minimum standards regarding the past," which are taken for granted in other countries (p. 18).

Anton Pelinka's essay takes a similar line of argument. To understand the EU-14's reaction it is crucial to comprehend the nature of the FPÖ. Pelinka describes the FPÖ as a party that both denies the European *Grundkonsens* (fundamental consensus) and contravenes basic European values with its "radically anti-European opposition and post-Nazi right-wing extremism" (p. 59). In contrast to the common belief in Austria that the FPÖ is a conventional right-wing party comparable to those in other European countries, Pelinka plausibly argues that the FPÖ is different. Within Europe, the FPÖ has always been regarded as a party purposefully and consistently playing down National Socialism. In the rest of Europe, it is considered as an incorrigible right-wing extremist party (p. 58). What is different between the FPÖ and all other xenophobic parties in Europe is its direct connection to the Nazi past by way of the VdU (*Verband der Unabhängigen*, Association of Independents), the FPÖ's predecessor party founded in 1949 by former Nazis (p. 56). In line with the peculiar "Austrian conditions," the VdU and later the FPÖ immediately became socially acceptable. Instead of building a *cordon sanitaire* around them like in other European countries, the ÖVP and the SPÖ had no reservations and cooperated with the former Nazis.

This can be regarded as an expression of Austria's sloppy handling of its inglorious Nazi past. Pelinka rightly stresses that Austria has always been abdicating responsibility by referring to the Moscow Declaration of 1943 and emphasizing victimhood (p. 55). Benz avers a "phenomenon of denial of history" (*Geschichtsverweigerung*) in Austria (p. 149). Sebastian Kurat explains in his article that with the proclamation of the Second Republic in 1945 the "myth of the victim" was elevated to a "*Staatsdoktrin*." Kurat argues that this myth enjoys constitutional status and has been consistently impeding the process of dealing with the past and Austrians' deeds during World War II (p. 112). Benz explains that the "internalization of the legend of the first victim of National Socialism" exempted the Austrian society from dealing with its history (p. 159). Along with the enfranchisement of former Nazis in 1949, according to Kurat, in the early 1950s Austrian politicians lobbied for an amnesty for felons previously convicted as war criminals. Even the active participation in the Holocaust was not regarded as justifying their ostracization. These practices and the general amnesty of Nazis in 1957 led to a "*Bagatellisierung*" (belittlement) of the crimes committed by National Socialism in the public (pp. 115-16).

The eleven essays in *Sanktionen* thus interpret the measures taken by the EU-14 within a wider framework: Austria's troubled relationship with its Nazi past, the suppression of guilt, the uncritical tolerance of Nazi ideas, the easy acceptance of populist xenophobia, and the pooh-poohing of the troubling character of the FPÖ. It is this ignorance about the nature of the FPÖ that allows for its successes in Austria. Strauß is right when he claims that in Austria clear lines of what is tolerable and what is not have never been drawn (p. 46ff.). Haider's numerous Nazi slogans never damaged his popularity. Martin Graf was elected the third president of the Nationalrat in 2008, even though his closeness to neo-Nazi circles is well-known. After his grave insults against the head of the Jewish religious community in Austria, he was not forced to step down. Barbara Rosenkranz with her ambivalent attitude toward Nazism[5] ran for the presidency in 2010. All of this would be unthinkable in Germany, France and other Western European countries and thus is a disgraceful Austrian specificity.

Another central thesis of the book is that the measures actually were more successful than is conventional wisdom in Austria. Frank argues that without the so-called "sanctions" of the EU-14, Haider would not have handed over the chairmanship of the FPÖ to Susanne Riess-Passer and withdrawn to Carinthia (p. 27). This is a bold assertion that is questionable. The FPÖ knew very well that the EU would never have accepted Haider as a member of government. It is more plausible that Haider, the embodiment of the populist opposition politician, never planned to join the coalition. One has to distinguish between the EU's pressure and the "sanctions" as such. With this in mind, it seems probable that even without the diplomatic measures Haider would not have entered the government. However, Frank is correct in his assessment that the "sanctions" accelerated the Schüssel coalition's comprehensive restitution policy, with the aim of shedding a positive light on the internationally isolated government.[6]

Pelinka insists that any assessment of the "sanctions" against the Austrian government has to include an assessment of the FPÖ.[7] This is certainly true and becomes evident in the report of the three wise men Martti Ahtisaari, Jochen Frowein and Marcelino Oreja. They received a mandate by the EU-14 to analyze both the Austrian government's respect for the common European values *and* the evolution of the political nature of the FPÖ. Nevertheless, not much attention has been paid to the latter point, which has never been a matter of serious debate in Austria. This explains why the report of the three wise men was generally interpreted as "an 'acquittal' after an unjustified indictment" (Pelinka, p. 61), and as a recognition by the EU that injustice was done to Austria (Rabinovici, p. 19). In reality, however, this was not the case. The report describes the FPÖ as a "right wing populist party with radical elements" that has "enforced xenophobic sentiments," which "must give rise to concern."[8] The wise men explicitly note positive effects of the measures. Nonetheless, there can be no doubt that they failed to accomplish their main goals: to avoid the FPÖ's participation in government and, more importantly, to literally wake up Austrians and to move them to adopt the European norms in dealing with right-wing extremism.

The eleven essays deliver a clear interpretation of the events in 2000, namely that the "sanctions" were justified, necessary and more successful than commonly claimed. In this respect the essays are one-sided. Critics of the EU's measures do not get a chance to speak. This, however, can also be seen as a strength of the book since the critical and denunciatory position toward the "sanctions" clearly dominates discourses in Austria on this matter. Other perspectives are rarely acknowledged. Strauß and Ströhle note in the preface that the great majority of publications on the EU's measures in 2000 released to date in Austria take up a negative attitude toward the "sanctions." By primarily discussing the (il)legal dimension of the measures, the alleged domestic political considerations by the EU-14 governments, and the EU's double standards in handling the Austrian case, most analyses fail to get to the very bottom of the matter.[9] The highly problematic nature of the FPÖ is ignored by almost all Austrian publications on the EU-14's measures. Hence, one might argue that the main reasons for the "sanctions" have never been understood by most Austrians. Herein lies a central merit of *Sanktionen*. By critically reflecting Austria's failure to come to terms with its Nazi past and the resulting political, societal, and the media's acceptance of the FPÖ as a conventional party, it contributes to a more complex understanding of the EU's diplomatic actions.

The book holds a mirror up to Austrians and their strange politics of history when it comes to World War II. The critique of Austria's insufficient sensitivity toward its Nazi past is accurate. There is a lack of awareness in the general public in Austria that any affinity to fascist or National Socialist ideas is unacceptable. We can only hope that the book's important message will become part of the political discourse. It is to be feared, however, that with reference to the authors, perceived as liberals and leftists by most Austrians, it will not be taken seriously and will be easily dismissed out of hand. The process of coming to terms with the past starting in the mid-1980s with the so-called "Waldheim affair," and developing a democratic culture that does not tolerate extremist ideas, is still ongoing. In the words of Pelinka, as long as the FPÖ is considered a conventional party, Austria "has not arrived in Europe" (p. 62). There is nothing to be added to this assessment.

Notes

1. For an overview of Austria's difficulties in dealing with its Nazi past see Günter Bischof, "Victims? Perpetrators? 'Punching Bags' of European Historical Memory? The Austrians and Their World War II Legacies," *German Studies Review 27* (Feb. 2004): 17-32.

2. Greene shows in a comparative case study of the FPÖ and the *Lega Nord* that the latter "has prompted its government to adopt more extreme right-wing ideologies and policies than the Freedom Party has in Austria, both before and after the parties' incorporation into their respective national governments." Referring to the EU's apparent double standards, Greene concludes, "If the Austrian diplomatic sanctions were an established precedent for how the EU should respond to extreme elements in its member nations [...] one would have expected a similar quarantine on Italy." See Megan Greene, "Right-Wing Movements in the European Union: A Case Study of the Austrian Freedom Party (FPÖ) and the Lega Nord (LN)," in *The Dollfuss/Schuschnigg Era in Austria: A Reassessment*, ed. Günter Bischof et al., Contemporary Austrian Studies 11 (New Brunswick, NJ: Transaction, 2003), 204.

3. In the ORF's (Austrian Broadcasting Corporation) TV program *Europastudio* of 25 April 2010, Michael Frank compared *Jobbik*'s Hungarian Guard, which has been outlawed but is still active, with the SA (*Sturmabteilung*), the Nazi Party's paramilitary organization. In the same broadcast, Ernst Gelegs labeled *Jobbik* a fascist, openly racist, and anti-Semitic party that would be unthinkable in Austria. Gelegs stated that in comparison to *Jobbik* the FPÖ would be a "left-liberal" party. *Jobbik* received 16.7 percent of the vote in Hungary's April 2010 general election. *Fidesz*, the conservative ruling party of Prime Minister Viktor Orbán, used an anti-Jewish language in its parliamentary election campaign "even Haider didn't dare utter." See Denis MacShane, "Europe's New Politics of Fear," *Newsweek*, 26 Apr. 2010. Despite—or due to?—its anti-Semitic campaign, *Fidesz* has won a two-thirds majority.

4. Sonja Puntscher-Riekmann, "Es ist vorbei. Ist es vorbei?," in *Eine europäische Erregung: Die "Sanktionen" der Vierzehn gegen Österreich im Jahr 2000 – Analysen und Kommentare*, ed. Erhard Busek and Martin Schauer (Vienna: Böhlau, 2003), 120.

5. According to a verdict of the European Court of Human Rights, it is legitimate to call Rosenkranz a "*Kellernazi*" ("basement Nazi"). Before being forced during the presidential campaign 2010 to admit the existence of gas chambers in the Third Reich's concentration and extermination camps, she called them into question.

6. This is confirmed by Günter Bischof and Michael S. Maier in "Reinventing Tradition and the Politics of History: Schüssel's Restitution and Commemoration Policies," in *The Schüssel Era in Austria*, ed. Günter Bischof and Fritz Plasser, Contemporary Austrian Studies 18 (New Orleans and Innsbruck: UNO Press and Innsbruck University Press, 2010), 212.

7. Anton Pelinka, "Österreich und Europa: Zur Isolierung eines Landes," in *Eine europäische Erregung*, 88.

8. Report by Martti Ahtisaari, Jochen Frowein, Marcelino Oreja (adopted in Paris on 8 September 2000), paragraphs 92 and 110; for the report in German see Busek and Schauer, eds., *Eine europäische Erregung*, 538-67; an English version of the report can be found under <www.mpg.de/pdf/commentsStatements/berichtOesterreich_en.pdf> (20 Apr. 2010).

9. See for example Michael Fleischhacker, *Wien, 4. Februar 2000 oder Die Wende zur Hysterie* (Vienna: Czernin, 2001); Waldemar Hummer and Anton Pelinka, eds., *Österreich unter "EU-Quarantäne": Die "Maßnahmen der 14" gegen die österreichische Bundesregierung aus politikwissenschaftlicher und juristischer Sicht – Chronologie, Kommentar, Dokumentation* (Vienna: Linde, 2002); Michael Gehler, "'Preventive Hammer Blow' or Boomerang? The EU 'Sanction'

Measures against Austria 2000," in *Austria in the European Union*, ed. Günter Bischof et al., Contemporary Austrian Studies 10 (New Brunswick, NJ: Transaction, 2002), 180-222; Busek and Schauer, eds., *Eine europäische Erregung*; Anton Pelinka's writings on this issue, which consistently discuss Austria's difficulties in dealing with its past and the FPÖ's specific nature, have to be mentioned as a notable exception among very few.

ANNUAL REVIEW

Austria 2009

Elections EU-Parliament in Austria
Elections in Upper Austria and in Vorarlberg
AUA and Hypo Group Alpe Adria
BZÖ, FPK and FPÖ
Economic and Statistical Data

Reinhold Gärtner

Elections EU-Parliament in Austria

The elections to the European Parliament were held in June 2009. Since 1979, all member states of the European Union elect their MPs directly. Before 1979 the MPs were sent to the EU Parliament by their countries. In June 2009, Austria had seventeen MPs. The SPÖ lost some 10 percent, and so the ÖVP could get the most seats. The FPÖ did not win as much as expected according to polls, and the *Liste Martin* was again vey successful—not only because of the enormous support of the *Kronen Zeitung*. Usually, the SPÖ would have gotten only four seats and the BZÖ no seat, but with the Reform Treaty of Lisbon, Austria got nineteen seats—one more for the SPÖ and the first one for the BZÖ. The voter turnout (46 percent) was a bit higher than in 2004 (42.4 percent). It had been 49.4 percent in 1999 and 67.7 percent in 1996.

Table 1: Elections to the European Parliament in June 2009 in Austria: Percentage - Seats

Year	SPÖ	ÖVP	FPÖ	Grüne	Liste Martin	Others
2009	23.7 – 5	30.0 - 6	12.7 – 2	9.9 – 2	17.7 – 3	4. 6* – 1
2004	33.3 – 7	32.7 – 6	6.3 – 1	12.9 – 2	14.0 – 2	
1999	31.7 – 7	30.6 – 7	23.4 – 5	9.3 – 2		
1996	29.2 – 6	29.7 – 7	27.5 – 6	6.8 – 1		4.3** – 1

*BZÖ; **LiF

The results for right-wing populist parties in these EU parliamentary elections were in some countries alarming. In the Netherlands, Geert Wilders and his PvV (*Partij voor de Vrijheid*; Freedom Party) got four seats; *Perussuomalaiset* (True Finns) from Finland got one seat; *Lega Nord* (Northern League; Italy) got nine; *Vlaams Belang* (Matters of the Flemish) in Belgium two; *Attak* in Bulgaria two and *Partidul Romania Mare* (Romania) three. Among the most radical of these parties is *Jobbik* (The better ones) in Hungary. The main target of the (anti-Semitic) party are Hungarian Roma. *Jobbik* is the political representative of the extremist Hungarian Guard, a paramilitary organization which reminds observers to the members of the fascist Hungarian Arrow Cross. *Jobbik*, too, has three MPs in the EU-Parliament.

The Reform Treaty of Lisbon came into effect in December 2009 after the pro-referendum in Ireland. In Austria, the Treaty was ratified by the Parliament in April 2008 already.

Elections in Upper Austria and in Vorarlberg

Elections were held in Vorarlberg and in Upper Austria on 27 September 2009. In Upper Austria elections are held every six years, in Vorarlberg (as in the other counties) every five years.

In Upper Austria there was a cooperation between the ÖVP and the Greens (*Grüne*) in the country's government, and the main question was whether the Greens would get enough votes to get a seat in the government again. The governments in Carinthia, Styria, Upper and Lower Austria and in the Burgenland are created according to the distribution of seats. All parties get at least one seat in the country government if they get more than some 9 to 10 percent. And with 9.2 percent, the Greens were successful. The election result was a disaster for the SPÖ: It lost more than 13 percent and eight of twenty-two seats. The FPÖ could not win all those who had voted for other parties in 2003, and the winner was the ÖVP. The ÖVP could get remarkable 46.9 percent, and Governor Josef Pühringer was stronger than any time before. Pühringer has been governor of Upper Austria since 1995.

Table 2: Election Results in Upper Austria by Percentage - Seats

	ÖVP	SPÖ	Grüne	FPÖ
2009	46.9 - 28	24.9 - 14	9.2 - 5	15.3 - 9
2003	43.4 - 25	38.3 - 22	9.1 - 5	8.4 - 4
1997	42.7 - 25	27.0 - 16	5.8 - 3	20.6 - 12
1991	45.2 - 26	31.4 - 19	5.7 - 0*	17.7 - 11

Source: Ministry of the Interior; *two Green parties ran for election

In Vorarlberg, there had been an ÖVP-FPÖ coalition for years. The election campaign of the FPÖ, though, brought an end to this coalition. The FPÖ's election campaign was xenophobic and producing scapegoats. But FPÖ-chairman Dieter Egger went one step further. During the campaign he was talking about Hanno Loewy, director of the Jewish Museum of Hohenems. Hohenems has a Jewish tradition that goes back centuries, and the Jewish Museum was opened in 1991. In 2009, Hanno Loewy criticized FPÖ's election campaign, and Dieter Egger commented this criticism: "*Der Exil-Jude aus Amerika in seinem hochsubventionierten Museum*" ("the exile Jew from America in his financially highly supported museum"). The German citizen Hanno Loewy was born in Frankfurt/Main (Germany). The remark of Egger was anti-Semitic and perfidious: "Jews from America" means financially strong and unscrupulous Jews; "exile" means those who could arrange to escape the Nazis and are not really seen as victims by the political extreme right. Governor Herbert Sausgruber (ÖVP) asked Egger to excuse himself for these remarks; otherwise he would not continue on the coalition with the FPÖ. Egger did not—and so the FPÖ is not member of the new government in Vorarlberg.

The loss of the ÖVP was comparatively moderate. The SPÖ, though, is with only 10 percent less and less visible in the country. The Greens managed to get at least a very small win, and the FPÖ won almost as much as the party had lost in 2004. Herbert Sausgruber is still governor of Vorarlberg (since 1997).

Table 3: Election Results in Vorarlberg by Percentage - Seats

	ÖVP	SPÖ	Grüne	FPÖ
2009	50.8 – 20	10.0 – 3	10.6 – 4	25.1 – 9
2004	54.9 – 21	16.9 – 6	10.2 – 4	12.9 – 5
1999	45.8 – 18	13.0 – 5	6.0 – 2	27.4 – 11
1994	49.9 – 20	16.2 – 6	7.7 – 3	18.4 – 7

Source: Ministry of the Interior

The next provincial elections will be held in the Burgenland (May 2010), Styria (September 2010) and in Vienna (October 2010). All three of them have SPÖ majorities and SPÖ governors at the moment.

AUA and Hypo Group Alpe Adria

The AUA (Austrian Airlines) had turbulent times in recent years. After severe losses, the AUA was looking for someone who could buy the sick airline. After some incompetent attempts of AUA's management, it was finally (in December 2009) bought by the German Lufthansa.

As other countries, Austria was affected by the worldwide financial and economic crisis. And the troubles of AUA were caused partly by this worldwide crisis, partly, though, by mismanagement.

Affected from the financial crisis were (some) Austrian banks, as well.

As in seven other Austrian countries, there is a Hypo bank in Carinthia, called Hypo Group Alpe Adria. In previous years, the *Hypothekenbanken* were owned by the countries; in recent years more and more of them were (partly) privatized. This happened in Carinthia, as well. One of the new owners was the *Bayerische Landesbank* (Germany). In 2009, it became more and more apparent that the Hypo Group Alpe Adria might collapse. So negotiations began, and in the end Austria took over the bank, which was close to bankruptcy. Otherwise the damage for Austria's bank system and for Austria's financial prestige might have been disastrous. In course of time it became clearer that the province of Carinthia and many political representatives of Carinthia (from the former governor Jörg Haider to his successor, Gerhard Dörfler) were responsible, too, for this fiasco.

BZÖ, FPK and FPÖ

The debacle of the Hypo Group led to a coup of the Carinthian BZÖ members. In summer 2009, Gerhard Dörfler (then BZÖ) said that the Viennese should vote for Michael Häupl and the SPÖ instead of Heinz-Christian Strache and the FPÖ in the forthcoming Viennese elections (autumn 2010), but in December 2009, Dörfler came back to the FPÖ. And so did other important members of the BZÖ in Carinthia (e.g. Uwe Scheuch). They announced the foundation of the FPK (*Freiheitliche Partei Kärntens*; Freedom Party of Carinthia) and that in future they would cooperate with Strache and the FPÖ again.

Economic and Statistical Data

Inflation in Austria was at 0.5 percent in 2009 (compared to 3.2 percent in 2008), and the Harmonized Index of Consumer Prices (HVPI) was at 0.4 percent (compared to 32.2 percent in 2008). The public deficit amounted to 3.4 percent in 2009 (0.4 percent in 2008), and public debts amounted to 66.5 percent in 2009 (62.5 percent in 2008).

In 2009, the Austrian GNP was at Euro 268 billion, a minus of € 5 billion in comparison to 2008 (Euro 33,090 per capita in 2009, compared to Euro 33,810 in 2008).

In 2008, imports amounted to Euro 119.57 billion (Euro 88.018 billion from the EU-27), and exports amounted to Euro 117.53 billion (Euro 84.798 billion to the European Union). Imports from NAFTA were at Euro 4.021 billion (Euro 4.394 billion in 2007); exports to NAFTA were at Euro 6.444 billion (Euro 7.043 billion in 2007).

In the fourth quarter of 2009, 4,088,900 people in Austria were employed (according to the Labor Force Concept; on average 4,097,900 were employed in 2008). Among them were 425,000 foreigners (428,200 in the fourth quarter of 2008); 182,600 of them were EU-27 citizens. The rate of unemployment was at 4.7 percent in the fourth quarter of 2009 (200.000 people; on average 4.0 percent in 2008).

At the beginning of 2009, 8,355,260 people were living in Austria; among them were 870,704 foreigners (and of them, 325,685 were from the EU-27 plus Switzerland). In 2008, 77,752 children were born alive in Austria, and 75,083 people died. Life expectancy is at 77.6 years (men) and 83 (women).

List of Authors

Gunda Barth-Scalmani is a professor at the Department of History and European Ethnology, University of Innsbruck.

Siegfried Beer is a professor of late modern and contemporary history and director of the Austrian Center for Intelligence, Propaganda and Security Studies (ACIPSS) at the University of Graz. He also serves as director of the Botstiber Institute for Austrian-American Studies (BIAAS) at Media, PA.

Peter Berger is chair and professor of economic and social history at the Vienna University of Economics and Business.

Günter Bischof is Marshall Plan Professor of History and the director of CenterAustria, University of New Orleans.

John W. Boyer is the Martin A. Ryerson Distinguished Service Professor in History and Dean of the College, University of Chicago.

Evan B. Bukey is Professor Emeritus of History at the University of Arkansas.

John Deak is an assistant professor in the Department of History as well as a Fellow of the Nanovic Institute for European Studies at the University of Notre Dame.

Reinhold Gärtner is a professor of political science at the University of Innsbruck.

Reinhard Heinisch is Chair of Austrian Politics and Head of the Department of Political Science at the University of Salzburg.

Patrick J. Houlihan is a Ph.D. candidate in the Department of History at the University of Chicago.

Ke-chin Hsia is a Ph.D. candidate in the Department of History at the University of Chicago.

William Johnston retired as Professor of History at the University of Massachusetts, Amherst in 1999 and lives in Melbourne.

Johannes Koll is a postdoctoral fellow at the Vienna University of Economics and Business.

Wolfgang Maderthaner is the director of the Labor History Association in Vienna.

Michael S. Maier is a doctoral candidate at the Department of Economic and Social History, University of Vienna.

Verena Pawlowsky, historian in Vienna, is engaged in different projects on the 18th–20th century history of Austria. See www.forschungsbuero.at.

Nicole M. Phelps is an assistant professor of history at the University of Vermont.

Fritz Plasser is professor of political science and Dean of the Faculty of Political Science and Sociology, University of Innsbruck.

Robert Pyrah is a postdoctoral research fellow at Oxford University.

Andreas Resch is professor of economic and social history at the Vienna University of Economics and Business.

Alexander Smith is the 2009/10 Ministry of Science Fellow at CenterAustria, University of New Orleans, and doctoral candidate in political science and economic history at the University of Innsbruck.

Julie Thorpe holds a research lectureship at the University of Western Sydney.

Andreas Weigl is head of the *Ludwig Boltzmann Institut für Stadtgeschichtsforschung* in Vienna and lecturer in economic and social history at the University of Vienna.

Harald Wendelin, historian in Vienna and founding member of the *Forschungsbüro*, is engaged in projects on the history of Austria.

Samuel R. Williamson, Jr. is Professor Emeritus of History and President/ Vice-Chancellor Emeritus of Sewanee: The University of the South.

Sara O.M. Yanovsky is a research fellow at Scholion – Interdisciplinary Research Center in Jewish Studies at the Hebrew University of Jerusalem.

Contemporary Austrian Studies

Günter Bischof and Fritz Plasser, Editors

Volume 1 (1993)
Austria in the New Europe

Volume 2 (1994)
The Kreisky Era in Austria
Oliver Rathkolb, Guest Editor

Volume 3 (1995)
Austria in the Nineteen Fifties
Rolf Steininger, Guest Editor

Volume 4 (1996)
Austro-Corporatism: Past—Present—Future

Volume 5 (1997)
Austrian Historical Memory & National Identity

Volume 6 (1998)
Women in Austria
Erika Thurner, Guest Editor

Volume 7 (1999)
The Vranitzky Era in Austria
Ferdinand Karlhofer, Guest Editor

Volume 8 (2000)
The Marshall Plan in Austria
Dieter Stiefel, Guest Editor

Volume 9 (2001)
Neutrality in Austria
Ruth Wodak, Guest Editor

Volume 10 (2002)
Austria and the EU
Michael Gehler, Guest Editor

Volume 11 (2003)
The Dollfuss/Schuschnigg Era in Austria: A Reassessment
Alexander Lassner, Guest Editor

Volume 12 (2004)
The Americanization/Westernization of Austria

Volume 13 (2005)
Religion in Austria
Hermann Denz, Guest Editor

Volume 14 (2006)
Austrian Foreign Policy in Historical Perspective
Michael Gehler, Guest Editor

Volume 15 (2007)
Sexuality in Austria
Dagmar Herzog, Guest Editor

Volume 16 (2008)
The Changing Austrian Voter

Volume 17 (2009)
New Perspectives on Austrians and World War II
Barbara Stelzl-Marx, Guest Editor

Volume 18 (2010)
The Schüssel Era in Austria

Also Available from UNO PRESS :

William Christenberry: Art & Family by J. Richard Gruber (2000)
The El Cholo Feeling Passes by Fredrick Barton (2003)
A House Divided by Fredrick Barton (2003)
Coming Out the Door for the Ninth Ward edited by Rachel Breunlin
from The Neighborhood Story Project series (2006)
The Change Cycle Handbook by Will Lannes (2008)
Cornerstones: Celebrating the Everyday Monuments & Gathering Places of New Orleans
edited by Rachel Breunlin, from The Neighborhood Story Project series (2008)
A Gallery of Ghosts by John Gery (2008)
Hearing Your Story: Songs of History and Life for Sand Roses by Nabile Farès
translated by Peter Thompson, from The Engaged Writers Series (2008)
The Imagist Poem: Modern Poetry in Miniature edited by William Pratt
from The Ezra Pound Center for Literature series (2008)
The Katrina Papers: A Journal of Trauma and Recovery by Jerry W. Ward, Jr.
from The Engaged Writers Series (2008)
On Higher Ground: The University of New Orleans at Fifty by Dr. Robert Dupont (2008)
Us Four Plus Four: Eight Russian Poets Conversing translated by Don Mager (2008)
Voices Rising: Stories from the Katrina Narrative Project edited by Rebeca Antoine (2008)
Gravestones (Lápidas) by Antonio Gamoneda, translated by Donald Wellman
from The Engaged Writers Series (2009)
The House of Dance and Feathers: A Museum by Ronald W. Lewis by Rachel Breunlin
& Ronald W. Lewis, from The Neighborhood Story Project series (2009)
I hope it's not over, and good-by: Selected Poems of Everette Maddox by Everette Maddox (2009)
Portraits: Photographs in New Orleans 1998-2009 by Jonathan Traviesa (2009)
Theoretical Killings: Essays & Accidents by Steven Church (2009)
Voices Rising II: More Stories from the Katrina Narrative Project edited by Rebeca Antoine (2010)
Rowing to Sweden: Essays on Faith, Love, Politics, and Movies by Fredrick Barton (2010)
Dogs in My Life: The New Orleans Photographs of John Tibule Mendes (2010)
Understanding the Music Business: A Comprehensive View edited by Harmon Greenblatt
& Irwin Steinberg (2010)
The Fox's Window by Naoko Awa, translated by Toshiya Kamei (2010)
A Passenger from the West by Nabile Farès, translated by Peter Thompson
from The Engaged Writers Series (2010)
The Schüssel Era in Austria: Contemporary Austrian Studies, Volume 18
edited by Günter Bischof & Fritz Plasser (2010)
The Gravedigger by Rob Magnuson Smith (2010)
Everybody Knows What Time It Is by Reginald Martin (2010)
When the Water Came: Evacuees of Hurricane Katrina by Cynthia Hogue & Rebecca Ross
from The Engaged Writers Series (2010)
Aunt Alice Vs. Bob Marley by Kareem Kennedy, from The Neighborhood Story Project series (2010)
Houses of Beauty: From Englishtown to the Seventh Ward by Susan Henry
from The Neighborhood Story Project series (2010)
Signed, The President by Kenneth Phillips, from The Neighborhood Story Project series (2010)
Beyond the Bricks by Daron Crawford & Pernell Russell
from The Neighborhood Story Project series (2010)
Green Fields: Crime, Punishment, & a Boyhood Between by Bob Cowser, Jr.,
from the Engaged Writers Series (2010)
New Orleans: The Underground Guide by Michael Patrick Welch & Alison Fensterstock (2010)
Writer in Residence: Memoir of a Literary Translater by Mark Spitzer (2010)
Open Correspondence: An Epistolary Dialogue by Abdelkébir Khatibi and Rita El Khayat, translated by
Safoi Babana-Hampton, Valérie K. Orlando, Mary Vogl

from The Engaged Writers Series (2010)
Black Santa by Jamie Bernstein (2010)
From Empire to Republic: Post-World-War-I Austria: Contemporary Austrian Studies, Volume 19 edited by Günter Bischof, Fritz Plasser and Peter Berger (2010)
Vegetal Sex (O Sexo Vegetal) by Sergio Medeiros, translated by Raymond L.Bianchi (2010)
Dream-crowned (Traumgekrönt) by Rainer Maria Rilke, translated by Lorne Mook (2010)
Wounded Days (Los Días Heridos) by Leticia Luna, translated by Toshiya Kamei (2010)
from The Engaged Writers Series (2010)

www.unopress.org